CAPTIVES OF ABB'S VALLEY

VOLUME II
OF THE BROWN, WOODWORTH EDITION

*with recent genealogies and histories
not included in Volume I*

BY ROBERT H. MOORE, JR.

Published by Robert H. Moore, Jr.

Printed by HeuleGordon, Inc.
1415 Plainfield Ave, N.E. • Grand Rapids, MI 49505

2007

TABLE OF CONTENTS

PREFACE

After some twelve years of time consuming and painstaking work, the updating of the James Moore, the "Captive," and Joseph Moore lineage was completed. Information on some branches is sparse because it was not possible to locate descendants and not everyone to whom I sent biographical sheets returned them. I am profoundly grateful to those who furnished information on their particular families and pictures. I wish to thank Nancy A. Nash (M64311312) for her most helpful advice.

Please let me know of typographical, factual errors, and omissions you may find in the up-date. I shall attempt to compile a file of such errors for a possible (but not probable) revision.

It has been a pleasure doing this work; I have enjoyed meeting family members as a result of this that I otherwise never would have.

Robert Henry Moore, Jr. (M622521)

INTRODUCTION

This supplement to Dr. Robert B. Woodworth's 1942 edition of <u>Captives of Abb's Valley</u> brings up to date the information on the Captain James Moore genealogy contained therein. This supplement also includes material on Captain Moore not in Dr. Woodworth's edition as well as material on the various branches of the James Moore, the "Captive," and Joseph Moore's descendants. An update of the descendants of Mary Moore was not attempted. I hope that a descendant will accomplish that. There are well over 500 names I have collected of the descendants of James and Joseph and I know I was not able to locate all.

The first part of the supplement covers, (1) general information on the descendants of James and Joseph, (2) some material on Captain Moore's war service, (3) an attempt to value his estate at death in current dollars based on the probate thereof (the probate of John Simpson's estate is given but not translated into dollars), (4) reprints of the write-up in the <u>Bluefield Daily Telegraph</u> of the celebration attending the dedication of the monument at the Moore farm of July 14, 1928, (5) Abb's Valley miscellaneous, i.e. location of graves in Moore cemetery, approximate location of Moore houses in the Valley, etc., and (6) a summary of the archeological findings from the excavation at the Moore Farm of October, 2000 that led to its being listed in the Commonwealth and National Registers of Historic Places.

The second part of the supplement gives the family trees of James Moore, the "Captive" and Joseph Moore, and a write-up on each branch of the families of these two men. An asterisk by the name of the descendant on the chart indicates that a biographical form was returned.

Finally, an index is appended.

I.

CAPTAIN JAMES MOORE FAMILY

Our ancestor, James Moore of County Down, Ireland, had at least 5 children. Those whose names we know are: Joseph and James who emigrated to Chester County, PA in 1726 and Rachael, John and Margaret who remained in Ireland. We don't know the name of their mother or mothers. In 1728 Joseph died here of consumption leaving only James in this country. In April 1734 James Moore married Jane Walker, also from County Down, who was one year younger: he was born in 1711 and she in 1712. They moved to Rockbridge County, VA with John Walker, Jane's brother, and settled on Walker's Creek near Jump Mountain, north and west of Lexington.

James and Jane had 10 children: John, who married his 1st cousin, Jane Walker; Mary, who was the great grandmother of Jeb Stuart; Rachel who married William McPheeters; Elizabeth who married Michael Coalter, one of whose sons, John, married a descendant of Pocahontas; Margaret who died as an infant; Captain James Moore who married Martha Poage whose brother-in-law, the Reverend Dr. Moses Hoge, was President of Hampden-Sydney College; Joseph who married his sister-in-law Margaret Coalter and later Eleanor Marquis; Jane who married Joseph Walker, possibly a relative of her mother; and Alexander and Samuel, both of whom died young. All of these families were closely affiliated with the Presbyterian Church.

Our direct ancestor, Captain James Moore, with his wife, Martha, settled in Abb's Valley, VA in southwest VA, around 1772 and had 9 children. On July 14, 1786, a band of 47 Shawnee Indians (as reported) from the Scioto valley in what is now Ohio, led by the notorious half-breed, Black Wolf, attacked the Moore homestead, killing Captain Moore, three of his children and a farm helper, John Simpson. Martha and the other children were taken by the Indians. Another son, James, was not there, having been captured by the self-same Black Wolf two years earlier and sold into slavery in Canada. A son, John, was killed on the 2nd day of the Indian raid. A daughter, Jane, along with her mother, tradition says, was burned at the stake near what is now Chillicothe, Ohio. She was about 14 years old then and her mother 44. The other children were, Joseph, who escaped the massacre, being in Rockbridge County with his grandparents and who married Christina Nicewander, and Mary, who was only 9 when captured. She later married the Rev. Samuel Brown by whom she had 11 children. Five sons were Presbyterian clergy; 3 were daughters, one of whom married a Presbyterian preacher and another a physician; one son was a Presbyterian Elder, one a physician and one died as in infant. The monument in memory of Mary Moore Brown and her husband in the cemetery at New Providence Church, Brownsville, Virginia where he was Pastor reads in part: "Through faith in God they reared a family including 5 ministers, 2 elders, the wife of a minister and the wife of a physician; "Though He slay me yet will I trust in Him."

Captain James Moore was born around 1740 making him 46 when he was killed. In 1771 before the Revolution, he visited Abb's Valley having learned of it from a Rockbridge County neighbor, Absolom Looney, taking along a man identified as an "English servant," John Simpson, probably an indentured servant. They put up a log cabin and the next year he moved there with his family who at that time was probably only John, described as "weak-minded and weak-bodied," and James who would have been 2 years old. Simpson came too. Moore's intent was to acquire the entire valley and raise horses but the Revolutionary War intervened. He volunteered for the Virginia militia, and served as a private at the battle of Point Pleasant where he was commissioned Captain of a company of riflemen on April 3, 1778. He is reported to have commanded a company at Cowpens, Alamance, Guilford Courthouse, and possibly Kings Mountain.

After the war he returned to Abb's Valley to raise Arabian horses from his magnificent stallion, Yorick. However, Shawnee Indians as reported earlier attacked the settlement with only James, Joseph and Mary of a family of 11, surviving. Also surviving was a young girl, Martha (Polly) Evans who was visiting.

James and Mary along with Martha Evans, were sold to French-Canadians by the Indians, rescued 3 years later (5 for James) by Thomas Evans, Martha's brother, and returned to Virginia. Martha married a Mr. Hummer and lived in Salem, VA, dying in 1827, 41 years after the ordeal. James returned to Abb's Valley, rebuilt the cabin burnt by the Indians in the raid, and died in his 81st year. Mary married the Rev. Samuel Brown and was widowed 20 years later. She was only 48 when she died, 6 years after her husband's death. The 3rd survivor, Joseph, returned to southwest Virginia to farm in Wright's Valley and died in 1848, probably around 73 years of age.

James, the "Captive," was born around 1770 at what is now known as Newell's Tavern near Natural Bridge, VA. He had 3 wives. The first was Barbara Taylor by whom he had 3 children, James Rutherford, Martha Poage, and William Taylor. She died shortly after William Taylor's birth. About a year later James married Nancy Shannon, born around 1783, daughter of Captain James Shannon by whom he had 9 children. They were married for some 20 years until her death whereupon he married Mary Robertson, née Price. She is reported to have left him and moved to Tennessee. They had no children. We don't know how long they were married but we do know that he lived some 27 years after his marriage to her, dying in 1851.

We don't know what happened to his oldest child, the 5th "James Moore." He is reported to have moved to Texas in 1845 after its admission to the Union, was a wealthy ranchman, and married an Indian woman.

Martha, the second child, married the Rev. Dr. Abraham Still, a Methodist minister and medical doctor. They moved to Kansas where he was a missionary to the Indian tribe that had killed his wife's grandparents and children. The Stills had 9 children, one of which, Andrew Taylor, was the founder of Osteopathy. Martha Still was 88 when she died.

William Taylor, the 3rd child, was married twice, first to Matilda Peery by whom he had 2 children, Lavinia and Elvira. Lavinia married Cyrus McDonald by whom she had 8 children. Elvira died as an infant. Two years after Matilda's death William Taylor, or "Squire" as he was called, married Mary Barns, by whom he had 9 children, one of whom, Robert Henry, died as a result of wounds received in the September 19, 1864 Civil War battle for Winchester. "Squire" Moore was 89 when he died; wife, Mary, lived an additional 6 years. It is through the Barns that "stiff fingers" (no joints in the fingers) is supposed to have come into the William Taylor line.

After William Taylor's mother's death, apparently in complication from his birth, he lived in Tennessee with her mother, Jane Walker Taylor, until he was 14, which would have been 1816. He then returned to Abb's Valley where he helped in working the family farm and which he later inherited from his father. When the Norfolk and Western Railway began developing the Pocahontas coalfield, he sold to them mineral rights to 1000 acres of the farm for coal development at $1.00 an acre. He is described as a zealous Methodist and contributor to the mission work in Africa of his cousin on his mother's side, Bishop Taylor.

The 4th child of James, the "Captive," was Sally Lain who married James Whitley by whom she had 8 children. It is not known Sally Lain's age at death. In a letter dated February 7, 1885, her brother, William Taylor, said that her son, Rufus Whitley, moved to Texas and that the rest of the family except one daughter went to Missouri "and did well." Daughter, Nancy, married Noah Bruce; Matilda married William Maxwell; Norman married Elizabeth Bowling; Rees married Elizabeth Witten; Barbara married James Gregory and Robert Crews; and William married Olivia Williams.

Joseph Addison, was the 5th child, and married his 1st cousin, Martha, daughter of his uncle Joseph, by whom he had 11 children. He lived in Wright's Valley where his uncle settled upon his return to Abb's Valley after the massacre. A son, William Taylor, was killed in the same battle at Winchester where his 1st cousin, Robert Henry, received his fatal wound. His other children were Nancy Jane, Martha Christine, Julia Ann, and Joseph Luther. He was 77 when he died.

Milton Ladd was the 6th child. He married Louisa Peery and moved to Missouri. No further information except a letter dated 2/28/1841 from him to his parents that is reproduced in the genealogical section on him.

The 6th child, Andrew Peery, married Nancy Cummings by whom he had 4 children, of which only 2 had children: John Columbus and Princess Palmyra. John married his 1st cousin, Mary Jane, daughter of his uncle, Isaac Quinn. Princess Palmyra married Charles Black and moved to California. Andrew was 61 when he died.

Mary Barns Moore, the 8th child, married William Whitley by whom she had five sons and one daughter. Each of the sons was a soldier in the C.S.A., one of whom was a Captain; daughter Emmaline married a C.S.A. soldier as well. Mary's age at date of death is not known.

Jane Shannon, the 9th child, married James Harvey Moore, her 1st cousin, son of her Uncle Joseph, by whom she had 3 children, and then married Charles Tiffany by who whom she had one child. Her daughter, Maria Tiffany, married Alexander St. Clair from whom the numerous "doctors" St. Clair of Bluefield a generation ago, were descended. Jane was 88 at her death.

The 10th child of James, the "Captive," was John Shannon Moore who married Margaret Whitley by whom he had 6 children and then married Emily Shannon by whom he had 5 more. Dr. Woodworth reports that the 3 younger children of Margaret Whitley Moore except Creed, which would be William Jackson, James, and David, went West after the War for Southern Independence with David settling near the Stills. Information about them is lost. Creed was killed in the 2nd battle of Winchester at which cousin, William Taylor, also was killed and cousin, Robert Henry, received his fatal wound. John Shannon Moore's age at death is not known.

Elizabeth, the 11th child, married the Rev. John Hoge; they had no children. Her age at death is not known.

The last and 12th child was Isaac Quinn who married Elizabeth Tabor by whom he had 8 children. Isaac Quinn was 72 when he died. Daughter, Mary Jane, married her 1st cousin, John, the son of her uncle Andrew. Three of the 8 children had no descendants. Nothing is known about descendants of Laura who married and moved to Ohio. Cosby married Charles Wilson; Edward Poage married Sarah Whitley and Myrtle Belcher, and Johnston Hoge married Lydia Compton.

Joseph, the 3rd surviving child of Captain James Moore, was born probably around 1773. After the massacre he lived with his mother's family in Rockbridge County, VA. until he was about 24 years of age when he moved back to southwestern Virginia to Wright's Valley. He married Christina Nicewander by whom he had 8 children, only 3 of which had children; James Harvey, Martha Poage, and Mary Brown. James Harvey married Jane Shannon Moore, his 1st cousin, by whom he had 3 children. After his death at an early age Jane married Charles Tiffany and had another child. Martha married the brother of her sister-in-law, her 1st cousin, by whom she had 11 children. Mary Brown married William V. Shannon, nephew of Nancy Shannon and grandson of Captain James Shannon. Joseph was probably around 75 at his death.

One final note: descendants of Captain James Moore in the C.S.A Army were 10, 4 of which were slain. There were a number of Still descendants in the Union Army but I do not have an accurate count.

HOW THE MOORES CAME TO AMERICA

Fincastle & Montgomery Counties Revolutionary War Record, 1775-1785, page 244, reports how our forbearer, James Moore, father of Captain James Moore, came to this country.

So far as Virginia is concerned from the first Colony in 1607 down to the present date, 1891, her age is not quite three centuries. It took 100 years for the infant settlement to extend as far out into the interior as the foot of the beautiful Blue Ridge. Beyond and over the ridge, so far as we know no eye of the white man had ever peered (save that of Capt. Bath and his little band in the year of 1670). The Valley of Virginia, Montgomery County (as it yet is) perched on the dividing crest, was a Terra incognita, or at least known only to the Red man. It was not until some time after Berkley, the Colonial Governor, and that remarkable man Nathaniel Bacon the revolutionist of 1675 that Governor Spottswood, at the head of a select Company, topped the Blue Ridge and sighted the valley at the head waters of the Shenandoah. It may well be supposed that after this many a hardy pioneer from the lowlands of Virginia, if for no more that adventures sake or mere hunting expeditions, followed in the wake of Spottswood and Bath and penetrated the lovely region at many an intermediate spot. Certain it is that in the year 1732 the tide of emigration began in reality to set in; from Pennsylvania in the Scotch Irish and Germans, the sternest and lordiest of men, the very sport of men upon whom, as a foundation, the country yet could be built. This was away down on the waters of the Potomac. It was about the 1734-5 that John Lewis (who had but lately landed from Ireland in Williamsburg, in company with John Mackey taking Salling as a guide) who had previously explored the country as far up as the James River, went as far as where Staunton now is and fixed a location eight miles below on which with his hardy family of 5 or 6 sons, Thomas, Andrew, Samuel, William, John and Charles he settled. On his return to Williamsburg he secured a grant from Governor Gooch of 100,000 acres, and met at the same time with Benjamin Borden, agent of Fairfax, just from England, who held a grant from James II of 500,000 acres to be located west of the Blue Ridge. It was this Borden who in the year 1737 returned to England and brought over 100 families, amongst whom were those excellent names the Alexanders, McDowells, Moores, McClung, McClures, Crawfords, Matthews, Archers, Pattons, Prestons, Trefords, et als, old settlers in old West Augusta.

A further description of how Southwest Virginia was settled appeared in an article by a Goodridge Wilson printed in The Clinch Valley News on 7/6/1941.

Two very large grants of land along the upper waters of the Shenandoah land were made, one to William Beverly and the other to Benjamin Burden (sic), on condition that the grantees settle a certain number of families upon them within a specified time. To meet that condition they induced a number of Scotch-Irish families to move down from Pennsylvania.

Foote's Sketches of Virginia, Volume II, has a chapter on New Providence, which contains an account of its origin by Rev. Samuel Houston, beginning with the grants to Beverly and Burden. He says: "The dividing line between their grants crossed the Valley near where New Providence church now stands. Those families that came first were nearly connected, or large families. For comfort and for safety they generally settled near each, and with the understanding that as soon as practicable they might have schools for their children, form religious societies and have places of public worship. These first settlers were near South Mountain, several of the name of Moore, others of Steel, McClung, Fulton, Beard; then a little farther on, my grandfather, John Houston, and his brother-in-law, John Montgomery, and some Eakens; near the middle of the valley on Kennedy's creek and its branches were the Kennedys, Wardlaws, Logans, another line of Steels, Edmundsons, Buchanans, Pattons, Millars, Stephensons; toward the North Mountain on Hays creek and Walkers creek were two families of Hays, four of Walkers, James Moore, two families of Robinson, one of Kelly, Hudson, Thompson, Smiley, and two Rheas; in the midst were three of the Berry family, one of Tedford, one McCampbell, two or three McCroskys and a Coalter family. In the course of a few years other families came and settled amongst them; their names were McNutt, Weir, Campbell, Wilson, Anderson, Culton, Henry, Lowry, another stock of Edmundsons, Todd, Stuart, Alexander, Crowder, Gray, Jamieson and two Pattons."

Captain James Moore, after winning an enviable reputation by his service during the Revolutionary war, moved from New Providence congregation and eventually found his way into Abb's Valley, Tazewell county. Here he was killed by Indians and his wife and children were killed or made captive. His daughter Mary, after being sold into servitude to a Canadian family, was rescued and brought back to relatives in the Valley. She married Rev. Samuel Brown, second pastor of New Providence, and is buried by his side in the old church graveyard. Her brother James went back to Abb's valley and many of his descendants are living in Southwest Virginia.

The House of Moore written by the Rev. Dr. William McPheeter (1778-1842) son of Rachel Moore & William McPheeter (she was a sister of Captain James Moore) gives further details on the early days of the James Moores in the new world:

My maternal grandfather was James Moore. He was born in Ireland, but of his parents I have received no information. It appears, however, that the family consisted of at least five children, viz: Joseph, James, John, Margaret, and Rachel.

James Moore, my grandfather, emigrated with his brother Joseph to America, state of Pennsylvania, sometime about the year 1726. John and his sisters Margaret and Rachel remained in Ireland. Joseph, the first named of this family, while in a course of preparation for the gospel ministry in Pennsylvania, died of consumption about the year 1727 or 1728.

My grandfather, after his arrival in America, married Jane Walker. She was also born in Ireland, and had emigrated to Pennsylvania some years after the emigration of my grandfather. They resided in Nottingham, a township in Chester County, Pennsylvania, until they removed to Walker's Creek, Rockbridge County, Virginia.

I have no recollection of my paternal grandparents, William McPheeter and Rebecca Thompson, but I have a distinct recollection of my maternal grandparents, James Moore and Jane Walker. In their advanced years they resided for some time at my father's house. My grandmother, owing to sickness or the infirmities of age, was confined pretty much to her room and bed. Both had long been members of the church and were, I believe, decidedly pious. I recollect that my grandfather used to retire regularly to his room upstairs, where, after closing the door, he used to remain for some time. Noticing this (when a small boy) and wishing to find out what he was about, I discovered through a small aperture under the door that he was on his knees engaged in prayer.

My grandfather, James Moore, died in Rockbridge County, Virginia, probably between the years of 1790 and 1796 and was buried in a graveyard on Walker's Creek, near Jump Mountain.

My grandmother lived, I think, a year or two after his death. She also died in Rockbridge County, south of Lexington, at the home of her daughter, (my aunt) Jane Walker.

Sometime before she died she remarked, "When I die I shall have a bonny easy death." Accordingly, during her last illness, some of the family were sitting in the room with her; she either turned herself over in the bed or was aided in doing so by someone present. Thus, lying still for some time, the remark was made: "Into what a fine, quiet sleep grandmother has fallen," (or words to that effect) but when after some time, her bed was approached, and her situation examined into, it was found that her spirit had quietly and without a struggle taken its flight to the unknown world. The remains were taken about 25 miles and buried beside her husband's grave.

EMINENT VIRGINIANS

The section of Dr. R.A. Brock's book, <u>Virginia and Virginians</u> subtitled "Eminent Virginians 1606-1888," on Tazewell County (he was Secretary of the Virginia Historical Society), had the following to say about some of our Moore ancestors:

James T. Moore

Born in Wrights Valley, Tazewell County, January 23, 1837, is a son of late Joseph A. Moore, a farmer of Abb's Valley, Blue Stone, and Wrights Valley, a grandson of James Moore who was captured by the Indians in Abb's Valley in early days, and a great-grandson of James Moore, whom the Indians killed in their massacre in the Valley. The mother of James T. is Martha P., daughter of Joseph Moore, a farmer, county clerk of Tazewell County, and who was a son of the James Moore above mentioned as escaping the massacre and carried away captive by the Indians.

James T. Moore entered service at Springville, Tazewell County, in 1861, in Company H, 45th Virginia Infantry, and participated in every movement of that company in the field until February, 1864. He then passed through the lines into Ohio, where he remained until May, 1865. His brother, William T. served in the same regiment until killed on the skirmish line near Winchester, in July 1864. Another brother, A.F., served a few months in the State Reserves.

John C. Moore

Was born on Christmas Day, 1852 in Abb's Valley near the place where his life was passed; was a farmer and lumberman, and a magistrate of the county; married in Tazewell County, October 15, 1874, Mary Jane Moore, and died on the 29th of March, 1887, leaving his widow with three children: Andrew Edward, Ida Maria and James Herbert. He was a son of the late Andrew Moore, a farmer of Abb's Valley, and a grandson of James Moore, also a farmer of the Valley. His mother was Nancy, daughter of John Cummings. Mrs. Mary J. Moore was born in the Blue Stone Valley, a daughter of Quinn Moore, who was a farmer of this county, and the son of the James Moore mentioned above. Her mother is Elizabeth, daughter of Daniel Tabor, a farmer of Blue Stone valley. Her father was in service in the Virginia militia during the late war.

Hon. William T. Moore

Was born March 7, 1802, on the old Moore homestead in Tazewell County where he still lives and which has always been his place of residence. He was for twenty-two years a magistrate of this county before the war, when what is now Bland, Mercer and McDowell counties were included in Tazewell County. Midnight often found him upon the Bench, so many were the cases brought before him, yet no appeal was ever taken from a decision he rendered. He married September 12, 1829 Matilda D., daughter of Thomas Peery, who was a planter of Abb's Valley, and whose father, George Peery, was a pioneer settler of that Valley. She was born January 26, 1811, and died January 1, 1842, having been the mother of two daughters, Lavinia W. and Elvira H., both deceased. He married secondly, at Wards Cove, September 12, 1844, Mary Barnes (sic), born at Wards Cove. Their children were nine, born in the order named: Robert, Henry, Matilda P., James Charles, Levisa W., Wm. Luther, Barbara J., Oscar B., Clinton D. and Mary E.

All are living but the first born, Robert Henry. This son, at the age of eighteen, entered the 45th Virginia Infantry, C.S.A., was wounded and made prisoner at Winchester, Virginia, September 19, 1864, and died of his wounds about three weeks later, at the house of the Rev. Mr. Eggleston. Mr. Moore had also three nephews killed in service.

William T. Moore is a son of the late James Moore who was captured by the Indians in Abb's Valley in 1784, in sight of his home, the Moore place, and taken to where Chillicothe, Ohio, now stands. They kept him two years, then sold him to the French for an old grey horse. The French held him prisoner three years, after which he was restored to his relatives. Two years after his capture the Indians returned to the Valley, killed his father and six of the family, captured the rest burned his mother and sister Jane at the stake. His father was Capt. James Moore, who served under General Greene in the Revolutionary war, and later discovered Abb's Valley, sometimes called "The beautiful valley of the sunless river." He was the first white man to settle there (sic), where he lived until massacred with his family on July 11 [sic], 1786. Six years later other settlers came to the Valley. The mother of Mrs. William T. Moore was Levicia, daughter of John Ward, whose father was the Major Ward who came from Ireland, served in the Revolutionary Army, and for whom Ward's Cove is named. Her father was the late William Barnes (sic), long a magistrate of Tazewell County, a son of Robert Barnes (sic) who came from Ireland, was one of the settlers of Ward's Cove, and a teacher there, a fine scholar.

HOWE'S HISTORY OF VIRGINIA

Howe in his <u>History of Virginia of 1865</u> wrote about Captain Moore's horses, particularly the stallion, Yorick. He had this to say:

> When Captain Moore and his family were massacred he had a splendid herd of about one hundred horses. A number of them were colts of Yorick, the Arabian stallion. Joseph Moore, a brother of the Captain, was then living in Kentucky. He came to Virginia and administered upon the estate of his deceased brother. When he returned to his home, he took a number of horses from Abb's Valley and disposed of them in Kentucky. It has been told, and it is a fact, the colts of Yorick had much to do with the production of the fine strain of horses from which Kentucky afterwards became famous. Some of Yorick's colts were left in Abb's Valley.

Howe's <u>History</u> has a picture of Rose, a grey mare who was 29 years old in 1918, the last known direct descendant of Yorick. Yorick killed 3 of the Indians who tried to ride him at the time of the massacre and was killed by the Indians when they could not subdue him. The picture has a young lad sitting on Rose who is Oscar Moore, Jr. 11/28/1911-3/28/1945.

Mrs. Helen B. Blankenship of Richlands, Virginia, sent me additional information on Yorick from Allison-Tayloe/Taylor research. A Charles Tayloe lived in Wrights Valley, being the son of Captain John Tayloe who surveyed Bristol in 1749. He was originally from Richmond County, Virginia. Captain James Moore bought Captain Tayloe's horse, Yorick, which had been raced in Richmond.

Mrs. Blankenship further said that her first cousin, Carl Myers, who lived in the Valley, was a friend of the "elder" Moore, whom I take to be Oscar Bascom. Carl told her that a farmer was plowing in a field (I presume in the Moore farm) and found the bones of a huge horse that was identified as Yorick. She believes that they were re-interned.

Howe's <u>History</u> also contains a write-up of Tazewell County. In it he describes the Moore massacre and ends this account with a dirge entitled "Moore's Lamentation" attributed to James Moore, the "Captive," written in memory of his slain mother. As a child, my great aunt, Mary Moore Davidson, sang it for me. I don't remember it as being especially tuneful. The words are as follows:

MOORE'S LAMENTATION

Assist me with words, Melpomene, assist me with skill to impart
The dolorous sorrow and pain that dwelt upon every heart,
When Moore and his infantile throng the savages cruel did slay,
His wife they led "Captive" along; with murmuring voice she did say:
"Farewell! Ye soft bowers so green, I'll traverse these valleys no more,

Beside yon murmuring stream lies bleeding the man I adore;
And with him my sweet innocent babes, these barbarous Indians have slain,
Were I but in one of their graves, then I would be free from my pain."
Once more on them she cast here eyes and bade them forever farewell.
Deep sobs from her bosom did rise, while she thus in anguish did wail.
The heathen her sorrows to crown, led her without further delay,
A victim to their Shawnee towns, and now comes her tragical day.
A council upon her was held, and she was condemned for to die;
On a rock they a fire did build, while she did their torments espy;
With splints of light wood they prepared to pierce in her body all round,
Her flesh for to mangle and tear. With sorrow she fell to the ground,
But her senses returning again, the mercy of God did implore.
"Thou Savior that for me wast slain and bathed in a bloody gore,
Have mercy now on me in death, and Heaven will sing forth thy praise
Soon as I have yielded my breath in a raging fiery blaze."
Then to her destruction proceeds each cruel bloodthirsty hellhound;
With lightwood they cause her to bleed, streaming from every wound.
The smoke from her body doth rise; she begs for their pity in vain:
These savages hear her cries, and with dancing laugh at her pain.
Three day in this manner she lay, tormented and bleeding the while,
But God His mercy displayed, and on her with pity did smile,
Growing angry at their cruel rage her soul would no longer confine.
Her torments He soon assuaged, and in praise she her breath did resign.
Let each noble, valorous youth, pity her deplorable end,
Awhile from your true loves part; join me each brother and friend,
For I have been where cannons roared and bullets did rapidly fly,
And yet I would venture once more, the Shawnees to conquer or die.

If it truly were written by James, it indicates that he was surprisingly well educated. The original of the dirge is at the Crab Orchard Museum, Tazewell, VA. Part of the letter sent to me with a copy of the dirge is paraphrased herewith:

It is reported that while captive among the Indians, James Moore learned their language, their ways, and their customs. He lived to be an old man and frequently visited the home of his young friends, Dr. Raleigh White Witten (1818-1898), and his wife Julie Virginia Harrison Witten, at Crab Orchard, now Pisgah. He would often entertain their children by donning his old Indian costume and dancing, whooping, and singing as he had seen the Indians do when he was a captive among them years before.

The original of the dirge was given to Dr. Witten's wife in 1844. In 1921, their daughter, Miss Marty Witten, gave it to Jeff Higginbotham of Pisgah.

Captives of Abbs Valley by The Rev. Dr. James Moore Brown on page 23 talks of the capture of James Moore:

About the middle of September, in the year above named (1784), he was sent after breakfast to bring a horse from the place where Mr. Poage had lived; the distance was about two miles. (He was fourteen years of age.) He had often gone there alone without fear; but on this occasion he had scarce lost sight of his father's house, when an unaccountable feeling of dread came over him; which became so distressing that he had at one time determined to go back, but was prevented from doing so by the fear of is father's displeasure. He never could explain this fear on any other ground, than that it was a strange presentiment of the evil, which was about to befall him. There is, however, one circumstance which I suppose makes the case entirely explicable without the necessity of having recourse to supernatural causes. He had spent the previous night till a late hour, reading the wild tale of <u>Valentine and Orson</u>, in which he was greatly interested; and the influence of the feeling of the past night still existed in his mind to some extent, though he knew not what it was. The account which he has since given of that matter, and which is here copied from his dictation, is that it was not dread of the Indians for he was not thinking of them. It was an undefined apprehension of some great calamity that would befall him; that perhaps some wild bear would devour him. (for full account, see <u>Howe's History of Virginia</u>, Sketches of Virginia by the Reverend Wm. Henry Foote, and reprint of James Moore's diary by James Douthart of Signal Mountain Press).

A copy of this book, <u>The Famous History of Valentine and Orson</u> is now owned by Historic Pocahontas Inc. for the Moore Family Association and is in its possession. It was procured by Robert H. Moore Jr., from a rare bookseller and donated to Historic Pocahontas for the Association. It is the 1738 edition published in England and could be of the same publication which James was reading. It is small, about the size of a pocket New Testament with very small type. Young James must have had excellent eyesight to read it! Obviously James was remarkably literate for someone at that time living in such an isolated place. It speaks well of the education he had or was receiving! The book will not be circulated.

THE JAMES MOORE APPLE TREE

The James Moore apple tree was considered one of the "Famous Trees of Virginia" and was the subject of an article by Irma Adams Gillespie, then of the Tazewell Study Circle. She recounts that the tree was planted by James Moore, the "Captive," in memory of his family members slain by the Indians. She describes it thus:

The apple scion that young James brought from the hills and planted in Abb's Valley developed into a tree that did not only yield well, but was a mark of beauty. The steady old tree stood for years and at the age of one hundred, it is said that it bore one hundred and sixteen bushels of delicious apples.

As time passed on the old tree began to disintegrate. Storms gradually broke limb after limb, but at a ripe old age it was at least four feet in diameter at the base of its trunk. Today it is no more. A few years ago the grand old tree had grown too old and too weak to resist the great pressure of the wind, the rain, and the snow. It fell, and great was its fall!

THE MARY MOORE CRADLE

The Rockbridge Historical Society of Lexington, VA has the cradle, made of walnut & poplar wood, six feet long, that Mary Moore slept in. It is described thusly (paraphrased):

> Invalid's (or Senility) Cradle
> Ca. 1800-20
> Walnut and poplar, six feel long
> Collection of the Rockbridge Historical Society, Lexington
>
> Mary Moore (1776-1824) is known in Virginia lore as the "Captive of Abb's Valley." During a raid on her Tazewell County home in 1786, Shawnee Indians massacred most of her family and abducted her. They took her to Ohio, where she was eventually sold into white slavery. After five years in Canada, Moore, at the age of fifteen, was rescued and returned to Virginia. She later married and became the mother of eleven children.
>
> As an older woman, perhaps haunted by her experiences in captivity, she slept in the large, specially constructed cradle-bed, in the effort to cure her insomnia. Similar cradles have been identified in collections in New York State and New England. Family tradition credits the crudely constructed bed to an unidentified cabinet maker in Brownsburg, VA.
>
> She was 48 when she died in 1824.

WILLIAM ANTHONY LATHROP

William Anthony Lathrop was a young engineer sent to Southwest Virginia with his new wife by the Southwest Virginia Improvement Company, predecessor of The Pocahontas Fuel Company, to develop the coal mine at Pocahontas, VA. The Norfolk and Western magazine of October, 1958 described the Lathrop's early adventures there. Below are excerpts:

> During their first two months in the region, the Lathrops lived in the home of a Squire Moore in Abb's Valley, which meant for the superintendent, "a horseback ride of seven miles night and morning," over the ridge to the forest-covered Laurel Valley, the site of the projected town of Pocahontas.
>
> The roads in winter were muddy almost beyond description. When their horses gave out, people rode mules, and one day the "lady from New York" saw a woman mounted, side saddle, on a cow. By summer the Lathrops had to take up mule riding while their horse was put out to grass for a while.
>
> Eager to see the beautiful country of blue grass, hill and valley, Mrs. Lathrop took her first riding lesson from the Squire's daughter, Barbara, a girl of her own age, and on

the old gentleman's pet horse "Rose." She wrote, "After my first sensation of being about 20 feet from the ground had passed, I enjoyed it very much. One ride in particular was about five miles away to which I called the Dividing Ridge between Virginia and West Virginia..... One could see the country for miles in every direction, not a sign of habitation, and all along the horizon the mountain, the bluest I ever saw.

2.

CAPTAIN MOORE'S WAR RECORD

Captain James Moore moved from Rockbridge County, Virginia to Abb's Valley in Tazewell County (then Montgomery County) in 1772. He was appointed a Lieutenant of Militia for Montgomery County five years later, February 26, 1777. He was 37 years of age.

The Revolutionary War Record of Fincastle and Montgomery Counties, 1775-1785, gives him as swearing allegiance to the state on October 5, 1777 along with others as follows:

A List of Persons Who Hath Sworn Allegiance to the State 1777

Oct. 5 1777

George Peerey
Joseph Turner
James Moore
Richard Grills
Thomas Ingles
William Hutchison
John Simpson
Thomas Poage

Source: Fincastle and Montgomery Counties Revolutionary War Record 1775-1785 page 66

The <u>War Record</u> gives the names of the persons in Captain Moore's Company, viz.:

A List of a Company of Militia in the County of Montgomery

Jas. Moore, Capt.	Wm. Kidd
George Peerey, 1st. Lieut.	John Peerey
Wm. McGuyer, 2d. Lieut.	John Simpson
Saml. Ferguson, Insign	John Howel Jones
Sutherlin Mayfield, Segt.	Jas. Cartmills
Solomon Struton, Segt.	Thos. Poage
Wm. Brown	John Compton, Junior
Nathaniel Man	Thos. Wiley
Absolam Staford	Jas. Shanon
Wm. Davidson	John Compton, Sen.
Jas. Mayfield	Wm. Peerey
Lou Brown	Wm. Watts
Shereld Atkins	Robt. Poage
Jno. English	Jno. Corder
John Lashley	John McGreyer
Uriah Stone	

Under Eighteen Years of Age

Henry Cartmill	Robt. Lasley
Joseph Davidson	

27 to be Drafted

Capt. Moore

Captain Moore's service was recognized in official reports as is shown by the by the listing, from the <u>War Record</u> account:

Names Mentioned in Military Accounts

Alex. Muley	Charles Deborax
John Gilliham	Coll. P. Love
Jas. Davis	John Gillion
Christian Shoults	Walter Carr
Hex. Chaney	Saml. Henley
Geo. Dougherty	Joseph McCormack
John Bark	John Tye
Robt. Young	Pat Henery
Matthews Little	Thos. Hughes
Wm. Ingram	Gideon Morris
Davd. Hukey	Jno. Miswaine
Jno. Cocks	John Burk
Wm. Ingram	John Malone
Jas. McCormack	John Swaine
John Drake	Geo. Little Thos. Reed
John Gibson	Wm Chary
James Moore	Jas. Maxell
Robert Moffell	
Wm. Maxwell	

Source: <u>Fincastle and Montgomery Counties Revolutionary War Record 1775-1785</u> page 166

Moore saw action in the battles of Point Pleasant, Cowpens, Alamance, Guilford Courthouse, and Kings Mountain, although that is not certain. The North Carolina DAR publication; <u>Biographical Sketches of Soldier Patriots in the Battle of Guilford Courthouse of March 15, 1781</u>, notes that he "led one of the frontier rifle companies at that hard fought battle." An account of that battle is given by Carolyn Szabad (M62154224), a Martha Poage Still descendent, as follows:

THE BATTLE OF GUILFORD COURTHOUSE

James led a rifle company of Virginia Militiamen, mostly mountaineers, under Col. William Campbell at the Battle of Guilford Courthouse on March 15, 1781. In this battle Nathaniel Greene with an assortment of American army and militia, engaged Cornwallis and his well trained regiments. Cornwallis and the British, attempting to break the gathering American strength in the south, had concentrated their efforts there since about 1778. By 1780 the British had substantial control of Georgia and South Carolina and were moving northward through the Carolinas to break into the more strongly held Virginia. The rugged militiamen, farmers and drovers who were not trained for war and were generally equipped only with their own personal gear had cost the British dearly at the Battle of Cowpens and at Kings Mountain. Nathaniel Greene, concerned that Cornwallis would succeed in positioning his troops north of him, assembled about 4,500 men, as many forces as he could muster, at Greensboro, NC with the goal of intercepting Cornwallis and breaking his military strength. He had the North Carolina and the Virginia Militia at the front lines waiting for the British arrival. Each militiaman was instructed that when the British got close enough to hit, he should fire off two rounds and then retreat. "By then, the enemy ranks were moving forward. Drums snapping, bagpipes skirling, bayonets glinting, they came at a measured pace across the cornfields toward the rail fence on which a thousand American guns rested. When they were 150 yards from the fence, the militia opened its first crashing round of fire. The British line, with great holes torn in it, staggered but re-formed and continued uphill, stepping over its dead" (From Guilford Courthouse Guide, National Park Service). The militia, as instructed, fired and withdrew, not necessarily in a very orderly manner, and the British just kept coming, battered by the militia and then by the Continental Army.

Captain Moore's company was responsible for the second-line confrontation. Because they were shooting from within trees and because of the shoot and withdraw plan, his company had dismounted and tied their horses out of rifle reach. When it was time for this company to retreat, they ran back (under fire) untied their horses, and withdrew. Captain Moore had trouble with his mettlesome horse, which was excited by the battle and wouldn't stand quiet enough for him to unite the reins. James' entire company was mounted and on the move by then, and mounted British Dragoons were charging them. James' thrifty Scots blood and frontier "make-do" attitude made him unwilling to cut the reins free, so he broke off the tree limb to which the reins were secured, swung up on his horse and tried to untangle the branch from the reins while in motion. The horse, already excited and now spooked by the dangling tree branch slapping its side, charged directly at the oncoming Dragoons, nearly reaching them before James was able to free the reins and turn his horse away.

Although the British were the victors in fact at Guilford Courthouse, it was a strategic loss for them, as they suffered very heavy losses. British strength in the South was indeed broken. Seven months later, in October, 1781, Cornwallis' surrender at Yorktown marked the formal end of British claim over the American colonies.

ANOTHER ACCOUNT OF MOORE'S SERVICE IN GUILFORD COURTHOUSE BATTLE

Another account of Captain Moore's service in the Battle of Guilford Courthouse is given in the application for a war pension by a Joseph Davidson. He states:

> In February 1781 there was a great alarm in the country from the supposed approach of the British army. The emergency was considered sufficiently important and pressing for Col. William Preston, who commanded the militia, to order out the men from the very borders of the settlements. Capt. Moore and his company were ordered into service and marched into North Carolina under Col. William Preston.

COMMANDANT OF DAVIDSON'S FORT AT COVE CREEK

In between these battles from 1777 and until his death, Captain Moore was Commandant of Davidson's Fort at Cove Creek. After his death, the Fort was commanded by Captain George Peery. Quoting from Joseph Davidson's application for a war pension is an incident describing Captain Moore's service as fort commander:

> Captain James Moore was charged with the defense of the neighborhood lying on Bluestone and Clinch rivers about their sources by Col. William Preston who was the colonel commandant of the militia in Montgomery County. He [Joseph Davidson] was very frequently called into service as an Indian scout or spy in the company of Capt. Moore. Early in the spring of 1776 Captain Moore, upon hearing that a strong party of Indians was lurking about the mountains of Guyandotte, summoned his men to an expedition. This was the first service of any note that he [Davidson] performed. He marched on this expedition as far as the Island of Guyandotte where it was said the Indians were encamped. They were, however gone before the whites arrived.

Prior to moving to Abb's Valley in 1772, it is reported that Moore had participated in the search for Mary Inglis who had been abducted by Indians in 1755. He would have been 15 years old then. His short life (he was 46 when killed) was filled with hardship and danger but of service to his community and country.

3.

ESTIMATE OF THE VALUATION OF CAPTAIN MOORE'S ESTATE

Given below is the appraisal ("Praisment") of Captain Moore's estate in pounds, shillings, and pence. It lists 43 horses and colts, 9 head of cattle, and miscellaneous items that survived the Indian raid. Converting the given currency into U.S. dollars at $1.43 to the pound, the present exchange rate, gives a value of $26,812.75, a rather handsome sum in those days!

Praisment of the Estate of Capt James More Dec.ᵈ

	£	Sᵒ	§
1 Bay Horse	12	0	0
1 Gray mare and yearling filley	17	0	0
1 Gray Horse	7	0	0
1 Brown mare	14	0	0
1 Chestnut sorrel horse	15	0	0
1 Gray Horse	7	0	0
1 Black mare and yearling	15	0	0
1 Spotted mare	10	0	0
1 Black mare	14	0	0
1 Bay horse	8	0	0
1 Black mare and Colt	5	0	0
1 Black horse	10	0	0
1 Black horse	9	0	0
1 Roan mare	5	10	0
1 Roan mare	8	0	0
1 White roan mare	7	0	0
1 Sorrel horse Coach	4	0	0
1 Roan horse	4	0	0
1 Mare yearling colt and bell	5	0	0
1 Bay yearling	5	10	0
1 Redroan mare and yearling	11	0	0
1 Black mare and yearling and bell	8	10	0
1 Black mare	6	0	0
Sundries of Iron utensils	2	15	0
9 yds Cloth	3	18	0
3 Sacks and nine Buckets salt	4	16	0
1 Gray mare	12	0	0
1 Black mare	10	0	0
1 Bay filley	4	10	0
1 Bay mare and yearling	14	0	0
1 Black mare and colt	10	0	0
1 Roan mare and yearling	6	0	0
1 Roan mare and yearling	14	0	0
1 Mare and colt	5	0	0
1 Gray mare and yearling	14	0	0
9 head of Cattle and a bell	18	0	0
1 Chist		8	0

Wm. Thompson
James Hoge   } Appraisers
Joseph Cloyd

At a court held for Montgomery County November 28ᵗ 1786
This inventory & Appraisment of the Estate of James Moore, Deceased
was returned to court & Ordered to be Recorded

List Abram Trigg ⁿᵐᶜ

It is curious that no valuation was placed on the land he owned. In a publication entitled <u>Land Speculation</u>, p138, in the Virginia Archives, Richmond, a James Moore is shown as owning in March, 1795 in Abb's Valley 259 acres according to a survey made by a Jesse Evans. This James Moore would be the "Captive" and the land must be what he had inherited. There is not a valuation on these acres. This publication notes that as of 6/17/1794 225,000 acres in an area near Roark's Gap was sold for $1570 or about 8 cents an acre. On Clear Fork of Wolf Creek it appears that on 3/20/1800 75,000 acres were sold for $14,000, indicating a value per acre of around 18 cents. The account in the publication does not say if the value of the dollars is current. Assuming the currency is in present dollars and averaging the above per acre sales prices, the 259 Abb's Valley acres listed above would have added $31.25 to the value of Captain Moore's estate.

John Simpson's estate was likewise appraised. It indicated that at death he owned 12 horses. I have not converted that into current dollars. No will is given for either Captain Moore or Simpson and I could not locate any further probate records. One wonders what disposition was made of Simpson's estate.

Joseph Moore, brother of Captain Moore, was appointed by the Court as "Executor and Administrator" of the estate of both Captain Moore and John Simpson. The orders directing this are found in the <u>Revolutionary War Records</u> in the Courthouse of Montgomery County in Christiansburg, VA. They are reproduced below.

Know all men, by these presents, that we Joseph Moore Andrew Moore David Sayers James Simpson & James Culton are held and firmly bound to Wm Davis Wm Love Thos Shannon Flower Swift & Joseph Cloyd, Gent. Justices of the court of Montgomery county, now setting in the sum of two thousand pounds Curr⁰ Money of Virg,ᵃ payment whereof, well and truly to be made to the said Justices, and their successors, we bind ourselves, and each of us, our, and each of our heirs, Executors, and administrators jointly and severally, firmly by these presents sealed, with our seals, this 22nd day of August in the year of our Lord one Thou-sand seven hunᵈ &eighty six and in the Tenth year of the Commonwealth.

The Condition of this Obligation is such that if the above bound Joseph Moor Administrator of all the goods, chattles, and credits of James Moor Deceased, do make or cause to be made, a true and perfect Inventory of all and singular the goods, chattles, and credits of the said Deceased which have or shall come to the hands, possession, or knowledge, of the said Joseph Moor or into the hands and possession of any other person or persons for him and the same so made do exhibit or cause to be exhibited, into the County Court of Montgomery at such time as he shall be thereunto required by the said court and the same goods, chattles, and credits, and all other the goods, chat-tles, and of the said Deceased, at the time of his Death, which at anytime after shall come to the hands or possession of the said Joseph or into the hands or possession of any Other person or persons for him do well and truly Administer according to Law; and farther do make a just and true account of all Actings and doings therein, when, thereto required, by the said Court: and all the rest and residue of the said goods, chattles and credits, which shall be found remain-ing upon the said Administrators Account the same being first Examined and allowed by the Justices of the court for the time being shall Deliver and pay unto such person or persons respectively, as the said Justices, by their Order, or Judgment, shall Direct pursuant to the Laws in that case made and provided. and if it shall hereafter appear that any Last will and Testament was made by the said Deceased and the Executor or Executors therein named do exhibit the same into the said Court, making request to have it allowed and approved accordingly, if the said Joseph Moore being thereunto required to render and Deliver up his Letters of Administration approbation of such Testament being had and made in the said Court then this Obligation to be void and of no Effect or else to remain in force and Virtue.
sealed and Delivered
in the presence of

}

Joseph Moore
Andrew Moore
David Sayer
James Simpson
James Culton

Because James after his return from captivity did not take up residence in Abb's Valley immediately but stayed with relatives in Rockbridge County, one must presume that he sold the horses, cattle, etc. that, he, Mary, and Joseph inherited from their father and divided the proceeds among them. I have found nothing that mentions this. Assuming that they received what the appraisal was, each would have gotten, if divided equally, some $9,000.00. James kept the land. Was an allowance given to Mary and Joseph for their share of that?

4.

CELEBRATION OF THE DEDICATION OF THE MOORE MONUMENT IN 1928

The <u>Bluefield Daily Telegraph</u> leading up to the Dedication of the Moore Monument in Abb's Valley on 7/14/1928, and on that day, had many accounts of the events that had occurred one hundred and fifty-two years before. The Dedication was also reported in the <u>Clinch Valley News</u>. It was a grand occasion! Below is given the 7/14/1928 and 7/15/1928 stories from the <u>Bluefield Daily Telegraph</u>.

BLUEFIELD DAILY TELEGRAPH
JULY 14, 1928

MOORE MONUMENT WILL BE UNVEILED

Immense Crowds Are Expected For Big Festival In Abbs Valley Today;
An Elaborate Program Is Planned

Just 142 years after an Indian band made an incursion into Abbs Valley, Tazewell county, Virginia, shot and killed Captain James Moore, a pioneer trail blazer and soldier of the Revolution, massacred other members of the Moore family, captured Moore's wife and several of their children and carried them away to undergo untold tortures and final death, a memorial in stately granite will be dedicated to the memory of these victims of the Shawnee tribe.

It was on July 14, 1786, that Captain James Moore was shot and killed in his yard while salting his stock. His cabin was attacked and burned by the Indians at the same time and this afternoon that tragic scene will be enacted on the same spot where the Moore cabin stood or nearly so. This will be carried out in mimic warfare by several Red Men, members of the various Red Men's lodges of the Bluefield region.

A human-like figure has been secured to represent Mrs. Moore. This will be tortured and burned as the savages engage in their war dance.

One of the largest assemblages of people seen in the east end of Tazewell county is expected to be present.

The towns have issued a proclamation declaring the day a holiday in commemoration of the dedication while various coal mines have issued orders to remain idle today.

Many distinguished people will attend the event, coming from hundreds of miles to be present.

The monument stands 14 feet high and is of granite. Bronze inscriptions will bear the name of the Moore Family and the date of the massacre.

A copper box will be enclosed in the shaft and in this box will be placed a number of relics. Several copies of newspapers dealing with the historic features of the dedication will be placed in the vault to be opened and read perhaps long after the present generation has passed away.

A large platform has been erected and covered, from which the speaking will take place. This stand is decorated with the Stars and Strips and bunting with two large American Flags waiving in the breeze nearby.

The program proper will be under the auspices of the American Legion Post of Pocahontas with the American Legion band furnishing the music.

The committee in charge has left nothing undone that would add to the comfort of the visitors. There is plenty of shade near by with ice water available for all. Numerous stands will be on the job to feed the hungry. Two large meadows have been thrown open for parking space.

The parade in Pocahontas will start at 9:30 o'clock and will wind its way into Abbs Valley, scene of the day's activities.

The program will be rendered on time and exactly as advertised. The unveiling of the monument will take place promptly at 1:30 o'clock. Governor Henry C. Stuart, of Russell county, scion of the Moore family, will act as master of ceremonies. Hon. J. W. Flanagan, of Dickenson county, will deliver an address, with short talks by several others. The committee does not desire to burden the crowd with too much speaking and will not do so.

Sherwood Anderson, who is known in every land and clime, will have a seat on the stage and no doubt will be called on for anything that he may desire to say. Mr. Anderson will be accompanied by Col. W. C. Pendleton, whose "History of Tazewell County" deals extensively with the Moore massacre.

Abbs Valley, scene of the dedication, is located on a hard surfaced road near Boissevain.

The place is reached from the east by Pocahontas and from the west by Tip Top.

Should the dirt roads be slick this morning it might be well to use the hard road by way of Pinnacle and Bramwell, but the Falls Mills road is in good shape and much used at this season.

Rain or shine the dedication will take place.

Bluefield Daily Telegraph
Sunday, July 15, 1928

Monument Honors Memory of Trail-Blazing Pioneers

Thousands Present for Moore Massacre Anniversary At Abbs Valley

Honorable J. W. Flannagan Makes Chief Address

Pageant Given By Red Men Depicts Events of Savage Raid; American Legion Has Charge of Program; Contests Feature All Day Fete

On a day far in the past the little "Valley of the Sunless River" resounded with the warwhoops of savages and the screams of their victims and the hillside was dyed with the blood of pioneers. But yesterday, 142 years later to a day, the valley echoed with the music of bands, the melody of the mountain man's fiddle, the chorus of men and women who sang that grand old hymn, "How Firm a Foundation," and the eloquence of silver-tongued orators.

And then, two daughters of the generations of today, deftly swept aside the white covering and a great granite monument marking the spot of the massacre of the Moore family in Abbs Valley by Black Wolf and his Shawnee tribe, was given to the sunlight.

It was a great occasion, and while the memorial may have been tardy as far as years are concerned, yet it is an accomplishment of which the whole section feels proud. There were many thousands present and the day was perfect for the purpose.

Marks Scene of Massacre

The monument marks the scene of the attack on the family of Captain James Moore by Shawnee Indians on the morning of July 14, 1786.

Captain Moore was shot, two children were tomahawked, another boy killed, a farm hand named Simpson shot. Mrs. Moore, Miss Evans, Jane and Mary Moore, John and the baby were taken away. The boy, John, was tomahawked and the baby's brains dashed out against a tree. Mrs. Moore and her daughter, Jane, were tortured with fire and burned at the stake. Out of the family of eleven persons, eight were murdered.

Monument is Near Highway

The monument has been placed near the public road on the site of the attack. It stands fourteen feet in height, counting the base. It is massive and bears an inscription on the side facing the highway.

The estate on which it is located is still in the Moore family, being owned by O.B. Moore, grandson of James Moore, II.

To the west of the monument a small stream flows down the valley and sinks at the foot of a hill and is said to pass underground for several miles, emerging near Pocahontas. This is why some one, according to Rev. W. C. Campbell, D.D., has called it the "Valley of the Sunless River." The proper name, however, is Abbs Valley, and it is one of the nicest sections of the splendid county of Tazewell.

The unveiling of the monument was under the direction and management of the Pocahontas Post of the American Legion, and a committee of which Dr. L.J. Stump was chairman and H.C. Callaway, secretary.

The big feature of the day's celebration was the unveiling of the monument and the pageant reproducing the tragic screams of 142 years ago.

Prominent People Participate

A large platform was erected near the monument and was occupied by prominent people of the section. Henry C. Callaway acted as chairman, ex Governor Henry C. Stuart being unable to attend on account of the death of a kinsman.

Lauds Pioneers

Hon J. W. Flannagan, of Clintwood, was the orator of the day, and he made a very fine address, reviewing the hardships and the bravery of the pioneer settlers, their contribution to the cause of liberty, and the making of this great republic. He paid them a fine tribute and declared on the foundation they had builded had been reared the greatest governmental structure of all times. He pointed out that strange and pernicious doctrines were making their appearance in the United States and expressed confidence that those who sprang from the pioneer stock would hold fast to the righteousness of old and the nation go on safely to greater achievement.

Chairman Callaway, on behalf of the descendants of the Moore family, presented Dr. L. J. Stump with a gold medal with an engraving of the monument on one side.

In response, Dr. Stump made an appropriate talk, expressing his appreciation.

At a signal from Chairman Callaway, Miss McDonald Moore, great-great-granddaughter of Cpt. James Moore, and whose home is on the old estate, and Mrs. Mary Moore Brown, also a great-great-granddaughter of the pioneer, drew the covering from the monument and a great cheer went up from the immense crowd.

The Red Men of Bluefield, Maybeury and Pocahontas enacted the tragedy, staging the scenes as on almost the exact spots where the various incidents actually occurred.

The cabin was destroyed and those who were left alive taken as prisoners. It was a very realistic battle. A reproduction of the cabin was burned and all the parts were faithfully portrayed by men and women of the neighborhood.

Thousand Present

A large field across the road from the monument was used as a parking ground and the traffic men in charge reported over two thousand automobiles. Various estimates were placed on the number attending, ranging from six to ten thousand. People came from all over the Clinch Valley and the neighboring counties in West Virginia and from distant states. Mayor Callaway and Dr. Stump and their aides handled the program in a masterly way in spite of the jam and confusion a great crowd occasions. There were no accidents, no misbehavior, and no event to mar the success of the day.

Edward Devors, of the Red Men, made an address at 11 a.m. He gave the history of the Red Men's order, its aims and purposes and its growth.

A group picture of the Moore descendants and connections was made. There were several hundred in this group.

Relics on Display

There was an all-day program of contests and races, prizes being offered for unusual exhibits and old and odd things. Among them were old newspapers, old automobiles.

The old fiddlers' contest was one of the interesting features of the all-day program. There were a number of ancient relics on display, among them Jim Moore's saddle, old time books and Indian relics. A large apple tree, brought from Rockbridge County and planted by James Moore, II, is still bearing fruit.

The Boy Scouts of Pocahontas and Bluefield, VA were most helpful in handling the crowds and doing turns for the convenience and comfort of the great crowd.

The traffic was in charge of a number of deputy vehicle commissioners under command of W.C. Breckinridge. The squad include E.H. Hedrick, Giles County; J.B. Boyd, Russell County; Charles Lee, Washington County. They were assisted by several police officers of Pocahontas.

Monument Was Long Advocated

The first suggestion that a monument to mark the scene of the Abbs Valley massacre was made by the late I. F. Johnson, president of the Norfolk and Western, and many times, at intervals, advocated by The Daily Telegraph. The monument is one of the handsomest marking a historic spot in the western-half of Virginia. It is of Georgia granite, and was made by Wright & Matthews of Bluefield, VA. The funds were provided by the descendants of the pioneer Moores. In a copper receptacle in the base of the monument is a list of the descendants who were present yesterday and registered, together with copies of The Daily Telegraph and Clinch Valley News, dated yesterday.

The beautiful and historic mansion house of the estate, owned by O.B. Moore, was thrown open to visitors and many parties ate their picnic dinners on the spacious lawn.

Many direct descendants were present, as evidenced by the photograph taken at the time. Thirty-four have been able to be identified.

Dedication of Moore Monument
July 14, 1928
Abb's Valley, Virginia

1. William Oscar Moore (Col.)	8. Trula McDowell	15. Edward Poage Moore	22. Samuel Elbert Mustard	29. McDonald Moore Mullins
2. Matilda Moore Mustard	9. Dr. Wade Hampton StClair	16. Myrtle Moore (Mrs. Edward Poage Moore)	23. Sally Wilson Moore (Mrs. O. B. Moore)	30. Mary Moore Wilson
3. Barbara Elvira Moore	10. Otis Eugene StClair	17. Paul Scott	24. Oscar Bascom Moore	31. Robert H. Moore, Jr.
4. Oscar Jasper Mustard	11. Rob Roy StClair	18. Florence Keister	25. Ora Virginia Moore Tabor	32. Byron Linwell Beamer
5. James William Moore	12. Robert Clinton Mustard	19. Margaret E. Moore	26. Margaret Emory Moore Scott	33. John Freeman Moore
6. John William Wilson	13. Margaret StClair Moore (Mrs. R. H. Moore)	20. Robert Henry Moore	27. Elizabeth Mustard Elmore	34. Andrew Edward Moore
7. Sidney Baxter Wilson	14. Glenn StClair	21. LaVicie Moore Higginbotham	28. Virginia Mustard Welch	

5.

ABB'S VALLEY MISCELLANEOUS

Grave locations in the Moore Family cemetery at the Moore farm.

I am indebted to Nancy A. Nash for identifying the grave locations and charting them. A copy of her work from which the drawing was made is below:

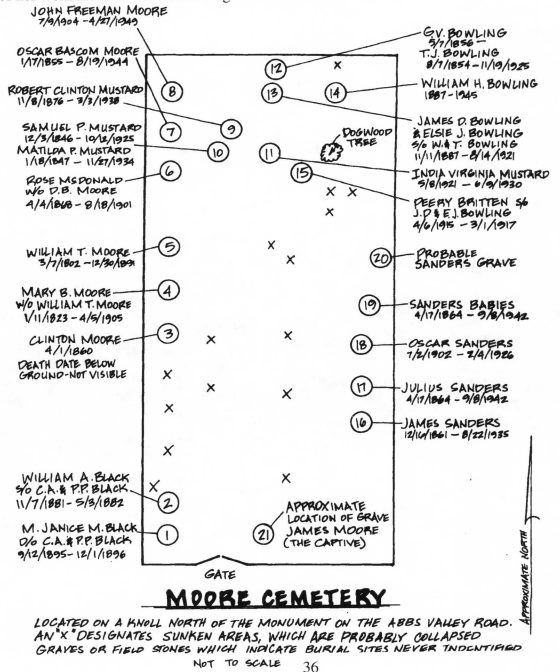

JOHN FREEMAN MOORE
7/9/1904 - 4/27/1949

OSCAR BASCOM MOORE
1/17/1855 - 8/19/1944

ROBERT CLINTON MUSTARD
11/8/1876 - 3/3/1938

SAMUEL P. MUSTARD
12/3/1846 - 10/12/1925

MATILDA P. MUSTARD
1/18/1847 - 11/27/1934

ROSE MCDONALD
W/O D.B. MOORE
4/4/1868 - 8/18/1901

WILLIAM T. MOORE
3/7/1802 - 12/30/1891

MARY B. MOORE
W/O WILLIAM T. MOORE
1/11/1823 - 4/5/1905

CLINTON MOORE
4/1/1860
DEATH DATE BELOW
GROUND - NOT VISIBLE

WILLIAM A. BLACK
S/O C.A. & P.P. BLACK
11/7/1881 - 5/3/1882

M. JANICE M. BLACK
D/O C.A. & P.P. BLACK
9/12/1895 - 12/1/1896

G.V. BOWLING
5/7/1856 -
T.J. BOWLING
8/7/1854 - 11/19/1925

WILLIAM H. BOWLING
1887 - 1945

JAMES D. BOWLING
& ELSIE J. BOWLING
S/O W. & T. BOWLING
11/11/1887 - 8/14/1921

DOGWOOD TREE

INDIA VIRGINIA MUSTARD
5/8/1921 - 6/9/1930

PEERY BRITTEN S/O
J.D & E.J. BOWLING
4/6/1915 - 3/1/1917

PROBABLE SANDERS GRAVE

SANDERS BABIES
4/17/1864 - 9/8/1942

OSCAR SANDERS
7/2/1902 - 2/4/1926

JULIUS SANDERS
4/17/1864 - 9/8/1942

JAMES SANDERS
12/16/1861 - 8/22/1935

APPROXIMATE
LOCATION OF GRAVE
JAMES MOORE
(THE CAPTIVE)

GATE

MOORE CEMETERY

LOCATED ON A KNOLL NORTH OF THE MONUMENT ON THE ABBS VALLEY ROAD. AN "X" DESIGNATES SUNKEN AREAS, WHICH ARE PROBABLY COLLAPSED GRAVES OR FIELD STONES WHICH INDICATE BURIAL SITES NEVER IDENTIFIED.

APPROXIMATE NORTH

NOT TO SCALE

Approximate location of Moore family homes in Abb's Valley in the 1800 and 1900's.

Seven home locations are given on the rough map below. The memory of a number of persons was drawn on to develop the map, which I trust is reasonably accurate.

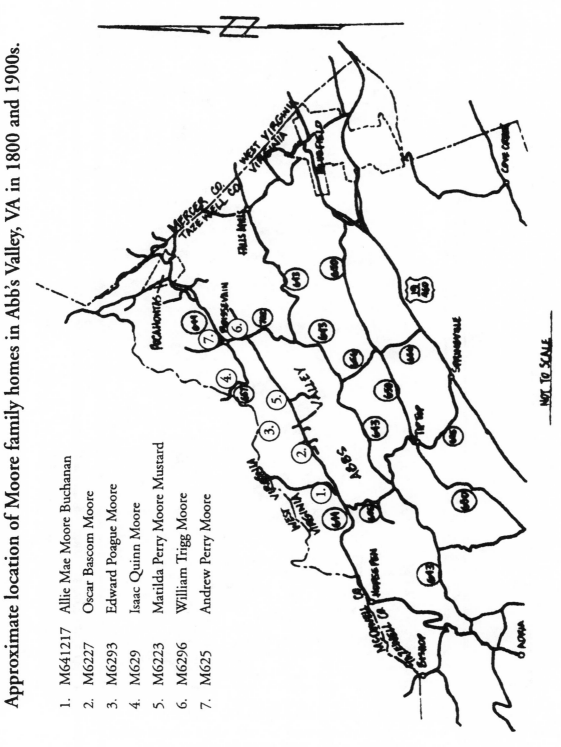

Approximate location of Moore family homes in Abb's Valley, VA in 1800 and 1900s.

1. M641217   Allie Mae Moore Buchanan
2. M6227   Oscar Bascom Moore
3. M6293   Edward Poague Moore
4. M629   Isaac Quinn Moore
5. M6223   Matilda Perry Moore Mustard
6. M6296   William Trigg Moore
7. M625   Andrew Perry Moore

Given below is a sketch of the Moore Farm in Abb's Valley.

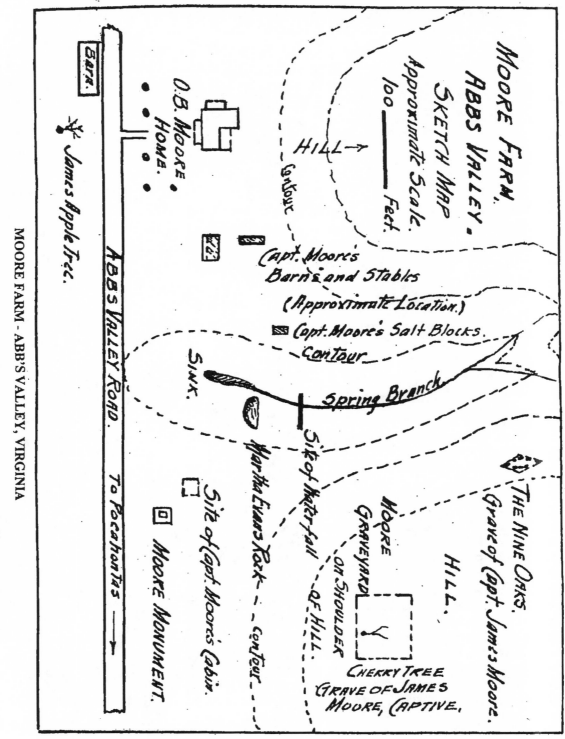

MOORE FARM - ABB'S VALLEY, VIRGINIA

This map shows the approximate location of the scenes of the massacre and modern conditions. On his permanent return to Tazewell County, James Moore, the captive, built his first house at the site of his father's cabin. But in 1822 he built two houses, large and small, on the site where Mr. Oscar Bascom Moore lived.

6.

MOORE FARM ARCHEOLOGICAL INVESTIGATION AND LISTING IN THE COMMONWEALTH AND NATIONAL REGISTERS OF HISTORIC PLACES

On October 26, 27, and 28, 2000, the Moore Family Association in connection with others, sponsored an archeological investigation of the Moore farm homestead to develop support for inclusion in the Commonwealth and National Registers of Historic Places. This was successful. The Association was informed that the "Captain James Moore Archeological site in Tazewell County, Virginia (VDHR file #092-5042) was officially listed on the Virginia Landmarks Register on 9/11/02 and on the National Register of Historic Places on 11/24/02."

The Abstract, Summary and Recommendations of the report of the investigation are given below.

Abstract

This report documents a preliminary archaeological investigation of the Capt. James Moore farmstead, 44TZ131, in Tazewell County, Virginia, conducted on October 26, 27, and 28, 2000. This site is located in Abb's Valley, along Route 644, about half a mile west of the Boissevain Elementary School. The project was sponsored by the Moore Family Association, working in cooperation with the Roanoke Regional Office of the Virginia Department of Historic Resources, Historic Pocahontas, Inc., and local citizens and school classes. The purpose of the investigation was to identify the precise location of the Capt. James Moore cabin, and other potential structures or activity areas, and to gather information to assess the site's eligibility for the National Register of Historic Places.

An area near a 1928 commemorative monument had been identified in Moore family tradition as the site of the Capt. James Moore family cabin. This area was thoroughly investigated, and 18th century ceramics and wrought nails were found in this spot. Other nearby areas were also investigated, but failed to produce artifacts overlying from this time period. An 13th century midden capped by a day fill, with early 19th century artifacts overlying the fill, was identified in the central portion of this area. Below the fill are artifacts from the original Moore family occupation, 1772 until the 1786 attack and burning of the cabin. Above the fill are remains from the 1798-1822 house of James Moore Jr. (James, the "Captive," in Moore family parlance). No architectural features were found from either cabin/house. The site also contains artifacts, and possibly two post molds, from a prehistoric occupation, with Late Archaic occupied indicated by Brewerton Side Notched projectile points, and a Late Woodland occupation indicated by Clarksville Triangular projectile points and Radford Ware ceramics.

It is our recommendation that the site has a high level of integrity and research potential and should be considered eligible for nomination to the National Register of Historic Places.

Summary and Recommendations

The 1786 attack of a large group of Shawnee on the Capt. James Moore family is well known in the history of southwestern Virginia, and is strongly commemorated by descendants, many of whom are active in the Moore Family Association. In 2000 this association sponsored an archaeological investigation to verify the location of the original Moore farmstead and cabin, and to assess the site's integrity for potential nomination to the National Register of Historic Places.

This investigation was conducted in October, 2000, and resulted in the location of sealed deposits containing 18th century artifacts, in the area identified by family history. Those deposits are sealed by a clay cap, over which are artifacts from the 1798-1822 occupation of James Moore Jr. (James, the "Captive"), who had returned to the homesite from which he himself had been captured in 1784. If the family history is also correct about the location of the original barns and outbuildings, these were located across the ravine, where James built his second house in 1822, and where at least two subsequent houses have been built. Thus they have likely been destroyed by the rebuilding episodes.

In contrast, the original cabin site seems to have been used only for agricultural purposes after 1822, with no mixing of later artifacts, and no substantial disturbances. While no 1772 or 1798 architectural features have been identified, the presence of two sealed short term historic middens, one 1772 to 1786 and the other 1798 to 1822, each connected with a rich family history, offers many opportunities to study the domestic life and material culture of the early Euro-American settlers to this area. The site also offers the potential to study the material culture and lifeways of earlier Indian inhabitants, since midden deposits containing Late Archaic and Late Woodland artifacts were identified below the 1772-1786 midden. These prehistoric deposits also contain at least two post molds, which could even represent a house, most likely from the Late Woodland occupation.

The integrity of these deposits is very high, and the significance of the site is also increased by its association with a person as locally famous as Capt. James Moore (a Revolutionary War hero) and an event, the 1786 attack on the Moore family, that has played such a prominent role in the history of southwestern Virginia. It is recommended that this site be carefully preserved for further study. A first step would be its nomination to the National Register of Historic Places. The site has been donated by the Moore family to Historic Pocahontas, Inc., for future safekeeping. If preservation easements or deed covenants are not already in place with this transfer, they might be considered. Additional archaeological investigations should include the excavation of a much larger area in large test units, possibly a large block style excavation, to look for structural features such as a chimney pad, or posts from piers which supported the cabin. The prehistoric component should also be investigated further, initially expanding out from the Unit I already completed, to provide more insight into the two posts and their association with other possible features.

Given the demonstrated interest of the local community, it is suggested that any future archaeological efforts include a public component, such as volunteer involvement in excavation, both by individuals and school classes, and the use of web sites to disseminate the information. We have found internet web sites to be a great way for large numbers of people to follow the progress of an excavation even if they cannot come to a site. Examples of recent web sites on frontier sites we have been involved with include those for Arbuckle's Fort in Greenbrier County, West Virginia (http:// www.greenbrierhistorical .org) maintained by the Greenbrier Historical Society, and Fort Edwards, in Mineral County, West Virginia (http://wwwfortcdwards.org), maintained by the Fort Edwards Foundation.

A copy of the complete report can be obtained from the Moore Family Association for a modest fee.

7.

THE MARTHA POAGE MOORE STILL LINE

Of the descendants of James Moore, "The Captive," the Martha Poage Moore Still line is probably the most interesting. She was born the 28th of January, 1800, and was the second child of James Moore, "The Captive." James, after his return from captivity, lived for a while in Kentucky with his mother's family, the Poages, and returned to Abbs Valley in March of 1789. He and Barbara Taylor, Martha's mother, were married on February 16, 1797. Martha married Abraham Still, a Methodist minister, on January 22, 1822 by whom she had nine children. See Woodworth's edition of The Captives of Abbs Valley for information on them. I shall attempt to bring that line up-to-date.

Abraham Still was born in Buncombe County, North Carolina, about 1797. The family moved to Tennessee where he was ordained as a preacher in the Holston Conference, Methodist Episcopal Church, and sent as a circuit rider to Tazewell County in the southwestern part of Virginia. While there he married Martha Moore. They soon moved to Lee County, Virginia, and then to New Market, Jefferson County, Tennessee. He was at one time Parson Brownlow's family physician at Knoxville, Tennessee, an ardent abolitionist.

Wanting to get into a new country where he could get land cheaply, the Rev. Still took a transfer from the Holston Conference, to the Missouri Conference of the M.E. Church. Moving from there he settled in Macon County, Missouri, near Bloomington, on May 2, 1837, and bought a land claim. Three years later he bought another claim in Schuyler County, and moved there. The family stayed there for five or six years, moving back to the same place in Macon County, about 1845. They remained in Macon County for some years, during which time the division in the Methodist Church took place. The Rev. Still, stayed with the old or Methodist Episcopal Church, which rendered him politically unpopular. Being a "free soiler" made it dangerous to his life; he asked the Methodist Conference for an appointment to a charge where he would be in less danger. He was sent to Kansas Territory to the Shawnee Mission about 1852, to the same Indians who massacred his wife's family, they having been transferred there by the United States Government. He found the same names among these Indians as those in the east and some of them remembered the event of his mother-in-law, Martha Poage Moore's, tragic death.

While in Missouri, the Rev. Still served the M.E. Church as circuit rider and presiding elder, and at the same time administered to the sick. "He would often have to stop in the fall season to attend the sick. His universal practice was to keep in his saddlebags with his Bible, a well filled-wallet of medicines in sections of cane stalks, as bottles were liable to break. Thus provided, he was prepared for the comfort of both soul and body." Adapted from notes by Dr. E.C. Still, the Rev. Abraham Still's son.

Martha and Abraham Still were ardent abolitionists and as such were caught up into the pro/anti slavery troubles in Kansas. For more about this, see Frontier Doctor,

<u>Medical Pioneer</u> by Charles E. Still, Jr. published by The Thomas Jefferson University Press at Northeast Missouri State University, Kirksville, Missouri, 1991. Fred Brown, one of John Brown's sons, who was shot by the pro-slavery men, is said to have died in Martha's arms. She was called the "Mother of Kansas." Biographical sheets on the descendants of Martha and Abraham Still follow the genealogical charts.

I am indebted to Lt.C. William L. Still, of Winchester, VA, a descendant of Thomas Chalmers Still, for information about his father, Mently F. Still. In a letter to me he wrote:

Dad was a remarkable man and was blind long before he even met my mother, and he never saw any of his children. However, he refused to admit defeat in any mechanical problem. I helped him deepen a neighbors well through solid rock, where he drilled the blast holes with a single-jack, set the charges, lit the fuse and then climbed out of the hole to wait for the blast. I saw him design and build an automatic load control system for home-built firewood saw without the availability of a machine shop. I saw him take over as foreman of a repair shop and get a company's logging trucks back on the road. I saw him virtually save a well from being abandoned when a tool was hung up in the hole.

Col. Still is a former newspaper editor and publisher and produced the syndicated radio program: "Health News." He has written a number of books on topics as varied as politics, finance, and health.

I am indebted also to Doreen Roden, daughter of Ernest Mently Still, for this history on the Thomas Chalmers Still line.

Dr. Thomas and Martha Still were living in Kansas near his parents. They went to California in 1863 in an oxen wagon train. Brother John and sister Cassandra and husband Dr. James McCollum came also. They had two sons, Abram and William, born in Kansas. Son, Edward, was born in Nebraska on the way. Thomas had a timber claim near Sabastopol. He owned a sawmill; Aruna Still was born there. Thomas moved to San Luis Obispo in 1867. Othor and Thomas Jr. were born there. He moved to Pozo Ortiga and homesteaded in 1872. Dabirma was born there. He built the first ever house there and half of it is still stands. Thomas and his son, William, helped build an irrigation canal in the valley about 100 miles from their home. That was in 1875.

Thomas moved to LaPanza, then a mining claim area, in 1879. Edward, Abram and William stayed in Pozo Ortiga and were partners in sheep herding. They decided to separate around 1895, with William moving to LaPanza. Abram married and owned property in Pozo Ortiga area. He had a post office and library in his house. The post office was named Annette. Edward's wife, Lelia Penwell, was the first teacher in a school called Antelope Valley School. It started in 1887 and closed in 1901. It was moved up-hill and renamed Annette School. Ernest,

Grace, Ellen, Eleanor, and Doreen went to this school. See the genealogical charts for this relationship. It closed in 1951. Edward married Lelia in 1896. They were sheep herders and raised sheep.

Thomas built a two-story house in LaPanza, in which he had a post office and grocery store. His daughter, Dabirma, took over the post office in 1900 until it was closed in 1935. Thomas and Martha had a place for people to eat and sleep. They were located on a road people traveled to go from McKitreck to San Luis Obispo. Thomas built part of this road. They also rented land and raised cattle. Their brand was 69. They had a dairy near their house. Their sons, Othor and William, helped them.

Thomas' daughter, Aruna, was 11 when they moved to LaPanza. She taught children in their house. There were many mines in the area. She could speak Spanish and so often served as an interpreter. She married Albert Davies who lived in the Annette area. He grew wheat also. They moved to the Northern part of California? and went into the car business. Ernest and Eleanor were close to them. I remember Aunt Runa.

In 1896 Thomas went to Kirksville, Mo. to study at his brother, Andrew Still's, school of Osteopathy, who was the founder of Osteopathy. He then opened an office in a hotel in San Luis Obispo, where his daughter, Dabirma, helped him. Martha, his wife, got sick so they returned to LaPanza. He always was the doctor in that area. Dabirma, called Birma, liked to take pictures. She and son, Othor, kept a family history. Daughters' Una and Ione were also interested in the family genealogy. Othor gave me the information I'm writing. I enjoyed visits with him and wish I had written down things he said. Ione was a very good painter. The horses she drew were perfect.

Dr. Thomas Still's Son, Mentley, lost his eyesight when he was 13. His wife, Anna, was a teacher at Annette School. She taught both my mother and father. Mentley repaired cars and made clocks from kits he got from Sears. Anna wrote the poetry that Mentley composed. They moved to the L.A. area and I am now in touch with his son, Abe. We are losing the Still name. He had two brothers that had sons. Abe has two daughters.

Edward carved "Rock of Ages Cleft for Me, Let Me Hide Myself in Thee - 1888 EMS" in a rock about 6 miles from where I live now. I have a picture of Grace, Paul, Eleanor, Ernest, Ellen and Glen Tabler above the carving.

Edward died in 1915. There was no high school here until 1920 so Lelia rented out the ranch in 1917 and moved to the San Jose area. She had there an orchard of walnuts, prunes, and apricots. A boy, Percy Catlin, had come from England to the area so he moved in with Edward and Lelia and was like a son to them. He helped Lelia with the orchard.

Ernest, (Doreen's father), went to high school in 1916 in New York. His mother's sister lived there. I still have the football he got from being on the team. We have many family things. He joined the army in World War I. His mother signed for him because he was not old enough. We have the discharge papers signed by Eisenhower. He then finished high school in San Jose. The ranch lease was up so he moved back to Annette and 3 years later married Eleanor. They grew wheat and raised cattle. They lived in the house built by Thomas (Edward, Lelia and their family lived there). I was about 5 years old when Ernest moved half of the house. The other half had a basement so it couldn't be moved. We lived in this house while he built an adobe house. The part he moved had two bedrooms and a hallway. He built an area on one side that was a kitchen/dining room and sitting room all in one. When we moved into the new house the other became the house for men working for us (called the Bunkhouse). Eleanor cooked 3 meals a day for men working the ranch. Ernest bought some other land down in the flat where I live now. Ernest drilled wells on this flat land and had a few spots to plant and irrigate. He was one of a group interested in a canal for irrigation. A canal of water has been brought from North California to L.A. for drinking water and is also used for irrigation. My husband, Bill, developed this land near where we live and we now have pistachios. He sold some of the land with irrigation rights where the owners have put in a large pistachio orchard and some grapes.

Grace and Paul Wallin, (Doreen's Aunt), lived in the Annette area and then in another area close by and later moved up North. Paul died so Grace moved in with Lelia, her mother, took care of her, and worked in that area. She put her two girls through school. She always loved the country life. She had a nice horse when she was young and won many horse races with it. She told me that she and Ernest liked to ride to LaPanza. She said her Grandma Martha was a good cook. Of course, I think that everyone in my family were good cooks. They sold the orchard and built a place to stay. Grace lived in it until recently. They sold all of it. Her daughter, Mim, took care of her there for 5 years. She lived to be 103 and I have enjoyed several visits with her.

Ellen Still became a teacher. She and her husband, Glenn, lived in the Annette area where she taught at the Annette School for two years. They moved to Arizona where they had a soda fountain. Both children were born there. She and her husband got a divorce and her children stayed with us. She became a teacher at another one room school nearby so I grew up very close to Elroy and Joyce, the children. They still seem like my own brother and sister. Ellen taught at the school from 1938 to 1957. She married Earl Newsom, a very nice person, who worked for Ernest. He could do many things - work with leather - weld water lines, etc. Edward and Lelia had donated the land to the Annette School so when it closed Lelia gave it to Ellen and Earl and they built a house there. Ellen moved to Nevada with her daughter, Joyce, after Earl died.

Jean Garlinghouse Witwer of Evergreen, Colorado has sent me a copy of the obituary of her uncle, Dr Richard E. Garlinghouse of Lincoln, Nebraska, which recounts an illustrious medical career:

A memorial service is scheduled for 1:30 p.m. Friday (1993) at Westminster Presbyterian Church, 2110 Sheridan Blvd., for longtime Lincoln physician, Dr. Richard E. Garlinghouse. He died Wednesday at age 83. Garlinghouse was elected president of the Nebraska State Medical Association in 1943 and was appointed to the state Board of Health in 1967. He was a founding fellow of the American College of Obstetrics and Gynecology. He also served as president of the Nebraska State Obstetrics and Gynecological Society and of the American College of Surgeons, Nebraska Chapter. A 1930 graduate of the University of Kansas, Garlinghouse graduated from the University of Pennsylvania College of Medicine in 1934, and began practicing medicine in Lincoln in 1937. He served as chief of staff at Bryan Memorial Hospital from 1953 to 1957.

Mrs. Witwer is married to Dr. John Witwer, who is the State Representative (R) from Evergreen on the Colorado Legislature. He practiced medicine for 30 years before getting into public service. He was a flight surgeon with the Army in Vietnam before retiring from the Army in 1996, specializing in radiology. He is on the Joint Budget Committee of the legistlature. His background in medicine makes him valuable on healthcare matters.

Biographical information on other Martha Poage Moore descendants is in the bio sheets following.

8.

THE MARTHA POAGE MOORE STILL LINE
GENEALOGICAL CHARTS

M621 *Martha Poage Moore - Abraham Still*

B. 1/28/1800   M. 8/21/1822   B. 8/25/1796
D. 12/25/1888   D. 12/31/1867

M6211 Edward Cox Still - Mary Susan Powell
B. 1/15/1824   B. 4/20/1848   B. 9/27/1824
D. 5/8/1906   D. 10/20/1882

M62111 - Fleetwood Churchill Still
B. 1/25/1849
D. 11/21/1853

M62112 - William Moore Still
B. 1/11/1851
D. 3/23/1851

M62113 - Joseph Maclise Still
B. 8/30/1852
D. 11/11/1853

M62114 - John Jay Still - Margaret Jones
B. 11/3/1854   M. 2/23/1881   B. _____
D. 8/22/1931   D. _____

M621141 - Annie Christine Still
B. 5/8/1887
D. _____

M621142 - Gladys Mary Still - Clair Wyman Ward
B. 11/13/1890   M. 2/20/1913   B. 1/26/1884
D. _____   D. _____

*Indicates that a bio is included.

M6211421 - Margaret Ward - Dale B. Lillywhite
    B. 2/14/1914   M. 7/24/1937   B. 7/17/1913
    D. _____   D. _____

M6211422 - Owen Jay Ward
    B. 5/30/1917
    D. _____

M6211423 - Janet Elizabeth Ward
    B. 9/28/1918
    D. _____

M62115 - James Edward Still
  B. 2/3/1857
  D. 4/7/1879

M62116 - Sarah Margaretta Still - Robert Harvey Dunnington
  B. 2/3/1857   M. 5/12/1880   B. 2/25/1847
  D. 12/24/1883   D. 10/4/1926

M621161 - Carl Still Dunnington - Nora Ellen Clarke
    B. 4/1/1882 M. 10/23/07   B. 2/12/1887
    D. _____   D. _____

M6211611 - Robert Clarke Dunnington - Gladys Marie Brown
    B. 8/11/1909   M. 9/9/1933   B. 11/3/1912
    D. _____   D. _____

*M62116111 - Patricia Louise Dunnington - Leroy Allen (Div.)
    B. 1/27/1935   M. 8/28/1955   B. 4/1/1934

M621161111 - Cynthia Ann Allen - Richard John Esmerian
    B. 11/13/1956   M. 6/20/1993   B. 1/18/1954

M6211611111 - Clarke Jarett Esmerian
    B. 5/4/1995

M6211611112 - Alexandria Elizabeth Esmerian
    B. 10/10/1996

M621161112 - Lisa Kay Allen - Timothy James Osse
    B. 12/7/1960   M. 8/9/1986   B. 10/25/1957

M621161113 - Mark Clarke Allen – Andrea G. Jopillo
    B. 8/2/1968   M. 11/24/2000   B. 12/1/1959

*M62116112 - Roberta Dunnington - James Edward Stuckey
    B. 1/5/1942   M. 2/28/1963   B. 10/3/1939

*M621161121 - Kimberly Dawn Stuckey
    B. 1/29/1974

*M62116113 - Annette Dunnington - Stanley Harrison
    B. 7/20/1944   M. 11/26/1968   B. 1/9/1946

*M621161131 - Stephanie Ann Harrison
    B. 3/31/1969

*M621161132 – Jason Earle Harrison
    B. 12/21/1973

M6211612 - William Glenn Dunnington - Ethel Emma Wolverton
    B. 9/5/1910   M. 10/1/1932   B. 1/7/1911
    D. 6/18/1993   D. 10/30/1969

M62116121 - Rachel Ann Dunnington - Bob Bondshu
    B. 8/29/1933   M. _____   B. _____

M621161211 - William Harold Bondshu
    B. _____

M621161212 - Coby Ann Bondshu
    B. _____

M621161213 - Frank Albert Bondshu
    B. _____

M621161214 - Krista Sue Bondshu
    B. _____

M62116122 - Marjorie Sue Dunnington - (1) Edward Dinges
    B. 2/26/1936   M.(1) _____   B. 4/5/1931
                    M.(2) _____   D. 1/16/1990

                                    (2) James Burpo
                                      B. 4/19/1934

*M621161221 - (1)Kristan Suzanne Dinges - Dale Eugene Hruby
    B. 11/24/1960   M. 2/25/1984   B. 6/16/1960

    *M6211612211 – Nathaniel Dale Hruby
        B. 1/31/1993

    *M6211612212 - Nicholas Glenn Hruby
        B. 10/7/1995

M621161222 - (1)Jennifer Elizabeth Dinges - Shon T. Erwin
    B. 4/10/1962   M. 5/22/1982   B. _____

    M6211612221 - Maeghan Sue Erwin
        B. 11/23/1982
        D. 12/17/1985

    M6211612222 - Dylan Dinges Erwin
        B. 12/18/1988

    M6211612223 – Haley Emma Erwin
        B. 6/27/1991

M621161223 - (1)Pamela Mitchell Dinges - Jay L. Davis
      B. 9/8/1968   M. 5/15/1993   B. _____

      M6211612231 – Allison Sue Davis
            B. 5/8/1996

      M6211612232 – Grant Louis Davis
            B. 8/20/1999

*M62116123 - Warren Harvey Dunnington - Elizabeth _____
    B. 4/17/1937   M._____   B. _____
    D. 8/18/1996

      *M621161231 - Melissa Ann Dunnington – Eric William Craven
          B. 4/29/1961   M. 5/28/1983   B. 3/5/1961

      M621161232 - Kathleen Elizabeth Dunnington
          B. 8/4/1965

      *M621161233 - Edward William Dunnington – Stefanie Ellen Walton
          B. 8/20/1969   M. 6/6/1992   B. 6/4/1969

    *M62116124 - Glenn Walter Dunnington - Margaret M. Lentine
      B. 9/17/1940   M. 11/22/1969   B. 3/12/1941

      *M621161241 - Cheryl Emma Dunnington - Troy J. Dunn
          B. 9/15/1972   M. 7/22/1995   B. 5/30/1960

      *M621161242 - Angela Marie Dunnington
          B. 6/13/1974

M6211613 - Ellen Still Dunnington - Lois Athel Smith
    B. 10/29/1912   M. 5/28/1932   B. 8/13/1908
    D. _____   D. _____

M62116131 - Carl Gene Smith - Henrianna _____
B. 2/24/1933   M. _____   B. _____

    M621161311 - Laura Ellen Smith
         B. _____

    M621161312 - Lee Ann Smith
         B. _____

    M621161313 - Glenn Robert Smith
         B. _____

    M621161314 - Holley Sue Smith
         B. _____

M62116132 - Jack Still Smith -   (1)Betty _____
B. 5/12/1935   M. (1) _____   B. _____
               M. (2) _____
                             (2)   Carol Jo _____
                                   B. _____

    M621161321 - (1)Zetta Loyce Smith
         B. _____

    M621161322 - (1)Joetta Still Smith
         B. _____

    M621161323 - (1)Kelvin Gene Smith
         B. _____

M62116133 - William Clarke Smith - Barbara Wessels
         B. _____   M. _____   B. _____

    M621161331 - Lois Ann Smith
         B. _____

    M621161332 - Lee Smith
         B. _____

M621161333 - William Clarke Smith, Jr.
    B. _____

M62116134 - Nancy Ellen Smith
    B. _____

M6211614 - Male
    B. 2/9/1919
    D. 2/10/1919

M6211615 - Mary Louise Dunnington - Alfred Raymond Barbour
    B. 8/19/1922   M. 12/30/1944   B. 12/6/1917
    D. 4/3/2000

   ***M62116151** - Melissa Ann Barbour - James Edward Sutton
        B. 10/17/1945   M. 6/22/1974   B. 5/5/1945

      M621161511 - Nora Barbour Sutton
            B. 1/9/1982

      M621161512 - Roberta Barbour Sutton
            B. 10/19/1984

   ***M62116152** - Mary Louise Barbour - (1) Michael Dunn
        B. 5/1/1950   (1) M. 5/6/1978   B. 6/4/1949
                              (2) M. 5/21/1988

                                (2) Charles Alexander Hatvany
                                B. 7/4/1950

      M621161521 - (2) Thomas Charles Hatvany
            B. 6/12/1990

   ***M62116153** - Alfred Dunnington Barbour - Mary Elizabeth Pearson
        B. 12/14/1955   M. 5/17/1980   B. 10/31/1955

      ***M621161531** – Anna Christina Barbour
            B. 7/27/1998

M62117 - Thomas Abraham Still - Clella Tula Richardson
    B. 12/20/1859   M. 1/11/1883   B. 12/14/1864
    D. 9/3/1911   D. 10/18/1919

M621171 - Edward Clark Still - June Blanch Marquith
    B. 11/10/1883   M. 12/25/1904   B. 6/7/1884
    D. _____   D. _____

M6211711 - Mabel Alvena Still - Alfred Neil Sharpe
    B. 11/25/1905   M. 6/25/1923   B. 12/3/1899
    D. _____   D. _____

M62117111 - Constance Lucille Sharpe
    B. 1/4/1925

M62117112 - Audrey Marquith Sharpe
    B. 8/12/1929

M6211712 - Frank Alva Still - Gladys Mae White
    B. 8/16/07 M. 10/15/1933 B. 1/18/1907
    D. _____   D. _____

M62117121 - Robert Edward Still
    B. 9/7/1934

M62117122 - John Marquith Still
    B. 7/23/1938

M62117123 - Jerold Marcus Still
    B. 7/23/1938

M6211713 - Blanch Jean Still - Ivan W. Bays
    B. 12/17/1909   M. 6/24/1925   B. _____
    D. _____   D. _____

M6211714 - Theodore Andrew Still
    B. 3/19/1921

M621172 - Della Jean Still
    B. 10/15/1885
    D. 8/22/1898

M621173 - Thomas Eugene Still
    B. 9/5/1887
    D. 2/5/1917

M621174 - Ruth Jane Still
    B. 11/20/1889
    D. 3/27/1935

M621175 - Mary Margaret Still - J. Samuel Lafferty
    B. 4/30/ 1893   M. _____   B. _____
    D. _____   D. _____

M621176 - Helen Dorothy Still - Frank Jones
    B. 8/9/1897 M. _____   B. _____
    D. _____   D. _____

M6212   James Moore Still - Rahab Mercy Saunders
    B.   2/5/1826   M. 7/18/1850   B. 5/15/1831
    D.   1/8/1907   D. 7/18/1907

M62121 - Martha Elizabeth Still
    B. 12/7/1851
    D. 1866

M62122 - Summerfield Saunders Still - Ella Daugherty
    B. 12/7/1851   M. 10/3/1877   B. 2/8/1856
    D. 11/20/1931   D. 6/21/1938

M621221 - George Anderson Still -   (1) Cora Cleophas
    B. 3/12/1882   M. (1) 6/1904   B. _____
    D. 11/23/1922   M. (2) 3/10/1906   D. 6/1904

(2) Ardella Dockery
B. 4/10/1879
D. _____

M621222 - Delia Frank Still - Guy B. Brunk
B. 7/24/1883   M. 6/27/1904   B. 4/15/1908
D. _____   D. _____

M6212221 - William Summerfield Brunk - Charlotte Marie Dickson
B. 4/9/1907   M. 7/6/1929   B. 4/15/1908
D. _____   D. _____

M62122211 - Charlotte Delia Judith Brunk
B. _____

M6212222 - Guy George Brunk - Sidney Mae Hines
B. 12/2/1910   M. 11/20/1937   B. 1/17/1912
D. _____   D. _____

M62122221 - Guy Edward Brunk
B. _____

M62123 - Susan Sorepta Still
B. 1853
D. As infant

M62124 - Mary Jane Findley Still - Anderson Craig
B. 1/11/1855   M. 12/17/1874   B. 6/23/1851
D. 2/22/1927   D. 4/26/1917

M621241 - Arthur Still Craig - Melle Rosimin Campbell
B. 9/9/1875   M.12/25/1900   B. 1876
D. _____   D. ____

M6212411 - Arthur Craig
  B. 1901
  D. 1902

M6212412 - Anderson Craig - _____
  B. 1904   M. _____   B. _____
  D. _____   D. _____

  M62124121 - Anderson Craig, Jr.
    B. 1938

M6212413 - Howard Campbell Craig - _____
  B. 1914   M. 1937   B. _____
  D. ____   D. _____

M621242 - Beulah R. Craig - Curtis Hammond Coe
  B. 9/11/1879   M. 10/25/1904   B. 9/26/1869
  D. _____   D. _____

  M6212421 - Mary Edna Coe - O.B. Lester
    B. 9/29/1905   M. 3/28/1925   B. _____
    D. _____   D. _____

  M6212422 - Curtis Craig Coe
    B. 2/16/1906
    D. _____

  M6212423 - Virginia Coe - Bernard LeDow Hamman
    B. 2/27/1915   M. 8/15/1937   B. _____
    D. _____   D. _____

M62125 - James Abram Still - Jennie Allen
  B. 11/8/1858   M. 6/17/1885   B. 7/22/1858
  D. 2/21/1914   D. _____

M621251 - Mary Gertrude Still - Charles James Ritchey
    B. 5/16/1891   M. 6/29/1916   B. 10/13/1885
    D. _____   D. _____

    M6212511 - Leslie McCaw Ritchey - Edith Margaret Ahern
        B. 12/19/1918   M. 5/22/1942   B. _____
        D. _____   D. _____

    M6212512 - Frances Arlene Ritchey
        B. 1/24/1923

M621252 - Virgil Farris Still - Hazel Elizabeth Dalziel
    B. 9/26/1897   M. 7/15/1924   B. 7/22/1900
    D. _____   D. _____

    M6212521 - Joanne Elizabeth Still
        B. 4/14/1926

    M6212522 - Allen Burt Still
        B. 3/5/1932

M6213 Andrew Taylor Still - (1) Mary Margaret Vaughan
    B. 8/6/1828   M. (1) 1/24/1849   B. _____
    D. 12/12/1917   M. (2) 11/25/1860   D. 9/29/1859

                            (2) Mary Elvira Turner
                                 B. 9/24/1834
                               D. 5/28/1910

M62131 - (1) Marusha Hale Still - John William Cowgill
    B. 12/8/1849   M. 12/6/1870   B. _____
    D. _____   D. _____

    M621311 - Marguerite Cowgill
        B. 9/12/1871
        D. 6/6/1897

M621312 - Janette Still Cowgill - Richard E. Hambeck
    B. 9/5/1872   M. 8/23/1900   B. _____
    D. _____   D. _____

M621313 - Henry Rutherford Cowgill - Zoe Ella Cooper
    B. 5/5/1876   M. 2/8/1905   B. _____
    D. _____   D. _____

    M6213131 - Elizabeth Aldeen Cowgill
        B. 12/27/1905
        D. _____

M621314 - Ralph E. Cowgill - Muriel Shaw
    B. 9/28/1877   M. _____   B. _____
    D. _____   D. _____

M621315 - Martha S. Cowgill - Purl Russell
    B. 3/6/1883   M. _____   B. _____
    D. _____   D. _____

    M6213151 - Zella Russell
        B. 10/20/1905
        D. _____

    M6213152 - Ruth Russell
        B. 12/4/1907
        D. _____

M621316 - Florence V. Cowgill - W.H. Remoly
    B. 3/10/1887   M. 3/1915 B. _____
    D. _____   D. _____

M621317 - Gertrude Cowgill - F.C. Martin
    B. 1/9/1890   M. 4/1915 B. _____
    D. _____   D. _____

M621318 - Alfred T. Cowgill - Laura Ranier
      B. 8/25/1892   M. _____   B. _____
      D. _____   D. _____

M62132 - **(1)** Abraham Price Still
     B. 11/12/1852
     D. 2/8/1864

M62132x - **(1)** George W. Still
     B. 3/9/1855
     D. 3/10/1855

M62133 - **(1)** Susan B. Still
     B. 4/11/1856
     D. 2/7/1864

M62133x - **(1)** Lorenzo Waugh Still
     B. 7/29/1859
     C. 8/4/1859

M62134 - **(2)** Dudley Turner Still
     B. 9/12/1861
     D. 11/2/1861

M62134x - **(2)** Marcia Ione Still
     B. 1/13/1863
     D. 2/23/1864

M62135 - **(2)** Charles Edward Still - Anna Florence Rider
     B. 1/7/1865   M. 7/30/1892   B. 12/19/1869
     D. _____   D. _____

M621351 - Harold Rider Still
     B. 4/11/1893
     D. 12/23/1893

M621352 - Helen Gladys Still
 B. 12/10/1894
 D. 9/3/1919

M621353 - Andrew Taylor Still
 B. 9/10/1897
 D. 10/3/1905

M621354 - Mary Elizabeth Still - Crawford Myles Easterline
 B. 11/1/1899 M. 2/11/1931 B. _____
 D. _____   D. _____

  M6213541 - Charles Still Easterline
   B. 7/22/1933

*M621355 - Charles Edward Still, Jr. - Dorris Shelton
 B. 3/26/1907 M. 6/9/1936 B. 8/25/1906
 D. _____   D. _____

  *M6213551 - Charles Shelton Still
   B. 2/16/1938

M62136 - **(2)** Herman Taylor Still -   (1) Bessie Updyke
 B. 5/25/1867 M. (1) 10/3/1893 B. 2/29/1876
 D. 10/25/1941 M. (2) 2/28/1918

             (2) Lottie Garrish
             B. _____

  M621361 - (1) Eugene Updyke Still - (1) Kathleen Sullivan
   B. 8/20/1898 M. (1) 8/10/1922 B. _____
   D. _____   M. (2) 12/20/1940 D. _____

            (2) Josephine Arnold
            B. 6/3/1914

   *M6213611 - (1) Eugene Updyke Still, Jr. – (1) Carlene Woodward (Div)
    B. 8/20/1941 M. (1) 10/10/1964 B. 6/3/1943
         M. (2) _____

(2) Susan_____
B. _____

*M621362 - (2) Herman Taylor Still, Jr.
B. 3/1920

M62137 - **(2)** Harry Mix Still - Nancy Miller
B. 5/25/1867   M.   10/7/1892   B. 7/28/1864
D. 7/28/1942   D. 10/30/1926

M621371 - Fred Mix Still - Blanche Laughlin McGinnis
B. 7/25   M.   2/10/1919   B.   2/7/1900

M6213711 - Andrew Taylor Still - Joice Page
B. _____   M. 3/17/1941   B. 6/10/1918
D. _____   D. _____

M6213712 - Harry Stanley Still
B. 4/10/1926

M621372 - Richard Harry Still - Frances Hamilton
B. 11/25/1903   M. 11/5/1930   B. 2/7/1904
D. _____   D. _____

M6213721 - Richard Harry Still, Jr. – (1) Gloria Lanza
B. 9/3/1931   M. (1)   _____   B. 12/25/1931
                 (2) 8/18/1973

(2) Roberta Elizabeth Sheffler
B.10/19/1946

*M62137211 - (1) Richard Harry Still, III – (1) Michele Cianci
B. 2/14/1953   M. (1) 6/30/1985   B. 10/11/1955
              M. (2) 3/19/2000

(2) Donna Geringer
B. 5/2/1966

M62137212 – (1) Mark Lanza Still
         B. 3/10/1959

M62137213 – (1) Adam Hamilton Still - _____
         B. 1/13/1963   M. _____   B. _____
         (Has 2 children)

M62137214 - (2) Boaz Alexander Still
         B. 1/9/1979

M62137215 - (2) Ann Taylor Still
         B. 7/20/1981

M62138 - **(2)** Fred Still
   B. 1/25/1874
   D. 6/6/1894

M62139 - **(2)** Martha Helen Blanche Still - George Mark Laughlin
         B. 1/5/1876   M. 4/11/1900   B. 1872
         D. 1957   D. 1948

M621391 - Mary Jane Laughlin - (1) John Stedman Denslow
         B. 1/17/1914   M (1) 8/22/1934   B. _____
         D. 1/15/1989   (2) 6/19/1976
                    (3) _____

                                (2) Martin Lowry
                                   B. _____

                                (3) James Wadlin
                                   B. _____

      M6213911 - (1) Martha Stedman Denslow - Calvin H. VanO'Linda (Div)
            B. 1/21/1937   M. 6/5/1956   B. 1965

M62139111 - Christopher Allen VanO'Linda - Lynda S. Wanwicke Hewitt
    B. 1/5/1957   M. 5/25/1983   B. _____

    M621391111 - Calvin VanO'Linda
        B. 10/1986

    M621391112 - Jessee Roy VanO'Linda
        B. 8/19/1987

    M621391113 - Katherine Rose VanO'Linda
        B. 8/19/1987

M6213912 - (1) Michael Taylor Denslow - Roberta Chornock
    B. 6/25/1939   M. 5/15/1971   B. _____
                                        D. 11/14/1998

    M62139121 - Jacquiline Michail Denslow
        B. 12/17/1973
        D. 6/28/1988

    M62139122 - Jennifer Catherine Denslow
        B. 12/17/1973

    M62139123 - John William Denslow
        B. 8/18/1983

M6213913 - (1) Peter Ross Denslow - Sharon Doran
    B. 1/21/1944   M. 1/24/1965   B. 7/7/1945

    M62139131 - Amy Denise Denslow - Greg Dimberg
        B. 1/30/1967   M. 2/22/1986   B. 3/5/1963

        M621391311 - Jena Leigh Dimberg
            B. 11/20/1987

        M621391312 - Cody Douglas Dimberg
            B. 1/15/1992

M62139132 - Michael Alan Denslow - Jennifer Faith
B. 11/21/1969   M. 6/1998 B. _____

M621391321 - Jacob Stedman Denslow
B. 1/13/1998

M621391322 - Madalyn Faith Denslow
B. 8/11/1999

M621392 - George Andrew Laughlin - V. Elizabeth Peterson
B. 6/17/1918   M. 6/7/1942   B. 5/6/1921
D. 10/1981

*****M6213921** - Patrick Andrew Laughlin - Susan Jacobson (Div)
B. 11/28/1943   M. 6/1964   B. 12/12/1942

*****M6213922** - Anne Lisabeth Laughlin - Carrold James Kempf
B. 12/16/1946   M. 4/1972   B. 10/2/1944

  *****M62139221** - Nathan Andrew Kempf – Renea Fredricksen
B. 11/17/1974   M. 7/19/2003   B. _____

  *****M62139222** - Joshua Paul Kempf
B. 2/25/1977

  *****M62139223** - Rachael Anne Kempf
B. 12/12/1978

  *****M62139224** - Aaron Matthew Kempf
B. 1/24/1984

*****M6213923** - Susan Denise Laughlin - Charles F. Hunter IV (Div)
B. 11/19/1948   M. 6/5/1970   B. 11/19/1946

*****M62139231** - Michael Brian Hunter - Molly Markway
B. 1/15/1971   M. 8/15/1995   B. 4/20/1973

*M621392311 - Grace Elizabeth Hunter
B. 8/20/2000

*M621392312 – Samuel Patrick Hunter
B. 3/21/2002

*M62139232 - Julianne Rebecca Hunter
B. 3/10/1973

M6214 Barbara Jane Poage Still - Frederick Philemon Vaughan
B. 11/29/1830   M. 1/23/1847   B. 11/7/1827
D.   3/4/1894   D. 10/24/1906

M62141 - Martha Moore Vaughan - Champ H. Graham
B. 11/3/1849   M. 1869   B. 2/15/1846
D. _____   D. 2/17/1916

M621411 - Edward Graham
Died as infant

M621412 - Katherine Graham
B. 9/19/1873
D. 11/17/1895

M621413 - Edith Barbia Graham - Page E. Hudson
B. 3/28/1876   M. 12/17/1902   B. 3/6/1874
D. 1/18/1917

M621414 - Finley Vaughan Graham - Josephine Wiggins
B. 3/8/1878   M. 6/20/1908   B. _____
D. _____   D. _____

M6214141 - Champ H. Graham, II
B. 4/17/1915
D. _____

M6214142 - Sarah Graham
B. 11/11/1918
D. _____

M621415 - Sylvia Graham
B. 1881
D. 1903

M621416 - Rose Graham - Ethelbert Jackson Hubbard
B. 5/18/1884   M. 12/6/1911   B. _____
D. _____   D. _____

    M6214161 - Jack Champ Hubbard
    B. 12/17/1913
    D. _____

    M6214162 - Martha Hubbard
    B. 12/5/1915
    D. 7/7/1916

    M6214163 - Rose Ethel Hubbard
    B. 7/2/1917
    D. _____

    M6214164 - David Graham Hubbard
    B. 10/5/1920
    D. _____

M621417 - Pansy Graham
B. 1885
D. 1887

M62142 - Catherine Connor Vaughan - Samuel Davidson Barnett
B. 1/25/1852   M. 8/23/1875   B. 2/7/1849
D. 12/18/1919   D. 10/12/1917

M621421 - Wilbur Carlyle Barnett
B. 12/24/1878
D. _____

M621422 - Samuel Arthur Barnett - Ethel Hannah Heryford
B. 12/20/1880   M. 4/6/1910   B. 7/13/1888
D. _____   D. _____

    M6214221 - Donald Arthur Barnett - Dorothy Elizabeth Ward
    B. 6/4/1915   M. 6/4/1938   B. 2/14/1915
    D. _____   D. _____

    M6214222 - Doris Elizabeth Barnett
    B. 6/9/1917
    D. _____

    M6214223 - Alvin Lee Barnett
    B. 11/14/1918
    D. _____

M621423 - Leta Winifred Barnett - Robert Lee Browning
B. 6/28/1883   M. 11/3/1909   B. 9/1/1885
D. 12/13/1930   D. _____

    M6214231 - Leota Vocile Browning - Robert Timothy Fairchild
    B. 11/9/1910   M. 6/22/1930   B. 7/16/1904
    D. _____   D. _____

        M62142311 - Robert Bertram Fairchild
        B. 5/12/1931

        M62142312 - Olive Rhae Fairchild
        B. 7/26/1932

        M62142313 - Patricia Louella Fairchild
        B. 8/30/1936

M6214232 - Virgil Lee Browning
    B. 11/1/1913
    D. 3/28/1921

M6214233 - Robert Lee Browning
    B. 4/5/1915
    D. _____

M621424 – Barbara Rosa Barnett - William Williamson Shelly
    B. 2/11/1889   M. 5/5/1928   B. 7/15/1880
    D. _____   D. _____

M621425 – Catherine Goldie Barnett
    B. 10/7/1832
    D. 8/7/1898

M62142x - Dudley Still Vaughan
    B. 5/27/1854
    D. 1859

M62143 - James Bradley Finley Vaughan
    B. 8/30/1856
    D. 1888

M62143x - William Vaughan
    B. 10/16/1858
    D. 1859

M62143y - Sarah C. Vaughan
    B. 9/5/1859
    D. 1859

M62144 - Frederick Philemon Vaughan - Stella Fluke
    B. 5/11/1861   M. _____   B._____
    D. _____   D. _____

D. _____   D. _____

M62145 - Winifred Marovia Vaughan - R. Douglas Fluke
B. 7/11/1863   M. _____   B. _____
D. 11/20/1926   D. _____

M62146 - Barbara Ann Frances Vaughan - Harvey Leander Kennedy
B. 10/26/1867   M. 5/9/1897   B. 11/10/1868
D. _____   D. 12/28/1937

M621461 - Harold Douglas Kennedy - Lela Cronin
B. 2/16/1898   M. 6/9/1919   B. _____
D. _____   D. _____

M6214611 - Mary Frances Kennedy
B. _____
D. 1926

M6214612 - James Cronin Kennedy
B. 8/8/1922

M6214613 - Elaine Kennedy
B. 7/1929

M621462 - Murray Vaughan Kennedy - Freda McDaniel
B. 11/30/1899   M. 11/1929   B. _____
D. _____   D. _____

M6214621 - Ken Kennedy
B. 4/4/1932

M621463 - Karl Leander Kennedy - Edyth Floyd
B. 5/12/1903   M. 1924   B. _____
D. _____   D. _____

M6214631 - Karen Ann Kennedy
B. 8/8/1927

M621464 - Barbara Jane Kennedy - Paul Richard Glanville
B.   6/25/1907   M.   2/1928   B. _____
D. _____   D. _____

    M6214641 - Barbara Ann Glanville
    B.   2/11/1932

    M6214642 - Jane Themaine Glanville
    B.   3/10/1935

M62147 - Abram Still Vaughan - Ida Caroline Amsden
B. 3/5/1871   M. 7/10/1895   B.   4/20/1872
D. _____   D. _____

    M621471 - Clara Caroline Vaughan - Philip James Thompson
    B.   3/31/1896   M.   8/16/1917   B. 12/6/1896
    D. _____   D. _____

        M6214711 - Neva Jean Thompson
        B. 4/22/1919
        D. 9/6/1919

    M621472 - Ida Geneva Vaughan - Russell W. Bentler, Jr.
    B.   5/12/1904   M.   8/1/1929   B.   3/22/1906
    D. _____   D. _____

    M621473 - Abram Still Vaughan, Jr. - Mildred Long
    B.   7/29/1907   M.   5/12/1928   B. _____
    D. _____   D. _____

        M6214731 - Gerald Ralph Vaughan
        B. 5/21/1929

M62148 - Icypheon Gertrude Vaughan
B. 9/21/1873
D. 11/15/1904

M6215   Thomas Chalmers Still - Martha Ann Allen
    B. 7/6/1833   M. 5/24/1858   B. 3/12/1838
    D. 8/20/1922   D. 9/9/1907

 M62151 - William Leonard Still
    B. 8/19/1852
    D. 3/14/1932

 M62152 - Abram Allen Still - Minnie Henrietta Wolf
    B. 12/13/1858   M. 4/14/1889   B. 12/6/1869
    D. 3/29/1937   D. 1/30/1932

  M621521 - Clarence Percy Still - Mabel Bernice Funk
    B. 12/23/1889   M. 9/23/1919   B. 9/2/1901
    D. 12/7/1980   D. 10/20/1987

  M6215211 - Elva Nadine Still - Carroll Martin
    B. 11/27/1921   M. _____   B. 7/1931
                                      D. 11/26/1985

   M62152111 - Gloria Martin - _____
    B. 6/3/1942   M. _____   B. _____

    M621521111 – Michelle _____
     B. _____

    M621521112 – Catherine _____
     B. _____

  M6215212 - Allan Alvin Still - Cora Mae Talley
    B. 11/25/1922   M. 3/15/1942   B. 7/1/1925
    D. 4/19/1984   D. 1/13/1989

   *M62152121 - Marilyn Ann Still – Perfecto Anthony Betita
    B. 12/18/1947   M. 9/1/1973   B. 1/14/1945

*M621521211 - Kevin Anthony Betita
    B. 6/28/1976

*M62152122 - Sharon Lee Still - (1) Robert Adam Grant, Jr.
    B. 10/10/1952   M. (1) 5/29/1976   B. 9/4_____
                         (2) 7/31/1984

                              (2) Steve Palmer
                                    B. 6/19/____

    *M621521221 - (1) Clayton Adam Grant
        B. 2/7/1979

    *M621521222 -(1) Corinne Lee Grant
        B. 12/14/1980

    *M621521223 - (2) Kaylee Jane Palmer
        B. 1/11/1987

M621522 - Infant son
    B. 1900
    D. 1900

    M621523 - Edith Dorothy Still - Harry Leslie Hatch
        B. 4/9/1895   M. 4/9/1914   B. 1886
        D. _____   D. _____

    M6215231 - Dorothy Henrietta Hatch - Herbert Walker Vieth
        B. 2/12/1915   M. 4/1/1933   B. _____
        D. _____   D. _____

    M6215232 - Helen Alice Hatch
        B. 3/26/1920
        D. _____

    M6215233 - Willard Leslie Hatch
        B. 11/20/1926

M62153 - Edward Marsden Still - Lelia E. Penwell
  B. 5/29/1863   M. 8/26/1896   B. 1/19/1866
  D. 10/19/1915   D. 7/1/1958

M621531 - Grace Still - Paul Wallin
  B. 8/27/1897   M. 10/30/1926   B. _____
  D. 11/13/2000   D. 2/1939

M6215311 - Miriam Wallin - Dwight Edward (Div.)
  B. 7/20/1930   M. 4/20/1963   B. 6/11/1930

M6215312 - Pauline Wallin - Jack Gerst
  B. 11/27/1933   M. 8/17/l952   B. 12/14/1930
                                             D. 12/12/1996

M62153121 - Randy Gerst - Gayle Wilson (Div.)
  B. 1/31/1956   M. 10/3/1981   B. 2/12/1957

M621531211 - Christopher Gerst
  B. 2/29/1988

M621531212 - Shelby Marie Gerst
  B. 1/16/1991

M62153122 - Linda Gerst - (1) Steve Votgelsanger (Div. 1/9/1990)
  B. 12/8/1957   M. (1) 11/13/1983   B. 10/27/1954
                        M.(2) 9/28/1994

                                     (2) Greg Aron (Div)
                                         B. 1/2/1960

M621531221 - (1) James Votgelsanger
  B. 2/18/1985

M621531222 - (2) Amanda Aron
  B. 1/5/1996

M62153123 - Dawn Gerst
    B. 3/9/1960

M621532 - Ernest Mently Still - Eleanor Twisselman
    B. 9/30/1898   M. 10/10/1925   B. 6/21/1905
    D. 1/18/1972   D. 4/3/1992

    M6215321 - Doreen Still - Billy Ray Roden
        B. 10/31/1932   M. 8/15/1951   B. 6/20/1931

        M62153211 - William Christian Roden–Karen Kay Moore
            B. 1/15/1953   M. 3/28/1981   B. 5/3/1952

            M62532111 - Matthew Christian Roden
                B. 5/2/1983

            M62532112 - Christina Doreen Roden
                B. 7/24/1986

        M62153212 - Sharon Lynn Roden
            B. 11/22/1955

    M6215322 - Edward M. Still
        B. 6/30/1934
        D. 12/15/1935

M621533 - Ellen Lelia Still - (1) Truman Glenn Tabler (Div. 1937)
    B. 8/16/1901   M. (1) 11/1926   B. 1/6/1901
    D. 10/2/1998   M. (2) 11/10/1942   D. 4/8/1972

                (2) Earl Maxwell Newson
                        B. 1/23/1908
                        D. 6/6/1987

    *M6215331 - (1) Joyce Bell Tabler (Newson) - Willard Eugene Bingeman
        B. 10/28/1931   M. 9/16/1950   B. 11/04/1916
                                          D. 6/6/1990

*M62153311 - Lea Naomi Bingeman - (1) Guy Early Anderson (Div. 1982)
B. 3/14/1957   M. (1) 11/29/1975   B. 2/10/1955
M. (2) 3/12/1983

(2) Roger Louis Shanahan
B. 10/14/1943

*M621533111 - (1) Stephanie Irene Anderson – David Price
B. 4/26/1976   M. 8/31/1996   B. 6/29/1976

*M621533112 - (2) Tara Rose Shanahan
Died as an infant 4/10/1983

*M621533113 - (2) Bridget Katherine Shanahan
B. 1/11/1984

*M62153312 - Sue Bingeman - (1) Robert Sutich (Div)
B. 11/21/1960   M. (1) 8/18/1979 B. 2/22/1959
M. (2) 2/14/1985

(2) Terry Greene
B. 5/12/1959

*M621533121 - (1) Travis Sutich – Greene
B. 6/23/1981

*M621533122 - (2) Christopher Greene
B. 2/23/1988

M62153313 - Jodi Bingeman - Guy Lemos
B. 12/26/1967   M. 10/10/1992   B. 12/9/1961

M6215332 - (1) Elroy Tabler (Newsom) - Adell Allison
B. 5/26/1935   M. 8/11/1956   B. 5/24/1937
D. 7/25/1998

M62153321 - Dan Newson
        B. 12/15/1957

M62153322 - Rhojean Newson
        B. 2/3/1963
        D. 2/3/1963

M62153323 - Mike Newsom
        B. 7/22/1965

M62154 - Aruna Grant Still - Albert Horace Minguay Davies
        B. 8/16/1865   M. 8/4/1887   B. 10/4/1863
        D. 10/29/1959

M621541 - Nelson Edward Davies - Lois Lydia Corey
        B. 5/23/1888   M. 4/4/1922   B. 8/12/1885
        D. _____   D. _____

M621542 - Helena Adelaide Davies - John Hannon Atkinson
        B. 5/23/1890   M. 6/24/1911   B. 7/9/1889
        D. 10/31/1918   D. 1/2/1953

M6215421 - Phayre Grace Atkinson - William Van Martyn Peck
        B. 2/12/1912   M. 11/3/1934   B. 1/10/1910
        D. 9/1998

M62154211 - William Peck - Leona _____
        B. 5/1/1939   M. _____   B. _____

M621542111 - James Peck
        B. _____

M621542112 - Cynthia Rose Peck
        B. _____

M62154212 - Edward Hannon Peck - (1) Luanna Fulton
    B. 5/31/1942   M. (1) _____   B. _____
                (2) 3/31/1962

                             (2) Verna Maw Stebbing
                                B. _____

M621542121 - (2) Stephen Christopher Peck - Laurie _____
    B. 4/12/1963   M. _____   B. _____

    M6215421211 - Christopher Peck
        B. _____

    M6215421212 - Joshua Peck
        B. _____

*M6215422 - Helena May Atkinson - (1) Milton William Melander
    B. 7/1/1913   M. (1) 7/10/1937   B. 4/13/1910
    D. 12/16/2003   M. (2) 6/22/1991   D. 12/19/1984
                M. (3) 2/15/2003

                        (2) Willis Renz
                            B. 4/12/1916
                            D. 12/9/1998

                        (3) Edgar McCann
                            B. _____

M62154221 - (2) Harold William Melander - Carole Janet Herschman
    B. 5/24/1939   M. 8/13/1966   B. 10/29/1943

    *M621542211 - Susan Carole Melander - Charles Lee Tiggs
        B. 6/16/1968   M. 7/10/1993   B. 3/3/1971

        *M6215422111 - Jonathan Karl Tiggs
            B. 9/1/1994

*M6215422112 - Deanna Kethry Tiggs
B. 4/22/1997

*M621542212 - Michael William Melander – Andrea Renee Janes
B. 10/7/1970   M. 12/18/1993   B. 6/30/1970

*M6215422121 - Matthew Melander
B. 5/8/1995

*M6215422122 - Stephen Michael Melander
B. 6/30/1999

*M6215422123 – Kimberley Paige Melander
B. 9/17/2001

*M621542213 - Eric John Melander – Melanie Joy Weinberg
B. 8/20/1973   M. 11/10/2001   B. 12/18/1975

*M62154222 - (2) Milton John Melander - Laura Leimer
B. 8/23/1941   M. 12/31/1994   B. 11/22/1945

*M62154223 - (2) Marilyn Louise Melander - (1) Eltje Johannes
Brunemeyer
B. 11/23/1943   M. (1) 6/20/1964 B. 2/14/1939
(2) 2/28/1976

(2) John Dougherty Tyson, II
B. 3/29/1939

*M6215432231 - (1) Timothy Allen Brunemeyer
B. 12/20/1964

*M6215432232 -(1) Thomas Andrew Brunemeyer - Audrey
Wai Lee (Div)
B. 4/6/1968   M. 5/23/1998   B. 3/11/1973

M62154224 - (2) Carolyn Grace Melander - Peter James Szabad
B. 8/1/1946   M. 6/29/68   B. _____

M621542241 - George M. Szabad, II
B. 11/10/1976

M62154225 - (2) Dorothy Jean Melander - John Stephen Wright
B. 9/14/1952   M. 8/2/1975   B. _____

M621542251 - Katherine Rae Wright
B. 2/18/1982

M621543 - Horatio Chalmers Davies - Lila May Stevenson
B. 12/12/1892   M. 5/2/1917   B. 4/9/1895
D. _____   D. _____

M6215431 - Edward Ivan Davies
B. 12/19/1921

M6215432 - Horatio Chalmers Davies, Jr.
B. 7/30/1923

M621544 - Harold Allen Davies - Bess Elizabeth Hocum
B. 4/26/1895   M. 6/23/1934   B. 4/11/1900
D. _____   D. _____

M621545 - Thomas Albert Davies - Rosalee Blexham
B. 1/1/1897   M. _____   B. _____
D. _____   D. _____

M621546 - Elva Birma Florence Davies - Edwin John Halcrow, Jr.
B. 7/30/1900   M. 6/12/1922   B. 3/11/1888
D. _____   D. _____

M6215461 - Edwin John Halcrow, III - Versia_____
B. 9/9/23   M. _____   B. _____

M62154611 – Patti Halcrow
B. _____

M6215462 - Elva Lois Halcrow
B. 6/21/1927

M6215463 - Lelia Grant Halcrow - _____ Pangborn
B. 5/12/1933   M. _____   B. _____

    M62154631 - Bobby Holcrow Pangborn
    B. _____

M6215464 - Mary Ann Halcrow - Allen R. Steen
B. 11/20/1937   M. _____   B. _____

M621547 - Albert Horace Minguay Davies, Jr. - Mary Virginia Long
B. 3/21/1905   M. 9/9/1933   B. 8/21/1910
D. _____   D. _____

    M6215471 - Virginia Maxie Davies - Joseph Biddle
    B. 11/17/1934   M. _____   B. _____

        M62154711 - Linda Biddle
        B. _____

        M62154712 - Kathleen Biddle - Michael Thomas Doran
        B. _____   M. _____   B. _____

        M62154713 - William Biddle
        B. _____

    M6215472 - Joan Adelaide Davies - Tim Downs
    B. 8/4/1936   M. _____   B. _____

        M62154721 - Tom Downs
        B. _____

        M62154722 - Al Downs
        B. _____

M6215473 - Gayle Aruna Davies - Frederick Jandry
    B. _____   M. _____   B. _____

M6215474 - Mary Alene Davies - David Hopkins
    B. _____   M. _____   B. _____

M62155 - Ruphus King Still
B. 11/8/1867
D. 6/2/1967

M62156 - Orthor Simpson Still
B. 5/8/1870
D. 2/15/1936

M62157 - Thomas Chalmers Still, Jr.
B. 12/25/1871
D. 12/28/1871

M62158 - Birma Harriet Still - John MacCullough MacLane
B. 3/20/1875   M. 12/21/1904   B. 9/17/1876
D. _____   D. _____

M621581 - Orthor Ione MacLane
B. 5/7/1909
C. _____
D.

M621582 - Birma Ione MacLane - John Samuel Bowman
B. 9/29/1910   M. 8/21/1933   B. 8/26/1897
D. _____   D. _____

M6215821 - Judy Bowman - Tom Foss
    B. 6/1/1941   M. _____   B. _____

M6215822 - Pat Bowman - Bill McDonald
    B. 9/10/1947   M. _____   B. _____

M62158221 - John Bowman McDonald
B. 5/1983   M. _____   B. _____

M6215823 – Mently Bowman
B. _____

M621583 - Mently MacCullough MacLane
B. 11/18/1911
C. _____
D.

M621584 - Duncan Still MacLane
B. 12/1/1913
D. _____

M621585 - Una May MacLane - Leonard O. Todd
B. 7/22/1915   M. 8/21/1933   B. 10/12/1911
D. _____   D. _____

M6215851 - Leonard MacLane Todd
B. 7/29/1936

M6215852 - James Samuel Todd
B. 2/2/1939

M6215853 - Lounis Todd
B. 11/1/1951

M62159 - Mently Frederick Still - Annabella Ross
B. 11/8/1879   M. 1/15/1915   B. 6/11/1877
D. _____   D. _____

M621591 - Abraham Craig Still - Marjorie Stockman
B. 1/1/1916   M. 1939   B. _____
D. _____   D. _____

M6215911 - Carolyn Still - Greef Takhar
B. 10/10/1941   M. _____   B. _____

M6215912 - Suzan Still
    B. 3/19/1947

M621592 - Thomas Clerill Still – Edith Elizabeth Huxtable
    B. 7/31/1918   M._____   B. 4/12/1919
    D. 4/28/1985   D. _____

    M6215921 – Thomas Chalmers Still - _____
        B. 10/9/1945   M. _____   B. _____

        M62159211 – Paul Anthony Still
            B. _____

*M6215922 – Frederick George Still – Mary Sue Davis
    B. 9/7/1950   M. 12/24/1972 B. 1/23/1952

    M62159221 – Kevin Natheniel Still – Joni Marie Moritz
        B. 8/1/1974   M. 8/11/2001   B. _____

    M62159222 – Kyle Christopher Still
        B. 2/26/1975

    M62159223 – Keith Michael Still
        B. 11/18/1977

    M62159224 – Carrie Anne Still
        B. 4/29/1980

    M62159225 – Katie Marie Still
        B. 10/12/1987

    M62159226 – Kelly Beth Still
        B. 6/17/1989

    M62159227 – Kimberly Joy Still
        B. 8/7/1991

M62159228 – Katrina Susanne Still
B. 1/22/1994

M62159229 – Kendra Michael Still
B. 11/29/1994

M621592-10 – Kirsty Noel Still
B. 1/5/1997

M6215923 – Duncan Ross Still
B. 7/24/1955

*M621593 - William Leonard Still - Mary Cathryne Wilson
B. 9/16/1919   M. 8/17/1945   B. 12/9/1920
D. _____   D. _____

*M6215931 - William Thomas Still - Cynthia Wheatly
B. 1/20/1948   M. 6/27/1981   B. 8/25/1957

*M62159311 - William S. Still
B. 11/5/1983

*M62159312 - Dara C. Still
B. 12/4/1987

*M62159313 - Noah Still
B. 6/19/1994

*M62159314 - Amanda Still
B. 12/5/1996

M6215932 - Robert John Still - Diane _____
B. 12/24/1949   M. _____   B. _____

M6215933 - Patricia Ann Still - Andrew Paulas, Jr.
B. 9/23/1951   M. 11/7/1983   B. _____

M62159331 - Wendy Catherine Paulas
B. 2/24/1985

M6216 John Wesley Still - Sophia Miller
B. 2/17/1836   M. 8/25/1867   B. 1/23/1839
D. 2/7/1888   D. 9/8/1918

    M62161 - Adaiah Still
    B. 7/21/1868
    D. _____

    M62162 - Jennie Tyler Still
    B. 3/23/1872
    D. 1/21/1874

    M62163 - Iva May Still - Merle Reed Wallace
    B. 6/13/1879   M. 1/1906   B. 10/26/1876
    D. _____   D. _____

        M621631 - Andrew Still Wallace - Dorothy Mildred Carpenter
        B. 10/16/1906   M. 8/8/1931   B. _____
        D. _____   D. _____

M6217 Mary Margarette Still - Thomas Madden Adams
B. 9/10/1838   M. 1863   B.
D. 1/23/1920   D. 6/16/1912

    M62171 - Abraham Alvah Adams - Elizabeth Roeder
    B. 3/24/1864   M. 1884   B. _____
    D. 3/1891

    M62172 - Edward Phillips Adams
    B. 6/1865
    D. 6/1866

M62173 - Martha E. Adams
   B. 1868
   D. 12/6/1891

M62174 - Hester Adams
   B. 1869
   D. as infant

M62175 - Frederick Vernon Adams - Marjorie Frances McLennan
   B. 4/16/1871   M. _____   B. 5/17/1881
   D. 7/7/1935   D. _____

   M621751 - Parks Madden Adams - Dorothy Whiting Doty
      B. 9/6/1910   M. 10/18/1935   B. _____
      D. _____   D. _____

      M6217511 - Parks Madden Adams, Jr.
         B. 12/4/1937

   M621752 - Emerson Still Adams - Ruth Peters
      B. 11/8/1912   M. _____   B. _____
      D. _____   D. _____

   M621753 - Stephen Andrews Adams - Elizabeth Dawson
      B. 3/6/1914   M. _____   B. _____
      D. _____   D. _____

M62176 - Edward J. Adams
   B. 4/16/1871
   D. 11/17/1891

M62177 - Elmer Adams - Margaret _____
   B. 5/31/1873   M. 10/25/1904   B. _____
   D. _____   D. _____

   M621771 - Wilbur Adams - Elsie Marie Schneider
      B. _____   M. _____   B. _____

M6217711 – Daughter -
    B. _____

M621772 - Margaretta Adams -
    B. _____

M6218   Marovia Marsden Still - Ezekiel Snider Clark
    B. 10/9/1844   M. 11/25/1869   B. 5/17/1845
    D. 8/8/1927   D. 3/13/1922

M62181 - Andrew Still Clark
    B. 7/20/1821
    D. 7/20/1821

M62182 - Pearl Amy Clark - Orestes Lucien Garlinghouse
    B. 7/21/1872   M. 9/27/1899   B. 6/18/1870
    D. 5/16/1968   D. 4/29/1949

M621821 - Marjorie Pearl Garlinghouse - Spencer Agassiz Gard
    B. 7/25/1900   M. 9/27/1924   B. 6/24/1898
    D. 9/24/1994   D. 11/21/1991

*M6218211 - Amy Lou Gard - Jack Brazil
    B. 12/2/1931   M. 8/2/1953   B. 5/6/1930
                                    D. 6/4/2002

*M62182111 - Christopher Shane Brazil - Rebecca A. Jarboe
    B. 10/30/1954   M. 11/11/1982   B. 3/4/1963

*M621821111 - Melina A. Brazil
    B. 7/14/1986

M621822 - Robert Orestes Garlinghouse - Esther Winifred Coghill
    B. 3/5/1910   M. 6/11/1934   B. 8/12/1907
    D. 3/6/1980   D. 10/2/1985

*M6218221 - Jean Garlinghouse - John Price Witwer
    B. 3/15/1939   M. 12/28/1968   B. 12/3/1940

    *M62182211 - Robert Earl Witwer - Heather Marie Hughes
        B. 2/10/1971   M. 12/29/1995   B. 10/4/1972

        *M621822111 - John Michael Witwer
            B. 2/9/2001

        *M621822112 – Robert James Witwer
            B. 12/8/2002

        *M621822113 - Jeffrey Bryant Witwer
            B. 1/3/2005

    *M62182212 - Elizabeth Anne Witwer - Mark Evan Feiner
        B. 7/11/1973   M. 2/19/2000   B. 2/13/1972

        *M621822121 - Rebecca Anne Feiner
            B. 6/6/2004

    *M6218222 - Jane Garlinghouse
        B. 6/26/1943

M621823 - Richard Earl Garlinghouse - Miriam Esther Thoroman
    B. 3/15/1910   M. 6/17/1934   B. 2/20/1909
    D. 11/17/1993   D. 11/10/1998

    *M6218231 - Richard Earl Garlinghouse, Jr. – Margaret Ann Pettus
        B. 4/12/1940   M. 9/23/1973   B. 6/9/1945

        *M62182311 – Sarah McCall Garlinghouse
            B. 9/26/1975

        *M62182312– Elizabeth Clark Garlinghouse
            B. 1/8/1978

*M62182313 – Katherine Monroe Garlinghouse
B. 12/23/1980

*M6218232 - Gretchen Ann Garlinghouse – Dennis Gregg Huddleston
B. 1/3/1947   M. 5/12/1974   B. 5/16/1949

*M62182321 – Zachary Clark Huddleston
B. 9/4/1984

M62183 - Earl Finley Clark - Ada Myrtle Hamilton
B. 2/2/1880   M. 7/2/1911   B. 8/19/1886
D. _____   D. _____

M621831 - Marovia Eldora Clark
B. 7/14/1916
D. 2/15/1917

M6219 – Cassandra Elliott Still - James Calvin McCollum
B. 10/10/1846   M. 1862   B. _____
D. 2/17/1888   D. 10/1900

M62191 - Mineola McCollum - Henry Bixby
B. 12/27/1863   M. 4/1883 B. 1863
D. _____   D. 1901

M621911 - Lillian McCollum Bixby
B. 1886
D. ____

M62192 - Loris McCollum - D.D. Johnson
B. 9/22/1881   M. _____   B. _____
D. 1915   D. _____

M621921 - Dellorice Johnson
B. _____

9.

<u>THE MARTHA POAGE MOORE STILL LINE</u>
<u>BIOGRAPHICAL CHARTS</u>

M62116111
Genealogical Number

Patricia Louise Dunnington   Kirkland, Washington
Name (including maiden name if applicable)   Town of Residence

Cherokee, Oklahoma   1/27/1935
Birthplace   Date of Birth   Date of Death   Where Buried

LeRoy Allen (Div)   Alva, Oklahoma   4/1/1934
Name of Spouse   Birthplace   Date of Birth   Date of Death

                            8/28/1955   Cherokee, Oklahoma
Where Buried   Date of Marriage   Place of Marriage

If married more than once:

Name of Spouse   Birthplace   Date of Birth   Date of Death

Where Buried   Date of Marriage   Place of Marriage

Parents of Spouse (with Mother's maiden name) 1st Marriage

Subsequent Marriage (if applicable)

Family Details

Schools attended, dates and degrees: Community, political work, etc.:

Descendant   Descendant

Spouse   Spouse

Basic Employment History: Clubs, Church Affiliations, etc.:

Descendant   Descendant

Spouse   Spouse

Military Service:

Descendant   Spouse

M62116112
Genealogical Number

Roberta Dunnington
Name (including maiden name if applicable)

Ponca City, Oklahoma
Town of Residence

Cherokee, OK
Birthplace

1/5/1942
Date of Birth

Date of Death

Where Buried

James Edward Stuckey
Name of Spouse

Cherokee, OK
Birthplace

10/3/1939
Date of Birth

Date of Death

Where Buried

2/28/1963
Date of Marriage

Norman, OK
Place of Marriage

If married more than once:

Name of Spouse

Birthplace

Date of Birth

Date of Death

Where Buried

Date of Marriage

Place of Marriage

Edward E. Stuckey, Ruth Frey Stuckey
Parents of Spouse (with Mother's maiden name) 1st Marriage

Subsequent Marriage (if applicable)

Family Details

Schools attended, dates and degrees:

Community, political work, etc.:

Descendant

Descendant

Spouse

Spouse

Basic Employment History:

Clubs, Church Affiliations, etc.:

Descendant

Descendant

Spouse

Spouse

Military Service:

Descendant

Spouse

M621161121
Genealogical Number

Kimberly Dawn Stuckey
Name (including maiden name if applicable)

Portland, OR
Town of Residence

Fort Sill, OK
Birthplace

1/29/1974
Date of Birth

Date of Death

Where Buried

Name of Spouse

Birthplace

Date of Birth

Date of Death

Where Buried

Date of Marriage

Place of Marriage

If married more than once:

Name of Spouse

Birthplace

Date of Birth

Date of Death

Where Buried

Date of Marriage

Place of Marriage

Parents of Spouse (with Mother's maiden name) 1st Marriage

Subsequent Marriage (if applicable)

Family Details

Schools attended, dates and degrees:

Community, political work, etc.:

Descendant

Descendant

Spouse

Spouse

Basic Employment History:

Clubs, Church Affiliations, etc.:

Descendant

Descendant

Spouse

Spouse

Military Service:

Descendant

Spouse

M62116113
Genealogical Number

Annette Dunnington
Name (including maiden name if applicable)

Amarillo, Texas
Town of Residence

Cherokee, OK
Birthplace

7/20/1944
Date of Birth

Date of Death

Where Buried

Stanley Harrison
Name of Spouse

Wellington, TX
Birthplace

1/9/1946
Date of Birth

Date of Death

Where Buried

11/26/1968
Date of Marriage

Amarillo, TX
Place of Marriage

If married more than once:

Name of Spouse

Birthplace

Date of Birth

Date of Death

Where Buried

Date of Marriage

Place of Marriage

Parents of Spouse (with Mother's maiden name) 1st Marriage

Subsequent Marriage (if applicable)

Family Details

Schools attended, dates and degrees:

Community, political work, etc.:

Descendant

Descendant

Spouse

Spouse

Basic Employment History:

Clubs, Church Affiliations, etc.:

Descendant

Descendant

Spouse

Spouse

Military Service:

Descendant

Spouse

M621161131
Genealogical Number

Stephanie Ann Harrison _____   Amarillo, TX _____
Name (including maiden name if applicable)   Town of Residence

Amarillo, TX _____   3/31/1969 _____   _____   _____
Birthplace   Date of Birth   Date of Death   Where Buried

_____   _____   _____   _____
Name of Spouse   Birthplace   Date of Birth   Date of Death

_____   _____   _____
Where Buried   Date of Marriage   Place of Marriage

If married more than once:

_____   _____   _____   _____
Name of Spouse   Birthplace   Date of Birth   Date of Death

_____   _____   _____
Where Buried   Date of Marriage   Place of Marriage

_____
Parents of Spouse (with Mother's maiden name) 1st Marriage

_____
Subsequent Marriage (if applicable)

Family Details

Schools attended, dates and degrees: Community, political work, etc.:

_____   _____
Descendant   Descendant

_____   _____
Spouse   Spouse

Basic Employment History: Clubs, Church Affiliations, etc.:

_____   _____
Descendant   Descendant

_____   _____
Spouse   Spouse

Military Service:

_____   _____
Descendant   Spouse

M621161132
Genealogical Number

Jason Earle Harrison
Name (including maiden name if applicable)

Houston, TX
Town of Residence

Amarillo, TX
Birthplace

12/21/1973
Date of Birth

Date of Death

Where Buried

Name of Spouse

Birthplace

Date of Birth

Date of Death

Where Buried

Date of Marriage

Place of Marriage

If married more than once:

Name of Spouse

Birthplace

Date of Birth

Date of Death

Where Buried

Date of Marriage

Place of Marriage

Parents of Spouse (with Mother's maiden name) 1st Marriage

Subsequent Marriage (if applicable)

Family Details

Schools attended, dates and degrees:

Community, political work, etc.:

Descendant

Descendant

Spouse

Spouse

Basic Employment History:

Clubs, Church Affiliations, etc.:

Descendant

Descendant

Spouse

Spouse

Military Service:

Descendant

Spouse

M621161221
Genealogical Number

Kristan Suzanne Dinges   Coppell, Texas
Name (including maiden name if applicable)   Town of Residence

West Point, NY   11/24/1960
Birthplace   Date of Birth   Date of Death   Where Buried

Dale Eugene Hruby, II   Frankfurt, Germany   6/16/1960
Name of Spouse   Birthplace   Date of Birth   Date of Death

                        2/25/1984   Fairfax, VA
Where Buried   Date of Marriage   Place of Marriage

If married more than once:

Name of Spouse   Birthplace   Date of Birth   Date of Death

Where Buried   Date of Marriage   Place of Marriage

Parents of Spouse (with Mother's maiden name) 1st Marriage

Subsequent Marriage (if applicable)

Family Details

Schools attended, dates and degrees: Community, political work, etc.:

Descendant   Descendant

Spouse   Spouse

Basic Employment History: Clubs, Church Affiliations, etc.:

Descendant   Descendant

Spouse   Spouse

Military Service:

Descendant   Spouse

M6211612211
Genealogical Number

Nathaniel Dale Hruby
Name (including maiden name if applicable)

Coppell, Texas
Town of Residence

Evanston, Illinois
Birthplace

1/31/1993
Date of Birth

Date of Death

Where Buried

Name of Spouse

Birthplace

Date of Birth

Date of Death

Where Buried

Date of Marriage

Place of Marriage

If married more than once:

Name of Spouse

Birthplace

Date of Birth

Date of Death

Where Buried

Date of Marriage

Place of Marriage

Parents of Spouse (with Mother's maiden name) 1st Marriage

Subsequent Marriage (if applicable)

Family Details

Schools attended, dates and degrees:

Community, political work, etc.:

Descendant

Descendant

Spouse

Spouse

Basic Employment History:

Clubs, Church Affiliations, etc.:

Descendant

Descendant

Spouse

Spouse

Military Service:

Descendant

Spouse

M6211612212
Genealogical Number

Nicholas Glenn Hruby   Coppell, Texas
Name (including maiden name if applicable)   Town of Residence

Irving, Texas   10/7/1995
Birthplace   Date of Birth   Date of Death   Where Buried

Name of Spouse   Birthplace   Date of Birth   Date of Death

Where Buried   Date of Marriage   Place of Marriage

If married more than once:

Name of Spouse   Birthplace   Date of Birth   Date of Death

Where Buried   Date of Marriage   Place of Marriage

Parents of Spouse (with Mother's maiden name) 1st Marriage

Subsequent Marriage (if applicable)

Family Details

Schools attended, dates and degrees: Community, political work, etc.:

Descendant   Descendant

Spouse   Spouse

Basic Employment History: Clubs, Church Affiliations, etc.:

Descendant   Descendant

Spouse   Spouse

Military Service:

Descendant   Spouse

M62116123
_____
Genealogical Number

Warren Harvey Dunnington
_____   _____
Name (including maiden name if applicable)   Town of Residence

Cherokee, OK   4-17-1937   8-18-1996   Arlington National Cemetary
_____   _____   _____   _____
Birthplace   Date of Birth   Date of Death   Where Buried

Elizabeth
_____   _____   _____   _____
Name of Spouse   Birthplace   Date of Birth   Date of Death

_____   _____   _____
Where Buried   Date of Marriage   Place of Marriage

If married more than once:

_____   _____   _____   _____
Name of Spouse   Birthplace   Date of Birth   Date of Death

_____   _____   _____
Where Buried   Date of Marriage   Place of Marriage

_____
Parents of Spouse (with Mother's maiden name) 1st Marriage

_____
Subsequent Marriage (if applicable)

Family Details

Schools attended, dates and degrees: Community, political work, etc.:

_____   _____
Descendant   Descendant

_____   _____
Spouse   Spouse

Basic Employment History: Clubs, Church Affiliations, etc.:

_____   _____
Descendant   Descendant

_____   _____
Spouse   Spouse

Military Service:

_____   _____
Descendant   Spouse

M621161231

Genealogical Number

Melissa Ann Dunnington   Greensboro, NC

Name (including maiden name if applicable)   Town of Residence

Fort Benning, GA   4-29-1961

Birthplace	Date of Birth	Date of Death	Where Buried
Eric William Craven	Munich, Germany	3-5-1961	
Name of Spouse	Birthplace	Date of Birth	Date of Death
	5-28-1983	St. Mary's Catholic Church, Fairfax, VA	
Where Buried	Date of Marriage	Place of Marriage	

If married more than once:

Name of Spouse	Birthplace	Date of Birth	Date of Death

Where Buried	Date of Marriage	Place of Marriage

Ronald Eric Craven & Barbara Snow Borden

Parents of Spouse (with Mother's maiden name) 1st Marriage

Subsequent Marriage (if applicable)

Family Details

Schools attended, dates and degrees: Community, political work, etc.:
B.J. FACS Education
James Madison University, 1979-1983

Descendant   Descendant

University of Virginia, 1979-1983, B.A.

Spouse   Spouse

Basic Employment History: Clubs, Church Affiliations, etc.:

Descendant   Descendant

Spouse   Spouse

Military Service:

                                       US Army, 1983 - 1993

Descendant   Spouse

M621161233
Genealogical Number

Edward William Dunnington
Name (including maiden name if applicable)

Seattle, WA
Town of Residence

Ft. Eustis, VA
Birthplace

8/20/1969
Date of Birth

Date of Death

Where Buried

Stefanie Elen Walton
Name of Spouse

Fayetteville, NC
Birthplace

6/4/1969
Date of Birth

Date of Death

Where Buried

6/6/1992
Date of Marriage

McLean, VA
Place of Marriage

If married more than once:

Name of Spouse

Birthplace

Date of Birth

Date of Death

Where Buried

Date of Marriage

Place of Marriage

Herbert Madison Walton, Jr. & Ellen Ruth Hall
Parents of Spouse (with Mother's maiden name) 1st Marriage

Subsequent Marriage (if applicable)

Family Details

Schools attended, dates and degrees:
Virginia Military Institute - 91 (BS-Math)
Covenant Theological Seminary -98 (Master of
Divinity)
Descendant
University of Virginia –
91 BA - Sociology
Spouse

Community, political work, etc.:

Descendant

Spouse

Basic Employment History:
Campus Minister in the Presbyterian Church (PCA) in
America at the University of Washington.
Descendant

Clubs, Church Affiliations, etc.:

Descendant

Spouse

Spouse

Military Service:
U.S. Army -(Field Art.) -91-94 Ft. Lewis, WA (2LT & 1LT)
94-98 Missouri Nat. Guard (1LT-CPT), 98-99 WA Nat. Guard (CPT)
Descendant

Spouse

M62116124
Genealogical Number

Glenn Walter Dunnington   Paris, Texas
Name (including maiden name if applicable)   Town of Residence

Cherokee, Oklahoma   9/17/1940
Birthplace   Date of Birth   Date of Death   Where Buried

Margaret Mary Lentine   Boston, MA   3/12/1941
Name of Spouse   Birthplace   Date of Birth   Date of Death

                          11/22/1969   Fairfax, VA
Where Buried   Date of Marriage   Place of Marriage

If married more than once:

Name of Spouse   Birthplace   Date of Birth   Date of Death

Where Buried   Date of Marriage   Place of Marriage

Anthony Lentine, Mary Martines Lentine
Parents of Spouse (with Mother's maiden name) 1st Marriage

Subsequent Marriage (if applicable)

Family Details

Schools attended, dates and degrees: Community, political work, etc.:

Univ. OK BS 1962, Univ. OK Med. School
MD 1966   Christus St. Joseph Hospital, Paris TX
Descendant   Descendant

Acton HS, Boston University   Republican Party
Spouse   Spouse

Basic Employment History: Clubs, Church Affiliations, etc.:
                                              Teach Sunday School
Tijerina-Dunnington - Le Urology Clinic   1st United Methodist Church
Descendant   Descendant
Business Manager of Tijerina Dunnington-Le   Volunteer taught Sunday School
Urology Clinic   1st United Methodist Church
Spouse   Spouse

Military Service:
17 Years US Army, Lt. Col Medical Corps.
Vietnam 1968-1969
Descendant   Spouse

M621161241
Genealogical Number

Cheryl Emma Dunnington
Name (including maiden name if applicable)

San Antonio, Texas
Town of Residence

Ft. Ord, California
Birthplace

9/15/1972
Date of Birth

Date of Death

Where Buried

Troy Joe Dunn
Name of Spouse

Lubbock, TX
Birthplace

5/30/1960
Date of Birth

Date of Death

Where Buried

7/22/1995
Date of Marriage

Paris, Texas
Place of Marriage

If married more than once:

Name of Spouse

Birthplace

Date of Birth

Date of Death

Where Buried

Date of Marriage

Place of Marriage

Parents of Spouse (with Mother's maiden name) 1st Marriage

Subsequent Marriage (if applicable)

Family Details

Schools attended, dates and degrees:
Paris High School (Grad. 1991)/Texas Christian University
(Grad. 1995) Bachelor in Social Work/Our Lady of the Lake
(Grad. 1996) Masters in Social Work
Descendant
Harding Simmons University - Bachelor in Counseling
Bachelor in Education
Spouse

Community, political work, etc.:

Descendant

Spouse

Basic Employment History:

Clubs, Church Affiliations, etc.:

School Social Worker
Descendant
Director of small Group Ministry &
Assimilation.
Spouse

Alamo Heights United Methodist Church
Descendant

Alamo Heights United Methodist Church
Spouse

Military Service:

Descendant

Spouse

M621161242
_____
Genealogical Number

Angela Mary Dunnington   Paris, TX
_____   _____
Name (including maiden name if applicable)   Town of Residence

Fort Ord, CA   6-13-1974
_____   _____   _____   _____
Birthplace   Date of Birth   Date of Death   Where Buried

_____   _____   _____   _____
Name of Spouse   Birthplace   Date of Birth   Date of Death

_____   _____   _____
Where Buried   Date of Marriage   Place of Marriage

If married more than once:

_____   _____   _____   _____
Name of Spouse   Birthplace   Date of Birth   Date of Death

_____   _____   _____
Where Buried   Date of Marriage   Place of Marriage

_____
Parents of Spouse (with Mother's maiden name) 1st Marriage

_____
Subsequent Marriage (if applicable)

Family Details

Schools attended, dates and degrees: Community, political work, etc.:
Paris High School; Oklahoma State
University, 1996 (Aviation Science)
_____   _____
Descendant   Descendant

_____   _____
Spouse   Spouse

Basic Employment History: Clubs, Church Affiliations, etc.:
Type Rated, Boeing 767, 797, 737
First Officer for United Airlines   Methodist
_____   _____
Descendant   Descendant

_____   _____
Spouse   Spouse

Military Service:

_____   _____
Descendant   Spouse

M62116151
Genealogical Number

Melissa Ann Barbour
Name (including maiden name if applicable)

Sacramento, CA
Town of Residence

Pittsburgh, PA
Birthplace

10/17/1945
Date of Birth

Date of Death

Where Buried

James Edward Sutton
Name of Spouse

Green Bay, Wisconsin
Birthplace

5/5/1945
Date of Birth

Date of Death

Where Buried

6/22/1974
Date of Marriage

Pittsburgh, PA
Place of Marriage

If married more than once:

Name of Spouse

Birthplace

Date of Birth

Date of Death

Where Buried

Date of Marriage

Place of Marriage

Nina Agamet Sutton and John Robert Sutton
Parents of Spouse (with Mother's maiden name) 1st Marriage

Subsequent Marriage (if applicable)

Family Details

Schools attended, dates and degrees:

North Eastern Univ. M.S. Biology, 1971
Hood College, B.A. Biology, 1967
Descendant
St. Norbert College, B.S. Biology - 1968
Stanford University, M.S. Biology - 1979
Spouse

Community, political work, etc.:

Spiritual Director
Descendant

Spouse

Basic Employment History:

Cytotechnology
Descendant

Environmental Specialist
Spouse

Clubs, Church Affiliations, etc.:

St. Francis of Assisi, Sacramento, CA
Descendant

St. Francis of Assisi, Sacramento, CA
Spouse

Military Service:

Descendant

Spouse

111

M62116152
Genealogical Number

Mary Louise Barbour
Name (including maiden name if applicable)

Arlington, MA
Town of Residence

Pittsburgh, PA
Birthplace

5/1/1950
Date of Birth

Date of Death

Where Buried

Charles Alexander Hatvany
Name of Spouse

Budapest, Hungary
Birthplace

7/4/1950
Date of Birth

Date of Death

Where Buried

5/21/1988
Date of Marriage

Sudbury, MA
Place of Marriage

If married more than once:

Michael Dunn
Name of Spouse

Philadelphia, PA
Birthplace

6/4/1949
Date of Birth

Date of Death

Where Buried

5/6/1978
Date of Marriage

Boston, MA
Place of Marriage

Parents of Spouse (with Mother's maiden name) 1st Marriage

Charles C. Hatvany and Eva Wlassics Hatvany
Subsequent Marriage (if applicable)

Family Details

Schools attended, dates and degrees:

B.S. Education, 1972, Wheelock College
Boston, MA
Descendant
B.S. Biology, 1972, Massachusetts Institute
of Technology, Boston, MA
Spouse

Community, political work, etc.:

Descendant

Spouse

Basic Employment History:
Vice President, Charles Hatvany and
Associates, Inc.
Descendant
President, Charles Hatvany and
Associates, Inc.
Spouse

Clubs, Church Affiliations, etc.:

Plymouth Congregational Church, Belmont, MA
Descendant
Deacon, Plymouth Congregational Church,
Belmont, MA
Spouse

Military Service:

Descendant

Spouse

M62116153
Genealogical Number

Alfred Dunnington Barbour
Name (including maiden name if applicable)

Gibsonia, PA
Town of Residence

Pittsburgh, PA
Birthplace

12/14/1955
Date of Birth

Date of Death

Where Buried

Mary Elizabeth Pearson
Name of Spouse

Minneapolis, MN
Birthplace

10/31/1955
Date of Birth

Date of Death

Where Buried

5/17/1980
Date of Marriage

New Providence, NJ
Place of Marriage

If married more than once:

Name of Spouse

Birthplace

Date of Birth

Date of Death

Where Buried

Date of Marriage

Place of Marriage

Earle and Diantha Sudor Pearson
Parents of Spouse (with Mother's maiden name) 1st Marriage

Subsequent Marriage (if applicable)

Family Details

Schools attended, dates and degrees:

Community, political work, etc.:

Boston University, 1979 BS Communications

Descendant
New York University , MBA 1984
University of Pittsburgh, 1981 B.A. Art History
Spouse

Descendant

Spouse

Basic Employment History:

Clubs, Church Affiliations, etc.:

Concast Metal Products Company
Descendant

Sewickley Presbyterian Church
Descendant

Spouse

Sewickley Presbyterian Church
Spouse

Military Service:

Descendant

Spouse

M621161531
Genealogical Number

Anna Christina Barbour   Gibsonia, PA
Name (including maiden name if applicable)   Town of Residence

St. Petersburg, Russia   7/27/1998
Birthplace   Date of Birth   Date of Death   Where Buried

Name of Spouse   Birthplace   Date of Birth   Date of Death

Where Buried   Date of Marriage   Place of Marriage

If married more than once:

Name of Spouse   Birthplace   Date of Birth   Date of Death

Where Buried   Date of Marriage   Place of Marriage

Parents of Spouse (with Mother's maiden name) 1st Marriage

Subsequent Marriage (if applicable)

Family Details

Schools attended, dates and degrees: Community, political work, etc.:

Descendant   Descendant

Spouse   Spouse

Basic Employment History: Clubs, Church Affiliations, etc.:

Descendant   Descendant

Spouse   Spouse

Military Service:

Descendant   Spouse

M621355
Genealogical Number

Charles Edward Still, Jr.
Name (including maiden name if applicable)   Town of Residence

                                    3/26/1907
Birthplace   Date of Birth   Date of Death   Where Buried

Dennis Shelton   8/25/1906
Name of Spouse   Birthplace   Date of Birth   Date of Death

                        6/9/1936
Where Buried   Date of Marriage   Place of Marriage

If married more than once:

Name of Spouse   Birthplace   Date of Birth   Date of Death

Where Buried   Date of Marriage   Place of Marriage

Parents of Spouse (with Mother's maiden name) 1st Marriage

Subsequent Marriage (if applicable)

Family Details

Schools attended, dates and degrees: Community, political work, etc.:

Descendant   Descendant

Spouse   Spouse

Basic Employment History: Clubs, Church Affiliations, etc.:

Descendant   Descendant

Spouse   Spouse

Military Service:

Descendant   Spouse

M6213551
Genealogical Number

Charles Shelton Still
Name (including maiden name if applicable)

Scottsdale, Arizona
Town of Residence

2/16/1938
Birthplace   Date of Birth   Date of Death   Where Buried

Name of Spouse   Birthplace   Date of Birth   Date of Death

Where Buried   Date of Marriage   Place of Marriage

If married more than once:

Name of Spouse   Birthplace   Date of Birth   Date of Death

Where Buried   Date of Marriage   Place of Marriage

Parents of Spouse (with Mother's maiden name) 1st Marriage

Subsequent Marriage (if applicable)

Family Details

Schools attended, dates and degrees:

Community, political work, etc.:

Descendant

Descendant

Spouse

Spouse

Basic Employment History:

Clubs, Church Affiliations, etc.:

Descendant

Descendant

Spouse

Spouse

Military Service:

Descendant

Spouse

M6213611
Genealogical Number

Eugene Updyke Still, Jr.
Name (including maiden name if applicable)

Near Scappouse, Oregon
Town of Residence

Chicago, Iliniois
Birthplace

8/20/1941
Date of Birth

Date of Death

Where Buried

Susan
Name of Spouse

Birthplace

Date of Birth

Date of Death

Where Buried

Date of Marriage

Place of Marriage

If married more than once:

Carlene Woodward
Name of Spouse

Walla Walla, WA
Birthplace

6/25/1943
Date of Birth

Date of Death

Where Buried

10/10/1964(Div)
Date of Marriage

Place of Marriage

Parents of Spouse (with Mother's maiden name) 1st Marriage

Subsequent Marriage (if applicable)

Family Details

Schools attended, dates and degrees:

Community, political work, etc.:

Descendant

Descendant

Spouse

Spouse

Basic Employment History:

Clubs, Church Affiliations, etc.:

Descendant

Descendant

Spouse

Spouse

Military Service:

Descendant

Spouse

M621362
Genealogical Number

Herman Taylor Still, Jr.
Name (including maiden name if applicable)

Town of Residence

3/1920
Birthplace | Date of Birth | Date of Death | Where Buried

Name of Spouse | Birthplace | Date of Birth | Date of Death

Where Buried | Date of Marriage | Place of Marriage

If married more than once:

Name of Spouse | Birthplace | Date of Birth | Date of Death

Where Buried | Date of Marriage | Place of Marriage

Parents of Spouse (with Mother's maiden name) 1st Marriage

Subsequent Marriage (if applicable)

Family Details

Schools attended, dates and degrees:

Community, political work, etc.:

Descendant

Descendant

Spouse

Spouse

Basic Employment History:

Clubs, Church Affiliations, etc.:

Descendant

Descendant

Spouse

Spouse

Military Service:

Descendant

Spouse

M62137211
Genealogical Number

Richard Harry Still, III
Name (including maiden name if applicable)

St. Louis, MO
Town of Residence

Nashville, Tenn.
Birthplace

2/14/1953
Date of Birth

Date of Death

Where Buried

Donna Geringer
Name of Spouse

Birthplace

5/2/1966
Date of Birth

Date of Death

Where Buried

3/19/2000
Date of Marriage

Hawaii
Place of Marriage

If married more than once:

Michele Cianci
Name of Spouse

NJ
Birthplace

10/11/1955
Date of Birth

Date of Death

Where Buried

6/30/1985
Date of Marriage

NJ
Place of Marriage

Parents of Spouse (with Mother's maiden name) 1st Marriage

Subsequent Marriage (if applicable)

Family Details

Schools attended, dates and degrees:

Community, political work, etc.:

Descendant

Descendant

Spouse

Spouse

Basic Employment History:

Clubs, Church Affiliations, etc.:

Descendant

Descendant

Spouse

Spouse

Military Service:

Descendant

Spouse

M6213921
Genealogical Number

Patrick Andrew Laughlin
Name (including maiden name if applicable)

Cascade, Idaho
Town of Residence

Kirksville, MO
Birthplace

11/28/1943
Date of Birth

Date of Death

Where Buried

Susan Jacobson
Name of Spouse

Duluth, MN
Birthplace

12/12/1942
Date of Birth

Date of Death

Where Buried

6/1964 (Div. 6/1969)
Date of Marriage

Duluth, MN.
Place of Marriage

If married more than once:

Name of Spouse

Birthplace

Date of Birth

Date of Death

Where Buried

Date of Marriage

Place of Marriage

Parents of Spouse (with Mother's maiden name) 1st Marriage

Subsequent Marriage (if applicable)

Family Details

Schools attended, dates and degrees:

Community, political work, etc.:

BS - 63 Ohio Wesleyan, Kirksville College of Osteopathic
Medicine - General Practitioner D.O.
Descendant

Descendant

Spouse

Spouse

Basic Employment History:

Clubs, Church Affiliations, etc.:

Portland Mi, Cascade, Id.
Descendant

Descendant

Spouse

Spouse

Military Service:

Descendant

Spouse

M6213922
Genealogical Number

Anne Lisabeth Laughlin
Name (including maiden name if applicable)

Washington, Ind.
Town of Residence

Kirksville, MO
Birthplace

12/16/1946
Date of Birth

Date of Death

Where Buried

Carrold James Kempf
Name of Spouse

Leola, SD
Birthplace

11/2/1949
Date of Birth

Date of Death

Where Buried

4/1972
Date of Marriage

Grinnell, Iowa
Place of Marriage

If married more than once:

Name of Spouse

Birthplace

Date of Birth

Date of Death

Where Buried

Date of Marriage

Place of Marriage

Ervin Kempf, Albena Hoffman
Parents of Spouse (with Mother's maiden name) 1st Marriage

Subsequent Marriage (if applicable)

Family Details

Schools attended, dates and degrees:

Community, political work, etc.:

Grinnell College B.S.; KCOM-D.O.
Descendant
N.D. State Univ. B.S. Kirksville College Osteopathic
Medicine, D.O. Surgeon
Spouse

Descendant

Spouse

Basic Employment History:

Clubs, Church Affiliations, etc.:

Osteopathic Physician, General Practioner
Descendant

Lutheran
Descendant

Osteopathic Physician Surgeon
Spouse

Spouse

Military Service:

Descendant

Spouse

M62139221
Genealogical Number

Nathan Andrew Kempf   Albuquerque, NM
Name (including maiden name if applicable)   Town of Residence

M. Clemens, Mich.   11/17/1974
Birthplace   Date of Birth   Date of Death   Where Buried

Renea Fredrickson   N.M.
Name of Spouse   Birthplace   Date of Birth   Date of Death

                         7/19/2003   Santa Fe, NM
Where Buried   Date of Marriage   Place of Marriage

If married more than once:

Name of Spouse   Birthplace   Date of Birth   Date of Death

Where Buried   Date of Marriage   Place of Marriage

Parents of Spouse (with Mother's maiden name) 1st Marriage

Subsequent Marriage (if applicable)

Family Details

Schools attended, dates and degrees: Community, political work, etc.:

University of New Mexico BS 1999
Descendant   Descendant

Spouse   Spouse

Basic Employment History: Clubs, Church Affiliations, etc.:

Satellite mapping   Lutheran
Descendant   Descendant

Spouse   Spouse

Military Service:

Descendant   Spouse

M62139222
Genealogical Number

Joshua Paul Kempf
Name (including maiden name if applicable)

So. Bend, IN
Town of Residence

Mt. Clemens, MI
Birthplace

2/25/1977
Date of Birth

Date of Death

Where Buried

Name of Spouse

Birthplace

Date of Birth

Date of Death

Where Buried

Date of Marriage

Place of Marriage

If married more than once:

Name of Spouse

Birthplace

Date of Birth

Date of Death

Where Buried

Date of Marriage

Place of Marriage

Parents of Spouse (with Mother's maiden name) 1st Marriage

Subsequent Marriage (if applicable)

Family Details

Schools attended, dates and degrees:

Community, political work, etc.:

Evergreen, Wi-BS Biology -1998
Descendant

Descendant

Spouse

Spouse

Basic Employment History:

Clubs, Church Affiliations, etc.:

Water Management Md, Maine
Descendant

Descendant

Spouse

Spouse

Military Service:

Descendant

Spouse

M62139223
Genealogical Number

Rachael Anne Kempf _____   Olympia Washington _____
Name (including maiden name if applicable)   Town of Residence

S. Bend, IN _____   12/12/1978   _____   _____
Birthplace   Date of Birth   Date of Death   Where Buried

_____   _____   _____   _____
Name of Spouse   Birthplace   Date of Birth   Date of Death

_____   _____   _____
Where Buried   Date of Marriage   Place of Marriage

If married more than once:

_____   _____   _____   _____
Name of Spouse   Birthplace   Date of Birth   Date of Death

_____   _____   _____
Where Buried   Date of Marriage Place of Marriage

_____
Parents of Spouse (with Mother's maiden name) 1st Marriage

_____
Subsequent Marriage (if applicable)

Family Details

Schools attended, dates and degrees: Community, political work, etc.:

Olympia, B.S. Spanish, 2002 _____   Environment _____
Descendant   Descendant

_____   _____
Spouse   Spouse

Basic Employment History: Clubs, Church Affiliations, etc.:

_____   _____
Descendant   Descendant

_____   _____
Spouse   Spouse

Military Service:

_____   _____
Descendant   Spouse

M62139224
Genealogical Number

Aaron Matthew Kempf
Name (including maiden name if applicable)

S. Bend, IN
Town of Residence

S. Bend, IN
Birthplace

1/24/1984
Date of Birth

Date of Death

Where Buried

Name of Spouse

Birthplace

Date of Birth

Date of Death

Where Buried

Date of Marriage

Place of Marriage

If married more than once:

Name of Spouse

Birthplace

Date of Birth

Date of Death

Where Buried

Date of Marriage

Place of Marriage

Parents of Spouse (with Mother's maiden name) 1st Marriage

Subsequent Marriage (if applicable)

Family Details

Schools attended, dates and degrees:

Community, political work, etc.:

U. of Ind. - Purdue - student
Descendant

Descendant

Spouse

Spouse

Basic Employment History:

Clubs, Church Affiliations, etc.:

Descendant

Descendant

Spouse

Spouse

Military Service:

Descendant

Spouse

M6213923
Genealogical Number

Susan Denise Laughlin
Name (including maiden name if applicable)

St. Louis, MO
Town of Residence

Kirksville, MO
Birthplace

11/19/1948
Date of Birth

Date of Death

Where Buried

Charles F. Hunter, II
Name of Spouse

Florida
Birthplace

11/19/1946
Date of Birth

Date of Death

Where Buried

6/5/1970 (Div. 1/91)
Date of Marriage

Valparaiso, IN
Place of Marriage

If married more than once:

Name of Spouse

Birthplace

Date of Birth

Date of Death

Where Buried

Date of Marriage

Place of Marriage

Parents of Spouse (with Mother's maiden name) 1st Marriage

Subsequent Marriage (if applicable)

Family Details

Schools attended, dates and degrees:

Valparaiso U.BA Elem. Ed/BSN St. Louis, U/
Law degree - St. Louis U.
Descendant

Spouse

Basic Employment History:
BSN - Shriner's Childrens Hospital, Health
Law - Kansas City, Apples Ct., St. Louis
Descendant

Spouse

Military Service:

Vietnam - Marines
Descendant

Community, political work, etc.:

Red Cross
Descendant

Spouse

Clubs, Church Affiliations, etc.:

Lutheran - Church of Christ
Descendant

Spouse

Spouse

M62139231
Genealogical Number

Michael Brian Hunter   St. Louis, MO
Name (including maiden name if applicable)   Town of Residence

Kirksville, MO   1/15/1971
Birthplace   Date of Birth   Date of Death   Where Buried

Molly Markway   Jefferson City, MO   4/21/1973
Name of Spouse   Birthplace   Date of Birth   Date of Death

                        8/15/1995   St. Louis, MO
Where Buried   Date of Marriage   Place of Marriage

If married more than once:

Name of Spouse   Birthplace   Date of Birth   Date of Death

Where Buried   Date of Marriage   Place of Marriage

Parents of Spouse (with Mother's maiden name) 1st Marriage

Subsequent Marriage (if applicable)

Family Details

Schools attended, dates and degrees: Community, political work, etc.:

U. of MO   BS: School of Law
Descendant   Descendant

Spouse   Spouse

Basic Employment History: Clubs, Church Affiliations, etc.:
Partner law Firm
                                               Church of Christ
Descendant   Descendant

Physical therapist -premature children
Spouse   Spouse

Military Service:

Descendant   Spouse

M621392311
Genealogical Number

Grace Elizabeth Hunter   St. Louis, MO
Name (including maiden name if applicable)   Town of Residence

                        8/20/2000
Birthplace   Date of Birth   Date of Death   Where Buried

Name of Spouse   Birthplace   Date of Birth   Date of Death

Where Buried   Date of Marriage   Place of Marriage

If married more than once:

Name of Spouse   Birthplace   Date of Birth   Date of Death

Where Buried   Date of Marriage   Place of Marriage

Parents of Spouse (with Mother's maiden name) 1st Marriage

Subsequent Marriage (if applicable)

Family Details

Schools attended, dates and degrees: Community, political work, etc.:

Descendant   Descendant

Spouse   Spouse

Basic Employment History: Clubs, Church Affiliations, etc.:

Descendant   Descendant

Spouse   Spouse

Military Service:

Descendant   Spouse

M621392312
Genealogical Number

Samuel Patrick Hunter   St. Louis, MO
Name (including maiden name if applicable)   Town of Residence

                              3/21/2002
Birthplace   Date of Birth   Date of Death   Where Buried

Name of Spouse   Birthplace   Date of Birth   Date of Death

Where Buried   Date of Marriage   Place of Marriage

If married more than once:

Name of Spouse   Birthplace   Date of Birth   Date of Death

Where Buried   Date of Marriage   Place of Marriage

Parents of Spouse (with Mother's maiden name) 1st Marriage

Subsequent Marriage (if applicable)

Family Details

Schools attended, dates and degrees: Community, political work, etc.:

Descendant   Descendant

Spouse   Spouse

Basic Employment History: Clubs, Church Affiliations, etc.:

Descendant   Descendant

Spouse   Spouse

Military Service:

Descendant   Spouse

M62139232
Genealogical Number

Julianne Rebecca Hunter   St. Louis, MO
Name (including maiden name if applicable)   Town of Residence

Kirksville, MO   3/10/1973
Birthplace   Date of Birth   Date of Death   Where Buried

Name of Spouse   Birthplace   Date of Birth   Date of Death

Where Buried   Date of Marriage   Place of Marriage

If married more than once:

Name of Spouse   Birthplace   Date of Birth   Date of Death

Where Buried   Date of Marriage   Place of Marriage

Parents of Spouse (with Mother's maiden name) 1st Marriage

Subsequent Marriage (if applicable)

Family Details

Schools attended, dates and degrees: Community, political work, etc.:

MO. Univ., St. Louis Univ, B.A./M.A.
Descendant   Descendant

Spouse   Spouse

Basic Employment History: Clubs, Church Affiliations, etc.:

Business office St. L. Med.
Descendant   Descendant

Spouse   Spouse

Military Service:

Descendant   Spouse

M62152121
Genealogical Number

Marilyn Ann Still
Name (including maiden name if applicable)

Arroyo Grande, California
Town of Residence

Atascadero, CA
Birthplace

12/18/1947
Date of Birth

Date of Death

Where Buried

Perfecto Anthony
Betita
Name of Spouse

San Luis Obispo, CA
Birthplace

1/14/1945
Date of Birth

Date of Death

Where Buried

9/1/1973
Date of Marriage

Reno, Nevada
Place of Marriage

If married more than once:

Name of Spouse

Birthplace

Date of Birth

Date of Death

Where Buried

Date of Marriage

Place of Marriage

Oliveira
Parents of Spouse (with Mother's maiden name) 1st Marriage

Subsequent Marriage (if applicable)

Family Details

Schools attended, dates and degrees:
Shandon High School Diploma 1965
Bakersfield Junior College 1965-67, California
Polytechnic State University BS Degree
Agricultural Business Management 1970
Descendant
Arroyo Grande High School Diploma 1963
Allan Hancock Community College 1963-1966
University of Nevada Reno, NV 1966-1967
Spouse

Community, political work, etc.:

Descendant
Played both High School & College
Football. Coach of Little League
& Babe Ruth Baseball. Helped to build
the local Babe Ruth field.
Spouse

Basic Employment History:

Freelance Photographer
Descendant
Floyd & Wells, Inc. Supervisor -
Drilling Dept.
Spouse

Clubs, Church Affiliations, etc.:

Catholic
Descendant
Filipino Community Club
Catholic
Spouse

Military Service:

Descendant

Spouse

M621521211
Genealogical Number

Kevin Anthony Betita   Arroyo Grande, CA
Name (including maiden name if applicable)   Town of Residence

Reno, Nevada   6/28/1976
Birthplace   Date of Birth   Date of Death   Where Buried

Name of Spouse   Birthplace   Date of Birth   Date of Death

Where Buried   Date of Marriage   Place of Marriage

If married more than once:

Name of Spouse   Birthplace   Date of Birth   Date of Death

Where Buried   Date of Marriage   Place of Marriage

Parents of Spouse (with Mother's maiden name) 1st Marriage

Subsequent Marriage (if applicable)

Family Details

Schools attended, dates and degrees: Community, political work, etc.:
Arroyo Grande High School - Diploma 1994
Allan Hancock Community College, Santa Maria, CA   DECA Club Placed at the National
AS Degree 2002   competition in Michigan
Descendant   Descendant

Spouse   Spouse

Basic Employment History: Clubs, Church Affiliations, etc.:
Floyd V. Wells Inc. Management Water Well   Archery Club
Drilling & Pump Co., Santa Maria, CA   Catholic
Descendant   Descendant

Spouse   Spouse

Military Service:

Descendant   Spouse

M62152122
Genealogical Number

Sharon Lee Still
Name (including maiden name if applicable)

Paso Robles, CA
Town of Residence

Paso Robles, CA
Birthplace

10/10/1952
Date of Birth

Date of Death

Where Buried

Robert Adam Grant, Jr.
Name of Spouse

Birthplace

9/4
Date of Birth

Date of Death

Where Buried

5/29/1976
Date of Marriage

Reno, NV
Place of Marriage

If married more than once:

Steve Palmer
Name of Spouse

Birthplace

Date of Birth

Date of Death

Where Buried

7/31/1984
Date of Marriage

Hawaii
Place of Marriage

Parents of Spouse (with Mother's maiden name) 1st Marriage

Subsequent Marriage (if applicable)

Family Details

Schools attended, dates and degrees:

Shandon High School Diploma
Fresno Denal Assistant Program - Diploma
Descendant

Community, political work, etc.:

Descendant

Spouse

Spouse

Basic Employment History:

Clubs, Church Affiliations, etc.:

Descendant

Descendant

Spouse

Spouse

Military Service:

Descendant

Spouse

M621521221
Genealogical Number

Clayton Adam Grant
Name (including maiden name if applicable)

Cholame, CA
Town of Residence

2/7/1979
Birthplace   Date of Birth   Date of Death   Where Buried

Name of Spouse   Birthplace   Date of Birth   Date of Death

Where Buried   Date of Marriage   Place of Marriage

If married more than once:

Name of Spouse   Birthplace   Date of Birth   Date of Death

Where Buried   Date of Marriage   Place of Marriage

Parents of Spouse (with Mother's maiden name) 1st Marriage

Subsequent Marriage (if applicable)

Family Details

Schools attended, dates and degrees:

Community, political work, etc.:

Paso Robles High School - Diploma
Descendant

Descendant

Spouse

Spouse

Basic Employment History:

Clubs, Church Affiliations, etc.:

Ranching - Championship Team Roper
Descendant

Descendant

Spouse

Spouse

Military Service:

Descendant

Spouse

M621521222
Genealogical Number

Corinne Lee Grant
Name (including maiden name if applicable)

Paso Robles, CA
Town of Residence

Templeton, CA
Birthplace

12/11/1980
Date of Birth

Date of Death

Where Buried

Name of Spouse

Birthplace

Date of Birth

Date of Death

Where Buried

Date of Marriage

Place of Marriage

If married more than once:

Name of Spouse

Birthplace

Date of Birth

Date of Death

Where Buried

Date of Marriage

Place of Marriage

Parents of Spouse (with Mother's maiden name) 1st Marriage

Subsequent Marriage (if applicable)

Family Details

Schools attended, dates and degrees:

Paso Robles High School - Diploma
Cuesta Community College
Descendant

Spouse

Basic Employment History:

Descendant

Spouse

Military Service:

Descendant

Community, political work, etc.:

Competed in horse shows and roping events.
Descendant

Spouse

Clubs, Church Affiliations, etc.:

Descendant

Spouse

Spouse

M62151223
Genealogical Number

Kaylee Jane Palmer   Paso Robles, CA
Name (including maiden name if applicable)   Town of Residence

Templeton, CA   1/19/1987
Birthplace   Date of Birth   Date of Death   Where Buried

Name of Spouse   Birthplace   Date of Birth   Date of Death

Where Buried   Date of Marriage   Place of Marriage

If married more than once:

Name of Spouse   Birthplace   Date of Birth   Date of Death

Where Buried   Date of Marriage   Place of Marriage

Parents of Spouse (with Mother's maiden name) 1st Marriage

Subsequent Marriage (if applicable)

Family Details

Schools attended, dates and degrees: Community, political work, etc.:

Descendant   Descendant

Spouse   Spouse

Basic Employment History: Clubs, Church Affiliations, etc.:

Descendant   Descendant

Spouse   Spouse

Military Service:

Descendant   Spouse

M6215331
Genealogical Number

Joyce Bell Tabler (Newsom)   Yerington, NV
Name (including maiden name if applicable)   Town of Residence

South Gate, California   10/28/1931
Birthplace   Date of Birth   Date of Death   Where Buried

Willard Eugene Bingeman   Wheeloch, ND   11/4/1916   6/6/1990
Name of Spouse   Birthplace   Date of Birth   Date of Death

                                                    St. James Episcopal Church,
Filer, Idaho   9/16/1950   Paso Robles, CA
Where Buried   Date of Marriage   Place of Marriage

If married more than once:

Name of Spouse   Birthplace   Date of Birth   Date of Death

Where Buried   Date of Marriage   Place of Marriage

Opal Naomi Willard & Winton Vivian Bingeman
Parents of Spouse (with Mother's maiden name) 1st Marriage

Subsequent Marriage (if applicable)

Family Details

Schools attended, dates and degrees: Community, political work, etc.:
Grad: Shandon High - Shandon, CA
1 yr. San Jose State College, San Jose, CA
Nursing Major   4-H Leader
Descendant   Descendant

8th Grade - Wheelock, N. Dakota
Spouse   Spouse

Basic Employment History: Clubs, Church Affiliations, etc.:
Office - South Lyon Hospital,
Yerington, NV   Episcopal Church
Descendant   Descendant
Cattle & grains - Carrisa Plains, CA
Rancher: Cattle & Alfalfa Hay, Yerington, NV   Episcopal Church
Spouse   Spouse

Military Service: US Army 1940-1945 with General Patton's
                                                    3rd Army in N. Africa and Europe
                                                    World War II
Descendant   Spouse

M62153311
Genealogical Number

Lea Naomi Bingeman
Name (including maiden name if applicable)

Hansen, Idaho
Town of Residence

Santa Barbara, CA
Birthplace

3/14/1957
Date of Birth

Date of Death

Where Buried

Roger Louis Shanahan
Name of Spouse

Great Falls, Montana
Birthplace

10/14/1943
Date of Birth

Date of Death

Where Buried

3/12/1983
Date of Marriage

Carson City, Nevada
Place of Marriage

If married more than once:

Guy Early Anderson
Name of Spouse

Coalinga, CA
Birthplace

2/10/1955
Date of Birth

Date of Death

Where Buried

11/29/1975
Date of Marriage

Yerington, Nevada
Place of Marriage

Frances Smith & Harold Anderson
Parents of Spouse (with Mother's maiden name) 1st Marriage

Lois Katherine Bisteaudeau & Patrick Shanahan
Subsequent Marriage (if applicable)

Family Details

Schools attended, dates and degrees:

Community, political work, etc.:

Grad. Yerington High, Yerington, NV
Descendant

Descendant

3 years college, Bozeman, Montana
Spouse

Spouse

Basic Employment History:

Clubs, Church Affiliations, etc.:

Office work
Descendant
Project Manager, Home Building
Industry
Spouse

Episcopal Church
Descendant

Catholic Church
Spouse

Military Service:

None
Descendant

None
Spouse

M621533111
Genealogical Number

Stephanie Irene Anderson   Riverdale, CA
Name (including maiden name if applicable)   Town of Residence

Carson City, Nevada   4/26/1976
Birthplace   Date of Birth   Date of Death   Where Buried

Dave Price   Searcy, Ark   6/29/1976
Name of Spouse   Birthplace   Date of Birth   Date of Death

                           8/31/1996   Virginia Beach, VA
Where Buried   Date of Marriage   Place of Marriage

If married more than once:

Name of Spouse   Birthplace   Date of Birth   Date of Death

Where Buried   Date of Marriage   Place of Marriage

Parents of Spouse (with Mother's maiden name) 1st Marriage

Subsequent Marriage (if applicable)

Family Details

Schools attended, dates and degrees: Community, political work, etc.:

Graduate of Sparks High, Sparks, Nevada
Descendant   Descendant

Grad: White County Central High, Judsonia, Ark.
Spouse   Spouse

Basic Employment History: Clubs, Church Affiliations, etc.:

Descendant   Descendant

Spouse   Spouse

Military Service:

US Navy (Jan '95-2000)   US Navy (July 1994 - present)
Descendant   Spouse

M621533112
Genealogical Number

Tara Rose Shanahan
Name (including maiden name if applicable)   Town of Residence

Reno, Nevada   4/10/1983   4/10/1983   Silver Springs, Nevada
Birthplace   Date of Birth   Date of Death   Where Buried

Name of Spouse   Birthplace   Date of Birth   Date of Death

Where Buried   Date of Marriage   Place of Marriage

If married more than once:

Name of Spouse   Birthplace   Date of Birth   Date of Death

Where Buried   Date of Marriage   Place of Marriage

Parents of Spouse (with Mother's maiden name) 1st Marriage

Subsequent Marriage (if applicable)

Family Details

Schools attended, dates and degrees: Community, political work, etc.:

Descendant   Descendant

Spouse   Spouse

Basic Employment History: Clubs, Church Affiliations, etc.:

Descendant   Descendant

Spouse   Spouse

Military Service:

Descendant   Spouse

M621533113
Genealogical Number

Bridget Katherine Shanahan   Hansen, Idaho
Name (including maiden name if applicable)   Town of Residence

Carson City, Nevada   1/11/1984
Birthplace   Date of Birth   Date of Death   Where Buried

Name of Spouse   Birthplace   Date of Birth   Date of Death

Where Buried   Date of Marriage   Place of Marriage

If married more than once:

Name of Spouse   Birthplace   Date of Birth   Date of Death

Where Buried   Date of Marriage   Place of Marriage

Parents of Spouse (with Mother's maiden name) 1st Marriage

Subsequent Marriage (if applicable)

Family Details

Schools attended, dates and degrees: Community, political work, etc.:

Graduated Hansen High – May 27, 2003
Descendant   Descendant

Spouse   Spouse

Basic Employment History: Clubs, Church Affiliations, etc.:

Descendant   Descendant

Spouse   Spouse

Military Service:

Descendant   Spouse

M62153312
Genealogical Number

Sue Bingeman
Name (including maiden name if applicable)

Twin Falls, Idaho
Town of Residence

Santa Barbara, CA
Birthplace

11/21/1960
Date of Birth

Date of Death

Where Buried

Terry Jay Greene
Name of Spouse

Twin Falls, Idaho
Birthplace

5/12/1959
Date of Birth

Date of Death

Where Buried

2/14/1985
Date of Marriage

Place of Marriage

If married more than once:

Robert Sutich
Name of Spouse

Minnesota
Birthplace

2/22/1959
Date of Birth

Date of Death

Where Buried

8/18/1979
Date of Marriage

Place of Marriage

Parents of Spouse (with Mother's maiden name) 1st Marriage

Conlie Lyle Greene & Erma Ruth Sullivan
Subsequent Marriage (if applicable)

Family Details

Schools attended, dates and degrees:

Community, political work, etc.:

Descendant

Descendant

Spouse

Spouse

Basic Employment History:

Clubs, Church Affiliations, etc.:

Descendant

Descendant

Spouse

Spouse

Military Service:

Descendant

Spouse

M621533121
Genealogical Number

Travis Sutich (Greene)
Name (including maiden name if applicable)

Twin Falls, Idaho
Town of Residence

Boise, Idaho
Birthplace

6/23/1981
Date of Birth

Date of Death

Where Buried

Name of Spouse

Birthplace

Date of Birth

Date of Death

Where Buried

Date of Marriage

Place of Marriage

If married more than once:

Name of Spouse

Birthplace

Date of Birth

Date of Death

Where Buried

Date of Marriage

Place of Marriage

Parents of Spouse (with Mother's maiden name) 1st Marriage

Subsequent Marriage (if applicable)

Family Details

Schools attended, dates and degrees:

Community, political work, etc.:

Descendant

Descendant

Spouse

Spouse

Basic Employment History:

Clubs, Church Affiliations, etc.:

Descendant

Descendant

Spouse

Spouse

Military Service:

USMC 3rd Battalian 7th Marines -serving in Iraq
Descendant

Spouse

M621533122
Genealogical Number

Christopher Greene
Name (including maiden name if applicable)

Twin Falls, Idaho
Town of Residence

Twin Falls, Idaho
Birthplace

2/23/1988
Date of Birth

Date of Death

Where Buried

Name of Spouse

Birthplace

Date of Birth

Date of Death

Where Buried

Date of Marriage

Place of Marriage

If married more than once:

Name of Spouse

Birthplace

Date of Birth

Date of Death

Where Buried

Date of Marriage

Place of Marriage

Parents of Spouse (with Mother's maiden name) 1st Marriage

Subsequent Marriage (if applicable)

Family Details

Schools attended, dates and degrees:

Community, political work, etc.:

Descendant

Descendant

Spouse

Spouse

Basic Employment History:

Clubs, Church Affiliations, etc.:

Descendant

Descendant

Spouse

Spouse

Military Service:

Descendant

Spouse

M6215422
Genealogical Number

Helena May Atkinson
Name (including maiden name if applicable)   Town of Residence
Please note new name: Helena Renz McCann

San Francisco, California   7/1/1913   12/16/2003
Birthplace   Date of Birth   Date of Death   Where Buried

Milton William Melander   San Francisco   4/13/1910   12/19/1984
Name of Spouse   Birthplace   Date of Birth   Date of Death

Palo Alto, CA   7/10/1937   San Francisco,CA
Where Buried   Date of Marriage   Place of Marriage

If married more than once:

William Renz   Ohio   4/12/1916   12/9/1998
Name of Spouse   Birthplace   Date of Birth   Date of Death

Ohio   6/22/1991   Austin, TX
Where Buried Date of Marriage   Place of Marriage

Maria Berglund Melander & Carl Gustav George Melander
Parents of Spouse (with Mother's maiden name) 1st Marriage

3rd marriage - Edgar McCann married 2/15/2003 in Austin, TX
Subsequent Marriage (if applicable)

Family Details

Schools attended, dates and degrees: Community, political work, etc.:

San Francisco State College AB degree May 1934
Descendant   Descendant

Spouse   Spouse

Basic Employment History: Clubs, Church Affiliations, etc.:

Descendant   Descendant

Spouse   Spouse

Military Service:

Descendant   Spouse

Harold William Melander married Carole Janet Hershman

Susan - Charles Tiggs
Michael - Andrea
Eric - Melanie

Milton John Melander - Laura Leimer

Marilyn Louise Melander 1. Eltje Brunemeyer

Timothy Brunemeyer 12/20/1964
Thomas Brunemeyer 4/6/19968

                       2. John Tyson

Carolyn Grace Melander Peter James Szabad
Dorothy Jean Melander Steven Wright

George Michael Szabad
Kati Rae Wright 2/18/1982

M621542211

Genealogical Number

Susan Carole Melander

Fort Worth, TX

Name (including maiden name if applicable)

Town of Residence

Fort Lee, VA   6-16-1968

Birthplace   Date of Birth   Date of Death   Where Buried

Charles Lee Tiggs, Jr   Amarillo, TX   3-3-1971

Name of Spouse   Birthplace   Date of Birth   Date of Death

7-10-1993   Lubboch, TX

Where Buried   Date of Marriage   Place of Marriage

If married more than once:

Name of Spouse   Birthplace   Date of Birth   Date of Death

Where Buried   Date of Marriage   Place of Marriage

Charles Lee Tiggs & Virginia Lloyd Gaines

Parents of Spouse (with Mother's maiden name) 1st Marriage

Subsequent Marriage (if applicable)

Family Details

Schools attended, dates and degrees: Texas Tech, B.S.- (Education)1989, M.ED.- 1992 Education deaf, blind, and hearing impaired
Descendant

Community, political work, etc.:
PTA Volunteer, Teacher
Descendant

Texas Tech, B.S. (Education)- 1993, M.ED.- 1996

Spouse   Spouse

Basic Employment History:
Teacher of Hearing & Visually Impaired; Internet Business

Clubs, Church Affiliations, etc.:
Catholic

Descendant Teacher of Hearing Impaired; Asst. Dean of Students, Texas Tech.; Data Base Coordinator Rochester Inst. of Tech.; Systems Analyst Express Docs

Descendant
None

Spouse   Spouse

Military Service:

Descendant   Spouse

147

M6215422111
_____
Genealogical Number

Jonathan Karl Tiggs

Fort Worth, TX
_____

Name (including maiden **name** if applicable)

Town of Residence

Lubbock, TX   9-1-1994
_____

Birthplace   Date of Birth   Date of Death   Where Buried

Name of Spouse   Birthplace   Date of Birth   Date of Death

Where Buried   Date of Marriage   Place of Marriage

If married more than once:

Name of Spouse   Birthplace   Date of Birth   Date of Death

Where Buried   Date of Marriage   Place of Marriage

Parents of Spouse (with Mother's maiden name) 1st Marriage

Subsequent Marriage (if applicable)

Family Details

Schools attended, dates and degrees: Community, political work, etc.:

Descendant   Descendant

Spouse   Spouse

Basic Employment History: Clubs, Church Affiliations, etc.:

Descendant   Descendant

Spouse   Spouse

Military Service:

Descendant   Spouse

M6215422112

Genealogical Number

Deanna Kethry Tiggs   Fort Worth, TX

Name (including maiden name if applicable)   Town of Residence

Lubbock, TX   4-22-1997

Birthplace   Date of Birth   Date of Death   Where Buried

Name of Spouse   Birthplace   Date of Birth   Date of Death

Where Buried   Date of Marriage   Place of Marriage

If married more than once:

Name of Spouse   Birthplace   Date of Birth   Date of Death

Where Buried   Date of Marriage   Place of Marriage

Parents of Spouse (with Mother's maiden name) 1st Marriage

Subsequent Marriage (if applicable)

Family Details

Schools attended, dates and degrees: Community, political work, etc.:

Descendant   Descendant

Spouse   Spouse

Basic Employment History: Clubs, Church Affiliations, etc.:

Descendant   Descendant

Spouse   Spouse

Military Service:

Descendant   Spouse

M621542212
_____
Genealogical Number

Michael William Melander　　　　　　　　　Diamond Bar, CA
_____　　　　_____
Name (including maiden name if applicable)　　Town of Residence

Honolulu, Hawaii　　　10-7-1970
_____　　_____　　_____　　_____
Birthplace　　　　　Date of Birth　　　　Date of Death　　　Where Buried

Andrea Renee Janes　Killeen, TX　　　　6-30-1970
_____　_____　　_____　　_____
Name of Spouse　　　Birthplace　　　　　Date of Birth　　　Date of Death

　　　　　　　　　12-18-1993　　　　Lubboch, TX
_____　　_____　　_____
Where Buried　　　　Date of Marriage　　Place of Marriage

If married more than once:

_____　　_____　　_____　　_____
Name of Spouse　　　Birthplace　　　　　Date of Birth　　　Date of Death

_____　　_____　　_____
Where Buried　　　　Date of Marriage　　Place of Marriage

Charles Dale Janes & Joanne Marie Underhill
_____
Parents of Spouse (with Mother's maiden name) 1st Marriage

_____
Subsequent Marriage (if applicable)

Family Details

Schools attended, dates and degrees:　　Community, political work, etc.:

Texas Tech, B.S. 1993 Mechanical Eng. Cal State M.B.A. 2003
_____
Descendant　　　　　　　　　　　　Descendant
Certification for Legal Secretary 1993
American Commercial College
_____　　　_____
Spouse　　　　　　　　　　　　　　Spouse

Basic Employment History: Porter Mfg., Eagle　Clubs, Church Affiliations, etc.:
Picher, Woods Equipment, (Eng. Manager) Varco International
(Eng. Designer)
_____　　　_____
Descendant　　　　　　　　　　　　Descendant

Kelly Services & Job Source, Secretary
_____　　　_____
Spouse　　　　　　　　　　　　　　Spouse

Military Service:

Army National Guard, July 1988 - April 2000
_____　　　_____
Descendant　　　　　　　　　　　　Spouse

M6215422121
_____
Genealogical Number

Matthew William Melander
_____
Name (including maiden name if applicable)

Town of Residence
_____

Lubbock, Texas	5-8-1995	4-15-2001	Keene Cemetery, Keene TX
Birthplace	Date of Birth	Date of Death	Where Buried

Name of Spouse	Birthplace	Date of Birth	Date of Death

Where Buried	Date of Marriage	Place of Marriage

If married more than once:

Name of Spouse	Birthplace	Date of Birth	Date of Death

Where Buried	Date of Marriage	Place of Marriage

Parents of Spouse (with Mother's maiden name) 1st Marriage
_____

Subsequent Marriage (if applicable)

Family Details

Schools attended, dates and degrees: Community, political work, etc.:

Descendant _____   Descendant _____

Spouse _____   Spouse _____

Basic Employment History: Clubs, Church Affiliations, etc.:

Descendant _____   Descendant _____

Spouse _____   Spouse _____

Military Service:

Descendant _____   Spouse _____

M6215422122
Genealogical Number

Stephen Michael Melander
Name (including maiden name if applicable)

Diamond Bar, CA
Town of Residence

Invine, CA
Birthplace

6/30/1999
Date of Birth

Date of Death

Where Buried

Name of Spouse

Birthplace

Date of Birth

Date of Death

Where Buried

Date of Marriage

Place of Marriage

If married more than once:

Name of Spouse

Birthplace

Date of Birth

Date of Death

Where Buried

Date of Marriage

Place of Marriage

Parents of Spouse (with Mother's maiden name) 1st Marriage

Subsequent Marriage (if applicable)

Family Details

Schools attended, dates and degrees:

Community, political work, etc.:

Descendant

Descendant

Spouse

Spouse

Basic Employment History:

Clubs, Church Affiliations, etc.:

Descendant

Descendant

Spouse

Spouse

Military Service:

Descendant

Spouse

M6215422123
_____
Genealogical Number

Kimberly Paige Melander   Diamond Bar, CA
_____   _____
Name (including maiden **name** if applicable)   Town of Residence

Invine, CA   9-17-2001
_____   _____   _____   _____
Birthplace   Date of Birth   Date of Death   Where Buried

_____   _____   _____   _____
Name of Spouse   Birthplace   Date of Birth   Date of Death

_____   _____   _____
Where Buried   Date of Marriage   Place of Marriage

If married more than once:

_____   _____   _____   _____
Name of Spouse   Birthplace   Date of Birth   Date of Death

_____   _____   _____
Where Buried   Date of Marriage   Place of Marriage

_____
Parents of Spouse (with Mother's maiden name) 1st Marriage

_____
Subsequent Marriage (if applicable)

Family Details

Schools attended, dates and degrees: Community, political work, etc.:

_____   _____
Descendant   Descendant

_____   _____
Spouse   Spouse

Basic Employment History: Clubs, Church Affiliations, etc.:

_____   _____
Descendant   Descendant

_____   _____
Spouse   Spouse

Military Service:

_____   _____
Descendant   Spouse

M621542213
_____
Genealogical Number

Eric John Melander   Adairsville, GA
_____   _____
Name (including maiden name if applicable)   Town of Residence

Honolulu, Hawaii   8-20-1973
_____   _____   _____   _____
Birthplace   Date of Birth   Date of Death   Where Buried

Melanie Joy Weinberg   Atlanta, GA   12-18-1975
_____ _____   _____   _____
Name of Spouse   Birthplace   Date of Birth   Date of Death

                        11-10-2001   Marietta, GA
_____   _____   _____
Where Buried   Date of Marriage   Place of Marriage

If married more than once:

_____ _____   _____   _____
Name of Spouse   Birthplace   Date of Birth   Date of Death

_____   _____   _____
Where Buried   Date of Marriage   Place of Marriage

Robert Wienberg & Kate Cohen
_____
Parents of Spouse (with Mother's maiden name) 1st Marriage

_____
Subsequent Marriage (if applicable)

Family Details

Schools attended, dates and degrees: Community, political work, etc.:

_____   _____
Descendant   Descendant

Georgia Southern University, 1994 - 1997
_____   _____
Spouse   Spouse

Basic Employment History: Clubs, Church Affiliations, etc.:

_____   _____
Descendant   Descendant

_____   _____
Spouse   Spouse

Military Service:

_____   _____
Descendant   Spouse

M62154222
Genealogical Number

Milton John Melander
Name (including maiden name if applicable)

Appleton, Wisc.
Town of Residence

San Francisco, California
Birthplace

8/23/1941
Date of Birth

Date of Death

Where Buried

Laura Leimer
Name of Spouse

Appleton, Wisc.
Birthplace

11/22/1945
Date of Birth

Date of Death

Where Buried

12/31/1994
Date of Marriage

Appleton, Wisc.
Place of Marriage

If married more than once:

Name of Spouse

Birthplace

Date of Birth

Date of Death

Where Buried

Date of Marriage

Place of Marriage

Parents of Spouse (with Mother's maiden name) 1st Marriage

Subsequent Marriage (if applicable)

Family Details

Schools attended, dates and degrees:

Community, political work, etc.:

University of Maine - BS Forestry
Descendant

Descendant
Chair person of Appleton Histories
Commission
Spouse

Layton School of Art - BS Fine Arts
Spouse

Basic Employment History:

Clubs, Church Affiliations, etc.:

Real Estate Broker
Descendant

Descendant

Real Estate Broker
Spouse

Spouse

Military Service:

US Air Force 1964-1968
Descendant

Spouse

M62154223
Genealogical Number

Marilyn Louise Melander   Greensboro, NC
Name (including maiden name if applicable)   Town of Residence

San Francisco, CA   11/23/1943
Birthplace   Date of Birth   Date of Death   Where Buried

John Dougherty Tyson, II   Lewistown, PA   3/29/1939
Name of Spouse   Birthplace   Date of Birth   Date of Death

                           2/28/1976   Englewood, NJ
Where Buried   Date of Marriage   Place of Marriage

If married more than once:

Eltje Johannes Brunemeyer Netherlands   2/14/1939
Name of Spouse   Birthplace   Date of Birth   Date of Death

                           6/20/1964   Bronxville, NY
Where Buried   Date of Marriage   Place of Marriage

John Tyson/Ruth Meek
Parents of Spouse (with Mother's maiden name) 1st Marriage

Subsequent Marriage (if applicable)

Family Details

Schools attended, dates and degrees: Community, political work, etc.:

Hunter College, BA 1965   Greensboro Choral Society
Descendant   Descendant
Dartmouth College, AB 1961
New York Univ. MBA 1974
Spouse   Spouse

Basic Employment History: Clubs, Church Affiliations, etc.:
United Jersey Bank 1978-1986   Starmount Presbyterian,
                                                  Junior League
Descendant   Descendant
Dupont 1965-1973, Burlington Industries 1973-1988 Starmount Presbyterian, Kiwanis, Mobile
Highland Industries 1988-2000   Meals Council
Spouse   Spouse

Military Service:

                                                  US Navy 1961-1965
Descendant   Spouse

M621542231
Genealogical Number

Timothy Allen Brunemeyer
Name (including maiden name if applicable)

Beachwood, NJ
Town of Residence

Hackensack, NJ
Birthplace

12/20/1964
Date of Birth

Date of Death

Where Buried

Name of Spouse

Birthplace

Date of Birth

Date of Death

Where Buried

Date of Marriage

Place of Marriage

If married more than once:

Name of Spouse

Birthplace

Date of Birth

Date of Death

Where Buried

Date of Marriage

Place of Marriage

Parents of Spouse (with Mother's maiden name) 1st Marriage

Subsequent Marriage (if applicable)

Family Details

Schools attended, dates and degrees:

Community, political work, etc.:

Central College 1982, Unity College 1984-1986
Luzerne County 1991
Descendant

Firefighter 8 years, EMT 9 years
Descendant

Spouse

Spouse

Basic Employment History:

Clubs, Church Affiliations, etc.:

Construction, Retail Sales
Descendant

Reformed Church of America
Descendant

Spouse

Spouse

Military Service:

Descendant

Spouse

M621542232
Genealogical Number

Thomas Andrew Brunemeyer   San Francisco, CA
Name (including maiden name if applicable)   Town of Residence

Kingston, NY   4/6/1968
Birthplace   Date of Birth   Date of Death   Where Buried

Audrey Wai Lee   Fresno, CA   3/11/1973
Name of Spouse   Birthplace   Date of Birth   Date of Death

                                5/23/1998   Tiburon, CA
Where Buried   Date of Marriage   Place of Marriage

If married more than once:

Name of Spouse   Birthplace   Date of Birth   Date of Death

Where Buried   Date of Marriage   Place of Marriage

Parents of Spouse (with Mother's maiden name) 1st Marriage

Subsequent Marriage (if applicable)

Family Details

Schools attended, dates and degrees: Community, political work, etc.:

Trinity College 1986-1990 B.A.
Descendant   Descendant

Spouse   Spouse

Basic Employment History: Clubs, Church Affiliations, etc.:
Paralegal Legal Strategies Group 1995-present
Remcho, Johnansen & Purcell 1991-1995
Descendant   Descendant

Spouse   Spouse

Military Service:

Descendant   Spouse

M6215922
Genealogical Number

Frederick (Rick) George Still
Name (including maiden name if applicable)

Hemet, CA
Town of Residence

Glendale, CA
Birthplace

9/7/1950
Date of Birth

Date of Death

Where Buried

Mary Sue Davis
Name of Spouse

Boulder, CO
Birthplace

1/23/1952
Date of Birth

Date of Death

Where Buried

12/24/1972
Date of Marriage

Highland Park, CA
Place of Marriage

If married more than once:

Name of Spouse

Birthplace

Date of Birth

Date of Death

Where Buried

Date of Marriage

Place of Marriage

Leland E. Davis & Gertrude B. Dickinson
Parents of Spouse (with Mother's maiden name) 1st Marriage

Subsequent Marriage (if applicable)

Family Details

Schools attended, dates and degrees:

Community, political work, etc.:

Over
Descendant

Descendant

Los Angeles City College, 1971-1972, A.A.
Spouse

Spouse

Basic Employment History:

Clubs, Church Affiliations, etc.:

Public Educator 1972-Present; Baptist Minister
1978-1980; Graphic Design 1990-1997
Descendant

Independent Baptist
Descendant

Homemaker; Homeschool Mother 1985-
present
Spouse

Independent Baptist
Spouse

Military Service:

Descendant

Spouse

Schools attended, etc.

Descendent:	Pasadena City College	A.A.	1968-1970
	Eastern Oregon College B.S.		1970-1972
	Cal. State San Bernadino M.A.		(in process) 1977-2003

Spouse:	Biola College		1970-1971
	Los Angeles City College A.A.		1971-1972

M621593
Genealogical Number

William Leonard Still
Name (including maiden name if applicable)

Winchester, VA
Town of Residence

La Panza, California
Birthplace

9/16/1919
Date of Birth

Date of Death

Where Buried

Mary Wilson
Name of Spouse

Denver, Colorado
Birthplace

12/9/1920
Date of Birth

Date of Death

Where Buried

8/17/1945
Date of Marriage

Denver, Colorado
Place of Marriage

If married more than once:

Name of Spouse

Birthplace

Date of Birth

Date of Death

Where Buried

Date of Marriage

Place of Marriage

Parents of Spouse (with Mother's maiden name) 1st Marriage

Subsequent Marriage (if applicable)

Family Details

Schools attended, dates and degrees:

Community, political work, etc.:

Airforce Institute of Tech. Masters - Control Engr.
Descendant

Descendant

Denver University
Spouse

Spouse

Basic Employment History:

Clubs, Church Affiliations, etc.:

USAF
Descendant

Descendant

Spouse

Spouse

Military Service:

USAF
Descendant

Spouse

M6215931
Genealogical Number

William Thomas Still   Winchester, VA
Name (including maiden name if applicable)   Town of Residence

Fairbourne, Ohio   1/20/1948
Birthplace   Date of Birth   Date of Death   Where Buried

Cynthia Wheatley   Lancaster, PA   8/25/1957
Name of Spouse   Birthplace   Date of Birth   Date of Death

                                                    Lincoln, VA
Where Buried   Date of Marriage   Place of Marriage

If married more than once:

Name of Spouse   Birthplace   Date of Birth   Date of Death

Where Buried   Date of Marriage   Place of Marriage

Samuel E. & Loya Lynn (Pigg) Wheatley
Parents of Spouse (with Mother's maiden name) 1st Marriage

Subsequent Marriage (if applicable)

Family Details

Schools attended, dates and degrees: Community, political work, etc.:
                                            Secretary of Frederick County Republican
                                            Committee, Author of 23 books & producer
Virginia Tech.   of 3 documentary videos. See attached sheet.
Descendant   Done over 1,000 radio & tv
                                            interviews on my books. Lifetime sales -
                                            250,000 + units.
Spouse   Descendant

Basic Employment History: Clubs, Church Affiliations, etc.:
                                            Winchester Kiwanis Club
Writer   Frederick County Personnel Committee
Descendant   Descendant
                                            President, Frederick County Woman's
Writer   Christian Book Club
Spouse   Spouse

Military Service:

Descendant   Spouse

M62159311
Genealogical Number

William S. Still
Name (including maiden name if applicable)

Winchester, VA
Town of Residence

Leesburg, VA
Birthplace

11/5/1983
Date of Birth

Date of Death

Where Buried

Name of Spouse

Birthplace

Date of Birth

Date of Death

Where Buried

Date of Marriage

Place of Marriage

If married more than once:

Name of Spouse

Birthplace

Date of Birth

Date of Death

Where Buried

Date of Marriage

Place of Marriage

Parents of Spouse (with Mother's maiden name) 1st Marriage

Subsequent Marriage (if applicable)

Family Details

Schools attended, dates and degrees:

Bridgewater College
Descendant

Spouse

Basic Employment History:
Won 3rd Place 2001 Virginia State Web Design Contest
Won 1st Place Virginia Regional Science Fair
Descendant

Spouse

Military Service:

Descendant

Community, political work, etc.:
Sherando H.S. Football Team,
Bridgwater College Football Team,
Dean's List @ Bridgewater College
Descendant

Spouse

Clubs, Church Affiliations, etc.:

Descendant

Spouse

Spouse

M62159312
Genealogical Number

Dara C. Still
Name (including maiden name if applicable)

Winchester, VA
Town of Residence

Eustis,FL
Birthplace

12/4/1987
Date of Birth

Date of Death

Where Buried

Name of Spouse

Birthplace

Date of Birth

Date of Death

Where Buried

Date of Marriage

Place of Marriage

If married more than once:

Name of Spouse

Birthplace

Date of Birth

Date of Death

Where Buried

Date of Marriage

Place of Marriage

Parents of Spouse (with Mother's maiden name) 1st Marriage

Subsequent Marriage (if applicable)

Family Details

Schools attended, dates and degrees:

Community, political work, etc.:

Descendant

Descendant

Spouse

Spouse

Basic Employment History:

Clubs, Church Affiliations, etc.:

Descendant

Descendant

Spouse

Spouse

Military Service:

Descendant

Spouse

M62159313
Genealogical Number

Noah Still   Winchester, VA
Name (including maiden name if applicable)   Town of Residence

Woodstock, VA   6/19/1994
Birthplace   Date of Birth   Date of Death   Where Buried

Name of Spouse   Birthplace   Date of Birth   Date of Death

Where Buried   Date of Marriage   Place of Marriage

If married more than once:

Name of Spouse   Birthplace   Date of Birth   Date of Death

Where Buried   Date of Marriage   Place of Marriage

Parents of Spouse (with Mother's maiden name) 1st Marriage

Subsequent Marriage (if applicable)

Family Details

Schools attended, dates and degrees: Community, political work, etc.:

Descendant   Descendant

Spouse   Spouse

Basic Employment History: Clubs, Church Affiliations, etc.:

Descendant   Descendant

Spouse   Spouse

Military Service:

Descendant   Spouse

M62159314
Genealogical Number

Amanda Still
Name (including maiden name if applicable)

Winchester, VA
Town of Residence

Winchester, VA
Birthplace

12/5/1996
Date of Birth

Date of Death

Where Buried

Name of Spouse

Birthplace

Date of Birth

Date of Death

Where Buried

Date of Marriage

Place of Marriage

If married more than once:

Name of Spouse

Birthplace

Date of Birth

Date of Death

Where Buried

Date of Marriage

Place of Marriage

Parents of Spouse (with Mother's maiden name) 1st Marriage

Subsequent Marriage (if applicable)

Family Details

Schools attended, dates and degrees:

Community, political work, etc.:

Descendant

Descendant

Spouse

Spouse

Basic Employment History:

Clubs, Church Affiliations, etc.:

Descendant

Descendant

Spouse

Spouse

Military Service:

Descendant

Spouse

M6218211

Genealogical Number

Amy Lou Gard   Dubois, WY

Name (including maiden name if applicable)   Town of Residence

Iola, Kansas   12-3-1931

Birthplace   Date of Birth   Date of Death   Where Buried

Jack Brazil   Eureka, Kansas   5-6-1930   6-4-2002

Name of Spouse   Birthplace   Date of Birth   Date of Death

Ashes scattered in WY 8-2-1953   Iola, Kansas

Where Buried   Date of Marriage   Place of Marriage

If married more than once:

_____

Name of Spouse   Birthplace   Date of Birth   Date of Death

Where Buried   Date of Marriage   Place of Marriage

Harry J. Brasil & Gertrude B. Mack

Parents of Spouse (with Mother's maiden name) 1st Marriage

Parents of Spouse (with Mother's maiden name) 1st Marriage

Subsequent Marriage (if applicable)

Family Details

Schools attended, dates and degrees: Community, political work, etc.:
Iola J.C. AA 1951;
University of WI, 1953, B.S. in Education   F.S. Volunteer, Campground Host 23 years

Descendant   Descendant
Eureka H.S. 1948; Emporia State University,
1956, B.S. Education   same as descendant

Spouse   Spouse

Basic Employment History: Clubs, Church Affiliations, etc.:

Science & Home Economics Teacher

Descendant   Descendant
Social Studies & American History/
Constitution Teacher

Spouse   Spouse

Military Service:

                                               Korean War Veteran, 1951-1953

Descendant   Spouse

M62182111
Genealogical Number

Christopher Shane Brazil   Wichita, KS
Name (including maiden name if applicable)   Town of Residence

Iola, KS   10/30/1954
Birthplace   Date of Birth   Date of Death   Where Buried

Rebecca A. Jarboe   Olathe, KS   3/4/1963
Name of Spouse   Birthplace   Date of Birth   Date of Death

                            11/11/1982   Iola, KS
Where Buried   Date of Marriage   Place of Marriage

If married more than once:

Name of Spouse   Birthplace   Date of Birth   Date of Death

Where Buried   Date of Marriage   Place of Marriage

Robert Jarboe & Delores Clayton
Parents of Spouse (with Mother's maiden name) 1st Marriage

Subsequent Marriage (if applicable)

Family Details

Schools attended, dates and degrees: Community, political work, etc.:
Wichita State Univ. Admin Justice 5-76
Elem-Burns, Leon, & Wichita, KS/Jr High-Hadley (Wichita)
High School - Wichita Heights. Allen Co. Com. College-Iola   NRA
Descendant   Descendant

Wichita State Univ. & Butler Co. Comm. College
Spouse   Spouse

Basic Employment History: Clubs, Church Affiliations, etc.:
Sedgwick Co. Sheriff - 85-present
79-10-80 Wichita Police, 1-81-6-81 Spring Hill
Ks. Police, 81-12/85 Wichita Co. Sheriff   NRA
Descendant   Descendant
Leoti Ks. Nursing Home
Presbyterian Manor Nursing Home
Sedgwick Co. Sheriff 90-present
Spouse   Spouse

Military Service:

1st Lt, 2nd 117th Infantry, 7th Inf. Division
Descendant   Spouse

M621821111
Genealogical Number

Melina A. Brazil
Name (including maiden name if applicable)

Wichita, KS
Town of Residence

Wichita, KS
Birthplace

7/14/1986
Date of Birth

Date of Death

Where Buried

Name of Spouse

Birthplace

Date of Birth

Date of Death

Where Buried

Date of Marriage

Place of Marriage

If married more than once:

Name of Spouse

Birthplace

Date of Birth

Date of Death

Where Buried

Date of Marriage

Place of Marriage

Parents of Spouse (with Mother's maiden name) 1st Marriage

Subsequent Marriage (if applicable)

Family Details

Schools attended, dates and degrees:

Community, political work, etc.:

Descendant

Descendant

Spouse

Spouse

Basic Employment History:

Clubs, Church Affiliations, etc.:

Descendant

Descendant

Spouse

Spouse

Military Service:

Descendant

Spouse

M6218221
_____
Genealogical Number

Jean Garlinghouse   Evergreen, CO
_____   _____
Name (including maiden **name** if applicable)   Town of Residence

Iowa City, Iowa   5-15-1939
_____   _____   _____   _____
Birthplace   Date of Birth   Date of Death   Where Buried

John Price Witwer, M.D. Pittsburgh, PA   12-3-1940
_____   _____   _____   _____
Name of Spouse   Birthplace   Date of Birth   Date of Death

                         12-28-1968   Vancouver, Washington
_____   _____   _____
Where Buried   Date of Marriage   Place of Marriage

If married more than once:

_____   _____   _____   _____
Name of Spouse   Birthplace   Date of Birth   Date of Death

_____   _____   _____
Where Buried   Date of Marriage   Place of Marriage

George Russell Witwer & Jane Hull Devenney
_____
Parents of Spouse (with Mother's maiden name) 1st Marriage

_____
Subsequent Marriage (if applicable)

Family Details

Schools attended, dates and degrees: Community, political work, etc.:

On Back   On Back
_____   _____
Descendant   Descendant

On Back   On Back
_____   _____
Spouse   Spouse

Basic Employment History: Clubs, Church Affiliations, etc.:

On Back   On Back
_____   _____
Descendant   Descendant

On Back   On Back
_____   _____
Spouse   Spouse

Military Service:

On Back
_____   _____
Descendant   Spouse

Schools attended, dates, and degrees:

Descendant:

University of Kansas	1960 A.B.
University of Kansas, Nursing	1965 B.S.
University of Washington	1966 M.N.

Spouse:

Amherst College	1962 A.B.
Cornell University Medical School	1966 M.D.
Intern at University of Washington	
Radiology Residency, University of Vermont	

Basic Employment History:

Descendant:

Staff Nurse
Instructor at University of Washington
Assistant Professor University of Oregon Medical School

Spouse:

Medical Staff, Lutheran Medical Center
Chairman, Radiology
President, Medical Staff

Miltary Service:

Descendant:

Captain, US Army 1967-1969
Vietnam Soldier, Commendation Medal with "V", Bronze Star, Air Medal

Community, political work, etc.:

Descendant:

Legislative Aide
Colorado State Capitol
Mount Evans Hospice Volunteer

Spouse:

Colorado State Representative (HD 25)
Joint Budget Committee

Clubs, Church Affliation, etc.:

Descendant:

Phi Beta Kappa
Pi Beta Phi
D.A.R.

M62182211

Genealogical Number

Robert Earl Witwer

Golden, CO

Name (including maiden name if applicable)

Town of Residence

Lincoln, NB | 2-10-1971

Birthplace | Date of Birth | Date of Death | Where Buried

Heather Marie Hughes | Patuxent River Naval Base, MD | 10-4-1972

Name of Spouse | Birthplace | Date of Birth | Date of Death

12-28-1995 | Washington, DC

Where Buried | Date of Marriage | Place of Marriage

If married more than once:

Name of Spouse | Birthplace | Date of Birth | Date of Death

Where Buried | Date of Marriage | Place of Marriage

Captain Michael Bryant Hughes Ph.D., & Shirley Marie Carlson

Parents of Spouse (with Mother's maiden name) 1st Marriage

Subsequent Marriage (if applicable)

Family Details

Schools attended, dates and degrees:

On Back

Descendant

On Back

Spouse

Community, political work, etc.:

On Back

Descendant

On Back

Spouse

Basic Employment History:

On Back

Descendant

On Back

Spouse

Clubs, Church Affiliations, etc.:

On Back

Descendant

On Back

Spouse

Military Service:

Descendant

Spouse

Schools attended, dates, and degrees:

Descendant: Amerhst College   1993 B.A.
University of Chicago Law School   1996 J.D.

Spouse: University of Pennsylvania   1994 B.S.
University of Chicago Law School   1997 J.D.

Basic Employment History:

Descendant: Hogan & Hartson Law Firm, Associate
Assistant Director - Department of Natural Resources, State of Colorado
Assistant General Counsel - Coors Brewing Company

Spouse: Private Law Practice
Deputy Counsel to Governor of Colorado

Community, politcal work, etc:

Descendant: Chief Counsel, State Republican Party
Board Member, Denver Central Shelter

Spouse: State Board of Equalization
Delegate to 2000 Republican National Convention
Colorado Reapportionment Commission

Clubs, Church Affiliation, etc.:

Descendant: Board of Trustees, Rockland Church
Editor,   *Amherst Spectator*
Second Place, National Speech Competition
Federalist Society

Spouse: University of Chicago Law Review
Federalist Society President
Alpha Phi President
USFSA Gold Medalist, Figure Skating

M621822111

Genealogical Number

John Michael Witwer   Golden, CO

Name (including maiden name if applicable)   Town of Residence

Wheat Ridge, CO   1-9-2001

Birthplace   Date of Birth   Date of Death   Where Buried

Name of Spouse   Birthplace   Date of Birth   Date of Death

Where Buried   Date of Marriage   Place of Marriage

If married more than once:

Name of Spouse   Birthplace   Date of Birth   Date of Death

Where Buried   Date of Marriage   Place of Marriage

Parents of Spouse (with Mother's maiden name) 1st Marriage

Subsequent Marriage (if applicable)

Family Details

Schools attended, dates and degrees: Community, political work, etc.:

Descendant   Descendant

Spouse   Spouse

Basic Employment History: **Clubs, Church Affiliations, etc.:**

Descendant   Descendant

Spouse   Spouse

Military Service:

Descendant   Spouse

M621822112

Genealogical Number

Robert James Witwer

Golden, CO

Name (including maiden name if applicable)

Town of Residence

Wheat Ridge, CO   12-8-2002

Birthplace   Date of Birth   Date of Death   Where Buried

Name of Spouse   Birthplace   Date of Birth   Date of Death

Where Buried   Date of Marriage   Place of Marriage

If married more than once:

Name of Spouse   Birthplace   Date of Birth   Date of Death

Where Buried   Date of Marriage   Place of Marriage

Parents of Spouse (with Mother's maiden name) 1st Marriage

Subsequent Marriage (if applicable)

Family Details

Schools attended, dates and degrees: Community, political work, etc.:

Descendant   Descendant

Spouse   Spouse

Basic Employment History: Clubs, Church Affiliations, etc.:

Descendant   Descendant

Spouse   Spouse

Military Service:

Descendant   Spouse

M621822113
Genealogical Number

Jeffrey Bryant Witwer   Golden, Co.
Name (including maiden name if applicable)   Town of Residence

Wheat Ridge, Co.   1/3/2005
Birthplace   Date of Birth   Date of Death   Where Buried

Name of Spouse   Birthplace   Date of Birth   Date of Death

Where Buried   Date of Marriage   Place of Marriage

If married more than once:

Name of Spouse   Birthplace   Date of Birth   Date of Death

Where Buried   Date of Marriage   Place of Marriage

Parents of Spouse (with Mother's maiden name) 1st Marriage

Subsequent Marriage (if applicable)

Family Details

Schools attended, dates and degrees: Community, political work, etc.:

Descendant   Descendant

Spouse   Spouse

Basic Employment History: Clubs, Church Affiliations, etc.:

Descendant   Descendant

Spouse   Spouse

Military Service:

Descendant   Spouse

M62182212

Genealogical Number

Elizabeth Anne Witwer   Norwalk, CT

Name (including maiden name if applicable)   Town of Residence

Denver, CO   7-11-1973

Birthplace   Date of Birth   Date of Death   Where Buried

Mark Evan Feiner   Middletown, NY   2-13-1972

Name of Spouse   Birthplace   Date of Birth   Date of Death

                      2-19-2000   Golden, CO

Where Buried   Date of Marriage   Place of Marriage

If married more than once:

Name of Spouse   Birthplace   Date of Birth   Date of Death

Where Buried   Date of Marriage   Place of Marriage

Dr. Frederick Steven Feiner & Judith Anne Ehrenfeld

Parents of Spouse (with Mother's maiden name) 1st Marriage

Subsequent Marriage (if applicable)

Family Details

Schools attended, dates and degrees: Community, political work, etc.:

On Back

Descendant   Descendant

On Back

Spouse   Spouse

Basic Employment History: Clubs, Church Affiliations, etc.:

On Back   On Back

Descendant   Descendant

On Back   Phi Beta Kappa

Spouse   Spouse

Military Service:

Descendant   Spouse

Schools attended, dates, and degrees:

Descendant: Amherst College
Breadloaf School of English At Middlebury College

Spouse: Brown University
Breadloaf School of English At Middlebury College

Basic Employment History:

Descendant: Maderia School, Holland Hall, Birch Wathen, Lenox School,
Greenwich Academy, English Teacher

Spouse: Flint Hills School, English Teacher
Greenwich Academy, Chairman, Department of English

Clubs, Church Affiliation, etc.:

Descendant: National Merit Scholar
1st Congregational Church of Norwalk

Spouse: Phi Beta Kappa

M621822121
Genealogical Number

Rebecca Anne Feiner
Name (including maiden name if applicable)

Norwalk, CT
Town of Residence

Greenwich, CT
Birthplace

6/6/2004
Date of Birth

Date of Death

Where Buried

Name of Spouse

Birthplace

Date of Birth

Date of Death

Where Buried

Date of Marriage

Place of Marriage

If married more than once:

Name of Spouse

Birthplace

Date of Birth

Date of Death

Where Buried

Date of Marriage

Place of Marriage

Parents of Spouse (with Mother's maiden name) 1st Marriage

Subsequent Marriage (if applicable)

Family Details

Schools attended, dates and degrees:

Community, political work, etc.:

Descendant

Descendant

Spouse

Spouse

Basic Employment History:

Clubs, Church Affiliations, etc.:

Descendant

Descendant

Spouse

Spouse

Military Service:

Descendant

Spouse

M6218222
_____
Genealogical Number

Jane Garlinghouse   Richmond, CA
_____   _____
Name (including maiden name if applicable)   Town of Residence

Owatowa, Minn.   6-26-1943
_____   _____   _____   _____
Birthplace   Date of Birth   Date of Death   Where Buried

_____   _____   _____   _____
Name of Spouse   Birthplace   Date of Birth   Date of Death

_____   _____   _____
Where Buried   Date of Marriage   Place of Marriage

If married more than once:

_____   _____   _____   _____
Name of Spouse   Birthplace   Date of Birth   Date of Death

_____   _____   _____
Where Buried   Date of Marriage   Place of Marriage

_____
Parents of Spouse (with Mother's maiden name) 1st Marriage

_____
Subsequent Marriage (if applicable)

Family Details

Schools attended, dates and degrees: Community, political work, etc.:
University of Kansas; Stanford University;
University of California, Davis 1976, B.S.   _____
Descendant   Descendant

_____   _____
Spouse   Spouse

Basic Employment History: Clubs, Church Affiliations, etc.:

Health Care Professional-Kaiser Permanente   _____
Descendant   Descendant

_____   _____
Spouse   Spouse

Military Service:

_____   _____
Descendant   Spouse

M6218231
Genealogical Number

Richard Earl Garlinghouse, Jr.   San Francisco, CA
Name (including maiden name if applicable)   Town of Residence

                   4/12/1940
Birthplace   Date of Birth   Date of Death   Where Buried

Margaret Ann Pettus   San Francisco, CA   6/9/1945
Name of Spouse   Birthplace   Date of Birth   Date of Death

                   9/23/1973   Atherton, CA
Where Buried   Date of Marriage   Place of Marriage

If married more than once:

Name of Spouse   Birthplace   Date of Birth   Date of Death

Where Buried   Date of Marriage   Place of Marriage

John Donald Pettus & Imelda
Parents of Spouse (with Mother's maiden name) 1st Marriage

Subsequent Marriage (if applicable)

Family Details

Schools attended, dates and degrees: Community, political work, etc.:

Stanford University BA, '62; M. ARCH. '67   Trustee; Convent of Sacred Heart
Descendant   Descendant

University of California at Berkeley '65
Spouse   Spouse

Basic Employment History: Clubs, Church Affiliations, etc.:

Architect & Real Estate Developer   Bohemian Club
Descendant   Descendant

Artist   California Tennis Club, Junior League
Spouse   Spouse

Military Service:

US Coast Guard
Descendant   Spouse

M62182312

Genealogical Number

Sarah McCall Garlinghouse   San Francisco, CA

Name (including maiden name if applicable)   Town of Residence

San Francisco, CA 9-26-1975

Birthplace Date of Birth Date of Death Where Buried

Name of Spouse Birthplace Date of Birth Date of Death

Where Buried Date of Marriage Place of Marriage

If married more than once:

Name of Spouse Birthplace Date of Birth Date of Death

Where Buried Date of Marriage Place of Marriage

Parents of Spouse (with Mother's maiden name) 1st Marriage

Subsequent Marriage (if applicable)

Family Details

Schools attended, dates and degrees: Community, political work, etc.:

University of PA, BA in 1999 & Columbia University, MS in 2003

Descendant   Descendant

Spouse   Spouse

Basic Employment History: Clubs, Church Affiliations, etc.:

Descendant   Descendant

Spouse   Spouse

Military Service:

Descendant   Spouse

M62182311
_____
Genealogical Number

Elizabeth Clark Garlinghouse   New York
                                           _____
Name (including maiden name if applicable)   Town of Residence

San Francisco, CA   1-8-1978
_____   _____   _____   _____
Birthplace   Date of Birth   Date of Death   Where Buried

_____   _____   _____   _____
Name of Spouse   Birthplace   Date of Birth   Date of Death

_____   _____   _____
Where Buried   Date of Marriage   Place of Marriage

If married more than once:

_____   _____   _____   _____
Name of Spouse   Birthplace   Date of Birth   Date of Death

_____   _____   _____
Where Buried   Date of Marriage   Place of Marriage

_____
Parents of Spouse (with Mother's maiden name) 1st Marriage

_____
Subsequent Marriage (if applicable)

Family Details

Schools attended, dates and degrees: Community, political work, etc.:

University of California at Berkeley, 1999
_____   _____
Descendant   Descendant

_____   _____
Spouse   Spouse

Basic Employment History: Clubs, Church Affiliations, etc.:

_____   _____
Descendant   Descendant

_____   _____
Spouse   Spouse

Military Service:

_____   _____
Descendant   Spouse

M62182313
_____
Genealogical Number

Katherine Monroe Garlinghouse   Washington, D.C.
_____   _____
Name (including maiden name if applicable)   Town of Residence

San Francisco, CA   12-23-1980
_____   _____   _____   _____
Birthplace   Date of Birth   Date of Death   Where Buried

_____   _____   _____   _____
Name of Spouse   Birthplace   Date of Birth   Date of Death

_____   _____   _____
Where Buried   Date of Marriage Place of Marriage

If married more than once:

_____   _____   _____   _____
Name of Spouse   Birthplace   Date of Birth   Date of Death

_____   _____   _____
Where Buried   Date of Marriage Place of Marriage

_____
Parents of Spouse (with Mother's maiden name) 1st Marriage

_____
Subsequent Marriage (if applicable)

Family Details

Schools attended, dates and degrees: Community, political work, etc.:

Tulane University, B.A., 2003
_____   _____
Descendant   Descendant

_____   _____
Spouse   Spouse

Basic Employment History: Clubs, Church Affiliations, etc.:

_____   _____
Descendant   Descendant

_____   _____
Spouse   Spouse

Military Service:

_____   _____
Descendant   Spouse

M6218232

Genealogical Number

Gretchen Ann Garlinghouse   Oakland, CA

Name (including maiden name if applicable)   Town of Residence

Lincoln, NB   1-3-1947

Birthplace   Date of Birth   Date of Death   Where Buried

Dennis Gregg Huddleston   Upland, CA   5-16-1949

Name of Spouse   Birthplace   Date of Birth   Date of Death

                              5-12-1974   Oakland, CA

Where Buried   Date of Marriage   Place of Marriage

If married more than once:

Name of Spouse   Birthplace   Date of Birth   Date of Death

Where Buried   Date of Marriage   Place of Marriage

William Roy Huddleston & Doris Imogen Rains

Parents of Spouse (with Mother's maiden name) 1st Marriage

Subsequent Marriage (if applicable)

Family Details

Schools attended, dates and degrees: Mills   Community, political work, etc.:
College, 1969, B.A.; Calif. College of Arts & Crafts,
1971: California Secondary Credential

Descendant   Descendant

University of California, Berkeley, 1972, B.A.

Spouse   Spouse

Basic Employment History: High School Art &   Clubs, Church Affiliations, etc.:
Photography Teacher Oakland Mus. Preparatory
School: Curatorial Asst. in Art and the College   Montclair Prebyterian Church; California Art & Education Assn.

Descendant   Descendant

Arborist   International Society of Arboriculture

Spouse   Spouse

Military Service:

                                                       Conscientious Objector, 2 Years Service as attendant to
                                                       handicapped.

Descendant   Spouse

185

M62182321
_____
Genealogical Number

Zachary Clark Huddleston   Oakland, CA
_____   _____
Name (including maiden name if applicable)   Town of Residence

Oakland, Califonia   9-4-1984
_____   _____   _____   _____
Birthplace   Date of Birth   Date of Death   Where Buried

_____   _____   _____   _____
Name of Spouse   Birthplace   Date of Birth   Date of Death

_____   _____   _____
Where Buried   Date of Marriage   Place of Marriage

If married more than once:

_____   _____   _____   _____
Name of Spouse   Birthplace   Date of Birth   Date of Death

_____   _____   _____
Where Buried   Date of Marriage   Place of Marriage

_____
Parents of Spouse (with Mother's maiden name) 1st Marriage

_____
Subsequent Marriage (if applicable)

Family Details

Schools attended, dates and degrees: Community, political work, etc.:
St. Mary's College High School, June '03
University of California, Santa Cruz, since Sep. 2003
_____   _____
Descendant   Descendant

_____   _____
Spouse   Spouse

Basic Employment History: Clubs, Church Affiliations, etc.:

_____   _____
Descendant   Descendant

_____   _____
Spouse   Spouse

Military Service:

_____   _____
Descendant   Spouse

10.

<u>THE MARTHA POAGE MOORE STILL LINE</u>
<u>PICTURES</u>

Martha Poage Moore Still
(M621)   B. 1/28/1800   D. 12/25/1888

Thomas Chalmers Still
(M6215)   B. 7/6/1833   D. 8/20/1922

Aruna Grant Still
(M62154)   B. 10/29/1865   D. 10/29/1959

Aruna Grant Still & Albert Davies Wedding
(M62154)   B. 8/16/1865   D. 10/29/1959

Helena Adelaide Davies & John Hannon Atkinson Wedding
(M621542)   B. 5/23/1890   D. 10/31/1918

Thomas Albert Davies
(M621545) B. 1/1/1897 D. _____

"Davies Boys at Still Ranch"

Still Family - LaPanza, CA about 1890

II.

THE WILLIAM TAYLOR MOORE LINE

The William Taylor Moore Line

William Taylor Moore was the third child of James, "The Captive" and the second child of Barbara Taylor Moore who died shortly after his birth. He lived until he was fourteen with his Taylor grandparents in Tennessee before returning to his father in Abbs' Valley. While there he made fast friendship with his Taylor cousin who became a Methodist Bishop and missionary to Africa. It is said that he regularly supported him in his work. Below are excerpts from an article about him that appeared in the Clinch Valley News in 1911.

This is a story of a simple Christian man whose life covered the greater part of the nineteenth century. His life was memorable rather for the immediate family history which preceded it, and for what he saw and heard, and for the things which occurred within its span, than for what he himself did. He lived in the wonder time of history. When he was born Jefferson was president, and Alexander Hamilton was in the zenith of his marvelous powers and in the shadow of the Republic's first martyrdom. Washington had been dead but three years and Patrick Henry but five. He remembered Napoleon on the imperial throne, Waterloo, and the death at St. Helena. His life encompassed the passing of the Lake School of poets, and the birth and death of nearly all the great lights of the Victorian era. He was nursed almost in the lap of the Revolution; he witnessed the rise and fall of the Confederacy; the birth and death of Lincoln and Lee, and the mighty clash of tongue and pen and sword with which their names are linked. In his time the pick of the archaeologist transfigured history, and the inspired revelations of geologist and astronomer Christianized science. The tallow dip was supplanted by the arc light, the sickle by the reaper and the flail by the thresher. He saw the map of the world changed and distance annihilated by steam and electricity. And along the little stream where in boyhood he had tracked elk and bear and deer he lived to see Corliss engines and palace cars and to hear a confusion of foreign tongues outdoing the perplexities of Babel.

Here March 7th, 1802, the subject of this sketch, William Taylor Moore, was born. What a romantic setting for the birth of one who was to travel to the gateway of the twentieth century! It's environment seems as far removed from the busy industrial scenes, the railways and the coke ovens of our Tazewell, as the times of good Haroun Alrishchid, when the childhood of another age was borne in shadow-sloops "by Bagdad's shrines of fretted gold." The crab apple and wild rose thickets of Abb's Valley were still ringing to the "flutes of Arcadia" and on the wilder frontier across the Ohio young barbarians were at play. There are no young barbarians now, simply little Indians in circumscribed and guarded settlements; but somewhere in the far borderlands, let us hope, the Arcadian wind harps still are playing.

But there was tragedy, as well as romance, in his coming, for his mother died when he was but a few days old. When he was about six weeks old his grandmother Taylor went on a visit to her kinsfolk in the middle Tennessee and took him with her. She was a member of the family which afterwards gave to Tennessee a brilliant Governor and Senator and to Methodism a distinguished missionary Bishop. This turned out to be a rather long visit, as the motherless boy remained there until he was fourteen years of age. Whether he had better school advantages there than his own neighborhood afforded is not known, but his education was not neglected, and he returned home well advanced in the elementary studies of that time.

In after years when this region became worthless as a hunting ground, Mr. Moore sold a thousand acres for one thousand dollars.

While, as a youth, he was fond of hunting, and spent much time at it, yet he did not neglect his duties. In the spring and summer he worked on the farm and in the fall and winter he attended school. The schoolhouse was six miles from his home and, although he walked, he attended so regularly and was so successful in his work that at an early age he was qualified to teach, which he did for several years. He was an earnest Christian, and in addition to his regular work, which was strenuous enough in those days, he taught on Sundays a community class of children and grown people, of all ages, in the wilds of McDowell County, about twelve miles from Abb's Valley. The curriculum of this heterogeneous school embraced almost everything from the primer to the Bible. School opened at sunrise and closed at sunset, and, as the teacher walked to and fro, it was necessary for him to start from home before dawn. It seems that long journeys afoot were of frequent occurrence. He was in the habit of thus attending court at Jeffersonville twenty odd miles away, and it was his custom to return the same day. He walked barefooted, his shoes slung by a string across his shoulder.

In the year 1826, at the age of twenty-four, he was married to Miss Matilda Peery, a daughter of George Peery. Of this union two daughters were born, one of whom died in infancy, the other, Lavinia, married Cyrus McDonald and moved with her husband to Missouri. He lost his wife about the year 1835.

In 1843 he married Miss Mary Barns, a member of the well-known Cove family. To them were born nine children, four daughters and five sons, one of whom, Clinton, died in infancy. Robert, the eldest son, enlisted in the army at the age of 16, and was killed at the battle of Winchester. He fills an unknown grave on that battlefield. (We now know that he is buried in the Confederate Cemetary in Winchester). His other sons, Charles, Luther and Oscar are still living. Charley, in Monroe county, W.Va; Squire Luther lives at Tazewell, and Oscar at the old home in Abb's Valley. The daughters all married natives of this county and are still living. They are Matilda, wife of Samuel Mustard, LaVicie, wife of

R.T. Higginbotham, Barbara, relict of Joseph Moss, and Mary, wife of Allen Davidson.

"Uncle Bill" Moore, as he was affectionately called by his friends, lived his entire life of ninety-one years, except the first fourteen, on the farm where he was born. Among his neighbors and acquaintances, throughout that long period, he "bore without abuse the grand old name of gentleman." He was a cordial host and many enjoyed the hospitality of his home. He was kind to the poor and one of his daughters bears witness that he never under any circumstances refused food or lodging to the passing stranger. He was a zealous member of the Methodist church, yet he delighted in entertaining ministers of all denominations. He was a member of the first missionary conference held in this part of the country, and beginning early in life, he contributed, on a yearly ascending scale, to the missionary cause. During his last years, he set apart Friday as a day of fasting that his offering might be more generous, and one of his last requests to the daughter who had been the stay and companion of his old age, was to send a remittance, after his death, to his cousin, the good Bishop Taylor, in Africa. He died December 29th, 1891, survived by his wife, who lived until the year 1906.

His descendants are many, and the story of his life, and of the heroism and sufferings of the pioneer family in Abb's Valley, will be handed down to succeeding generations far into the future. He was the last connecting link between the old order and the new. He sleeps amid the scenes where in tranquility and beneficience his long life was spent. Many who have not yet reached middle age remember the kindly face and have heard with delight, around a grandfather's fireside, the stories of his romantic boyhood and the bedtime prayer of simple faith and hope. And one of these has stood at evening time on the little pastoral hillock where he is at rest, and heard the bold call of the subconscious pioneer, and has seen a magic reel unroll shadowy films of that far away time when the fires were lighted in the Indian camp hardby, and the treble call of the panther was heard in the gorge beyond.

William Taylor was involved indirectly with the opening of the famed Pocahontas Coalfield. In 1881, William Arthur Lathrop was sent to the Abb's Valley area to open up those coalfields. An account of this was given in a Bluefield, W.VA. paper as follows:

"Mr. Lathrop, a 27-year-old mining engineering graduate of LeHigh University, and his 24-year-old bride, Harriet, left New York in November of 1881, bound for the wilds of southwestern Virginia. On November 22, they reached the end of the N&W line (at that time) in Dublin, VA., and travelled by carriage to Pearisburg, to Princeton, then on to Pocahontas.

Since the area was then primarialy wilderness, the Lathrops spent their first few days in the area at the Squire Moore home in Abb's Valley (named for Absalom Looney. The town of Tazewell was then known as Jeffersonville.)

However, their "northern" ways were vastly different from those of the Moore's, and the Lathrops immediately searched for their own temporary housing.

Around the first of February, the Lathrops moved from the Moore's home and established a home in another Abb's Valley dwelling they shared with the Spotts family. "As soon as possible," Mrs. Lathrop wrote in a letter to her children, "we settled in two rooms, and started housekeeping, a happy couple."

The second child of William Taylor was Robert Henry Moore. He was wounded at Winchester, VA. in the battle of 9/19/84 and died 11/17/84. He is in the <u>Roster of Confederate Soldiers buried in Stonewall Cemetery, Winchester, Virginia</u> compiled by the Turner Ashby Chapter #54 of the United Daughters of the Confederacy on page 47 and buried in plot #328 in that cemetary. In "Notes by Amanda Barns Sutherland" printed in the September, 1999 newsletter of the Tazewell County Historical Society, this account was given of his death:

When the Civil War came on he (Oscar Fitzallen, believed to be a relative of Robert Henry's mother, Mary Barns Moore) returned to Tazewell to join the Confederate Army. He planned to come back by way of Cape of Good Hope. Fortunately, for some reason he did not take the boat as planned. It was wrecked. Later he came by way of the Isthmus of Panama. He joined the Army and was made Lieutenant. He spent some time in camp near Lewisburg, West Virginia; was captured at Winchester while carrying Robert Moore, his wounded nephew, off the battlefield. I think he was held prisoner 'till the close of the war.

I am indebted to Jim Fredlock, (M6223121), great-grandson of William Taylor Moore and grandson of Matilda Moore Mustard, (M6223) fourth child of William Taylor, for the history below of the Mustard family:

Early in the 18th century the Mustards lived in a town called Freedown, in Ireland. It was from the family home in Freedown that the first came to America. The events which led to the first Mustard leaving the land of his birth is an often told tale which has been handed down from one generation to another. However, the legend has been verified by an old Irish lady, a Mrs. Groggin, who was born and grew up in the town of Freedown, Ireland. This lady, now of San Antonio, Texas related that when she was a girl she often ate apples from the "old Mustard orchard." The lady was brought up by her grandfather, who was an Irish sea captain. She remembers hearing her grandfather tell the "Tale of the Corpse," it being a story of much interest, since the events took place in their home community. The story goes:

In the area of Freedown, Ireland, about the middle of the 18th century, there was much interest due to religious persecution. There was friction between the Protestant and Catholic peoples. A Frenchman, who was a Catholic, died in Freedown, and a wake was held. The Priest was unable to come until the following day, so the people of the neighborhood gathered to continue the observance of the wake.

Among those who attended were three young boys, aged 16 years, William Mustard, Robert Barns, and another, name unknown. The boys, full of mischief, decided to play a trick on the priest. Sometime during the early morning hours the women of the group went to the kitchen to prepare food for themselves and to have everything in readiness upon the arrival of the priest. The older men had become tired of talking and had gone to sleep, leaving the corpse unattended. The boys found this to be the perfect time to carry out their plan. They took the corpse from the coffin, tied some ropes around it and pulled it up into the chimney through the fireplace. The ropes were then passed through the chimney and fastened to a door or window on the outside of the house.

In the morning the priest came, and was in the midst of his prayers when the three pranksters lowered the corpse from the interior of the soot filled chimney. The sight of the soot covered corpse nearly frightened the poor priest out of his wits, not to mention the others present. Since it was a serious offense to molest a corpse, the young boys made a speedy department to America, to safety and freedom.

After some years the two boys, William Mustard and Robert Barnes, married sisters, Brown. It was from the wife of William that the peculiarity of the structure of the hands known as "straight fingers" came into the Mustard family and continues even in the seventh generation. To William Mustard and his wife were born two sons, William and James. When the sons were small, the family returned to Ireland on a visit. Upon returning to the US, the father fell from a gang plank at Norfolk, VA and was drowned. The mother and her sons returned to their home in what is now Giles County where the mother died in a short time. While herding cattle in Tazewell County for Mr. Brown, their uncle, one cold winter the brothers became lost in the woods and William was frozen to death. Thus there remained only James Mustard from whom are descended the many branches of the Mustard family as we know it at present.

We know nothing more of the events in the life of James until his marriage to Sarah Munsey at Mechanicsburg, Virginia, on May 4, 1791. The story is told of how the couple were returning from a flax "scutching" party when they met the minister and asked him to marry them, which he did on the spot in a downpour of rain. To them were born 8 children: William, John, Joshua, James, Elisha, Polly, Julia and Sally. Three of the sons married Patterson sisters, who were the daughters of Issac and Agnes (Patton) Patterson, a prominent family of the Cove section of Wythe Country.

William, who married Annah Patterson, was the father of Sarah, Nancy, Matilda, Joseph, J. Thomas, Harvey R, Wesley Newton, William Gratton, J. Jasper and Samuel P.

All his sons, except Joseph, who died young, served in the Confderate Army. William was reportedly the first manufacturer of gun powder in the area. The shop stood on the farm now owned by Mrs. Hiram Stowers at Mechanicsburg, VA. William Gratton was the first Bland County surveyor.

John, who married Dicie Patterson, was the father of James Harvey, William P., Josh, Elisha, Elizabeth, Maddie, Mary, Tommy, Jane, Allen, Anne, and Kenny. He was one of the six commissioners appointed upon the formation of the County to lay off the County into four magisterial districts. Three of his sons are known to have served in the Confederate army.

Sharon Mustard (M6223322), granddaughter of Matilda Moore Mustard, married Douglas J. Katz who had an illustrious career in the U.S. Navy. The Bluefield Daily Telegraph (Katz is a native of Bluefield, W.VA) described the retirement ceremony of Admirial Katz, who retired from the Navy in August of 1997:

Although he referred to it as his "last hurrah" during his command change speech Friday aboard the USS LaBoon, Vice Admiral Douglas Katz, USN, may have more cheers remaining to add to his distinguished 32-year career as an officer in the U.S. Navy.

Katz, rather slight of build but possessing a most commanding powerful voice, struggled vocally and emotionally a couple times as he talked about the resourcefulness of the "American Blue Jackets" and as he read from a hand-written note on the command change program.

"Surface warfare, in every aspect, has been our life from the people and family services to war, fighting and even planning and budgeting," he said. "We've seen ships come and go; now it's our turn.

"We leave knowing we have given our all and can only hope the Navy is better of for us having served." Getting out that final line was, perhaps, the most difficult words he had had to deliver. Katz was the eighth commander of the U.S. Atlantic Surface Fleet, and served at that post from September of 1994 until Friday.

Always humorous and always filled with respect for his family, his Bluefield roots, the Naval Academy and all those he served with, Katz was obviously not surrendering his flag, but rather repositioning for the three months between "six June" and his retirement on "one August." During the ceremony, he fired-off a few well-laced salvos in the direction of Congress and the Pentagon.

Flanked by "side boys" posted on the bunting-bedecked dais of the LaBoon, Katz expressed his regrets that Rear Admiral Collins Griffin III was not confirmed by the U.S. Senate in time for the ceremony, and was thus unable to participate in the command change ceremony.

"The Senate was just unable to get Hank confirmed in time," Katz said.

The shot aimed for the Senate was tame in comparison to the volley Katz lobbed in the direction of Capitol Hill in general. "I do have concerns with today's budget cuts," he said. "I'm reminded of the commercial that says: Pay me now or pay me later. It's the pay me later that bothers me. We can make 'just in time readiness' work, but we must maintain our ships to do it."

There was a note of lamentation when Katz referred to a discussion he had with his father, Leroy Katz, before his death. In a way, that discussion indirectly led to the command change aboard the LaBoon.

Katz said his father discussed burial at sea and although the favorite ship of his son's diverse command had been the battleship USS New Jersey, he said: "The New Jersey is already gone and the (carrier, USS) America will be gone soon. The (destroyer USS) Deyo was the only ship I had commanded still in action." "Make it Deyo," he said to me. "She'll be around for a while."

Katz said he had met Captain John Francis "Jake" LaBoon, a fellow Naval Academy graduate (1944) who served in the Chaplain Corps. In addition, Katz's son, Ensign Robert Katz, is operations officer aboard the LaBoon. "I'd give him my sword, even though he's got one newer and better," Katz said.

At two points during his speech, Katz referred to Bluefield. First to recognize the smatering of Bluefielders among the 500 or 600 people attending the ceremony, then again to thank the community "for our up-bringing."

His mother and father, Leroy and Wayne Katz passed away within a year of each other in 1994. During the ceremony, Katz presented flowers to his wife, Sharon, his sister, Leslie Katz, and his daughter-in-law, Melanie Katz. His daughter, Erica, and son-in-law, Walter Nathaniel Perkins, were unable to attend because Erica was in Charlottesville, VA., expecting the birth of her daughter Saturday.

"FTD should be delivering her flowers at this very moment," Katz said. As a naval officer, he expects precision.

"I don't know how they do it," Leslie Katz said during the reception that followed the ceremony. "Ensigns come and pick us up at Doug and Sharon's quarters, bring us to the events, then when it's time to go, someone just walks over to me, touches me on the arm and says: 'It's time to go.'

"I wonder how they know it's me they're supposed to touch on the arm, " Leslie thought out loud. "They must be well trained."

After receiving the third Distinguished Service Cross of his career during the ceremony, Katz assumed the podium. "Ought Oh!" he said. "We accept awards on behalf of the people who make it happen for us," Katz said, referring to both his medal and to the Meritorious Public Service Award presented to his wife.

"I served with Admiral Katz in Bahrain and again the Gulf," 10-year veteran Navy Seaman and combat videographer, Jeff Russell, said just prior to the ceremony. "He was a good officer. He always put the sailors under his command first."

Admiral Charles R. "Chuck" Larson, superindendent of the U.S. Naval Academy made the same observation during his key-note address. Larson said Katz created the Academy's "Professional Development Department" on one tour in Annapolis, then directed the program during a second placement there.

"He made Midshipmen look forward to the Surface Fleet," Larson said.

Larson went into detail about how Katz, as a gunnersmate aboard the John Paul Jones in 1970, personally effected repairs on a gun mount to enable the ship to lay cover fire for a combined Navy Seal/South Vietnamese Army landing force. Larson said "he welded the gun mount" despite the fact that there were live rounds of ammunition in the turret.

"I got off to a fiery start," Katz later commented. "In Vietnam, I think I grew up."

Larson also spoke of Sharon's role in creating Ombudsmen services for Navy spouses, creating scholarship foundations and leaving a lasting impression during her husband's career. "You have the toughest job in the Navy, " Larson said to Sharon. "To Doug and Sharon; wherever you go; Fair winds and following seas."

William Luther Moore (M6225), fifth child of William Taylor, known as "Squire Moore," died in 1926. A resolution passed by the Alexander St.Clair Memorial Bible Class on his death is reproduced below:

RESOLUTION

First: That by the death of Honorable W.L. Moore, Tazewell County lost one of its most distinguished, influential and successful citizens and one who had faithfully served it as Representative in the Virginia Legislature, as Justice of the Peace, and School Trustee, and who from young manhood to death had been an important factor in the affairs of the County.

Second: That Esquire Moore was blessed in having a long line of Christian ancestors, from who he inherited an abiding Christian faith, and this inheritance grew and became firmly fixed with the passing years of a long and useful life.

Third: That the kindness of heartwarm sympathy, cordiality and humor, of Esquire Moore endeared him to all who know him intimately, and his cordial and pleasant greetings were sunny spots in the daily lives of many grown folks and children.

Fourth: That Esquire Moore was a zealous member of this, the Alexander St. Clair Memorial Bible Class, and prompt and regular in his attendance upon, and support of this class.

Fifth: That the members of this class lost a friend by the death of Esquire Moore, and that they tender to his widow and family their sincere sympathy for their bereavement.

Sixth: That a copy of this resolution be delivered to the widow and family and be published in the Clinch Valley News.

> JNO. S. BOTTIMORE
> S.M.B. COULLING,
> GEO. C. PEERY, Committee

Oscar Bascom Moore (M6227), the seventh child of William Taylor, died in 1964. His extensive obituary is given below:

Death Marks Passing Of One Of Surviving
Members Of Moore Family Of Abb's Valley
Massacre Fame

Oscar Bascom Moore, 89, prominent farmer and grazier and decsendant of Captain James Moore, most of whose family were murdered in the Abb's Valley massacre of 1786, died at 1 o'clock yesterday morning in Abb's Valley. He had been an invalid for the past ten months.

His death marked the passing of one of the two last surviving direct decendants of the famous Revolutionary war soldier, Captain Moore, who settled in Abb's Valley after the close of the war and whose fights against the Indians is one of the highlights of the pioneer history of Tazewell County.

O.B. Moore was born January 18, 1855, and had lived and reared his family on the Moore farm in a house built across the ravine from the original Moore cabin. Despite his advanced age Mr. Moore retained a clear and active mind which was retentive in memory. He had furnished most of the data which has been compiled by a number of writers on the early history of Tazewell and particularly concerning the Abb's Valley massacre. He was a zealous Methodist, a very successful farmer and grazier and for years had been a director in the Bank of Pocahontas. He had served as special assessor of Tazewell County and once was a candidate for the state legislature on the Farmers' Alliance ticket. He was held in high esteem and his genial hospitality as attested by the hundreds of persons who made visits to his home to get acquainted at first hand with the scenes among which their ancestors lived.

Mr. Moore was twice married. His first wife was Miss Rose McDonald, a native of Martinsburg, Mo. To this union two children were born, WilliamTaylor Moore, of Baileysville, W.VA., and Mrs. Randolph Marshall, of Charlottesville, Va. Some time after the death of his first wife he married Miss Sallie Wilson, of Abb's Valley and to this union three children survive, Freeman Moore of Abb's Valley, Mrs. J. Roy Mullin, 710 Parkway, this city, and Oscar B. Moore, Jr., who is now with the armed forces in France. Besides his second wife and children he is survived by one sister, Mrs. Mary Davidson of Tazewell, a number of nephews and nieces. Among his nephews are Robert H. Moore, of Liberty Street, Bluefield, and W.L. Mustard, Heatherwood Road, this city.

Active pallbearers will be nephews of the deceased.

Honorary pallbears: N.J. Morre, George Gillespie, Charles Duy, L.B. Crawford, W.A. Bishop, W.O. Scruggs, J.K. Sult, R.O. Crockett, Dr. Charles T. StClair, sr., R.M. Baldwin, Dr. M.B. Crockett, Joe Barnes, M.H. Kiser, Joe Wainwright, Sidney Block, C.C. Frazier, Ancil Davidson, R.P. Johnson, Tyler Frazier, Herbert Butt, J.B. Mullin, H.Elmer Kiser, Christie Dennen, Hampton Crawford, Junius Ellett, M. Harvey, Glen Mullin, C.P. Painter, Frank St.Clair, Alex St.Clair, Sonny Thompson, Frank Ellett, C.W. Butt, Ben T. Graham, B.K. Tabor, Baxter Wilson, Will Wilson, C. Maxey, John St.Clair, W.L. Painter, Shel Surface, Dr. Rufus Copenhaver, Buddy Britain, R.A. Tabor, C.T. Bowen, Clint Moss, John W. Buchannan, George Rosenbaum, Judge A.C. Buchanan, James H. Harman, W.F. Dennen, Sol Baach, L. Magrill, J.P. Curtis, A.V. Sproles, J.C. Leister, F.E. Wagner, sr., J.K. Peters, W.J. German, Dr. H.A. Porter, Dr Wade S. St.Clair, Dr. C.J. Reynolds, R.C. Brown, R.C. Harrison and Rev. S.W. Moore.

And, finally, reprinted herewith are excerpts from the obituary of Alfred Leroy Mowery, husband of May Moore Mowery (M622741) granddaughter of Oscar Bascom. Dr. Mowery had an outstanding career in the early stages of the space missions.

Alfred Leroy Mowery, 70, passed away August 26, 2004 at the Methodist Hospital in Houston after a lengthy illness that he met with great determination and courage. Born on August 14, 1934 in Augusta, Georgia, he was a graduate of the Academy of Richmond County. He earned his B.S. degree from Duke University and continued his education at North Carolina State University where he earned his Master's Degree in Nuclear Engineering and Doctorate in Engineering Physics. He was a member of Phi Kappa Phi, Sigma Xi, and Pi Mu Epsilon.

Dr. Mowery's distinguished career began at Los Alamos Scientific Laboratory, followed by his work on the NERVA Program at the Westinghouse Astronuclear Laboratory in Pittsburgh, Pa. He then worked for the original Atomic Energy Commission in Space Nuclear Systems, both in Cleveland and Washington, DC, the Department of State, and Department of Energy. While at DOE, his work focused on nuclear safety and risk assessment programs for both the Galileo and Ulysses missions.

He demonstrated the safety of the RTG's and was granted a patent to be used in future missions. He received citations for his contributions to both the Voyager and Galileo programs. After his retirement, he and Dr. David Black worked on several projects and publications for American Nuclear Society, and conferences on propulsion and space nuclear power. Together they developed a basic design for a compact nuclear rocket, SPARS, and presented the paper at AIAA. He and Dr. Dave McCutchan were writing a book on statistics that we still plan to publish.

He was preceded in death by his parents, Elba Norris Madebach and Alfred Leroy Mowery, Sr. He is survived by his wife of forty-nine years, Mary Moore Mullin Mowery of Las Vegas, Nevada, three children and four grandchildren; son, Mark Wayland Mowery, his wife Beverly and their children, Jeffrey and Melissa of Centreville, VA.; a son, Alfred Leighton Mowery of Houston; a daughter, Cynthia Lacretia Mowery Philistine, her husband Jim and their children, Kyle and Kristen of Houston; and a sister, Michael Nathanson of Houston.

Al and Mary retired to Hilton Head Island, S.C. and then moved to Las Vegas in 1999 in a Sun City community. Al was active in the Sun City Photography Club and Computer Club. He was an avid photographer all his life and published a CD on digital photography.

There are other William Taylor Moore descendants who have had full and interesting lives whose abbreviated biographies are in the biographical section of this book.

12.

THE WILLIAM TAYLOR MOORE LINE
GENEALOGICAL CHARTS

M622 William Taylor Moore - (1) Mathilda Peery
B.3/7/1802   (1)M.9/10/1829   B.1/29/1813
D.12/30/1891   (2) M.9/12/1844   D.12/28/1842

- (2) Mary Bowen Barns
B.1/11/1823
D.4/5/1905

M6221 - Lavinia Walker Moore (1) - Cyrus McDonald
B.8/29/1830   M.9/14/1852   B.8/15/1826
D.1/1/1888   D.11/22/1905

M62211 - William Jackson McDonald - Katherine Maitland
B.6/30/1853   M.10/14/1880   B.4/11/1854
D.10/2/1927   D.4/18/1929

M622111 - Ruth McDonald
B.10/10/1885

M62212 - Charles Black McDonald
B.2/8/1855
D.9/12/1880

M62213 - Rush McDonald
B.6/19/1857
D.6/20/1891

M62214 - Robert McDonald
B.1/17/1859
D. As infant

M62215 - Bud McDonald
B.12/6/1860
D. As infant

*Indicates that a bio is included.

M62216 - Walter Crockett McDonald - Mary Violett
B.2/11/1864   M.12/30/1896   B.5/8/1873
D._____   D._____

  M622161 - Frank Cobb McDonald - Margaret Lucille Heimbach
  B.3/19/1898   M.6/22/1930   B.7/5/1907
  D._____   D._____

    M6221611 - Marylin McDonald
    B.5/24/1933

    M6221612 - Frank Alan McDonald
    B.11/11/1937

  M622162 - Mamie Violette McDonald - Jeremiah Stephen Fruin
  B.2/26/1900   M.5/30/1924   B.2/12/1895
  D._____   D._____

  M6221621 - Robert McDonald Fruin
  B.4/10/1925

  M622163 - Anna Margaret McDonald
  B.11/14/1917
  D._____

M62217 - Olive Moore McDonald - Lee M. Rannabarger
B.2/10/1869   M.10/25/1888   B.11/7/1863
D.5/13/1931   D._____

  M622171 - Mary Lavenia Rannabarger - Walter William Shackelford
  B.2/22/1894   M.2/21/1913   B._____
  D._____   D._____

  M6221711 - Mary Genevieve Shackelford - John Vance Neale
  B.12/10/1915   M.6/27/1937   B.12/25/1909
  D._____   D._____

M6221712 - Kenneth Lee Shackelford - Sara Jane Handley
B.11/1/1917   M._____   B.5/13/1916
D._____   D.4/13/1997

*M62217121** - Kenneth Lee Shackelford, Jr. – Carol Donnelly
B.4/17/1945   M._____   D._____

*M62217122** -   Lavenia Kay Shackelford – Charles Robert Henry
B.4/12/1947   M._____   B.1/1/46

*M622171221** - Kristin Kay Henry - Elston Breen Arntz
B.10/18/1970   M.5/3/1997   B._____

*M622171222** - Jason Charles Henry
B.5/26/1973

*M622171223** - Ryan Patrick Henry
B.8/19/1976

*M622171224** - Courtney Robyn Henry
B.3/18/1980

*M62217123** - Stephen Roy Shackelford – Mary Ellen _____
B.11/6/1949   M. 5/5/1979   B. 12/9/1953

*M6221713** - Donald William Shackelford
B.11/12/1919
D. _____

*M6221714** - Marjorie Lou Shackelford
B.3/11/1921

M622172 - Arthur Rannabarger - Grace Clements
B.5/12/1899   M.5/19/1924   B.2/2/1903
D._____   D._____

M6221721 - Richard Arthur Rannabarger
B.3/28/1925

M6221722 - Robert Lee Rannabarger
B.10/9/1926

M6221723 - Charles Edward Rannabarger
B.9/20/1928

M6221724 - Glen Russell Rannabarger
B.6/17/1932
D.2/17/1933

M6221725 - Juanita Joanne Rannabarger
B.6/10/1934

M6221726 - Mary Lou Rannabarger
B.1/6/1939

M6221727 - Marvin Ray Rannabarger
B.1/6/1939

M622173 - Annie Fields Rannabarger - Allie Wyett
B.1/24/1901   M.1926   B._____
D._____   D._____

M62218 - James Emmett McDonald - Susie Jones
B.9/15/1870   M.9/21/1891   B.2/1871
D._____   D._____

M622181 - John Rush McDonald - Katherine Mayfield
B.9/5/1892   M.6/4/1931   B.5/28/1903
D._____   D._____

M6221811 - Susan Mary McDonald
B.7/20/1932

M6221812 - James Andrew McDonald
B.8/31/1936

M622182 - Maurine McDonald
    B.3/18/1897
    D.7/23/1899

M622183 - W. Huston McDonald - Mary Blakey
    B.1/11/1901   M.5/10/1924   B.12/3/1901
    D._____   D._____

M6221x - Elvira H. Moore (1)
    B.7/7/1832
    D. In Youth

M6222 - Robert Henry Moore (2)
    B.1/16/1845
    D.11/17/1864

M6223 - Matilda Peery Moore(2) - Samuel Patterson Mustard
    B.1/18/1847   M.10/3/1873   B.12/3/1846
    D.11/26/1934   D.10/12/1915

M62231 - William Luther Mustard - Nancy Elizabeth Barns
    B.8/5/1874   M.9/3/1902   B.6/24/1879
    D.11/17/1949   D.12/10/1944

    M622311 - Mary Matilda Mustard - Andrew Wolf McThenia
        B.9/26/1903   M.9/3/1928   B. 1/5/1897
        D. 12/14/1989   D. 12/8/1983

        *M6223111 - Mary Amanda McThenia - Don Robert Iodice
            B.9/8/1933   M.6/10/61   B. 5/22/1928

            *M62231111 - Don Robert Iodice, Jr. - Deborah Forslin
                B. 2/15/1963   M._____   B. 4/22/1955

*M622311111 - Amanda Ruthe Iodice
B.3/29/1986

M62231112 - James Michael Iodice - Rebecca Brackett
B.3/7/1967   M.9/8/91   B. 6/5/1967

M622311121 - Landon Anthony Iodice
B.10/1/1999

M622311122 – McKenna Saige Iodice
B. 4/27/2001

*M6223112 - Andrew Wolf McThenia, Jr. - Anne Whitley
B.8/15/1935   M.2/1962   B.3/25/1938

M62231121 - Paige Barns McThenia - Kirk Bazler Melnikoff
B.4/4/1963   M.8/3/1996   B. 4/5/1969

M62231122 - Andrew Wolf McThenia, III – Gretchen Bell
B.2/26/1965   M. 5/10/1997   B. 8/23/1967

M622311221 – Whitley Wolf McThenia
B. 1/29/2000

M622311222 – Emma Grace McThenia
B. 12/13/2001

M62231123 - William Talmadge McThenia
B.6/1967

M622312 - Elizabeth Barns Mustard - James Ray Fredlock
B.10/14/1905   M.4/6/1928   B.1/27/1901
D.2/15/1986   D.10/11/1989

*M6223121 - James William Fredlock - Jacqueline Joy Hyre
B.9/17/1929   M.6/16/1957   B.5/28/1935

M62231211 - James Herold Fredlock - Shirley Jane Copen
B.2/20/1958   M.12/29/1979   B.2/21/1960

M622312111 - Caitlin Elizabeth Fredlock
B.8/15/1992

M622312112 – Bailie Rebecca Fredlock
B. 1/14/1998

M62231212 - Michael Wilson Fredlock - Jana Leigh Gettlefinger
B.6/26/1959   M.7/24/1993   B.12/20/1964

M622312121 - Kara Wilson Fredlock
B.12/11/1994

M622312122 – Michael L. Fredlock
B. 5/23/1998

M62231213 - John Andrew Fredlock
B.3/28/1962

M6223122 - Joe Barns Fredlock - (1) Arlene Marie Bussey (Div)
B.10/14/1933   (1) M.   B.4/23/1934
                    (2) M.
                    (3) M. 8/22/1992
                              (2) Molly Pickett
                              B._____

                              (3) Anne Carol Holt
                              B. 7/9/1943

*__M62231221__ - (1) Amy Barns Fredlock - Michael John Mintz
B.6/4/1958   M.6/4/1988   B.10/20/1960

*__M622312211__ - Aaron Barns Mintz
B.6/24/1989

*M622312212 - Anna Johnston Mintz
B.5/21/1991

M62231222 - (1) Jenny Elizabeth Fredlock - Mark Stanley Franczak
B.5/9/1961   M.6/4/1988   B.2/14/1957

M622312221 - Amanda Rae Franczak
B.1/6/1990

M622312222 - Marlee Whitman Franczak
B.11/6/91

M622312223 - Ian Mark Franczak
B.4/10/95

M62232 - Robert Clinton Mustard - **M62243** - Margaret Virginia Moore
B.11/21/1876   M.2/24/1915   B.8/21/1879
D.3/3/1938   D._____

M62233 - Grattan Floyd Mustard - **M62916** - Jennie Rebecca Wilson
B.3/13/1879   M.1/21/1914   B.8/7/1886
D._____   D._____

*M622331 - Barnes Samuel Mustard - Mellie Virginia Cassell
B.12/12/1914   M.6/2/1937   B.5/23/1915
D.4/29/1989   D.3/31/1995

*M6223311 - Rebecca Glyn Mustard - Oral Vernon Jones
B.9/5/1938   M. 5/26/1955   B.4/18/1935

*M62233111 - Diana Glyn Jones - Ted Ray Gardner
B.9/13/1958   M.8/2/80   B.3/31/1954

*M622331111 - Laura Allison Gardner
B.12/20/1983

*M622331112 - Thomas Barnes Gardner
B.5/2/1986

*M622331113 - John Sanders Gardner
B.3/28/1990

M62233112 - Samuel Vernon Jones - Lisa Lee Dean
B.6/20/1960   M.8/15/1987   B.4/24/1965

M622331121 - Meredith Hope Jones
B.10/13/1989

M622331122 - Hunter Addison Jones
B.4/19/1993

M6223312 - Nancy Barnes Mustard - Lanny Leck Sparks
B.6/27/1941   M. 6/2/1962   B.5/16/1941

M62233121 - Blenna Rae Sparks - James Mark Patterson
B.7/27/1965   M.10/7/1989   B. 5/5/1956

M622331211 - Ryan Mark Patterson
B.4/21/1993

M622331212 - Leah Rae Patterson
B.5/8/1996

*M62233122 - Lanny Leck Sparks, Jr. - Mary Wood Spencer
B.12/31/1966   M.10/9/1994   B.9/1/1969

*M622331221 - Monroe Spencer Sparks
B.9/20/1997

M622331222 – Jenna Katherine Sparks
B. 8/3/1999

M6223313 - Arden Jane Mustard - William Wayne Seay
B.8/11/1952   M._____   B.3/21/1949

M62233131 - Jonathan Bransford Seay
    B.4/8/1986

M622332 - Clinton Luther Mustard - Geneva Mea Croye
    B.2/8/1916   M.12/24/1937   B.10/28/1918
    D.7/12/1997   D.8/1/1984

M6223321 - Brenda Mustard - Barry A. Noll
    B.7/25/1939   M._____   B.2/5/1939

M62233211 - David Alan Noll - Robyn _____
    B.1/31/1962   M.8/7/1993   B._____

M62233212 - Diane Noll - _____ Knight (Div)
    B.11/24/1964   M._____   B._____

*__M6223322__ - Sharon Lynne Mustard - Douglas J. Katz
    B.1/19/1944   M.6/11/1965   B.5/1/1942

*__M62233221__ - Robert Douglas Katz - Melanie Bell
    B.3/13/1967   M.7/1/1995   B. 8/25/1969

*__M622332211__ – Cameron Robert Katz
    B. 9/9/1998

*__M622332212__ – Cayla Alexis Katz
    B. 3/16/2001

*__M62233222__ - Erica Lynne Katz - Walter Nathaniel Dow Perkins
    B.9/18/1970   M.8/17/1991   B. 6/14/1969

*__M622332221__ - Walter Douglas Dow Perkins
    B.8/18/1994

*__M622332222__ - Sharon Brie-Anna Perkins
    B.6/14/1997

M6223323 - Carol Mustard - _____ Lester
B.8/13/1945   M._____   B._____
D.10/27/1991

    M62233231 - Michael L. Lester
    B.6/26/1970

M6223324 - Clinton Luther Mustard, Jr - Ruth _____
B.3/26/1956   M._____   B._____

M622333 - Grattan Floyd Mustard, Jr. - Dorothy Lawson
B.10/13/1917   M._____   B._____
D._____   D._____

    M6223331 - Karen Mustard - James Kanagy
    B.8/2/1962   M._____   B.6/3/1960

        M62233311 - Katherine Mustard Kanagy
        B.7/12/1989

        M62233312 - Khristina Mustard Kanagy
        B.11/15/1990

        M62233313 - Kimberly Mustard Kanagy
        B.8/21/1992

        M62233314 - James Gregory Kanagy
        B.4/14/1994

M622334 - India Mustard
B.5/8/1921
D.6/9/1930

M62234 - Barbara India Mustard
B.3/21/1882
D.11/5/1887

*M62235 - Oscar Jasper Mustard - Alma Marguerite Leister
  B.4/10/1883   M.9/22/1922   B.8/2/1893
  D.6/24/1945   D.5/21/1987

  *M622351 - Jean Ann Mustard - Richard Lee Whitt, Jr.
    B.7/25/1928   M. 6/5/1948   B.1/30/1921
                                     D.6/10/2002

    M6223511 - Richard Darrell Whitt - Ruth Raney Lewis
      B.7/29/1952   M.11/1/1980   B. 10/27/1959

  *M622352 - Alma Marguerite Mustard - (1) Joseph Anthony Pupello (Div)
    B.7/19/1930   (1) M. 5/2/1951   B. 9/26/1932
                     (2) M.6/9/1997

                                     (2)Thomas Joseph Senn
                                     B.9/9/1928
                                     D.8/12/1997

    M6223521 - Marcia Ann Pupello (1) - Lawrence Smith
      B.12/26/1953   M.1/7/1989   B. 3/2/1954

*M62236 - Samuel Elbert Mustard - Margaret Elizabeth Buchanan
  B.6/16/1889   M.10/14/1915   B.6/14/1891
  D.8/22/1960   D.5/10/1962

  M622361 - Mary Virginia Mustard - (1) Sam Poindexter
    B.10/27/1916   (1) M. 1950   B.
    D.1/20/1999   (2) M. 2/2/1954

                                     (2) Gene Welch (Div)
                                     B. 8/31/1928
                                     D. 9/2000

*M622362 - Elizabeth Barnes Mustard – Eugene E. Elmore
      B.5/13/1923   M. 6/16/1949   B.7/14/1913
                                                 D.12/24/1974

M6224 - James Charles Moore (2) - Sarah Elizabeth Taylor
      B.4/1/1849   M.12/24/1872   B.1/12/1845
      D.4/14/1926   D.5/5/1931

M62241 - William Oscar Moore - Ella Catharine Wylie
      B.11/20/1874   M. 5/28/1911   B.11/7/1889
      D.2/2/1964   D.11/12/1964

    M622411 - Robert Taylor Moore
          B.5/8/1912
          D. 1999

    M622412 - William Oscar Moore, Jr.
          B.12/22/1913
          D.5/27/1989

    M622413 - James Milton Moore
          B. 3/14/1916
          D.5/14/1969

   *M622414 - Elizabeth Brown Moore - Joseph Kirk Peters
          B.7/12/1919   M._____   B.6/15/1892
          D.6/6/2000   D.8/22/1962

   *M622415 - John Clinton Moore
          B.12/30/1923

    M622416 - Nancy Ellen Moore - Glenn Thomas Medford
          B.5/23/1929   M. 2/3/1956   B.4/30/1929
                                            D.4/21/2000

M62242 - Mary India Moore
    B.12/27/1876
    D.2/1/1952

M62243 - Margaret Virginia Moore - **M62232** Robert Clinton Mustard
    B.8/22/1879   M.2/24/1915   B.11/21/1876
    D.7/27/1968   D.3/3/1938

M62244 - Barbara Elvira Moore
    B.3/4/1881
    D.6/3/1966

M62245 - Sallie Matilda Moore - Roy Stennett Beamer
    B.9/26/1883   M.10/29/1913   B.4/7/1881
    D.9/21/1972   D.11/5/1952

    M622451 - Byron Linwell Beamer
        B.7/10/1914
        D.1/11/1975

    M622452 - Charles Madison Beamer
        B.9/21/1915
        D.4/4/1986

    M622453 - Robert Anderson Beamer - Kathryn Ruth Causey
        B.1/27/1919   M._____   B.3/20/1929
        D. _____   D. _____

        M6224531 - Robert Arthur Beamer - Elizabeth Smith
            B.5/22/1953   M._____   B._____

            M62245311 - Rachael Rogers Beamer
            B.6/23/1980

        M6224532 - Sara Kay Beamer - John Andrew Broaddus Holt, III
            B.11/11/1955   M._____   B.6/13/1951

M62245321 - John Andrew Broaddus Holt, IV
B.1/6/1986

M62245322 - Rush Madison Holt
B.12/20/1987

M62245323 - Tristan Asa Holt
B.9/16/1993

M6224533 - Margaret Anita Beamer
B.7/29/1957

M6224534 - Asa Brown Beamer
B.5/20/1959

M6224535 - William Andrew Beamer
B.1/13/1961

M622454 - William Taylor Beamer
B.5/19/1922
D.1977

M622455 - Mary Moore Beamer - William Talbert McNeil
B.10/29/1925   M._____   B.8/10/1917
                                         D._____

M6224551 - Charles Richard McNeil
B.9/8/1951

M6224552 - Barbara Jean McNeil - (1) Dan Belcher (Div)
B.3/24/1954   M._____   B._____
                   M._____

                                (2) William Holesapple
                                     B._____

M62245521 – (1) Michele Ranee Belcher
B.9/5/1978

M62245522 – (1) Todd McNeil Belcher
    B._____

M622456 - Asa Glen Beamer
    B.4/4/1927
    D.10/13/2002

M62246 - Ella Brown Moore
    B.10/3/1886
    D.8/5/1975

M6225 - William Luther Moore (2) - (1) India Taylor
    B.3/31/1851   (1)M.7/2/1879   B.4/2/1850
    D.11/14/1926   (2)M.3/19/1885   D.4/19/1881

                        - (2)Mildred Smith
                            B.11/5/1863
                            D.5/30/1935

M62251 - (1) India Moore - Rufus Pierce Copenhaver
    B.9/10/1880   M.8/7/1907   B.7/31/1875
    D.12/5/1968   D.2/17/1945

    M622511 - Virginia S. Copenhaver
        B.5/31/1908
        D.1/26/1993

    M622512 - John William Copenhaver - Ruth Marie Van Winkle
        B.10/27/1910   M. 7/3/1940   B. 5/4/1915
        D. 1/3/1988   D.12/31/1998

        M6225121 – John William Copenhaver, Jr. – (1) Christina Vestling
            B. 9/8/1942   (1) M. _____   B. 10/7/1943
                       (2) M. _____

                                 (2) Suzanne Mary Novak
                                 B. 11/14/1949

M62251211 –**(1)** – Catherine Anne Copenhaver – Stephen David Martin
      B. 2/28/1971   M. 8/25/1995   B. _____

    M622512111 – Stephen Carl Martin
      B. 8/5/1999

    M622512112 – Catherine Meredith Martin
      B. 2/4/2002

M62251212 – **(1)** – John Carl Copenhaver
    B. 12/14/1973

M6225122 – Mary India Copenhaver
    B. _____

M6225123 – Kathryn Hart Copenhaver
    B. _____

M6225124 – Timothy Taylor Copenhaver
    B. _____

M622513 - Margaret Barns Copenhaver - A.H. Phillips
    B.12/5/1913   M._____   B. 9/14/1917
    D. 4/15/1997   D. 5/1/1977

    M6225131 - Margaret Phillips
      B.11/3/1945
      D.9/16/1949

M622514 - Rufus Pierce Copenhaver, Jr. - Edna Louise Pruden
    B.9/14/1917   M._____   B._____
    D.12/5/1956   D._____

    M6225141 - Taylor Pierce Copenhaver
      B.6/3/1947

M62252 - (2) Robert Henry Moore - Margaret Huston StClair
    B.6/10/1887   M.12/1/1920   B.1/14/1896
    D.7/18/1948   D.3/19/1981

*M622521 - Robert Henry Moore, Jr. - (1) Patricia Hewittson-Fisher (Div)
    B.4/17/1923   (1)M.12/7/1960   B.4/5/1938
                   (2)M.7/26/1995

                                   (2) Judith Dressel
                                    B.6/26/1941

*M6225211 - (1) Robert Henry Moore, III - Lisa Weinberger
      B.10/28/1962   M.9/13/1987   B. 11/9/1965

*M62252111 - Elizabeth Margaret Moore
        B.10/10/1991

*M62252112 - Robert Henry Moore, IV
        B.3/15/1994

*M6225212 - (1) Turner Cronin Moore
      B.2/9/1969

*M622522 - George Walker StClair Moore - Alice Hobson
    B.10/13/1924   M. 6/20/1945   B.1/20/1925
                               D.2/5/2001

*M6225221 - Mary Berkeley Moore - Eric Courtney (Div)
      B.9/8/1946   M._____   B._____
      D.1/27/1995

*M62252211 - Ian Berkeley Courtney
        B.7/20/1983

*M6225222 - George Walker StClair Moore, Jr. - (1) Sandra Lee Adams (Div)
      B.10/29/1949   (1) M. 5/1975   B.10/26/1950
                  (2) M. 4/20/1985

                                              (2) Sandra Harris Cornow
                                                 B.3/27/1949

    *M62252221 - (1) Alyson Adams Moore
        B.3/30/1978

    *M62252222 - (2) George Walker StClair Moore, III
        B.5/14/1991

*M6225223 - Margaret StClair Moore - Dana Miquelle (Div)
    B.9/19/1951   M.5/27/1973   B. 5/16/1951

    *M62252231 - Jessica George Miquelle - Edward Romero
    B.12/8/1977   **M.8/12/2006**   **B.12/26/1971**

    *M62252232 - Dana Lisa Miquelle
        B.10/31/1980

*M6225224 - Robert Barnes Moore - Eileen Therese Walsh
    B.3/18/1954   M. 6/11/1983   B. 6/14/1952

    *M62252241 - Jonathan Tyler Moore
        B.10/1/1984

    *M62252242 - Christopher James Moore
        B.3/30/1987

*M622523 - James Rutherford Moore - (1) Erika Nauman
    B.6/13/1928   (1) M. 7/23/1955 B. 10/21/1934
    D.7/12/2004   (2) M. 3/18/1978
                        (2) Barbara White
                        B. 2/2/1937

*M6225231 - (1) Erika Kehding Moore - Frederick Ward Price
    B.5/30/1956   M._____   B.7/1/1953

    *M62252311 - Frederick Ward Price, Jr.
        B.5/16/1986

*M62252312 - Robert Henry Price
B.10/23/1989

*M6225232 - (1) James Rutherford Moore, Jr. - Linda Lee Bender
B. 4/1//1958   M. 11/3/1990   B. 10/3/1960

*M62252321 - James Rutherford Moore, III
B. 9/27/1992

*M62252322 - Alexandra Wilson Moore
B. 10/27/1994

*M6225233 - (1) Ann-Huston Moore - Raymond Parker
B. 12/20/1960   M. 5/22/1982   B. 3/16/1959

*M62252331 – Maria St.Clair Parker
B. 11/13/1985

*M62252332 – Rebecca Katharine Parker
B. 1/31/1987

*M62252333 – Ann-Margaret Parker
B. 7/25/1989

*M62252334 - Elizabeth Nelson Parker
B. 4/14/1994

*M6225234 - (1) Katharine Tierney Moore
B. 12/18/1962

*M6225235 - (1) Eric St.Clair Moore - Robin Esther Barnett
B. 1/26/1965   M. 10/1/1992   B. 3/16/1965

*M62252351 Elliott Nauman Moore
B. 10/23/1994

*M62252352 Jacob Reynolds Moore
B. 2/19/2001

*M622524 - Margaret St.Clair Moore - Richard Ripley (Div)
B. 5/12/1931   M. 6/22/1957   B.3/17/1930
D. 9/21/2005

*M6225241 - St.Clair Ripley
B.6/28/1959

*M6225242 - Huston Ripley - Catalina Meija
B.10/18/1961   M.5/21/2005   B.11/16/1974

*M6225243 - Timothy Regan Ripley
B.2/28/1963

M62253 - (2) Mary Ellen Moore - Charles Robert Brown, Jr.
B.12/24/1893   M.5/18/1921   B.12/5/1892
D.2/14/1986   D.5/30/55

M62254 - (2) Barnes Thompson Moore - Otelia June Simmons
B.1/28/1899   M.4/18/1929   B.10/7/1900
D.7/7/1975   D.10/25/1984

*M622541 - June Archer Moore - (1) Duncan Dallas McDuffie (Div)
B.9/5/1931 (1) M. 6/16/1951   B.6/11/1928
          (2) M. 10/6/1979

                        (2) William Henry Smith
                            B. 7/9/1923
                            D. 5/17/1987

*M6225411 - (1) Infant Son
B.8/25/1952
D.8/25/1952

*M6225412 - (1) Susan Cameron McDuffie - Michael Joseph Pechar
B.4/21/1954   M.9/23/1987   B.1/29/1948

*M62254121 - Matthew Dallas Pechar
B.10/8/1988

*M6225413 - (1) Mary Moore McDuffie - Mark Patrick Cary (Div)
B.8/14/1955   M.3/2/1980   B.1/11/1955

*M62254131 - Cameron Mary Ellen Cary
B.11/7/1982

*M62254132 - Sara Michelle Cary
B.9/23/1986

*M6225414 - (1) Elizabeth Archer McDuffie - Duane Alan Kitchings
B.4/23/1959   M.5/14/1989   B.5/5/1955

*M62254141 - James Alan Kitchings
B.6/9/1995

*M62254142 - Joshua David Kitchings
B.1/16/2001

M6226 - Levicie Barnes Moore (2) - Reese Thompson Higginbotham
B.1/1/1853   M.11/25/1875   B.8/16/1841
D._____   D.3/16/1912

M62261 - Mary Amanda Higginbotham
B.9/21/1876
D._____

M62262 - William Moore Higginbotham - **M628113** - Margaret Elizabeth Morton
B.9/7/1878   M.1/7/1915   B.7/21/1878
D.10/20/1972   D.5/13/1966

M622621 - William Moore Higginbotham, Jr. - Lula Burnett
B.8/28/1920   M.10/21/1944   B. 2/8/1923
D.9/24/1987

M6226211 - William Moore Higginbotham, III
    B. 6/15/1945

*M6226212 – Margaret Elizabeth Higginbotham - Stephen Douglas Snyder
    B. 8/13/1947   M. 7/11/1970   B. 11/2/1947

    *M62262121 - Stephen Douglas Snyder, Jr. – (1) Beverly _____
        B. 1/23/1975   (1) M. _____ B. _____
                     (2) M. 9/12/2002

                                (2) Kelly Darby
                                B. 1/20/1981

        *M622621211 – (1) Natalie Elizabeth Snyder
           B. 11/16/2000

    *M62262122 - Michael William Snyder
        B. 11/24/1983

*M6226213 – Charles Andrew Higginbotham - Carla Lee Smith
    B. 12/3/1950   M. 6/7/1975   B. 8/23/1949

    *M62262131 – Charles Russell Higginbotham
        B. 2/15/1981

    *M62262132 - Joshua Moore Higginbotham
        B. 12/27/1984

M6226214 – Lucy Virginia Higginbotham - (1) Samuel Eugene Banton
    B. 12/1/1957   M. 7/6/1975   B. _____

                                (2) Ben Tuckwiller
                                B. 2/1/1965

    M62262141 - (1) Anthony Reed Banton
        B._____

        M62262142 - (1) Megan Elizabeth Banton
           B._____

M62263 - Barbara Letitia Higginbotham - Charles Green Rader
    B.1/1/1881   M.12/14/1911   B._____
    D._____   D._____

    M622631 - Virginia June Rader - Earl W. Kidd
        B.6/10/1918   M._____   B._____
        D.2/24/2004   D._____

        M6226311 - Linda Jane Kidd - Robert F. Rodgers
           B._____   M._____   B._____

           M62263111 - William Thornton Rodgers
              B._____

           M62263112 - Robert Earl Rodgers
              B._____

           M62263113 - Brian Frank Rodgers
              B._____

        M6226312 - Charlotte Ann Kidd
           B. 1/3/1950

        M6226313 - Sara Louise Kidd - William E. Irons
           B._____   M._____   B._____

           M62263131 - Amanda Irons
              B. _____

           M62263132 - J. Oliver Irons
              B._____

           M62263133 - Molly Irons
              B._____

M62263134 - Anny Irons
B. 10/1/1987

*M6226314 - Susan Rebecca Kidd - Mark B. Goode
B. 8/31/1956   M. 7/22/1978   B. 2/16/1956

*M62263141 - Joshua Goode
B. 4/22/1981

*M62263142 - Zachary Goode
B. 1/12/1984

*M62263143 - Caleb Goode
B. 6/1/1987

*M62263144 - Isaac Goode
B. 11/12/1989

M62264 - Laura Matilda Higginbotham - Cecil C. Rodgers
B.1/16/1883   M.11/24/1920   B.8/25/1886
D._____   D._____

M62265 - Sally Alice Higginbotham
B.4/7/1885
D.5/15/1904

M62266 - Lavinia Brown Higginbotham
B.5/19/1887
D.7/13/1889

M62267 - Oscar Donald Higginbotham
B.11/16/1889
D _____

M62268 - India Allen Higginbotham - Raymond Edgar Bright
B.1/14/1893   M.5/1/1926   B.4/8/1899
D. 1975   D. 1986

M622681 - Nancy Ellen Bright - (1)Edwin Boone Wilson
    B.11/21/1927   (1) M._____   B.1928
    D.8/11/1999   (2) M._____D._____

                   (2)Carey Moore Hayes
                      B.1923
                      D.1994

*M6226811 - (1)Charles Edwin Wilson - (1)Debra Michelle Lilly
    B.1/7/1950   (1) M. 7/23/1971 B.1/6/1954
               (2) M. 7/18/1992

                     (2)Janet Ellen McDowell
                     B.1/28/1954

*M62268111 - (1)Tracy Elizabeth Wilson
    B.2/20/1972

*M622681111 – Kristen Bailey Rojo
    B. 8/19/2000

*M62268112 - (1)Jesse Price Wilson – Shauna Brott
    B.7/30/1975   M.6/21/1997   B. 3/14/1975

*M6281121 – Reid David Wilson
    B. 10/13/2002

M6226812 - (1)William Edgar Wilson
    B.12/2/1950

M6226813 - (1)Thomas Lynn Wilson
    B. 5/3/1952

*M62269 - Clynta LeVici Higginbotham - Robert Moore Baldwin
     B.7/6/1896   M.6/7/1920 B.7/4/1896
     D._____   D._____

M6227 - Oscar Bascom Moore (2) - (1) Rose McDonald
   B.1/17/1855 M.2/26/1896 B.4/4/1866
   D.8/25/1944 M.9/23/1903 D.8/18/1902

             - (2) **M62913** - Sarah Elizabeth Wilson
                B.10/11/1878
                D._____

M62271 - William Taylor Moore, II(1) - Etta Morgan
   B.12/28/1896 M.8/26/1928 B.11/4/1907
   D.10/25/1972   D.11/23/1983

  M622711 - William Taylor Moore, III - Virginia Shields
     B.2/4/1930   M.5/28/1949 B.5/12/1932

   M6227111 - Jeffrey Taylor Moore
     B.4/10/1955

  M622712 - Barbara Rebecca Rose Moore - (1)Robert Miller
     B.10/10/1932 (1) M.10/8/1955 B.1/16/1924
     D.9/8/1997   (2) M.5/16/1986 D.5/24/1980

                (2)James Calvin Fox
                B._____

   *M6227121 - Linda Elaine Miller(1) - Dirk Christian Baltzly
     B.10/11/1963 M.9/3/1988 B.8/24/1963

M62272 - Mary Elizabeth Moore(1) - Randolph Macon Marshall
    B.5/23/1899   M.6/16/1923   B.6/29/1897
    D.2/25/1959   D._____

    M622721 - Barbara Moore Marshall
        B.2/18/1925
        D.11/22/1977

*M62273 - John Freeman Moore(2)
    B.7/9/1904
    D.4/1949

*M62274 - Rose McDonald Moore(2) - **M624621** John Roy Mullin
    B.10/20/1906   M.10/2/1931   B.2/1/1900
    D. 7/8/1989   D.4/3/1962

    *M622741 - Mary Moore Mullin – Alfred LeRoy Mowery, Jr.
        B.10/29/1934   M. 9/2/1955   B. 8/14/1934
                                        D. 8/26/2004

        *M6227411 – Mark Wayland Mowery – Beverly Jean Phillips
            B. 7/11/1957   M. 6/13/1981   B. 10/24/1959

            *M62274111 – Jeffrey Phillips Mowery
                B. 12/7/1989

            *M62274112 – Melissa Moore Mowery
                B. 4/30/1992

        *M6227412 – Alfred Leighton Mowery
            B. 6/26/1960

        *M6227413 – Cynthia Lucretia Mowery – James Philistine
            B. 4/1/1963   M. 1/11/1986   B. 6/26/1960

            *M62274131 – Kristen Rose Philistine
                B. 6/6/1991

*M62274132 – Kyle James Philistine
B. 4/12/1994

*M622742 – John Roy Mullin, Jr. – (1) Alice Darlene Van Kirk (Div)
B.3/10/1941   (1) M. _____   B. 10/31/1942
              (2) M. 6/17/1990

                  (2) Trudy Joyce Tomlinson
                    B. 6/4/1949

*M6227421 – (1) Melanie Michael Mullin – Michael Rourke Levy (Div)
B. 8/4/1968   M. 12/30/1994   B. 9/13/1959

*M62274211 – Christopher Michael Levy
B. 6/18/1995

*M62274212 – Zachary Rourke Levy
B. 1/2/1997

*M6227422 – (1) Carrie Beth Mullin – Charles Felder McMichael
B. 2/21/1974   M. 4/1/2000   B. 8/17/1972

*M62274221 – Caroline Rae McMichael
B. 11/30/2004

* M62275 – Oscar Barnes Moore(2)
B.11/28/1911
D. 3/28/1945

M6228 – Barbara Jane Moore (2) – Joseph S. Moss
B.9/10/1857   M.11/25/1896   B.9/23/1836
D.1/15/1944   D.3/7/1905

M6228x – Clinton Barnes Moore (2)
B.4/1/1860
D.10/17/1863

M6229 - Mary Eliza Moore (2) - William Allen Davidson
    B.5/15/1863   M.10/14/1891   B.1/17/1858
    D._____   D.1/5/1925

13.

<u>The William Taylor Moore Line</u>
<u>Biographical Charts</u>

M62217121
Genealogical Number

Kenneth Lee Shackelford, Jr.   Park City, Utah
Name (including maiden name if applicable)   Town of Residence

                                    4/17/1945
Birthplace   Date of Birth   Date of Death   Where Buried

Carol Donnelly
Name of Spouse   Birthplace   Date of Birth   Date of Death

Where Buried   Date of Marriage   Place of Marriage

If married more than once:

Name of Spouse   Birthplace   Date of Birth   Date of Death

Where Buried   Date of Marriage   Place of Marriage

Parents of Spouse (with Mother's maiden name) 1st Marriage

Subsequent Marriage (if applicable)

Family Details

Schools attended, dates and degrees: Community, political work, etc.:

Descendant   Descendant

Spouse   Spouse

Basic Employment History: Clubs, Church Affiliations, etc.:

Descendant   Descendant

Spouse   Spouse

Military Service:

Descendant   Spouse

M62217122
Genealogical Number

Lavinia Kay Shackelford   Pasadena, CA
Name (including maiden name if applicable)   Town of Residence

Pontiac, IN   7/12/1947
Birthplace   Date of Birth   Date of Death   Where Buried

Charles Robert Henry   Los Angeles   1/1/1946
Name of Spouse   Birthplace   Date of Birth   Date of Death

Where Buried   Date of Marriage   Place of Marriage

If married more than once:

Name of Spouse   Birthplace   Date of Birth   Date of Death

Where Buried   Date of Marriage   Place of Marriage

Parents of Spouse (with Mother's maiden name) 1st Marriage

Subsequent Marriage (if applicable)

Family Details

Schools attended, dates and degrees: Community, political work, etc.:

Descendant   Descendant

Spouse   Spouse

Basic Employment History: Clubs, Church Affiliations, etc.:

Descendant   Descendant

Spouse   Spouse

Military Service:

Descendant   Spouse

M622171221
Genealogical Number

Kristin Kay Henry   Henderson, NV
Name (including maiden name if applicable)   Town of Residence

_____   10/18/1970   _____   _____
Birthplace   Date of Birth   Date of Death   Where Buried

Elston Breen Arntz   _____   _____
Name of Spouse   Birthplace   Date of Birth   Date of Death

_____   5/3/1997   _____
Where Buried   Date of Marriage   Place of Marriage

If married more than once:

_____   _____   _____   _____
Name of Spouse   Birthplace   Date of Birth   Date of Death

_____   _____   _____
Where Buried   Date of Marriage   Place of Marriage

Parents of Spouse (with Mother's maiden name) 1st Marriage

Subsequent Marriage (if applicable)

Family Details

Schools attended, dates and degrees: Community, political work, etc.:

_____   _____
Descendant   Descendant

_____   _____
Spouse   Spouse

Basic Employment History: Clubs, Church Affiliations, etc.:

_____   _____
Descendant   Descendant

_____   _____
Spouse   Spouse

Military Service:

_____   _____
Descendant   Spouse

M622171222
Genealogical Number

Jason Charles Henry
Name (including maiden name if applicable)   Town of Residence

Pasadena, California   5/26/1973
Birthplace   Date of Birth   Date of Death   Where Buried

Name of Spouse   Birthplace   Date of Birth   Date of Death

Where Buried   Date of Marriage   Place of Marriage

If married more than once:

Name of Spouse   Birthplace   Date of Birth   Date of Death

Where Buried   Date of Marriage   Place of Marriage

Parents of Spouse (with Mother's maiden name) 1st Marriage

Subsequent Marriage (if applicable)

Family Details

Schools attended, dates and degrees: Community, political work, etc.:

Descendant   Descendant

Spouse   Spouse

Basic Employment History: Clubs, Church Affiliations, etc.:

Descendant   Descendant

Spouse   Spouse

Military Service:

Descendant   Spouse

M622171223
Genealogical Number

Ryan Patrick Henry
Name (including maiden name if applicable)   Town of Residence

Pasadena, California   8/19/1976
Birthplace   Date of Birth   Date of Death   Where Buried

Name of Spouse   Birthplace   Date of Birth   Date of Death

Where Buried   Date of Marriage   Place of Marriage

If married more than once:

Name of Spouse   Birthplace   Date of Birth   Date of Death

Where Buried   Date of Marriage   Place of Marriage

Parents of Spouse (with Mother's maiden name) 1st Marriage

Subsequent Marriage (if applicable)

Family Details

Schools attended, dates and degrees: Community, political work, etc.:

Descendant   Descendant

Spouse   Spouse

Basic Employment History: Clubs, Church Affiliations, etc.:

Descendant   Descendant

Spouse   Spouse

Military Service:

Descendant   Spouse

M622171224
Genealogical Number

Courtney Robyn Henry
Name (including maiden name if applicable)   Town of Residence

Highland Park, IN   3/18/1980
Birthplace   Date of Birth   Date of Death   Where Buried

Name of Spouse   Birthplace   Date of Birth   Date of Death

Where Buried   Date of Marriage   Place of Marriage

If married more than once:

Name of Spouse   Birthplace   Date of Birth   Date of Death

Where Buried   Date of Marriage   Place of Marriage

Parents of Spouse (with Mother's maiden name) 1st Marriage

Subsequent Marriage (if applicable)

Family Details

Schools attended, dates and degrees: Community, political work, etc.:

Descendant   Descendant

Spouse   Spouse

Basic Employment History: Clubs, Church Affiliations, etc.:

Descendant   Descendant

Spouse   Spouse

Military Service:

Descendant   Spouse

M62217123
Genealogical Number

Stephen Roy Shackelford   St. Charles, IL
Name (including maiden name if applicable)   Town of Residence

Atascadero, CA   11/6/1949
Birthplace   Date of Birth   Date of Death   Where Buried

Mary Ellen   Iowa   12/9/1953
Name of Spouse   Birthplace   Date of Birth   Date of Death

                           5/5/1979   Phoenix, AZ
Where Buried   Date of Marriage   Place of Marriage

If married more than once:

Name of Spouse   Birthplace   Date of Birth   Date of Death

Where Buried   Date of Marriage   Place of Marriage

Parents of Spouse (with Mother's maiden name) 1st Marriage

Subsequent Marriage (if applicable)

Family Details

Schools attended, dates and degrees: Community, political work, etc.:

Descendant   Descendant

Spouse   Spouse

Basic Employment History: Clubs, Church Affiliations, etc.:

Descendant   Descendant

Spouse   Spouse

Military Service:

Descendant   Spouse

M6221713
Genealogical Number

Donald William Shackelford
Name (including maiden name if applicable)

Town of Residence

Birthplace

11/12/1919
Date of Birth

Date of Death

Where Buried

Name of Spouse

Birthplace

Date of Birth

Date of Death

Where Buried

Date of Marriage

Place of Marriage

If married more than once:

Name of Spouse

Birthplace

Date of Birth

Date of Death

Where Buried

Date of Marriage

Place of Marriage

Parents of Spouse (with Mother's maiden name) 1st Marriage

Subsequent Marriage (if applicable)

Family Details

Schools attended, dates and degrees:

Community, political work, etc.:

Descendant

Descendant

Spouse

Spouse

Basic Employment History:

Clubs, Church Affiliations, etc.:

Descendant

Descendant

Spouse

Spouse

Military Service:

Descendant

Spouse

M6221714
Genealogical Number

Marjorie Lou Shackelford
Name (including maiden name if applicable)

Town of Residence

3/11/1921

Birthplace — Date of Birth — Date of Death — Where Buried

Name of Spouse — Birthplace — Date of Birth — Date of Death

Where Buried — Date of Marriage — Place of Marriage

If married more than once:

Name of Spouse — Birthplace — Date of Birth — Date of Death

Where Buried — Date of Marriage — Place of Marriage

Parents of Spouse (with Mother's maiden name) 1st Marriage

Subsequent Marriage (if applicable)

Family Details

Schools attended, dates and degrees:

Community, political work, etc.:

Descendant

Descendant

Spouse

Spouse

Basic Employment History:

Clubs, Church Affiliations, etc.:

Descendant

Descendant

Spouse

Spouse

Military Service:

Descendant

Spouse

M6223111
Genealogical Number

Mary Amanda McThenia
Name (including maiden name if applicable)

Rochester Hills, Mich.
Town of Residence

Montgomery, W.VA
Birthplace

9/8/1933
Date of Birth

Date of Death

Where Buried

Don Robert Iodice
Name of Spouse

Providence, RI
Birthplace

5/22/1928
Date of Birth

Date of Death

Where Buried

6/10/1961
Date of Marriage

Alderson, WV
Place of Marriage

If married more than once:

Name of Spouse

Birthplace

Date of Birth

Date of Death

Where Buried

Date of Marriage

Place of Marriage

James Anthony Iodice/Eileen McGuire
Parents of Spouse (with Mother's maiden name) 1st Marriage

Subsequent Marriage (if applicable)

Family Details

Schools attended, dates and degrees:

University of Geneva, Switzerland
Stuart Hall, Staunton-Sweet Briar College BA
Descendant

Yale - BA & MA Sorbonne - France
Spouse

Basic Employment History:

Paralegal
Descendant

Professor of French & Linguistics
Spouse

Military Service:

Descendant

Community, political work, etc.:

Much Volunteer
Descendant

School Board. Much Volunteer
Spouse

Clubs, Church Affiliations, etc.:

Served on many boards.
Descendant

Served on many boards.
Spouse

Spouse

M62231111
Genealogical Number

Don Robert Iodice, Jr.   Everett, WA
Name (including maiden name if applicable)   Town of Residence

Hinsdale, ILL   2/15/1963
Birthplace   Date of Birth   Date of Death   Where Buried

Debroah Forslin   4/22/1955
Name of Spouse   Birthplace   Date of Birth   Date of Death

Where Buried   Date of Marriage   Place of Marriage

If married more than once:

Name of Spouse   Birthplace   Date of Birth   Date of Death

Where Buried   Date of Marriage   Place of Marriage

Clarence Fry - Ruthe Chase
Parents of Spouse (with Mother's maiden name) 1st Marriage

Subsequent Marriage (if applicable)

Family Details

Schools attended, dates and degrees: Community, political work, etc.:

Pomfret, CT - Oakland U. California Maritime
Descendant   Descendant

Spouse   Spouse

Basic Employment History: Clubs, Church Affiliations, etc.:

Descendant   Descendant

Spouse   Spouse

Military Service:

Descendant   Spouse

M622311111
Genealogical Number

Amanda Ruthe Iodice
Name (including maiden name if applicable)

Everett, WA
Town of Residence

Kodiak, Alaska
Birthplace

3/29/1986
Date of Birth

Date of Death

Where Buried

Name of Spouse

Birthplace

Date of Birth

Date of Death

Where Buried

Date of Marriage

Place of Marriage

If married more than once:

Name of Spouse

Birthplace

Date of Birth

Date of Death

Where Buried

Date of Marriage

Place of Marriage

Parents of Spouse (with Mother's maiden name) 1st Marriage

Subsequent Marriage (if applicable)

Family Details

Schools attended, dates and degrees:

Community, political work, etc.:

Descendant

Descendant

Spouse

Spouse

Basic Employment History:

Clubs, Church Affiliations, etc.:

Descendant

Descendant

Spouse

Spouse

Military Service:

Descendant

Spouse

M6223112
Genealogical Number

Andrew Wolfe McThenia, Jr.
Name (including maiden name if applicable)

Lexington, VA
Town of Residence

Alderson, W.VA
Birthplace

8/15/1935
Date of Birth

Date of Death

Where Buried

Anne Whitley
Name of Spouse

Birthplace

March, 1937
Date of Birth

Date of Death

Where Buried

Feb. 1962
Date of Marriage

Memphis, TN
Place of Marriage

If married more than once:

Name of Spouse

Birthplace

Date of Birth

Date of Death

Where Buried

Date of Marriage

Place of Marriage

William & Sara Whitley
Parents of Spouse (with Mother's maiden name) 1st Marriage

Subsequent Marriage (if applicable)

Family Details

Schools attended, dates and degrees:

Community, political work, etc.:

Descendant

Descendant

Spouse

Spouse

Basic Employment History:

Clubs, Church Affiliations, etc.:

Descendant

Descendant

Spouse

Spouse

Military Service:

Descendant

Spouse

M6223121
Genealogical Number

James William Fredlock
Name (including maiden name if applicable)

Morgantown, W.VA
Town of Residence

Morgantown, W.VA   9/17/1929
Birthplace   Date of Birth   Date of Death   Where Buried

Jacqueline Joy Hyre   Morganstown, W.VA   5/28/1935
Name of Spouse   Birthplace   Date of Birth   Date of Death

                          6/16/1957   Morgantown, W.VA
Where Buried   Date of Marriage   Place of Marriage

If married more than once:

Name of Spouse   Birthplace   Date of Birth   Date of Death

Where Buried   Date of Marriage   Place of Marriage

Harold Martiney Hyre/Dollie Wilson
Parents of Spouse (with Mother's maiden name) 1st Marriage

Subsequent Marriage (if applicable)

Family Details

Schools attended, dates and degrees:

W.VA School Pharmacy BS 1951
Descendant

Spouse

Basic Employment History:
Self-employed - owned 3 drug stores at
one time.
Descendant

Spouse

Military Service:
24 Inf. Div. US Army Japan 1951/1953
45 Inf. Div. - Korea
Descendant

Community, political work, etc.:
City Council: Sanitary Board, Cancer Board,
United Way Board, Parking Authority
Descendant

Spouse

Clubs, Church Affiliations, etc.:

Descendant
Suncrest Garden Club
School teacher.
Spouse

Spouse

M62231221
Genealogical Number

Amy Barns Fredlock   Herndon, VA
Name (including maiden name if applicable)   Town of Residence

Morgantown, W.VA   6/4/1958
Birthplace   Date of Birth   Date of Death   Where Buried

Michael John Mintz   Chicago, ILL   10/20/1960
Name of Spouse   Birthplace   Date of Birth   Date of Death

                          6/4/1988   Morgantown, W.VA
Where Buried   Date of Marriage   Place of Marriage

If married more than once:

Name of Spouse   Birthplace   Date of Birth   Date of Death

Where Buried   Date of Marriage   Place of Marriage

John Michael Mintz/Janice Johnston
Parents of Spouse (with Mother's maiden name) 1st Marriage

Subsequent Marriage (if applicable)

Family Details

Schools attended, dates and degrees: Community, political work, etc.:

J.D. West Virginia University
Descendant   Descendant

J.D. West Virginia University
Spouse   Spouse

Basic Employment History: Clubs, Church Affiliations, etc.:
Attorney retired.
A happy stay-at-home mama   Floris United Methodist Church
Descendant   Descendant

Shaw, Pittman - Law firm   Floris United Methodist Church
Spouse   Spouse

Military Service:

Descendant   Spouse

M622312211
Genealogical Number

Aaron Barns Mintz
Name (including maiden name if applicable)

Herndon, VA
Town of Residence

Herndon, VA   6/24/1989
Birthplace   Date of Birth   Date of Death   Where Buried

Name of Spouse   Birthplace   Date of Birth   Date of Death

Where Buried   Date of Marriage   Place of Marriage

If married more than once:

Name of Spouse   Birthplace   Date of Birth   Date of Death

Where Buried   Date of Marriage   Place of Marriage

Parents of Spouse (with Mother's maiden name) 1st Marriage

Subsequent Marriage (if applicable)

Family Details

Schools attended, dates and degrees: Community, political work, etc.:

Descendant   Descendant

Spouse   Spouse

Basic Employment History: Clubs, Church Affiliations, etc.:

Descendant   Descendant

Spouse   Spouse

Military Service:

Descendant   Spouse

M622312212
Genealogical Number

Anna Johnston Mintz
Name (including maiden name if applicable)

Herndon, VA
Town of Residence

Herndon, VA
Birthplace

5/21/1991
Date of Birth

Date of Death

Where Buried

Name of Spouse

Birthplace

Date of Birth

Date of Death

Where Buried

Date of Marriage

Place of Marriage

If married more than once:

Name of Spouse

Birthplace

Date of Birth

Date of Death

Where Buried

Date of Marriage

Place of Marriage

Parents of Spouse (with Mother's maiden name) 1st Marriage

Subsequent Marriage (if applicable)

Family Details

Schools attended, dates and degrees:

Community, political work, etc.:

Descendant

Descendant

Spouse

Spouse

Basic Employment History:

Clubs, Church Affiliations, etc.:

Descendant

Descendant

Spouse

Spouse

Military Service:

Descendant

Spouse

M622331
Genealogical Number

Barnes Samuel Mustard
Name (including maiden name if applicable)

Town of Residence

Abbs Valley	12/12/1914	4/29/1989	Woodlawn, Bl
Birthplace	Date of Birth	Date of Death	Where Buried

Mellie Virginia Cassell	Switchback, W.VA	5/23/1915	3/31/1995
Name of Spouse	Birthplace	Date of Birth	Date of Death

Woodlawn, Bluefield	6/2/1937	Bland, VA
Where Buried	Date of Marriage	Place of Marriage

If married more than once:

Name of Spouse	Birthplace	Date of Birth	Date of Death

Where Buried	Date of Marriage	Place of Marriage

Hubert Arthur Cassell/Bertha Ross
Parents of Spouse (with Mother's maiden name) 1st Marriage

Subsequent Marriage (if applicable)

Family Details

Schools attended, dates and degrees:

Community, political work, etc.:

Bluefield College & WV Business
College 1934
Descendant

Descendant

Concord College 1934
Spouse

Spouse

Basic Employment History:
Book-keeper Pocahontas Fuel Co.
Bishop
Descendant

Clubs, Church Affiliations, etc.:

Methodist
Descendant

School Teacher
Spouse

Methodist
Spouse

Military Service:

Descendant

Spouse

M6223311
Genealogical Number

Rebecca Glyn Mustard   Wytheville, VA
Name (including maiden name if applicable)   Town of Residence

Bishop, VA   9/5/1938
Birthplace   Date of Birth   Date of Death   Where Buried

Oral Vernon Jones   Bradshaw, W.VA   4/18/1935
Name of Spouse   Birthplace   Date of Birth   Date of Death

                              5/26/1955   Tazewell, VA
Where Buried   Date of Marriage   Place of Marriage

If married more than once:

Name of Spouse   Birthplace   Date of Birth   Date of Death

Where Buried   Date of Marriage   Place of Marriage

Bernie Jones/Ochel Lycans
Parents of Spouse (with Mother's maiden name) 1st Marriage

Subsequent Marriage (if applicable)

Family Details

Schools attended, dates and degrees: Community, political work, etc.:

Business School 1956
Descendant   Descendant

Marshall College 1954-55
Spouse   Spouse

Basic Employment History: Clubs, Church Affiliations, etc.:

Book-keeper - Secretary   Methodist
Descendant   Descendant

Real Estate Broker   Methodist
Spouse   Spouse

Military Service:

Descendant   Spouse

M62233111
Genealogical Number

Diana Glynn Jones
Name (including maiden name if applicable)

Wytheville, VA
Town of Residence

Bluefield, W.VA
Birthplace

6/13/1958
Date of Birth

Date of Death

Where Buried

Ted Ray Gardner
Name of Spouse

Galax, VA
Birthplace

3/31/1954
Date of Birth

Date of Death

Where Buried

8/2/1980
Date of Marriage

Wytheville, VA
Place of Marriage

If married more than once:

Name of Spouse

Birthplace

Date of Birth

Date of Death

Where Buried

Date of Marriage

Place of Marriage

Iva June Dalton and Loris Clyde Gardner
Parents of Spouse (with Mother's maiden name) 1st Marriage

Subsequent Marriage (if applicable)

Family Details

Schools attended, dates and degrees:

Community, political work, etc.:

Radford University Grad 5/80 BSN-Nursing
Descendant
Virginia Tech. Grad 1972 BA History
Wytheville Comm. College 1980 AD-Nursing
Spouse

Descendant

Spouse

Basic Employment History:

Clubs, Church Affiliations, etc.:

Registered nurse/case manager
Descendant
Registered nurse - CED Home Medical
Equipment Company
Spouse

St. Paul United Methodist Church
Descendant

St. Paul United Methodist Church
Spouse

Military Service:

Descendant

Spouse

M622331111
Genealogical Number

Laura Allison Gardner						Wytheville, VA
Name (including maiden name if applicable)			Town of Residence

Bristol, Tenn.			12/20/1983
Birthplace			Date of Birth			Date of Death			Where Buried

Name of Spouse			Birthplace			Date of Birth			Date of Death

Where Buried			Date of Marriage			Place of Marriage

If married more than once:

Name of Spouse			Birthplace			Date of Birth			Date of Death

Where Buried			Date of Marriage			Place of Marriage

Parents of Spouse (with Mother's maiden name) 1st Marriage

Subsequent Marriage (if applicable)

Family Details

Schools attended, dates and degrees:				Community, political work, etc.:

Virginia Tech. - currently attending.
Descendant								Descendant

Spouse									Spouse

Basic Employment History:						Clubs, Church Affiliations, etc.:

									St. Paul United Methodist Church
Descendant								Descendant

Spouse									Spouse

Military Service:

Descendant								Spouse

M622331112
Genealogical Number

Thomas Barnes Gardner
Name (including maiden name if applicable)

Wytheville, VA
Town of Residence

Bristol, Tenn.   5/2/1986
Birthplace   Date of Birth   Date of Death   Where Buried

Name of Spouse   Birthplace   Date of Birth   Date of Death

Where Buried   Date of Marriage   Place of Marriage

If married more than once:

Name of Spouse   Birthplace   Date of Birth   Date of Death

Where Buried   Date of Marriage   Place of Marriage

Parents of Spouse (with Mother's maiden name) 1st Marriage

Subsequent Marriage (if applicable)

Family Details

Schools attended, dates and degrees: Community, political work, etc.:

George Wythe High School - Senior
Descendant   Descendant

Spouse   Spouse

Basic Employment History: Clubs, Church Affiliations, etc.:

                                              St. Paul United Methodist Church
Descendant   Descendant

Spouse   Spouse

Military Service:

Descendant   Spouse

265

M622331113
Genealogical Number

John Sanders Gardner   Wytheville, VA
Name (including maiden name if applicable)   Town of Residence

Wytheville, VA   3/28/1990
Birthplace   Date of Birth   Date of Death   Where Buried

Name of Spouse   Birthplace   Date of Birth   Date of Death

Where Buried   Date of Marriage   Place of Marriage

If married more than once:

Name of Spouse   Birthplace   Date of Birth   Date of Death

Where Buried   Date of Marriage   Place of Marriage

Parents of Spouse (with Mother's maiden name) 1st Marriage

Subsequent Marriage (if applicable)

Family Details

Schools attended, dates and degrees: Community, political work, etc.:

Scott Memorial Middle School - 8th Grade
Descendant   Descendant

Spouse   Spouse

Basic Employment History: Clubs, Church Affiliations, etc.:

                                               St. Paul United Methodist Church
Descendant   Descendant

Spouse   Spouse

Military Service:

Descendant   Spouse

M62233122
Genealogical Number

Lanny Leck Sparks, Jr.
Name (including maiden name if applicable)

Abingdon, VA
Town of Residence

Roanoke,VA
Birthplace

12/31/1966
Date of Birth

Date of Death

Where Buried

Mary Wood Spencer
Name of Spouse

Greensboro, NC
Birthplace

9/1/1969
Date of Birth

Date of Death

Where Buried

10/9/1994
Date of Marriage

Tarboro, NC
Place of Marriage

If married more than once:

Name of Spouse

Birthplace

Date of Birth

Date of Death

Where Buried

Date of Marriage

Place of Marriage

Parents of Spouse (with Mother's maiden name) 1st Marriage

Subsequent Marriage (if applicable)

Family Details

Schools attended, dates and degrees:

Community, political work, etc.:

VA Tech B.S. Forestry & Wildlife Mgmt.
Graduated 1990
Descendant

Descendant

Meredith College B.S. Graduated Interior Design and
Graphic Art
Spouse

Spouse

Basic Employment History:

Clubs, Church Affiliations, etc.:

VA - Dept. of Environmental Quality
Descendant

Grace Christian Fellowship
Descendant

Graphic Art - Homemaker
Spouse

Grace Christian Fellowship
Spouse

Military Service:

Descendant

Spouse

M622331221
Genealogical Number

Monroe Spencer Sparks   Abingdon, VA
Name (including maiden name if applicable)   Town of Residence

Abingdon, VA   9/2/1997
Birthplace   Date of Birth   Date of Death   Where Buried

Name of Spouse   Birthplace   Date of Birth   Date of Death

Where Buried   Date of Marriage   Place of Marriage

If married more than once:

Name of Spouse   Birthplace   Date of Birth   Date of Death

Where Buried   Date of Marriage   Place of Marriage

Parents of Spouse (with Mother's maiden name) 1st Marriage

Subsequent Marriage (if applicable)

Family Details

Schools attended, dates and degrees: Community, political work, etc.:

Descendant   Descendant

Spouse   Spouse

Basic Employment History: Clubs, Church Affiliations, etc.:

Descendant   Descendant

Spouse   Spouse

Military Service:

Descendant   Spouse

M6223322
Genealogical Number

Sharon Lynne Mustard
Name (including maiden name if applicable)

Annapolis, MD
Town of Residence

Washington, DC
Birthplace

1/9/1944
Date of Birth

Date of Death

Where Buried

Douglas J. Katz
Name of Spouse

Madison, Wisc.
Birthplace

5/1/1942
Date of Birth

Date of Death

Where Buried

6/11/1965
Date of Marriage

Place of Marriage

If married more than once:

Name of Spouse

Birthplace

Date of Birth

Date of Death

Where Buried

Date of Marriage

Place of Marriage

Parents of Spouse (with Mother's maiden name) 1st Marriage

Subsequent Marriage (if applicable)

Family Details

Schools attended, dates and degrees:

Community, political work, etc.:

Descendant

Descendant

Spouse

Spouse

Basic Employment History:

Clubs, Church Affiliations, etc.:

Descendant

Descendant

Spouse

Spouse

Military Service:

Descendant

Spouse

M62233221
Genealogical Number

Robert Douglas Katz
Name (including maiden name if applicable)

Chula Vista, CA
Town of Residence

Jacksonville, Fla.
Birthplace

3/13/1967
Date of Birth

Date of Death

Where Buried

Melanie Bell
Name of Spouse

Norfolk, VA
Birthplace

8/25/1969
Date of Birth

Date of Death

Where Buried

7/1/1995
Date of Marriage

Norfolk, VA
Place of Marriage

If married more than once:

Name of Spouse

Birthplace

Date of Birth

Date of Death

Where Buried

Date of Marriage

Place of Marriage

Parents of Spouse (with Mother's maiden name) 1st Marriage

Subsequent Marriage (if applicable)

Family Details

Schools attended, dates and degrees:
Univ. of South Carolina BS -Engineering '90
Navy Post-Graduate School - MS Financial
Management '95
Descendant
Radford University BS-Psychology &Sociology '92
Central Michigan Univ. MSA - Administration '01
Spouse

Community, political work, etc.:

Descendant

Spouse

Basic Employment History:

US Navy - Naval Officer
Descendant

Homemaker & Long Term Care & Activity Consultant
Spouse

Military Service:

Descendant

Clubs, Church Affiliations, etc.:

Descendant

Spouse

Spouse

M622332211
Genealogical Number

Cameron Robert Katz   Chula Vista, CA
Name (including maiden name if applicable)   Town of Residence

                          9/9/1998
Birthplace   Date of Birth   Date of Death   Where Buried

Name of Spouse   Birthplace   Date of Birth   Date of Death

Where Buried   Date of Marriage   Place of Marriage

If married more than once:

Name of Spouse   Birthplace   Date of Birth   Date of Death

Where Buried   Date of Marriage   Place of Marriage

Parents of Spouse (with Mother's maiden name) 1st Marriage

Subsequent Marriage (if applicable)

Family Details

Schools attended, dates and degrees: Community, political work, etc.:

Descendant   Descendant

Spouse   Spouse

Basic Employment History: Clubs, Church Affiliations, etc.:

Descendant   Descendant

Spouse   Spouse

Military Service:

Descendant   Spouse

M622332212
Genealogical Number

Cayla Alexis Katz _____   Chula Vista, CA _____
Name (including maiden name if applicable)   Town of Residence

_____ 3/16/2001   _____   _____
Birthplace   Date of Birth   Date of Death   Where Buried

_____ _____   _____   _____
Name of Spouse   Birthplace   Date of Birth   Date of Death

_____ _____   _____
Where Buried   Date of Marriage   Place of Marriage

If married more than once:

_____ _____   _____   _____
Name of Spouse   Birthplace   Date of Birth   Date of Death

_____ _____   _____
Where Buried   Date of Marriage   Place of Marriage

_____
Parents of Spouse (with Mother's maiden name) 1st Marriage

_____
Subsequent Marriage (if applicable)

Family Details

Schools attended, dates and degrees: Community, political work, etc.:

_____   _____
Descendant   Descendant

_____   _____
Spouse   Spouse

Basic Employment History: Clubs, Church Affiliations, etc.:

_____   _____
Descendant   Descendant

_____   _____
Spouse   Spouse

Military Service:

_____   _____
Descendant   Spouse

M62233222
Genealogical Number

Erica Lynne Katz
Name (including maiden name if applicable)

Charlottesville, VA
Town of Residence

Long Beach, California
Birthplace

9/18/1970
Date of Birth

Date of Death

Where Buried

Walter Nathaniel Dow Perkins
Name of Spouse

Charlottesville, VA
Birthplace

6/14/1970
Date of Birth

Date of Death

Where Buried

8/17/1991
Date of Marriage

Charleston, S.C.
Place of Marriage

If married more than once:

Name of Spouse

Birthplace

Date of Birth

Date of Death

Where Buried

Date of Marriage

Place of Marriage

Parents of Spouse (with Mother's maiden name) 1st Marriage

Subsequent Marriage (if applicable)

Family Details

Schools attended, dates and degrees:

Community, political work, etc.:

Descendant

Descendant

Spouse

Spouse

Basic Employment History:

Clubs, Church Affiliations, etc.:

Descendant

Descendant

Spouse

Spouse

Military Service:

Descendant

Spouse

M622332221
Genealogical Number

Walter Douglas Dow Perkins
Name (including maiden name if applicable)

Charlottesville, VA
Town of Residence

Bluefield, W.VA
Birthplace

8/18/1994
Date of Birth

Date of Death

Where Buried

Name of Spouse

Birthplace

Date of Birth

Date of Death

Where Buried

Date of Marriage

Place of Marriage

If married more than once:

Name of Spouse

Birthplace

Date of Birth

Date of Death

Where Buried

Date of Marriage

Place of Marriage

Parents of Spouse (with Mother's maiden name) 1st Marriage

Subsequent Marriage (if applicable)

Family Details

Schools attended, dates and degrees:

Community, political work, etc.:

Descendant

Descendant

Spouse

Spouse

Basic Employment History:

Clubs, Church Affiliations, etc.:

Descendant

Descendant

Spouse

Spouse

Military Service:

Descendant

Spouse

M622332222
Genealogical Number

Sharon Brie-Anna Perkins
Name (including maiden name if applicable)

Charlottesville, VA
Town of Residence

Charlottesville, VA   6/14/1997
Birthplace   Date of Birth   Date of Death   Where Buried

Name of Spouse   Birthplace   Date of Birth   Date of Death

Where Buried   Date of Marriage   Place of Marriage

If married more than once:

Name of Spouse   Birthplace   Date of Birth   Date of Death

Where Buried   Date of Marriage   Place of Marriage

Parents of Spouse (with Mother's maiden name) 1st Marriage

Subsequent Marriage (if applicable)

Family Details

Schools attended, dates and degrees: Community, political work, etc.:

Descendant   Descendant

Spouse   Spouse

Basic Employment History: Clubs, Church Affiliations, etc.:

Descendant   Descendant

Spouse   Spouse

Military Service:

Descendant   Spouse

M62235
Genealogical Number

Oscar Jasper Mustard
Name (including maiden name if applicable)   Town of Residence

Machanicsville, VA   4/10/1883   6/24/1945   Bluefield, W.V
Birthplace   Date of Birth   Date of Death   Where Buried
                            Wards Cove
Alma Marguerite Leister   Taz. Cty VA   8/2/1893   5/21/1987
Name of Spouse   Birthplace   Date of Birth   Date of Death

Tazewell, VA   9/22/1922   Welch, W.VA
Where Buried   Date of Marriage   Place of Marriage

If married more than once:

Name of Spouse   Birthplace   Date of Birth   Date of Death

Where Buried   Date of Marriage   Place of Marriage

James Henry Leister/Eliza Whitter Dorbins
Parents of Spouse (with Mother's maiden name) 1st Marriage

Subsequent Marriage (if applicable)

Family Details

Schools attended, dates and degrees: Community, political work, etc.:

Tazewell County Schools, Graduate
Emory Henry College, Religion 1901-1904   Shriner & Masionic Lodge 32 degree
Descendant   Descendant
Tazewell County Schools, Graduate 1918
Business College - 1918-1919   Eastern Star Lodge
Spouse   Spouse

Basic Employment History: Clubs, Church Affiliations, etc.:
Engineer & Coal Inspector - Pocahontas
Fuel Co.   Methodist
Descendant   Descendant
Worked in various law offices in Tazewell, VA.
Later, Pocahontas Fuel Co, Pocahontas VA, Secretary Methodist
Spouse   Spouse

Military Service:

Descendant   Spouse

M622351
Genealogical Number

Jean Ann Mustard   Danville, VA
Name (including maiden name if applicable)   Town of Residence

Pocahontas, VA   7/25/1928
Birthplace   Date of Birth   Date of Death   Where Buried

Richard Lee Whitt, Jr.   McDowell County, W.VA   1/30/1921   6/10/2002
Name of Spouse   Birthplace   Date of Birth   Date of Death
Danville Memorial Gardens
Danville, VA   6/5/1948   Richlands, VA
Where Buried   Date of Marriage   Place of Marriage

If married more than once:

Name of Spouse   Birthplace   Date of Birth   Date of Death

Where Buried   Date of Marriage   Place of Marriage

Richard Lee Whitt/Reba Dillion Whitt
Parents of Spouse (with Mother's maiden name) 1st Marriage

Subsequent Marriage (if applicable)

Family Details

Schools attended, dates and degrees: Community, political work, etc.:

Pocahontas VA, June 1946, Graduate
Descendant   Descendant

Gary W.VA June 1939 Graduate
Spouse   Spouse

Basic Employment History: Clubs, Church Affiliations, etc.:
Pocahontas VA 1944-1958
1. Chief Operator, General Telephone Co. S.E.
2. Front End Manager, Kroger Co. Danville, VA-1960-1984   Methodist
Descendant   Descendant
1938-1960 Pocahontas Fuel Co. (coal mine).
Electrician, Machine Operator Jenkinjones W.VA
1960-1973 City of Danville, VA - Electrician & Plant
Electrician & Plant Operator Brantly Steam Plant   Methodist
Spouse   Spouse

Military Service:

                                     U.S. Navy
Descendant   Spouse

M622352
Genealogical Number

Alma Marguerite Mustard   Danville, VA
Name (including maiden name if applicable)   Town of Residence

Tazewell, VA   7/19/1930
Birthplace   Date of Birth   Date of Death   Where Buried

Thomas Joseph Senn   Pittsburg, PA   9/9/1928   8/12/1997
Name of Spouse   Birthplace   Date of Birth   Date of Death

Fort Knox, KY   6/9/1997   Clearwater, FL
Where Buried   Date of Marriage   Place of Marriage

If married more than once:

Joseph Anthony Pupello (Div.)   Brockton, Mass   9/26/1932
Name of Spouse   Birthplace   Date of Birth   Date of Death

                                5/2/1951   Washington, DC
Where Buried   Date of Marriage   Place of Marriage

Nicholas Marie Pupello/Anna Spagna Pupello
Parents of Spouse (with Mother's maiden name) 1st Marriage

John Carroll Senn/Matilda Boyle Senn
Subsequent Marriage (if applicable)

Family Details

Schools attended, dates and degrees: Community, political work, etc.:

Pocahontas High School, VA/Diploma 1944-48
West VA Business College Bluefield, W.VA 1950-51
Descendant   Descendant
Catholic High School, Philadelphia, PA 1942-46
St. Benedict College, Atchison KS
Spouse #2   Spouse

Basic Employment History: Clubs, Church Affiliations, etc.:

US Government - 30 years   Methodist
Descendant   Descendant
#1-Special Agent, US Treasury Dept. (AFT) (Retired)   Catholic
#2-US Army, Lt. Colonel (Retired)   Catholic
Spouses   Spouse

Military Service:

                                                  #1 - U.S. Air Force/1949-1953
                                                  #2 - Military Service U.S. Army - 1946-1976
Descendant   Spouse

M62236
Genealogical Number

Samuel Elbert Mustard
Name (including maiden name if applicable)   Town of Residence

Abbs Valley, VA   6/6/1889   8/22/1960   Pocahontas, \
Birthplace   Date of Birth   Date of Death   Where Buried

Margaret Elizabeth Buchanan   Tazewell, VA   6/14/1891   5/10/1962
Name of Spouse   Birthplace   Date of Birth   Date of Death

Pocahontas, VA   Oct 14 1915   Tazewell, VA
Where Buried   Date of Marriage   Place of Marriage

If married more than once:

Name of Spouse   Birthplace   Date of Birth   Date of Death

Where Buried   Date of Marriage   Place of Marriage

John Witter Buchanan/Mary Elizabeth Peery
Parents of Spouse (with Mother's maiden name) 1st Marriage

Subsequent Marriage (if applicable)

Family Details

Schools attended, dates and degrees: Community, political work, etc.:

Descendant   Descendant

Spouse   Spouse

Basic Employment History: Clubs, Church Affiliations, etc.:

Descendant   Descendant

Spouse   Spouse

Military Service:

Descendant   Spouse

M622362
Genealogical Number

Elizabeth Barnes Mustard   La Porte, IN
Name (including maiden name if applicable)   Town of Residence

Abbs Valley, VA   5/13/1923
Birthplace   Date of Birth   Date of Death   Where Buried

Eugene E. Elmore   Saltville, VA   7/14/1913   12/24/1974
Name of Spouse   Birthplace   Date of Birth   Date of Death
Woodlawn
Bluefield, W. VA.   6/16/1949   Pocahontas, VA
Where Buried   Date of Marriage   Place of Marriage

If married more than once:

Name of Spouse   Birthplace   Date of Birth   Date of Death

Where Buried   Date of Marriage   Place of Marriage

Parents of Spouse (with Mother's maiden name) 1st Marriage

Subsequent Marriage (if applicable)

Family Details

Schools attended, dates and degrees: Community, political work, etc.:

Descendant   Descendant

Spouse   Spouse

Basic Employment History: Clubs, Church Affiliations, etc.:

Descendant   Descendant

Spouse   Spouse

Military Service:

Descendant   Spouse

M622414
Genealogical Number

Elizabeth Browne Moore
Name (including maiden name if applicable)

Pocahontas, VA
Town of Residence

Sinks Grove, W.VA
Birthplace

7/19/1919
Date of Birth

6/6/2000
Date of Death

Where Buried

Joseph Kirk Peters
Name of Spouse

Bramwell, W.VA
Birthplace

10/151892
Date of Birth

8/22/1962
Date of Death

Ceres
Where Buried

Date of Marriage

Place of Marriage

If married more than once:

Name of Spouse

Birthplace

Date of Birth

Date of Death

Where Buried

Date of Marriage

Place of Marriage

Parents of Spouse (with Mother's maiden name) 1st Marriage

Subsequent Marriage (if applicable)

Family Details

Schools attended, dates and degrees:

Community, political work, etc.:

Union High School graduated 1945
Descendant

Descendant

Spouse

Mayor of Pocahontas
Spouse

Basic Employment History:

Clubs, Church Affiliations, etc.:

Company Store Clerk - housewife
Descendant

Pocahontas Methodist Church
Descendant

Pocahontas Fuel
Spouse

Pocahontas Methodist Church
Spouse

Military Service:

Descendant

Spouse

M622415
Genealogical Number

John Clinton Moore   Sinks Grove, W.VA
Name (including maiden name if applicable)   Town of Residence

Sinks Grove, W.VA   12/30/1923
Birthplace   Date of Birth   Date of Death   Where Buried

Name of Spouse   Birthplace   Date of Birth   Date of Death

Where Buried   Date of Marriage   Place of Marriage

If married more than once:

Name of Spouse   Birthplace   Date of Birth   Date of Death

Where Buried   Date of Marriage   Place of Marriage

Parents of Spouse (with Mother's maiden name) 1st Marriage

Subsequent Marriage (if applicable)

Family Details

Schools attended, dates and degrees: Community, political work, etc.:

Descendant   Descendant

Spouse   Spouse

Basic Employment History: Clubs, Church Affiliations, etc.:

Descendant   Descendant

Spouse   Spouse

Military Service:

Descendant   Spouse

M622521
Genealogical Number

Robert H. Moore, Jr.
Name (including maiden name if applicable)

Easton, MD
Town of Residence

Bluefield, W.VA
Birthplace

4/17/1923
Date of Birth

Date of Death

Where Buried

Judith Ann Dressel
Name of Spouse

Breese, ILL.
Birthplace

6/26/1941
Date of Birth

Date of Death

Where Buried

7/26/1995
Date of Marriage

Fairfax, VA.
Place of Marriage

If married more than once:

Patricia Hewittson-Fisher
Name of Spouse

London, Eng.
Birthplace

4/5/1938
Date of Birth

Date of Death

Where Buried

12/7/1960
Date of Marriage

Bluefield, W.VA
Place of Marriage

Hewittson-Fisher/Mona Turner
Parents of Spouse (with Mother's maiden name) 1st Marriage

Glen Allen Dressel/Murlene Monaghan
Subsequent Marriage (if applicable)

Family Details

Schools attended, dates and degrees:
McCallie School, 1940. W&L BA 1944; Cert. in
Commerce 1946; Harvard Bus School MBA 1951; Clev.
State Univ JD 1963
Descendant

Community, political work, etc.:
Dir. Bluefield State College Foundation;
Vol. Prison Fellowship Ministries

Descendant
Defense Advisory Committee for Women in
Military. National Governors Association-
Technology Warfare
Spouse

Northwestern University BA 63
Univ. of Chicago MA 1967
Spouse

Basic Employment History:
Jewell Ridge Coal Co; Pittsburgh Consolidation Co;
Otis & Co; Aquarium Systems & related Cos; Aqualife
Research Corp. Pocahontas Mining Co.
Descendant
Kodak 80-92 NIB-PresidentCEO 92-96
Chauncey Group President/CEO 97-2002
LaserGrade Testing Co. - CEO/President
Spouse

Clubs, Church Affiliations, etc.:
 Union, Skating Club, Clev, Ohio; Fincastle
Country Club, Bluefield, VA. Harvard Club, NYC.
Westminister Pres. Church
Descendant

Army & Navy Club, Nassau Club
Spouse

Military Service:
US Navy 1942-1946
Descendant

Spouse

Descendant:

Clubs: Army & Navy Club Washington, D.C. Westminister
Pres. Church, Bluefield, WVA; Prison Fellowship
Volunteer, Moore Family Association, Library Friends Bluefield, WVA

M6225211
Genealogical Number

Robert Henry Moore, III
Name (including maiden name if applicable)

Seattle, Washington
Town of Residence

Cleveland, Ohio
Birthplace

10/23/1962
Date of Birth

Date of Death

Where Buried

Lisa Weinberger
Name of Spouse

Cleveland, Ohio
Birthplace

11/9/1965
Date of Birth

Date of Death

Where Buried

Date of Marriage

Place of Marriage

If married more than once:

Name of Spouse

Birthplace

Date of Birth

Date of Death

Where Buried

Date of Marriage

Place of Marriage

Zoltan Weinberger and Rella Silverman
Parents of Spouse (with Mother's maiden name) 1st Marriage

Subsequent Marriage (if applicable)

Family Details

Schools attended, dates and degrees:

Community, political work, etc.:

Univ. of Minnesota, BS 1988
Descendant
Kent State Univ. MA 1993
Univ. of Minnesota, BA 1988 Art History
Spouse

Habitat for Humanity
Descendant

Habitat for Humanity
Spouse

Basic Employment History:
V.P. Municipal Trading Manager
Seattle - NW Securities Corp.
Descendant
Art/History Teacher, Kent State
Manatee Comm. College
Spouse

Clubs, Church Affiliations, etc.:
Washington Athletic Club, Seattle
Temple Beth AM
Descendant

Temple Beth AM
Spouse

Military Service:

Descendant

Spouse

M62252111
Genealogical Number

Elizabeth Margaret Moore
Name (including maiden name if applicable)

Seattle, Washington
Town of Residence

Cleveland, Ohio
Birthplace

10/10/1991
Date of Birth

Date of Death

Where Buried

Name of Spouse

Birthplace

Date of Birth

Date of Death

Where Buried

Date of Marriage

Place of Marriage

If married more than once:

Name of Spouse

Birthplace

Date of Birth

Date of Death

Where Buried

Date of Marriage

Place of Marriage

Parents of Spouse (with Mother's maiden name) 1st Marriage

Subsequent Marriage (if applicable)

Family Details

Schools attended, dates and degrees:

Community, political work, etc.:

Descendant

Descendant

Spouse

Spouse

Basic Employment History:

Clubs, Church Affiliations, etc.:

Descendant

Descendant

Spouse

Spouse

Military Service:

Descendant

Spouse

M62252112
Genealogical Number

Robert Henry Moore, IV
Name (including maiden name if applicable)

Seattle, Washington
Town of Residence

Cleveland, Ohio
Birthplace

3/15/1994
Date of Birth

Date of Death

Where Buried

Name of Spouse

Birthplace

Date of Birth

Date of Death

Where Buried

Date of Marriage

Place of Marriage

If married more than once:

Name of Spouse

Birthplace

Date of Birth

Date of Death

Where Buried

Date of Marriage

Place of Marriage

Parents of Spouse (with Mother's maiden name) 1st Marriage

Subsequent Marriage (if applicable)

Family Details

Schools attended, dates and degrees:

Community, political work, etc.:

Descendant

Descendant

Spouse

Spouse

Basic Employment History:

Clubs, Church Affiliations, etc.:

Descendant

Descendant

Spouse

Spouse

Military Service:

Descendant

Spouse

M6225212
Genealogical Number

Turner Cronin Moore   Sarasota, Fla.
Name (including maiden name if applicable)   Town of Residence

Cleveland, Ohiio   2/9/1959
Birthplace   Date of Birth   Date of Death   Where Buried

Name of Spouse   Birthplace   Date of Birth   Date of Death

Where Buried   Date of Marriage   Place of Marriage

If married more than once:

Name of Spouse   Birthplace   Date of Birth   Date of Death

Where Buried   Date of Marriage   Place of Marriage

Parents of Spouse (with Mother's maiden name) 1st Marriage

Subsequent Marriage (if applicable)

Family Details

Schools attended, dates and degrees: Community, political work, etc.:

Hampden Sydney College -
BA 1992
Descendant   Descendant

Spouse   Spouse

Basic Employment History: Clubs, Church Affiliations, etc.:
Financial Advisor, Morgan Stanley
& Co.
Descendant   Descendant

Spouse   Spouse

Military Service:

Descendant   Spouse

M622522
Genealogical Number

George Walker St. Clair Moore
Name (including maiden name if applicable)

Venice, FL
Town of Residence

Bluefield, W.VA
Birthplace

10/13/1925
Date of Birth

Date of Death

Where Buried

Alice Hobson
Name of Spouse

Bluefield, W.VA
Birthplace

1/20/1925
Date of Birth

2/5/2001
Date of Death

Florida
Where Buried

6/20/1945
Date of Marriage

Bluefield, W.VA
Place of Marriage

If married more than once:

Name of Spouse

Birthplace

Date of Birth

Date of Death

Where Buried

Date of Marriage

Place of Marriage

Jennings Wise Hobson, Mary Louise Hobson nee Berkeley
Parents of Spouse (with Mother's maiden name) 1st Marriage

Subsequent Marriage (if applicable)

Family Details

Schools attended, dates and degrees:

Community, political work, etc.:

W&L, Duke, Penn Med.
Descendant

Descendant

Spouse

Spouse

Basic Employment History:

Clubs, Church Affiliations, etc.:

Physician in Newcastle, PA
Descendant

Descendant

Spouse

Spouse

Military Service:

USN
Descendant

Spouse

M6225221
Genealogical Number

Mary Berkeley Moore
Name (including maiden name if applicable)

Town of Residence

Maplewell Cemetery
Tazewell, VA
Where Buried

Bluefield, W.VA
Birthplace

9/8/1946
Date of Birth

1/27/1995
Date of Death

Eric Courtney (Div.)
Name of Spouse

Birthplace

Date of Birth

Date of Death

Where Buried

Date of Marriage

Place of Marriage

If married more than once:

Name of Spouse

Birthplace

Date of Birth

Date of Death

Where Buried

Date of Marriage

Place of Marriage

Parents of Spouse (with Mother's maiden name) 1st Marriage

Subsequent Marriage (if applicable)

Family Details

Schools attended, dates and degrees:

Community, political work, etc.:

Duke - 1968 BA
Descendant

Descendant

Spouse

Spouse

Basic Employment History:

Clubs, Church Affiliations, etc.:

Descendant

Descendant

Spouse

Spouse

Military Service:

Descendant

Spouse

M62252211
Genealogical Number

Ian Berkeley Courtney   Waquoit, Mass.
Name (including maiden name if applicable)   Town of Residence

                              7/20/1983
Birthplace   Date of Birth   Date of Death   Where Buried

Name of Spouse   Birthplace   Date of Birth   Date of Death

Where Buried   Date of Marriage   Place of Marriage

If married more than once:

Name of Spouse   Birthplace   Date of Birth   Date of Death

Where Buried   Date of Marriage   Place of Marriage

Parents of Spouse (with Mother's maiden name) 1st Marriage

Subsequent Marriage (if applicable)

Family Details

Schools attended, dates and degrees: Community, political work, etc.:

Descendant   Descendant

Spouse   Spouse

Basic Employment History: Clubs, Church Affiliations, etc.:

Descendant   Descendant

Spouse   Spouse

Military Service:

Descendant   Spouse

M6225222
Genealogical Number

George Walker St. Clair Moore, Jr.   Centreville, VA
Name (including maiden name if applicable)   Town of Residence

Bluefield, W.VA   10/29/1949
Birthplace   Date of Birth   Date of Death   Where Buried

Sandra Harris Cornow   Philadelphia, PA   3/27/1949
Name of Spouse   Birthplace   Date of Birth   Date of Death

                                          4/20/1985
Where Buried   Date of Marriage   Place of Marriage

If married more than once:

Sandra Lee Adams   Newcastle, PA   10/26/1950
Name of Spouse   Birthplace   Date of Birth   Date of Death

                                          5/1975
Where Buried   Date of Marriage   Place of Marriage

Roland and Betty Adams
Parents of Spouse (with Mother's maiden name) 1st Marriage

Frank and Doris Cornow
Subsequent Marriage (if applicable)

Family Details

Schools attended, dates and degrees: Community, political work, etc.:

Penn State '73 BA   BSA
Descendant   Descendant

Temple '78   Guiding Eyes for the Blind
Spouse   Spouse

Basic Employment History: Clubs, Church Affiliations, etc.:

Exxon Mobil   Church of The Epiphany
Descendant   Descendant

CPA - enjoying Motherhood
Spouse   Spouse

Military Service:

Descendant   Spouse

M62252221
Genealogical Number

Alyson Adams Moore
Name (including maiden name if applicable)

Columbia, SC
Town of Residence

Newcastle, PA
Birthplace

3/30/1978
Date of Birth

Date of Death

Where Buried

Name of Spouse

Birthplace

Date of Birth

Date of Death

Where Buried

Date of Marriage

Place of Marriage

If married more than once:

Name of Spouse

Birthplace

Date of Birth

Date of Death

Where Buried

Date of Marriage

Place of Marriage

Parents of Spouse (with Mother's maiden name) 1st Marriage

Subsequent Marriage (if applicable)

Family Details

Schools attended, dates and degrees:

Community, political work, etc.:

Clemson 2000 BA, Clemson 2001 MBA
Descendant

Descendant

Spouse

Spouse

Basic Employment History:

Clubs, Church Affiliations, etc.:

Descendant

Descendant

Spouse

Spouse

Military Service:

Descendant

Spouse

M62252222
<u>Genealogical Number</u>

George Walker St. Clair Moore, III   Centreville, VA
<u>Name (including maiden name if applicable)</u>   <u>Town of Residence</u>

Newport Beach, CA   5/14/1991
<u>Birthplace</u>   <u>Date of Birth</u>   <u>Date of Death</u>   <u>Where Buried</u>

<u>Name of Spouse</u>   <u>Birthplace</u>   <u>Date of Birth</u>   <u>Date of Death</u>

<u>Where Buried</u>   <u>Date of Marriage</u>   <u>Place of Marriage</u>

If married more than once:

<u>Name of Spouse</u>   <u>Birthplace</u>   <u>Date of Birth</u>   <u>Date of Death</u>

<u>Where Buried</u>   <u>Date of Marriage</u>   <u>Place of Marriage</u>

<u>Parents of Spouse (with Mother's maiden name) 1st Marriage</u>

<u>Subsequent Marriage (if applicable)</u>

Family Details

Schools attended, dates and degrees: Community, political work, etc.:

<u>Descendant</u>   <u>Descendant</u>

<u>Spouse</u>   <u>Spouse</u>

Basic Employment History: Clubs, Church Affiliations, etc.:

                                                    Boy Scouts
<u>Descendant</u>   <u>Descendant</u>

<u>Spouse</u>   <u>Spouse</u>

Military Service:

<u>Descendant</u>   <u>Spouse</u>

M6225223
Genealogical Number

Margaret St. Clair Moore
Name (including maiden name if applicable)

Waquoit, Mass.
Town of Residence

Cherry Point, NC
Birthplace

9/19/1951
Date of Birth

Date of Death

Where Buried

Dana Miquelle (Div)
Name of Spouse

Stoneham, MA
Birthplace

5/16/1951
Date of Birth

Date of Death

Where Buried

5/27/1973
Date of Marriage

Bernardsville, NJ
Place of Marriage

If married more than once:

Name of Spouse

Birthplace

Date of Birth

Date of Death

Where Buried

Date of Marriage

Place of Marriage

Jean (Bryer) Miquelle & Claude Hector Miquelle
Parents of Spouse (with Mother's maiden name) 1st Marriage

Subsequent Marriage (if applicable)

Family Details

Schools attended, dates and degrees:

St. Catherine's School, Richmond, Drew University
Madison, NJ 1973 Religion
Descendant
Willston Academy, Drew University
1973 Religion
Spouse

Basic Employment History:
Swim Instructor/coach, Bookkeeping
Accounting
Descendant

Spouse

Military Service:

Descendant

Community, political work, etc.:

Descendant

Spouse

Clubs, Church Affiliations, etc.:

Descendant

Spouse

Spouse

M62252231
Genealogical Number

Jessica George Miquelle   Easthampton , MA
Name (including maiden name if applicable)   Town of Residence

Falmouth, MA   12/8/1977
Birthplace   Date of Birth   Date of Death   Where Buried

Edward Romero   Columbia, S.A.   12/26/1971
Name of Spouse   Birthplace   Date of Birth   Date of Death

                        8/12/2006   Cape Cod, MA
Where Buried   Date of Marriage   Place of Marriage

If married more than once:

Name of Spouse   Birthplace   Date of Birth   Date of Death

Where Buried   Date of Marriage   Place of Marriage

Parents of Spouse (with Mother's maiden name) 1st Marriage

Subsequent Marriage (if applicable)

Family Details

Schools attended, dates and degrees: Community, political work, etc.:

UMASS, Amherst Finance 5/25/03
Descendant   Descendant

Spouse   Spouse

Basic Employment History: Clubs, Church Affiliations, etc.:

Just starting
Descendant   Descendant

Spouse   Spouse

Military Service:

Descendant   Spouse

M62252232
Genealogical Number

Dana Lisa Miquelle   Mashpee, MA
Name (including maiden name if applicable)   Town of Residence

Falmouth, MA   10/31/1980
Birthplace   Date of Birth   Date of Death   Where Buried

Name of Spouse   Birthplace   Date of Birth   Date of Death

Where Buried   Date of Marriage   Place of Marriage

If married more than once:

Name of Spouse   Birthplace   Date of Birth   Date of Death

Where Buried   Date of Marriage   Place of Marriage

Parents of Spouse (with Mother's maiden name) 1st Marriage

Subsequent Marriage (if applicable)

Family Details

Schools attended, dates and degrees: Community, political work, etc.:

Hollins University, Psychology 5/25/02
Descendant   Descendant

Spouse   Spouse

Basic Employment History: Clubs, Church Affiliations, etc.:

Early childcare
Descendant   Descendant

Spouse   Spouse

Military Service:

Descendant   Spouse

M6225224
Genealogical Number

Robert Barnes Moore   Freehold, NJ
Name (including maiden name if applicable)   Town of Residence

Danville, PA   3/18/1954
Birthplace   Date of Birth   Date of Death   Where Buried

Eileen Walsh   Chicago, IL   6/14/1952
Name of Spouse   Birthplace   Date of Birth   Date of Death

                                6/11/1983   Cedar Crest, NM
Where Buried   Date of Marriage   Place of Marriage

If married more than once:

Name of Spouse   Birthplace   Date of Birth   Date of Death

Where Buried   Date of Marriage   Place of Marriage

Ray Walsh & Lillian (Whiteford)
Parents of Spouse (with Mother's maiden name) 1st Marriage

Subsequent Marriage (if applicable)

Family Details

Schools attended, dates and degrees: Community, political work, etc.:

Adrian College, BA Psychology,
BA Accounting   Church Consistory
Descendant   Descendant
                                                   PTO, Open Door Fund Pantry, Other
University of New Mexico   volunteer work, Sunday School Teacher
Spouse   Spouse

Basic Employment History: Clubs, Church Affiliations, etc.:

Currently employed by AT&T   Colts Neck Reformed Church
Descendant   Descendant

Formerly employed by Gortex Industries   Colts Neck Reformed Church
Spouse   Spouse

Military Service:

Descendant   Spouse

M62252241
Genealogical Number

Jonathan Tyler Moore   Freehold, NJ
Name (including maiden name if applicable)   Town of Residence

Stamford, CT   10/1/1984
Birthplace   Date of Birth   Date of Death   Where Buried

Name of Spouse   Birthplace   Date of Birth   Date of Death

Where Buried   Date of Marriage   Place of Marriage

If married more than once:

Name of Spouse   Birthplace   Date of Birth   Date of Death

Where Buried   Date of Marriage   Place of Marriage

Parents of Spouse (with Mother's maiden name) 1st Marriage

Subsequent Marriage (if applicable)

Family Details

Schools attended, dates and degrees: Community, political work, etc.:

St. John Vianney H.S.
Richard Stockton College of NJ
Descendant   Descendant

Spouse   Spouse

Basic Employment History: Clubs, Church Affiliations, etc.:

Descendant   Descendant

Spouse   Spouse

Military Service:

Descendant   Spouse

M62252242
Genealogical Number

Christopher James Moore
Name (including maiden name if applicable)

Freehold, NJ
Town of Residence

Red Bank, NJ
Birthplace

3/30/1987
Date of Birth

Date of Death

Where Buried

Name of Spouse

Birthplace

Date of Birth

Date of Death

Where Buried

Date of Marriage

Place of Marriage

If married more than once:

Name of Spouse

Birthplace

Date of Birth

Date of Death

Where Buried

Date of Marriage

Place of Marriage

Parents of Spouse (with Mother's maiden name) 1st Marriage

Subsequent Marriage (if applicable)

Family Details

Schools attended, dates and degrees:

Community, political work, etc.:

St. John Vianney H.S.
Descendant

Descendant

Spouse

Spouse

Basic Employment History:

Clubs, Church Affiliations, etc.:

Descendant

Descendant

Spouse

Spouse

Military Service:

Descendant

Spouse

M622523
Genealogical Number

James Rutherford Moore
Name (including maiden name if applicable)

Richmond, VA
Town of Residence

Bluefield, W.VA
Birthplace

6/13/1928
Date of Birth

7/12/2004
Date of Death

Where Buried

Barbara Ann White
Name of Spouse

Ashland, VA
Birthplace

2/2/1937
Date of Birth

Date of Death

Where Buried

3/18/1978
Date of Marriage

Richmond, VA
Place of Marriage

If married more than once:

Erika Nauman
Name of Spouse

Port-au-Prince Haiti
Birthplace

10/21/1934
Date of Birth

Date of Death

Where Buried

7/23/1955
Date of Marriage

Bluefield, W.VA
Place of Marriage

Parents of Spouse (with Mother's maiden name) 1st Marriage

Subsequent Marriage (if applicable)

Family Details

Schools attended, dates and degrees:

Community, political work, etc.:

Descendant

Descendant

Spouse

Spouse

Basic Employment History:

Clubs, Church Affiliations, etc.:

Descendant

Descendant

Spouse

Spouse

Military Service:

Descendant

Spouse

M6225231
Genealogical Number

Erika Kehding Moore   Charlotte, NC
Name (including maiden name if applicable)   Town of Residence

Richmond, VA   5/30/1956
Birthplace   Date of Birth   Date of Death   Where Buried

Frederick Ward Price   7/1/1953
Name of Spouse   Birthplace   Date of Birth   Date of Death

Where Buried   Date of Marriage   Place of Marriage

If married more than once:

Name of Spouse   Birthplace   Date of Birth   Date of Death

Where Buried   Date of Marriage   Place of Marriage

Parents of Spouse (with Mother's maiden name) 1st Marriage

Subsequent Marriage (if applicable)

Family Details

Schools attended, dates and degrees: Community, political work, etc.:

Descendant   Descendant

Spouse   Spouse

Basic Employment History: Clubs, Church Affiliations, etc.:

Descendant   Descendant

Spouse   Spouse

Military Service:

Descendant   Spouse

M62252311
Genealogical Number

Frederick Ward Price, Jr.   Charlotte, NC
Name (including maiden name if applicable)   Town of Residence

Charlotte, N.C.   5/16/1986
Birthplace   Date of Birth   Date of Death   Where Buried

Name of Spouse   Birthplace   Date of Birth   Date of Death

Where Buried   Date of Marriage   Place of Marriage

If married more than once:

Name of Spouse   Birthplace   Date of Birth   Date of Death

Where Buried   Date of Marriage   Place of Marriage

Parents of Spouse (with Mother's maiden name) 1st Marriage

Subsequent Marriage (if applicable)

Family Details

Schools attended, dates and degrees: Community, political work, etc.:

Descendant   Descendant

Spouse   Spouse

Basic Employment History: Clubs, Church Affiliations, etc.:

Descendant   Descendant

Spouse   Spouse

Military Service:

Descendant   Spouse

M62252312
Genealogical Number

Robert Henry Price   Charlotte, NC
Name (including maiden name if applicable)   Town of Residence

Charlotte, N.C.   10/23/1989
Birthplace   Date of Birth   Date of Death   Where Buried

Name of Spouse   Birthplace   Date of Birth   Date of Death

Where Buried   Date of Marriage   Place of Marriage

If married more than once:

Name of Spouse   Birthplace   Date of Birth   Date of Death

Where Buried   Date of Marriage   Place of Marriage

Parents of Spouse (with Mother's maiden name) 1st Marriage

Subsequent Marriage (if applicable)

Family Details

Schools attended, dates and degrees: Community, political work, etc.:

Descendant   Descendant

Spouse   Spouse

Basic Employment History: Clubs, Church Affiliations, etc.:

Descendant   Descendant

Spouse   Spouse

Military Service:

Descendant   Spouse

M6225232
Genealogical Number

James Rutherford Moore, Jr.
Name (including maiden name if applicable)

Mechanicsville, VA
Town of Residence

Richmond, VA
Birthplace

4/1/1958
Date of Birth

Date of Death

Where Buried

Linda Lee Bender
Name of Spouse

Arlington, VA
Birthplace

10/3/1960
Date of Birth

Date of Death

Where Buried

11/3/1990
Date of Marriage

Richmond, VA
Place of Marriage

If married more than once:

Name of Spouse

Birthplace

Date of Birth

Date of Death

Where Buried

Date of Marriage

Place of Marriage

Parents of Spouse (with Mother's maiden name) 1st Marriage

Subsequent Marriage (if applicable)

Family Details

Schools attended, dates and degrees:

Community, political work, etc.:

Washington & Lee University
Descendant

Descendant

Spouse

Spouse

Basic Employment History:

Clubs, Church Affiliations, etc.:

Davenport & Co. LLC
Descendant

Second Baptist Church
Descendant

Janet E. Brown, Esq.
Spouse

Second Baptist Church
Spouse

Military Service:

Descendant

Spouse

<u>M62252321</u>
Genealogical Number

<u>James Rutherford Moore, III</u>
Name (including maiden name if applicable)

<u>Mechanicsville, VA</u>
Town of Residence

<u>Richmond, VA</u>
Birthplace

<u>9/27/1992</u>
Date of Birth

Date of Death

Where Buried

Name of Spouse

Birthplace

Date of Birth

Date of Death

Where Buried

Date of Marriage

Place of Marriage

If married more than once:

Name of Spouse

Birthplace

Date of Birth

Date of Death

Where Buried

Date of Marriage

Place of Marriage

Parents of Spouse (with Mother's maiden name) 1st Marriage

Subsequent Marriage (if applicable)

Family Details

Schools attended, dates and degrees:

Community, political work, etc.:

Descendant

Descendant

Spouse

Spouse

Basic Employment History:

Clubs, Church Affiliations, etc.:

Descendant

Descendant

Spouse

Spouse

Military Service:

Descendant

Spouse

M62252322
Genealogical Number

Alexandra Wilson Moore
Name (including maiden name if applicable)

Mechanicsville, VA
Town of Residence

Richmond, VA
Birthplace

10/27/1994
Date of Birth

Date of Death

Where Buried

Name of Spouse

Birthplace

Date of Birth

Date of Death

Where Buried

Date of Marriage

Place of Marriage

If married more than once:

Name of Spouse

Birthplace

Date of Birth

Date of Death

Where Buried

Date of Marriage

Place of Marriage

Parents of Spouse (with Mother's maiden name) 1st Marriage

Subsequent Marriage (if applicable)

Family Details

Schools attended, dates and degrees:

Community, political work, etc.:

Descendant

Descendant

Spouse

Spouse

Basic Employment History:

Clubs, Church Affiliations, etc.:

Descendant

Descendant

Spouse

Spouse

Military Service:

Descendant

Spouse

M6225233
Genealogical Number

Anne-Huston Moore   Richmond, VA
Name (including maiden name if applicable)   Town of Residence

Richmond, VA   12/20/1960
Birthplace   Date of Birth   Date of Death   Where Buried

Raymond Parker
Name of Spouse   Birthplace   Date of Birth   Date of Death

Where Buried   Date of Marriage   Place of Marriage

If married more than once:

Name of Spouse   Birthplace   Date of Birth   Date of Death

Where Buried   Date of Marriage   Place of Marriage

Parents of Spouse (with Mother's maiden name) 1st Marriage

Subsequent Marriage (if applicable)

Family Details

Schools attended, dates and degrees: Community, political work, etc.:

Descendant   Descendant

Spouse   Spouse

Basic Employment History: Clubs, Church Affiliations, etc.:

Descendant   Descendant

Spouse   Spouse

Military Service:

Descendant   Spouse

M62252331
Genealogical Number

Maria St.Clair Parker
Name (including maiden name if applicable)

Richmond, VA
Town of Residence

Richmond, VA
Birthplace

11/13/1985
Date of Birth

Date of Death

Where Buried

Name of Spouse

Birthplace

Date of Birth

Date of Death

Where Buried

Date of Marriage

Place of Marriage

If married more than once:

Name of Spouse

Birthplace

Date of Birth

Date of Death

Where Buried

Date of Marriage

Place of Marriage

Parents of Spouse (with Mother's maiden name) 1st Marriage

Subsequent Marriage (if applicable)

Family Details

Schools attended, dates and degrees:

Community, political work, etc.:

Descendant

Descendant

Spouse

Spouse

Basic Employment History:

Clubs, Church Affiliations, etc.:

Descendant

Descendant

Spouse

Spouse

Military Service:

Descendant

Spouse

M622523332
Genealogical Number

Rebecca Katharine Parker   Richmond, VA
Name (including maiden name if applicable)   Town of Residence

Richmond, VA   1/31/1987
Birthplace   Date of Birth   Date of Death   Where Buried

Name of Spouse   Birthplace   Date of Birth   Date of Death

Where Buried   Date of Marriage   Place of Marriage

If married more than once:

Name of Spouse   Birthplace   Date of Birth   Date of Death

Where Buried   Date of Marriage   Place of Marriage

Parents of Spouse (with Mother's maiden name) 1st Marriage

Subsequent Marriage (if applicable)

Family Details

Schools attended, dates and degrees: Community, political work, etc.:

Descendant   Descendant

Spouse   Spouse

Basic Employment History: Clubs, Church Affiliations, etc.:

Descendant   Descendant

Spouse   Spouse

Military Service:

Descendant   Spouse

M62252333
Genealogical Number

Ann-Margaret Parker   Richmond, VA
Name (including maiden name if applicable)   Town of Residence

Richmond, VA   7/25/1989
Birthplace   Date of Birth   Date of Death   Where Buried

Name of Spouse   Birthplace   Date of Birth   Date of Death

Where Buried   Date of Marriage   Place of Marriage

If married more than once:

Name of Spouse   Birthplace   Date of Birth   Date of Death

Where Buried   Date of Marriage   Place of Marriage

Parents of Spouse (with Mother's maiden name) 1st Marriage

Subsequent Marriage (if applicable)

Family Details

Schools attended, dates and degrees: Community, political work, etc.:

Descendant   Descendant

Spouse   Spouse

Basic Employment History: Clubs, Church Affiliations, etc.:

Descendant   Descendant

Spouse   Spouse

Military Service:

Descendant   Spouse

M62252334
Genealogical Number

Elizabeth Nelson Parker
Name (including maiden name if applicable)

Richmond, VA
Town of Residence

Richmond, VA
Birthplace

4/14/1994
Date of Birth

Date of Death

Where Buried

Name of Spouse

Birthplace

Date of Birth

Date of Death

Where Buried

Date of Marriage

Place of Marriage

If married more than once:

Name of Spouse

Birthplace

Date of Birth

Date of Death

Where Buried

Date of Marriage

Place of Marriage

Parents of Spouse (with Mother's maiden name) 1st Marriage

Subsequent Marriage (if applicable)

Family Details

Schools attended, dates and degrees:

Community, political work, etc.:

Descendant

Descendant

Spouse

Spouse

Basic Employment History:

Clubs, Church Affiliations, etc.:

Descendant

Descendant

Spouse

Spouse

Military Service:

Descendant

Spouse

M6225234
Genealogical Number

Katharine Tierney Moore
Name (including maiden name if applicable)

Richmond, VA
Town of Residence

Richmond, VA
Birthplace

12/18/1962
Date of Birth

Date of Death

Where Buried

Name of Spouse

Birthplace

Date of Birth

Date of Death

Where Buried

Date of Marriage

Place of Marriage

If married more than once:

Name of Spouse

Birthplace

Date of Birth

Date of Death

Where Buried

Date of Marriage

Place of Marriage

Parents of Spouse (with Mother's maiden name) 1st Marriage

Subsequent Marriage (if applicable)

Family Details

Schools attended, dates and degrees:

University of Cincinnati-Masters in
Social Work 1997
Descendant

Community, political work, etc.:

Henrico County Mental Health
Descendant

Spouse

Spouse

Basic Employment History:

Clubs, Church Affiliations, etc.:

Descendant

Descendant

Spouse

Spouse

Military Service:

Descendant

Spouse

M6225235
Genealogical Number

Eric St. Clair Moore   Richmond, VA
Name (including maiden name if applicable)   Town of Residence

Richmond, VA   1/25/1965
Birthplace   Date of Birth   Date of Death   Where Buried

Robin Esther Barnett   3/1/1965
Name of Spouse   Birthplace   Date of Birth   Date of Death

Where Buried   Date of Marriage   Place of Marriage

If married more than once:

Name of Spouse   Birthplace   Date of Birth   Date of Death

Where Buried   Date of Marriage   Place of Marriage

Michael Philip Barnett and Sarah Lynn Reynolds
Parents of Spouse (with Mother's maiden name) 1st Marriage

Subsequent Marriage (if applicable)

Family Details

Schools attended, dates and degrees: Community, political work, etc.:

Descendant   Descendant

Spouse   Spouse

Basic Employment History: Clubs, Church Affiliations, etc.:

Descendant   Descendant

Spouse   Spouse

Military Service:

Descendant   Spouse

M62252351
Genealogical Number

Elliott Nauman Moore   Richmond, VA
Name (including maiden name if applicable)   Town of Residence

Richmond, VA   10/23/1994
Birthplace   Date of Birth   Date of Death   Where Buried

Name of Spouse   Birthplace   Date of Birth   Date of Death

Where Buried   Date of Marriage   Place of Marriage

If married more than once:

Name of Spouse   Birthplace   Date of Birth   Date of Death

Where Buried   Date of Marriage   Place of Marriage

Parents of Spouse (with Mother's maiden name) 1st Marriage

Subsequent Marriage (if applicable)

Family Details

Schools attended, dates and degrees: Community, political work, etc.:

Descendant   Descendant

Spouse   Spouse

Basic Employment History: Clubs, Church Affiliations, etc.:

Descendant   Descendant

Spouse   Spouse

Military Service:

Descendant   Spouse

M62252352
Genealogical Number

Jacob Reynolds Moore   Richmond, VA
Name (including maiden name if applicable)   Town of Residence

Richmond, VA   2/19/2001
Birthplace   Date of Birth   Date of Death   Where Buried

Name of Spouse   Birthplace   Date of Birth   Date of Death

Where Buried   Date of Marriage   Place of Marriage

If married more than once:

Name of Spouse   Birthplace   Date of Birth   Date of Death

Where Buried   Date of Marriage   Place of Marriage

Parents of Spouse (with Mother's maiden name) 1st Marriage

Subsequent Marriage (if applicable)

Family Details

Schools attended, dates and degrees: Community, political work, etc.:

Descendant   Descendant

Spouse   Spouse

Basic Employment History: Clubs, Church Affiliations, etc.:

Descendant   Descendant

Spouse   Spouse

Military Service:

Descendant   Spouse

M622524
Genealogical Number

Margaret St.Clair Moore
Name (including maiden name if applicable)

Morristown, NJ
Town of Residence

Bluefield, W.VA
Birthplace

5/21/1931
Date of Birth

9/21/2005
Date of Death

Tazewell, VA
Where Buried

Richard Ripley (Div.)
Name of Spouse

New Haven, Conn.
Birthplace

3/17/1930
Date of Birth

Date of Death

Where Buried

Date of Marriage

Place of Marriage

If married more than once:

Name of Spouse

Birthplace

Date of Birth

Date of Death

Where Buried

Date of Marriage

Place of Marriage

Parents of Spouse (with Mother's maiden name) 1st Marriage

Subsequent Marriage (if applicable)

Family Details

Schools attended, dates and degrees:

Nat'l Cathedral School; BA 1952 Sweet Briar College
Sorbonne, Paris 1953
Descendant

Community, political work, etc.:
Junior League, one of organizers of the
center for women return to school
employment. Literacy volunteer of America
Descendant

Spouse

Spouse

Basic Employment History:

Center for Int'l Studies, MIT
Descendant

Clubs, Church Affiliations, etc.:
1953 Ping Pong Champion of Paris.
American Students & Artists Center.
Presbyterian
Descendant

Spouse

Spouse

Military Service:

Descendant

Spouse

<u>M6225241</u>
Genealogical Number

<u>St. Clair Ripley</u>   <u>NY, NY</u>
Name (including maiden name if applicable)   Town of Residence

<u>New York, NY</u>   <u>6/28/1959</u>   _____   _____
Birthplace   Date of Birth   Date of Death   Where Buried

_____   _____   _____   _____
Name of Spouse   Birthplace   Date of Birth   Date of Death

_____   _____   _____
Where Buried   Date of Marriage   Place of Marriage

If married more than once:

_____   _____   _____   _____
Name of Spouse   Birthplace   Date of Birth   Date of Death

_____   _____   _____
Where Buried   Date of Marriage   Place of Marriage

_____
Parents of Spouse (with Mother's maiden name) 1st Marriage

_____
Subsequent Marriage (if applicable)

Family Details

Schools attended, dates and degrees: Community, political work, etc.:

Kent School, Columbia Univ. Trained as an
actor in London, England.
Descendant   Descendant

_____   _____
Spouse   Spouse

Basic Employment History: Clubs, Church Affiliations, etc.:

_____   _____
Descendant   Descendant

_____   _____
Spouse   Spouse

Military Service:

_____   _____
Descendant   Spouse

M6225242
Genealogical Number

Huston Ripley   Philadelphia, PA
Name (including maiden name if applicable)   Town of Residence

Morristown, NJ   10/18/1961
Birthplace   Date of Birth   Date of Death   Where Buried

Catalina Mejia Restrepo   Medellin, Colombia   11/16/1974
Name of Spouse   Birthplace   Date of Birth   Date of Death

                           5/21/2005   Philadelphia, PA
Where Buried   Date of Marriage   Place of Marriage

If married more than once:

Name of Spouse   Birthplace   Date of Birth   Date of Death

Where Buried   Date of Marriage   Place of Marriage

Alberto Leon Mejia & Rosario Restrepo de Mejia
Parents of Spouse (with Mother's maiden name) 1st Marriage

Subsequent Marriage (if applicable)

Family Details

Schools attended, dates and degrees: Community, political work, etc.:
George School; PA Academy of Fine Arts
BFA Cum Laude, Univ. of Penn: MFA
Pratt Institute
Descendant   Descendant
San Jose de las Vegas (Medellin, Colombia), Universidad
Nacional de Colombia: BFA (Medellin), The School of
The Art Institute of Chicago MFA
Spouse   Spouse

Basic Employment History: Clubs, Church Affiliations, etc.:
Visual Artist. Has exhibited
his artwork extensively.   Pen and Pencil Club, Philadelphia.
Descendant   Descendant
Visual and Performance Artist. Has
exhibited her work in Colombia and USA.
Spouse   Spouse

Military Service:

Descendant   Spouse

319

M6225243
Genealogical Number

Timothy Regan Ripley   Randolph, NJ
Name (including maiden name if applicable)   Town of Residence

Morristown, NJ   2/28/1963
Birthplace   Date of Birth   Date of Death   Where Buried

Name of Spouse   Birthplace   Date of Birth   Date of Death

Where Buried   Date of Marriage   Place of Marriage

If married more than once:

Name of Spouse   Birthplace   Date of Birth   Date of Death

Where Buried   Date of Marriage   Place of Marriage

Parents of Spouse (with Mother's maiden name) 1st Marriage

Subsequent Marriage (if applicable)

Family Details

Schools attended, dates and degrees: Community, political work, etc.:

Gill-St. Bernard's; Bradford College;
Arizona State Univ. BS
Descendant   Descendant

Spouse   Spouse

Basic Employment History: Clubs, Church Affiliations, etc.:

Computer Analyst
Descendant   Descendant

Spouse   Spouse

Military Service:

Descendant   Spouse

M622541
Genealogical Number

June Archer Moore
Name (including maiden name if applicable)

Matthews, N.C.
Town of Residence

Richmond, VA
Birthplace

9/5/1931
Date of Birth

Date of Death

Where Buried

William Henry Smith
Name of Spouse

Lee County, S.C.
Birthplace

7/9/1923
Date of Birth

4/17/1987
Date of Death

Forest Lawn Cemetery
Union County, N.C.
Where Buried

10/6/1979
Date of Marriage

Charlotte, N.C.
Place of Marriage

If married more than once:

Duncan Dallas McDuffie (Div.)
Name of Spouse

Ft. Sam Houston, TX
Birthplace

6/11/1928
Date of Birth

Date of Death

Where Buried

6/16/1951
Date of Marriage

Tazewell, VA
Place of Marriage

Jasper Kemper & Elizabeth Hoofnagle McDuffie
Parents of Spouse (with Mother's maiden name) 1st Marriage

Subsequent Marriage (if applicable)

Family Details

Schools attended, dates and degrees:

Converse College - 1948-1950
Pan American School, Richmond VA - 1951-1951
Descendant

Queens College
Spouse

Basic Employment History:

Former Owner - Jubilee Advertising Specialties
Descendant

Westinghouse Electric
Spouse

Military Service:

Descendant

Community, political work, etc.:
See overleaf.

Descendant

Spouse

Clubs, Church Affiliations, etc.:

Matthews United Methodist
Descendant

Spouse

U.S. Army 1941-1945
Spouse

June Archer(Moore) Smith

Community Work: Local Projects Chairman - Junior Woman's Club -Winston-Salem, NC
Volunteer in Music Dept. Matthews United Methodist Church each week.
Librarian for Senior Community Choir - Matthews, NC
President – The Moore Family Association

William Henry Smith

Community Work: At the beginning of the Polio epidemic in the late 1940's Bill and one of
his best friends maintained all of the iron lungs in the city of Charlotte,
Mecklenburg County and western North Carolina, traveling thousands of
miles. He continued this service many years after the epidemic was over.

He was awarded the following:

    March of Dimes Service Award for Outstanding
    Humanitarian Award to the Disabled.

    Sertoma International Service to Mankind Award

M6225411
Genealogical Number

Infant Son McDuffie
Name (including maiden name if applicable)

Town of Residence

Winston-Salem, NC
Birthplace

8/25/1952
Date of Birth

8/25/1952
Date of Death

Jeffersonville Cemetery
Tazewell, VA
Where Buried

Name of Spouse

Birthplace

Date of Birth

Date of Death

Where Buried

Date of Marriage

Place of Marriage

If married more than once:

Name of Spouse

Birthplace

Date of Birth

Date of Death

Where Buried

Date of Marriage

Place of Marriage

Parents of Spouse (with Mother's maiden name) 1st Marriage

Subsequent Marriage (if applicable)

Family Details

Schools attended, dates and degrees:

Community, political work, etc.:

Descendant

Descendant

Spouse

Spouse

Basic Employment History:

Clubs, Church Affiliations, etc.:

Descendant

Descendant

Spouse

Spouse

Military Service:

Descendant

Spouse

M6225412
Genealogical Number

Susan Cameron McDuffie
Name (including maiden name if applicable)

Concord, Ohio
Town of Residence

Winston-Salem, N.C.
Birthplace

4/21/1954
Date of Birth

Date of Death

Where Buried

Michael Joseph
Name of Spouse

Pechar
Birthplace

1/'29/1948
Date of Birth

Date of Death

Where Buried

9/23/1987
Date of Marriage

Las Vegas, NV
Place of Marriage

If married more than once:

Name of Spouse

Birthplace

Date of Birth

Date of Death

Where Buried

Date of Marriage

Place of Marriage

Parents of Spouse (with Mother's maiden name) 1st Marriage

Subsequent Marriage (if applicable)

Family Details

Schools attended, dates and degrees:

Community, political work, etc.:

N.C. State - BS Elec.
Eng. 1976
Descendant

Descendant

Spouse

Spouse

Basic Employment History:

Clubs, Church Affiliations, etc.:

Descendant

Baptist
Descendant

Spouse

Spouse

Military Service:

Descendant

Spouse

M62254121
Genealogical Number

Matthew Dallas Pechar
Name (including maiden name if applicable)

Concord, Ohio
Town of Residence

Painesville, Ohio
Birthplace

10/8/1988
Date of Birth

Date of Death

Where Buried

Name of Spouse

Birthplace

Date of Birth

Date of Death

Where Buried

Date of Marriage

Place of Marriage

If married more than once:

Name of Spouse

Birthplace

Date of Birth

Date of Death

Where Buried

Date of Marriage

Place of Marriage

Parents of Spouse (with Mother's maiden name) 1st Marriage

Subsequent Marriage (if applicable)

Family Details

Schools attended, dates and degrees:

Community, political work, etc.:

Descendant

Descendant

Spouse

Spouse

Basic Employment History:

Clubs, Church Affiliations, etc.:

Descendant

Descendant

Spouse

Spouse

Military Service:

Descendant

Spouse

M6225413
Genealogical Number

Mary Moore McDuffie
Name (including maiden name if applicable)

Matthews, N.C.
Town of Residence

Winston-Salem, N.C.
Birthplace

8/14/1955
Date of Birth

Date of Death

Where Buried

Mark Patrick Casey (Div.)
Name of Spouse

Birthplace

1/4/1955
Date of Birth

Date of Death

Where Buried

3/2/1980
Date of Marriage

Charlotte, N.C.
Place of Marriage

If married more than once:

Name of Spouse

Birthplace

Date of Birth

Date of Death

Where Buried

Date of Marriage

Place of Marriage

Parents of Spouse (with Mother's maiden name) 1st Marriage

Subsequent Marriage (if applicable)

Family Details

Schools attended, dates and degrees:

Community, political work, etc.:

East Carolina Univ. - BS Indus.
Tech. 1971
Descendant

Descendant

Spouse

Spouse

Basic Employment History:

Clubs, Church Affiliations, etc.:

Electronics
Descendant

Methodist
Descendant

Spouse

Spouse

Military Service:

Descendant

Spouse

M62254131
Genealogical Number

Cameron Mary Ellen Cary
Name (including maiden name if applicable)

Matthews, NC
Town of Residence

Raleight, NC
Birthplace

11/7/1982
Date of Birth

Date of Death

Where Buried

Name of Spouse

Birthplace

Date of Birth

Date of Death

Where Buried

Date of Marriage

Place of Marriage

If married more than once:

Name of Spouse

Birthplace

Date of Birth

Date of Death

Where Buried

Date of Marriage

Place of Marriage

Parents of Spouse (with Mother's maiden name) 1st Marriage

Subsequent Marriage (if applicable)

Family Details

Schools attended, dates and degrees:

Community, political work, etc.:

Descendant

Descendant

Spouse

Spouse

Basic Employment History:

Clubs, Church Affiliations, etc.:

Descendant

Descendant

Spouse

Spouse

Military Service:

Descendant

Spouse

M62254132
Genealogical Number

Sara Michelle Cary
Name (including maiden name if applicable)

Matthews, NC
Town of Residence

Raleigh, NC
Birthplace

9/23/1986
Date of Birth

Date of Death

Where Buried

Name of Spouse

Birthplace

Date of Birth

Date of Death

Where Buried

Date of Marriage

Place of Marriage

If married more than once:

Name of Spouse

Birthplace

Date of Birth

Date of Death

Where Buried

Date of Marriage

Place of Marriage

Parents of Spouse (with Mother's maiden name) 1st Marriage

Subsequent Marriage (if applicable)

Family Details

Schools attended, dates and degrees:

Community, political work, etc.:

Descendant

Descendant

Spouse

Spouse

Basic Employment History:

Clubs, Church Affiliations, etc.:

Descendant

Descendant

Spouse

Spouse

Military Service:

Descendant

Spouse

M6225414
Genealogical Number

Elizabeth Archer McDuffie
Name (including maiden name if applicable)

St. Matthews, S.C.
Town of Residence

Winston-Salem, N.C.
Birthplace

4/23/1959
Date of Birth

Date of Death

Where Buried

Duane Alan Kitchings
Name of Spouse

Birthplace

5/5/1955
Date of Birth

Date of Death

Where Buried

5/14/1989
Date of Marriage

Aiken, S.C.
Place of Marriage

If married more than once:

Name of Spouse

Birthplace

Date of Birth

Date of Death

Where Buried

Date of Marriage

Place of Marriage

Parents of Spouse (with Mother's maiden name) 1st Marriage

Subsequent Marriage (if applicable)

Family Details

Schools attended, dates and degrees:

Community, political work, etc.:

Univ. of N.C. at Greensboro
Descendant

Descendant

Spouse

Spouse

Basic Employment History:

Clubs, Church Affiliations, etc.:

Sales
Descendant

Baptist
Descendant

Sales
Spouse

Baptist
Spouse

Military Service:

Descendant

Spouse

M62254141
Genealogical Number

James Alan Kitchings St. Matthews, S.C.
Name (including maiden name if applicable) Town of Residence

Orangeburg, S.C. 6/9/1995
Birthplace Date of Birth Date of Death Where Buried

Name of Spouse Birthplace Date of Birth Date of Death

Where Buried Date of Marriage Place of Marriage

If married more than once:

Name of Spouse Birthplace Date of Birth Date of Death

Where Buried Date of Marriage Place of Marriage

Parents of Spouse (with Mother's maiden name) 1st Marriage

Subsequent Marriage (if applicable)

Family Details

Schools attended, dates and degrees: Community, political work, etc.:

Descendant Descendant

Spouse Spouse

Basic Employment History: Clubs, Church Affiliations, etc.:

Descendant Descendant

Spouse Spouse

Military Service:

Descendant Spouse

M62254142
_____
Genealogical Number

Joshua Davis Kitchings
_____
Name (including maiden name if applicable)

St. Matthews, S.C.
_____
Town of Residence

Columbia, S.C.
_____
Birthplace

1/16/2001
_____
Date of Birth

_____
Date of Death

_____
Where Buried

_____
Name of Spouse

_____
Birthplace

_____
Date of Birth

_____
Date of Death

_____
Where Buried

_____
Date of Marriage

_____
Place of Marriage

If married more than once:

_____
Name of Spouse

_____
Birthplace

_____
Date of Birth

_____
Date of Death

_____
Where Buried

_____
Date of Marriage

_____
Place of Marriage

_____
Parents of Spouse (with Mother's maiden name) 1st Marriage

_____
Subsequent Marriage (if applicable)

Family Details

Schools attended, dates and degrees:

Community, political work, etc.:

_____
Descendant

_____
Descendant

_____
Spouse

_____
Spouse

Basic Employment History:

Clubs, Church Affiliations, etc.:

_____
Descendant

_____
Descendant

_____
Spouse

_____
Spouse

Military Service:

_____
Descendant

_____
Spouse

M6226212
Genealogical Number

Margaret Elizabeth Higginbotham
Name (including maiden name if applicable)

Tyler, TX
Town of Residence

Frankford, W. VA
Birthplace

8/13/1947
Date of Birth

Date of Death

Where Buried

Stephen Douglas Snyder, Sr.
Name of Spouse

White Sulphur
Springs, W.VA
Birthplace

11/2/1947
Date of Birth

Date of Death

Where Buried

7/11/1970
Date of Marriage

Place of Marriage

If married more than once:

Name of Spouse

Birthplace

Date of Birth

Date of Death

Where Buried

Date of Marriage

Place of Marriage

Parents of Spouse (with Mother's maiden name) 1st Marriage

Subsequent Marriage (if applicable)

Family Details

Schools attended, dates and degrees:

Graduated Frankford High School - 1965
Attended Concord College (1 year) - 1966
Descendant

Community, political work, etc.:

Descendant

Spouse

Spouse

Basic Employment History:
1967-RBS Inc. 1968-69 W.VA Dept. Highways.
Housewife since 1970
Descendant

Clubs, Church Affiliations, etc.:

Active in local church.
Descendant
Active in local church.
Ham radio operator

Spouse

Spouse

Military Service:

Descendant

Spouse

M62262121
Genealogical Number

Stephen Douglas Snyder, Jr.
Name (including maiden name if applicable)

Tyler, TX
Town of Residence

Baltimore, MD
Birthplace

1/23/1975
Date of Birth

Date of Death

Where Buried

Kelly Darby
Name of Spouse

Tyler, TX
Birthplace

1/20/1981
Date of Birth

Date of Death

Where Buried

9/12/2002
Date of Marriage

Place of Marriage

If married more than once:

Beverly
Name of Spouse

Birthplace

Date of Birth

Date of Death

Where Buried

Date of Marriage

Place of Marriage

Parents of Spouse (with Mother's maiden name) 1st Marriage

Subsequent Marriage (if applicable)

Family Details

Schools attended, dates and degrees:

Robert E. Lee High School - 1993 Graduate
Descendant

Jacksonville High School, TX - 1999
Spouse

Basic Employment History:

Whitehouse Police Dept.
Descendant

Darby Green Houses
Spouse

Military Service:

Marines
Descendant

Community, political work, etc.:

Descendant

Spouse

Clubs, Church Affiliations, etc.:
First United Methodist Church,
Jacksonville, TX
Descendant

Spouse

Spouse

M62262121
Genealogical Number

Natalie Elizabeth Snyder
Name (including maiden name if applicable)

Tyler, Texas
Town of Residence

	11/16/2000		
Birthplace	Date of Birth	Date of Death	Where Buried

Name of Spouse	Birthplace	Date of Birth	Date of Death

Where Buried	Date of Marriage	Place of Marriage

If married more than once:

Name of Spouse	Birthplace	Date of Birth	Date of Death

Where Buried	Date of Marriage	Place of Marriage

Parents of Spouse (with Mother's maiden name) 1st Marriage

Subsequent Marriage (if applicable)

Family Details

Schools attended, dates and degrees:

Community, political work, etc.:

Descendant

Descendant

Spouse

Spouse

Basic Employment History:

Clubs, Church Affiliations, etc.:

Descendant

Descendant

Spouse

Spouse

Military Service:

Descendant

Spouse

M62262122
Genealogical Number

Michael William Snyder
Name (including maiden name if applicable)

Tyler, TX
Town of Residence

Portsmouth, OH
Birthplace

11/24/1983
Date of Birth

Date of Death

Where Buried

Name of Spouse

Birthplace

Date of Birth

Date of Death

Where Buried

Date of Marriage

Place of Marriage

If married more than once:

Name of Spouse

Birthplace

Date of Birth

Date of Death

Where Buried

Date of Marriage

Place of Marriage

Parents of Spouse (with Mother's maiden name) 1st Marriage

Subsequent Marriage (if applicable)

Family Details

Schools attended, dates and degrees:

Graduated High School - May 2002
Tyler Jr. College - Present
Descendant

Community, political work, etc.:

Descendant

Spouse

Spouse

Basic Employment History:

Student
Descendant

Clubs, Church Affiliations, etc.:

Tyler Gospel Chapel, Tyler, TX
Descendant

Spouse

Spouse

Military Service:

Descendant

Spouse

M6226213
Genealogical Number

Charles Andrew Higginbotham   Frankford, W.VA
Name (including maiden name if applicable)   Town of Residence

Frankford, W.VA   12/3/1950
Birthplace   Date of Birth   Date of Death   Where Buried

Carla Lee Smith   Ronceverte, W.VA   8/23/1949
Name of Spouse   Birthplace   Date of Birth   Date of Death

                             6/7/1975
Where Buried   Date of Marriage   Place of Marriage

If married more than once:

Name of Spouse   Birthplace   Date of Birth   Date of Death

Where Buried   Date of Marriage   Place of Marriage

Parents of Spouse (with Mother's maiden name) 1st Marriage

Subsequent Marriage (if applicable)

Family Details

Schools attended, dates and degrees: Community, political work, etc.:

Graduated - Greenbrier East High School -1969
Attended WVU-Community College 1969-70   Asst. Chief - Frankford Vol. Fire Dept.
Descendant   Descendant
Lewisburg High School 1967
St. Mary's School of Nursing - RN 1967-70
Spouse   Spouse

Basic Employment History: Clubs, Church Affiliations, etc.:
Sunrise Farm 1969-72 (Family Farm). Kyle's Garage
1973-74. WV Dept. Highways 1974-85. Greenbrier
Respiratory Care Services 1985 - present   Lewisburg United Methodist Church
Descendant   Descendant
                                                  Lewisburg United Methodist Church. Board
                                                  Member - Greenbrier Valley Hospice.
Greenbrier Valley Medical Center 1974 to present. Greenbrier Interagency Council
Spouse   Spouse

Military Service:

Descendant   Spouse

email: Chigg@mail.WVNET.EDU

M62262131
Genealogical Number

Charles Russell Higginbotham
Name (including maiden name if applicable)

Frankford, W. VA
Town of Residence

Fairlea, W.VA
Birthplace

2/15/1981
Date of Birth

Date of Death

Where Buried

Name of Spouse

Birthplace

Date of Birth

Date of Death

Where Buried

Date of Marriage

Place of Marriage

If married more than once:

Name of Spouse

Birthplace

Date of Birth

Date of Death

Where Buried

Date of Marriage

Place of Marriage

Parents of Spouse (with Mother's maiden name) 1st Marriage

Subsequent Marriage (if applicable)

Family Details

Schools attended, dates and degrees:

Graduated - Greenbrier East High School - 1999
Attending - Greenrbier Community College - Present
Descendant

Community, political work, etc.:

2nd Lieutenant - Frankford Vo. Fire Dept.
Descendant

Spouse

Spouse

Basic Employment History:
S.J. Neathawk Lumber - 2000
John Bell Co. 2000 - present
Descendant

Clubs, Church Affiliations, etc.:

Lewisburg United Methodist Church
Descendant

Spouse

Spouse

Military Service:

Descendant

Spouse

M62262132
Genealogical Number

Joshua Moore Higginbotham
Name (including maiden name if applicable)

Frankford, W. VA
Town of Residence

Ronceverte, W.VA
Birthplace

12/27/1984
Date of Birth

Date of Death

Where Buried

Name of Spouse

Birthplace

Date of Birth

Date of Death

Where Buried

Date of Marriage

Place of Marriage

If married more than once:

Name of Spouse

Birthplace

Date of Birth

Date of Death

Where Buried

Date of Marriage

Place of Marriage

Parents of Spouse (with Mother's maiden name) 1st Marriage

Subsequent Marriage (if applicable)

Family Details

Schools attended, dates and degrees:

Greenbrier East High School - 2003
West Virginia University-enrolled Fall 2003
Descendant

Community, political work, etc.:

Descendant

Spouse

Spouse

Basic Employment History:

Clubs, Church Affiliations, etc.:

Student
Descendant

Lewisburg United Methodist Church
Descendant

Spouse

Spouse

Military Service:

Descendant

Spouse

M6226314
Genealogical Number

Susan Rebecca Kidd
Name (including maiden name if applicable)

Huddleston, VA
Town of Residence

Ronceverte, W.VA
Birthplace

8/31/1956
Date of Birth

Date of Death

Where Buried

Mark B. Goode
Name of Spouse

Bedford, VA
Birthplace

2/16/1956
Date of Birth

Date of Death

Where Buried

7/22/1978
Date of Marriage

Maxwelton, W.VA
Place of Marriage

If married more than once:

Name of Spouse

Birthplace

Date of Birth

Date of Death

Where Buried

Date of Marriage

Place of Marriage

Parents of Spouse (with Mother's maiden name) 1st Marriage

Subsequent Marriage (if applicable)

Family Details

Schools attended, dates and degrees:

Community, political work, etc.:

VA Tech. BS '78 Radford Univ. BS '94
Radford Univ. MSN '99
Descendant

Descendant

VA Tech. BS '78
Spouse

Spouse

Basic Employment History:
Family Nurse Practitioner -
Carilion Health System
Descendant

Clubs, Church Affiliations, etc.:

Bedford Presbyterian Church
Descendant

Self employed - Double Good Farm
Spouse

Spouse

Military Service:

Descendant

Spouse

M62263141
_____
Genealogical Number

Joshua Goode
_____
Name (including maiden name if applicable)

Huddleston, VA
_____
Town of Residence

Roanoke, VA
_____
Birthplace

4/22/1981
_____
Date of Birth

_____
Date of Death

_____
Where Buried

_____
Name of Spouse

_____
Birthplace

_____
Date of Birth

_____
Date of Death

_____
Where Buried

_____
Date of Marriage

_____
Place of Marriage

If married more than once:

_____
Name of Spouse

_____
Birthplace

_____
Date of Birth

_____
Date of Death

_____
Where Buried

_____
Date of Marriage

_____
Place of Marriage

_____
Parents of Spouse (with Mother's maiden name) 1st Marriage

_____
Subsequent Marriage (if applicable)

Family Details

Schools attended, dates and degrees:

Community, political work, etc.:

Virginia Tech (present)
_____
Descendant

_____
Descendant

_____
Spouse

_____
Spouse

Basic Employment History:

Clubs, Church Affiliations, etc.:

_____
Descendant

_____
Descendant

_____
Spouse

_____
Spouse

Military Service:

_____
Descendant

_____
Spouse

M62263142
Genealogical Number

Zachary Goode
Name (including maiden name if applicable)

Huddleston, VA
Town of Residence

Roanoke, VA
Birthplace

1/12/1984
Date of Birth

Date of Death

Where Buried

Name of Spouse

Birthplace

Date of Birth

Date of Death

Where Buried

Date of Marriage

Place of Marriage

If married more than once:

Name of Spouse

Birthplace

Date of Birth

Date of Death

Where Buried

Date of Marriage

Place of Marriage

Parents of Spouse (with Mother's maiden name) 1st Marriage

Subsequent Marriage (if applicable)

Family Details

Schools attended, dates and degrees:

Community, political work, etc.:

Duke Univ. (present)
Descendant

Descendant

Spouse

Spouse

Basic Employment History:

Clubs, Church Affiliations, etc.:

Descendant

Descendant

Spouse

Spouse

Military Service:

Descendant

Spouse

M62263143
Genealogical Number

Caleb Goode
Name (including maiden name if applicable)

Huddleston, VA
Town of Residence

Roanoke, VA
Birthplace

6/1/1987
Date of Birth

Date of Death

Where Buried

Name of Spouse

Birthplace

Date of Birth

Date of Death

Where Buried

Date of Marriage

Place of Marriage

If married more than once:

Name of Spouse

Birthplace

Date of Birth

Date of Death

Where Buried

Date of Marriage

Place of Marriage

Parents of Spouse (with Mother's maiden name) 1st Marriage

Subsequent Marriage (if applicable)

Family Details

Schools attended, dates and degrees:

Community, political work, etc.:

Staunton River High (present)
Descendant

Descendant

Spouse

Spouse

Basic Employment History:

Clubs, Church Affiliations, etc.:

Descendant

Descendant

Spouse

Spouse

Military Service:

Descendant

Spouse

M62263144
Genealogical Number

Isaac Goode
Name (including maiden name if applicable)

Huddleston, VA
Town of Residence

Roanoke, VA
Birthplace

11/12/1989
Date of Birth

Date of Death

Where Buried

Name of Spouse

Birthplace

Date of Birth

Date of Death

Where Buried

Date of Marriage

Place of Marriage

If married more than once:

Name of Spouse

Birthplace

Date of Birth

Date of Death

Where Buried

Date of Marriage

Place of Marriage

Parents of Spouse (with Mother's maiden name) 1st Marriage

Subsequent Marriage (if applicable)

Family Details

Schools attended, dates and degrees:

Community, political work, etc.:

Staunton River Middle (present)
Descendant

Descendant

Spouse

Spouse

Basic Employment History:

Clubs, Church Affiliations, etc.:

Descendant

Descendant

Spouse

Spouse

Military Service:

Descendant

Spouse

M6226811
Genealogical Number

Charles Edwin Wilson   Cleburne, Texas
Name (including maiden name if applicable)   Town of Residence

Washington, DC   1/7/1950
Birthplace   Date of Birth   Date of Death   Where Buried

Janet Ellen McDowell   Ft. Worth, TX   1/28/1954
Name of Spouse   Birthplace   Date of Birth   Date of Death

                        7/18/1992   Colleyville, TX
Where Buried   Date of Marriage   Place of Marriage

If married more than once:

Debra Michelle Lilly   Pulaski, VA   1/6/1954
Name of Spouse   Birthplace   Date of Birth   Date of Death

                        7/23/1971   Clifton Forge, VA
Where Buried   Date of Marriage   Place of Marriage

Paul Ryan Lilly - Ollie Page
Parents of Spouse (with Mother's maiden name) 1st Marriage

Robert Mervyn McDowell - Mary Helen Simmons
Subsequent Marriage (if applicable)   (2nd Marriage)

Family Details

Schools attended, dates and degrees: Community, political work, etc.:

_____   _____
Descendant   Descendant

_____   _____
Spouse   Spouse

Basic Employment History: Clubs, Church Affiliations, etc.:

_____   _____
Descendant   Descendant

_____   _____
Spouse   Spouse

Military Service:

_____   _____
Descendant   Spouse

M62268111
Genealogical Number

Tracy Elizabeth Wilson
Name (including maiden name if applicable)

Duncanville, Texas
Town of Residence

Ronceverte, W. VA
Birthplace

2/20/1972
Date of Birth

Date of Death

Where Buried

Name of Spouse

Birthplace

Date of Birth

Date of Death

Where Buried

Date of Marriage

Place of Marriage

If married more than once:

Name of Spouse

Birthplace

Date of Birth

Date of Death

Where Buried

Date of Marriage

Place of Marriage

Parents of Spouse (with Mother's maiden name) 1st Marriage

Subsequent Marriage (if applicable)

Family Details

Schools attended, dates and degrees:

Community, political work, etc.:

Descendant

Descendant

Spouse

Spouse

Basic Employment History:

Clubs, Church Affiliations, etc.:

Descendant

Descendant

Spouse

Spouse

Military Service:

Descendant

Spouse

M622681111
Genealogical Number

Kristin Bailey Rojo   Duncanville, Texas
Name (including maiden name if applicable)   Town of Residence

Dallas, Texas   8/9/2000
Birthplace   Date of Birth   Date of Death   Where Buried

Name of Spouse   Birthplace   Date of Birth   Date of Death

Where Buried   Date of Marriage   Place of Marriage

If married more than once:

Name of Spouse   Birthplace   Date of Birth   Date of Death

Where Buried   Date of Marriage   Place of Marriage

Parents of Spouse (with Mother's maiden name) 1st Marriage

Subsequent Marriage (if applicable)

Family Details

Schools attended, dates and degrees: Community, political work, etc.:

Descendant   Descendant

Spouse   Spouse

Basic Employment History: Clubs, Church Affiliations, etc.:

Descendant   Descendant

Spouse   Spouse

Military Service:

Descendant   Spouse

M62268112
Genealogical Number

Jesse Price Wilson
Name (including maiden name if applicable)

Franklin, TN
Town of Residence

Pottstown, PA
Birthplace

7/20/1975
Date of Birth

Date of Death

Where Buried

Shauna Elaine Brott
Name of Spouse

Dallas, Texas
Birthplace

3/14/1975
Date of Birth

Date of Death

Where Buried

6/21/1997
Date of Marriage

Denton, Texas
Place of Marriage

If married more than once:

Name of Spouse

Birthplace

Date of Birth

Date of Death

Where Buried

Date of Marriage

Place of Marriage

Parents of Spouse (with Mother's maiden name) 1st Marriage

Subsequent Marriage (if applicable)

Family Details

Schools attended, dates and degrees:

Community, political work, etc.:

Descendant

Descendant

Spouse

Spouse

Basic Employment History:

Clubs, Church Affiliations, etc.:

Descendant

Descendant

Spouse

Spouse

Military Service:

Descendant

Spouse

M6281121
Genealogical Number

Reid David Wilson						Franklin, Tenn.
Name (including maiden name if applicable)			Town of Residence

							10/13/2002
Birthplace						Date of Birth			Date of Death			Where Buried

Name of Spouse					Birthplace			Date of Birth			Date of Death

Where Buried					Date of Marriage			Place of Marriage

If married more than once:

Name of Spouse					Birthplace			Date of Birth			Date of Death

Where Buried					Date of Marriage			Place of Marriage

Parents of Spouse (with Mother's maiden name) 1st Marriage

Subsequent Marriage (if applicable)

Family Details

Schools attended, dates and degrees:				Community, political work, etc.:

Descendant							Descendant

Spouse								Spouse

Basic Employment History:					Clubs, Church Affiliations, etc.:

Descendant							Descendant

Spouse								Spouse

Military Service:

Descendant							Spouse

M62269
Genealogical Number

Clynta Le Vici Higginbotham
Name (including maiden name if applicable)   Town of Residence

                                    7/6/1896
Birthplace   Date of Birth   Date of Death   Where Buried

Robert Moore Baldwin, Sr.   7/4/1896
Name of Spouse   Birthplace   Date of Birth   Date of Death

                                    6/7/1920
Where Buried   Date of Marriage   Place of Marriage

If married more than once:

Name of Spouse   Birthplace   Date of Birth   Date of Death

Where Buried   Date of Marriage   Place of Marriage

Parents of Spouse (with Mother's maiden name) 1st Marriage

Subsequent Marriage (if applicable)

Family Details

Schools attended, dates and degrees: Community, political work, etc.:

Descendant   Descendant

Spouse   Spouse

Basic Employment History: Clubs, Church Affiliations, etc.:

Descendant   Descendant

Spouse   Spouse

Military Service:

Descendant   Spouse

M6227121
Genealogical Number

Linda Elaine Miller   Australia
Name (including maiden name if applicable)   Town of Residence

                          10/11/1963
Birthplace   Date of Birth   Date of Death   Where Buried

Dirk Christian Baltzly   8/24/1963
Name of Spouse   Birthplace   Date of Birth   Date of Death

                          9/3/1988
Where Buried   Date of Marriage   Place of Marriage

If married more than once:

Name of Spouse   Birthplace   Date of Birth   Date of Death

Where Buried   Date of Marriage   Place of Marriage

Parents of Spouse (with Mother's maiden name) 1st Marriage

Subsequent Marriage (if applicable)

Family Details

Schools attended, dates and degrees: Community, political work, etc.:

Descendant   Descendant

Spouse   Spouse

Basic Employment History: Clubs, Church Affiliations, etc.:

Descendant   Descendant

Spouse   Spouse

Military Service:

Descendant   Spouse

M62273
Genealogical Number

John Freeman Moore
Name (including maiden name if applicable)

Town of Residence

Abbs Valley, VA
Birthplace

7/9/1904
Date of Birth

April, 1949
Date of Death

Abbs Valley
Where Buried

Name of Spouse

Birthplace

Date of Birth

Date of Death

Where Buried

Date of Marriage

Place of Marriage

If married more than once:

Name of Spouse

Birthplace

Date of Birth

Date of Death

Where Buried

Date of Marriage

Place of Marriage

Parents of Spouse (with Mother's maiden name) 1st Marriage

Subsequent Marriage (if applicable)

Family Details

Schools attended, dates and degrees:

Community, political work, etc.:

Descendant

Descendant

Spouse

Spouse

Basic Employment History:

Clubs, Church Affiliations, etc.:

Descendant

Descendant

M62274
Genealogical Number

Rose McDonald Moore
Name (including maiden name if applicable)   Town of Residence

                                                                    Monte Vista P
Abbs Valley, VA   10/20/1906   7/8/1989   Bluefield, W.V
Birthplace   Date of Birth   Date of Death Where Buried

John Roy Mullin (M624621)   Nemours, W.VA   2/1/1900   4/3/1962
Name of Spouse   Birthplace   Date of Birth   Date of Death

Monte Vista Park   10/2/1931
Where Buried   Date of Marriage   Place of Marriage

If married more than once:

_____   _____   _____   _____
Name of Spouse   Birthplace   Date of Birth   Date of Death

_____   _____   _____
Where Buried   Date of Marriage   Place of Marriage

Javin Baldwin Mullin/Sara Poage Karr (M62462)
Parents of Spouse (with Mother's maiden name) 1st Marriage

_____
Subsequent Marriage (if applicable)

Family Details

Schools attended, dates and degrees: Community, political work, etc.:

_____   _____
Descendant   Descendant

_____   _____
Spouse   Spouse

Basic Employment History: Clubs, Church Affiliations, etc.:

_____   _____
Descendant   Descendant

M622741
Genealogical Number

Mary Moore Mullin
Name (including maiden name if applicable)

Las Vegas, NV
Town of Residence

Bluefield, W. VA
Birthplace

10/29/1934
Date of Birth

Date of Death

Where Buried

Alfred LeRoy Mowery, Jr.
Name of Spouse

Augusta, GA
Birthplace

8/14/1934
Date of Birth

8/26/2004
Date of Death

Where Buried

9/2/1955
Date of Marriage

Bluefield, W.VA
Place of Marriage

If married more than once:

Name of Spouse

Birthplace

Date of Birth

Date of Death

Where Buried

Date of Marriage

Place of Marriage

Parents of Spouse (with Mother's maiden name) 1st Marriage

Subsequent Marriage (if applicable)

Family Details

Schools attended, dates and degrees:
U. of Richmond - 1952-54
McClain Bus. College -1955

Community, political work, etc.:

Descendant
Duke U. BS 1955,NC State U. MS 1957
NC State PhD Eng. Physics
Spouse

Descendant

Spouse

Basic Employment History:

Clubs, Church Affiliations, etc.:

19 years Dentistry - retired
Descendant

Sun City Dance Club 1999-present
Descendant
Sun City Computer Club
Sun City Photography Club
Spouse

Dept of Energy - retired
Spouse

Military Service:

None
Descendant

Spouse

M6227411
Genealogical Number

Mark Wayland Mowery
Name (including maiden name if applicable)

Centreville, VA
Town of Residence

Bluefield, W.VA
Birthplace

7/11/1957
Date of Birth

Date of Death

Where Buried

Beverly Jean Phillips
Name of Spouse

Baltimore, MD
Birthplace

6/24/1959
Date of Birth

Date of Death

Where Buried

6/13/1981
Date of Marriage

Stevensville, VA
Place of Marriage

If married more than once:

Name of Spouse

Birthplace

Date of Birth

Date of Death

Where Buried

Date of Marriage

Place of Marriage

Parents of Spouse (with Mother's maiden name) 1st Marriage

Subsequent Marriage (if applicable)

Family Details

Schools attended, dates and degrees:

Community, political work, etc.:

Descendant

Descendant

Spouse

Spouse

Basic Employment History:

Clubs, Church Affiliations, etc.:

Descendant

Descendant

Spouse

Spouse

Military Service:

Descendant

Spouse

M62274111
Genealogical Number

Jeffrey Phillip Mowery
Name (including maiden name if applicable)

Centreville, VA
Town of Residence

Fairfax, VA
Birthplace

12/7/1989
Date of Birth

Date of Death

Where Buried

Name of Spouse

Birthplace

Date of Birth

Date of Death

Where Buried

Date of Marriage

Place of Marriage

If married more than once:

Name of Spouse

Birthplace

Date of Birth

Date of Death

Where Buried

Date of Marriage

Place of Marriage

Parents of Spouse (with Mother's maiden name) 1st Marriage

Subsequent Marriage (if applicable)

Family Details

Schools attended, dates and degrees:

Community, political work, etc.:

Descendant

Descendant

Spouse

Spouse

Basic Employment History:

Clubs, Church Affiliations, etc.:

Descendant

Descendant

Spouse

Spouse

Military Service:

Descendant

Spouse

M62274112
Genealogical Number

Melissa Moore Mowery
Name (including maiden name if applicable)

Centreville, VA
Town of Residence

Fairfax, VA
Birthplace

4/30/1992
Date of Birth

Date of Death

Where Buried

Name of Spouse

Birthplace

Date of Birth

Date of Death

Where Buried

Date of Marriage

Place of Marriage

If married more than once:

Name of Spouse

Birthplace

Date of Birth

Date of Death

Where Buried

Date of Marriage

Place of Marriage

Parents of Spouse (with Mother's maiden name) 1st Marriage

Subsequent Marriage (if applicable)

Family Details

Schools attended, dates and degrees:

Community, political work, etc.:

Descendant

Descendant

Spouse

Spouse

Basic Employment History:

Clubs, Church Affiliations, etc.:

Descendant

Descendant

Spouse

Spouse

Military Service:

Descendant

Spouse

M6227412
Genealogical Number

Alfred Leighton Mowery
Name (including maiden name if applicable)

Houston, TX
Town of Residence

Raleigh, NC
Birthplace

6/26/1960
Date of Birth

Date of Death

Where Buried

Name of Spouse

Birthplace

Date of Birth

Date of Death

Where Buried

Date of Marriage

Place of Marriage

If married more than once:

Name of Spouse

Birthplace

Date of Birth

Date of Death

Where Buried

Date of Marriage

Place of Marriage

Parents of Spouse (with Mother's maiden name) 1st Marriage

Subsequent Marriage (if applicable)

Family Details

Schools attended, dates and degrees:

Community, political work, etc.:

U. of Md. BS EE 1981
Descendant

Descendant

Spouse

Spouse

Basic Employment History:

Clubs, Church Affiliations, etc.:

Computer Chip Manuf. & Development.
Descendant

Descendant

Spouse

Spouse

Military Service:

Descendant

Spouse

M6227413
Genealogical Number

Cynthia Lucretia Mowery   Houston, TX
Name (including maiden name if applicable)   Town of Residence

Los Alamos, NM   4/1/1963
Birthplace   Date of Birth   Date of Death   Where Buried

James Philistine   Baltimore, MD   6/26/1960
Name of Spouse   Birthplace   Date of Birth   Date of Death

                           1/11/1986   Potomac, MD
Where Buried   Date of Marriage   Place of Marriage

If married more than once:

Name of Spouse   Birthplace   Date of Birth   Date of Death

Where Buried   Date of Marriage   Place of Marriage

Parents of Spouse (with Mother's maiden name) 1st Marriage

Subsequent Marriage (if applicable)

Family Details

Schools attended, dates and degrees: Community, political work, etc.:

Univ. of Md (12/85). Florida Institute of
Tech. 12/91 (not yet graduated)
Descendant   Descendant

Westwood College of Aviation 4/04
Spouse   Spouse

Basic Employment History: Clubs, Church Affiliations, etc.:
The Boeing Company 5/89-now –
International Space Station   Episcopal Church
Descendant   Descendant

Various Aerospace Companies   Episcopal Church
Spouse   Spouse

Military Service:

                                                    US Navy 1979-83
Descendant   Spouse

M62274131
Genealogical Number

Kristen Rose Philistine   Houston, TX
Name (including maiden name if applicable)   Town of Residence

Huntsville, AL   6/6/1991
Birthplace   Date of Birth   Date of Death   Where Buried

Name of Spouse   Birthplace   Date of Birth   Date of Death

Where Buried   Date of Marriage   Place of Marriage

If married more than once:

Name of Spouse   Birthplace   Date of Birth   Date of Death

Where Buried   Date of Marriage   Place of Marriage

Parents of Spouse (with Mother's maiden name) 1st Marriage

Subsequent Marriage (if applicable)

Family Details

Schools attended, dates and degrees: Community, political work, etc.:

Descendant   Descendant

Spouse   Spouse

Basic Employment History: Clubs, Church Affiliations, etc.:

Descendant   Descendant

Spouse   Spouse

Military Service:

Descendant   Spouse

M62274132
Genealogical Number

Kyle James Philistine   Huston, TX
Name (including maiden name if applicable)   Town of Residence

Huntsville, AL   4/12/1994
Birthplace   Date of Birth   Date of Death   Where Buried

Name of Spouse   Birthplace   Date of Birth   Date of Death

Where Buried   Date of Marriage   Place of Marriage

If married more than once:

Name of Spouse   Birthplace   Date of Birth   Date of Death

Where Buried   Date of Marriage   Place of Marriage

Parents of Spouse (with Mother's maiden name) 1st Marriage

Subsequent Marriage (if applicable)

Family Details

Schools attended, dates and degrees: Community, political work, etc.:

Descendant   Descendant

Spouse   Spouse

Basic Employment History: Clubs, Church Affiliations, etc.:

Descendant   Descendant

Spouse   Spouse

Military Service:

Descendant   Spouse

M622742
Genealogical Number

John Roy Mullin, Jr.
Name (including maiden name if applicable)

Lawrenceville, GA
Town of Residence

Bluefield, W.VA
Birthplace

3/10/1941
Date of Birth

Date of Death

Where Buried

Trudy Joyce Tomlinson
Name of Spouse

Tuscumbia, AL
Birthplace

6/4/1949
Date of Birth

Date of Death

Where Buried

6/17/1990
Date of Marriage

Jamaica
Place of Marriage

If married more than once:

Alice Darlene Van Kirk (Div.)
Name of Spouse

Monongahela, PA
Birthplace

10/31/1942
Date of Birth

Date of Death

Where Buried

Date of Marriage

Place of Marriage

Parents of Spouse (with Mother's maiden name) 1st Marriage

Subsequent Marriage (if applicable)

Family Details

Schools attended, dates and degrees:

West Virginia University - Doctor of
Dental Surgery
Descendant

Spouse

Basic Employment History:

Dental practice (private) 1970-1998
Descendant

Spouse

Military Service:
Captain - U.S. Army 1968-1970
1 year Vietnam
Descendant

Community, political work, etc.:

Descendant

Spouse

Clubs, Church Affiliations, etc.:

Descendant

Spouse

Spouse

M6227421
Genealogical Number

Melanie Michael Mullin   Roswell, GA
Name (including maiden name if applicable)   Town of Residence

Augusta, GA   8/4/1968
Birthplace   Date of Birth   Date of Death   Where Buried

Michael Rourke Levy   Tampa, FL   9/13/1959
Name of Spouse   Birthplace   Date of Birth   Date of Death

                            12/30/1994   Atlanta, GA
Where Buried   Date of Marriage   Place of Marriage

If married more than once:

Name of Spouse   Birthplace   Date of Birth   Date of Death

Where Buried   Date of Marriage   Place of Marriage

Parents of Spouse (with Mother's maiden name) 1st Marriage

Subsequent Marriage (if applicable)

Family Details

Schools attended, dates and degrees: Community, political work, etc.:

University of Alabama 86-90 Management Degree
Descendant   Descendant

Spouse   Spouse

Basic Employment History: Clubs, Church Affiliations, etc.:

Post Properties Inc. (Manager) 11 years   Northpoint Community Church
Descendant   Descendant

Spouse   Spouse

Military Service:

Descendant   Spouse

M62274211
Genealogical Number

Christopher Michael Levy
Name (including maiden name if applicable)

Roswell, GA
Town of Residence

Atlanta Northside Hospital
Birthplace

6/18/1995
Date of Birth

Date of Death

Where Buried

Name of Spouse

Birthplace

Date of Birth

Date of Death

Where Buried

Date of Marriage

Place of Marriage

If married more than once:

Name of Spouse

Birthplace

Date of Birth

Date of Death

Where Buried

Date of Marriage

Place of Marriage

Parents of Spouse (with Mother's maiden name) 1st Marriage

Subsequent Marriage (if applicable)

Family Details

Schools attended, dates and degrees:

Community, political work, etc.:

Descendant

Descendant

Spouse

Spouse

Basic Employment History:

Clubs, Church Affiliations, etc.:

Descendant

Descendant

Spouse

Spouse

Military Service:

Descendant

Spouse

M62274212
Genealogical Number

Zachary Rourke Levy
Name (including maiden name if applicable)

Roswell, GA
Town of Residence

Atlanta Northside Hospital
Birthplace

1/2/1997
Date of Birth

Date of Death

Where Buried

Name of Spouse

Birthplace

Date of Birth

Date of Death

Where Buried

Date of Marriage

Place of Marriage

If married more than once:

Name of Spouse

Birthplace

Date of Birth

Date of Death

Where Buried

Date of Marriage

Place of Marriage

Parents of Spouse (with Mother's maiden name) 1st Marriage

Subsequent Marriage (if applicable)

Family Details

Schools attended, dates and degrees:

Community, political work, etc.:

Descendant

Descendant

Spouse

Spouse

Basic Employment History:

Clubs, Church Affiliations, etc.:

Descendant

Descendant

Spouse

Spouse

Military Service:

Descendant

Spouse

M6227422
Genealogical Number

Carrie Beth Mullin
Name (including maiden name if applicable)

Roswell, GA
Town of Residence

Atlanta, GA
Birthplace

2/21/1974
Date of Birth

Date of Death

Where Buried

Charles Felder McMichael III
Name of Spouse

Slidell, LA
Birthplace

8/17/1972
Date of Birth

Date of Death

Where Buried

4/1/2000
Date of Marriage

Atlanta, GA
Place of Marriage

If married more than once:

Name of Spouse

Birthplace

Date of Birth

Date of Death

Where Buried

Date of Marriage

Place of Marriage

Catherine Zimmerman & Charles Felder McMichael, Jr.
Parents of Spouse (with Mother's maiden name) 1st Marriage

Subsequent Marriage (if applicable)

Family Details

Schools attended, dates and degrees:
Univ. Of Georgia-Environmental Health
Univ. of Alabama at Birmingham - Masters
in Industrial Hygiene
Descendant
Louisiana State Univ. - Baton Rouge
Univ. of Alabama -Birmingham-Masters in
Industrial Hygiene
Spouse

Community, political work, etc.:

Descendant

Spouse

Basic Employment History:
Amoco, BP Amoco, Solvay Advanced
Polymers, Health & Safety work
Descendant

Clubs, Church Affiliations, etc.:

Descendant

Georgia Pacific - Health & Safety work
Spouse

Spouse

Military Service:

Descendant

Spouse

M62274221
Genealogical Number

Caroline Rae McMichael   Roswell, GA
Name (including maiden name if applicable)   Town of Residence

                          11/30/2004
Birthplace   Date of Birth   Date of Death   Where Buried

Name of Spouse   Birthplace   Date of Birth   Date of Death

Where Buried   Date of Marriage   Place of Marriage

If married more than once:

Name of Spouse   Birthplace   Date of Birth   Date of Death

Where Buried   Date of Marriage   Place of Marriage

Parents of Spouse (with Mother's maiden name) 1st Marriage

Subsequent Marriage (if applicable)

Family Details

Schools attended, dates and degrees: Community, political work, etc.:

Descendant   Descendant

Spouse   Spouse

Basic Employment History: Clubs, Church Affiliations, etc.:

Descendant   Descendant

Spouse   Spouse

Military Service:

Descendant   Spouse

M62275
Genealogical Number

Oscar Barnes Moore,
Name (including maiden name if applicable)   Town of Residence

Abbs Valley, VA	11/28/1911	3/28/1945	Monte Vista C
Birthplace	Date of Birth	Date of Death	Where Buried

Not married			
Name of Spouse	Birthplace	Date of Birth	Date of Death

Where Buried	Date of Marriage	Place of Marriage

If married more than once:

Name of Spouse	Birthplace	Date of Birth	Date of Death

Where Buried	Date of Marriage	Place of Marriage

Parents of Spouse (with Mother's maiden name) 1st Marriage

Subsequent Marriage (if applicable)

Family Details

Schools attended, dates and degrees: Community, political work, etc.:

Descendant   Descendant

Spouse   Spouse

Basic Employment History: Clubs, Church Affiliations, etc.:

Descendant   Descendant

Spouse   Spouse

Military Service:

Died World War II
Descendant   Spouse

367

14.

The William Taylor Moore Line
Pictures

William Taylor Moore
(M622)   B. 3/7/1802   D. 12/30/1891

Virginia & Margaret Copenhaver
(M622511)   B. 5/3/1908   D. 1/26/1993
(M622513)   B. 12/5/1913   D. 4/15/1997

Dr. Rufus P. Copenhaver
(M622514)   B. 9/14/1917   D. 12/5/1956

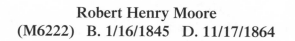

Robert Henry Moore
(M6222)   B. 1/16/1845   D. 11/17/1864

William Luther Moore (M6225)
India Moore Copenhaver (M62251)
Robert Henry Moore (M62252)

B. 3/31/1851 D. 11/14/1926
B. 9/10/1880 D. 12/5/1968
B. 6/10/1887 D. 7/18/1948

William Luther Moore
(M6225)   B. 3/31/1851   D. 11/14/1926

Mary Moore and Others
(M62253)   B. 12/24/1893   D. 2/14/1986

Barnes Moore and Others
(M62254)   B. 1/28/1899   D. 7/7/1975

Oscar Bascom Moore (M6227)   B. 1/17/1855 D. 8/25/1944

Barbara Jane Moore Moss (M6228)   B. 9/10/1857 D. 1/15/1940

Mary Eliza Moore Davidson (M6229)   B. 5/15/1863 D. _____

15.

THE SALLY LAIN MOORE LINE

The Sally Lain Moore Line

Sally Lain was the fourth child of James, the "Captive." She married James Whitley and I am indebted to Cora Whitley Bertram (M6233271), great-granddaughter of Sally Lain, for the update of information on the Rufus C. Whitley descendants (the third child of Sally Lain).

Mrs. Bertram has in her possession a photograph (tin-type) that is purported to be of James "The Captive." This is possible because James died in 1851 and the first daquerreotypes were taken in 1815. It seems unusual, though, that a photographer could make it to southwest Virginia by 1851 considering how remote and sparsely populated that area was then. Could James have made a trip to Rockbridge County and have been photographed there? Mrs. Bertram's account of how her family came to possess the picture is reproduced below:

It has always been in the Whitley's home - and being told by my "gran," Nancy E. Meacham Whitley (Mrs. C.T.), who he was - it is what I call a "tin type" and is faded and pitted. After I got interested in genealogy, I took it and had it copied - was rather expensive because they would not touch the picture itself - afraid that they might use the wrong thing on it. They photographed it then took that neg. and picture (copy) and an artist touched it up slightly - really just made it a little darker where he was sure of the lines and cleaned the spots and face; then they made a photo of that. I still have the original in my possession; in fact it is framed and hanging on my upstairs hallway wall. I have made a family tree there with old photo's. I have just always known who it was.

My great grandfather Rufus Whitley had it in his possession and then my grandmother Nancy had it in her side of the house on the wall and when she died - my dad had it. I do not know if Rufus C. brought it to Texas in 1859 or if he got it from his mother at a later date. He could have even gotten it on any of his trips back to Tazwell. He lived to 91 and was a very active man and made several trips back to Tazewell. Also my grandfather (Rufus C.S. , oldest son) Charles T. went back to Tazewell several times and was sent to school for a couple of years in Missouri. Also Charles T. was a cowboy and drove cattle on trail drives up to Missouri after he was well grown (until he married) whilst he was building his own herd of cattle.

Biographical information on other Sally Lain descendants is in the bio sheets following.

16.

THE SALLY LAIN MOORE LINE
GENEALOGICAL CHARTS

M623   *Sally Lain Moore – James Whitley*
B. 1/22/1804   M. 1822   B. 6/1/1797
D. 4/16/1890   D. 8/23/1845

M6231   Nancy Lane Whitley - Noah Bruce
B. _____   M. _____   B. _____
D. _____   D. _____

M62311 - Garland S. Bruce - _____
B. 9/4/1842   M. _____   B. _____
D. 10/10/1921   D. _____

M623111 - Frank L. Bruce
B. 10/26/1867
D. 8/11/1940

M6232   Matilda B. Whitley - William P. Maxwell
B. _____   M. _____   B. _____
D. _____   D. _____

M62321 - James A. Maxwell
B. 1847
D. _____

M62322 - Rufus C. Maxwell
B. 3/1/849
D. 9/11/1853

M62323 - Sarah J. Maxwell
B. 7/7/1851
D. 7/27/1853

*Indicates that a bio is included.

M62324 - Hannibal Maxwell
B. 1857
D. _____

M62325 - Lavina B. Maxwell
B. 1862
D. _____

M62326 - Veda M. Maxwell
B. 1864
D. _____

M62327 - William H. Maxwell
B. 1867
D. _____

M6233 Rufus C. Whitley - Elizabeth H. Gregory
B. _____   M. _____   B. _____
D. _____   D. _____

M62331 - Mary L. Whitley - T. B. McMurray
B. 6/10/1853   M. _____   B. _____
D. 5/3/1883   D. _____

M623311 - Lulora H. McMurray   Courthouse burned: no records
B. _____
D. _____

M623312 - Louis T. McMurray
B. _____
D. _____

M623313 - Rufus J. McMurray
    B. _____
    D. _____

M62332 - Charles Tiffany Whitley - Nancy Emaline Meacham
    B. 2/27/1859   M. 10/9/1887   B. 8/30/1866
    D. 8/19/1911   D. 3/25/1938

    M623321 - Captain Loyd Whitley - May Vance
        B. 11/6/1888   M. 4/17/1911   B. _____
        D. 12/23/1918   D. _____

        M6233211 - Infant Son
            B. 1918
            D. 1918

    M623322 - William Rufus Whitley - Althea Owens
        B. 2/8/1891   M. 5/3/1913   B. _____
        D. 5/16/1964

        M6233221 - Robert Owen Whitley
            B. 2/27/1914
            D. 6/1/1914

        M6233222 - William Rufus Whitley, Jr. - Lois Craddock
            B. 4/4/1918   M. 3/1941   B. _____
            D. _____   D. _____

            M62332221 - William Loyd Whitley - Judy Gean
                B. 5/7/1948   M. 4/1970   B. _____

M623322211 - Amy Whitley
B. 8/13/1976

M623322212 - Mary Whitley
B. 9/27/1978

M6233223 - Loyd George Whitley - Louise Rumley
B. 11/1922   M. 11/18/1948   B. _____

M62332231 - Rufus Joseph Whitley
B. 12/6/1949

M62332232 - Loyd George Whitley, Jr.
B. 6/6/1952

M623323 - Beulah B. Whitley
B. 9/18/1893
D. 5/26/1894

M623324 - Vesta Elizabeth Whitley - John Thomas White
B. 4/7/1895   M. 8/23/1916   B. _____
D. 2/16/1969   D. _____

M6233241 - Frances Nan White - Paul P. Rose
B. 1/2/1919   M. _____   B. _____
D. _____   D. _____

M62332411 - J. T. Rose - Sandra K. Roland
B. 8/20/1943   M. 9/5/1969   B. _____

M623324111 - Melanie Ann Rose
B. 5/11/1972

M623324112 - Leah Nan Rose
B. 7/9/1973

M623324113 - Lynnelle Renee Rose
B. 8/9/1978

M623325 - Charles T. Whitley, Jr.
B. 12/7/1897
D. 1/2/1901

M623326 - Martha Whitley
B. 7/26/1900
D. 5/9/1904

M623327 - James Oliver Whitley - Gladys Katheryn Maxwell
B. 8/29/1903   M. 4/29/1926   B. 5/5/1908
D. 9/25/1979   D. _____

M6233271 - Cora Elizabeth Whitley - Jack Lloyd Bertram
B. 2/23/1927   M. 7/12/1945   B. 9/21/1926

M62332711 - Patricia Jean Bertram
B. 3/29/1948

M62332712 - James Porter Bertram - Janet Rounsville-Smith
B. 10/16/1949   M. 8/15/1987   B. 8/5/1955

M6233272 - James Oliver Whitley, Jr. - Mary Ann North
B. 5/21/1932   M. 8/18/1951   B. _____

M62332721 - Elizabeth Ann Whitley
B. 7/5/1958

M623328 - Infant Girl
B. 8/3/1906
D. 8/3/1906

M62333 - James Rufus Whitley - Mary J. Chesher
B. 8/26/1867   M. _____   B. _____
D. 1953   D. _____

M623331 - Milton Whitley
B. 1890
D. _____

M623332 - Cora Whitley
B. 1891
D. _____

M623333 - George Whitley
B. 1894
D. _____

M623334 - William Whitley
B. 1897
D. _____

M623335 - Paul Whitley
    B. 1904
    D. _____

M623336 - Virginia Whitley - John Cozart
    B. 1907   M. _____   B. _____
    D. 10/29/1988   D. _____

    M6233361 - Larry J. Cozart
        B. _____

    M6233362 - John L. Cozart
        B. _____

M62334 - John L. Whitley
    B. 1/28/1876
    D. 11/11/1877

M6234   Norman S. Whitley - Elizabeth Bowling
    B. _____   M. _____   B. _____
    D. _____   D. _____

    M62341 - James S. Whitley
        B. 1864
        D. _____

    M62342 - Sarah L. Whitley
        B. 1865
        D. _____

    M62343 - Annie Whitley
        B. _____
        D. _____

M6235   Rees B. Whitley - Elizabeth Whitten
B. _____   M. _____   B. _____
D. _____   D. _____

M62351 - James Samuel Whitley - Mary E. Wynn
B. 4/1864   M. 1/2/1901   B. _____
D. 1930   D. _____

M62352 - Kirby G. Whitley - Ida Hines
B. 1866   M. 11/12/1885   B. _____
D. _____   D. _____

M62353 - Sarah Fanny Whitley - Stephen Peery
B. 1869   M. _____   B. _____
D. _____   D. _____

M62354 - William E. Whitley - Amelia E. Fee
B. _____   M. 9/12/1898   B. _____
D. 3/2/1955   D. _____

M62355 - Thomas F. Whitley - Lena Davis
B. 1873   M. 3/19/1896   B. _____
D. _____   D. _____

M62356 - Nancy J. Whitley - Frank Griffith
B. 9/30/1876   M. 1892   B. _____
D. 1/1/1959   D. _____

M62357 - Charles H. Whitley - Mabel Williams
    B. 4/1879   M. 1/9/1902   B. _____
    D. 3/3/1965   D. _____

M62358 - Henry H. Whitley
    B. 5/17/1888
    D. _____

M6236 Peggy (Margaret) Whitley - Mathias Harman Beavers
    B. _____   M. _____   B. _____
    D. _____   D. _____

M62361 - Sarah Lavine Beavers
    B. 4/29/1851
    D. 8/27/1853

M62362 - Eleanor P. Beavers - Charles Henry Peery
    B. 9/21/1853   M. 1/28/1873   B. 1852
    D. 2/15/1923   D. 1935

    M623621 - John David Peery - Treulean Crockett
        B. 1874   M. _____   B. 1876
        D. 1936   D. 1959

        M6236211 - Charles David Peery - **M626123** Margaret Whitley
            B. _____   M. _____   B. _____

        M62362111 - Treulean Ann Peery
            B. _____

        M62362112 - Cosby Harrison Peery
            B. _____

M62362113 - William Whitley Peery
    B. _____

M62362114 - Charles David Peery, Jr.
    B. _____

M62362115 - Jeannette Peery
    B. _____

M62362116 – William Whitley Peery
    B. _____

M62362117 - Nan Peery
    B. _____

M6236212 - Glen Clay Peery - Mary Kiser
    B. 1901   M. _____   B. 10/7/1900
    D. 1963   D. 11/17/2002

M62362121 - Glen Clay Peery, Jr. – Martha Josephine
                                              Thompson
        B. 6/24/1923   M. 11/21/1945   B. 10/24/1923
        D. 6/13/1970

    *M623621211 - Michael Thompson Peery - Linda Jean
                                                Thacker
        B. 9/23/1947   M. 6/21/1973   B. 6/20/1948

        *M6236212111 - Leslie Katherine Peery–Lance Reid
                                                    Allen
          B. 1/19/1976 M. 5/23/1999 B. 12/13/1977

*M62362121111 – Mary Paige Allen
B. 10/13/1999

*M62362121112 – Thomas David Allen
B. 12/24/2001

*M6236212112 - Michael David Peery
B. 4/17/1977

*M6236212113 - Sarah Elizabeth Peery
B. 10/23/1979

*M623621212 - John Clay Peery - (1) Charlene Patricia
Robertson (Div)
B. 7/13/1950   (1) M. _____   B. 1/10/1952
(2) M. 7/2/1983

(2) Alice Jo Buchanan (Div)
B. 9/24/1957

*M6236212121 – (2) Samuel Clay Peery
B. 10/1/1984

*M6236212122 – (2) Andrew David Peery
B. 8/15/1986

*M623621213 - Stephen Preston Peery - (1) Pamela Jane
Mitchum (Div)
B. 11/23/1953   (1) M. 6/24/1977 B. _____
(2)M. 8/6/1988

(2) Rita Inez Casey
B. 7/17/1957

*M6236212131 - (1) Stephen Preston Peery, Jr.
B. 10/26/1979

*M6236212132 - (2) Stuart Samuel Peery
B. 3/28/1989

M623621214 - Mary Bowen Peery - (1) William Joseph Yeatts
Horton (Div)
B. 7/7/1955   M. 9/23/1974   B. 11/15/1954
M. 12/31/1999

(2) Ronald Lee Calley
B. 12/6/1956

M6236212141 - (1) Jennifer Josephine Horton
B. 5/9/1975

M6236212142 - (1) William Henry Clay Horton –
Megan Renee Brown
B. 7/21/1980   M. 7/6/2002   B.12/4/1981

M6236212143 - (1) John Bowen Horton
B. 8/4/1988

M62362122 -   John Kiser Peery
B. 7/2/1929
D. 4/1948

M6236213 - Elizabeth Peery – John R. Boggess
B. _____   M. _____   B. _____
D. _____   D. _____

M62362131 – Bill Johnny Boggess
    B. _____

M623621312 - Betty Boggess
    B. _____

M6236214 - Ruth Christian Peery – Keith Thompson
    B. _____   M. _____   B. _____

M623622 - Joseph Grattan Peery - Mollie Rosenbaum
    B. _____   M. _____   B. _____
    D. 1/18/1908   D. _____

M6236221 - Charles Henry Peery – Eleanor Pheobe Beavers
    B. 6/1/1851   M. _____   B. 9/21/1853
    D. 1/19/1935   D. 2/15/1923

M6236222 - Harold Peery
    B. _____

M6236223 - Margaret Peery
    B. _____

M623623 - Lena D. Peery - (1)George P. Hall
    B. _____   M. _____   B. _____
                       M. _____

                     (2)H. George McCall
                           B. _____

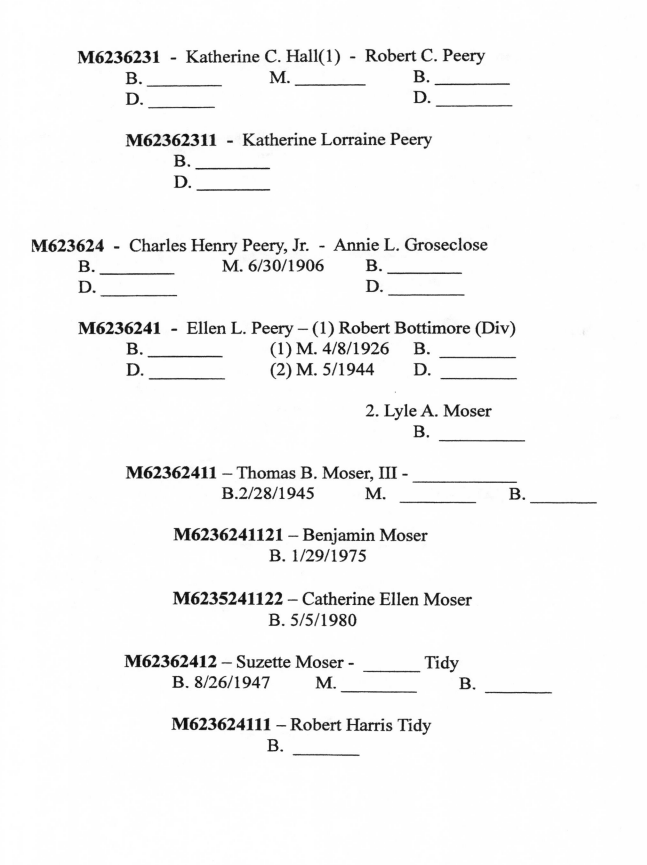

M6236231 - Katherine C. Hall(1) - Robert C. Peery
    B. _____   M. _____   B. _____
    D. _____   D. _____

    M62362311 - Katherine Lorraine Peery
        B. _____
        D. _____

M623624 - Charles Henry Peery, Jr. - Annie L. Groseclose
    B. _____   M. 6/30/1906   B. _____
    D. _____   D. _____

    M6236241 - Ellen L. Peery – (1) Robert Bottimore (Div)
        B. _____   (1) M. 4/8/1926   B. _____
        D. _____   (2) M. 5/1944   D. _____

                                    2. Lyle A. Moser
                                         B. _____

    M62362411 – Thomas B. Moser, III - _____
        B.2/28/1945   M. _____   B. _____

        M6236241121 – Benjamin Moser
            B. 1/29/1975

        M6235241122 – Catherine Ellen Moser
            B. 5/5/1980

    M62362412 – Suzette Moser - _____ Tidy
        B. 8/26/1947   M. _____   B. _____

        M623624111 – Robert Harris Tidy
            B. _____

M6236242 - Lena Louise Peery
    B. _____

M6236243 - Charles Henry Peery, III – Martha Josephine Thompson
    B. 1/4/1922   M. 10/17/1985   B. 10/24/1923
    D. 7/23/1994

M623625 - Maggie C. Peery
    B. _____
    D. _____

M623626 - Kate Louise Peery
    B. _____
    D. _____

M623627 - Letitia Ward Peery - Charles Henry Harman
    B. _____   M. _____   B. _____
    D. _____   D. _____

    M6236271 - Eleanor Amelia Harman – (1) Allen Brown Carter
        B. _____   (1) M. _____   B. _____
        D. _____   (2) M. _____   D. _____

                                      (2) Thomas C. Brewer
                                            B. _____
                                            D. _____

        M62362711 – Amelia Suzanne Carter – (1) Cy H. Lemaire
            B. 1929   (1) M. _____   B. _____
                       (2) M. _____

                                      2 _____ Sloan
                                            B. _____

M62362712 – William Henry Carter - _____
     B. 1931   M. _____   B. _____

M6236272 - Lillian Margaret Harman – Martin L. Harman
     B. 10/21/1912   M. 1931   B. 5/4/1905
     D. 10/1974   D. 8/1944

     *M62335562721 – Martin L. Harman, Jr. – (1) Margaret Hardy
          B. 10/17/1933 (1) M. _____   B. _____
                      (2) M. _____
                                 (2) Jean Klay
                                 B. _____

          M623627211 – Lynn Harman
               B. _____

          M623627212 – Kaye Harman - _____ Stine
               B. _____   M. _____   B. _____

               M6236272121 - Carolyn Ashley Stine
                    B. _____

               M6236272122 – Kathryn Lynn Stine
                    B. _____

M6236273 - William French Harman - _____
     B. _____   M. _____   B. _____
     D. _____   D. _____

     M62362731 – William F. Harman, III
          B. _____

     M62362732 – David S. Harman
          B. _____

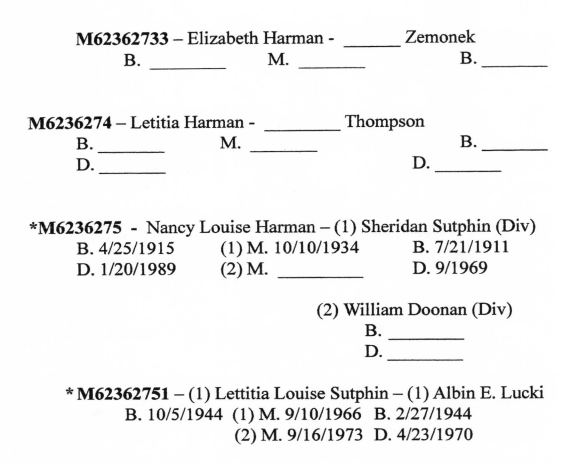

M62362733 – Elizabeth Harman - _____ Zemonek
      B. _____   M. _____   B. _____

M6236274 – Letitia Harman - _____ Thompson
      B. _____   M. _____   B. _____
      D. _____   D. _____

*M6236275 - Nancy Louise Harman – (1) Sheridan Sutphin (Div)
      B. 4/25/1915   (1) M. 10/10/1934   B. 7/21/1911
      D. 1/20/1989   (2) M. _____   D. 9/1969

                            (2) William Doonan (Div)
                                    B. _____
                                    D. _____

    * M62362751 – (1) Lettitia Louise Sutphin – (1) Albin E. Lucki
        B. 10/5/1944 (1) M. 9/10/1966 B. 2/27/1944
                    (2) M. 9/16/1973 D. 4/23/1970

                                 (2) Carolton S. Littell
                                    B. 10/10/1934

      *M623622511 - (2) Albin Earl Lucki Littell
           B. _____

M6236276 - Catherine Peery Harman
      B. _____

M6236277 - Charles Henry Harman, Jr. – Gladys _____
      B. _____   M. _____   B. _____
      D. 9/2001   D. _____

M62363 - William Grattan Beavers - Letitia Ellen Crockett
B. 7/9/1855   M. 10/18/1877   B. _____
D. 9/6/1887   D. _____

M623631 - Eliza Pearl Beavers
B. _____

M62364 - Dexter Estel Beavers - Eliza Caroline Kiser
B. 10/31/1857   M. 9/27/1882   B. _____
D. 8/19/1931   D. _____

M623640 - Eugene Bertram Beavers - Lucy Archer
B. _____   M. _____   B. _____

M6236401 - Elmer Beavers
B. _____

M6236402 - Bertram Bruce Beavers
B. _____

M6236403 - Lucille Beavers
B. _____

M623641 - Walter Summerfield Beavers - Dora Roberts
B. _____   M. _____   B. _____

M6236411 - Roy Kent Beavers
B. _____

M6236412 - Mildred Beavers
B. _____

M6236413 - Lillian Grey Beavers
B. _____

M6236414 - Ernest Beavers
B. _____

M6236415 - Curtis Beavers
B. _____

M6236416 - Mary Virginia Beavers
B. _____

M6236417 - Cecil Beavers
B. _____

M6236418 - David Beavers
B. _____

M623642 - Allie Mae Beavers - James S. Letton
B. _____   M. _____   B. _____

M6236421 - James Wendell Letton
B. _____

M6236422 - Joseph S. Letton
B. _____

M6236423 - Frances Elizabeth Letton
    B. _____

M6236424 - Virginia Trula Letton
    B. _____

M623643 - William Grattan Beavers - Carnie Culbertsons
    B. _____   M. _____   B. _____

M6236431 - Carlisle Beavers
    B. _____

M6236432 - Helen P. Beavers
    B. _____

M6236433 - Glenn Beavers
    B. _____

M6236434 - Virginia Katherine Beavers
    B. _____

M6236435 - Elaine Beavers
    B. _____

M623644 - Annie Gertrude Beavers - Frank Field
    B. _____   M. _____   B. _____

M6236441 - Thelma Gertrude Field
      B. _____

M6236442 - Edith Neel Field
      B. _____

M6236443 - Katherine Field
      B. _____

M6236444 - Earl Field
      B. _____

M623645 - Charles Claude Beavers - Lillian Ratcliff
      B. _____   M. _____   B. _____

M6236451 - Charles Claude Beavers, Jr.
      B. _____

M6236452 - Loraine Beavers
      B. _____

M6236453 - Eugene Beavers
      B. _____

M623646 - Virgie Irene Beavers - Garfield Morley
      B. _____   M. _____   B. _____

M6236461 - Sayers French Morley
     B. _____

M6236462 - Raymond Carr Morley
     B. _____

M623647 - Ethel Glenn Beavers - James Chapin
     B. _____   M. _____   B. _____

M6236471 - Edna Cleo Chapin
     B. _____

M6236472 - William Chapin
     B. _____

M6236473 - Jennings Chapin
     B. _____

M6236474 - Betty Lou Chapin
     B. _____

M6236475 - Emma Miller Chapin
     B. _____

M6236476 - Nancy Caroline Chapin
     B. _____

M6236477 - Joseph Mongul Chapin
     B. _____

M623648 - Otis Howard Beavers - Florence Bohrer
B. _____   M. _____   B. _____

M623648l – Betty Beavers
B. _____

M6236482 - Edwin Howard Beavers
B. _____

M623649 - Eva Gray Beavers - John Bise
B. _____   M. _____   B. _____

M6236491 - Daryle Ester Bise
B. _____

M6236492 - Earl Saxton Bise
B. _____

M6236493 - Ralph Bise
B. _____

M6236494 - Frank Bise
B. _____

M62365 - George Francis Beavers - Elvira Compton
B. 5/4/1860   M. _____   B. _____
D._____   D. _____

M62366 - Sterling Price Beavers
    B. 4/1/1863
    D. 11/18/1927

M62367 - Charles Paris Beavers - Betty Mae Brown
    B. 1/1/1866   M. _____   B. _____
    D. _____   D. _____

        M623671 - Mary Beavers
            B. _____

M62368 - Gallie Leo Beavers - Hetty Roberts
    B. 11/21/1868   M. _____   B. _____
    D. 1/10/1937   D. _____

        M623681 - Wilford Beavers
            B. _____

M62369 - Summerfield Still Beavers
    B. 11/12/1871
    D. 9/26/1876

M62369x - Edward Stanley Beavers
    B. 12/6/1876
    D.11/4/1937

M6237 Barbara J. Whitley - (1) James A. Gregory
    B. _____   M. (1) _____   B. _____
    D. _____   M. (2) _____   D. _____

(2) Robert Crews
B. _____
D. _____

M62371 - (1) Sarah A. Gregory - George H. Turner
    B. 2/1859   M. 8/21/1876   B. _____
    D. _____   D. _____

M62372 - (1) Rosa T. Gregory - N. A. Quice (7 children)
    B. 4/1861   M. 11/25/1875   B. _____
    D. _____   D. _____

M62373 - (2) William Carleton Crews - Josephine Baldwin
    B. 1/7/1866   M. 12/20/1885   B. _____
    D. 2/6/1911   D. _____

    M623731 - Steve A. Crews - Lilly M. Allen
        B. 12/7/1892   M. 1919   B. _____
        D. 2/5/1939   D. _____

        M6237311 - Elizabeth Ruth Crews - Dale L. Pidgeon
            B. 1929   M. 9/2/1950   B. _____

            M62373111 - Juvenne Elizabeth Pidgeon - Tim Van Clezie
                                          (3 children)
                B. 5/22/1949   M. 11/28/1969   B. _____

M62374 - (2) Charlie P. Crews - Elizabeth Corbin
    B. 6/12/1872   M. 12/2/1896   B. _____
    D. 2/1/1947

M62375 - (2) Grover Crews
    B. 1875
    D. _____

M62376 - (2) Jennie Jordan Crews - Charlie Hutsell
    B. 8/23/1876   M. 11/10/1897   B. _____
    D. 11/9/1949   D. _____

    M623761 - Jewell Hutsell - James E. Jarvies
        B. 8/1899   M. _____   B. _____
        D. _____   D. _____

        M6237611 - Jeannette Jarvies
            B. _____

        M6237612 - Harold Jarvies
            B. _____

M6238   Mary P. Whitley
            B. 6/25/1842
            Died as infant.

M6239   William A. Whitley - Olivia C. Williams
            B. 11//17/1844   M. 2/28/1867   B. _____
            D. 2/10/1888   D. _____

14.

The Sally Lain Moore Line
Biographical Charts

M623621211
_____
Genealogical Number

Michael Thompson Peery   Stuart's Draft, VA
_____   _____
Name (including maiden name if applicable)   Town of Residence

Tazewell, VA   7-23-1947
_____   _____   _____   _____
Birthplace   Date of Birth   Date of Death   Where Buried

Linda Jean Thacker
_____   _____   _____   _____
Name of Spouse   Birthplace   Date of Birth   Date of Death

                                          6-21-1973
_____   _____   _____
Where Buried   Date of Marriage   Place of Marriage

If married more than once:

_____   _____   _____   _____
Name of Spouse   Birthplace   Date of Birth   Date of Death

_____   _____   _____
Where Buried   Date of Marriage   Place of Marriage

_____
Parents of Spouse (with Mother's maiden name) 1st Marriage

_____
Subsequent Marriage (if applicable)

Family Details

Schools attended, dates and degrees: Community, political work, etc.:

_____   _____
Descendant   Descendant

_____   _____
Spouse   Spouse

Basic Employment History: Clubs, Church Affiliations, etc.:

_____   _____
Descendant   Descendant

_____   _____
Spouse   Spouse

Military Service:

_____   _____
Descendant   Spouse

M6236212111
_____

Genealogical Number

Leslie Katherine Peery
_____

Name (including maiden name if applicable) Town of Residence

Tazewell County, VA   1-19-1976
_____

Birthplace   Date of Birth   Date of Death   Where Buried

_____

Name of Spouse   Birthplace   Date of Birth   Date of Death

_____

Where Buried   Date of Marriage   Place of Marriage

If married more than once:

_____

Name of Spouse   Birthplace   Date of Birth   Date of Death

_____

Where Buried   Date of Marriage   Place of Marriage

_____

Parents of Spouse (with Mother's maiden name) 1st Marriage

_____

Subsequent Marriage (if applicable)

Family Details

Schools attended, dates and degrees: Community, political work, etc.:

_____

Descendant   Descendant

_____

Spouse   Spouse

Basic Employment History: Clubs, Church Affiliations, etc.:

_____

Descendant   Descendant

_____

Spouse   Spouse

Military Service:

_____

Descendant   Spouse

M62362121111
Genealogical Number

Mary Paige Allen
Name (including maiden name if applicable)   Town of Residence

_____   10/13/1999   _____   _____
Birthplace   Date of Birth   Date of Death   Where Buried

_____   _____   _____   _____
Name of Spouse   Birthplace   Date of Birth   Date of Death

_____   _____   _____
Where Buried   Date of Marriage   Place of Marriage

If married more than once:

_____   _____   _____   _____
Name of Spouse   Birthplace   Date of Birth   Date of Death

_____   _____   _____
Where Buried   Date of Marriage   Place of Marriage

Parents of Spouse (with Mother's maiden name) 1st Marriage

Subsequent Marriage (if applicable)

Family Details

Schools attended, dates and degrees: Community, political work, etc.:

_____   _____
Descendant   Descendant

_____   _____
Spouse   Spouse

Basic Employment History: Clubs, Church Affiliations, etc.:

_____   _____
Descendant   Descendant

_____   _____
Spouse   Spouse

Military Service:

_____   _____
Descendant   Spouse

M62362121112
Genealogical Number

Thomas David Allen
Name (including maiden name if applicable)

Town of Residence

Birthplace

12/24/2001
Date of Birth

Date of Death

Where Buried

Name of Spouse

Birthplace

Date of Birth

Date of Death

Where Buried

Date of Marriage

Place of Marriage

If married more than once:

Name of Spouse

Birthplace

Date of Birth

Date of Death

Where Buried

Date of Marriage

Place of Marriage

Parents of Spouse (with Mother's maiden name) 1st Marriage

Subsequent Marriage (if applicable)

Family Details

Schools attended, dates and degrees:

Community, political work, etc.:

Descendant

Descendant

Spouse

Spouse

Basic Employment History:

Clubs, Church Affiliations, etc.:

Descendant

Descendant

Spouse

Spouse

Military Service:

Descendant

Spouse

M6236212112
_____
Genealogical Number

Michael David Peery
_____   _____
Name (including maiden name if applicable)   Town of Residence

Tazewell County, VA   4-17-1977
_____ _____   _____   _____
Birthplace   Date of Birth   Date of Death   Where Buried

_____ _____   _____   _____
Name of Spouse   Birthplace   Date of Birth   Date of Death

_____ _____   _____
Where Buried   Date of Marriage   Place of Marriage

If married more than once:

_____ _____   _____   _____
Name of Spouse   Birthplace   Date of Birth   Date of Death

_____ _____   _____
Where Buried   Date of Marriage   Place of Marriage

_____
Parents of Spouse (with Mother's maiden name) 1st Marriage

_____
Subsequent Marriage (if applicable)

Family Details

Schools attended, dates and degrees: Community, political work, etc.:

_____   _____
Descendant   Descendant

_____   _____
Spouse   Spouse

Basic Employment History: Clubs, Church Affiliations, etc.:

_____   _____
Descendant   Descendant

_____   _____
Spouse   Spouse

Military Service:

_____   _____
Descendant   Spouse

M6236212113

Genealogical Number

Sarah Elizabeth Peery

Name (including maiden name if applicable)   Town of Residence

10-23-1979

| Birthplace | Date of Birth | Date of Death | Where Buried |

| Name of Spouse | Birthplace | Date of Birth | Date of Death |

| Where Buried | Date of Marriage | Place of Marriage |

If married more than once:

| Name of Spouse | Birthplace | Date of Birth | Date of Death |

| Where Buried | Date of Marriage | Place of Marriage |

Parents of Spouse (with Mother's maiden name) 1st Marriage

Subsequent Marriage (if applicable)

Family Details

Schools attended, dates and degrees: Community, political work, etc.:

Descendant   Descendant

Spouse   Spouse

Basic Employment History: Clubs, Church Affiliations, etc.:

Descendant   Descendant

Spouse   Spouse

Military Service:

Descendant   Spouse

M623621212
_____
Genealogical Number

John Clay Peery   Andersonville, TN
_____   _____
Name (including maiden name if applicable)   Town of Residence

Tazewell, VA   7-13-1950
_____   _____   _____   _____
Birthplace   Date of Birth   Date of Death   Where Buried

Alice Jo Buchanan   Divorced
_____   _____   _____   _____
Name of Spouse   Birthplace   Date of Birth   Date of Death

                     7-2-1982
_____   _____   _____
Where Buried   Date of Marriage   Place of Marriage

If married more than once:

Charlene Patricia Robertson   1-9-1952
_____   _____   _____   _____
Name of Spouse   Birthplace   Date of Birth   Date of Death

_____   _____   _____
Where Buried   Date of Marriage   Place of Marriage

_____
Parents of Spouse (with Mother's maiden name) 1st Marriage

_____
Subsequent Marriage (if applicable)

Family Details

Schools attended, dates and degrees: Community, political work, etc.:

_____   _____
Descendant   Descendant

_____   _____
Spouse   Spouse

Basic Employment History: Clubs, Church Affiliations, etc.:

_____   _____
Descendant   Descendant

_____   _____
Spouse   Spouse

Military Service:

_____   _____
Descendant   Spouse

M6236212121
_____
Genealogical Number

Samuel Clay Buchanan Peery
_____
Name (including maiden name if applicable)

_____
Town of Residence

10-1-1984
_____
Birthplace   Date of Birth   Date of Death   Where Buried

Name of Spouse   Birthplace   Date of Birth   Date of Death

Where Buried   Date of Marriage   Place of Marriage

If married more than once:

Name of Spouse   Birthplace   Date of Birth   Date of Death

Where Buried   Date of Marriage   Place of Marriage

Parents of Spouse (with Mother's maiden name) 1st Marriage

Subsequent Marriage (if applicable)

Family Details

Schools attended, dates and degrees: Community, political work, etc.:

Descendant   Descendant

Spouse   Spouse

Basic Employment History: Clubs, Church Affiliations, etc.:

Descendant   Descendant

Spouse   Spouse

Military Service:

Descendant   Spouse

M6236212122
_____
Genealogical Number

Andrew David Peery
_____   _____
Name (including maiden **name** if applicable)   Town of Residence

           8-15-1986

Birthplace	Date of Birth	Date of Death	Where Buried

Name of Spouse	Birthplace	Date of Birth	Date of Death

Where Buried	Date of Marriage	Place of Marriage

If married more than once:

Name of Spouse	Birthplace	Date of Birth	Date of Death

Where Buried	Date of Marriage	Place of Marriage

_____
Parents of Spouse (with Mother's maiden name) 1st Marriage

_____
Subsequent Marriage (if applicable)

Family Details

Schools attended, dates and degrees: Community, political work, etc.:

Descendant	Descendant

Spouse	Spouse

Basic Employment History: Clubs, Church Affiliations, etc.:

Descendant	Descendant

Spouse	Spouse

Military Service:

Descendant	Spouse

M623621213
_____
Genealogical Number

Stephen Preston Peery   Tazewell, VA
_____   _____
Name (including maiden name if applicable)   Town of Residence

Tazewell, VA   11-23-1953
_____ _____ _____ _____
Birthplace   Date of Birth   Date of Death   Where Buried

Rita Inez Casey   7-17-1957
_____ _____ _____ _____
Name of Spouse   Birthplace   Date of Birth   Date of Death

                    8-6-1988
_____ _____ _____
Where Buried   Date of Marriage   Place of Marriage

If married more than once:

Pamela Jane Mitchen (DIV)
_____ _____ _____ _____
Name of Spouse   Birthplace   Date of Birth   Date of Death

                    6-24-1987
_____ _____ _____
Where Buried   Date of Marriage   Place of Marriage

_____
Parents of Spouse (with Mother's maiden name) 1st Marriage

_____
Subsequent Marriage (if applicable)

Family Details

Schools attended, dates and degrees: Community, political work, etc.:

_____   _____
Descendant   Descendant

_____   _____
Spouse   Spouse

Basic Employment History: Clubs, Church Affiliations, etc.:

_____   _____
Descendant   Descendant

_____   _____
Spouse   Spouse

Military Service:

_____   _____
Descendant   Spouse

M6236212131
_____
Genealogical Number

Stephen Preston Peery, Jr.
_____   _____
Name (including maiden name if applicable)   Town of Residence

                    10-26-1979
_____   _____   _____   _____
Birthplace   Date of Birth   Date of Death   Where Buried

_____   _____   _____   _____
Name of Spouse   Birthplace   Date of Birth   Date of Death

_____   _____   _____
Where Buried   Date of Marriage   Place of Marriage

If married more than once:

_____   _____   _____   _____
Name of Spouse   Birthplace   Date of Birth   Date of Death

_____   _____   _____
Where Buried   Date of Marriage   Place of Marriage

_____
Parents of Spouse (with Mother's maiden name) 1st Marriage

_____
Subsequent Marriage (if applicable)

Family Details

Schools attended, dates and degrees: Community, political work, etc.:

_____   _____
Descendant   Descendant

_____   _____
Spouse   Spouse

Basic Employment History: Clubs, Church Affiliations, etc.:

_____   _____
Descendant   Descendant

_____   _____
Spouse   Spouse

Military Service:

_____   _____
Descendant   Spouse

M6236212132
_____
Genealogical Number

Stuart Samuel Peery
_____
Name (including maiden name if applicable)

Town of Residence

3-20-1990
_____
Birthplace   Date of Birth   Date of Death   Where Buried

Name of Spouse   Birthplace   Date of Birth   Date of Death

Where Buried   Date of Marriage   Place of Marriage

If married more than once:

Name of Spouse   Birthplace   Date of Birth   Date of Death

Where Buried   Date of Marriage   Place of Marriage

Parents of Spouse (with Mother's maiden name) 1st Marriage

Subsequent Marriage (if applicable)

Family Details

Schools attended, dates and degrees: Community, political work, etc.:

Descendant   Descendant

Spouse   Spouse

Basic Employment History: Clubs, Church Affiliations, etc.:

Descendant   Descendant

Spouse   Spouse

Military Service:

Descendant   Spouse

M62362721

Genealogical Number

Martin L. Harman, Jr.		Winter Haven, FLA	
Name (including maiden name if applicable)		Town of Residence	

Richlands, VA	10-17-1933				
Birthplace	Date of Birth	Date of Death	Where Buried

Jean Klay	Tampa, FLA	4-21-1928	
Name of Spouse	Birthplace	Date of Birth	Date of Death

	6-19-1979	Lake Wales, FLA	
Where Buried	Date of Marriage	Place of Marriage	

If married more than once:

Margaret Hardy	Bluefield, W.VA.	10-14-1936	
Name of Spouse	Birthplace	Date of Birth	Date of Death

Where Buried	Date of Marriage	Place of Marriage	

Parents of Spouse (with Mother's maiden name) 1st Marriage

Joe & Marian Klay

Subsequent Marriage (if applicable)

Family Details

Schools attended, dates and degrees:
Radford College, M.C., V.P.I.; Greenbrier
Military School; Concord College, BA

Descendant

Florida State University

Spouse

Basic Employment History:

College Professor & Coach; Travel Agent

Descendant

Spouse

Military Service:

Descendant

Community, political work, etc.:

YMCA

Descendant

Spouse

Clubs, Church Affiliations, etc.:

Presbyterian Church

Descendant

Spouse

Spouse

M6236275
_____
Genealogical Number

Nancy Louise Harman   Deceased
_____   _____
Name (including maiden name if applicable)   Town of Residence

Tazewell, VA   4-25-1915   1-20-1989   Tucson, AZ
_____   _____   _____   _____
Birthplace   Date of Birth   Date of Death   Where Buried

Sheridan Sutphin   Princeton, West VA   7-21-1911   9-1969
_____   _____   _____   _____
Name of Spouse   Birthplace   Date of Birth   Date of Death

Beckley, West VA   10-10-1934   Tazewell, VA
_____   _____   _____
Where Buried   Date of Marriage   Place of Marriage

If married more than once:

William Doonan   Boston, MA   Deceased ?
_____   _____   _____   _____
Name of Spouse   Birthplace   Date of Birth   Date of Death

                                          Tucson, AZ
_____   _____   _____
Where Buried   Date of Marriage   Place of Marriage

Charles Henry Harman & Letitia Ward Peery Harman
_____
Parents of Spouse (with Mother's maiden name) 1st Marriage

_____
Subsequent Marriage (if applicable)

Family Details

Schools attended, dates and degrees: Community, political work, etc.:
 Arlington Hall & Salem Academy
_____   _____
Descendant   Descendant

_____   _____
Spouse   Spouse

Basic Employment History: Clubs, Church Affiliations, etc.:

_____   _____
Descendant   Descendant

_____   _____
Spouse   Spouse

Military Service:

_____   _____
Descendant   Spouse

M62362751
Genealogical Number

Letticia Louise Sutphin   Tucson, AZ
Name (including maiden name if applicable)   Town of Residence

Beckley, W.VA   10/5/1944
Birthplace   Date of Birth   Date of Death   Where Buried

Carlton S. Littell   Buffalo, NY   10/10/1934
Name of Spouse   Birthplace   Date of Birth   Date of Death

                 9/16/1973   Tucson, AZ
Where Buried   Date of Marriage   Place of Marriage

If married more than once:

Albin E. Lucki   Toledo, OH   2/27/1944   4/23/1970
Name of Spouse   Birthplace   Date of Birth   Date of Death

Lost in Southeast Asia   9/10/1966   Tucson, AZ
Where Buried   Date of Marriage   Place of Marriage

Emili Lucki & Pauline Hnatiuk
Parents of Spouse (with Mother's maiden name) 1st Marriage

Hardin H. Littell & Jane Goodyear
Subsequent Marriage (if applicable)

Family Details

Schools attended, dates and degrees: Community, political work, etc.:

University of Arizona, 1966, B.S.
Descendant   Descendant

Spouse   Spouse

Basic Employment History: Clubs, Church Affiliations, etc.:

Descendant   Descendant

Spouse   Spouse

Military Service:

M623627511
Genealogical Number

Albin Earl Lucki Littell
Name (including maiden name if applicable)

Town of Residence

Birthplace	Date of Birth	Date of Death	Where Buried

Kristen Miller
Name of Spouse

Birthplace	Date of Birth	Date of Death

Where Buried	Date of Marriage	Place of Marriage

If married more than once:

Name of Spouse	Birthplace	Date of Birth	Date of Death

Where Buried	Date of Marriage	Place of Marriage

Parents of Spouse (with Mother's maiden name) 1st Marriage

Subsequent Marriage (if applicable)

Family Details

Schools attended, dates and degrees:

Community, political work, etc.:

Descendant

Descendant

Spouse

Spouse

Basic Employment History:

Clubs, Church Affiliations, etc.:

Harris Trust Co. Tucson, AZ
Descendant

Descendant

Spouse

Spouse

Military Service:

Descendant

Spouse

17.

The Joseph Addison Moore Line

Joseph Addison Moore was the fifth child of James Moore, the "Captive." Mr John Greene of San Jose, California (M6242232) sent me a copy of "random notes" by Frances St.Clair Wagner Johnson ca 1975, his aunt. John Greene is a descendent of Joseph Addison Moore:

In thinking of the 175th birthdate of Tazewell Co. it came to my mind that there is a Confederate soldier buried in an old cemetery on my place in Abb's Valley. Now there is very little evidence of what was once a cemetery. It is located on a very high knoll that commands a good view of the valley and the highway.

I remember as a child, the cemetery having a broken-down paling fence around it which was nearly all gone at that time. The headstones for the graves were native fieldstone.

Mr. Oscar Moore told me many years ago about a Confederate soldier being buried there. He said he was a very small boy at that time and he remembered seeing the young soldier who had been slung across the back of a horse which conveyed him to this vicinity for burial after he had been killed near Nemours or what is called the Mouth of Abb's Valley.

Mr. Moore said the party who was conveying the soldier here stopped at his house to rest and refresh themselves.

He and some small boys who were playing together lifted the cape that had been thrown over the young solider so that they might have a look at him. He said he appeared to be a very handsome young man with black hair and a flowing moustache. He said he learned his name was George Oatz or Utz and his home was in Ky.

I think Pendleton's History gives his name as Utz.

Many, many years later the nephews/grandsons (and neighbor's boys) of my family loved to go to this spot and camp over night and have an early morning breakfast. One nephew particularly liked to go to "Soldier Hill" for an outing.

He was so impressed with the story of the Confederate soldier that he nicknamed the spot "Soldier Hill" and "Soldier Hill" it has been called ever since. Now those boys who grew up so playful and carefree have served their country and some have fought in wars.

Biographical information on other Joseph Addison descendants is in the bio sheets following.

18.

The Joseph Addison Moore Line
Genealogical Charts

M624 *Joseph Addison Moore*   M642 *Martha Poage Moore*

B. 9/29/1805   M. 8/30/1831   B. 5/1/1811
D. 5/5/1882   D. 8/7/1890

M6241 - Augustus Fulton Moore – Sally Sayers
    B. 1832   M. 2/16/1860   B. _____
    D. 1908   D. 12/17/1912

    M62411 - Mary Louise Moore - Robert Daniel Brown
        B. 1/23/1861   M. 12/29/1880   B. _____
        D. 5/6/1937   D. 3/20/1920

        M624111 - Charles Fudge Brown - Essie Amanda Anderson Smoot
            B. 10/25/1881   M. 2/4/1903   B. 10/14/1881
            D. 5/20/1906   D. _____

        M624112 - Grace Reeves Brown - Robert Hutton Snodgrass
            B. 5/31/1884   M. 6/24/1903   B. _____
            D. _____   D. _____

            M6241121 - Charles Brown Snodgrass - Eloise Legard Craig
                B. 12/12/1906   M. 8/8/1935   B. 8/14/1909
                D. _____   D. _____

            M6241122 - Robert Hutton Snodgrass, Jr.
            B. 9/20/1913
             D. _____

            *M6241123 - Harold William Snodgrass – Helen Marie Szczepanski
                B. 6/15/1918   M. 6/1945   B. 3/27/1924
                D. 12/28/2003   D. 10/28/1997

*Indicates that a bio is included.

*M62411231 – Mary Brown Snodgrass- (1) John Leon Freeman
    B. 12/11/1946   (1) M. _____   B. 3/45
                  (2) M. _____

                (2) Richard Brent Newton
                B. 6/6/1947

*M624112311 – (1) John Benjamin Freeman
    B. 11/12/1971

*M62411312 – Nils Martin Freeman
    B. 4/25/1973

*M62411232 – Sandra Jane Snodgrass
    B. 4/27/1954

M624112x - Mattie Lou Brown
  B. 12/19/1886
  D. 7/19/1888

M624113 - Robert Luther Brown - Mattie M. Clark
  B. 10/22/1888   M. 12/26/1907   B. _____
  D. _____   D._____

M6241131 - Mary Joe Brown - Leslie Gregory
  B. _____   M. _____   B. _____
  D. 8/12/1999   D. 11/16/1995

M6241132 - Ernest Brown - Pearl Thompson
  B. _____   M. _____   B. _____

M62411321 - Joan Brown
  B. 1938

M624114 - Clara Rebecca Brown - Thomas Montgomery Preston
    B. 7/13/1891   M. 2/10/1915   B. 3/23/1887
    D. _____   D. 3/12/1927

M6241141 - Isabella Moore Preston - (1) Lynn D. Sweet
    B. 3/9/19   (1)M. 9/5/1937 B. _____
    D. ____   (2)M. 5/17/1948 D. _____

                     (2)Burnham Phillip Jackson
                     B. 3/27/1921
                     D. 9/23/1989

M62411411 - Linda Rebecca Sweet(1) - Thomas Nemia
    B. 6/8/1939   M. _____   B. _____

M624114111 - Clara Rebecca Nemia - Seward Lawlor
    B. 2/8/1969   M. 1991   B. 1953

M6241141111 - Claire Rebecca Lawlor
    B. 7/13/1994

M62411412 - Burnham P. Jackson, Jr.(2) - (1) Jane Fix
    B. 5/7/1942   (1) M. _____ B. _____
              (2) M. 1985

                     (2)Diana Holbrook
                     B. 4/20/1961

M624114121 - Burnham P. Jackson, III (1)
    B. 1976

M624114122 - Christopher Jackson (2)
    B. 9/1985

M624114123 - Jessica Jackson (2)
      B. 12/7/1990

M6241142 - Thomas Ballard Preston – (1) Judith Ann Jackson
      B. 11/16/1921   (1) M. _____   B. _____
      D. 11/12/1992   (2) M. _____   D. 10/26/1985

                           (2) Martha Clark Iresor
                                 B. _____

    M62411421 – (1) Mary Helen Preston
          B. _____

    M62411422 – (1) Thomas Montgomery Preston
          B. _____

    M62411423 – Jack Preston
          B. _____

    M62411424 - Judith Ann Jackson Preston
          B. _____
          D. Deceased

M6241143 - Irene Brown Preston – Malcolm Marvin Brown, Jr.
      B. 3/1/1927   M. _____   B. _____

    M62411431 – Malcolm Marvin Brown, III – Sharon Rouse
          B. _____   M. _____   B. _____

        M624114311 – Malcolm Marvin Brown, IV
              B. _____

    M62411432 – Clara Rebecca Brown – (1) Glenn Willoughby
          B. _____   (1)M. _____   B. _____
                       (2)M. _____
                       (3)M. _____

                                               (2) William Askew
                                                     B. _____

                                               (3) Patrick Rankin
                                                     B. _____

M624115 - Blanche Louise Brown - Charles Marvin McGraw
      B. 11/12/1892   M. 9/27/1911   B. 10/16/1889
      D. _____   D. _____

     M6241151 - Charles Marvin McGraw - Julie Brown
           B. 8/10/1912   M. 1939   B. _____
           D. _____   D. _____

          M62411511 - Michael McGraw
                B. _____

     M6241152 - Infant
           B. 1918
           D. 1918

     M6241153 - Mary Moore McGraw
           B. 6/14/1920

     M6241154 - Lyle Gillespie McGraw
           B. 2/13/1922
           D. 2/24/1922

     M6241155 - Janet Irene McGraw - John Miles Bender
           B. 6/19/1925   M. 9/18/1941   B. _____

M624116 - Banner B. Brown - Della Mae Willis
B. 9/15/1894　　M. 1/30/1932　　B. _____
D. _____　　　　　　　　　　　　D. _____

　　M6241161 - Banner B. Brown, Jr.
　　　　B. _____

　　M6241162 - Barbara Brenda Brown
　　　　B. _____

M624117 - Vivian Gertrude Brown - Walter Porter Jackson
B. 12/25/1897　　M. 10/8/1917　　B. 5/3/1893
D. _____　　　　　　　　　　　　D. 12/1/1968

　　M6241171 - Mary Porter Jackson - James Eugene Steffey
　　　　B. 9/2/1918　　M. 10/4/1936　　B. 6/14/1913
　　　　D. 6/30/1994　　　　　　　　　　　D. 7/26/1983

　　　　M62411711 - Infant
　　　　　　B. 12/23/1939
　　　　　　D. 12/23/1939

　　　　M62411712 - James Porter Steffey - Kathy Mitchell
　　　　　　B. 10/19/1942　　M. _____　　B. _____
　　　　　　D. 5/28/1994

　　　　*M62411713 - Cassandra Gene Steffey - Gerald David Thomas
　　　　　　B. 10/1/1946　　M. 10/24/1969　　B. 4/26/1943

　　　　*M624117131 - Robert Brown Thomas - Susan Elizabeth
　　　　　　　　　　　　　　　　　　　　　　　　Sherman
　　　　　　B. 2/16/1967　　M. 11/23/1992　　B. 6/26/1968

*M6241171311- Megan Elizabeth Thomas
B. 2/21/1997

*M6241171312 - Morgan Alexandra Thomas
B. 2/21/1997

*M6241171313 - David Joseph Thomas
B. 1/28/2000

*M624117132 - Mary Alexandra Thomas – Timothy Andrew
Holck
B. 3/4/1971   M. 5/17/2003   B. 11/29/1966

*M624117133 - William Gerald Thomas – Amy Joyce
Wooten
B. 10/15/1976   M. 4/20/2002   B. 1/2/1975

*M62411714 - Stephen Early Steffey – (1) Lisa Gail Wood (Div)
B. 6/21/1949   M. (1) 5/17/1979   B. 3/9/1956
M. (2) 11/18/2000

(2) Shannon C.C. Perotti
B. 7/12/1945

*M624117141 - (2) Allison Leigh Steffey
B. 9/2/1981

*M6241172 - Robert Floyd Jackson – Ethel Marie Goad
B. 5/21/1921   M. 6/14/1943   B. _____
D. _____   D. _____

M62411721 – Robert Floyd Jackson, Jr. – Iris Lorrene Bagley
B. 4/30/1944   M. 1/29/1965   B. _____

M624117211 – Matthew Charles Jackson –Tracy Lynn Miller
B. 11/29/1969   M. 5/21/1984   B. _____

M6241172111 – Cole Lewis Jackson
B. 6/10/2000

M6241172112 – Riley Marie Jackson
B. 4/23/2003

M624117212 – Dana Robert Jackson
B. 10/26/1971

M62411722 – Martha Susan Jackson – (1) Mel Lipton (Div)
B. 9/30/1946   (1)M. 6/21/1969   B. _____
                     (2)M. 8/22/1992
                                    (2) Robert E. Mills
                                    B. _____

M624117221 - Timothy Todd Lipton
B. 2/12/1970

M62411723 – Margaret Ellen Jackson – Ralph Jefferson Martin, Jr.
B. 12/29/1948   M. 6/11/1971   B. _____

M624117231 - Robert Sutherland Martin – Lisa Michelle
                                    Groff (Div)
         B. 3/2/1975   M. 6/15/1996   B. _____

M6241172311 – Brittany Sue Martin
B. 12/10/1996

M6241172312 – Kimberly Marie Martin
B. 8/2/1997

*M6241173 - Rush Cecil Jackson – Seawillow Henderson Umberger
     B. 9/11/1922   M. 3/16/1946   B. 12/18/1925

*M62411731 - Patricia Kay Jackson - Mark W. Mangus
     B. 12/30/1953   M.8/13/1977   B. 1/18/1952

*M624117311 - Mark W. Mangus, Jr.
     B. 2/17/1981

*M624117312 - Kimberly Faith Mangus
     B. 3/21/1982

M62411732 – Rush Cecil Jackson, Jr.
     B. 11/7/1962

M6241174 - Vivian Gertrude Brown – Walter Porter Jackson
     B. 12/25/1897   M. 10/8/1917   B. 15/3/1893
     D. 7/29/1966   D. 12/1/1968

*M62411741 – Vivian Brown Jackson – (1) Arthur M.Jones
     B. 7/26/1928   (1)M. 10/16/1948   B. 2/21/1928
                           (2)M. 6/3/1961   D. 6/14/1973
                           (3)M. 5/24/1974

                                              (2) Clarence Junior Schall
                                                   B. 3/13/1935
                                                   D. 3/26/1973

                                              (3) John R. Lukas, M.D.
                                                   B. 1/23/1913
                                                   D. 4/24/1992

*M624117411 - (1) Vivian Lee Jones – (1) Howard Travis
                                                    Bramblett (Div)
B. 6/3/1951 (1)M. 12/15/1972 B. 7/6/1951
              (2)M. 7/25/1981

                              (2) Edward Frank Garrity (Div)
                                  B. 8/8/1953

*M624117411 – (1) Kristopher Travis Bramblett
                        B. 9/8/1974

*M624117412 – (2) Marc Mahlon Bramblett
                        B. 2/6/1977

*M62411742 – (1) Preston Arthur Jones – (1) Charlotte Looney
                                                    Atherton (Div)
B. 10/4/1952   (1)M. _____1972   B. 4/24/1954
                    (2)M. 9/26/1981

                              (2) Cynthia L. Barnhart
                                  B. 3/17/1960

*M624117421 - (1) Preston Arthur Jones, Jr.
                        B. 8/8/1973

*M624117422 – (2) Christina Marie Jones
                        B. 2/25/1983

*M62411743 – (1) Patrick Gheen Jones
        B. 10/16/1954
        D. 3/26/1973

*M62411744 – (2) Barbara Jo Schall – (1) Phillip Lamar Beatty
                B. 1/20/1962   (1)M. 4/18/1986 B. 11/24/1960
                                    (2)M. 9/1/1990   D. 11/27/1989

(2) Michael Greg Jarrard
B. 10/22/1962

*M624117441 – (1) Kyle Lamarr Beatty-Jarrard
B. 5/31/1986

*M624117442 – (1) Brittany Nicole Beatty-Jarrard
B. 1/20/1988

*M624117443 – (2) Katlyn Tiffinay Jarrard
B. 6/26/1992

M624118 - Hayter Crocket Brown - Gladys Ritchie
B. 1/22/1900   M. 11/23/1921   B. _____
D. 12/6/1969   D. 3/7/1987

M6241181 - Frances Brown
B. _____

M6241182 - Heyter Crocket Brown, Jr.
B. _____

M6241183 - Mary Louise Brown - _____ Baker
B. _____   M. _____   B. _____
D. 12/21/1994

M6241184 - Robert Daniel Brown
B. _____

M6241185 - Charles Luther Brown
B. _____

M624119 - Robert Daniel Brown, Jr. - Vivian Virginia Prince
B. 10/21/1907   M. 10/17/1937   B. 10/15/1915
D. _____   D. _____

    M6241191 - Barbara Kent Brown
      B. 12/18/1938

    M6241192 - Robert Adair Brown
      B. 1/24/1940

M62412 - Rebecca Moore - L.C. Neel
B. 4/27/1870   M. 11/ /1894   B. 4/17/1874
D. 6/13/1900   D. 2/9/1940

    M624121 - Clarence Neel
    B. 9/12/1895
    D. _____

    M624122 - Luther Bishop Neel - Byrd Litton
    B. 7/10/1897   M. 1927   B. _____
    D. _____   D. _____

      M6241221 - Luther Bishop Neel, Jr.
      B. 5/1929

    M624123 - Carl Francis Neel - Pauline Pasley
    B. 5/16/1901   M. 1933   B. _____
    D. _____   D. _____

M62413 - Bettie Moore - Benjamin Reed
B. _____   M. _____   B. _____

M62414 - Elvira Moore
       B. _____

M62415 - Buse Harman Moore
       B. _____

M6242 — Martha Amanda Moore — William Bailey
    B. 1834   M. 7/24/1856   B. _____
    D. _____   D. _____

M62420 - Mary J. Bailey
    B. 4/16/1857
    D. _____

M62421 - Jane Annabel Bailey - Charles Alexander Wagner
    B. 3/12/1859   M. 5/30/1877   B. _____
    D. 9/25/1937   D. _____

    M624211 - James Hoge Wagner - Lillian A. Brown
        B. 3/12/1877   M. 6/21/1901   B. _____
        D. 9/13/1951   D. _____

    M624212 - Sue Georgia Wagner - Evans Newberry Williams
        B. 9/1/1880   M. 12/20/1905   B. _____
        D. 7/16/1968

        M6242121 - Roy J. Williams - Mary E. Morgan
            B. 12/19/1906   M. _____   B. _____
            D. _____   D. _____

            M62421211 - Eva Sue Williams - Thomas A. Murray
                B. 4/17/1941   M. 11/24/1962   B. 1/18/1939

M624212111 - Susan Annetta Murray - Mack Bowers
B. 1/10/1964   M. _____   B. _____

M6242121111 - William Thomas Bowers
B. 11/2/1992

M624212112 - Jeffrey Aaron Murray
B. 9/11/1966

M6242122 - Dan Wagner Williams - Hazel I. Burk
B. 2/18/1909   M. 8/11/1944   B. _____
D. 1/28/1973

M62421221 - Virginia Ruth Williams - Don Greenwood
B. 1/17/1948   M. _____   B. _____

M624212211 - Ursula Diane Greenwood
B. 5/6/1972

M624212212 - Eric Joseph Greenwood
B. 1/30/1974

M62421222 - Danny Grattan Williams
B. 1/25/1953
D. 7/30/1966

M62421223 Leslie Kenneth Williams - Jean Knickerbocker
B. 8/4/1954   M. _____   B. _____

M624212231 - Holly Opal Williams
B. 2/19/1980

M624212232 - Brandon Burke Williams
    B. 1/18/1983

M624212233 - Valerie Blanch Williams
    B. 2/18/1985

M624212234 - Emily Marie Williams
    B. 6/9/1988

M6242123 - Anabelle Williams - Joe Michael Williams
    B. 6/9/1911   M. _____   B. 2/11/1898
    D. 8/13/1984   D. 1/12/1963

M62421231 - Bobbie Joe Williams - Rita Clarone Opdahl
    B. 6/15/1934   M. 6/2/1962   B. _____

M624212311 - Michael Joseph Williams
    B. 10/4/1963

M624212312 - Mark Jason Williams
    B. 3/25/1965

M624212313 - Max Justin Williams
    B. 8/31/1969

M6242124 - Georgia H. Williams
    B. 11/22/1914
    D. _____

M6242125 - Garnet Porter Williams - Evelyn Lucille Robertson
    B. 10/5/1916   M. _____   B. 9/23/1913
    D. 3/15/1990   D. _____

M62421251 - Garnet Porter Williams, Jr. - Donna Kegley
    B. 12/3/1947   M. 11/24/1971   B. _____

M6242126 - Mildred M. Williams – James E. Stevenson
    B. 4/4/1923   M. _____   B. _____

M624213 - Edward Mustard Wagner - Gladys Smith
    B. 1/28/1884   M. _____   B. _____
    D. 7/9/1936

M6242131 - Robert Charles Wagner - Nancy Sue Calhoun
    B. 5/22/1920   M. _____   B. _____
    D. 5/12/1944

M6242311 - Charles Edward Wagner (1) Mary R. Fain
    B. 11/7/1942   M. _____   B. _____
                        M. _____

                        (2) Beverly Broncale
                        B. _____

M624213111 - (2) Robert Charles Wagner
    B. _____

M624213112 - (2) Amy Elizabeth Wagner
    B. _____

M624213113 - (2) Jennifer Wagner
    B. _____

M624213114 - (2) Jason Wagner
    B. _____

M62421312 - Jefferson Calhoun Wagner - Edith Harris
    B. 11/11/1944   M. _____   B. _____

      M624213121 - Michael Lamar Wagner
        M. _____

      M624213122 - Steven Andrew Wagner
        M. _____

M6242132 - Kathryn Wagner - Clyde W. Byrge
    B. 12/17/1922   M. _____   B. _____
    D. _____   D. _____

      M62421321 - Robert Earl Byrge – Carol L. Hanks
        B. 6/1/1959   M. _____   B. _____

M6242133 - James Edward Wagner - Bernice Hawkins
    B. 3/22/1924   M. _____   B. _____

M6242134 - Paul Keith Wagner
    B. 10/2/1930
    D. 12/7/1931

M624214 - Amanda Ella Wagner - William Tabor
    B. 2/14/1887   M. _____   B. _____
    D. 3/20/1920   D. _____

    M6242141 - Lillian B. Tabor - George Hodock
      B. _____   M. _____   B. _____

M62421411- Thomas J. Hodock, II - Katherine J. Boone
    B. 4/19/1949   M. _____   B. _____

    M624124111 Thomas J. Hodock, III - Donna R. Dawson
        B. 5/29/1969   M. _____   B. _____

        M6242141111 - Timothy W. Hodock
            B. 1/30/1973

        M6242141112 - Tanya J. Hodock
            B. 12/14/1976

        M6242141113 - Brett A. Hodock
            B. 5/1/1979

        M624214112 - Donald Hodock
            B. _____

    M6242142 - Kenneth Tabor
        B. _____

M624215 - Lillie Mae Wagner - Arch W. Ruble
    B. 1/8/1891   M. 2/9/1916   B. _____
    D. 3/12/1966   D. _____

    M6242151 - Charles Ruble - Eva Pauline Patton
        B. _____   M. _____   B. 8/9/1916

    M62421511 - Sandra Mae Ruble - (1) David Leedy (Div)
        B. 11/21/1947   M. _____   B. _____
                        M. 6/26/1993

(2) James West
B. _____

M624215111 - (1) Melissa Leedy - Keith Akens
B. 10/1/1967   M. _____   B. _____

M6242151111 - Chyna Akens
B. _____

M62421512 - Charles Ervin Ruble - Karen Brown
B. 2/10/1960   M. 2/17/1990   B. _____

M6242152 - A. W. Ruble
B. _____

M624216 - Jeanie Pearl Wagner - David R. Carter
B. 2/27/1895   M. 2/17/1916   B. _____
D. 10/25/1972   D. _____

M6242161 - Beatrice Frazier Carter - Glenn Drexel Hatcher
B. 9/9/1916   M. _____   B. 11/14/1905
D. 5/5/1988   D. _____

M62421611 - Thomas Clark Hatcher - Mary Winifred Strong
B. 8/6/1939   M. 8/13/1965   B. 8/2/1942

M624216111 - Mary Kathryn Hatcher - Kenneth Jones
B. 8/25/1968   M. 1/5/1992   B. _____

M6242161111 - Zachary Kenneth Jones
B. 5/14/1993

M624216112 - Elizabeth Ann Hatcher
B. 5/10/1970

M624216113 - John Thomas Hatcher - Rebecca Click
B. 8/28/1975   M. _____   B. _____

M6242161131 - Jonathan Randall Clark Hatcher
B. 6/20/2000

M62421612 - Jenny Lynn Hatcher - Frank A. Roncella
B. 6/6/1941   M. _____   B. 7/2/1940

M624216121 - Frank Roncella - Tammie Crockett
B. 3/14/1961   M. _____   B. 1/14/1971

M6242161211 - Crystal S. Roncella
B. 3/18/1986

M6242161212 - Tara L. Roncella
B. 9/4/1989

M624216122 - Anthony J. Roncella - Mishell Billings
B. 8/2/1965   M. _____   B. 1/31/1963

M6242161221 - Stephanie N. Roncella
B. 8/18/1989

M62421613 - James Edward Hatcher - J. Jennifer Davis
        B. 4/17/1945   M. 5/9/1966   B. _____

M624216131 - James Edward Hatcher, Jr. - Kathi Renee Young
        B. 12/12/1965   M. 12/18/1993   B. _____

M624216132 - Tara D. Hatcher
        B. 3/12/1969

M624216133 - Kristen Noel Hatcher
        B. 12/18/1970

M6242162 - Daniel R. Carter, Jr. - Alta Goodman
        B. 11/9/1918   M. _____   B. _____
        D. 8/3/1988

M62421621 - Roger Dale Carter (1) Patricia Barker
        B. 6/21/1952   M. _____   B. _____
                            M. _____

                                    (2) Alice Stapleton
                                        B. _____

        M624216211 - (1) Jodi Carter
                B. _____

        M624216212 - (1) Amy M. Carter
                B. _____

        M624216213 - (2) Daniel J. Carter
                B. 5/16/1977

M624216214 - (2) Loann M. Carter
　　　　B. 5/2/1978

M62421622 - Gloria D. Carter - Ricki Cline
　　　　B. 10/16/1957　　M. _____　　　B. _____

　　M624216221 - Eric T. Cline
　　　　B. 2/16/1979

　　M624216222 - Whitney M. Cline
　　　　B. 12/21/1988

M6242163 - James Edward Carter - Helen Wagner Martin
　　　B. 1/31/1921　　M. _____　　B. _____
　　　D. 1992

M6242164 - William Kyle Carter - Olen Collins
　　　B. 2/2/1923　　M. _____　　B. _____
　　　D. 10/19/1987

　　M62421641 - William D. Carter (1) Brenda Kirby
　　　　B. 2/13/1946　　M. _____　　　B. _____
　　　　　　　　　　M. _____

　　　　　　　　　　(2) Bernice Liming
　　　　　　　　　　　B. _____

　　M624216411 - (1) William E. Carter
　　　　B. 3/31/1968

M624216412 - (1) Michael D. Carter
      B. 12/23/1969

M62421642 - Michael T. Carter - Eleanor Samuel
      B. 3/38/1947   M. _____   B. _____

M62421643 - Mary E. Carter - Brian P. Balderson
      B. 6/26/1954   M. _____   B. _____

    M624216431 - Kathryn L. Balderson
          B. 9/6/1984

M62421644 - Jenny L. Carter - Marks S. Pourier
      B. 8/27/1957   M. _____   B. _____

    M624216441 - Jenny Pourier
          B. _____

M6242165 - Ben Reese Carter - G. Laverne Chaffin (Div)
    B. 1/4/1927   M. _____   B. _____
    D. 11/6/1978

    M62421651 - Ben Reese Carter, Jr. - Iris Newman
          B. 11/19/1949   M. _____   B. _____

    M624216511 - Jennifer E. Carter
          B. 5/30/1973

    M624216512 - Michael R. Carter
          B. 1/25/1977

M62421652 - Debra S. Carter - L. Linn Day
    B. 3/18/1951   M. _____   B. _____

    M624216521 - Ashley L. Day
        B. 9/30/1981

    M624216522 - Devin C. Day
        B. 1/27/1986

M6242166 - Mary Ann Carter
    B. 1/4/1927
    D. 1927

M6242167 - Harry Lee Carter - Ellie Baker
    B. 11/15/1928   M. 2/2/1984   B. _____

M624217 - Rosa Mariah Wagner - William Guy French
    B. 1/10/1896   M. _____   B. 10/8/1894
    D. 3/7/1974   D. _____

M6242171 - William H. French - Helen Worley
    B. 6/26/1922   M. _____   B. _____
    D. 7/15/1974

M62421711 - Richard H. French - (1) Regina Ealy
    B. 5/19/1945   M. _____   B. _____
                   M. _____

                      (2) Susan Annette Bales
                      B. 12/24/1953

M624217111 - (1) Richard H. French, Jr.
B. 2/16/1967

M624217112 - (1) Sherry L. French
B. 10/7/1971

M624217113 - (2) Amanda R. French
B. 8/19/1977

M624217114 - (2) Brenda R. French
B. 3/6/1980

M62421712 - James G. French - Rebecca Danley
B. 7/16/1954   M. _____   B. 5/14/1951

M624217121 - Jerri Lynn French
B. 3/8/1974

M624217122 - Jami Beth French
B. 9/8/1982

M624217123 - Jennifer Leanne French
B. _____

M624218 - Lena Flournoy Wagner - Robert L. Caudill
B. 6/20/1901   M. _____   B. _____
D. 7/25/1985   D. _____

M6242181 - Robert L. Caudill, Jr.
B. 9/13/1924
D. 9/22/1988

M6242182 - Gene B. Caudill - JoAnn Boyd
B. 6/14/1930   M. _____   B. _____

　　M62421821 - Teresa L. Caudill - Jason L. Harry, Jr.
　　B. 1/10/1953   M. _____   B. _____

　　　　M624218211 - Steven K. Harry
　　　　B. 12/21/1971

　　　　M624218212 - Lynn M. Harry
　　　　B. 8/5/1976

　　　　M624218213 - Lisa D. Harry
　　　　B. 3/18/1978

　　*****M62421822** - Angela J. Caudill - Ronald E. McCall
　　B. 12/16/1954   M. 5/7/1977   B. 12/19/1949

　　M62421823 - Mark S. Caudill
　　B. 2/4/1959
　　D. 6/21/1977

　　M62421824 - Craig E. Caudill – Sarah Jane Bean
　　B. _____   M. 5/19/2001   B. _____

M6242183 - David Franklin Caudill
B. 2/11/1937

M6242184 - M. Ann Caudill - James W. Rebuck
    B. 8/22/1939   M. _____   B. _____

    M62421841 - Allen Wayne Rebuck - Helen F. Dillard
        B. 3/27/1959   M. _____   B. _____

    M62421842 - John Wallace Rebuck - Vivian L. Widetrup
        B. 3/2/1964   M. _____   B. _____

M62422 - Martha Alice Bailey - Elias Green Wagner
    B. 11/11/1867   M. _____   B. 7/16/1859
    D. 12/19/1895   D. 3/24/1938

    M624221 - William David Wagner – Margaret Eugenia Hetherington
        B. 5/2/1882   M. _____   B. 1882
        D. 4/10/1961   D. 1942

        M6242211 - William Garnet Wagner
            B. 9/14/1906
            D. 5/13/1973

        M6242212 - Julia Alice Wagner - Modock McKenzie
            B. 7/8/1908   M. _____   B. 7/21/1902
            D. 12/1975   D. _____

            M62422121 - Margaret Eugenia McKenzie - Jackson M. McClain
                B. 10/23/1934   M. _____   B. 9/21/1934

                M624221211 - Kevin Thomas McClain - Donna King
                    B. 10/1/1962   M. _____   B. _____

M6242212111 - Cara Megan McClain
B. 10/2/1991

M624221212 - Laura Lynn McClain-William Lewis Schmithorst, Jr.
B. 8/1/1965   M. _____   B. _____

M62422122 - Alice Lynn McKenzie
B. 6/30/1938

M6242213 - Joseph Green Wagner - Irene Armstrong
B. 10/10/1912   M. _____   B. 6/23/1926
D. _____   D. 8/8/1977

M62422131 - Linda Sue Wagner - James Chambers
B. 8/26/1948   M. _____   B. _____

M624221311 - Kimberly Chambers
B. 6/29/1973

M624221312 - Tracy Chambers
B. 12/22/1974

M624221313 - Amanda Chambers
B. 6/20/1978

M62422132 - Joseph Dell Wagner
B. 12/18/1949

M62422133 - Betty Ann Wagner
B. 6/5/1952

M6242214 - Helen Wagner - (1) Ed Martin
    B. 1915   M. _____   B. _____
    D. _____   M. _____   D. _____

                (2) James Edward Carter
                B. _____

M62422141 - (1) James David Martin
    B. _____

M6242215 - James Paul Wagner - Gladys Patterson Bailey
    B. 8/7/1916   M. 5/2/1944   B. 3/3/1928
    D. 1/19/1996

M62422151 - James Paul Wagner, Jr. - Linda Neely
    B. 4/18/1945   M. _____   B. 1/6/1947

M624221511 - Patricia Sue Wagner
    B. 10/15/1974

M6242216 - Eleanor Wagner - Alan J. Duncan
    B. 3/17/1920   M. _____   B. _____

M62422161 - Barry Allyn Duncan
    B. _____

M62422162 - Stephen Kent Duncan
    B. _____

M6242217 - Ruth Wagner
    B. _____
    D. 1928

M624222 - Samuel Oscar Wagner - Margaret Ellen Harrison
    B. 4/3/1884   M. _____   B. 11/19/1885
    D. 7/15/1931   D. 8/12/1972

        M6242221 - Mildred Harrison Wagner - Sank Smith
              B. 11/29/1906   M. _____   B. _____
              D. 9/1/1966   D. _____

        M6242222 - Frances St.Clair Wagner - Frank James Johnson
              B. 1908   M. _____   B. _____
              D. 1992   D. _____

        M6242223 - Jean Merle Wagner - Alpha Everette Greene
              B. 1910   M. _____   B. 2/26/1912
              D. 6/3/1991   D. _____

              M62422231 - Jane Ellen Greene - James Arthur
                    B. 10/18/1934   M. _____   B. _____

                  M624222311 - James Frederick Arthur - Debbie Abell
                        B. _____   M. _____   B. _____

                      M6242223111 - James Arthur
                          B. _____

M6242223112 - Justin Arthur
    B. _____

M6242223113 - Joel Arthur
    B. _____

M624222312 - Judith Lynn Arthur - Dale Rawlings
    B. _____   M. _____   B. _____

    M6242223121 - Louis Rawlings
        B. _____

    M6242223122 - Loren Rawlings
        B. _____

    M6242223123 - Genevieve Rawlings
        B. _____

    M6242223124 - Chase Rawlings
        B. 1991

M624222313 - John Arthur
    B. _____

M62422232 - John David Greene - Teresa Elizabeth Stichter
    B. 4/15/1939   M. 2/25/1967   B. 9/27/1943

M624222321 - Loraine Dawn Greene – Shanti McCormick
    B. 2/23/1970   M. _____   B. _____

    M6242223211 – Amber Rose McCormick
        B. 12/6/1997

M624222322 - Deborah Ann Greene
B. 11/27/1972

M62422233 - Hoge Milton Greene - Gustie Lancaster
B. 3/3/1942   M. _____   B. _____

M624222331 - Christopher Greene
B. 1970

M62422234 - Stephen Greene
B. _____

M6242224 - Bernice Mescal Wagner - Campbell Houston Chrisman, II
B. 8/11/1914   M. _____   B. 3/15/1915
D. 21/1981

M62422241 - Campbell Houston Chrisman, III - Iris Tuck
B. 1/13/1945   M. 9/18/1965   B. 1/13/1943

M624222411 - Craig Michael Chrisman - Amy _____
B. 8/24/1968   M. 9/22/1990   B. _____

M624222412 - Cindy Marie Chrisman
B. 10/8/1975

M624222413 - Mark Allen Chrisman
B. 8/25/1977

M62422242 - Nancy Gray Chrisman - Louis Lindsay Osborne
B. 1/12/1949   M. _____   B. _____

M624222421 - David Louis Osborne
B. 3/1/1971

M624222422 - Lori Susan Osborne
B. 6/21/1982

M62422243 - Alice Lynn Chrisman - _____Nordin (Div)
B. 2/24/1955   M. _____   B. _____

M624222431 - Claes Hakan Nordin
B. 6/10/1984

M6242225 - Margaret Eunice Wagner - Ralph George Lively
B. 9/11/1926   M. 9/25/1945   B. 3/8/1924
                                                            D. In the 70's

M62422251 - Samuel Richard Lively - Cheryl Lowry
B. 10/13/1947   M. _____   B. _____

M62422252 - Frances Ellen Lively - Gerald Perez
B. 7/6/1950   M. _____   B. _____

M624222521 - Michael Perez
B. _____

M624222522 - Laura Perez
B. _____

M62422253 - George Thomas Lively - Kristina Boren
B. 11/9/1959   M. _____   B. _____

M624222531 - Wayne Lively
  B. _____

M624222532 - Zane Michael Lively
  B. _____

M624223 - Ozella Gray Wagner - Robert King Carr
  B. 6/16/1886 M. _____ B. 9/5/1884
  D. 5/20/1966   D. 5/4/1941

  M6242231 - John Elias Carr
    B. 5/28/1907
    D. 1/26/1909

  M6242232 - Ella Sue Wagner Carr
    B. 9/4/1910
    D. _____

M624224 - James Pierce Wagner - (1) Louise Martin
  B. 8/1888 M. _____ B. _____
  D. 9/22/1964 M. _____ D. _____

         (2) Lillian Myrtle Tieche
            B. _____
            D. 1976
No information on which was mother of three children

  M6242241 - Janella Lee Wagner - Percy Estes Talley
    B. 3/21/1912 M. _____ B. _____
    D. _____   D. _____

  M6242242 - Albert Carl Wagner - Frances Erlene Harris
    B. 4/22/1915 M. 9/25/1937 B. 11/26/1916
    D. _____   D. _____

M62422421- Carlton Lee Wagner - Patsy Cook
   B. 12/18/1938   M. 1/1959   B. _____

   M624224211 - Barbara Ann Wagner - Jeffrey Drewry
      B. 8/31/1959   M. 1/28/1989   B. _____

   M624224212 - Gary Lee Wagner - Teresa Lurics
      B. 6/19/1967   M. _____   B. _____

   M624224213 - Debra Jo Wagner
      B. 4/27/1972

M62422422 - Beverly Ann Wagner - Samuel E. Richardson
   B. 4/25/1941   M. 1962   B. 1/9/1941

   M624224221 - Todd Carl Richardson
      B. 7/1/1962

   M624224222 - Scott E. Richardson - _____ Hills
      B. 2/22/1963   M. _____   B. _____

M62422423 - Alice Kathryn Wagner - Thomas B. Trott
   B. 9/28/1944   M. 6/1965   B. _____

   M624224231 - Lynn Trott - Edward E. Campbell, Jr.
      B. 11/19/1965   M. 6/9/1990   B. _____

   M624224232 - Allison Tyler Trott
      B. 11/4/1973

M6242243 - Curtis Pierce Wagner - Evelyn Martin
B. 3/28/1920   M. _____   B. _____
D. _____   D. _____

M624225 - Tyler Frazier Wagner - Hallie/Hattie Groseclose
B. 4/8/1894   M. _____   B. _____
D. 12/9/1960   D. _____

M624226 - Claude Wagner - Pearle Mustard
B. 9/1/1890   M. _____   B. 12/13/1886
D. 12/28/1969   D. 4/1/1971

M624227 - Mariah Clarica Wagner
B. 10/16/1897
D. 11/14/1903

M624228 - Nancy Georgia Wagner - Wilbur W. Fleenor
B. 12/27/1898   M. 5/20/1923   B. 3/20/1899
D. 2/18/1989   D. 6/6/1977

M6242281 - Wilbur Winston Fleenor, Jr. - Martha Jane Sparks
B. 5/5/1926   M. _____   B. _____
D. 11/28/1990

M62422811 - Carol Lynn Fleenor
B. 12/28/1948

M62422812 - John Winston Fleenor
B. 11/25/1952

M62422813 - Scott Wade Fleenor
B. 3/8/1956

M6242282 - Mary Ann Fleenor Hassell Grey Marberry
    B. 6/12/1932   M. _____   B. _____

M62422821 - Katherine Lee Marberry
    B. 11/9/1955

M62422822 - Shirley Ann Marberry - Ronald Craver
    B. 9/29/1960   M. _____   B. _____

    M624228221 - Jason Thomas Craver
        B. 11/4/1986

    M624228222 - Jennifer Ann Craver
        B. 2/14/1988

M6242283 - Jane Wagner Fleenor - Warren Comer Lower
    B. 9/9/1937   M. 2/13/1960   B. _____

    M62422831 - David Comer Lower - Tami Sue Monroe
        B. 3/20/1961   M. 9/12/1992   B. _____

    M62422832 - Amy Beth Lower - Clayton Evans Pierce
        B. 1/11/1965   M. 6/16/1990   B. _____

M624229 - Martha Alice Wagner
    B. 10/23/1900
    D. 10/18/1920

M62422-10 - St.Clair Wagner - Edna Wagner Rowe
    B. 2/22/1902   M. _____   B. _____
    D. 10/6/1985   D. _____

M62422-10-1 - Roger Wolson Wagner - Rhonda Louise Fix
B. 4/12/1933   M. 8/15/1957   B. _____

M62422-10-1-1 - Amanda Wagner
B. 9/16/1980

M62422-11 - Charles Deaton Wagner - Sudie Self
B. 10/12/1903   M. _____   B. _____
D. 6/30/1977

M62422-11-1 - Jack Wagner
B. _____

M62422-l1-2 - Ule Wagner
B. _____

M62422-12 - Myrtle Addington Wagner - Curtis Etter
B. 2/12/1905   M. _____   B. _____
D. 5/30/1971

M62422-12-1 - Curtis Etter, Jr. - Barbara Lilley
B. 1/13/1937   M. _____   B. _____

M62422-13 - Eula Green Wagner - Merle Givens Lockridge
B. 8/29/1907   M. 8/26/1930   B. 10/30/1894
D. _____   D. 4/28/1984

M62422-13-1 - Janet Mae Lockridge - Dennis Lee Crutchfield
B. 11/11/1930   M. _____   B. 9/23/1927

M62422-13-1-1 - Kevin Scott Crutchfield
  B. 3/16/1961

M62422-13-1-2 - Gary Brent Crutchfield
  B. 3/18/1964

M62422-14 - Mae Brown Wagner - Claude Robertson
  B. 12/10/1908 M. _____   B. _____
  D. 10/1/1980   D. _____

M62422-15 - Robert King Wagner - Ida Frances Davis
  B. 11/28/1910 M. 11/30/1935 B. 2/26/1914
  D. _____   D. 4/12/1985

M62422-15-1 - Robert King Wagner, Jr. - Patricia Staubers
   B. 11/10/1936 M. 2/14/1957 B. _____

M62422-15-2 - Charlotte Ann Wagner - Harry Arthur Swartzel
   B. 11/3/1938 M. 6/22/1956 B. _____

M62422-15-3 - Barbara Lee Wagner - (1) Joe Bailey Snivley (Div)
   B. 9/6/1940 (1)M. 3/27/1959 B. _____
        (2)M. 2/20/1976

             (2) Michael Dole Lawrence
             B. _____

M62422-15-4 - Ella Sue Wagner - Charles David Reese
   B. 11/12/1942 M. 6/16/1960 B. _____

M62422-15-5 - David Franklin Wagner - (1) Carol Young
    B. 4/5/1945   (1)M. _____   B. _____
    D. 11/21/1979   (2)M. 3/29/1972

                    (2) Josephine Rennie
                    B. _____

M62422-15-6 - Mary Frances Wagner - Kenneth Michael Armstrong
    B. 4/5/1945   M. 11/14/1964   B. _____

M62422-15-7 - Charles Davis Wagner - Elizabeth Fletcher
    B. 11/10/1946   M. 10/20/1973   B. _____

M62422-15-8 - John Randolph Wagner - Sandi Duclos
    B. 2/17/1948   M. 5/9/1969   B. _____

M62422-15-9 - Rebecca Hope Wagner - Francis Harold Breen
    B. 6/13/1950   M. 5/19/1990   B. _____

M62422-15-10 - William Thomas Wagner
    B. 6/8/1952
    D. 6/8/1952

M62422-15-11 - Virginia Belle Wagner - William Virgil Simmons
    B. 12/22/1953   M. 12/22/1972   B. _____

M62422-16 - Virginia Bogle Wagner - Charles Richard Beadle
    B. 3/10/1910   M. _____   B. 4/5/1919
    D. _____   D. _____

M62422-16-1 - Suzanne Doshia Beadle - Ralph Edward Kilpatrick
      B. 1/24/1949   M. 9/18/1971   B. _____

M62422-17 - Frances Lacine Wagner - Sam Buchanan
      B. 2/12/1914   M. _____   B. _____
      D. _____   D. _____

M62422-17-1 - Donnie E. Buchanan - Mary Sue Nutty
      B. 7/7/1937   M. _____   B. 11/19/1940

M62423 - Joseph Garland Bailey - Vicie Virginia Wagner
      B. 11/20/1870   M. 9/13/1899   B. 6/15/1880
      D. 6/14/1933   D. 2/26/1961

M624231 - Paris Johnson Bailey - Opie Litton
      B. 7/17/1900   M. _____   B. 1/16/1896
      D. 4/23/1970   D. 11/21/1986

M6242311 - Paris Johnson Bailey, Jr. - June Heldreth
      B. 1/9/1922   M. _____   B. _____

M624232 - William Tracie Bailey - Viola Mae Chandler
      B. 11/20/1901   M. 10/31/1922   B. 10/30/1904
      D. 6/16/1971

M6242321 - Joseph Garland Bailey - Fannie Ellis Baker
      B. 3/22/1924   M. _____   B. _____

M6242322 - Ellis Pyott Bailey - Lucy Patton
      B. 6/6/1926   M. _____   B. _____

M62423221 - Arthur Wendell Bailey
    B. 5/1947

M62423222 - Terry W. Bailey
    B. 6/2/1949

M6242323 - Laleen Opie Bailey - Frank A. Forbes
    B. 3/23/1931   M. 4/25/1951   B. 2/25/1929
                                              D. 8/23/1989

M62423231 - Anita Gail Forbes - John R. Bucchi
    B. 7/5/1952   M. 10/17/1970   B. 5/29/1952

    M624232311 - John Stevens Bucchi - Pam Murphy
        B. 6/18/1971   M. _____   B. _____

    M624232312 - Amy Lynn Bucchi
        B. 10/5/1972

    M624232313 - Michael Paul Bucchi
        B. 12/2/1977

    M624232314 – Jena Marie Bucchi
        B. 9/4/1980

M6242324 - Dallas T. Bailey - Elizabeth Lester
    B. 5/5/1936   M. _____   B. _____

M6242325 - Donald P. Bailey – Bonnie Howard
    B. 6/25/1939   M. _____   B. _____

M6242326 - Carrie Elizabeth Taylor Bailey - Clarence Lee Pace
 B. 10/9/1947   M. _____   B. 4/2/1948

M62423261 - Gregory Lee Pace - Valerie Rice
 B. 1/30/1973   M. 10/20/1992   B. _____

M62423262 - Kevin Michael Pace
 B. 2/15/1976

M624233 - James Elwood Bailey - Edna Moorefield
 B. 11/26/1907   M. 9/11/1934   B. 5/9/1913
 D. 5/13/1969   D. 3/24/1964

M6242331 - James Elwood Bailey, Jr. - Betty Sarver
 B. 11/4/1938   M. 7/7/1958   B. _____
 D. 12/21/1991

  M62423311 - Darrell Bailey
   B. _____

  M62423312 – Male
   B. _____

M6242332 - Glen Robert Bailey - Hanna Cecil
 B. _____   M. _____   B. _____

M6242333 - Wanda Jeanette Bailey - James Rorrer
 B. 4/16/1945   M. _____   B. _____
 D. 10/11/1992

M6242334 - Charles David Bailey - Billie Puckett
B. _____   M. _____   B. _____

M624234 - Paul Bailey - Florence Jones
B. 10/9/1922   M. _____   B. 2/1/1924
D. 9/22/1985

M6242341 - Paul Allan Bailey (1) Jane Tabor
B. 2/20/1948   M. _____   B. _____
M. _____

(2) Helen Diane Davis
B. 5/15/1947

M62423411 - (1) Michael Allan Bailey - April Lynn Perriello
B. 8/27/1970   M. _____   B. _____

M62423412 - (2) Tammy Michelle Bailey
B. 8/27/1978

M6242342 - Barbara Ann Bailey - George Allen Lester
B. 12/19/1952   M. _____   B. _____

M624234121 - Victor Allen Lester
B. 4/1/1973

M624234122 - Adam Keith Lester
B. 3/4/1976

M6242343 – Lois Eve Bailey
B. 2/16/1959
D. 1973

M624235 - Frank Bailey - Pauline Patton
    B. _____   M. _____   B._____
    D. 1936(?)

M624236 - Gabriel Bailey
    Died in infancy

M62424 - Margaret A. Bailey - Lee Mays
    B. 1868   M. _____   B. _____
    D. _____   D. _____

M62425 - James William Bailey - (1) Sally Lou Wallace
    B. 3/21/1873   (1)M. _____   B. 1873
    D. 11/28/1964   (2)M. 12/26/1912   D. 1911
                      (3)M. 10/5/1940

                                  (2) Dora Lee Bowman
                                       B. 4/9/1873
                                       D. 8/19/1939

                                  (3) Beulah B. Dillon
                                       B. _____
                                       D. 1/1/1985

M624251 - **(1)** Minnie Gertrude Bailey - John Greever Leedy
    B. 3/23/1896   M. 9/30/1914   B. 2/13/1884
    D. 4/5/1986   D. 9/6/1949

    M6242511 - Mary Alice Leedy - Paul Alexander Sells
        B. 7/5/1915   M. 2/22/1936   B. _____
        D. 5/6/1987

M62425111 - John Paul Rutledge Sells - Lynn Elizabeth Duggan
    B. 2/6/1937   M. 12/28/1956   B. _____
    D. 2/18/1991

    M624251111 - John Paul Alexander Sells
        B. 8/12/1963

    M624251112 - Mary Lori Sells - _____ Denny
        B. 10/15/1965   M. _____   B. _____

        M6242511121 - Brandon Taylor Denny
            B. _____

    M624251113 - Mary Amy Sells
    Died soon after birth

M62425112 - Thomas Michael Sells - (1)Candy Texter(Div)
    B. 10/13/1943   (1)M. _____   B. _____
            (2)M. 4/26/1979

                  (2) Scarlett Harkleroad
                    Bogart
                  B. _____

***M62425113** - James Edward Sells - Becky Campbell (Div)
    B. 7/13/1945   M. _____   B. _____

    M624251131 - Clinton Edward Sells
        B. 4/6/1979

M6242512 - Lois Annette Leedy
  B. 2/24/1917
  D. 1/21/1921

M6242513 - Ruth Greer Leedy - (1) Gerry Adamson (Div)
  B. 9/27/1919   M. _____   B. _____
  D. 9/27/1979   M. _____   D. _____

                              (2) Charles E. Bond
                                 B. _____
                                 D. 9/15/1985

    M62425131 - (1) John William Adamson
      B. 7/29/1948
      D. 7/30/1948

M6242514 - John Clark Leedy - Ruth Robert Hassen
  B. 5/8/1922   M. 4/19/1947   B. _____
  D. 5/8/1964

    M62425141 - Patricia Jean Leedy - Greg Olson
      B. 4/7/1948   M. _____   B. _____

        M624251411 - Norman Clark Olson
          B. _____

        M624251412 - Nicholas Dean Olson
          B. _____

    M62425142 - Janet Leedy - Art Warren
      B. 4/21/1950   M. _____   B. _____

M624251421 - Scott Warren
    B. _____

M624251422 - Kenny Warren
    B. _____

M624251423 - Brad Warren
    B. _____

M62425143 - Chris Elizabeth Leedy - Danny Farris
    B. 12/11/1951   M. _____   B. _____

    M624251431 - Amber Dawn Farris
        B. _____

M62425144 - John Robert Leedy
    B. 11/29/1954

M6242515 - Jimmy Eleanor Leedy - Carl Johnny Wajick
    B. 7/4/1925   M. 9/7/45   B. _____
    D. 4/27/1973   D. 12/13/1976

*M62425151 - Margaret Ann Wajick - (1) Arthur Norris (Div.)
    B. 8/6/1948   (1)M. 1/13/1964 B. 1/3/1944
                (2)M. 10/9/1982

                        (2) Charlie Green Lowery.
                             B. 9/29/1940

    M624251511 - (1) John Thomas Norris – Debbie N. Bain
        B. 7/6/1964   M. 2/2000 B. 4/23/1966

M624251512 - (1) Lisa Carol Norris - Joseph Randolph
B. 11/9/1966   M. 9/15/1990   Wamsley
                                  B. 2/8/1970

M6242515121 - Kyle Hunter Wamsley
B. 7/26/1992

M6242515122 - Travis Reed Wamsley
B. 11/18/1993

M62425152 - Carl Johnny Wajick, II - Iris Renee Stewart
B. 7/13/1950   M. 2/8/1971   B. 12/7/1949

M624251521 - Leslie Michelle Wajick
B. 10/2/1972

M624251522 - Stephanie Lynn Wajick
B. 3/1/1974

M624251523 - Brian David Wajick
B. 11/11/1976

M62425153 - Alice Ruth Wajick - James David Taylor
B. 1/25/1952   M. 11/24/1972   B. _____

M624251531 - Rebecca Eleanor Taylor
B. 4/12/1979

M6242516 - Doris Jean Leedy - Robert Hilton Anthony
   B. 8/14/1927   M. 3/8/1954   B. _____
   D. 6/6/1988   D. _____

   M62425161 - Jeffrey Lynn Anthony - Ann Marie Turner (Div)
   B. 12/24/1958   M. _____   B. _____

      M624251611 - Amy Lynn Anthony
   B. 4/28/1977

      M624251612 - Alice Annette Anthony
   B. 2/20/1979

*M6242517 - Margaret Baugh Leedy - William Harrison Rosen
   B. 1/26/1930   M. 7/7/1951   B. 5/5/1923
                                          D. 1/5/1992

   *M62425171 - Trudy Susan Rosen
   B. 10/20/1952

   *M62425172 - Rebecca Dawn Rosen - Richard Earl Saunders
   B. 4/18/1957   M. 7/2/1977   B. 7/31/1955

      *M624251721 - Jessica Nicole Saunders
   B. 9/29/1983

      *M624251722 - Sara Amanda Saunders
   B. 9/29/1983

M62425173 - Mary Gay Rosen
   B. 6/17/1960
   D. 6/17/1960

*M62425174 - Wendy Gail Rosen
  B. 6/18/1961

M624252 - (1) Willie Mabel Bailey
  B. 1898
  D. 1898

M624253 - (2) Alma Sue Bailey - Howard D. Vaughan
  B. 8/22/1902   M. 3/19/1923   B. 9/19/1898
  D. 3/8/1995   D. 4/14/1976

M624254 - (2) William Paul Bailey - Eva Myrtle Neff
  B. 2/18/1904   M. 9/4/1925   B. 11/14/1906
  D. 4/15/1993   D. 10/19/2000

M624255 - (2) Margaret Isabel Bailey - Walter Jackson Neff
  B. 6/28/1910   M. 11/12/1935   B. 3/17/1906
  D. 5/6/1998   D. 3/1/1991

M62426 - Thomas Brown Bailey - Mahola Frances Carter
  B. 11/23/1866   M. 9/6/1886   B. 6/6/1867
  D. _____   D. 9/6/1934

M624261 - George Alexander Bailey - Lula Rowe (Div)
  B. _____   M. _____   B. _____

  M6242611 - Frances Bailey
  B. _____

M6242612 - Pauline Bailey
    B. _____

M6242613 - Kermit Carter Bailey
    B. _____

M624262 - William Lee Bailey - Stella Felicia Harman
    B. 2/1889   M. _____   B. _____
    D. 2/19/1971   D. _____

  M62426221 - Ben Tom Bailey - Leora Stinson
      B. 8/30/1913   M. _____   B. _____
      D. _____   D. _____

    M62426211 - Ben Tom Bailey, Jr. - Madge Neece
        B. _____   M. _____   B. _____

      M624262111 - Ben Tom Bailey, III
          B. _____

      M624262112 - Sherry Bailey
          B. _____

    M62426212 - Peggy Bailey - Jason Pyott Tiller, Jr.
        B. _____   M. _____   B. _____

      M624262121 - Jason Pyott Tiller, III
          B. _____

    M62426213 - Betty Bailey - _____
        B. _____

M624262131 - Dustin _____
    B. _____

M624262132 - Lindsey _____
    B. _____

M62426214 - Ron Bailey - Brenda Farley
    B. _____   M. _____   B. _____
    M624262141 - Ron Bailey, Jr.
    B. _____

M6242622 - Lee Stuart Bailey - Virgie Ellis
    B. _____   M. _____   B. _____

M6242623 - William George Bailey
    B. _____

M6242624 - Frank Gray Bailey - Louise Angles
    B. 1/29/1928   M. _____   B. _____

    M62426241 - Frank Bailey
    B. _____

    M62426242 - Wanda Bailey
    B. _____

M6242625 - Mary Jackson Bailey - L.E. Puckett
    B. 3/26/1932   M. 1/21/1951   B. _____

    M62426251 - Lee Ed Puckett, Jr. - Mary Lynn Thomas
    B. 7/28/1952   M. _____   B. _____

M624262511 - Mary Kristen Puckett
B. 10/4/1981

M624262512 - Kelly Nicole Puckett
B. 10/25/1983

M62426251 - John Franklin Puckett - Donna Lynn Orander
B. 4/13/1955   M. _____   B. _____

M624262521 - Erinn Michelle Pucket
B. 7/17/1985

M624262522 - Michael Puckett
B. 7/17/1989

M624262523 - Bruce Allen Puckett
B. 10/20/1992

M6242626 - Frances Arnett Bailey - (1) Archie Bennett
B. 2/17/1934   M.(1) _____   B. _____
                   M.(2) _____

                          (2) Howard Shannon
                          B. _____

M62426261 - (1) Michael Bennett
B. _____

M62426262 - (1) Terry Ward Bennett
B. _____

M62426263 - (1) Martin Bennett
                            B. _____

M6242X – William Taylor Moore
        B. 1835
        D. 9/19/1864

M6243 James Tivis Moore - Sarah A.W. Caldwell
            B. 1/23/1837   M. 12/18/1867   B. 10/22/1846
            D. 8/15/1920   D. 8/13/1930

    M62431 - Martha India Moore - Samuel Howe Wingo
            B. 12/29/1868   M. 9/15/1885   B. 9/10/1862
            D. _____   D. 11/20/1932

        M624311 - Macye Moore Wingo - (1)Thomas Emory Leffel
            B. 10/25/1886   (1)M.12/11/1904 B. 8/12/1883
            D. _____   (2)M. 4/12/1911 D. 2/24/1908

                                    (2)Bunyan Webster Dillon
                                        B. 3/8/1882
                                        D. _____

        M6243111 - Will Tom Leffel(1) - Annabel Thompson
            B. 12/6/1905   M. 9/15/1936   B. _____
            D. _____   D. _____

        M6243112 - Sarah India Dillon(2) - Emil Dwight Hill
            B. 7/19/1912   M. 11/21/1936   B. _____
            D. _____   D. _____

        M6243113 - Bunyan Webster Dillon, Jr.(2) - Hazel Belle Albert
            B. 10/7/1913   M. 4/28/1934   B. _____
            D. _____   D. _____

M62431131 - Martha Moore Dillon
B. 6/29/1936

M6243114 - James Moore Dillon(2) - Elizabeth McQueen
B. 9/6/1915   M. 12/18/1941   B. _____
D. _____   D. _____

M6243115 - Samuel Jesse Dillon(2)
B. 6/2/1920
D. _____

M62432 - Margaret Emory Moore - Matthew Scott
B. 12/16/1870   M. 9/23/1888   B. _____
D. _____   D. 2/12/1923

M624321 - John Tivis Scott - Ruth Bennett
B. 10/6/1889   M. _____   B. 5/1/1894
D. 8/l958   D. 10/5/1957

M6243211 - Margaret Ellen Scott - Martin Lunsford
B, 9/22/1916   M. 9/16/1939   B. 1/14/1909
D. 3/1/2000   D. 1992

*M62432111 - Nancy Scott Lunsford - James Russell Miltenberger
B. 10/3/1942   M. 5/81965   B. 9/6/1936

*M624321111 - William Martin Miltenberger
B. 12/8/1967

M624321112 - Sharon Ann Miltenberger - Douglas M.
Garrou
B. 7/31/1969   M. 9/12/1992   B. 7/31/1966

M6243211121 - Thomas S. Garrou
B. 11/13/1997

M6243211122 - James M. Garrou
B. 11/13/1997

M6243211123 – Daniel D. Garrou
B. 7/21/2002

M6243212 - John Tivis Scott, Jr. - (1)Mary Jane Towers
B. 6/29/1924   (1)M. _____B. 8/25/1927
(2)M. 10/18/1952 D. 11/25/1951

- (2)Viola Dorothy Atkinson
B. 10/5/1933

M62432121 - John Tivis Scott, III(1) - Leslie Shannon
B. 6/14/1950   M. 6/26/1971   B. 8/2/1947

M624321211 - Sara Shannon Scott
B. 6/5/ 1976

M624321212 - Amy Towers Scott
B. 7/28/1977

M624321213 - Rachael Elizabeth Scott
B. 8/22/1980

*M62432122 - Deborah Ruth Scott(2) - Lawrence George
Queenin
B. 2/14/1954   M. 5/9/1981   B. 5/10/1945

M62432123 - Steven Michael Scott(2) - (1) Jodia F. Chin (Div)
   B. 12/27/1960   (1)M. 5/20/1989 B. 8/12/___
                     (2)M. 8/6/1994

                          - (2) Marlene Yvonne Melendez
                            B. 6/9/1961

M6243213 - David Moore Scott - Beatrice Iverna Barker
   B. 5/13/1927   M. 11/23/1946   B. 6/8/1926
   D. 9/4/1978

   M62432131 - Frances Kay Scott - James Edward Elswick
      B. 11/24/1947   M. 10/16/1966   B. 10/26/1946

      M624321311 - Eric Shayne Elswick - Jessica _____
         B. 11/3/1967   M. 8/15/1990   B. 9/13/1969

         M6243213111 - Eric Shayne Elswick, Jr.
            B. 11/17/1991

      M624321312 - Sherry Lee Elswick
         B. 2/10/1972

   M62432132 - David Moore Scott, Jr.
      B. 6/23/1951

   M62432133 - Delores Jean Scott - Emil Cornett Evans
      B. 6/23/1951   M. 12/27/1970   B. 2/9/1951

      M624321331 - Elizabeth Wynn Evans - Peter Paul Hudak
         B. 8/9/1972   M. 6/24/1995   B. 7/20/1972

M6243213311 - Christian Tyler Hudak
B. 5/14/1995

M624321332 - Mollie Bea Evans
B. 12/19/1977

M624321333 - Emil Cornett Evans, Jr.
B. 6/3/1980

M62432134 - Dwight Barker Scott
B. 10/8/1958

M6243214 - William Bennett Scott
B. 5/15/1931
D. 6/18/1950

M6243215 - Thomas Bennett Scott - June Ann Conn
B. 5/28/1935   M. 6/7/1958   B. 6/4/1935

M62432151 - Susan Elaine Scott - Glenn Paul Childress
B. 1/1/1961   M. 7/11/1987   B. 11/7/1962

M624321511 - Rebecca Jane Childress
B. 12/20/1993

M62432152 - Keith Conn Scott
B. 10/1/1963

M624322 - Willie Gladys Scott
B. 7/24/1891
D. 11/2/1928

M624323 - Sidney Martin Scott - Mary Elizabeth Muncy
    B. 4/27/1893   M.   12/24/1914   B. 8/9/1897
    D. 6/5/1964   D. 4/26/1953

M6243231 - James Muncy Scott - Corrine Touchberry
    B. 5/13/1916   M. 1/5/1942   B. 12/31/1919
    D. 10/5/1971

M62432311 - James Muncy Scott, Jr. - Elizabeth Stuart Haley
    B. 6/17/1946   M. 6/1/1968   B. 8/17/1946

M624323111 - James Muncy Scott, III
    B. 6/18/1969

M624323112 - Rosemary Corrine Scott - Matthew
                                       Franklin Moore
    B. 1/13/1972   M. 3/11/1995   B. 1/13/1970

M6243231121 – Haley Corrine Moore
    B. 9/17/1995

M62432312 - Lynda Marie Scott - Roland Gert Munique (Div)
    B. 4/10/1948   M. 1/31/1971   B. 4/1/1947

M624323121 - Roland Christopher Munique – April N. Neri
    B. 3/26/1975   M. 7/13/2002   B. _____

M624323122 - Caroline Heidi Munique
    B. 3/6/1976

M62432313 - Ruth Diane Scott - John David Knapp
    B. 10/9/1949   M. 1/27/1973   B. 9/1/1946

M624323131 - Jacob Samuel Knapp
    B. 1/21/1976

M624323132 - Jennifer Marie Knapp
    B. 3/18/1977

M624323133 - Ezra John Knapp
    B. 2/8/1982

M6243232 - Sidney Martin Scott, Jr. - Ruth Ilene Christine Hall
    B. 6/21/1919   M. 8/4/1940   B. 2/19/1922
    D. _____   D. 3/15/2002

  M62432321 - Sidney Martin Scott, III - Linda Gail Cruikshank
      B. 8/2/1941   M. 10/6/1967   B. 3/14/1940

    M624323211 - Kelly Leigh Scott - William Sweatt
        B. 4/5/1968   M. 1992   B. _____

    M624323212 - Sidney Martin Scott, IV - Rebecca Morgan
        B. 10/21/1969   M. 9/11/1993   B. 12/30/1968

      M6243232121 – Grace Morgan Scott
        B. 4/15/2000

      M6243232122 – Andrew Jonathon Scott
        B. 4/6/2003

  *M62432322 - Judith Ann Scott - Warren Pratt Self
      B. 1/20/1945   M. 6/3/1966   B. 2/26/1943

M624323221 - Christina Rene Self - (1) Louis Stockwell
(Div)
B. 6/21/1968   (1)M. 4/14/1991   B. _____
                (2)M. 9/7/2003

(2) John Michael Hatherly
B. 4/2/1961

M6243232211 – (2) Celine Michelle Hatherly
B. 11/6/2000

***M624323222** - Michelle Leigh Self - Mark Thomas Rackley
B. 11/21/1970   M. 8/13/1994   B. 12/15/1968

***M6243232221** – Sarah Catherine Rackley
B. 8/6/2000

***M6243232222** – Paul William Rackley
B. 6/30/2002

***M62432323** - Cynthia Rose Scott - Thomas Craddock
B. 8/26/1949   M. 1/19/1974   B. 4/30/1952

***M624323231** - Katrina Rose Craddock
B. 2/24/1986

M624324 - Luther George Scott - Mildred _____
B. 9/17/1895   M. _____   B. _____
D. 1975

M6243241 - Russell E. Scott
B. 3/7/1920
D. 1940

M6243242 - Lois Ann Scott
B. 1940

M624325 - Paul Mitchell Scott - Rene Roberts
     B. 10/18/1897   M. 10/25/1923   B. 7/7/1899
     D. 6/6/1980   d. 3/13/1988

M6243251 - Paul Mitchell Scott, Jr. - Elizabeth Edgar Johnson
     B. 11/1/1928   M. 6/15/1968   B. 8/12/1932

M624326 - Matthew Emory Scott - Dorothy _____
     B. 11/19/1899   M. _____   B. _____
     D. _____   D. _____

M6243261 - Hubert Emory Scott - Leah _____
     B. 1942   M. _____   B. _____

     M62432611 - Tracy Scott
          B. _____

     M62432612 - Brad Scott
          B. _____

     M62432613 - Kelly Scott
          B. _____

M624327 - Algene Stewart Scott - Goldie Barth
     B. 7/19/1904   M. 10/26/1928   B. 9/17/1904
     D. 10/30/1975   D. 10/19/1996

*M6243271 - Patricia Ann Scott - Neal Holloway Jones
     B. 8/4/1934   M. 6/5/1952   B. 9/15/1931

M62432711 - Judith Lee Jones - Ronald Lester Raglin
B. 3/10/1953   M. 10/22/1978   B. 9/19/1953

    M624327111 - Bradley Ronald Raglin
      B. 3/6/1982

    M624327112 - Jonathan Travis Raglin
      B. 4/30/1986

*M62432712** - Neal Scott Jones - Julia Linda Murphy
B. 6/8/1955 M. 6/10/1979   B. 2/12/1958

    *M624327121** - Jennifer Susan Jones
      B. 2/14/1981

    *M624327122** - Meghan Rose Jones
      B. 1/14/1988

M62432713 - Joanne Patricia Jones - Donald Brooke Marshall
B. 3/18/1959   M. 7/11/1982   B. 4/4/1957

    M624327131 - Kristen Brooke Marshall
      B. 3/22/1986

    M624327132 - Lauren Patricia Marshall
      B. 6/4/1989

M624328 - James Rudolph Scott - (1)Elizabeth Twining
B. 10/1909   (1)M. _____ B. 7/2/1914
D. 1986   (2)M. _____ D. 10/5/1961

              (2)Laura Banker
              B. _____

M6243281 - James Rudolph Scott, Jr. - _____(Div)
    B. 4/5/1941   M. _____   B. _____

M6243282 - Robert Twining Scott - (1)Dorothy Zucko
    B. 2/5/1944   (1)M. 6/1966   B. _____
                    (2)M. 1976

                                  (2)Carolyn Lea Seaman
                                       B. 6/22/1945

      M62432821 - David Christopher Scott(1) - _____
         B. 9/20/1971   M. _____   B. _____

      M62432822 - Suzanne Elizabeth Scott(2)
         B. 1/19/1977

M6243283 - Sarah Ann Scott - Willis Francis Thompson (Div)
    B. 7/23/1954   M. 7/7/1974   B. _____

      M62432831 - Laura Elizabeth Thompson
         B. 1/24/1981

      M62432832 - Bradley William Thompson
         B. 5/15/1985

      M62432833 - Alicia Ann Thompson
         B. 1/28/1988

M62433 - Ora Virginia Moore - Sidney J. Tabor
    B. 1872   M. _____   B. _____
    D. _____   D. _____

M624331 - Irving Moore Tabor
    B. _____

M6244 Nancy Jane Moore - William Elgin Neel
    B. 8/5/1837   M. _____   B. 1817
    D. 1903   D. 1889

    M62441 - Charles Brown Neel - Mary Mariah Bailey
        B. 8/5/1878   M. 10/11/1899   B. 2/14/1880
        D. 1/11/1936   D. _____

        M624411 - William Alexander Neel - Trula Ann Kennedy
            B. 8/5/1900   M. 7/4/1931   B. _____
            D. _____   D. _____

            M6244111 - Elizabeth Ann Neel
                B. 4/16/1938

        M624412 - Virginia Neel
            B. 7/24/1905
            D. _____

        M624413 - Bailey Moore Neel - Martha Robinson Callison
            B. 4/5/1907   M. 9/7/1935   B. _____
            D. _____   D. _____

            M6244131 - Mary Moore Neel
                B. 5/30/1936

            M6244132 - Charles Bailey Neel
                B. 8/5/1938

    M62442 - James Luther Neel - Margaret Aston Hicks
        B. 2/24/1881   M. 9/4/1907   B. 9/30/1882
        D. 7/19/1921   D. _____

M624421 - Mary Moore Neel
  B. 8/16/1908
  C. 9/16/1912

M624422 - Elizabeth Ward Neel
  B. 10/11/1910
  D. 10/24/1912

M6245 - Martha Christine Moore - David Chapman Stafford
    B. 11/18/1841   M. 5/10/1866   B. 3/31/1839
    D. 2/19/1917   D. 2/17/1900

M62451 - James Addison Stafford - Sally Bane
    B. 2/26/1867   M. _____   B. _____
    D. 11/14/1933   D. _____

M624511 - _____ Stafford - R.C. Allen
    B. _____   M. _____   B. _____

M624512 - _____ Stafford - S.M. Flanagan
    B. _____   M. _____   B. _____

M624513 - Dewey Chapman Stafford
    B. _____

M624514 - _____ - Jack Rock
    B. _____   M. _____   B. _____

M624515 - James William Stafford
    B. _____

M62452 - Tyler Hoge Stafford - (1) Laura Belle Sands
    B. 10/26/1868   (1)M. 6/10/1891   B. 6/28/1869
    D. _____   (2)M. 12/26/1900   D. 11/13/1896
                (3)M. 10/22/1931

                (2) Ida Jane Bones
                    B. 5/23/1877
                    D. 5/15/1926

                (3) Grace Lucy Minnick
                    B. 9/24/1893
                    D. _____

M624521 - (1) Laura Mae Stafford Lawrence James Morehead
    B. 5/1/1892   M. 7/20/1910   B. 1/30/1888
    D. _____   D. _____

    M6245211 - Hazel Mae Morehead - Hartwell Sizer
        B. 7/24/1911   M. _____   B. _____
        D. _____   D. _____

    M6245212 - Dorothy Belle Morehead - Garnett Stafford
        B. 2/6/1914   M. _____   B. _____
        D. _____   D. _____

        M62452121 - Robert Lee Stafford
            B. 9/27/1936

    M6245213 - Henry Lawrence Morehead - Patty Louise Kier
        B. 9/14/1916   M. _____   B. _____
        D. _____   D. _____

M6245214 - Donald Jackson Morehead
      B. 8/17/1921
      D. _____

M624522 - (2) Roy Edward Stafford - Sarah Jane Bryant
      B. 9/20/1902   M. 10/20/1927   B. 4/19/1903
      D. _____   D. _____

     M6245221 - Charles Draper Stafford
          B. 11/28/1928

     M6245222 - Ellen Jane Stafford
          B. 3/25/1930

     M6245223 - Crystal Mae Stafford
          B. 10/15/1931

M624523 - (2) Ida Faith Stafford - Gilbert Lee Mitchell
      B. 1/1/1917   M. 11/11/1933   B. _____
      D. _____   D. _____

     M6245231 - Iris Elaine Mitchell
          B. 9/5/1935

     M6245232 - Richard Earl Mitchell
          B. 12/19/1937

     M6245233 - Eldred Duane Mitchell
          B. 6/5/1941

M62453 - Roberta Jane Stafford
     B. 2/1871
     D. 2/6/1910

M62454 - Margaret Julia Stafford - Edgar Christian
    B. 1/7/1873   M. _____   B. _____
    D. 7/18/1904

    M624541 - Homer T. Christian
        B. _____

M62455 - Elizabeth Dora Lee Stafford - Edward Astor Deaton
    B. 1/28/1875   M. 4/30/1902   B. 7/22/1870
    D. _____   D. _____

M62456 - Robert Luther Brown Stafford - Frances Blanche Kelley
    B. 5/5/1877   M. 4/16/1915   B. 2/18/1891
    D. _____   D. _____

    M624561 - Margie Kathleen Stafford
        B. 2/19/1916
        D. _____

    M624562 - Hazel Irene Stafford
        B. 12/6/1917
        D. _____

    M624563 - Carrie Lucille Stafford
        B. 3/6/1921
        D. _____

    M624564 - David Orville Stafford
        B. 2/27/1923

M62457 - Dailey Van Buren Stafford - Pearl Josephine Johnston
    B. 8/27/1879   M. 11/6/1902   B. _____
    D. _____   D. _____

M62458 - Nellie Grant Stafford - John C. Vest
    B. 11/8/1881   M. 5/18/1904   B. _____
    D. 12/30/1905   D. _____

    M624581 - Clara Lucille Vest - William A. Buchanan
        B. 3/10/1905   M. 8/12/1933   B. _____
        D. _____   D. _____

        M6245811 - William A. Buchanan, Jr.
          B. 6/27/1934

        M6245812 - Mary Elizabeth Buchanan
          B. 6/1/1938

M62459 - Stacy Pink Stafford
    B. 10/19/1883
    D. 9/11/1905

M62459x - Grace Pearl Stafford
    B. 10/19/1883
    D. 6/24/1904

M6245X – Attila Moore – _____ Reynolds
    B. _____   M. _____   B. _____
    D. _____   D. _____

M6246 - Octavia Columbus Moore - Giles Rufus Karr
    B. 1/11/1849   M. 1/9/1872   B. 12/7/1843
    D. 1932   D. 1928

M62461 - Charles Robert Karr - (1)Rachel Davis
    B. 4/5/1874   (1)M. _____   B. _____
    D. 3/13/1951   (2)M. _____   D. 1/24/1948

                            (2)Annie Davis
                                B. 8/16/1887
                                D. 12/1984

M62462 - Sarah Poage Karr - Javin Baldwin Mullin
    B. 1/2/1876   M. 10/5/1898   B. 7/28/1872
    D. 7/13/1962   D. 2/20/1945

For this line see **M62274**

M624622 - Giles Austin Mullin - Naomi Clair Jones
    B. 3/6/1901   M. 6/21/1930   B. 5/8/1908
    D. 1969   D. 11/24/1987

M6246221 - Joan Patricia Mullin - William Snead, Jr. (Has children)
    B. 3/23/1934   M. _____   B. _____

M6246222 - Anita Clair Mullin - James Mayo (Has children)
    B. 1/2/1938   M. _____   B. _____
    D. 1993

M624623 - Walter Lee Mullin - Mabel Dennis
    B. 8/29/1903   M. 10/9/1936   B. _____
    D. _____   D. 8/1985

M6246231 - Walter Lee Mullin, Jr.
    B. 1952
    D. 1962

M624624 - Glenn Baldwin Mullin - **M641216** Mary Mildred Moore
    B. 7/3/1904   M. 6/12/1936   B. 8/12/1908
    D. _____

    M6246241 - James Oscar Mullin
        B. 10/23/1940

M624625 - Cecil Karr Mullin - Emma Lou Davis
    B. 6/27/1907   M. 6/29/1940   B. _____
    D. _____

    M6246251 - Wayne Mullin
        B. _____

M624626 - Javin Luther Mullin - Margaret Shrader
    B. 12/27/1914   M. _____   B. _____
    D. _____

    M6246261 - Larry Mullin - _____ (Has children)
        B. 1951   M. _____   B. _____
        D. 1982

M62463 - Margaret Frazier Karr - Wirt H. Bailey
    B. 1/19/1878   M. 1905   B.   4/4/1873
    D. 3/19/1957   D.   7/23/1957

M624631 - Virginia Catherine Bailey
  B. 4/30/1906
  D. 1/22/2000

M624632 - Baby Girl
  B. 6/14/1907
  D. 6/14/1907

M62464 - William Luther Karr - (1)Violet Owens
  B. 8/1880   (1)M. _____   B. _____
  D. 6/1956   (2)M. _____

                    (2)Billie Counts
                      B. 9/11/1881
                      D. _____

M62465 - James Wirt Karr - Pauline Bailey
  B. 2/18/1883   M. _____   B. _____
  D. 2/18/1957   D. 4/1978

M62466 - Frank King Karr - Leola French
  B. 8/25/1887   M 5/21/1924   B. 12/18/1903
  D. 5/14/1960   D. 6/28/1991

M62467 - Jesse Moore Karr - Lynwood Stafford
  B. 1/29/1891   M. _____   B. 9/15/1893
  D. 8/9/1956   D. 1/13/1997

  M624671 - Mary Moore Karr - Walter Franklin Borkey
    B. 7/25/1930   M. 11/19/1955   B. 7/31/1931

    M6246711 - Karen Leigh Borkey - Ricky Lynn Bowman
      B. 2/15/1958   M. 3/17/1984   B. 10/27/1955

      M62467111 - Mary Katelyn Bowman
        B. 10/23/1986

M6246712 - Walter Franklin Borkey, Jr. - (1) Elizabeth Morgan
    B. 2/6/1963   (1)M. 1/20/1990 B. 5/10/1963
                   (2)M. 2/13/1998

                              (2) Kathleen Graf
                                  B. 2/16/1967

       M62467121 - Elizabeth Cameron Borkey(1)
          B. 1/9/1991

       M62467122 - John Franklin Borkey(2)
          B. 9/25/1992

M62468 - Nida Jane Karr - James Roy Brown
    B. 4/12/1897   M. 11/29/1916   B. 6/1890
    D. Oct 196?   D. 11/4/1981

    M624681 - James Roy Brown, Jr.
       B. 9/27/1917
       D. 7/29/1918

    M624682 - Nelson Clark Brown - Iva Gaye Taylor
       B. 7/20/1919   M. 6/30/1948   B. 5/5/1927
       D. 5/31/1972

       M6246821 - Nelson Clark Brown, Jr. - Judy Gail Fulcher
          B. 8/17/1949   M. 8/7/1976   B. 7/4/1955

          M62468211 - Caleb Fulcher Brown
             B. 4/6/1985

       *M6246822 - Robin Taylor Brown - Jonathan Dudley Merchant
          B. 5/13/1964   M. 8/18/1990   B. 4/17/1963

*M62468221 - Jeffrey Thomas Merchant
B. 11/2/1995

*M62468222 - Christopher Scott Merchant
B. 2/29/2000

M624683 - James Elwood Brown - Geneva Grego
B. 7/21/1924   M. 6/27/1944   B. 2/28/1923
D. 12/22/1993

M6246831 - James Elwood Brown, Jr. - Sharon _____
B. 3/9/1948   M. _____   B. _____

M62468311 - Steven James Brown
B. _____

*M6246832 - Michael Fortunato Brown - Wanda Chapman
B.10/9/1951   M. 6/18/1972   B. 3/24/1954

*M62468321 - Christie Michelle Brown - Ples John Breazeale, III
B.1/24/1977   M. 12/7/1995   B. _____

*M624683211 - Ples John Breazeale, IV.
B. 11/6/1996

*M624683212 – Allissa Genevieve Breazeale
B. 11/23/1997

*M62468322 - Robert Michael Brown – Bobbie Jo Bailey
B. 12/16/1978   M. 12/19/2001   B. 1/11/1981

M6247 Elizabeth Tennessee Moore - James Howard Hendrickson
       B. 1/2/1851   M. 5/10/1873   B. _____
       D. 9/20/1881   D. _____

M62471 - Effie Virginia Hendrickson - Robert Stephans
       B. 4/12/1874   M. _____ B. _____
       D. _____   D. _____

M624711 - Ottie Mabel Stephans - Laurel Everett Carter
       B. 2/16/1897   M. 7/10/1918 B. 7/11/1889
       D. _____   D. _____

    M6247111 - Shirley Ann Carter
        B. 5/3/1922

    M6247112 - Francis Gray Carter
        B. 4/16/1928
        D. 4/16/1928

M624712 - Carrie Lee Stephens - George Francis Powell
       B. 10/28/1898   M. 6/5/1920 B. 1/18/1893
       D. _____   D. _____

    M6247121 - Emma Virginia Powell
        B. 4/3/1921
        D. _____

    M6247122 - George Robert Powell
        B. 5/3/1923

    M6247123 - Dorothy Lee Powell
        B. 11/22/1925

    M6247124 - Joy Ann Powell
        B. 5/2/1928

M6247125 - Harley Ray Powell
    B. 11/11/1930

M624713 - Binnie Catherine Stephens - George Vernan Zeiders
    B. 11/9/1901   M. 7/22/1929   B. 3/29/1906
    D. _____   D. _____

    M6247131 - Phyllis Loraine Zeiders
        B. 3/22/1930

    M6247132 - Edith Elene Zeiders
        B. 4/3/1932

    M6247133 - Thomas Doyle Zeiders
        B. 3/21/1936

    M6247134 - Lois Janice Zeiders
        B. 10/3/1937

M624714 - William Edward Stephens - Eleanor Gladys Anderson
    B. 9/19/1903   M. 9/30/1939   B. 4/18/1910
    D. _____   D. _____

M624715 - Robert Roosevelt Stephens
    B. 6/5/1905
    D. _____

M624716 - Sidney Beltrans Stephens
    B. 9/24/1907
    D. _____

M624717 - Ada Lee Stephens - Anund Moen
    B. 8/19/1910   M. 12/8/1936   B. 1/21/1908
    D. _____   D. _____

M62472 - Binnie Frazier Hendrickson - Charles Washington Gill
    B. 12/2/1875   M. 4/15/1897   B. 7/23/1872
    D. 3/7/1942   D. _____

M624721 - Lena Mariah Gill - John Dewey Johnson
    B. 3/10/1898   M. 3/15/1921   B. 9/19/1898
    D. _____   D. _____

    M6247211 - Eva Lorraine Johnson
        B. 12/23/1922

M624722 - Howard Hounsell Gill - (1) M628181 Virginia Irene Crocket(Div)
    B. 7/22/1899   (1)M. 7/12/1924   B. 5/29/1900
    D. _____   (2)M. 9/27/1936   D. _____

                             (2) Willie Gladys Mullin
                               B. 7/11/1901
                               D. _____

    M6247221 - Douglas Leon Gill(1)
        B. 7/6/1925

    M6247222 - George Ronald Gill(2)
        B. 3/24/1939

    M6247223 - James Howard Gill(2)
        B. 8/31/1940

M624723 - Charles Henry Gill - (1) _____
    B. 4/5/1901   (1) M. _____   B. _____
    D. _____   (2) M. 12/23/1933   D. _____

(2) Virginia Aileen Buchanan
B. 2/12/1908
D. _____

M6247231 - (1) Peggy Henderson Gill
B. 5/13/1923

M6247232 - (1) Betty Ann Gill
B. 5/23/1926

M6247233 - (2) Charles Henry Gill, Jr.
B. 2/6/1936

M6247234 - (2) Mary Gill
B. 11/23/1937
D. 11/23/1937

M6247235 - (2) David Buchanan Gill
B. 11/2/1940

M624724 - Sam William Gill - Bannie Melissa Sanders
B. 3/2/1903   M. 3/28/1932   B. 1/5/1905
D. _____   D. _____

M6247241 - Sam William Gill
B. 9/7/1935

M6247242 - Aneva Alice Gill
B. 11/6/1938

M6247243 - Sue Ellen Gill
B. 5/15/1940

M62473 - James Moore Hendrickson - Lola Lee Wells
    B. 10/11/1877   M. 9/26/1900   B. _____
    D. _____   D. _____

  M624731 - Annie Wells Hendrickson - _____ Macan
      B. 11/18/1901   M. _____   B. _____
      D. _____   D. _____

    M6247311 - Douglas Macan
        B. 1921

    M6247312 - _____ Macan (male)
        B. 1923

  M624732 - John Robert Moore Hendrickson
      B. 8/8/1903
      D. 2/1940

  M624733 - Mary Isabel Hendrickson - Bruce R. Trimble
      B. 11/28/1906   M. _____   B. _____
      D. _____   D. _____

    M6247331 - Donald Trimble
        B. 1926

    M6247332 - Markley Trimble
        B. 1933

  M624734 - Pauline Maud Trimble - Arthur Bridgeman
      B. 6/29/1909   M. _____   B. _____
      D. _____   D. _____

M624735 - Frank James Hendrickson - Sylvia Marie Boggs
    B. 9/27/1911   M. 5/25/1932   B. _____
    D. _____   D. _____

    M6247351 - Cora Janet Hendrickson
        B. 9/18/1932

    M6247352 - Frank Erwin Hendrickson
        B. 3/27/1934

    M6247353 - Jaqueline Lee Hendrickson
        B. 11/24/1940

M624736 - Charles Maurice Hendrickson - Helen Doggett
    B. 11/4/1913   M. 2/1/1939   B. _____
    D. _____   D. _____

    M6247361 - Charles Maurice Hendrickson, Jr.
        B. 1940

M624737 - Mildred Lee Hendrickson - Arvel Long Murphy
    B. 10/3/1918   M. 9/9/1940   B. 1/9/1917
    D. _____   D. _____

    M6247371 - Addison Moore Murphy
        B. 6/5/1941

M6248 - Julia Ann Moore - Andrew Hounshell
    B. 2/22/1854   M. 7/31/1879   B. 10/21/1839
    D. 8/1/1925   D. _____

M62481 - Mary Moore Hounshell - Jesse Lafayette Massey
     B. 2/27/1882   B. 12/23/1897   B. 11/2/1872
     D. _____   D. 1/18/1931

     M624811 - Robert Dewey Massey - Nell Francis Wheelock
          B. 10/3/1899   M 9/5/1923   B. _____
          D. _____   D. _____

M62482 - Sarah Elizabeth Hounshell - Benjamin Reeves Firestone
     B. 9/21/1887   M. 3/28/1906   B. 2/21/1884
     D. _____   D. _____

     M624821 - infant
          B. 8/22/1907
          D. 8/25/1907

     M624822 - Thelma Louise Firestone - Robert Lee Hogg
          B. 3/16/1910   M. 10/4/1939   B. _____
          D. _____   D. _____

          M6248221 - Barbara Virginia Hogg
               B. 11/25/1941

     M624823 - Benjamin Reeves Firestone, Jr.
          B. 6/10/1920
          D. 6/13/1920

     M624824 - Barbara Moore Firestone
          B. 10/13/1935

M62483 - Robert Andrew Hounshell - Johnnie Ades Rambo
     B. 12/11/1890   M. 4/21/1912   B. 1/19/1889
     D. 3/29/1938   D. _____

M624831 - Howard Andrew Hounshell
    B. 6/1/1914
    D. _____

M624832 - Billie Reeves Hounshell - (male)
    B. 6/10/1921

M6249 — Joseph Luther Moore
    B. 4/18/1856
    D. 5/6/1880

17.

The Joseph Addison Moore Line
Biographical Charts

M6241123

Genealogical Number

Harold William Snodgrass

Stafford, TX

Name (including maiden name if applicable)

Town of Residence

Glade Spring, VA	6-15-1918	12-28-2003	Miami, FLA
Birthplace	Date of Birth	Date of Death	Where Buried

Helen Marie Szczepanski	Monessen, PA	3-27-1924	10-28-1997
Name of Spouse	Birthplace	Date of Birth	Date of Death

Miami, FLA	June 1945	Wisconsin	
Where Buried	Date of Marriage	Place of Marriage	

If married more than once:

Name of Spouse	Birthplace	Date of Birth	Date of Death

Where Buried	Date of Marriage	Place of Marriage	

Stanley Szczepanski & Mary Putco

Parents of Spouse (with Mother's maiden name) 1st Marriage

Subsequent Marriage (if applicable)

Family Details

Schools attended, dates and degrees:

Community, political work, etc.:

Medical College of Virginia, M.D.

Descendant   Descendant

University of Wisconsin

Spouse   Spouse

Basic Employment History: Clubs, Church Affiliations, etc.:

Physician

Descendant   Descendant

Housewife

Spouse   Spouse

Military Service:

US Army

Descendant   Spouse

M62411231
Genealogical Number

Mary Snodgrass   Missouri City, TX
Name (including maiden name if applicable)   Town of Residence

_____   11/11/1946   _____   _____
Birthplace   Date of Birth   Date of Death   Where Buried

Richard Brent Newton   _____   6/6/1947   _____
Name of Spouse   Birthplace   Date of Birth   Date of Death

_____   _____   _____
Where Buried   Date of Marriage   Place of Marriage

If married more than once:

John Leon Freeman   _____   3/1945   _____
Name of Spouse   Birthplace   Date of Birth   Date of Death

_____   _____   _____
Where Buried   Date of Marriage   Place of Marriage

_____
Parents of Spouse (with Mother's maiden name) 1st Marriage

_____
Subsequent Marriage (if applicable)

Family Details

Schools attended, dates and degrees: Community, political work, etc.:

_____   _____
Descendant   Descendant

_____   _____
Spouse   Spouse

Basic Employment History: Clubs, Church Affiliations, etc.:

_____   _____
Descendant   Descendant

_____   _____
Spouse   Spouse

Military Service:

_____   _____
Descendant   Spouse

M624112311
Genealogical Number

John Benjamin Freeman
Name (including maiden name if applicable)   Town of Residence

_____   11/12/1971   _____   _____
Birthplace   Date of Birth   Date of Death   Where Buried

_____   _____   _____   _____
Name of Spouse   Birthplace   Date of Birth   Date of Death

_____   _____   _____
Where Buried   Date of Marriage   Place of Marriage

If married more than once:

_____   _____   _____   _____
Name of Spouse   Birthplace   Date of Birth   Date of Death

_____   _____   _____
Where Buried   Date of Marriage   Place of Marriage

_____
Parents of Spouse (with Mother's maiden name) 1st Marriage

_____
Subsequent Marriage (if applicable)

Family Details

Schools attended, dates and degrees: Community, political work, etc.:

_____   _____
Descendant   Descendant

_____   _____
Spouse   Spouse

Basic Employment History: Clubs, Church Affiliations, etc.:

_____   _____
Descendant   Descendant

_____   _____
Spouse   Spouse

Military Service:

_____   _____
Descendant   Spouse

M624112312

Genealogical Number

Nils Martin Freeman

Name (including maiden name if applicable)   Town of Residence

4-25-1973

Birthplace   Date of Birth   Date of Death   Where Buried

Name of Spouse   Birthplace   Date of Birth   Date of Death

Where Buried   Date of Marriage   Place of Marriage

If married more than once:

Name of Spouse   Birthplace   Date of Birth   Date of Death

Where Buried   Date of Marriage   Place of Marriage

Parents of Spouse (with Mother's maiden name) 1st Marriage

Subsequent Marriage (if applicable)

Family Details

Schools attended, dates and degrees: Community, political work, etc.:

Descendant   Descendant

Spouse   Spouse

Basic Employment History: Clubs, Church Affiliations, etc.:

Descendant   Descendant

Spouse   Spouse

Military Service:

Descendant   Spouse

M62411232

Genealogical Number

Sandra Jane Snodgrass

Name (including maiden name if applicable)   Town of Residence

4-27-1954

| Birthplace | Date of Birth | Date of Death | Where Buried |

| Name of Spouse | Birthplace | Date of Birth | Date of Death |

| Where Buried | Date of Marriage | Place of Marriage |

If married more than once:

| Name of Spouse | Birthplace | Date of Birth | Date of Death |

| Where Buried | Date of Marriage | Place of Marriage |

Parents of Spouse (with Mother's maiden name) 1st Marriage

Subsequent Marriage (if applicable)

Family Details

Schools attended, dates and degrees: Community, political work, etc.:

Descendant   Descendant

Spouse   Spouse

Basic Employment History: Clubs, Church Affiliations, etc.:

Descendant   Descendant

Spouse   Spouse

Military Service:

Descendant   Spouse

M62411713
Genealogical Number

Cassandra Steffey
Name (including maiden name if applicable)

Jonesborough, TN
Town of Residence

Johnson City, TN
Birthplace

10/1/1946
Date of Birth

Date of Death

Where Buried

Gerald David Thomas
Name of Spouse

Meadowview, VA
Birthplace

4/26/1943
Date of Birth

Date of Death

Where Buried

10/24/1969
Date of Marriage

Johnson City, TN
Place of Marriage

If married more than once:

Name of Spouse

Birthplace

Date of Birth

Date of Death

Where Buried

Date of Marriage

Place of Marriage

Naomi Van Lear Thomas
Parents of Spouse (with Mother's maiden name) 1st Marriage

Subsequent Marriage (if applicable)

Family Details

Schools attended, dates and degrees:

Community, political work, etc.:

ESTU 1970-1971 BS & MA;
VPI & SU 1974
Descendant

Descendant

Spouse

Spouse

Basic Employment History:

Clubs, Church Affiliations, etc.:

Descendant

Descendant

Spouse

Spouse

Military Service:

Descendant

US Navy
Spouse

M624117131
_____
Genealogical Number

Robert Brown Thomas   Baton Rouge, FLA
_____   _____
Name (including maiden name if applicable)   Town of Residence

Johnson City, TN   2-16-1967
_____ _____   _____   _____
Birthplace   Date of Birth   Date of Death   Where Buried

Susan Elizabeth Sherman New Orleans, LA   6-26-1968
_____ _____   _____   _____
Name of Spouse   Birthplace   Date of Birth   Date of Death

                        11-23-1992
_____ _____   _____
Where Buried   Date of Marriage   Place of Marriage

If married more than once:

_____ _____   _____   _____
Name of Spouse   Birthplace   Date of Birth   Date of Death

_____ _____   _____
Where Buried   Date of Marriage   Place of Marriage

_____
Parents of Spouse (with Mother's maiden name) 1st Marriage

Lady Pat Patterson & Irving Julius Sherman
_____
Subsequent Marriage (if applicable)

Family Details

Schools attended, dates and degrees: Community, political work, etc.:

_____   _____
Descendant   Descendant

_____   _____
Spouse   Spouse

Basic Employment History: Clubs, Church Affiliations, etc.:

_____   _____
Descendant   Descendant

_____   _____
Spouse   Spouse

Military Service:

_____   _____
Descendant   Spouse

M6241171311
_____
Genealogical Number

Megan Elizabeth Thomas   Johnson City, TN
_____   _____
Name (including maiden name if applicable)   Town of Residence

Baton Rouge, LA   2-21-1997
_____   _____   _____
Birthplace   Date of Birth   Date of Death   Where Buried

_____   _____   _____
Name of Spouse   Birthplace   Date of Birth   Date of Death

_____   _____
Where Buried   Date of Marriage   Place of Marriage

If married more than once:

_____   _____   _____
Name of Spouse   Birthplace   Date of Birth   Date of Death

_____   _____
Where Buried   Date of Marriage   Place of Marriage

_____
Parents of Spouse (with Mother's maiden name) 1st Marriage

_____
Subsequent Marriage (if applicable)

Family Details

Schools attended, dates and degrees: Community, political work, etc.:

_____   _____
Descendant   Descendant

_____   _____
Spouse   Spouse

Basic Employment History: Clubs, Church Affiliations, etc.:

_____   _____
Descendant   Descendant

_____   _____
Spouse   Spouse

Military Service:

_____   _____
Descendant   Spouse

M6241171312
_____
Genealogical Number

Morgan Alexandra Thomas   Johnson City, TN
_____   _____
Name (including maiden name if applicable)   Town of Residence

Baton Rouge, LA   2-21-1997
_____   _____   _____   _____
Birthplace   Date of Birth   Date of Death   Where Buried

_____   _____   _____   _____
Name of Spouse   Birthplace   Date of Birth   Date of Death

_____   _____   _____
Where Buried   Date of Marriage   Place of Marriage

If married more than once:

_____   _____   _____   _____
Name of Spouse   Birthplace   Date of Birth   Date of Death

_____   _____   _____
Where Buried   Date of Marriage   Place of Marriage

_____
Parents of Spouse (with Mother's maiden name) 1st Marriage

_____
Subsequent Marriage (if applicable)

Family Details

Schools attended, dates and degrees: Community, political work, etc.:

_____   _____
Descendant   Descendant

_____   _____
Spouse   Spouse

Basic Employment History: Clubs, Church Affiliations, etc.:

_____   _____
Descendant   Descendant

_____   _____
Spouse   Spouse

Military Service:

_____   _____
Descendant   Spouse

M6241171313
_____
Genealogical Number

David Joseph Thomas   Johnson City, TN
_____   _____
Name (including maiden name if applicable)   Town of Residence

Baton Rouge, LA   1-28-2000
_____   _____   _____   _____
Birthplace   Date of Birth   Date of Death   Where Buried

_____   _____   _____   _____
Name of Spouse   Birthplace   Date of Birth   Date of Death

_____   _____   _____
Where Buried   Date of Marriage   Place of Marriage

If married more than once:

_____   _____   _____   _____
Name of Spouse   Birthplace   Date of Birth   Date of Death

_____   _____   _____
Where Buried   Date of Marriage   Place of Marriage

_____
Parents of Spouse (with Mother's maiden name) 1st Marriage

_____
Subsequent Marriage (if applicable)

Family Details

Schools attended, dates and degrees: Community, political work, etc.:

_____   _____
Descendant   Descendant

_____   _____
Spouse   Spouse

Basic Employment History: Clubs, Church Affiliations, etc.:

_____   _____
Descendant   Descendant

_____   _____
Spouse   Spouse

Military Service:

_____   _____
Descendant   Spouse

527

M624117132
_____
Genealogical Number

Mary Alexandra Thomas   Morrisville, NC
_____   _____
Name (including maiden name if applicable)   Town of Residence

Johnson City, TN   3-4-1971
_____   _____   _____   _____
Birthplace   Date of Birth   Date of Death   Where Buried

Timothy Andrew Holck   Willoughby, OH   11-29-1966
_____   _____   _____   _____
Name of Spouse   Birthplace   Date of Birth   Date of Death

                        5-17-2003   Johnson City, TN
_____   _____   _____   _____
Where Buried   Date of Marriage   Place of Marriage

If married more than once:

_____   _____   _____   _____
Name of Spouse   Birthplace   Date of Birth   Date of Death

_____   _____   _____
Where Buried   Date of Marriage   Place of Marriage

Miriam Irja Anlgren &Frederick George Holck
_____
Parents of Spouse (with Mother's maiden name) 1st Marriage

_____
Subsequent Marriage (if applicable)

Family Details

Schools attended, dates and degrees: Community, political work, etc.:
  Wofford College 1992 B.S.
_____   _____
Descendant   Descendant

Wofford College 1990 B.S.; Clemson 1992 MBA
_____   _____
Spouse   Spouse

Basic Employment History: Clubs, Church Affiliations, etc.:

_____   _____
Descendant   Descendant

_____   _____
Spouse   Spouse

Military Service:

_____   _____
Descendant   Spouse

M624117133
_____
Genealogical Number

William Gerald Thomas
_____
Name (including maiden name if applicable)

Johnson City, TN   10-15-1976
_____
Birthplace   Date of Birth

Johnson City, TN
_____
Town of Residence

Date of Death   Where Buried

Amy Joyce Wooten   Nashville, TN   1-2-1975
_____
Name of Spouse   Birthplace   Date of Birth   Date of Death

Where Buried   Date of Marriage   Place of Marriage

If married more than once:

Name of Spouse   Birthplace   Date of Birth   Date of Death

Where Buried   Date of Marriage   Place of Marriage

Thomas Edward Wooten & Margaret Eloise McCall
_____
Parents of Spouse (with Mother's maiden name) 1st Marriage

_____
Subsequent Marriage (if applicable)

Family Details

Schools attended, dates and degrees: Community, political work, etc.:
East Tennessee State University 1998 B.S.
_____
Descendant   Descendant
East Tennessee State University 1998 B.S.
_____
Spouse   Spouse

Basic Employment History: Clubs, Church Affiliations, etc.:

Descendant   Descendant

Spouse   Spouse

Military Service:

Descendant   Spouse

M62411714
_____
Genealogical Number

Stephen Early Steffey   Denver, CO
_____   _____
Name (including maiden name if applicable)   Town of Residence

Washington, D.C.   6-21-1949
_____ _____   _____   _____
Birthplace   Date of Birth   Date of Death   Where Buried

Sharron CC Perotti   Colorado Springs, CO   7-12-1945
_____ _____   _____   _____
Name of Spouse   Birthplace   Date of Birth   Date of Death

                     11-18-2000   Denver, CO
_____ _____   _____
Where Buried   Date of Marriage   Place of Marriage

If married more than once:

Lisa Gail Wood   Johnson City, TN   3-9-1956
_____ _____   _____   _____
Name of Spouse   Birthplace   Date of Birth   Date of Death

                     5-17-1979   Johnson City, TN
_____ _____   _____
Where Buried   Date of Marriage   Place of Marriage

Paul Wood & June Daughty
_____
Parents of Spouse (with Mother's maiden name) 1st Marriage

Lawrence Perotti & Eileen Quinn
_____
Subsequent Marriage (if applicable)

Family Details

Schools attended, dates and degrees: Community, political work, etc.:
ETSU, 1980, B.S. Electronics
_____   _____
Descendant   Descendant
Seattle Univ., 1967, BA;
University of Denver, 1987, MS
_____   _____
Spouse   Spouse

Basic Employment History: Clubs, Church Affiliations, etc.:

_____   _____
Descendant   Descendant

_____   _____
Spouse   Spouse

Military Service:
US Navy 1968-1972
_____   _____
Descendant   Spouse

M624117141
_____
Genealogical Number

Allison Leigh Steffey   Atlanta, GA
_____   _____
Name (including maiden name if applicable)   Town of Residence

Elizabethton, TN   9-2-1981
_____   _____   _____   _____
Birthplace   Date of Birth   Date of Death   Where Buried

_____   _____   _____   _____
Name of Spouse   Birthplace   Date of Birth   Date of Death

_____   _____   _____
Where Buried   Date of Marriage   Place of Marriage

If married more than once:

_____   _____   _____   _____
Name of Spouse   Birthplace   Date of Birth   Date of Death

_____   _____   _____
Where Buried   Date of Marriage   Place of Marriage

_____
Parents of Spouse (with Mother's maiden name) 1st Marriage

_____
Subsequent Marriage (if applicable)

Family Details

Schools attended, dates and degrees: Community, political work, etc.:

_____   _____
Descendant   Descendant

_____   _____
Spouse   Spouse

Basic Employment History: Clubs, Church Affiliations, etc.:

_____   _____
Descendant   Descendant

_____   _____
Spouse   Spouse

Military Service:

_____   _____
Descendant   Spouse

M6241172

Genealogical Number

Robert Floyd Jackson   Salem, VA

Name (including maiden name if applicable)   Town of Residence

Saltville, VA	5-21-1921		
Birthplace	Date of Birth	Date of Death	Where Buried
Ethel Marie Goad	Hillsville, VA	1-9-1922	
Name of Spouse	Birthplace	Date of Birth	Date of Death

Where Buried	Date of Marriage	Place of Marriage

If married more than once:

Name of Spouse	Birthplace	Date of Birth	Date of Death

Where Buried	Date of Marriage	Place of Marriage

Parents of Spouse (with Mother's maiden name) 1st Marriage

Subsequent Marriage (if applicable)

Family Details

Schools attended, dates and degrees: Community, political work, etc.:

Medical College of VA, School of Dentistry (Honors)

Descendant	Descendant

Spouse	Spouse

Basic Employment History: Clubs, Church Affiliations, etc.:
Navy Dental Corp, 1945-6; Retired from Private
Dental Practice 1983

Descendant	Descendant

Spouse	Spouse

Military Service:
Navy Dental Corp in Korea
Navy Reserve 38 years

Descendant	Spouse

M6241173

Genealogical Number

Rush Cecil Jackson   San Antonio, TX

Name (including maiden name if applicable)   Town of Residence

Emory, VA   9-11-1922

Birthplace   Date of Birth   Date of Death   Where Buried

Seawillow Umbarger Henderson   Wytheville, VA   7-18-1925

Name of Spouse   Birthplace   Date of Birth   Date of Death

                       3-16-1946

Where Buried   Date of Marriage   Place of Marriage

If married more than once:

Name of Spouse   Birthplace   Date of Birth   Date of Death

Where Buried   Date of Marriage   Place of Marriage

Parents of Spouse (with Mother's maiden name) 1st Marriage

Subsequent Marriage (if applicable)

Family Details

Schools attended, dates and degrees: Community, political work, etc.:

Descendant   Descendant

Spouse   Spouse

Basic Employment History: Clubs, Church Affiliations, etc.:

Descendant   Descendant

Spouse   Spouse

Military Service:

Merchant Marines 1941-1946

Descendant   Spouse

M62411731

Genealogical Number

Patricia Kay Jackson   San Antonio, Texas

Name (including maiden name if applicable)   Town of Residence

Roanoke, VA   12/30/1953

Birthplace   Date of Birth   Date of Death   Where Buried

Mark W. Mangus   Detroit, MI   1/18/1952

Name of Spouse   Birthplace   Date of Birth   Date of Death

                     8/13/1977   San Antonio, TX

Where Buried   Date of Marriage   Place of Marriage

If married more than once:

N/A

Name of Spouse   Birthplace   Date of Birth   Date of Death

Where Buried   Date of Marriage   Place of Marriage

Robert Stacey Mangus, Sr. & Lois Dupuis

Parents of Spouse (with Mother's maiden name) 1st Marriage

Subsequent Marriage (if applicable)

Family Details

Schools attended, dates and degrees: Community, political work, etc.:

On Back   Cystic Fibrosis Foundation

Descendant   Descendant

On Back   Cystic Fibrosis Foundation, EFFORTS

Spouse   Spouse

Basic Employment History: Clubs, Church Affiliations, etc.:

On Back   Church of Reconciliation

Descendant   Descendant

On Back   Church of Reconciliation

Spouse   Spouse

Military Service:

                                                U.S. Air Force 1970-1974

Descendant   Spouse

Schools attended, dates and degrees:

Descendant:	Washington & Lee High School	1968-1972	
	Mary Washington College	1972-1974	Pre-Nursing
	George Mason University	1974-1976	B.S. Nursing

Spouse:	Finey High School	1964-1970	
	San Antonio College	1975-1978	A.A.
	University of Texas, San Antonio	1978-1980	
	St. Phillips College	1980-1981	Certified in Res
	San Antonio College	1982-1984	Associate of Sc
	University of Texas, Health Science Center at San Antonio	1997-2000	B.S. in Respiral

Basic Employment Details:

Descendant:	Christus Santa Rosa Healthcare	1980-1990
	Travelers/Conservco	1991-1996
	Prudential Healthcare	1997-2000
	Christus Santa Rosa Healthcare	2000-present

Spouse:	Christus Santa Rosa Healthcare	1979-present

M624117311
Genealogical Number

Mark W. Mangus, Jr.   San Antonio, Texas
Name (including maiden name if applicable)   Town of Residence

San Antonio, Texas   2-17-1981
Birthplace   Date of Birth   Date of Death   Where Buried

Name of Spouse   Birthplace   Date of Birth   Date of Death

Where Buried   Date of Marriage   Place of Marriage

If married more than once:

Name of Spouse   Birthplace   Date of Birth   Date of Death

Where Buried   Date of Marriage   Place of Marriage

Parents of Spouse (with Mother's maiden name) 1st Marriage

Subsequent Marriage (if applicable)

Family Details

Schools attended, dates and degrees: Community, political work, etc.:

John Marshall High School 1995-1999
San Antonio College, 1999-2001   JROTC in High School
Descendant   Descendant

Spouse   Spouse

Basic Employment History: Clubs, Church Affiliations, etc.:
Starbucks, California Pizza Kitchen,   Church of Reconciliation, Lead singer for
Kinko's   the band - Losing Streak
Descendant   Descendant

Spouse   Spouse

Military Service:

Descendant   Spouse

M624117312
Genealogical Number

Kimberly Faith Mangus   San Antonio, Texas
Name (including maiden name if applicable)   Town of Residence

San Antonio, Texas   3/21/1982
Birthplace   Date of Birth   Date of Death   Where Buried

Name of Spouse   Birthplace   Date of Birth   Date of Death

Where Buried   Date of Marriage   Place of Marriage

If married more than once:

Name of Spouse   Birthplace   Date of Birth   Date of Death

Where Buried   Date of Marriage   Place of Marriage

Parents of Spouse (with Mother's maiden name) 1st Marriage

Subsequent Marriage (if applicable)

Family Details

Schools attended, dates and degrees: Community, political work, etc.:

John Marshall High School, 1996-1999
San Antonio College, 1999-Present   JROTC in High School
Descendant   Descendant

Spouse   Spouse

Basic Employment History: Clubs, Church Affiliations, etc.:
Souper Salads, Sonic, Starbucks,
Old Navy   Phi Theta Kappa
Descendant   Descendant

Spouse   Spouse

Military Service:

Descendant   Spouse

M6241174
Genealogical Number

Vivian Brown Jackson   Ocala, FLA
Name (including maiden name if applicable)   Town of Residence

Saltville, VA   7/26/1928
Birthplace   Date of Birth   Date of Death   Where Buried

John R. Lukas, MD   Detroit, Mich.   1/23/1913   4/24/1992
Name of Spouse   Birthplace   Date of Birth   Date of Death

Ocala, FLA   5/24/1974   Ocala, FLA
Where Buried   Date of Marriage   Place of Marriage

If married more than once:
Arthur M. Jones (Div)   Saltville, VA   2/21/1928   6/14/1973
Clarence Junior Schall   Kittanning, PA   3/13/1935   3/26/1973
Name of Spouse   Birthplace   Date of Birth   Date of Death

Marion, VA   10/16/1948   Alexandria, VA
Ocala, FLA   6/3/1961   Ocala, FLA
Where Buried   Date of Marriage   Place of Marriage

Arthur Jones & Lucy Shelley
Clarence Schall & Lillie
Parents of Spouse (with Mother's maiden name) 1st Marriage

_____
Subsequent Marriage (if applicable)

Family Details

Schools attended, dates and degrees: Community, political work, etc.:

_____   _____
Descendant   Descendant

_____   _____
Spouse   Spouse

Basic Employment History: Clubs, Church Affiliations, etc.:

_____   _____
Descendant   Descendant

_____   _____
Spouse   Spouse

Military Service:

_____   _____
Descendant   Spouse

M62411741
_____

Genealogical Number

Vivian Lee Jones   Jupiter, FLA
_____   _____
Name (including maiden name if applicable)   Town of Residence

Everett, Mass.   6-3-1951
_____   _____   _____   _____
Birthplace   Date of Birth   Date of Death   Where Buried

Edward Frank Garrity (DIV) Germany   8-8-1953
_____   _____ _____   _____
Name of Spouse   Birthplace   Date of Birth   Date of Death

                            7-25-1981   Gainesville, FLa
_____   _____ _____
Where Buried   Date of Marriage   Place of Marriage

If married more than once:

Howard Travis Bramblett(DIV) Dayton, Ohio   7-6-1951
_____   _____ _____   _____
Name of Spouse   Birthplace   Date of Birth   Date of Death

                              12-15-1972   Dunnellon, FLA
_____   _____ _____
Where Buried   Date of Marriage   Place of Marriage

_____
Parents of Spouse (with Mother's maiden name) 1st Marriage

_____
Subsequent Marriage (if applicable)

Family Details

Schools attended, dates and degrees: Community, political work, etc.:

_____   _____
Descendant   Descendant

_____   _____
Spouse   Spouse

Basic Employment History: Clubs, Church Affiliations, etc.:

_____   _____
Descendant   Descendant

_____   _____
Spouse   Spouse

Military Service:

_____   _____
Descendant   Spouse

539

M624117411
_____
Genealogical Number

Kristopher Travis Bramblett   Jupiter, FLA
_____   _____
Name (including maiden name if applicable)   Town of Residence

Fayetteville, NC   9-8-1974
_____   _____   _____   _____
Birthplace   Date of Birth   Date of Death   Where Buried

_____   _____   _____   _____
Name of Spouse   Birthplace   Date of Birth   Date of Death

_____   _____   _____
Where Buried   Date of Marriage   Place of Marriage

If married more than once:

_____   _____   _____   _____
Name of Spouse   Birthplace   Date of Birth   Date of Death

_____   _____   _____
Where Buried   Date of Marriage   Place of Marriage

_____
Parents of Spouse (with Mother's maiden name) 1st Marriage

_____
Subsequent Marriage (if applicable)

Family Details

Schools attended, dates and degrees: Community, political work, etc.:
Jupiter High School
_____   _____
Descendant   Descendant

_____   _____
Spouse   Spouse

Basic Employment History: Clubs, Church Affiliations, etc.:
Valentine Aquatics, Jupiter, FLA
_____   _____
Descendant   Descendant

_____   _____
Spouse   Spouse

Military Service:
US Army 1993-1996 (Bosnia & Mannheim, Germany
_____   _____
Descendant   Spouse

M624117412
_____
Genealogical Number

Marc Mahlon Bramblett   Jupiter, FLA
_____   _____
Name (including maiden name if applicable)   Town of Residence

Ocala, FLA   2-6-1977
_____   _____   _____   _____
Birthplace   Date of Birth   Date of Death   Where Buried

_____   _____   _____   _____
Name of Spouse   Birthplace   Date of Birth   Date of Death

_____   _____   _____
Where Buried   Date of Marriage   Place of Marriage

If married more than once:

_____   _____   _____   _____
Name of Spouse   Birthplace   Date of Birth   Date of Death

_____   _____   _____
Where Buried   Date of Marriage   Place of Marriage

_____
Parents of Spouse (with Mother's maiden name) 1st Marriage

_____
Subsequent Marriage (if applicable)

Family Details

Schools attended, dates and degrees: Community, political work, etc.:
Jupiter High School
_____   _____
Descendant   Descendant

_____   _____
Spouse   Spouse

Basic Employment History: Clubs, Church Affiliations, etc.:
Valentine Aquatics; Jupiter, FLA
_____   _____
Descendant   Descendant

_____   _____
Spouse   Spouse

Military Service:

_____   _____
Descendant   Spouse

M62411742
_____
Genealogical Number

Preston Arthur Jones   Lewisburg, TN
_____   _____
Name (including maiden name if applicable)   Town of Residence

Syracuse, NY   10-4-1952
_____   _____   _____   _____
Birthplace   Date of Birth   Date of Death   Where Buried

Cynthia L. Barnhart   Flint, Michigan   3-17-1960
_____   _____   _____   _____
Name of Spouse   Birthplace   Date of Birth   Date of Death

                    9-26-1981   Flint, Michigan
_____   _____   _____
Where Buried   Date of Marriage   Place of Marriage

If married more than once:

Charlotte L. Atherton (DIV)   Garden City, Michigan   2-24-1954
_____   _____   _____   _____
Name of Spouse   Birthplace   Date of Birth   Date of Death

                    1972   Aurora, CO
_____   _____   _____
Where Buried   Date of Marriage   Place of Marriage

_____
Parents of Spouse (with Mother's maiden name) 1st Marriage

_____
Subsequent Marriage (if applicable)

Family Details

Schools attended, dates and degrees: Community, political work, etc.:

_____   _____
Descendant   Descendant

_____   _____
Spouse   Spouse

Basic Employment History: Clubs, Church Affiliations, etc.:

_____   _____
Descendant   Descendant

_____   _____
Spouse   Spouse

Military Service:

_____   _____
Descendant   Spouse

M624117421

Genealogical Number

Preston Arthur Jones, Jr.   Flint, Michigan

Name (including maiden **name** if applicable)   Town of Residence

Tampa, FLA   8-8-1973

Birthplace   Date of Birth   Date of Death   Where Buried

Name of Spouse   Birthplace   Date of Birth   Date of Death

Where Buried   Date of Marriage   Place of Marriage

If married more than once:

Name of Spouse   Birthplace   Date of Birth   Date of Death

Where Buried   Date of Marriage   Place of Marriage

Parents of Spouse (with Mother's maiden name) 1st Marriage

Subsequent Marriage (if applicable)

Family Details

Schools attended, dates and degrees: Community, political work, etc.:

Mott Community College; Flint, Michigan

Descendant   Descendant

Spouse   Spouse

Basic Employment History: **Clubs, Church Affiliations, etc.:**

Descendant   Descendant

Spouse   Spouse

Military Service:

Descendant   Spouse

M624117422
_____
Genealogical Number

Christina Marie Jones   Lewisburg, TN
_____   _____
Name (including maiden name if applicable)   Town of Residence

Flint, Michigan   2-25-1983   3-26-1973   Ocala, FLA
_____   _____   _____   _____
Birthplace   Date of Birth   Date of Death   Where Buried

_____   _____   _____   _____
Name of Spouse   Birthplace   Date of Birth   Date of Death

_____   _____   _____
Where Buried   Date of Marriage Place of Marriage

If married more than once:

_____   _____   _____   _____
Name of Spouse   Birthplace   Date of Birth   Date of Death

_____   _____   _____
Where Buried   Date of Marriage Place of Marriage

_____
Parents of Spouse (with Mother's maiden name) 1st Marriage

_____
Subsequent Marriage (if applicable)

Family Details

Schools attended, dates and degrees: Community, political work, etc.:
Junior at University of Memphis, TN
_____   _____
Descendant   Descendant

_____   _____
Spouse   Spouse

Basic Employment History: Clubs, Church Affiliations, etc.:

_____   _____
Descendant   Descendant

_____   _____
Spouse   Spouse

Military Service:

_____   _____
Descendant   Spouse

M62411743
_____
Genealogical Number

Patrick Gheen Jones
_____
Name (including maiden name if applicable)

_____
Town of Residence

Syracuse, NY   10-16-1954   3-26-1973   Ocala, FLA
_____   _____   _____
Birthplace   Date of Birth   Date of Death   Where Buried

_____   _____   _____   _____
Name of Spouse   Birthplace   Date of Birth   Date of Death

_____   _____   _____
Where Buried   Date of Marriage   Place of Marriage

If married more than once:

_____   _____   _____   _____
Name of Spouse   Birthplace   Date of Birth   Date of Death

_____   _____   _____
Where Buried   Date of Marriage   Place of Marriage

_____
Parents of Spouse (with Mother's maiden name) 1st Marriage

_____
Subsequent Marriage (if applicable)

Family Details

Schools attended, dates and degrees: Community, political work, etc.:

_____   _____
Descendant   Descendant

_____   _____
Spouse   Spouse

Basic Employment History: Clubs, Church Affiliations, etc.:

_____   _____
Descendant   Descendant

_____   _____
Spouse   Spouse

Military Service:

_____   _____
Descendant   Spouse

M62411744
_____
Genealogical Number

Barbara Jo Schall   Gainesville, GA
_____   _____
Name (including maiden name if applicable)   Town of Residence

Ocala, FLA   1-20-1962
_____   _____   _____   _____
Birthplace   Date of Birth   Date of Death   Where Buried

Michael Greg Jarrard   Gainesville, FLA   10-22-1962
_____   _____   _____   _____
Name of Spouse   Birthplace   Date of Birth   Date of Death

                       9-1-1990   Gainesville, GA
_____   _____   _____
Where Buried   Date of Marriage   Place of Marriage

If married more than once:

Phillip Lamar Beatty   Gainesville, FLA   11-24-1960   11-27-1989
_____   _____   _____   _____
Name of Spouse   Birthplace   Date of Birth   Date of Death

Gainesville, GA   4-18-1986   Gainesville, GA
_____   _____   _____
Where Buried   Date of Marriage   Place of Marriage

Edward Lamar Beatty / Ruby Neil Landrum
_____
Parents of Spouse (with Mother's maiden name) 1st Marriage

_____
Subsequent Marriage (if applicable)

Family Details

Schools attended, dates and degrees: Community, political work, etc.:

_____   _____
Descendant   Descendant

_____   _____
Spouse   Spouse

Basic Employment History: Clubs, Church Affiliations, etc.:

_____   _____
Descendant   Descendant

_____   _____
Spouse   Spouse

Military Service:

_____   _____
Descendant   Spouse

M624117441
Genealogical Number

Kyle Lamar Beatty-Jarrard
Name (including maiden name if applicable)

Gainesville, GA
Town of Residence

Gainesville, GA   5/31/1986
Birthplace   Date of Birth

Date of Death   Where Buried

Name of Spouse   Birthplace   Date of Birth   Date of Death

Where Buried   Date of Marriage   Place of Marriage

If married more than once:

Name of Spouse   Birthplace   Date of Birth   Date of Death

Where Buried   Date of Marriage   Place of Marriage

Parents of Spouse (with Mother's maiden name) 1st Marriage

Subsequent Marriage (if applicable)

Family Details

Schools attended, dates and degrees: Community, political work, etc.:

Senior at Chestatee H.S., Gainesville, GA
Descendant   Descendant

Spouse   Spouse

Basic Employment History: Clubs, Church Affiliations, etc.:

Descendant   Descendant

Spouse   Spouse

Military Service:

Descendant   Spouse

M624117442
Genealogical Number

Brittany Nicole Beatty-Jarrad
Name (including maiden name if applicable)

Gainesville, GA
Town of Residence

Gainesville, GA   1/20/1988
Birthplace   Date of Birth

Date of Death   Where Buried

Name of Spouse   Birthplace   Date of Birth   Date of Death

Where Buried   Date of Marriage   Place of Marriage

If married more than once:

Name of Spouse   Birthplace   Date of Birth   Date of Death

Where Buried   Date of Marriage   Place of Marriage

Parents of Spouse (with Mother's maiden name) 1st Marriage

Subsequent Marriage (if applicable)

Family Details

Schools attended, dates and degrees: Community, political work, etc.:

Sophmore at Chestatee H.S.,
Gainesville, GA
Descendant   Descendant

Spouse   Spouse

Basic Employment History: Clubs, Church Affiliations, etc.:

Descendant   Descendant

Spouse   Spouse

Military Service:

Descendant   Spouse

M624117443
Genealogical Number

Katlyn Tiffany Jarrard
Name (including maiden name if applicable)

Gainesville, GA
Town of Residence

Gainesville, GA
Birthplace

6/26/1982
Date of Birth

Date of Death

Where Buried

Name of Spouse

Birthplace

Date of Birth

Date of Death

Where Buried

Date of Marriage

Place of Marriage

If married more than once:

Name of Spouse

Birthplace

Date of Birth

Date of Death

Where Buried

Date of Marriage

Place of Marriage

Parents of Spouse (with Mother's maiden name) 1st Marriage

Subsequent Marriage (if applicable)

Family Details

Schools attended, dates and degrees:

Community, political work, etc.:

Student at Sardi's Elementary School, Gainesville, GA
Descendant

Descendant

Spouse

Spouse

Basic Employment History:

Clubs, Church Affiliations, etc.:

Descendant

Descendant

Spouse

Spouse

Military Service:

Descendant

Spouse

M62421822
_____
Genealogical Number

Angela J. Caudill   Bluefield, West VA
_____   _____
Name (including maiden name if applicable)   **Town of Residence**

Bluefield, West VA   12-16-1954
_____   _____   _____   _____
Birthplace   **Date of Birth**   **Date of Death**   **Where Buried**

Ronald B. McCall   Bluefield, West VA   12-19-1949
_____   _____   _____   _____
Name of Spouse   **Birthplace**   **Date of Birth**   **Date of Death**

                       5-7-1977   Bluefield, West VA
_____   _____   _____
Where Buried   **Date of Marriage**   **Place of Marriage**

If married more than once:

_____   _____   _____   _____
Name of Spouse   **Birthplace**   **Date of Birth**   **Date of Death**

_____   _____   _____
Where Buried   **Date of Marriage**   **Place of Marriage**

Gene B & Jo Ann (Boyd) Caudill
_____
Parents of Spouse (with Mother's maiden name) 1st Marriage

_____
Subsequent Marriage (if applicable)

Family Details

Schools attended, dates and degrees:	Community, political work, etc.:
Bluefield High School	Chamber of Commerce
Descendant	Descendant
Graham High School	Westminster Brass
Spouse	Spouse

Basic Employment History:	Clubs, Church Affiliations, etc.:
Frontier	Westminster Presbyterian
Descendant	Descendant
Airgas Mid-Am	Westminster Presbyterian
Spouse	Spouse

Military Service:

_____   _____
Descendant   Spouse

M62425113
_____
Genealogical Number

James E. Sells   Bristol, TN
_____   _____
Name (including maiden name if applicable)   Town of Residence

Princeton, West VA   7-13-1945
_____   _____   _____   _____
Birthplace   Date of Birth   Date of Death   Where Buried

Becky Campbell - (Div.)
_____   _____   _____   _____
Name of Spouse   Birthplace   Date of Birth   Date of Death

_____   _____   _____
Where Buried   Date of Marriage   Place of Marriage

If married more than once:

_____   _____   _____   _____
Name of Spouse   Birthplace   Date of Birth   Date of Death

_____   _____   _____
Where Buried   Date of Marriage   Place of Marriage

_____
Parents of Spouse (with Mother's maiden name) 1st Marriage

_____
Subsequent Marriage (if applicable)

Family Details

Schools attended, dates and degrees: Community, political work, etc.:

East Tennesse State University, 1972, B.S.
_____   _____
Descendant   Descendant

_____   _____
Spouse   Spouse

Basic Employment History: Clubs, Church Affiliations, etc.:
Commonwealth Community Bank, VP Real Estate Division, 5 years
Charter Federal Savings Bank, 25 years
_____   _____
Descendant   Descendant

_____   _____
Spouse   Spouse

Military Service:

US Army, 1966 - 1969
_____   _____
Descendant   Spouse

M62425151
Genealogical Number

Margaret Ann Wajick   Petersburg, VA
Name (including maiden name if applicable)   Town of Residence

                              8/6/1948
Birthplace   Date of Birth   Date of Death   Where Buried

Charles Green Lowrey   South Boston, VA   9/29/1940
Name of Spouse   Birthplace   Date of Birth   Date of Death

                              10/9/1982   Petersburg, VA
Where Buried   Date of Marriage   Place of Marriage

If married more than once:

Arthur Norris (Div)   Greene County, NC   1/3/1944
Name of Spouse   Birthplace   Date of Birth   Date of Death

                              1/13/1964   Prince George, VA
Where Buried   Date of Marriage   Place of Marriage

Walter Elmer Norris & Early Frizzell
Parents of Spouse (with Mother's maiden name) 1st Marriage

Subsequent Marriage (if applicable)

Family Details

Schools attended, dates and degrees: Community, political work, etc.:

Descendant   Descendant

Spouse   Spouse

Basic Employment History: Clubs, Church Affiliations, etc.:

Descendant   Descendant

Spouse   Spouse

Military Service:

Descendant   Spouse

M6242517
Genealogical Number

Margaret Baugh Leedy
Name (including maiden name if applicable)

Richmond, VA
Town of Residence

Vivian, West VA
Birthplace

1/26/1930
Date of Birth

Date of Death

Where Buried

William Harrison Rosen
Name of Spouse

Buckingham, VA
Birthplace

5/5/1923
Date of Birth

1/5/1992
Date of Death

Chesterfield, VA
Where Buried

7/7/1951
Date of Marriage

Salem, VA
Place of Marriage

If married more than once:

Name of Spouse

Birthplace

Date of Birth

Date of Death

Where Buried

Date of Marriage

Place of Marriage

William Henry Rosen & Mary Florence Garrett
Parents of Spouse (with Mother's maiden name) 1st Marriage

Subsequent Marriage (if applicable)

Family Details

Schools attended, dates and degrees:

Welch W.VA High School 1947; Graduated Lewis
Gale Hospital School of Nursing as RN
Descendant

Buckingham High School
Spouse

Basic Employment History:
Virginia Veterans Hospital and Chesterfield
Nursing Home
Descendant
Dupont
American Tobacco Company, 32 years.
Spouse

Military Service:

Descendant

Community, political work, etc.:

DAR (Scotchtown Chapter)
DAR#676965
Descendant

Spouse

Clubs, Church Affiliations, etc.:

Methodist
Descendant

Baptist/Methodist
Spouse

Army Air Corp & WWII Veteran
Spouse

M62425171
_____
Genealogical Number

Trudy Susan Rosen   Richmond, VA
_____   _____
Name (including maiden name if applicable)   Town of Residence

Richmond, VA   10-20-1952
_____   _____   _____   _____
Birthplace   Date of Birth   Date of Death   Where Buried

_____   _____   _____   _____
Name of Spouse   Birthplace   Date of Birth   Date of Death

_____   _____   _____
Where Buried   Date of Marriage   Place of Marriage

If married more than once:

_____   _____   _____   _____
Name of Spouse   Birthplace   Date of Birth   Date of Death

_____   _____   _____
Where Buried   Date of Marriage   Place of Marriage

_____
Parents of Spouse (with Mother's maiden name) 1st Marriage

_____
Subsequent Marriage (if applicable)

Family Details

Schools attended, dates and degrees: Community, political work, etc.:
Meadowbrook High School, Chesterfield, 1971
Virginia Commonwealth University, 1976, B.S. (Educ.)   DAR - Scotchtown Chapter; DAR # 681423
_____   _____
Descendant   Descendant

_____   _____
Spouse   Spouse

Basic Employment History: Clubs, Church Affiliations, etc.:
Health & PE Teacher, Gill School 1976-1979 & Philip Morris
1979-Present Supervisor, Analyst   Methodist
_____   _____
Descendant   Descendant

_____   _____
Spouse   Spouse

Military Service:

_____   _____
Descendant   Spouse

M62425172

Genealogical Number

Rebecca Dawn Rosen

Name (including maiden name if applicable)

Midlothian, VA

Town of Residence

Richmond, VA   6-18-1957

Birthplace   Date of Birth   Date of Death   Where Buried

Richard Earl Saunders   Richmond, VA   7-31-1955

Name of Spouse   Birthplace   Date of Birth   Date of Death

7-2-1977   Richmond, VA

Where Buried   Date of Marriage   Place of Marriage

If married more than once:

Name of Spouse   Birthplace   Date of Birth   Date of Death

Where Buried   Date of Marriage   Place of Marriage

Parents of Spouse (with Mother's maiden name) 1st Marriage

Subsequent Marriage (if applicable)

Family Details

Schools attended, dates and degrees: Community, political work, etc.:

Graduated Meadowbrook High School, 1975

Descendant   Descendant

Graduated Kennedy High School,1976

Spouse   Spouse

Basic Employment History: Clubs, Church Affiliations, etc.:

Descendant   Descendant

Spouse   Spouse

Military Service:

Descendant   Spouse

M624251721
_____
Genealogical Number

Jessica Nicole Saunders   Midlothian, VA
_____   _____
Name (including maiden name if applicable)   Town of Residence

Richmond, VA   9-29-1983
_____   _____   _____   _____
Birthplace   Date of Birth   Date of Death   Where Buried

_____   _____   _____   _____
Name of Spouse   Birthplace   Date of Birth   Date of Death

_____   _____   _____
Where Buried   Date of Marriage   Place of Marriage

If married more than once:

_____   _____   _____   _____
Name of Spouse   Birthplace   Date of Birth   Date of Death

_____   _____   _____
Where Buried   Date of Marriage   Place of Marriage

_____
Parents of Spouse (with Mother's maiden name) 1st Marriage

_____
Subsequent Marriage (if applicable)

Family Details

Schools attended, dates and degrees: Community, political work, etc.:
Graduated Manchester High School, 2003
Student - Longwood University
_____   _____
Descendant   Descendant

_____   _____
Spouse   Spouse

Basic Employment History: Clubs, Church Affiliations, etc.:
                                               Jobs Daughters, PHQ & M.M.
                                               Belmont United Methodist, Farmville United Methodist
_____   _____
Descendant   Descendant

_____   _____
Spouse   Spouse

Military Service:

_____   _____
Descendant   Spouse

M624251722
_____
Genealogical Number

Sara Amanda Saunders   Midlothian, VA
_____   _____
Name (including maiden name if applicable)   Town of Residence

Richmond, VA   9-29-1983
_____   _____   _____   _____
Birthplace   Date of Birth   Date of Death   Where Buried

_____   _____   _____   _____
Name of Spouse   Birthplace   Date of Birth   Date of Death

_____   _____   _____
Where Buried   Date of Marriage   Place of Marriage

If married more than once:

_____   _____   _____   _____
Name of Spouse   Birthplace   Date of Birth   Date of Death

_____   _____   _____
Where Buried   Date of Marriage   Place of Marriage

Parents of Spouse (with Mother's maiden name) 1st Marriage

_____
Subsequent Marriage (if applicable)

Family Details

Schools attended, dates and degrees: Community, political work, etc.:
Graduated Manchester High School, 2003
Student, Longwood University
_____   _____
Descendant   Descendant

_____   _____
Spouse   Spouse

Basic Employment History: Clubs, Church Affiliations, etc.:
                                           Jobs Daughters, PHQ & M.M.
                                           Belmont United Methodist, Farmville United Methodist
_____   _____
Descendant   Descendant

_____   _____
Spouse   Spouse

Military Service:

_____   _____
Descendant   Spouse

557

M62425174
Genealogical Number

Wendy Gail Rosen   Richmond, VA
Name (including maiden name if applicable)   Town of Residence

Richmond, VA   6/18/1961
Birthplace   Date of Birth   Date of Death   Where Buried

Name of Spouse   Birthplace   Date of Birth   Date of Death

Where Buried   Date of Marriage   Place of Marriage

If married more than once:

Name of Spouse   Birthplace   Date of Birth   Date of Death

Where Buried   Date of Marriage   Place of Marriage

Parents of Spouse (with Mother's maiden name) 1st Marriage

Subsequent Marriage (if applicable)

Family Details

Schools attended, dates and degrees: Community, political work, etc.:
J.G. Hening Elem., Falling Creek Middle
Meadowbrook High School
Virginia Commonwealth University 1984 B.M.E. (Music Educ.)
Virginia Commonwealth University 2002 M.M.E. (Music Educ.)
Descendant   Descendant

Spouse   Spouse

Basic Employment History: Clubs, Church Affiliations, etc.:
Marymount School - 3 Years
Chesterfield County Public Elementary   Belmont United Methodist Church,
Schools 13 Yrs. (Music Specialist)   Youth Member of Sing Out South.
Descendant   Descendant

Spouse   Spouse

Military Service:

Descendant   Spouse

M62432111

Genealogical Number

Nancy Scott Lunsford

Name (including maiden name if applicable)

Fogelsville, PA

Town of Residence

Washington, D.C.	10-3-1942		
Birthplace	Date of Birth	Date of Death	Where Buried

James Russell Miltenberger	Johnston, PA	9-6-1936	
Name of Spouse	Birthplace	Date of Birth	Date of Death

Where Buried	Date of Marriage	Place of Marriage

If married more than once:

Name of Spouse	Birthplace	Date of Birth	Date of Death

Where Buried	Date of Marriage	Place of Marriage

Parents of Spouse (with Mother's maiden name) 1st Marriage

Subsequent Marriage (if applicable)

Family Details

Schools attended, dates and degrees:

Muhlenberg College, 1984, B.A.

Community, political work, etc.:

Descendant	Descendant

Penn State University, 1958, B.S.; RPA Master in Management 1970

Spouse	Spouse

Basic Employment History:

Realtor, 1984 - Present

Clubs, Church Affiliations, etc.:

Asbury United Methodist Church

Descendant	Descendant

Retired Military (20 Years) & Retired Engineer w/PPL Utility   Asbury United Methodist Church

Spouse	Spouse

Military Service:

Retired Navy Commander

Descendant	Spouse

M624321111
_____
Genealogical Number

William Martin Miltenberger   Los Angeles, CA
_____   _____
Name (including maiden name if applicable)   Town of Residence

Springfield, MA   12-8-1967
_____   _____   _____   _____
Birthplace   Date of Birth   Date of Death   Where Buried

_____   _____   _____   _____
Name of Spouse   Birthplace   Date of Birth   Date of Death

_____   _____   _____
Where Buried   Date of Marriage   Place of Marriage

If married more than once:

_____   _____   _____   _____
Name of Spouse   Birthplace   Date of Birth   Date of Death

_____   _____   _____
Where Buried   Date of Marriage   Place of Marriage

_____
Parents of Spouse (with Mother's maiden name) I^st Marriage

_____
Subsequent Marriage (if applicable)

Family Details

Schools attended, dates and degrees: Community, political work, etc.:

Penn State University, 1989
_____   _____
Descendant   Descendant

_____   _____
Spouse   Spouse

Basic Employment History: Clubs, Church Affiliations, etc.:

Marketing
_____   _____
Descendant   Descendant

_____   _____
Spouse   Spouse

Military Service:

_____   _____
Descendant   Spouse

M62432122
Genealogical Number

Deborah Ruth Scott
Name (including maiden name if applicable)

Ft. Lauderdale, FL
Town of Residence

Baltimore, MD
Birthplace

2/14/1954
Date of Birth

Date of Death

Where Buried

Lawrence George Queenin
Name of Spouse

Staten Island, NY
Birthplace

5/10/1945
Date of Birth

Date of Death

Where Buried

5/9/1981
Date of Marriage

Timonium, MD
Place of Marriage

If married more than once:

Name of Spouse

Birthplace

Date of Birth

Date of Death

Where Buried

Date of Marriage

Place of Marriage

Frances E. Cofer and Marre A. Queenin
Parents of Spouse (with Mother's maiden name) 1st Marriage

Subsequent Marriage (if applicable)

Family Details

Schools attended, dates and degrees:

Community, political work, etc.:

Descendant

Descendant

Spouse

Spouse

Basic Employment History:

Clubs, Church Affiliations, etc.:

Descendant

Descendant

Spouse

Spouse

Military Service:

Descendant

Spouse

M62432322
_____
Genealogical Number

Judith Ann Scott   Christiansburg, VA
_____   _____
Name (including maiden name if applicable)   Town of Residence

Washington, D.C.   1-20-1945
_____   _____   _____   _____
Birthplace   Date of Birth   Date of Death   Where Buried

Warren Pratt Self   Fredericksburg, VA   2-26-1943
_____   _____   _____   _____
Name of Spouse   Birthplace   Date of Birth   Date of Death

                        6-3-1966   Lithia, VA
_____   _____   _____
Where Buried   Date of Marriage   Place of Marriage

If married more than once:

_____   _____   _____   _____
Name of Spouse   Birthplace   Date of Birth   Date of Death

_____   _____   _____
Where Buried   Date of Marriage   Place of Marriage

Frank Matthew & Arline Oceil Smith Self
_____
Parents of Spouse (with Mother's maiden name) 1st Marriage

_____
Subsequent Marriage (if applicable)

Family Details

Schools attended, dates and degrees: Community, political work, etc.:

Please see back   5 Books published about teaching English or writing
_____   _____
Descendant   Descendant

Please see back
_____   _____
Spouse   Spouse

Basic Employment History: **Clubs, Church Affiliations, etc.:**

Please see back   Phi Kappa Phi, Anglican Church
_____   _____
Descendant   Descendant

 Please see back
_____   _____
Spouse   Spouse

Military Service:

                            1st Lieutenant for US Army, Vietnam Veteran 1967 - 1969
_____   _____
Descendant   Spouse

Schools attended, dates and degrees:

| Descendant: | Radford College | B.S. |
| | Radford College | M.S. |

Spouse:	VMI	1965 B.A. English
	University of Virginia	1967 M.A. English Lit.
	Virginia Tech	1978 E.D.D. Higher Educati

Basic Employment History:

Descendant: Teacher - 15 years
State Regional, local education administration - 15 years

Spouse:	Radford University:	1968-1984	Professor of English
		1984-1989	Department Chair
		1989-2002	Assistant Vice President
		2002-Now	VP for Academic Affairs

M624323222
Genealogical Number

Michelle Leigh Self   Rydal, GA
Name (including maiden name if applicable)   Town of Residence

Radford, VA   1/21/1970
Birthplace   Date of Birth   Date of Death   Where Buried

Mark Thomas Rackley   Austin, Texas   12/15/1968
Name of Spouse   Birthplace   Date of Birth   Date of Death

                        8/13/1994   Emory, VA
Where Buried   Date of Marriage   Place of Marriage

If married more than once:

Name of Spouse   Birthplace   Date of Birth   Date of Death

Where Buried   Date of Marriage   Place of Marriage

Frank & Johnnye Zumwalt Rackley
Parents of Spouse (with Mother's maiden name) 1st Marriage

Subsequent Marriage (if applicable)

Family Details

Schools attended, dates and degrees: Community, political work, etc.:

Please see back   _____
Descendant   Descendant

Please see back   _____
Spouse   Spouse

Basic Employment History: Clubs, Church Affiliations, etc.:
Minister, Cowan Presbyterian Church
(Tenn.) Homemaker Presently.   _____
Descendant   Descendant
Minister, Bartow Presbyterian Church
(GA)   _____
Spouse   Spouse

Military Service:

_____   _____
Descendant   Spouse

Schools attended, dates, and degrees:

Descendant:

Emory & Henry College	1990 B.A.
Union Theological Seminary	1994 MDIV
Presbyterian School of Christian Education	1994 M.S.

Spouse:

Bethel College	1988 B.S.
Union Theological Seminary	1993 MDIV
Presbyterian School of Christian Education	1993 M.S.

M6243232221
_____
Genealogical Number

Sarah Catherine Rackley   Rydal, GA
_____   _____
Name (including maiden name if applicable) Town of Residence

                        8-6-2000
                     _____
_____   _____   _____   _____
Birthplace   Date of Birth   Date of Death   Where Buried

_____   _____   _____   _____
Name of Spouse Birthplace   Date of Birth   Date of Death

_____   _____   _____
Where Buried   Date of Marriage   Place of Marriage

If married more than once:

_____   _____   _____   _____
Name of Spouse Birthplace   Date of Birth   Date of Death

_____   _____   _____
Where Buried   Date of Marriage   Place of Marriage

_____
Parents of Spouse (with Mother's maiden name) 1st Marriage

_____
Subsequent Marriage (if applicable)

Family Details

Schools attended, dates and degrees: Community, political work, etc.:

_____   _____
Descendant   Descendant

_____   _____
Spouse   Spouse

Basic Employment History: Clubs, Church Affiliations, etc.:

_____   _____
Descendant   Descendant

_____   _____
Spouse   Spouse

Military Service:

_____   _____
Descendant   Spouse

M6243232222
Genealogical Number

Paul William Rackley
Name (including maiden name if applicable)

Rydal, Ga.
Town of Residence

Birthplace

6/30/2002
Date of Birth

Date of Death

Where Buried

Name of Spouse

Birthplace

Date of Birth

Date of Death

Where Buried

Date of Marriage

Place of Marriage

If married more than once:

Name of Spouse

Birthplace

Date of Birth

Date of Death

Where Buried

Date of Marriage

Place of Marriage

Parents of Spouse (with Mother's maiden name) 1st Marriage

Subsequent Marriage (if applicable)

Family Details

Schools attended, dates and degrees:

Community, political work, etc.:

Descendant

Descendant

Spouse

Spouse

Basic Employment History:

Clubs, Church Affiliations, etc.:

Descendant

Descendant

Spouse

Spouse

Military Service:

Descendant

Spouse

M62432323

Genealogical Number

Cynthia Rose Scott   Roanoke, VA

Name (including maiden name if applicable)   Town of Residence

Pearisburg, VA   8-26-1949

Birthplace   Date of Birth   Date of Death   Where Buried

Thomas Craddock   Roanoke, VA   4-30-1952

Name of Spouse   Birthplace   Date of Birth   Date of Death

                    1-19-1974   Trinity Episcopal Church; Buchanan, VA

Where Buried   Date of Marriage Place of Marriage

If married more than once:

Name of Spouse   Birthplace   Date of Birth   Date of Death

Where Buried   Date of Marriage Place of Marriage

Byron & Ann (Baier) Craddock

Parents of Spouse (with Mother's maiden name) 1st Marriage

Subsequent Marriage (if applicable)

Family Details

Schools attended, dates and degrees: Community, political work, etc.:
Buchanan Elem.; James River High School;
National Business College   Volunteer in school & sports for children
Descendant   Descendant
Northside High School
Virginia Western Community College   Volunteer in school & sports for children
Spouse   Spouse

Basic Employment History: Clubs, Church Affiliations, etc.:

Social Service Work   St. Philip Lutheran Church

Descendant   Descendant

Sales - Dental Equipment   St. Philip Lutheran Church

Spouse   Spouse

Military Service:

                                               Virginia National Guard, 10 years

Descendant   Spouse

M624323231
Genealogical Number

Katrina Craddock
Name (including maiden name if applicable)

Roanoke, VA
Town of Residence

Roanoke, VA
Birthplace

2/24/1986
Date of Birth

Date of Death

Where Buried

Name of Spouse

Birthplace

Date of Birth

Date of Death

Where Buried

Date of Marriage

Place of Marriage

If married more than once:

Name of Spouse

Birthplace

Date of Birth

Date of Death

Where Buried

Date of Marriage

Place of Marriage

Parents of Spouse (with Mother's maiden name) 1st Marriage

Subsequent Marriage (if applicable)

Family Details

Schools attended, dates and degrees:

Cloverdale Elem; Read Mountain Middle
Currently at James River High School
Descendant

Community, political work, etc.:
Girls State; Yousav
Traveled Abroad
Volunteer at Nursing Home,
Descendant

Spouse

Spouse

Basic Employment History:

Clubs, Church Affiliations, etc.:

Descendant

St. Philip Lutheran Church
Descendant

Spouse

Spouse

Military Service:

Descendant

Spouse

M6243271
_____

Genealogical Number

Patricia Ann Scott   Trappe, MD
_____   _____
Name (including maiden name if applicable)   Town of Residence

Baltimore, MD   8-4-1934
_____   _____   _____   _____
Birthplace   Date of Birth   Date of Death   Where Buried

Neal Holloway Jones   New Castle, PA   9-15-1931
_____   _____   _____   _____
Name of Spouse   Birthplace   Date of Birth   Date of Death

                       6-5-1952   Elkton, MD
_____   _____   _____
Where Buried   Date of Marriage   Place of Marriage

If married more than once:

_____   _____   _____   _____
Name of Spouse   Birthplace   Date of Birth   Date of Death

_____   _____   _____
Where Buried   Date of Marriage   Place of Marriage

_____
Parents of Spouse (with Mother's maiden name) 1st Marriage

_____
Subsequent Marriage (if applicable)

Family Details

Schools attended, dates and degrees: Community, political work, etc.:

 High School
_____   _____
Descendant   Descendant

 High School
_____   _____
Spouse   Spouse

 Basic Employment History: **Clubs, Church Affiliations, etc.:**
 Retired from Bank of America, 30 years   Quota International - Cambridge; Pres. UMW,
 Part-time Dorchester Chamber of Commerce   St. Marks, Easton
_____   _____
Descendant   Descendant
Retired from Eastern Airlines 30 years & from
MAD, (13 Yrs.) BWI Airport
_____   _____
Spouse   Spouse

 Military Service:

                                                US Army - Korean War
_____   _____
Descendant   Spouse

M62432712

Genealogical Number

N. Scott Jones

Name (including maiden name if applicable)

Bowie, MD

Town of Residence

Baltimore, MD   6-18-1955

Birthplace   Date of Birth   Date of Death   Where Buried

Julia L. Murphy   Cambridge, MD   2-12-1958

Name of Spouse   Birthplace   Date of Birth   Date of Death

                         6-10-1979   Cambridge, MD

Where Buried   Date of Marriage   Place of Marriage

If married more than once:

Name of Spouse   Birthplace   Date of Birth   Date of Death

Where Buried   Date of Marriage   Place of Marriage

Parents of Spouse (with Mother's maiden name) 1ˢᵗ Marriage

William E. Murphy, Jr. & Phyllis Gordon

Subsequent Marriage (if applicable)

Family Details

Schools attended, dates and degrees: Community, political work, etc.:

Descendant   Descendant

Spouse   Spouse

Basic Employment History: Clubs, Church Affiliations, etc.:

Descendant   Descendant

Spouse   Spouse

Military Service:

Descendant   Spouse

M624327121

Genealogical Number

Jennifer S. Jones   Bowie, MD

Name (including maiden name if applicable)   Town of Residence

Silver Spring, MD   2-14-1981

Birthplace   Date of Birth   Date of Death   Where Buried

Name of Spouse   Birthplace   Date of Birth   Date of Death

Where Buried   Date of Marriage   Place of Marriage

If married more than once:

Name of Spouse   Birthplace   Date of Birth   Date of Death

Where Buried   Date of Marriage   Place of Marriage

Parents of Spouse (with Mother's maiden name) 1st Marriage

Subsequent Marriage (if applicable)

Family Details

Schools attended, dates and degrees: Community, political work, etc.:

Descendant   Descendant

Spouse   Spouse

Basic Employment History: Clubs, Church Affiliations, etc.:

Descendant   Descendant

Spouse   Spouse

Military Service:

Descendant   Spouse

M624327122

Genealogical Number

Meghan R. Jones

Name (including maiden name if applicable)

Bowie, MD

Town of Residence

Silver Spring, MD   1-14-1988

| Birthplace | Date of Birth | Date of Death | Where Buried |

| Name of Spouse | Birthplace | Date of Birth | Date of Death |

| Where Buried | Date of Marriage | Place of Marriage |

If married more than once:

| Name of Spouse | Birthplace | Date of Birth | Date of Death |

| Where Buried | Date of Marriage | Place of Marriage |

Parents of Spouse (with Mother's maiden name) 1st Marriage

Subsequent Marriage (if applicable)

Family Details

Schools attended, dates and degrees: Community, political work, etc.:

Descendant   Descendant

Spouse   Spouse

Basic Employment History: Clubs, Church Affiliations, etc.:

Descendant   Descendant

Spouse   Spouse

Military Service:

Descendant   Spouse

M6246822
_____
Genealogical Number

Robin Taylor Brown   Vinton, VA
_____   _____
Name (including maiden name if applicable)   Town of Residence

Roanoke, VA   5-13-1964
_____   _____   _____   _____
Birthplace   Date of Birth   Date of Death   Where Buried

Jonathan Dudley Merchant Richmond, VA   4-17-1963
_____   _____   _____   _____
Name of Spouse   Birthplace   Date of Birth   Date of Death

                          8-18-1990   Roanoke, VA
_____   _____   _____
Where Buried   Date of Marriage   Place of Marriage

If married more than once:

_____   _____   _____   _____
Name of Spouse   Birthplace   Date of Birth   Date of Death

_____   _____   _____
Where Buried   Date of Marriage   Place of Marriage

Alton Merchant & Linda Schultz
_____
Parents of Spouse (with Mother's maiden name) 1st Marriage

_____
Subsequent Marriage (if applicable)

Family Details

Schools attended, dates and degrees: Community, political work, etc.:

University of Virginia B.A. 1987   PTA
_____   _____
Descendant   Descendant

VA Western Community College A.A. & A.S. 1985   Cub Scout Den Leader
_____   _____
Spouse   Spouse

Basic Employment History: Clubs, Church Affiliations, etc.:
Children Coordinator at Battered Womens Shelter   Community Advent Christian Church
Music Teacher
_____   _____
Descendant   Descendant

Automotive Mechanic   Community Advent Christian Church
_____   _____
Spouse   Spouse

Military Service:

                                                  US Army, Texas, 1980s
_____   _____
Descendant   Spouse

M62468221
_____
Genealogical Number

Jeffrey Thomas Merchant　　　　　Vinton, VA
_____　　　　　_____
Name (including maiden name if applicable)　　Town of Residence

Roanoke, VA　　　11-2-1995
_____　_____　　_____　_____
Birthplace　　　Date of Birth　　Date of Death　　Where Buried

_____　_____　　_____　_____
Name of Spouse　　Birthplace　　　Date of Birth　　Date of Death

_____　_____　　_____
Where Buried　　Date of Marriage　　Place of Marriage

If married more than once:

_____　_____　　_____　_____
Name of Spouse　　Birthplace　　　Date of Birth　　Date of Death

_____　_____　　_____
Where Buried　　Date of Marriage　　Place of Marriage

_____
Parents of Spouse (with Mother's maiden name) 1st Marriage

_____
Subsequent Marriage (if applicable)

Family Details

Schools attended, dates and degrees:　　　Community, political work, etc.:

_____　　　　　_____
Descendant　　　　　　　Descendant

_____　　　　　_____
Spouse　　　　　　　　Spouse

Basic Employment History:　　　　Clubs, Church Affiliations, etc.:

_____　　　　　_____
Descendant　　　　　　　Descendant

_____　　　　　_____
Spouse　　　　　　　　Spouse

Military Service:

_____　　　　　_____
Descendant　　　　　　　Spouse

575

M62468222
Genealogical Number

Christopher Scott Merchant   Vinton, VA
Name (including maiden name if applicable)   Town of Residence

Salem, VA   2-29-2000
Birthplace   Date of Birth   Date of Death   Where Buried

Name of Spouse   Birthplace   Date of Birth   Date of Death

Where Buried   Date of Marriage   Place of Marriage

If married more than once:

Name of Spouse   Birthplace   Date of Birth   Date of Death

Where Buried   Date of Marriage   Place of Marriage

Parents of Spouse (with Mother's maiden name) 1st Marriage

Subsequent Marriage (if applicable)

Family Details

Schools attended, dates and degrees: Community, political work, etc.:

Descendant   Descendant

Spouse   Spouse

Basic Employment History: Clubs, Church Affiliations, etc.:

Descendant   Descendant

Spouse   Spouse

Military Service:

Descendant   Spouse

M6246832
_____

Genealogical Number

Michael Fortunato Brown

Welch, West VA
_____

Name (including maiden name if applicable)

Town of Residence

Kimball, West VA   10-9-1951
_____

Birthplace   Date of Birth   Date of Death   Where Buried

Wanda Chapman   Saltville, VA   3-24-1954

Name of Spouse   Birthplace   Date of Birth   Date of Death

6-18-1972   Kimball, West VA
_____

Where Buried   Date of Marriage   Place of Marriage

If married more than once:

_____

Name of Spouse   Birthplace   Date of Birth   Date of Death

_____

Where Buried   Date of Marriage   Place of Marriage

Clyde H. & Verna Hattie Woodard Chapman
_____

Parents of Spouse (with Mother's maiden name) 1st Marriage

_____

Subsequent Marriage (if applicable)

Family Details

Schools attended, dates and degrees:
Kimball Elem.; Keystone & Kimball Jr. High;
Welch High School
_____

Descendant

Welch Elem, Jr. High & High School
_____

Spouse

Community, political work, etc.:

Kimball Fire Dept 35 years, Chief for 16 years
_____

Descendant

_____

Spouse

Basic Employment History:
School Bus Driver, Coal Prep. Plant Operator;
Apprentice Funeral Director
_____

Descendant

Secretary
_____

Spouse

Clubs, Church Affiliations, etc.:

Carswell Community Church, Member & Asst. Pastor
_____

Descendant

Carswell Community Church
_____

Spouse

Military Service:

_____

Descendant

_____

Spouse

M62468321
Genealogical Number

Christie Michelle Brown   Virginia Beach, VA
Name (including maiden name if applicable)   Town of Residence

Bluefield, West VA   1-24-1977
Birthplace   Date of Birth   Date of Death   Where Buried

John Breazeale, III
Name of Spouse   Birthplace   Date of Birth   Date of Death

                            12-7-1995
Where Buried   Date of Marriage   Place of Marriage

If married more than once:

Name of Spouse   Birthplace   Date of Birth   Date of Death

Where Buried   Date of Marriage   Place of Marriage

Parents of Spouse (with Mother's maiden name) 1st Marriage

Subsequent Marriage (if applicable)

Family Details

Schools attended, dates and degrees: Community, political work, etc.:

Descendant   Descendant

Spouse   Spouse

Basic Employment History: Clubs, Church Affiliations, etc.:

Descendant   Descendant

Spouse   Spouse

Military Service:

Descendant   Spouse

M624683211
Genealogical Number

Ples John Breazeale, IV
Name (including maiden name if applicable)

Salamanca, NY
Town of Residence

Virginia Beach, VA
Birthplace

11/6/1996
Date of Birth

Date of Death

Where Buried

Name of Spouse

Birthplace

Date of Birth

Date of Death

Where Buried

Date of Marriage

Place of Marriage

If married more than once:

Name of Spouse

Birthplace

Date of Birth

Date of Death

Where Buried

Date of Marriage

Place of Marriage

Parents of Spouse (with Mother's maiden name) 1st Marriage

Subsequent Marriage (if applicable)

Family Details

Schools attended, dates and degrees:

Community, political work, etc.:

Descendant

Descendant

Spouse

Spouse

Basic Employment History:

Clubs, Church Affiliations, etc.:

Descendant

Descendant

Spouse

Spouse

Military Service:

Descendant

Spouse

M62483212
Genealogical Number

Allissa Genevieve Breazeale   Salamanca, NY
Name (including maiden name if applicable)   Town of Residence

Virginia Beach, VA   11-23-1997
Birthplace   Date of Birth   Date of Death   Where Buried

Name of Spouse   Birthplace   Date of Birth   Date of Death

Where Buried   Date of Marriage   Place of Marriage

If married more than once:

Name of Spouse   Birthplace   Date of Birth   Date of Death

Where Buried   Date of Marriage   Place of Marriage

Parents of Spouse (with Mother's maiden name) 1st Marriage

Subsequent Marriage (if applicable)

Family Details

Schools attended, dates and degrees: Community, political work, etc.:

Descendant   Descendant

Spouse   Spouse

Basic Employment History: Clubs, Church Affiliations, etc.:

Descendant   Descendant

Spouse   Spouse

Military Service:

Descendant   Spouse

M62468322
Genealogical Number

Robert Michael Brown   Glen Daniels, West VA
Name (including maiden name if applicable)   Town of Residence

Bluefield, West VA   12-16-1978
Birthplace   Date of Birth   Date of Death   Where Buried

Bobbie Jo Bailey   1-11-1981
Name of Spouse   Birthplace   Date of Birth   Date of Death

                            12-19-2001   Williamsburg, VA
Where Buried   Date of Marriage   Place of Marriage

If married more than once:

Name of Spouse   Birthplace   Date of Birth   Date of Death

Where Buried   Date of Marriage   Place of Marriage

Parents of Spouse (with Mother's maiden name) 1st Marriage

Subsequent Marriage (if applicable)

Family Details

Schools attended, dates and degrees: Community, political work, etc.:
Kimball Elem; Welch Jr. High School;
Mount View High School
Descendant   Descendant

Spouse   Spouse

Basic Employment History: Clubs, Church Affiliations, etc.:

US Navy, Machinist Mining Company   Kimbell Methodist Church
Descendant   Descendant

Spouse   Spouse

Military Service:

US Navy, 4 years
Descendant   Spouse

18.

THE JOSEPH ADDISON MOORE LINE
PICTURE

Martha Amanda Moore Bailey (M6242)   B. 1834 D._____

Picture taken in 1860

19.

The Milton Ladd Moore Line

The Milton Ladd Moore Line

Milton Ladd Moore was the sixth child of James Moore. Mr. John Greene of San Jose, California (M6242232) sent me a copy of an interesting letter of which I am reproducing part. The writer is Milton Moore, brother of Joseph Addison, and "Isaac" is the youngest child of James, the "Captive," Isaac Quinn.

When I was in Tazewell County in early July, my aunt, Margaret Wagner Lively gave me a letter that someone gave to her sister when the old Moore house was torn down. It appears to me to have been written by Milton Moore, in Missouri, to his father and mother, James and Nancy Moore in Abb's Valley.

I will copy it here (as written) but would like to know if the Tazewell County Historical Society would have some interest in having the letter. It is in pretty good shape except it has a tendency to tear where it is folded.

Bluff Grove Mo

March 19

> Mr James Moore Abbs Valley
> Tazewell County
> Virginia

Grundy County Mo Feb 28th 1841

Dear Father & Mother

At this late period I take my pen in hand to write to you for the first time.

I look back and recon time I find that ~~find that~~ four years and six months has roll'd round since I left the land of my nativity. Several excuses might be offored for not writing sooner. First I did not know where to direct my letter that it would find you. First I heart (sic) you had left the valley and mooved to russel (the next) from there to Sandy and I supposed you were still living there till ~~the~~ last fall the emegrants from Tazewell in formed me better. I have nothing new or particular to write. I suppose it is needless for me to descrite our country for you have heard the description so often and by different ones that it would be like telling over an old story let it suffise to say that in my opinion we have a first rate country and I believe a much better country than Tazewell. The soil is far superior and the face of the country is so smooth that it is a pleasant task to till the soil here in stid (sic)of a ~~task~~ burthen (sic). We can raise more grain of all kinds to the same quantity of ground and good for vegetables of all kinds.

I raised upwards of seven hundred bushels of corn this year under unfavorable circ umstances and without any assistance.

We have no rough rugged mountains to climb over and inter cept (sic) between neighborhoods but if we wish to visit a distant neighborhood we can steer our course through the prairie now and then crossing a skirt of timber without the use of a road. not withstanding our country cannot be called a level country the bluffs from the river and creeks rise from one to two hundred feet then opens out the prairie gradually spreading over the high divides which is our best farming land. I have 240 acres of land 160 in the prairie and 80 in the timber I live just in at the edge of the timber and farm entirely in the prairie if I was so minded I could fence the whole quarter (which is 160 acres) in one square field and plow the (sic) whole of it without the least inconveanance (sic). And as to health I believe we have the healthiest of the two countries for I have heard of five deaths ~~to one in~~ Tazewell to one here. I have been trying to farm since I have been in this country but I may engage in the brick r????? for the prep for work is considerable I am clear of debt have 240 acres of land 3 head of horses 7 head of cattle 34 head of hogs 7 head of sheep and a few chickens which composes my fortune. And I would add two of the finest little girls you ever saw. Virginia Columbus and Nancy Jane. The former is as fast as a pig and the ????? smartest thing on foot and with the tongue you ever saw, and her knowledge about domestic concerns surpasses those of riper years. The friends are all well and well pleased with the exception of Minor Winn he complains a little. James and Minor has bought joining 2 & 1/2 miles from here Minor got 240 acres for which he gave $1200 he has entered some 3 or 4 eighties at congress (?) price James got 560 acres at 24 hundred dollars and has entered some for 5 hundred acres more James is well pleased and sends his compliments to you Gibson bought 8 miles west on Sugarcreek.

Dr Still lives about 50 miles East I have not heard from them since last August they were well then.

I think if Isaac (younger brother) would come to this country it would by far be the best thing he could do, there the country is old and worn out and again a man with no property there has a dull chance to gather any particularly when he is unsettled and ~~again~~ a further he ~~can~~ cannot associate with the highest class of man for a man there without propety is look'd at with a degraded eye. Here it is entirely different, the country is fresh and so much superior wages is high anything of a hand can get from 12 to 16 dollars a month, party spirit does not run so high here if a man will act honorable (if he has not so much property) he is received in the best company. If he will come I think I can give him such a chance that in a few years he can purchase a cumfortable (sic) home which will be a great support in the decline of life (there I am sure he cannot procure such a home) James Winn will return to Virginia next fall and he can have a verry good chance for company, I expect to engage in the brick

This is the end of the page and the end of the material I have. I have tried to copy the letter exactly as it is written. If you would like to preserve the letter let me know. I think it is of historical signficance to Tazewell County and should be preserved. If there is a safe way of sending it let me know.

(The letter was sent to the Tazewell County Library in Tazewell, VA and lost!).

20.

THE MILTON LADD MOORE LINE
GENEALOGICAL CHART

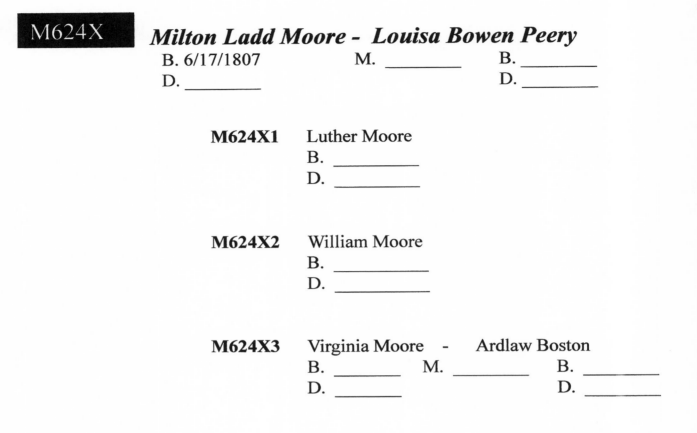

M624X   *Milton Ladd Moore - Louisa Bowen Peery*

B. 6/17/1807   M. _____   B. _____

D. _____   D. _____

M624X1   Luther Moore

B. _____

D. _____

M624X2   William Moore

B. _____

D. _____

M624X3   Virginia Moore   -   Ardlaw Boston

B. _____   M. _____   B. _____

D. _____   D. _____

21.

THE ANDREW PEERY MOORE LINE
GENEALOGICAL CHARTS

M625   *Andrew Peery Moore - Nancy Cummings*
B . 6/5/1808   M. 1/28/1841   B. 9/18/1819
D. 2/1/1869   D. 11/7/1899

M6251 - Flavins Joseph Moore
B. 3/16/1842
D. 8/6/1851

M6252 - John Columbus Moore - **M6292** Mary Jane Moore
B. 12/24/1852   M. 10/15/1874   B. 10/4/1852
D. 3/29/1887   D. 4/27/1937

M62521 - Andrew Edward Moore
B. 3/13/1876
D. 3/12/1930.

M62522 - Ida Marie Moore - **M62911** Hugh Edward Wilson
B. 4/7/1878   M. 11/25/1908   B. 3/17/1874
D. _____   D. _____

M625221 - Hazel Virginia Wilson
B. 11/9/1910
D. _____

M625222 - Mary Moore Wilson
B. 6/2/1913
D. _____

M62523 - James Herbert Moore - Sallie May Moss
B. 4/13/1882   M. _____   B. 3/12/1874
D. _____   D. 8/5/1931

M6253 - George Montraville Moore
B. 3/17/1855
D. 2/15/1884

M6254 - Princess Palmyra Moore - Charles Alexander Black
B. 6/13/1858   M. 11/17/1880   B. 8/2/1851
D. _____   D. 10/10/1937

M62541 - William Arthur Black
B. 12/7/1881
D. 5/31/1882

M62542 - Ora Lee Black - Henry William Stille
B. 5/7/1883   M. 6/10/1910   B. 8/17/1877
D. _____   D. 1/29/1919

M625421 - Charles Henry Stille - Laura Louise Perrin
    B. 12/22/1911   M. 4/1/1934   B. _____
    D. _____   D. _____

M6254211 - Charlene Louise Stille
    B. 8/31/1937

M62543 - Andrew Glen Black - Ethel Gertrude Thornton
    B. 6/22/1886   M. 1911   B. _____
    D. _____   D. _____

M62544 - Mary Jane Moore Black
    B. 9/12/1895
    D. 11/1/1896

M62545 - Charles Clinton Black - (#1) Vernon Donna Steele
    B. 3/25/1899   M. 6/1919   B. _____
    D. _____   M. 6/22/1935   D. _____

                         - (#2) Edith Margie Comstock
                              B. 10/21/1905
                              D. _____

M625451 - (#1) Bruce Beverly Black
    B. 12/31/1920

M625452 - (#1) Barbara Beryl Black
    B. 10/4/1922

21.

THE MARY B. MOORE LINE
GENEALOGICAL CHARTS

M626   ***Mary B. Moore - William Whitley***
B. 8/2/1810   M. 11/12/1829   B. _____
D. _____   D. _____

     M6261 - Elgan Lane Whitley - Frances Ann Whitman
         B. 8/28/1830   M. 2/12/1861   B. 1/20/1842
         D. 1917   D. _____

         M62611 - Ella Jackson Whitley - Robert Hendricks Ireson
             B. 1/11/1862   M. 2/29/1880   B. _____
             D. _____   D. _____

             M626111 - Robert Lane Ireson - (1) Laura Hall
                 B. _____   M. _____   B. _____
                 D. _____   D. _____

                           (2) Lettie Lauder
                                 B. _____
                                 D. _____

                 M6261111 - Earl Ireson(1)
                      B. _____
                      D. _____

             M626112 - Annie Lou Ireson
                 B. _____
                 D. _____

             M626113 - Eva May Ireson - Perle Thompson
                 B. _____   M. _____   B. _____
                 D. _____   D. _____

             M626114 - William Moore Ireson - (1) Nannie Denny
                 B. _____   (1)M. _____   B. _____
                 D. _____   (2)M. _____   D. _____

*Indicates that a bio is included.

             (2) Julia Fawbush
                 B. _____
                 D. _____

M626115 - Harvey Peery Ireson - Amelia Peery
     B. _____   M. _____   B. _____
     D. _____   D. _____

M626116 - Robert StClair Ireson
     B. _____
     D. _____

M626117 - Janie Gray Ireson - (1) Charles F. Yates
     B. _____   (1)M. _____   B. _____
     D. _____   (2)M. _____   D. _____

             (2) Jay A. Robins
                 B. _____
                 D. _____

M626118 - Rosalie StClair Ireson
     B. _____
     D. _____

M62612 - William Addison Whitley - Cosby Harrison
   B. 9/23/1864   M. 9/10/1885   B. 1867
   D. _____   D. _____

M626121 - Fannie Ann Whitley - C.G. Williamson
       B. 8/7/1886   M. _____   B. _____
       D. 2/13/1912   D. _____

M626122 - Nellie Rose Whitley - H.A. Vawter
      B. 3/1890   M. 6/24/1914   B. _____
      D. _____   D. _____

M6261221 - Nancy Rose Vawter
    B. 1/28/1918
    D. _____

M6261222 - Margaret Cosby Vawter
    B. 9/26/1923
    D. _____

M626123 - Margaret May Whitley - **M6231111** Charles David Peery
    B. 3/27/1895   M. 9/1918   B. _____
    D. _____   D. _____

M6261231 - Trula Ann Peery
    B. 9/15/1921
    D. _____

M6261232 - Cosby Harrison Peery
    B. 6/6/1923
    D. _____

M6261233 - William Whitley Peery
    B. _____
    D. _____

M6261234 - Charles David Peery, Jr.
    B. _____
    D. _____

M6261235 - Jeannette Peery
    B. _____
    D. _____

M6261236 - Nan Peery
    B. _____
    D. _____

M626124 - Nannie Belle Whitley
B. 5/3/1896
D. 8/3/1917

M6262   Wesley Price Whitley - (1) Margaret R. Peery
B. 1832   (1)M. 11/12/1853   B. _____
D. _____   (2)M. _____   D. _____

(2) Kate Lawrence
B. _____
D. _____

M62621 - Polly Whitley(2)
B. _____
D. _____

M62622 - Mary Price Whitley(2)
B. _____
D. _____

M6263   James Shannon Whitley - Margaret Peery Witten
B. 1/17/1834   M. 1/11/1854   B. 7/22/1828
D. 6/3/1916   D. 1/7/1908

M62631 - Mary Alice Whitley - Archibald Thompson Graham
B. 12/9/1854   M. 1875   B. 6/17/1851
D. 1/13/1916   D. 11/17/1925

M626311 - James William Graham - Leora Boishe Vaiden
B. _____   M. _____   B. _____
D. _____   D. _____

M6263111 - Warren Graham
B. _____
D. _____

M6263112 - Spencer Graham
    B. _____
    D. _____

M626312 - Robert Newton Graham - (1) Mattie Jessee
    B. _____   (1)M. _____   B. _____
    D. _____   (2)M. _____   D. _____

                                   (2) Leah Fanning
                                         B. _____
                                         D. _____

    M6263121 - Alice Ann Graham (Mother not given)
        B. _____
        D. _____

M626313 - Archibald Thompson Graham, Jr.
    B. _____
    D. _____

M626314 - Mabel Graham - William Meshac White
    B. 4/16/1879   M. 10/25/1899   B. 10/17/1879
    D. _____   D. _____

    M6263141 - Clair Graham White – W.M. Cumbow
        B. 7/27/1900   M. _____   B. _____
        D. _____   D. _____

    M6263142 - Hubert Stuart White - Sarah Humphrey
        B. 11/8/1902   M. _____   B. _____
        D. _____   D. _____

        M62631421 - Hubert Stuart White, Jr.
            B. _____
            D. _____

M6263143 - Gorman Thurston White - Geneva Porterfield
B. 10/5/1903   M. _____   B. _____
D. _____   D. _____

    M62631431 - Robert White
    B. _____
    D. _____

M6263144 - Arnold Brown White - Lucille White
B. 5/15/1906   M. _____   B. _____
D. _____   D. _____

    M62631441 - Orville Brown White
    B. _____
    D. _____

M6263145 - Buford Thompson White - Minnie White
B. 1/12/1910   M. _____   B. _____
D. _____   D. _____

    M62631451 - Thomas White
    B. _____

M6263146 - Mary Rachel White - William Thompson
B. 8/25/1911   M. _____   B. _____
D. _____   D. _____

    M62631461 - William S. Thompson
    B. _____

    M62631462 - Geneva Anne Thompson
    B. _____

M626315 - Margaret Louisa Graham - Walter Edward Bundy
B. 3/9/1886   M. 10/3/1908   B. 4/5/1883
D. _____   D. _____

M6263151 - Margaret Naomi Bundy
B. 6/24/1909
D. _____

M6263152 - Henry Carter Bundy - Ruby Long
B. 11/7/1911   M. 1/1937   B. _____
D. _____   D. _____

M6263153 - Eunice Jean Bundy
B. 3/30/1913
D. _____

M6263154 - Mary Candler Bundy - Leon Dickerson
B. 1/17/1916   M. 12/24/1938   B. _____
D. _____   D. _____

M6263155 - Walter Edward Bundy, Jr.
B. 5/16/1919
D. _____

M62632 - Sarah Rebecca Whitley - **M6293** Edward Poage Moore **(see M6293)**
B. 10/9/1856   M. 1882   B. 12/19/1854
D. 9/17/1918   D. 1/9/1939

M62633 - Reese Jackson Whitley - Rachel White Witten
B. 3/14/1859   M. 3/17/1887   B. 12/14/1861
D. 7/13/1934   D. _____

M626331 - Margaret Catherine Whitley - Vernan C. Smith
B. 1888   M. 9/13/1911   B. _____
D. _____   D. _____

M6263311 - Harold Whitley Smith - Nell Remines
B. _____   M. _____   B. _____
D. _____   D. _____

M626332 - Mary Blanche Whitley - Walter Bernard McCall
B. 7/16/1890   M. 1/19/1912   B. 10/15/1890
D. _____   D. _____

M6263321 - Kathryn Elizabeth McCall
B. 10/31/1912
D. _____

M6263322 Mary Jean McCall
B. 2/9/1916
D. _____

M626332x - William Reese Whitley
B. 9/23/1892
D. 3/16/1907

M626333 - James Robert Whitley - Ethel Robina Collins
B. 9/13/1893   M. 6/4/1921   B. 1/5/1893
D. _____   D. _____

M6263331 - James Robert Whitley, Jr.
B. 10/17/1923
D. _____

M626334 - Sarah Virginia Whitley - Frank M. Shelton
B. 9/3/1896   M. 11/2/1918   B. 11/18/1899
D. _____   D. _____

M6263341 - Francis Witten Shelton
B. 10/14/1919
D. _____

M6263342 - William Reese Shelton
B. 11/24/1921
D. _____

M6263343 - Kent Fulton Shelton
    B. 6/13/1927
    D. _____

M626335 - Janie Florence Whitley - John Wellington Mundy, Jr.
    B. 6/11/1898   M. 10/1/1919   B. 1/12/1898
    D. _____   D. 1/30/1928

    M6263351 - Garnet Jackson Mundy
        B. 3/21/1920
        D. _____

    M6263352 - Charles William Mundy
        B. 10/8/1922
        D. _____

    M6263353 - James Whitley Mundy
        B. 11/15/1924
        D. _____

M626336 - Walter Whitley - Lena Lawson
    B. 6/15/1900   M. _____   B. _____
    D. _____   D. _____

    M6263361 - Sharon Rose Whitley
        B. _____
        D. _____

    M6263362 - Jana Grace Whitley
        B. _____
        D. _____

M626337 - Ebb Keister Whitley - Pearl Long
    B. 4/16/1902   M. 11/16/1922   B. _____
    D. _____   D. _____

M6263372 - Phyllis Brook Whitley
      B. _____
      D. _____

M6263373 - Ebb Keister Whitley, Jr.
      B. _____
      D. _____

M626338 - Joseph Garnett Whitley - Julia Gray Wallace
      B. 6/28/1904   M. 10/25/1936   B. 4/23/1912
      D. _____   D. _____

    M6263381 - Reese Jackson Whitley II
          B. 8/7/1937
          D. _____

    M6263382 - Irene Patterson Whitley
          B. 1/22/1939
          D. _____

M626339 - Rosalyn Whitley
      B. 3/26/1908
      D. _____

M62634 - Margaret E. Whitley - William Henry Witten
    B. 6/18/1862   M. 7/22/1880   B. 7/17/1859
    D. 9/17/1945   D. 12/12/1923

    M626341 - James Graham Witten
        B. 5/31/1881
        D. 11/31/1883

    M626342 - Margaret Matilda Witten - Grattan Billips
        B. 1/28/1884   M. _____   B. _____
        D. 8/30/1915   D. _____

M6263421 - Margaret Billips
    B. _____
    D. _____

M6263422 - Alice Billips
    B. _____
    D. _____

M626343 - Cynthia Rebecca Witten - Walter M. Hoilman
    B. 3/28/1886   M. 10/26/1904   B. 2/22/1877
    D. _____   D. _____

M6263431 - Hazel Audrine Hoilman - Lewis Andrew Rutherford
    B. 3/12/1906   M. 7/9/1933   B. 4/29/1909
    D. 9/27/1968   D. 2/3/1975

    M62634311 - Martha Lou Rutherford - Eugene Farrell Warren
                                                          (Div)
        B. 6/5/1935   M. 8/18/1957   B. _____

        M626343111 - Becky Jo Warren - Morehead
            B. _____   M. _____   B. _____

        M626343112 - Hazel Marie Warren - James Leroy
                                                Coen, Jr. (Div)
            B. 7/27/1963   M. _____   B. 1/17/1948

            M6263431121 - Brittany Elizabeth Warren Coen
            B. 8/28/1983

M6263432 - Margaret Sue Hoilman - Howard M. Collins
    B. 5/23/1912   M. 7/18/1930   B. 1/30/1907
    D. 11/1/1997   D. 12/23/1993

*M62634321 - Melinda Lou Collins - John Merton Larson, M.D.
    B. 7/28/1944   M. 10/26/1968   B. 3/16/1934

*M626343211 - Kelly Michelle Larson, M.D. - Andrew Jay
                                                    Denson, Ph.D.
        B. 11/27/1969   M. 1/16/1998   B. 10/4/1969

*M626343212 - Michael Collins Larson
        B. 12/27/1974

M6263433 - Annie Lucille Hoilman - James Samuel Turner
    B. 3/4/1918   M. 7/18/1945   B. 5/22/1920
    D. 2/5/1996   D. 8/4/1978

M62634331 - Rebecca Sue Turner - Theodore Ward (Div)
        B. 12/14/1946   M. _____   B. _____

M626344 - Hattie Mae Witten - Rawl Yost
    B. 12/4/1888   M. _____   B. _____
    D. 11/21/1910   D. _____

M626345 - Ella Lucile Witten - Robert Walter Johnson
    B. 7/11/1891   M. 1/4/1909   B. 3/6/1881
    D. _____   D. _____

M6263451 - Lillian Rebecca Johnson - Garland R. Lowe
    B. 6/25/1910   M. 7/10/1935   B. 11/21/1900
    D. _____   D. _____

M6263452 - Robert Wilson Johnson - Mabel Ellis
B. 5/14/1917   M. 10/12/1936   B. 12/19/1917
D. _____   D. _____

M62634521 - Joe Ellis Johnson
B. 7/14/1937

M626346 - Samuel Edward Witten - Edith Johnson
B. 1/20/1894   M. _____   B. _____
D. _____   D. _____

M6263461 - Helen Lucile Witten
B. _____
D. _____

M6263462 - William Witten
B. _____
D. _____

M626347 - Mary Bea Witten - Leed Adkins
B. 5/22/1896   M. 7/15/1913   B. _____
D. _____   D. _____

M6263471 - Robert Walter Adkins
B. 4/2/1915
D. _____

M6263472 - Mary Virginia Adkins
B. 3/6/1918
D. _____

M6263473 - Samuel Edward Adkins
B. 3/12/1920
D. _____

M6263474 - William Earl Adkins
B. 12/24/1924
D. _____

M626348 - Luther Reis Witten
     B. 2/25/1903
     D._____

M626349 - John Andrew Witten
     B. 5/21/1906
     D. _____

M62635 - Louisa Whitley - Joseph H. Jones
     B. 6/9/1865   M. 6/23/1886   B. 7/16/1864
     D. _____   D. _____

M626351 - Maude Louise Jones - (1) Allen Jennings Hurdle
     B. 6/24/1890   (1)M. 1/4/1911   B. 1/12/1881
     D. _____   (2)M. 1/2/1930   D. 10/25/1917

                    (2) Peter Joseph Chevurout
                    B. 6/25/1873
                    D. _____

    M6263511   (1) Louise Elizabeth Hurdle
          B. 10/21/1911
          D. _____

    M6263512   (1) Mildred Jeanette Hurdle - Donald John Hickey
          B. 2/2/1913   M. 5/26/1934   B. _____
          D. _____   D. _____

    M6263513   (1) Allen Jennings Hurdle, Jr. - Helen Frances Dutton
          B. 8/4/1917   M. 11/6/1937   B. 3/17/1918
          D. _____   D. _____

M626352 - Joseph Claude Jones - Lucile Maud Stamey
     B. 6/24/1890   M. 1/14/1921   B. 6/7/1902
     D. _____   D. _____

M6263521 - Hazel Lou Jones
       B. 8/22/1923

M6263522 - Ora Jeanette Jones
       B. 9/22/1926

M62636 - Florence Jeannette Whitley - George Walter Keister
       B. 10/19/1872   M. 6/7/1899   B. 5/4/1865
       D. _____   D. 1/1/1915

    M626361 - Louise Gay Keister - Cyrene Boyle Jessee
           B. 4/2/1900 M. 12/11/1917   B. 3/31/1892
           D. _____   D. _____

        M6263611 - Vara Jeanette Jessee - Mattison Hess Evans
               B. 12/7/1919   M. 11/20/1937   B. 8/15/1914
               D. _____   D. _____

        M6263612 - Margaret June Jessee
               B. 8/13/1925

    M626362 - Blanchard Osborne Keister - Cecilia Anita Rock
           B. 7/2/1902   M. 1/11/1926   B. 10/22/1904
           D. _____   D. _____

        M6263621 - Emmy Jean Keister - Noland Edward Dennison
               B. 9/21/1928   M. _____   B. _____

            M62636211 - Noland Edward Dennison, Jr. - Ruth Ferree
                  B. _____   M. _____   B. _____

M626362111 - Cecia Mare Dennison
   B. _____
   D. _____

M626362112 - Nathan Ward Dennison
   B. _____
   D. _____

M62636212 - Virginia Dennison
   B. _____
   D. _____

M62636213 - Diane K. Dennison
   B. _____
   D. _____

M6263622 - Phyllis Carolyn Keister
   B. 2/15/1932

M62464 -Hugh J. Whitley - Elvira N. Neal
   B. _____   M. _____   B. _____
   D. _____   D. _____

M6265 John H. Whitley - Eleanor Whitman
   B. 1/18/1842   M. 10/30/1865   B. _____
   D. 9/17/1918   D. _____

M62651 - Annie Cora Whitley - J. Raleigh Peery
   B. 5/26/1868   M. 12/20/1893   B. _____
   D. 12/25/1895   D. _____

M62652 - Hugh Price Whitley
   B. 1869
   D. 1883

M62653 - John Whitman Whitley - (1) Nannie Peery
          B. 2/12/1871   M. 11/8/1893   B. 1868
          D. _____   M. _____   D. 1935

                            (2) Sarah Elizabeth Beavers
                                    B. _____
                                    D. _____

M626531 - (1) Nannie Rose Whitley - Isaac Walter Miller, Jr.
          B. 3/27/1895   M. 8/5/1925   B. 5/15/1899
          D. _____   D. _____

M626532 - (1) Stewart French Whitley - Martha Rebecca Beavers
          B. 10/2/1899   M. 12/24/1922   B. 8/2/1903
          D. _____   D. _____

M626533 - (1) John David Whitley - Margaret Hawkins
          B. _____   M. 2/6/1925   B. _____
          D. _____   D. _____

M626534 - (1) Ellen Mary Whitley
          B. 1906
          D. 1/31/1920

M62654 - Elgan Lane Whitley - Hadley Lucile Speer
          B. 4/13/1874   M. 10/2/1903   B. 2/24/1887
          D. 1/19/1925   D. _____

M626541 - E. Lane Whitley, Jr.
          B. 4/1/1911
          D. _____

M62655 - William Neel Whitley - Gertrude Burnett
          B. 12/24/1875   M. 9/7/1904   B. 2/3/1876
          D. _____   D. _____

M626551 - Theron Jennings Whitley
  B. 5/15/1906
  D. 9/6/1907

M626552 - William Gerald Whitley - Louise Emeline Anderson
  B. 11/23/1907   M. 9/22/1934   B. _____
  D. _____   D. _____

  M6265521 - Virginia Geraldine Whitley
    B. 6/26/1935

M626553 - George Lockhart Whitley
  B. 10/13/1910
  D. _____

M626554 - Dorothy Whitley - Herbert Leroy Churchman
  B. 2/13/1913   M. 10/18/1934   B. 12/16/1908
  D. _____   D. _____

  M6265541 - Nora Irene Churchman
    B. 1/6/1938

  M626555 - Virginia Ellen Whitley
    B. 12/19/1914
    D. _____

M62656 - Mary Naomi Whitley
  B. 8/14/1878
  D. _____

M62657 - Nellie Rose Whitley
  B. _____
  D. as infant

M62658 - Minnie Whitley
> B. _____
> D. as infant

M6266   Emmaline V. Whitley - (1) Thomas J. Crockett
> B. _____   (1)M. 10/30/1865   B. _____
> D. 1892   (2)M. _____   D. _____

(2) James Ireson
> B. _____
> D. _____

M62661 - William Crockett(1)
> B. _____
> D. _____

M62662 - Sally Crockett(1)
> B. _____
> D. _____

M62663 - Molly Crockett(1)
> B. _____
> D. _____

M62664 - Margaret Crockett(1)
> B. _____
> D. _____

M62665 - Thomas Crockett(1)
> B. _____
> D. _____

M62666 - Grace Crockett(1)
> B. _____
> D. _____

M62667 - Alma Lackie Crockett(1)
    B. _____
    D. _____

23.

THE MARY B. MOORE LINE
BIOGRAPHICAL CHARTS

M62634321
Genealogical Number

Melinda Lou Collins   Marco Island, Collier Co., FL
Name (including maiden name if applicable)   Town of Residence

Washington, D.C.   7/28/1944
Birthplace   Date of Birth   Date of Death   Where Buried

John Merton Larson, M.D.   Ottawa, IL   3/16/1934
Name of Spouse   Birthplace   Date of Birth   Date of Death

                            10/26/1968   La Grange, Cook Co., IL
Where Buried   Date of Marriage   Place of Marriage

If married more than once:

Name of Spouse   Birthplace   Date of Birth   Date of Death

Where Buried   Date of Marriage   Place of Marriage

Merton Edmund Larson/Julia Edvarda Hagerup Larson (maiden name)
Parents of Spouse (with Mother's maiden name) 1st Marriage

Subsequent Marriage (if applicable)

Family Details

Schools attended, dates and degrees: Community, political work, etc.:

R.N, Alexandria Hosp. School of Nursing
Descendant   Descendant

Physician, Univ of Illinois, Speciality - Anesthesia
Spouse   Spouse

Basic Employment History: Clubs, Church Affiliations, etc.:
                                                       DAR, UDC

Descendant   Descendant

Spouse   Spouse

Military Service:
US Nurse Corps   US Navy Medical Corps

Descendant   Spouse

M626343211
Genealogical Number

Kelly Michelle Larson
Name (including maiden name if applicable)   Town of Residence

<table>
<tr><td></td><td>11/27/1969</td><td></td><td></td></tr>
<tr><td>Birthplace</td><td>Date of Birth</td><td>Date of Death</td><td>Where Buried</td></tr>
</table>

<table>
<tr><td>Andrew Jay Denson</td><td></td><td>10/4/1969</td><td></td></tr>
<tr><td>Name of Spouse</td><td>Birthplace</td><td>Date of Birth</td><td>Date of Death</td></tr>
</table>

<table>
<tr><td></td><td>1/16/1998</td><td></td></tr>
<tr><td>Where Buried</td><td>Date of Marriage</td><td>Place of Marriage</td></tr>
</table>

If married more than once:

<table>
<tr><td></td><td></td><td></td><td></td></tr>
<tr><td>Name of Spouse</td><td>Birthplace</td><td>Date of Birth</td><td>Date of Death</td></tr>
</table>

<table>
<tr><td></td><td></td><td></td></tr>
<tr><td>Where Buried</td><td>Date of Marriage</td><td>Place of Marriage</td></tr>
</table>

Parents of Spouse (with Mother's maiden name) 1st Marriage

Subsequent Marriage (if applicable)

Family Details

Schools attended, dates and degrees: Community, political work, etc.:

Descendant   Descendant

Spouse   Spouse

Basic Employment History: Clubs, Church Affiliations, etc.:

M.D.
Descendant   Descendant

Ph.D.
Spouse   Spouse

Military Service:

Descendant   Spouse

M626343212
Genealogical Number

Michael Collins Larson   Westmont, IL
Name (including maiden name if applicable)   Town of Residence

La Grange, IL   12/27/1974
Birthplace   Date of Birth   Date of Death   Where Buried

Name of Spouse   Birthplace   Date of Birth   Date of Death

Where Buried   Date of Marriage   Place of Marriage

If married more than once:

Name of Spouse   Birthplace   Date of Birth   Date of Death

Where Buried   Date of Marriage   Place of Marriage

Parents of Spouse (with Mother's maiden name) 1st Marriage

Subsequent Marriage (if applicable)

Family Details

Schools attended, dates and degrees: Community, political work, etc.:
Univ. of Iowa, Benedictine Univ.

Descendant   Descendant

Spouse   Spouse

Basic Employment History: Clubs, Church Affiliations, etc.:
Asst. Manager, Accounting Dept, Nordstrom's
Oak Brook, IL.

Descendant   Descendant

Spouse   Spouse

Military Service:

Descendant   Spouse

24.

THE MARY B. MOORE LINE
PICTURES

Margaret Emeline Whitley Witten (M62634)   B. 6/16/1862   D. 9/17/1945

Margaret Emeline Whitley Witten (M62634)   B. 6/16/1862   D. 9/17/1945
Cynthia Rebecca Whitten Hoilman (M626343)   B. 3/28/1886   D. _____
Margaret Sue Hoilman Collins (M6263432)   B. 5/23/1912   D. 11/1/1997
Melinda Lou Collins Larson (M62634321)   B. 7/28/1944

25.

The Jane Shannon Moore Line

The Jane Shannon Moore Line

Jane Shannon Moore was the 8th child of James Moore, the "Captive." She was married twice, first to her cousin James Harvey Moore (M641) son of Joseph Moore (M64) and Christina Nicewander, and second to Charles Fitzgerald Tiffany. Her first child by Tiffany, fourth child in all, was Maria Jane Tiffany (M6274) who married Alexander St.Clair from whom the renown numerous doctors St.Clair in Bluefield were descended. Reproduced below is the obituary of Jane Shannon Moore Tiffany of 12/21/1900 from the Clinch Valley News of Tazewell, VA.

Mrs. Tiffany Dead
Was a daughter of James Moore, who was abducted by Indians.

> Mrs. Jane Tiffany, relict of the late Charles Tiffany, died
> Saturday night at the home of her son in law, State Senator
> Alexander St.Clair, at Bluestone, Tazewell county, VA.

> Mrs. Tiffany was a daughter of James Moore, of Abb's Valley,
> who, together with his father and sister Mary, was captured by
> Indians in Abb's Valley and taken to Canada. The young man
> eventually effected his escape and, rescuing his sister, brought
> her back to her home in safety.

> Mrs. Tiffany was twice married, and is survived by three
> children - Mrs. Alexander St.Clair, of Bluestone; Mrs. Charles
> T. Gillespie, of Kentucky, and Samuel Moore, of Wright's
> Valley.

> Mrs. Tiffany was noted for her gentle and refined manners. In
> 1826 she connected herself with the Methodist church, and has
> ever since lived a beautiful Christian life, and was greatly
> beloved in the community.

I am indebted to Richard Otis St.Clair (M627461), great-grandson of Jane Moore Tiffany, for the interesting obituary of his brother, C. Wade St.Clair (M627462), who died on 11/8/2002:

> Native of Welch, Wade St.Clair graduated from Kentucky
> Military Institute and Duke University. He served in Korea in
> the Air Force during the Korean War, and then joined the staff
> of WBT/WBTV in Charlotte, N.C. He became a Program
> Director of WBT Radio, where he performed improvisational
> comedy with Owen Spamm and Ty Boyd for radio and
> television. Wade was then recruited by NASA, where he

distinguished himself in both the broadcast and public services mediums. His career began with NASA in 1963 when he was given the responsibility of developing the Aeronautics and Space Report, a weekly radio show about current events at NASA. The show was distributed to hundreds of radio stations across the nation and featured Willard Scott, who did the narration. When NASA needed a proven veteran to take over its public services division for the Apollo lunar landing program, it turned to Wade, who organized a group that would be responsible for handling public requests for exhibits, speakers, and appearances by astronauts. It was his plan to invite and accommodate thousands of people to the Apollo launches at Cape Kennedy, which was perhaps his most important contribution.

In the weeks following the successful splashdown of the Apollo 11 astronauts, Wade was given the responsibility to go to Houston and brief Neil Armstrong, Mike Collins, and Buzz Aldrin about NASA's plans for their public appearances. Wade, at the White House request, planned and commandeered a two month, around the world tour of 40 countries for the astronauts. He worked with the White House, State Department, and U.S. Information Agency in pulling together a public affairs support team to advance and staff the trip. It was a monumental task which he was required to complete in a very short time.

In what was to become one of Wade's last major assignments, he was called upon to plan a two week tour by the Apollo 13 astronauts to Iceland, Switzerland, Greece, Malta and Ireland. The trip was a huge success and set the stage for similar trips by succeeding Apollo astronauts.

In early 1971, Wade left NASA to accept a position with the National Center for Resource Recovery where he again applied his talents in putting together an effective public affairs organization dedicated to educate Americans on the need to protect and preserve the environment.

He then served as the Director of Development for Reading Is Fundamental (RIF) for 18 years. During his time at RIF, he increased the organization's income fourfold. Wade retired in 1998, and devoted his time to family, friends, travel and music through participation in his church, the NOVA Singers, and the New Dominion Chorale.

The widow of Dr. Wade Hampton St. Clair, the former Mary Louise Archer (M627431) died on May 8, 2005 in Charlottesville, Va. at 98 years of a full and interesting life. She had written three books: <u>An American Girl</u>, <u>Interlude: Letters from a Foreign Correspondent</u>, and <u>A Knock on the Door</u>. The books are largely autobiographical and are a pleasure to read.

Biographical information on other Jane Shannon Moore descendants in the bio sheets following.

26.

THE JANE SHANNON MOORE LINE
GENEALOGICAL CHARTS

M627   *Jane Shannon Moore - (1) James Harvey Moore (See M641)*
B. 7/19/1812   (1)M. 9/11/1832   B. _____
D. 12/21/1900   (2)M. 1/6/1853   D. 1846

(2) Charles Fitzgerald Tiffany
B. 6/6/1800
D. 2/9/1876

M6274 - Maria Jane Tiffany(2) - Alexander St.Clair
B.12/24/1853   M. 9/26/1871   B. 4/17/1845
D. 1/3/1940   D. 10/21/1921

M62741 - Charles Tiffany St.Clair - Rosa Lee Snidow
B. 5/27/1873   M. 6/7/1897   B. 5/21/1878
D. 11/17/1946   D. _____

M627411 - Charles Tiffany St.Clair, Jr. - Natalie Virginia Maynard
B. 5/31/1899   M. 9/6/1927   B. 11/30/1907
D. 6/7/1965   D. 11/30/1961

*M6274111 - Charles Tiffany St.Clair, III - Delores L. Davis
B. 10/7/1928   M. 5/13/1950 B. 1/20/1933

M62741111 - Beverly Virginia St.Clair - John Baird
B. 2/7/1951   M. 8/19/1979   B. 1/29/1945

M62741112 - Charles Tiffany St.Clair, IV
B. 8/24/1953

M62741113 - Joseph Davis St.Clair
B. 3/29/1955

*M6274112 - Marea Norvell St.Clair   (1) George Dudley Sutherland, Jr.(Div)
B. 4/12/1941   (1)M. 8/8/1959   B. 1/15/1941
(2)M. 4/23/1994

*Indicates that a bio is included.

(2) Gordon Lockwood Douglas, Jr.
B. 11/20/1937

*M62741121 - (1) Marjorie St.Clair Sutherland - Roger Patterson Sither
B. 8/16/1960   M. 3/24/1979   B. 6/20/1956

*M627411211 - Marea Nicole Sither
B. 9/17/1979

*M62741122- (1) George Dudley Sutherland, III - Julia Tripp King
B. 7/15/1961   M. 4/30/1989   B. 6/29/1962

*M627411221 - Linden Crockett Sutherland
B. 8/18/1995

*M627411222 - Rebecca Lindsey Sutherland
B. 10/7/1997

*M627411223 - Nathalie Lynn Sutherland
B. 11/23/1998

*M62741123 - (1) Katheryn Marea Sutherland - Todd Slayter Everett
B. 11/1/1966   M.5/30/1992   B. 10/2/1963

*M627411231 – Tyler Shane Everett
B. 10/3/2000

*M627411232 – Tiffany Sutherland Everett
B. 3/25/2002

M62742 - John Alexander St.Clair - Nannie Hanson Harman
B. 2/5/1875   M. 3/2/1904   B. 10/30/1881
D. _____   D. _____

M627421 - Maria Tiffany St.Clair - Walter Murray Elswick
B. 2/5/1905   M. 1/6/1934   B. 5/9/1899
D. 6/15/1992   D. _____

M627422 - Sarah Elizabeth St.Clair - Walter Bass Perkins
      B. 12/20/1906   M. 10/11/1930   B. 9/23/1903
      D. _____   D. _____

      M6274221 - Gordon St.Clair Perkins
            B. 2/20/1935
            D. 10/26/1989

M627423 - Jane Elwood St.Clair - Lilburn Everett Ward, Jr.
      B. 12/20/1906   M. 6/12/1937   B. 4/12/1909
      D. 1/1/1985   D. 6/15/1992

      *****M6274231** - Lilburn Everett Ward, III - Kitty Lou Tinnell
            B. 11/28/1938   M. 11/22/1961   B. 12/22/1939

            M62742311 - Everett St.Clair Ward - Maria Garnett
                  B. 5/21/1962   M. 4/16/1994   B. _____

                  M627423111 - Jane Ketner Ward
                      B. 11/28/1998

                  M627423112 - Everett St.Clair Ward, Jr.
                      B. 7/4/2000

            *****M62742312** - Stacey Tinnel Ward - Harry David Halpert
                  B. 8/25/1967   M. 7/25/1992   B. 2/6/1967

                  *****M627423121** - John Turner Halpert
                      B. 5/30/1996

                  *****M627423122** - Charles London Halpert
                      B. 3/9/1999

                  M627423123 – Wallace Ward Halpert
                      B. 8/15/2001

            M62742313 - Kimberly Ann Ward - Nestor Sanchez
                  B. 5/21/1969   M. 7/24/1997   B. 7/18/1953

M627423131 - Jon Marco Sanchez
 B. 1/27/1999

M627423132 – Eli Gabriel Sanchez
 B. 9/15/2000

M627424 - Nancy Harman St.Clair - John Edward Traynham, Jr.
 B. 1/10/1909 M. 5/18/1935 B. 2/25/1910
 D. 9/6/1990   D. 2/16/1985

 *M6274241 - Ann Tiffany Traynham - Larry Klappenbach
  B. 5/30/1936 M. 11/30/1957 B. 1/23/1934

  *M62742411 - David Edward Klappenbach – Elizabeth Dawn Hatfield
   B. 9/3/1958 M. 8/4/1990 B. 6/27/1968

   *M627424111 Preston Michael Klappenbach
    B. 9/9/2000

  *M62742412 – Brian Dale Klappenbach
   B. 7/10/1960

  *M62742413 – Bruce Douglas Klappenbach – Shannon Andrea Sellers
   B. 2/3/1963 M. 1/20/1996 B. 8/20/1969

   *M627424131 - Andrew Bean Klappenbach
    B. 4/4/1998

   *M627424132 – Charles Mitchell Klappenbach
    B. 2/16/2000

   *M627424133 – Elliott Boone Klappenbach
    B. 3/4/2002

 *M6274242 - John Edward Traynham, III - _____ (Div)
  B. 3/23/1940 M. _____ B. _____
  4 Children

 *M6274243 - Nancy St.Clair Traynham - William Gordon Johnston
  B. 7/15/1946 M. 2/15/1975 B. _____
  3 Children

M62743 - Wade Hampton St.Clair - Elizabeth Alexine Armstrong
    B. 4/18/1877   M. 6/6/1906   B. _____
    D. _____   D. _____

    M627431 - Wade Hampton St.Clair, Jr. – Mary Louise Archer
        B. 7/20/1908   M. _____   B. 1907
        D. 6/25/1987   D. 5/8/2005

        M6274311 – Elizabeth Armstrong St.Clair
            B. 3/22/1940

        M6274312 - Mary Archer St.Clair - Thomas Biddle Harvey Jr.
            B. 9/22/1942   M. _____   B. _____

            M62743121 - Thomas Biddle Harvey III
                B. 2/23/1971

    M627432 - Alexander Armstrong St.Clair, II
        B. 7/24/1911
        D. 1944

M62744 - Glenn Moore St.Clair - Julia Leonard Pendleton
    B. 8/23/1879   M. 2/15/1907   B. 5/2/1882
    D. 5/6/1966   D. 7/30/1938

    M627441 - Julia Tiffany St.Clair - Chase Morison Adkins
        B. 12/2/1907   M. 8/28/1937   B. 3/20/1904
        D. 12/21/2000   D. 3/31/1959

        M6274411 - Chase Morison Adkins, Jr. – Carolyn Elizabeth Redd
            B. 6/20/1938   M. 5/4/1968   B. 3/15/1946

            M62744111 - Stephen Girard Adkins, III – Lisa Yvonne Thomas
                B. 6/4/1975   M. 12/8/2001   B. 12/25/1979

            M62744112 - Elizabeth Chase Adkins
                B. 9/20/1983

M627442 - Rosalinda Blow St.Clair - Frank Graham Farrier
      B. 12/20/1908   M. 1/20/1940   B. 9/17/1906
      D. 12/15/2000   D. 4/18/1907

*M6274421 - Rosalinda Graham Farrier – (1) James F. Vaughn (Div.)
      B. 3/25/1942 (1)M. _____   B. _____
                 (2)M. 8/30/1991   D. 1986

                                 (2) James N. Daughtrey
                                    B. 10/29/1932
                                    D. 7/26/1996

*M6274422 - Frank Graham Farrier, Jr. - Patricia Martin (Div)
      B. 10/15/1943   M. 6/10/1971   B. _____

      M62744221 - Frank Graham Farrier, III - Lisha Young
             B. 9/26/1972   M. 4/1998   B. 10/18/1974

           M627442211 - Lola Grace Farrier
                 B. 8/22/2000

      M6274423 - Martin Pence Farrier, III - Sallie Allen
             B. 10/12/1945   M. 6/73   B. 7/31/1952
                                            D. 6/15/1989

      M62744231 - Jenny Grogan Farrier
             B. 10/18/1974

      M62744232 - Martin Pence Farrier, IV
             B. 5/22/1977

M627443 - Pauline Bittle St.Clair - Samuel Campbell Wilson
      B. 6/20/1917   M. 9/5/1938   B. 7/4/1912
      D. 4/19/1971   D. 10/7/1975

      M6274431 - Julia Kate Wilson - (1) Daniel T. Gilreath (Div)
             B. 7/7/1950   M. _____   B. _____
                            M. 2000

(2) Robert L. Jensen, Jr.
B. 3/1/1941

M62744311 - (1) Daniel Jeffrey Gilreath
B. 5/10/1974

M62744312 - (1) Kate Elizabeth Gilreath
B. 12/11/1978

*M627444 - Jacqueline Pendleton St.Clair - Kenneth John Brown
B. 2/25/1919   M. 3/9/1943   B. 1/30/1922
D. 7/28/2005   D. 11/8/1990

*M6274441 - Jacqueline St.Clair Brown - David A. Pilawski (Div)
B. 1/4/1944   M. 4/28/1973   B. 3/24/1943

*M62744411 - Renee Dawn Pilawski
B. 6/2/1975

* M62744412 - Chad Louis Pilawski
B. 2/8/1978

*M6274442 - Kenneth John Brown Jr. - Chiara Michele Yenyo
B. 6/4/1945   M. 6/17/1989   B. 7/22/1958

*M62744421 - Candice Michele Brown
B. 3/16/1993

*M6274443 - Nancy Tiffany Brown - Fred Sven Berg
B. 8/12/1952   M. 10/10/1981   B. 7/13/1952

*M62744431 - Michelle Tiffany Berg
B. 9/16/1982

*M62744432 - Sean Sven Berg
B. 4/30/1986

*M627445 - Glenn St.Clair - Desle O.H. Miller
B. 2/23/1922   M. 12/10/1943   B. 8/5/1922

M6274451   - Robert D. Miller – Jill Junene Jaspers
B. 1/11/1947   M. 9/1/1979   B. 6/14/1946

M62744511 - Katherine Jaspers Miller
B. 12/14/1980

*M6274452   - Julia St.Clair Miller – (1) Jeffrey Mason Reynolds (Div)
B. 4/22/1949   (1)M. 9/2/1972   B. 10/26/1950
                      (2)M. 5/24/2002

                      (2) James Michael Keating
                      B. 8/7/1946

*M62744521 – (1) Benjamin Mason Reynolds – Heide Marie Scheel Nogel
B. 5/28/1977   M. 8/18/2001   B. 5/10/1979

M627445211 – Alexander Mason Reynolds Scheel
B. 2/17/2002

*M62744522 - (1)Edric Scott Reynolds
B. 9/29/1980

M62745 - Frank Tabler St.Clair - Hersilia Susan Crockett
B. 11/20/1881   M. 4/26/1905   B. 11/17/1882
D. _____   D. _____

M627451 - Frank Tabler St.Clair, Jr. - Tommy Leady Baldwin
B. 3/30/1911   M. _____   B. _____
D. 12/5/1953   D. _____

M62746 - Otis Eugene St.Clair - Lillian Bess Pryor
     B. 1/11/1884   M. 10/25/1923   B. 3/13/1896
     D. 12/13/1978   D. 12/9/1964

    *M627461 - Richard Otis St.Clair - Mary Kate Stockner
        B. 3/16/1926   M. 12/29/1950   B. 9/9/28

        *M6274611 - Allison Leigh St.Clair - Thomas Legge Schildwachter, M.D.
           B. 10/3/1953 M. 8/28/1976   B. 3/13/1949

           *M62746111 - Brooke Ashton Schildwachter
               B. 3/20/1979

           *M62746112 - Meredith Donnel Schildwachter
               B. 11/5/1980

           *M62746113 - Hayes St.Clair Schildwachter
               B. 5/8/1984

    M627462 - Charles Wade St.Clair - Patricia George Coley (Div)
        B. 4/14/1930   M. _____   B. 6/9/31
        D. 11/8/2002   D. _____

        M6274621 - Jane Pryor St.Clair
           B. 1/13/1959

        *M6274622 - Amy (Amey) Rowe St.Clair – Burke Harold Moeller
           B. 8/27/1962   M. 6/30/2001   B. 5/21/1968

M62747 - Rob Roy St.Clair - Catherine Cecil Peery
     B. 6/7/1886   M. 7/17/1916   B. _____
     D. _____   D. _____

    M627471 - Catherine Cecil St.Clair
        B. _____
        D. _____

M627472 - Rob Roy St.Clair, Jr. - Grace Parnell
    B. 5/28/1920   M. _____   B. _____
    D. _____   D. _____

M62747x - Martha Jane St.Clair
    B. 10/31/1888
    D. 6/21/1890

M62748 - Alexander St.Clair, III - **M 628163** - Ruth Jane Crockett
    B. 1/4/1891   M. 1/7/1937   B. 12/18/1898
    D. 1/11/1974   D. 5/1947

    M627481 - Alexander St.Clair, IV - Phyllis Carol Short
        B. 1/13/940   M. 6/16/1961   B. 1/24/1938

        M6274811 - Frank Sterling St.Clair
            B. 12/13/1971

        M6274812 - Judean Annette St.Clair - Greg Barton Hines
            B. 8/2/1972   M. 6/19/1999   B. 6/15/1969

    *M627482 - Wade Tiffany St.Clair – (1) Kathryn Louise Bowen
        B. 10/27/1941   (1)M. 8/10/1968   B. 7/23/1948
                       (2)M. 3/18/1988

                            (2) Nora Louise Bryant
                               B. 8/31/1945

        *M6274821 – (1) Kathryn Tiffany St.Clair
            B. 2/10/1973

M62749 - Sarah Maria St.Clair - Henry Thomas Haley
    B. 10/12/1894   M. 3/14/1922   B. 3/1/1891
    D. 10/1968   D. _____

M62749x - Rosalinda Blow St.Clair
    B. 12/14/1896
    D. 11/25/1908

27.

THE JANE SHANNON MOORE LINE
BIOGRAPHICAL CHARTS

M6274111
Genealogical Number

Charles Tiffany St. Clair, III   Columbus, Ohio
Name (including maiden name if applicable)   Town of Residence

Richmond, VA   10/7/1928
Birthplace   Date of Birth   Date of Death   Where Buried

Delores L. Davis   Jenkins, KY   1/20/1933
Name of Spouse   Birthplace   Date of Birth   Date of Death

                                 5/13/1950   Bristol, Tenn.
Where Buried   Date of Marriage   Place of Marriage

If married more than once:

Name of Spouse   Birthplace   Date of Birth   Date of Death

Where Buried   Date of Marriage   Place of Marriage

Parents of Spouse (with Mother's maiden name) 1st Marriage

Subsequent Marriage (if applicable)

Family Details

Schools attended, dates and degrees: Community, political work, etc.:

Descendant   Descendant

Spouse   Spouse

Basic Employment History: Clubs, Church Affiliations, etc.:

Descendant   Descendant

Spouse   Spouse

Military Service:

Descendant   Spouse

M6274112
Genealogical Number

Marea Norvell St. Clair
Name (including maiden name if applicable)

N. Ft. Myers, FL
Town of Residence

Bluefield, W. VA
Birthplace

4/12/1941
Date of Birth

Date of Death

Where Buried

Gordon Lockwood Douglas, Jr.
Name of Spouse

Morristown, N.J.
Birthplace

11/20/1937
Date of Birth

Date of Death

Where Buried

4/23/1994
Date of Marriage

N. Fort Myers, FL
Place of Marriage

If married more than once:

George Dudley Sutherland, Jr.
Name of Spouse

McComas. W.VA
Birthplace

1/15/1941
Date of Birth

Date of Death

Where Buried

8/8/1959
Date of Marriage

Bristol, VA
Place of Marriage

Mr. & Mrs. George Dudley Sutherland (Evans - mothers maiden name)
Parents of Spouse (with Mother's maiden name) 1st Marriage

Subsequent Marriage (if applicable)

Family Details

Schools attended, dates and degrees:

Community, political work, etc.:

W. VA Univ. 59-60 - Palm Beach JR.College-
AS Nursing
Descendant

Descendant

Univ. of Bridgeport, CT 1956-60
Spouse

Spouse

Basic Employment History:

Clubs, Church Affiliations, etc.:

Registered Critical Care Nurse
Descendant

Presbyterian
Descendant

Financial Services - 40 years
Spouse

Presbyterian
Spouse

Military Service:

Descendant

Spouse

M62741121
Genealogical Number

Marjorie St. Clair Sutherland   Palm Beach Gardens, FL
Name (including maiden name if applicable)   Town of Residence

Bluefield, W.VA   8/16/1960
Birthplace   Date of Birth   Date of Death   Where Buried

Roger Patterson Sither   Harvey, Illinois   6/20/1956
Name of Spouse   Birthplace   Date of Birth   Date of Death

                           3/24/1979   North Palm Beach, Florida
Where Buried   Date of Marriage   Place of Marriage

If married more than once:

Name of Spouse   Birthplace   Date of Birth   Date of Death

Where Buried   Date of Marriage   Place of Marriage

Gordon Bennett Sither and Elizabeth Bedford Steele
Parents of Spouse (with Mother's maiden name) 1st Marriage

Subsequent Marriage (if applicable)

Family Details

Schools attended, dates and degrees: Community, political work, etc.:

Univ. of FL. 1979, AA - Business
Descendant   Descendant

Univ. of FL. 1979, Finance BA/BS
Spouse   Spouse

Basic Employment History: Clubs, Church Affiliations, etc.:

Mass Mutual Life Insurance   First Presbyterian
Descendant   Descendant

Pratt & Whitney - U/C
Spouse   Spouse

Military Service:

Descendant   Spouse

M627411211
Genealogical Number

Marea Nicole Sither
Name (including maiden name if applicable)

Palm Beach Gardens, FL
Town of Residence

Palm Beach Gardens, FL   9/17/1979
Birthplace   Date of Birth

Date of Death   Where Buried

Name of Spouse   Birthplace   Date of Birth   Date of Death

Where Buried   Date of Marriage   Place of Marriage

If married more than once:

Name of Spouse   Birthplace   Date of Birth   Date of Death

Where Buried   Date of Marriage   Place of Marriage

Parents of Spouse (with Mother's maiden name) 1st Marriage

Subsequent Marriage (if applicable)

Family Details

Schools attended, dates and degrees: Community, political work, etc.:

Univ. of FL.
Descendant   Descendant

Spouse   Spouse

Basic Employment History: Clubs, Church Affiliations, etc.:

Presbyterian
Descendant   Descendant

Spouse   Spouse

Military Service:

Descendant   Spouse

M62741122
Genealogical Number

George Dudley Sutherland, III
Name (including maiden name if applicable)   Town of Residence

              7/15/1961
Birthplace   Date of Birth   Date of Death   Where Buried

Julia Tripp King   6/29/1962
Name of Spouse   Birthplace   Date of Birth   Date of Death

              4/30/1989
Where Buried   Date of Marriage   Place of Marriage

If married more than once:

Name of Spouse   Birthplace   Date of Birth   Date of Death

Where Buried   Date of Marriage   Place of Marriage

Parents of Spouse (with Mother's maiden name) 1st Marriage

Subsequent Marriage (if applicable)

Family Details

Schools attended, dates and degrees: Community, political work, etc.:

Descendant   Descendant

Spouse   Spouse

Basic Employment History: Clubs, Church Affiliations, etc.:

Descendant   Descendant

Spouse   Spouse

Military Service:

Descendant   Spouse

M627411221
Genealogical Number

Linden Crockett Sutherland

Name (including maiden name if applicable)   Town of Residence

8/18/1995

Birthplace   Date of Birth   Date of Death   Where Buried

Name of Spouse   Birthplace   Date of Birth   Date of Death

Where Buried   Date of Marriage   Place of Marriage

If married more than once:

Name of Spouse   Birthplace   Date of Birth   Date of Death

Where Buried   Date of Marriage   Place of Marriage

Parents of Spouse (with Mother's maiden name) 1st Marriage

Subsequent Marriage (if applicable)

Family Details

Schools attended, dates and degrees: Community, political work, etc.:

Descendant   Descendant

Spouse   Spouse

Basic Employment History: Clubs, Church Affiliations, etc.:

Descendant   Descendant

Spouse   Spouse

Military Service:

Descendant   Spouse

M627411222
Genealogical Number

Rebecca Lindsey Sutherland
Name (including maiden name if applicable)   Town of Residence

_____   10/7/1997
Birthplace   Date of Birth   Date of Death   Where Buried

Name of Spouse   Birthplace   Date of Birth   Date of Death

Where Buried   Date of Marriage   Place of Marriage

If married more than once:

Name of Spouse   Birthplace   Date of Birth   Date of Death

Where Buried   Date of Marriage   Place of Marriage

Parents of Spouse (with Mother's maiden name) 1st Marriage

Subsequent Marriage (if applicable)

Family Details

Schools attended, dates and degrees: Community, political work, etc.:

Descendant   Descendant

Spouse   Spouse

Basic Employment History: Clubs, Church Affiliations, etc.:

Descendant   Descendant

Spouse   Spouse

Military Service:

Descendant   Spouse

M627411223
Genealogical Number

Nathalie Lynn Sutherland
Name (including maiden name if applicable)   Town of Residence

                          11/23/1998
Birthplace   Date of Birth   Date of Death   Where Buried

Name of Spouse   Birthplace   Date of Birth   Date of Death

Where Buried   Date of Marriage   Place of Marriage

If married more than once:

Name of Spouse   Birthplace   Date of Birth   Date of Death

Where Buried   Date of Marriage   Place of Marriage

Parents of Spouse (with Mother's maiden name) 1st Marriage

Subsequent Marriage (if applicable)

Family Details

Schools attended, dates and degrees: Community, political work, etc.:

Descendant   Descendant

Spouse   Spouse

Basic Employment History: Clubs, Church Affiliations, etc.:

Descendant   Descendant

Spouse   Spouse

Military Service:

Descendant   Spouse

M62741123
Genealogical Number

Katheryn Marea Sutherland
Name (including maiden name if applicable)   Town of Residence

                                    11/1/1966
Birthplace   Date of Birth   Date of Death   Where Buried

Todd Slayter Everett   10/2/1964
Name of Spouse   Birthplace   Date of Birth   Date of Death

                                    5/30/1992
Where Buried   Date of Marriage   Place of Marriage

If married more than once:

Name of Spouse   Birthplace   Date of Birth   Date of Death

Where Buried   Date of Marriage   Place of Marriage

Parents of Spouse (with Mother's maiden name) 1st Marriage

Subsequent Marriage (if applicable)

Family Details

Schools attended, dates and degrees: Community, political work, etc.:

Descendant   Descendant

Spouse   Spouse

Basic Employment History: Clubs, Church Affiliations, etc.:

Descendant   Descendant

Spouse   Spouse

Military Service:

Descendant   Spouse

M627411231
Genealogical Number

Tyler Shane Everett
Name (including maiden name if applicable)   Town of Residence

                         10/3/2000
Birthplace   Date of Birth   Date of Death   Where Buried

Name of Spouse   Birthplace   Date of Birth   Date of Death

Where Buried   Date of Marriage   Place of Marriage

If married more than once:

Name of Spouse   Birthplace   Date of Birth   Date of Death

Where Buried   Date of Marriage   Place of Marriage

Parents of Spouse (with Mother's maiden name) 1st Marriage

Subsequent Marriage (if applicable)

Family Details

Schools attended, dates and degrees: Community, political work, etc.:

Descendant   Descendant

Spouse   Spouse

Basic Employment History: Clubs, Church Affiliations, etc.:

Descendant   Descendant

Spouse   Spouse

Military Service:

Descendant   Spouse

M627411232
Genealogical Number

Tiffany Sutherland Everett
Name (including maiden name if applicable)   Town of Residence

                                 3/25/2003
Birthplace   Date of Birth   Date of Death   Where Buried

Name of Spouse   Birthplace   Date of Birth   Date of Death

Where Buried   Date of Marriage   Place of Marriage

If married more than once:

Name of Spouse   Birthplace   Date of Birth   Date of Death

Where Buried   Date of Marriage   Place of Marriage

Parents of Spouse (with Mother's maiden name) 1st Marriage

Subsequent Marriage (if applicable)

Family Details

Schools attended, dates and degrees: Community, political work, etc.:

Descendant   Descendant

Spouse   Spouse

Basic Employment History: Clubs, Church Affiliations, etc.:

Descendant   Descendant

Spouse   Spouse

Military Service:

Descendant   Spouse

M6274231
Genealogical Number

Lilburn Everett Ward, III
Name (including maiden name if applicable)

Roanoke, VA
Town of Residence

New Brunswick, NJ   11/28/1938
Birthplace   Date of Birth

Date of Death   Where Buried

Kitty Lou Tinnell   Roanoke, VA   12/2/1939
Name of Spouse   Birthplace   Date of Birth

Date of Death

Where Buried

11/22/1961
Date of Marriage

Roanoke, Virginia
Place of Marriage

If married more than once:

Name of Spouse   Birthplace   Date of Birth   Date of Death

Where Buried   Date of Marriage   Place of Marriage

Parents of Spouse (with Mother's maiden name) 1st Marriage

Subsequent Marriage (if applicable)

Family Details

Schools attended, dates and degrees:

Community, political work, etc.:

UVA-VA Tech BA Business Admin
Descendant

Descendant

Spouse

Spouse

Basic Employment History:
NCR - Reynolds Metal - Chesapeake Corp.
Commonwealth Builders Inc.
Descendant

Clubs, Church Affiliations, etc.:

Presbyterian
Descendant

Spouse

Spouse

Military Service:

USA Army 1959-1961
Descendant

Spouse

M62742312
Genealogical Number

Stacey Tinnell Ward   Baltimore, MD
Name (including maiden name if applicable)   Town of Residence

Richmond, VA   8/25/1967
Birthplace   Date of Birth   Date of Death   Where Buried

Harry D. Halpert   Baltimore, MD   2/6/1967
Name of Spouse   Birthplace   Date of Birth   Date of Death

                      7/25/1992   Roanoke, VA
Where Buried   Date of Marriage   Place of Marriage

If married more than once:

Name of Spouse   Birthplace   Date of Birth   Date of Death

Where Buried   Date of Marriage   Place of Marriage

Parents of Spouse (with Mother's maiden name) 1st Marriage

Subsequent Marriage (if applicable)

Family Details

Schools attended, dates and degrees: Community, political work, etc.:

University of Virginia, 1989 BA,
1990 M. of Teaching
Descendant   Descendant

Washington: Lee, 1989 BA.
Spouse   Spouse

Basic Employment History: Clubs, Church Affiliations, etc.:

Teacher   First Presbytarian Chruch
Descendant   Descendant

President - Merchants Terminal Corp. -
(Frozen Food Warehouse)   Chiznk Amuno Synagogue
Spouse   Spouse

Military Service:

Descendant   Spouse

M627423121
Genealogical Number

John "Jack" Turner Halpert
Name (including maiden name if applicable)

Baltimore, MD
Town of Residence

Baltimore, MD   5/30/1996
Birthplace   Date of Birth   Date of Death   Where Buried

Name of Spouse   Birthplace   Date of Birth   Date of Death

Where Buried   Date of Marriage   Place of Marriage

If married more than once:

Name of Spouse   Birthplace   Date of Birth   Date of Death

Where Buried   Date of Marriage   Place of Marriage

Parents of Spouse (with Mother's maiden name) 1st Marriage

Subsequent Marriage (if applicable)

Family Details

Schools attended, dates and degrees: Community, political work, etc.:

Descendant   Descendant

Spouse   Spouse

Basic Employment History: Clubs, Church Affiliations, etc.:

Descendant   Descendant

Spouse   Spouse

Military Service:

Descendant   Spouse

M627423122
Genealogical Number

Charles London Halpert   Baltimore, MD
Name (including maiden name if applicable)   Town of Residence

Baltimore, MD   3/9/1999
Birthplace   Date of Birth   Date of Death   Where Buried

Name of Spouse   Birthplace   Date of Birth   Date of Death

Where Buried   Date of Marriage   Place of Marriage

If married more than once:

Name of Spouse   Birthplace   Date of Birth   Date of Death

Where Buried   Date of Marriage   Place of Marriage

Parents of Spouse (with Mother's maiden name) 1st Marriage

Subsequent Marriage (if applicable)

Family Details

Schools attended, dates and degrees: Community, political work, etc.:

Descendant   Descendant

Spouse   Spouse

Basic Employment History: Clubs, Church Affiliations, etc.:

Descendant   Descendant

Spouse   Spouse

Military Service:

Descendant   Spouse

M6274241
Genealogical Number

Ann Tiffany Traynham
Name (including maiden name if applicable)

Mount Gilead, NC 27306
Town of Residence

Bluefield, W.VA
Birthplace

5/30/1936
Date of Birth

Date of Death

Where Buried

Larry Klappenbach
Name of Spouse

Wadena, Minn.
Birthplace

1/23/1934
Date of Birth

Date of Death

Where Buried

11/30/1957
Date of Marriage

Waynesboro, VA.
Place of Marriage

If married more than once:

Name of Spouse

Birthplace

Date of Birth

Date of Death

Where Buried

Date of Marriage

Place of Marriage

August William Klappenbach - Anna Marie Becker
Parents of Spouse (with Mother's maiden name) 1st Marriage

Subsequent Marriage (if applicable)

Family Details

Schools attended, dates and degrees:

Community, political work, etc.:

Waynesboro High School - 1953
Descendant

Descendant

University of Idaho BSEE 1956
Spouse

Spouse

Basic Employment History:

Clubs, Church Affiliations, etc.:

Descendant

First Lutheran Church, Albemarle, NC.
Descendant

Electrical Engineer-General Electric
Spouse

First Lutheran Church
Spouse

Military Service:

Descendant

Spouse

David Edward Klappenbach
b. Sept. 3, 1958 m. Elizabeth Dawn Hatfield 8/4/1990
Tampa, FL. b. June 27, 1968, Kentucky
Lutheran Pastor - grad. Lutheran Southern Theological Seminary 1998
Malinta, Oh. - 1998-Present
1. Preston Michael Klappenbach   b. Sept 9, 2000 - Malinta, Oh.

Brian Dale Klappenbach
b. July 10, 1960
Tampa, FL
Graduated NC State 1983, BSEE
Elec. Engineer, Raleigh, NC

Bruce Douglas Klappenbach
b. Feb 3, 1963   m. Shannon Andrea Sellers Jan 20 1996
Tampa, FL   b. Aug 10, 1969 - Raleigh, NC
Civil Engineer NC DOT   1st grade School Teacher
Raleigh, NC.

1. Andrew Beam Klappenbach
b. April 4, 1998, Raleigh

2. Charles Mitchell Klappenbach
b. Feb 16, 2000, Raleigh

3. Elliott Boone Klappenbach
b. March 4, 2002, Raleigh

M62742411
Genealogical Number

David Edward Klappenbach
Name (including maiden name if applicable)

Malinta, Ohio
Town of Residence

Tampa, FL
Birthplace

9/31/1958
Date of Birth

Date of Death

Where Buried

Elizabeth Dawn Hatfield
Name of Spouse

Kentucky
Birthplace

6/27/1968
Date of Birth

Date of Death

Where Buried

8/4/1990
Date of Marriage

Place of Marriage

If married more than once:

Name of Spouse

Birthplace

Date of Birth

Date of Death

Where Buried

Date of Marriage

Place of Marriage

Parents of Spouse (with Mother's maiden name) 1st Marriage

Subsequent Marriage (if applicable)

Family Details

Schools attended, dates and degrees:

Community, political work, etc.:

1998 Lutheran Southern Theological Seminary
Descendant

Descendant

Spouse

Spouse

Basic Employment History:

Clubs, Church Affiliations, etc.:

Lutheran Pastor
Descendant

Descendant

Spouse

Spouse

Military Service:

Descendant

Spouse

M627424111
Genealogical Number

Preston Michael Klappenbach   Malinta, Ohio
Name (including maiden name if applicable)   Town of Residence

Malinta, Ohio   9/9/2000
Birthplace   Date of Birth   Date of Death   Where Buried

Name of Spouse   Birthplace   Date of Birth   Date of Death

Where Buried   Date of Marriage   Place of Marriage

If married more than once:

Name of Spouse   Birthplace   Date of Birth   Date of Death

Where Buried   Date of Marriage   Place of Marriage

Parents of Spouse (with Mother's maiden name) 1st Marriage

Subsequent Marriage (if applicable)

Family Details

Schools attended, dates and degrees: Community, political work, etc.:

Descendant   Descendant

Spouse   Spouse

Basic Employment History: Clubs, Church Affiliations, etc.:

Descendant   Descendant

Spouse   Spouse

Military Service:

Descendant   Spouse

M62742412
Genealogical Number

Brian Dale Klappenbach   Raleigh, NC
Name (including maiden name if applicable)   Town of Residence

Tampa, FL   7/10/1960
Birthplace   Date of Birth   Date of Death   Where Buried

Name of Spouse   Birthplace   Date of Birth   Date of Death

Where Buried   Date of Marriage   Place of Marriage

If married more than once:

Name of Spouse   Birthplace   Date of Birth   Date of Death

Where Buried   Date of Marriage   Place of Marriage

Parents of Spouse (with Mother's maiden name) 1st Marriage

Subsequent Marriage (if applicable)

Family Details

Schools attended, dates and degrees: Community, political work, etc.:

NC State 1983 - BSEE
Descendant   Descendant

Spouse   Spouse

Basic Employment History: Clubs, Church Affiliations, etc.:

Electric Engineer, Raleigh, NC.
Descendant   Descendant

Spouse   Spouse

Military Service:

Descendant   Spouse

M62742413
Genealogical Number

Bruce Douglas Klappenbach   Raleigh, NC
Name (including maiden name if applicable)   Town of Residence

Tampa, FL   2/3/1963
Birthplace   Date of Birth   Date of Death   Where Buried

Shannon Andrea Sellers   Raleigh, NC   8/20/1969
Name of Spouse   Birthplace   Date of Birth   Date of Death

     1/20/1996
Where Buried   Date of Marriage   Place of Marriage

If married more than once:

Name of Spouse   Birthplace   Date of Birth   Date of Death

Where Buried   Date of Marriage   Place of Marriage

Parents of Spouse (with Mother's maiden name) 1st Marriage

Subsequent Marriage (if applicable)

Family Details

Schools attended, dates and degrees: Community, political work, etc.:

Descendant   Descendant

Spouse   Spouse

Basic Employment History: Clubs, Church Affiliations, etc.:

Civil Engineer, NCDOT
Descendant   Descendant

1st Grade School Teacher
Spouse   Spouse

Military Service:

Descendant   Spouse

M627424131
Genealogical Number

Andrew Beam Klappenbach
Name (including maiden name if applicable)

Raleigh, NC
Town of Residence

Raleigh, NC
Birthplace

4/4/1998
Date of Birth

Date of Death

Where Buried

Name of Spouse

Birthplace

Date of Birth

Date of Death

Where Buried

Date of Marriage

Place of Marriage

If married more than once:

Name of Spouse

Birthplace

Date of Birth

Date of Death

Where Buried

Date of Marriage

Place of Marriage

Parents of Spouse (with Mother's maiden name) 1st Marriage

Subsequent Marriage (if applicable)

Family Details

Schools attended, dates and degrees:

Community, political work, etc.:

Descendant

Descendant

Spouse

Spouse

Basic Employment History:

Clubs, Church Affiliations, etc.:

Descendant

Descendant

Spouse

Spouse

Military Service:

Descendant

Spouse

M627424132
Genealogical Number

Charles Mitchell Klappenbach
Name (including maiden name if applicable)

Raleigh, NC
Town of Residence

Raleigh, NC
Birthplace

2/16/2000
Date of Birth

Date of Death

Where Buried

Name of Spouse

Birthplace

Date of Birth

Date of Death

Where Buried

Date of Marriage

Place of Marriage

If married more than once:

Name of Spouse

Birthplace

Date of Birth

Date of Death

Where Buried

Date of Marriage

Place of Marriage

Parents of Spouse (with Mother's maiden name) 1st Marriage

Subsequent Marriage (if applicable)

Family Details

Schools attended, dates and degrees:

Community, political work, etc.:

Descendant

Descendant

Spouse

Spouse

Basic Employment History:

Clubs, Church Affiliations, etc.:

Descendant

Descendant

Spouse

Spouse

Military Service:

Descendant

Spouse

M627424133
Genealogical Number

Elliott Boone Klappenbach
Name (including maiden name if applicable)

Raleigh, NC
Town of Residence

Raleigh, NC   3/4/2002
Birthplace   Date of Birth   Date of Death   Where Buried

Name of Spouse   Birthplace   Date of Birth   Date of Death

Where Buried   Date of Marriage   Place of Marriage

If married more than once:

Name of Spouse   Birthplace   Date of Birth   Date of Death

Where Buried   Date of Marriage   Place of Marriage

Parents of Spouse (with Mother's maiden name) 1st Marriage

Subsequent Marriage (if applicable)

Family Details

Schools attended, dates and degrees: Community, political work, etc.:

Descendant   Descendant

Spouse   Spouse

Basic Employment History: Clubs, Church Affiliations, etc.:

Descendant   Descendant

Spouse   Spouse

Military Service:

Descendant   Spouse

M6274242
Genealogical Number

John Edward Traynham, III   Bedford, VA.
Name (including maiden name if applicable)   Town of Residence

Waynesboro, VA   2/23/1940
Birthplace   Date of Birth   Date of Death   Where Buried

Divorced
Name of Spouse   Birthplace   Date of Birth   Date of Death

Where Buried   Date of Marriage   Place of Marriage

If married more than once:

Name of Spouse   Birthplace   Date of Birth   Date of Death

Where Buried   Date of Marriage   Place of Marriage

Parents of Spouse (with Mother's maiden name) 1st Marriage

Subsequent Marriage (if applicable)

Family Details

Schools attended, dates and degrees: Community, political work, etc.:

VMI - graduated 1962
Medical Degree UVA - 1966
Descendant   Descendant

Spouse   Spouse

Basic Employment History: Clubs, Church Affiliations, etc.:

Orthopedist
Descendant   Descendant

Spouse   Spouse

Military Service:

Stationed in Japan - Vietnam War
Descendant   Spouse

M6274243
Genealogical Number

Nancy St. Clair Traynham
Name (including maiden name if applicable)

Centerville, Mass.
Town of Residence

Staunton, VA
Birthplace

7/15/1946
Date of Birth

Date of Death

Where Buried

Willam Gordan Johnston
Name of Spouse

Birthplace

Date of Birth

Date of Death

Where Buried

2/15/1975
Date of Marriage

Charlottesville, VA
Place of Marriage

If married more than once:

Name of Spouse

Birthplace

Date of Birth

Date of Death

Where Buried

Date of Marriage

Place of Marriage

Parents of Spouse (with Mother's maiden name) 1st Marriage

Subsequent Marriage (if applicable)

Family Details

Schools attended, dates and degrees:

Community, political work, etc.:

Descendant

Descendant

Spouse

Spouse

Basic Employment History:

Clubs, Church Affiliations, etc.:

Pharmacist
Descendant

Descendant

Urologist
Spouse

Spouse

Military Service:

Descendant

Vietnam
Spouse

M6274421
Genealogical Number

Rosalinda Graham Farrier
Name (including maiden name if applicable)

Virginia Beach, VA
Town of Residence

Bluefield, WVA
Birthplace

3/25/1942
Date of Birth

Date of Death

Where Buried

James H. Daughtrey
Name of Spouse

Suffolk, VA
Birthplace

10/29/1932
Date of Birth

7/26/1996
Date of Death

Suffolk, VA
Where Buried

8/30/1991
Date of Marriage

Virginia Beach, VA
Place of Marriage

If married more than once:

James F. Vaughan
Name of Spouse

Norfolk, VA
Birthplace

Date of Birth

Date of Death

Virginia Beach, VA
Where Buried

Date of Marriage

Virginia Beach, VA
Place of Marriage

Parents of Spouse (with Mother's maiden name) 1st Marriage

Subsequent Marriage (if applicable)

Family Details

Schools attended, dates and degrees:

Community, political work, etc.:

ODU Masters
Longwood College BS
Descendant

Descendant

Spouse

Spouse

Basic Employment History:

Clubs, Church Affiliations, etc.:

Chesapeake Public Schools
Descendant

Memorial United Methodist
Descendant

Spouse

Spouse

Military Service:

Descendant

Spouse

M6274422
Genealogical Number

Frank Graham Farrier, Jr.
Name (including maiden name if applicable)

Newport, VA
Town of Residence

Newport, Giles County, VA
Birthplace

10/15/1943
Date of Birth

Date of Death

Where Buried

Patricia Martin (Div.)
Name of Spouse

Birthplace

Date of Birth

Date of Death

Where Buried

6/10/1971
Date of Marriage

Place of Marriage

If married more than once:

Name of Spouse

Birthplace

Date of Birth

Date of Death

Where Buried

Date of Marriage

Place of Marriage

Parents of Spouse (with Mother's maiden name) 1st Marriage

Subsequent Marriage (if applicable)

Family Details

Schools attended, dates and degrees:

Community, political work, etc.:

Descendant

Descendant

Spouse

Spouse

Basic Employment History:

Clubs, Church Affiliations, etc.:

Descendant

Descendant

Spouse

Spouse

Military Service:

Descendant

Spouse

M627444
Genealogical Number

Jacqueline Pendleton St. Clair	Fairfax, VA
Name (including maiden name if applicable)	Town of Residence

Tazewell, VA	2/25/1919	7/28/2005	Arlington National Cemetary
Birthplace	Date of Birth	Date of Death	Where Buried

Kenneth John Brown	Bronx, NY	1/30/1922	11/8/1990
Name of Spouse	Birthplace	Date of Birth	Date of Death

Arlington National Cemetary	3/9/1943	Coeur d'Alene, Idaho
Where Buried	Date of Marriage	Place of Marriage

If married more than once:

Name of Spouse	Birthplace	Date of Birth	Date of Death

Where Buried	Date of Marriage	Place of Marriage

John Joseph Brown and Lillian Zne Brown
Parents of Spouse (with Mother's maiden name) 1st Marriage

Subsequent Marriage (if applicable)

Family Details

Schools attended, dates and degrees:

Sulin College, Bristol, VA
Bowling Green Business Univ. Bowling Green, KY
Descendant
Various college courses through the Air Force
also Business School
Spouse

Basic Employment History:

City of Fairfax 1965-1979 Assessment Dept.
Descendant
U.S. Air Force and Federal
Gvmt - Defense Intelligence Agency
Spouse

Military Service:

U.S. Air Force - 30 years combined service.
Descendant

Community, political work, etc.:

Volunteer Prince Wm. County
Library
Descendant

Spouse

Clubs, Church Affiliations, etc.:
Tazewell Methodist - Lifetime member
Charter member Jeffersonville Women's Club.
Descendant

Reserve Officers' Club. Lions Club
Spouse

Spouse

M6274441
Genealogical Number

Jacqueline St. Clair Brown
Name (including maiden name if applicable)

Royal Palm Beach, FL.
Town of Residence

Bluefield, W.VA
Birthplace

1/4/1944
Date of Birth

Date of Death

Where Buried

David A. Pilawski (Div)
Name of Spouse

Cleveland, Ohio
Birthplace

3/24/1943
Date of Birth

Date of Death

Where Buried

4/28/1973
Date of Marriage

Arlington Hall, Arlington, VA
Place of Marriage

If married more than once:

Name of Spouse

Birthplace

Date of Birth

Date of Death

Where Buried

Date of Marriage

Place of Marriage

Louis Anthony Pilawski - Stella M.
Parents of Spouse (with Mother's maiden name) 1st Marriage

Subsequent Marriage (if applicable)

Family Details

Schools attended, dates and degrees:

Community, political work, etc.:

Medical College of VA, B.S, 1966
Descendant

Descendant

Spouse

Spouse

Basic Employment History:

Clubs, Church Affiliations, etc.:

School Teacher
Descendant

Descendant

Spouse

Spouse

Military Service:

Descendant

Command Sergeant Major - Retired US Army
Spouse

M62744411
Genealogical Number

Renee Dawn Pilawski							Military
Name (including maiden name if applicable)				Town of Residence

Miami, FL.						6/2/1975
Birthplace					Date of Birth			Date of Death			Where Buried

Name of Spouse					Birthplace			Date of Birth			Date of Death

Where Buried					Date of Marriage			Place of Marriage

If married more than once:

Name of Spouse					Birthplace			Date of Birth			Date of Death

Where Buried					Date of Marriage			Place of Marriage

Parents of Spouse (with Mother's maiden name) 1st Marriage

Subsequent Marriage (if applicable)

Family Details

Schools attended, dates and degrees:					Community, political work, etc.:

Descendant									Descendant

Spouse										Spouse

Basic Employment History:						Clubs, Church Affiliations, etc.:

Descendant									Descendant

Spouse										Spouse

Military Service:

Sgt. U.S. Army
Descendant									Spouse

M62744412
Genealogical Number

Chad Louis Pilawski
Name (including maiden name if applicable)

Ft. Lauderdale, FL
Town of Residence

Miami, FL   2/8/1978
Birthplace   Date of Birth

Date of Death   Where Buried

Name of Spouse   Birthplace   Date of Birth   Date of Death

Where Buried   Date of Marriage   Place of Marriage

If married more than once:

Name of Spouse   Birthplace   Date of Birth   Date of Death

Where Buried   Date of Marriage   Place of Marriage

Parents of Spouse (with Mother's maiden name) 1st Marriage

Subsequent Marriage (if applicable)

Family Details

Schools attended, dates and degrees: Community, political work, etc.:

Descendant   Descendant

Spouse   Spouse

Basic Employment History: Clubs, Church Affiliations, etc.:

Delta Airlines
Descendant   Descendant

Spouse   Spouse

Military Service:

Descendant   Spouse

M6274442
Genealogical Number

Kenneth John Brown, Jr.   Marietta, GA
Name (including maiden name if applicable)   Town of Residence

Orlanda, FL   6/4/1945
Birthplace   Date of Birth   Date of Death   Where Buried

Chiaria Michelle Yenyo   7/22/1958
Name of Spouse   Birthplace   Date of Birth   Date of Death

                               6/17/1989
Where Buried   Date of Marriage   Place of Marriage

If married more than once:

Name of Spouse   Birthplace   Date of Birth   Date of Death

Where Buried   Date of Marriage   Place of Marriage

Edward Yenyo - Fay
Parents of Spouse (with Mother's maiden name) 1st Marriage

Subsequent Marriage (if applicable)

Family Details

Schools attended, dates and degrees: Community, political work, etc.:

Descendant   Descendant

Spouse   Spouse

Basic Employment History: Clubs, Church Affiliations, etc.:

Descendant   Descendant

Spouse   Spouse

Military Service:

Descendant   Spouse

M62744421
Genealogical Number

Candice Michelle Brown   Marietta, GA
Name (including maiden name if applicable)   Town of Residence

_____   _____   _____   _____
Birthplace   Date of Birth   Date of Death   Where Buried

_____   _____   _____   _____
Name of Spouse   Birthplace   Date of Birth   Date of Death

_____   _____   _____
Where Buried   Date of Marriage   Place of Marriage

If married more than once:

_____   _____   _____   _____
Name of Spouse   Birthplace   Date of Birth   Date of Death

_____   _____   _____
Where Buried   Date of Marriage   Place of Marriage

_____
Parents of Spouse (with Mother's maiden name) 1st Marriage

_____
Subsequent Marriage (if applicable)

Family Details

Schools attended, dates and degrees: Community, political work, etc.:

_____   _____
Descendant   Descendant

_____   _____
Spouse   Spouse

Basic Employment History: Clubs, Church Affiliations, etc.:

_____   _____
Descendant   Descendant

_____   _____
Spouse   Spouse

Military Service:

_____   _____
Descendant   Spouse

M6274443
Genealogical Number

Nancy Tiffany Brown
Name (including maiden name if applicable)

Fairfax, VA
Town of Residence

Tazewell, VA   8/12/1952
Birthplace   Date of Birth

Date of Death   Where Buried

Fred Sven Berg   Chelsea, MA   2/13/1952
Name of Spouse   Birthplace   Date of Birth   Date of Death

                        10/10/1981   Manassas, VA
Where Buried   Date of Marriage   Place of Marriage

If married more than once:

Name of Spouse   Birthplace   Date of Birth   Date of Death

Where Buried   Date of Marriage   Place of Marriage

Fredrick H. Berg - Alice McQuestin
Parents of Spouse (with Mother's maiden name) 1st Marriage

Subsequent Marriage (if applicable)

Family Details

Schools attended, dates and degrees:

George Mason Univ. BS in Educ. .
Marymount Univ. Masters Legal Admin.
Descendant

Community, political work, etc.:

Descendant

Spouse

Spouse

Basic Employment History:

Intellectual Property Law Firm Manager
Descendant

Clubs, Church Affiliations, etc.:

Descendant

Custom Home Carpenter/Builder
Spouse

Spouse

Military Service:

Descendant

Spouse

M62744431
Genealogical Number

Michelle Tiffany Berg   Fairfax, VA
Name (including maiden name if applicable)   Town of Residence

Fairfax, VA   9/6/1982
Birthplace   Date of Birth   Date of Death   Where Buried

Name of Spouse   Birthplace   Date of Birth   Date of Death

Where Buried   Date of Marriage   Place of Marriage

If married more than once:

Name of Spouse   Birthplace   Date of Birth   Date of Death

Where Buried   Date of Marriage   Place of Marriage

Parents of Spouse (with Mother's maiden name) 1st Marriage

Subsequent Marriage (if applicable)

Family Details

Schools attended, dates and degrees: Community, political work, etc.:

Bradford Univ. - Upcoming Senior
Descendant   Descendant

Spouse   Spouse

Basic Employment History: Clubs, Church Affiliations, etc.:

Descendant   Descendant

Spouse   Spouse

Military Service:

Descendant   Spouse

M62744432
_____
Genealogical Number

Sean Sven Berg   Fairfax, VA
_____   _____
Name (including maiden name if applicable)   Town of Residence

Fairfax, VA   4/30/1986
_____   _____   _____   _____
Birthplace   Date of Birth   Date of Death   Where Buried

_____   _____   _____   _____
Name of Spouse   Birthplace   Date of Birth   Date of Death

_____   _____   _____
Where Buried   Date of Marriage   Place of Marriage

If married more than once:

_____   _____   _____   _____
Name of Spouse   Birthplace   Date of Birth   Date of Death

_____   _____   _____
Where Buried   Date of Marriage   Place of Marriage

_____
Parents of Spouse (with Mother's maiden name) 1st Marriage

_____
Subsequent Marriage (if applicable)

Family Details

Schools attended, dates and degrees: Community, political work, etc.:

_____   _____
Descendant   Descendant

_____   _____
Spouse   Spouse

Basic Employment History: Clubs, Church Affiliations, etc.:

_____   _____
Descendant   Descendant

_____   _____
Spouse   Spouse

Military Service:

_____   _____
Descendant   Spouse

M627445
Genealogical Number

Glenn St. Clair   Geneva, ILL
Name (including maiden name if applicable)   Town of Residence

Tazewell, VA   2/23/1922
Birthplace   Date of Birth   Date of Death   Where Buried

Desle O.H. Miller   Geneseo, ILL   8/5/1922
Name of Spouse   Birthplace   Date of Birth   Date of Death

                          12/10/1943
Where Buried   Date of Marriage   Place of Marriage

If married more than once:

Name of Spouse   Birthplace   Date of Birth   Date of Death

Where Buried   Date of Marriage   Place of Marriage

Harry & Alma Licke Miller
Parents of Spouse (with Mother's maiden name) 1st Marriage

Subsequent Marriage (if applicable)

Family Details

Schools attended, dates and degrees: Community, political work, etc.:

Sullins College - 1939-41
Descendant   Descendant

U. of ILL. graduated 1943
Spouse   Spouse

Basic Employment History: Clubs, Church Affiliations, etc.:

Secretarial   Congregational Church
Descendant   Descendant

Farm Equipment Industry   same - Lions
Spouse   Spouse

Military Service:

Army Air Corps - WWII
Descendant   Spouse

M6274452
Genealogical Number

Julia St. Clair Miller
Name (including maiden name if applicable)

Golden, CO
Town of Residence

Moline, ILL
Birthplace

4/22/1949
Date of Birth

Date of Death

Where Buried

James Michael Keating
Name of Spouse

Birthplace

8/7/1946
Date of Birth

Date of Death

Where Buried

5/24/2003
Date of Marriage

Golden, CO
Place of Marriage

If married more than once:

Jeffrey Mason Reynolds
Name of Spouse

Sydney, NY
Birthplace

10/26/1950
Date of Birth

Date of Death

Where Buried

9/2/1972
Date of Marriage

Bettendorf, Iowa
Place of Marriage

Parents of Spouse (with Mother's maiden name) 1st Marriage

Subsequent Marriage (if applicable)

Family Details

Schools attended, dates and degrees:
Univ. Of Colo.-Denver- M.S. - 1988
Univ. Of Colo. - BA 1971. Colo. School of
Mines - M.S. - 1992
Descendant

Community, political work, etc.:

Descendant

Oregon State Univ - BS 1988, MS 1994
Spouse

Spouse

Basic Employment History:
Research Chemist 1971-73, Teacher 1974-77,
Environmental Scientist 1989-present
Descendant

Clubs, Church Affiliations, etc.:

Descendant

Environmental Engineer
Spouse

Spouse

Military Service:

Descendant

Spouse

M62744521
Genealogical Number

Benjamin Mason Reynolds
Name (including maiden name if applicable)

Golden, CO
Town of Residence

Denver, CO
Birthplace

5/28/1977
Date of Birth

Date of Death

Where Buried

Heidi Marie Scheel Nagel
Name of Spouse

Concepcion, Chile
Birthplace

5/10/1979
Date of Birth

Date of Death

Where Buried

8/18/2001
Date of Marriage

Golden, CO
Place of Marriage

If married more than once:

Name of Spouse

Birthplace

Date of Birth

Date of Death

Where Buried

Date of Marriage

Place of Marriage

Gerardo Adolfo Scheel Zambrano, Patricia Andrea Nagel Sbatbaro
Parents of Spouse (with Mother's maiden name) 1st Marriage

Subsequent Marriage (if applicable)

Family Details

Schools attended, dates and degrees:

Hamilton College/1995-99/Bachelor of Arts
English/History
Descendant

San Juan de Las Condes High School 1999
Spouse

Basic Employment History:

English teacher in Chile/teacher in CO
Descendant

Homemaker/mother/spanish teacher
Spouse

Military Service:

Descendant

Community, political work, etc.:

Descendant

Spouse

Clubs, Church Affiliations, etc.:

ex-Christian Scientist
Descendant

ex-Catholic
Spouse

Spouse

M62744522
Genealogical Number

Edric Scott Reynolds
Name (including maiden name if applicable)

Golden, CO
Town of Residence

Aspen, CO
Birthplace

9/24/1980
Date of Birth

Date of Death

Where Buried

Name of Spouse

Birthplace

Date of Birth

Date of Death

Where Buried

Date of Marriage

Place of Marriage

If married more than once:

Name of Spouse

Birthplace

Date of Birth

Date of Death

Where Buried

Date of Marriage

Place of Marriage

Parents of Spouse (with Mother's maiden name) 1st Marriage

Subsequent Marriage (if applicable)

Family Details

Schools attended, dates and degrees:

Community, political work, etc.:

Univ. of Colorado - Boulder 1999-present
Descendant

Descendant

Spouse

Spouse

Basic Employment History:

Clubs, Church Affiliations, etc.:

Descendant

Descendant

Spouse

Spouse

Military Service:

Descendant

Spouse

M627461
Genealogical Number

Richard Otis St. Clair
Name (including maiden name if applicable)

Fairfax, VA
Town of Residence

Welch, W. VA
Birthplace

3/16/1926
Date of Birth

Date of Death

Where Buried

Mary Kate Stockner
Name of Spouse

Havaco, W.VA
Birthplace

9/9/1928
Date of Birth

Date of Death

Where Buried

12/29/1950
Date of Marriage

Welch, W.VA
Place of Marriage

If married more than once:

Name of Spouse

Birthplace

Date of Birth

Date of Death

Where Buried

Date of Marriage

Place of Marriage

Raymond Early Stachner - Alma Hayes
Parents of Spouse (with Mother's maiden name) 1st Marriage

Subsequent Marriage (if applicable)

Family Details

Schools attended, dates and degrees:

Virginia Tech 1950-BS in Electrical Engineering.
University of Colorado 1969-Communications
Engineering.
Descendant
Lees McRae College - 1946-48
Concord College - 1948-50-BS in Education
Spouse

Basic Employment History:
Western Electric/Bell Telephone Labs 1950-1966.
AT&T Company 1966-1982. MITRE Corporation
1982-1987. Retired 1987.
Descendant

Social Studies and Librarian (School)

Professional
Community, political work, etc.:
Subsection Chairman, Inst. of Electrical &
Electronic Engineers IEEE. Subsection Vice-
Chairman, American Inst. of Electrical Engin
AIEE. Spanish Interpreter for Community Se
Descendant
Fish volunteer (For Immediate Sympathe
Help)
Spouse

Clubs, Church Affiliations, etc.:

Deacon, Presbyterian Church.
Ham Radio Associations
Descendant

Presbyterian - Deacon of Elder

M6274611
Genealogical Number

Allison Leigh St. Clair
Name (including maiden name if applicable)

Charlottesville, VA
Town of Residence

Winston- Salom, NC   10/3/1953
Birthplace   Date of Birth

Date of Death   Where Buried

Thomas Schildwachter, MD   Baltimore, MD   3/13/1949
Name of Spouse   Birthplace   Date of Birth   Date of Death

8/28/1976
Where Buried   Date of Marriage   Place of Marriage

If married more than once:

Name of Spouse   Birthplace   Date of Birth   Date of Death

Where Buried   Date of Marriage   Place of Marriage

Thomas Donnell Schildwachter - Edith Ashton Schildwachter
Parents of Spouse (with Mother's maiden name) 1st Marriage

Subsequent Marriage (if applicable)

Family Details

Schools attended, dates and degrees:

Univ. of VA (Charlottesville) - BS 1975
Vanderbilt Univ. (Nashville TN) MA 1976
Descendant

Univ. of VA (Charlottesville) - BA 1971
Univ. of VA Medical School MD - 1975
Spouse

Basic Employment History:

'Towers' - UVA Hospital, Charlottesville City
Schools. Charlottesville YMCA
Descendant

Self-employed - Orthopedic Surgery Practice
Spouse

Military Service:

Descendant

Community, political work, etc.:

St. Anne's Belfield School Parent Auxiliary work
Martha Jefferson Hospital Women's Committee
Charlottesville Garden Club
Descendant
U.S. Lacrosse Foundation
Charlottesville Lacrosse Foundation, Seminole
 Lacrosse League Coach, Christ Episcopal Church
Volunteer Coach, St. Anne's Belfield School
Spouse

Clubs, Church Affiliations, etc.:

Christ Episcopal Church
Descendant
Farmington Country Club Committee
Christ Episcopal Church
Spouse

Spouse

M62746111
Genealogical Number

Brooke Ashton Schildwachter
Name (including maiden name if applicable)

Charlottesville, VA - permanent
(Chapel Hill NC, Student)
Town of Residence

Charlottesville, VA   3/20/1979
Birthplace   Date of Birth   Date of Death   Where Buried

Name of Spouse   Birthplace   Date of Birth   Date of Death

Where Buried   Date of Marriage   Place of Marriage

If married more than once:

Name of Spouse   Birthplace   Date of Birth   Date of Death

Where Buried   Date of Marriage   Place of Marriage

Parents of Spouse (with Mother's maiden name) 1st Marriage

Subsequent Marriage (if applicable)

Family Details

Schools attended, dates and degrees:
St. Anne's Belfield School 1997
Univ. of NC - Chapel Hill - BA 2001 American Studies/
Communications double major. Postgraduate work - present.
(Applying to Medical Schools).
Descendant

Community, political work, etc.:

Descendant

Spouse

Spouse

Basic Employment History:
UNC Dept. of Alcohol Studies - Lab

(present with post grad classes)
Descendant

Clubs, Church Affiliations, etc.:
UNC Lax team volunteer coordinator, UNC Women's
Lacrosse Team. Phi Betta Kappa-UNC.
Durham Academy Lacrosse Coach, ACT volunteer
Descendant

Spouse

Spouse

Military Service:

Descendant

Spouse

M62746112
Genealogical Number

Charlottesville, VA - permanent
Fort Collins, CO (student)
Meredith Donnell Schildwachter
Name (including maiden name if applicable)   Town of Residence

Charlottesville, VA   11/5/1980
Birthplace   Date of Birth   Date of Death   Where Buried

Name of Spouse   Birthplace   Date of Birth   Date of Death

Where Buried   Date of Marriage   Place of Marriage

If married more than once:

Name of Spouse   Birthplace   Date of Birth   Date of Death

Where Buried   Date of Marriage   Place of Marriage

Parents of Spouse (with Mother's maiden name) 1st Marriage

Subsequent Marriage (if applicable)

Family Details

Schools attended, dates and degrees: Community, political work, etc.:
St. Anne's Belfield School 1999
Loyola University Baltimore MD 1999-2000
Bond University (Australia) 2000   Loyola Women's Lacrosse Team
Colorado State University 2001-present-graduate   1999-2000
(May 2004) Landscape Horticultural Design   Descendant
Descendant

Spouse   Spouse

Basic Employment History: Clubs, Church Affiliations, etc.:
Nanny for UVA Women's Lacrosse Coach
J.W. Townsend Landscape Services 2002
Landscape Design Firm (Co.) 2003
Descendant   Descendant

Spouse   Spouse

Military Service:

Descendant   Spouse

M62746113
Genealogical Number

Hayes St. Clair Schildwachter

Charlottesville, VA - permanent
Nashville, TN (Student

Name (including maiden name if applicable)

Town of Residence

Charlottesville, VA   5/8/1984
Birthplace   Date of Birth   Date of Death   Where Buried

Name of Spouse   Birthplace   Date of Birth   Date of Death

Where Buried   Date of Marriage   Place of Marriage

If married more than once:

Name of Spouse   Birthplace   Date of Birth   Date of Death

Where Buried   Date of Marriage   Place of Marriage

Parents of Spouse (with Mother's maiden name) 1st Marriage

Subsequent Marriage (if applicable)

Family Details

Schools attended, dates and degrees: Community, political work, etc.:

St. Anne;s Belfield School 2002
Vanderbilt University 2002 - present
Descendant   Descendant

Spouse   Spouse

Basic Employment History: Clubs, Church Affiliations, etc.:

Taylor, Zuka, Milnor, Carter Law Firm "runner" presently
Sloan's Restaurant, Benzinger Lawn Service, Total
Body Fitness - PT aide.
Descendant   Descendant

Spouse   Spouse

Military Service:

Descendant   Spouse

M6274622
Genealogical Number

Amy (Amey) Rowe St. Clair (kept maiden name)   Alexandria, VA
Name (including maiden name if applicable)   Town of Residence

Charlotte, NC   8/27/1962
Birthplace   Date of Birth   Date of Death   Where Buried

Burke Harold Moeller   Walla Walla, Wash.   5/21/1968
Name of Spouse   Birthplace   Date of Birth   Date of Death

                           6/30/2001   Blowing Rock, NC
Where Buried   Date of Marriage   Place of Marriage

If married more than once:

Alan Mandy (Div.)   South Africa   9/8/1973
Name of Spouse   Birthplace   Date of Birth   Date of Death

                           5/8/1998   Johannesburg, South Africa
Where Buried   Date of Marriage   Place of Marriage

Parents of Spouse (with Mother's maiden name) 1st Marriage

Subsequent Marriage (if applicable)

Family Details

Schools attended, dates and degrees: Community, political work, etc.:

UNC. Chapel Hill - BA 1984
Int'l Relations & Philosophy (Double Major)
Descendant   Descendant
Pitzer Univ. Claremont, Calif.
BA - Political Studies
Spouse   Spouse

Basic Employment History: Clubs, Church Affiliations, etc.:
Planning and Liaison Engineer at
the Dept. of State
Descendant   Descendant

Writer and Producer for NBC
Spouse   Spouse

Military Service:

Descendant   Spouse

M627482
Genealogical Number

Wade Tiffany St. Clair
Name (including maiden name if applicable)

Bluefield, VA
Town of Residence

Bluefield, W. VA
Birthplace

10/27/1941
Date of Birth

Date of Death

Where Buried

Nora Louise Bryant
Name of Spouse

Raysal, W.VA
Birthplace

8/31/1945
Date of Birth

Date of Death

Where Buried

3/18/1988
Date of Marriage

Bluefield, VA
Place of Marriage

If married more than once:

Kathryn Louise Bowen
Name of Spouse

Tazewell, VA
Birthplace

7/23/1948
Date of Birth

Date of Death

Where Buried

8/10/1968
Date of Marriage

Tazewell, VA
Place of Marriage

Parents of Spouse (with Mother's maiden name) 1st Marriage

Subsequent Marriage (if applicable)

Family Details

Schools attended, dates and degrees:

Community, political work, etc.:

Descendant

Descendant

Spouse

Spouse

Basic Employment History:

Clubs, Church Affiliations, etc.:

Descendant

Descendant

Spouse

Spouse

Military Service:

Descendant

Spouse

M6274821
Genealogical Number

Kathryn Tiffany St. Clair   Atlanta, GA
Name (including maiden name if applicable)   Town of Residence

Bluefield, W.VA   2/10/1973
Birthplace   Date of Birth   Date of Death   Where Buried

Name of Spouse   Birthplace   Date of Birth   Date of Death

Where Buried   Date of Marriage   Place of Marriage

If married more than once:

Name of Spouse   Birthplace   Date of Birth   Date of Death

Where Buried   Date of Marriage   Place of Marriage

Parents of Spouse (with Mother's maiden name) 1st Marriage

Subsequent Marriage (if applicable)

Family Details

Schools attended, dates and degrees: Community, political work, etc.:

1995 - BA - Hollins College
2001 MBA - Georgia State Univ.
Descendant   Descendant

Spouse   Spouse

Basic Employment History: Clubs, Church Affiliations, etc.:

Descendant   Descendant

Spouse   Spouse

Military Service:

Descendant   Spouse

28.

THE JANE SHANNON MOORE LINE
PICTURES

Alex StClair Family

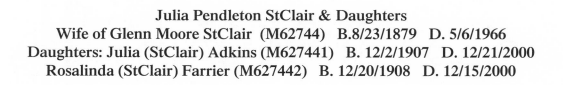

Julia Pendleton StClair & Daughters
Wife of Glenn Moore StClair (M62744)   B.8/23/1879   D. 5/6/1966
Daughters: Julia (StClair) Adkins (M627441)   B. 12/2/1907   D. 12/21/2000
Rosalinda (StClair) Farrier (M627442)   B. 12/20/1908   D. 12/15/2000

29.

THE JOHN SHANNON MOORE LINE
GENEALOGICAL CHARTS

M628 *John Shannon Moore - (1) Margaret A. Whitley*
B. 7/25/1814   M. 12/19/1833   B. _____
D. _____   M. 10/3/1853   D. _____

(2) Emily Shannon
B. _____
D. _____

M6281 – (1) Eliza Jane Moore - Robert Crockett
B. 9/19/1834   M. 6/27/1853   B. 3/2/1819
D. 11/9/1901   D. 5/7/1895

M62811 - Margaret Jane Crockett - William Benjamin Morton
B. 7/23/1855   M. 11/18/1874   B. 1/22/1852
D. 5/8/1935   D. 10/18/1934

M628111 - James Edward Morton - (1) Eugenia Johnson
B. 1/30/1876   M. 1900   B. _____
D. _____   M. _____   D. 4/9/1932

(2) Edith Sheridan Foster
B. _____
D. _____

M6281111 - Margaret Ellen Morton - Clarke E. Fife
(Mother not given)
B. 4/4/1905   M. 6/26/1933   B. 6/13/1904
D. _____   D. _____

M62811111 - Stephen Edward Fife
B. 6/22/1938

M628112 - Alice Eliza Morton - Elliot Barnabas Johnson
B. 7/14/1877   M.10/17/1900   B. 8/3/1875
D. _____   D. _____

ᵏIndicates that a bio is included.

M6281121 - Elliott Morton Johnson
    B. 12/7/1906
    D. _____

M628113 - Margaret Elizabeth Morton - **M62262** William M. Higginbotham
    B. 7/21/1878   M. 1/7/1915   B. 9/7/1878
    D. _____   D. _____

    M622621 - William Moore Higginbotham, Jr.
        B. 8/28/1920
        D. _____

M628114 - Robert Kemp Morton - Julia Ward Davidson
    B. 1/25/1880   M. 10/7/1909   B. 7/24/1886
    D. _____   D. _____

    M6281141 - Robert Kemp Morton, Jr. - Eleanor Warren Rucker
        B. 8/10/1910   M. 8/7/1937   B. 12/21/1915
        D. _____   D. _____

        M62811411 - Robert Kemp Morton, III
            B. 3/7/1938

    M6281142 - Margaret Elizabeth Morton
        B. 9/2/1912
        D. _____

    M6281143 - William Benjamin Morton
        B. 9/1/1916
        D. _____

M628114x - Charles St.Clair Morton
    B. 1/19/1882
    D. 12/8/1923

M628115 - Nancy Letitia Morton - Frank Buchanan Stafford
      B. 6/29/1884   M. 9/4/1925   B. 6/11/1890
      D. _____   D. _____

M628116 - William Benjamin Morton, Jr. - Myrtle Atkinson
      B. 7/25/1887   M. 8/10/1913   B. 3/31/1888
      D. _____   D. _____

M628117 - Verna Rochette Morton
      B. 2/19/1889
      D. _____

M628118 - Arthur Price Morton - Lillian George Wright
      B. 5/30/1893   M. 11/26/1921   B. _____
      D. _____   D. _____

    M6281181 - Charles Wright Morton
          B. 10/16/1925
          D. _____

    M6281182 - Arthur Price Morton, Jr.
          B. 8/4/1930
          D. 4/28/1935

    M6281183 - George Calvin Morton
          B. _____
          D. _____

M628119 - Mary Moore Morton - (1) James Martin Edwards (Div)
      B. 4/6/1900   M. 12/19/1919   B. 10/6/1899
      D. _____   M. 6/8/1935   D. _____

                        (2) Jack Downs Knight
                            B. 5/23/1900
                            D. _____

M6281191 - **(1)** James Martin Edwards, Jr.
B. 10/16/1920
D. _____

M6281192 - **(1)** William Morton Edwards
B. 6/15/1922
D. _____

M6281193 - **(1)** David Crockett Edwards
B. 9/1/1923
D. _____

M62812 - Letitia Ellen Crockett - **M62312** William Grattan Beavers
B. 5/12/1857   M. _____   B. 6/9/1855
D. 12/20/1911   D. 9/6/1887

  M623121 - Eliza Pearl Beavers
    B. _____ M. _____ B. _____
    D. _____   D. _____

M62813 - Nancy Caroline Crockett - H. Wade Beavers
B. _____ M. _____   B. _____
D. _____   D. _____

  M628131 - Robert G. Beavers - Nora McCall
    B. _____ M. _____ B. _____
    D. _____   D. _____

    M6281311 - H. Wade Beavers, II
      B. _____
      D. _____

  M628132 - Elmer Lee Beavers
    B. _____
    D. As infant

M62814 - David Titus Crockett - Capitola Peery
    B. 9/2/1862   M. 9/20/1882   B. 6/30/1860
    D. 10/14/1895   D. 12/23/1895

    M628141 - Permelia Letitia Crockett
        B. 1//12/1884
        D. 8/6/1887

    M628142 - Anne Olive Crockett
        B. 2/25/1892
        D. _____

M62815 - Elizabeth Crockett - Benjamin Porter
    B. 2/17/1865   M. 3/21/1886   B. 9/1861
    D. _____   D. 6/30/1936

    M628151 - Robert Minister Porter
        B. 4/29/1888
        D. _____

    M628152 - Nancy Letitia Porter
        B. 9/23/1896
        D. _____

    M628153 - William Benjamin Porter - Delilah Adkins Walker
        B. 10/31/1904   M. 11/8/1925   B. 1/10/1906
        D. _____   D. _____

        M6281531 - Thadryl Trevell Porter
            B. 1/28/1931
            D. 1/28/1931

    M628154 - Eliza Porter
        B. _____
        D. As infant

M62816 - Robert Addison Crockett - (1) Annie Bell Crockett
    B. 6/1/1870   (1)M. 4/19/1893 B. 7/29/1876
    D. 10/6/1937   (2)M. 3/7/1917 D. 3/27/1915

                  (2) Ella Sue Wright
                    B. 6/5/1898
                    D. _____

M628161 - Harry Wade Crockett(1) - (1) Blanche Williams
    B. 9/8/1894   M. _____   B. _____
    D. _____   M. _____   D. _____

                  (2) Elizabeth Stoples
                    B. _____
                    D. _____

M6281611 - Robert Jackson Crockett(1)
    B. 10/19/1916
    D. _____

M6281612 - Benjamin Quintus Crockett(1)
    B. 10/1916
    D. 11/6/1918

M628162 - Rose Annie Crockett(1) - Montelle Hatchett
    B. 8/13/1896   M. _____   B. 3/13/1882
    D. _____   D. 2/12/1921

M628163 - Ruth Jane Crockett(1) - (1) Eugene Fox
    B. 12/18/1898 M. 6/2/1920 B. _____
    D. _____   M. 1/7/1937 D. _____

                  (2) **M62748** Alexander St.Clair, III
                    B. 1/4/1891
                    D. 1/11/1924

For this line see M62748

M628164 - Robert Addison Crockett, Jr.(1) - Lottie Perdue
B. 6/10/1903   M. 3/3/1932 B. 9/12/1909
D. _____   D. _____

M6281641 - Robert Addison Crockett, III
B. 12/25/1932
D. _____

M628165 - Sidney Emil Crockett(1)
B. 5/7/1905
D. _____

M628166 - Nancie Lettie Crockett(1) - Raymond S. Harry
B. 4/22/1907   M. _____   B. _____
D. _____   D. _____

M6281661 - Nancie Ann Harry
B. 5/1935

M628167 - Stillbirth(1)
D. 3/2/1909

M628168 - David Thomas Crockett(1) - Stella Looney
B. 4/3/1904   M. 11/24/1938   B. _____
D. _____   D. _____

M628169 - Myra Loraine Crockett(2)
B. 11/23/1917
D. _____

M62817 - Helen Louvenia Crockett - Charles Frank Kitts
     B. 3/14/1873   M. 5/25/1892   B. 9/12/1865
     D. _____   D. _____

  M628171 - Robert Ernest Kitts - Nellie Mae Hoke
       B. 10/8/1893   M. 7/22/1931   B. 5/29/1909
       D. _____   D. _____

    M6281711 - Elizabeth Louvenia Kitts
         B. 8/20/1932

  M628172 - David Roscoe Kitts - Lula Kate Lowe
       B. 1/13/1895   M. 10/1/1922   B. 11/16/1895
       D. _____   D. _____

  M628173 - Ruth Alice Kitts - Glen Dunlap
       B. 11/16/1896   M. 5/2/1923   B. 7/30/1895
       D. _____   D. _____

    M6281731 - Glenna Ruth Dunlap
         B. 3/30/1924
         D. _____

  M628173x - Stillborn
       D. 2/27/1898

  M628174 - Newell Jane Kitts - Nye Britts
       B. 5/29/1901   M. 9/10/1924   B. 6/22/1890
       D. _____   D. 9/4/1931

  M628175 - Nancy Ethel Kitts
       B. 3/23/1903
       D. _____

  M628175x - Stillborn
       D. 4/8/1904

M628176 - William Moore Kitts
    B. 1/19/1911
    D. _____

M628177 - Charles Frank Kitts, Jr.
    B. 1/31/1911
    D. 10/13/1937

M628178 - Homer Morton Kitts
    B. 1/23/1915
    D. _____

M62818 - William Jackson Crockett - Rose Ella Neel
    B. 9/8/1875 M. 7/5/1899   B. 6/15/1877
    D. _____   D. _____

  M628181 - Virginia Irene Crockett - Howard Hounshell Gill
      B. 5/29/1900   M. 7/12/1924   B. 7/22/1899
      D. _____   D. _____

    M6281811 - Douglas Leon Gill
        B. 7/6/1925

  M628182 - Nan Rose Crockett - Lee Alexander Harman
      B. 10/22/1902   M. 9/4/1931   B. 7/13/1895
      D. _____   D. _____

M6282   (1) Nancy Lane Moore - David Allen Daugherty
      B. 10/28/1836   M. 10/22/1858   B. 6/14/1836
      D. 5/18/1918   D. 10/17/1904

  M62821 - Sarah Elizabeth Daugherty - James Collins Nutty
      B. 8/22/1859   M. 9/30/1880   B. 1846
      D. 11/9/1922   D. 11/9/1922

M628211 - Nancy Lane Nutty
B. 1881
D. _____

M628212 - Hattie Blanche Nutty
B. 1883
D. _____

M628213 - Stillborn
D. _____

M628214 - Son (died as infant)
D. _____

M628215 - James Collins Nutty, Jr.
B. 1892
D. 4/1936

M628216 - William Allen Nutty
B. 1897
D. _____

M628217 - George Daugherty Nutty
B. 1901
D. _____

M62822 - Harriet Letcher Daugherty - Matthias Fox Neel
B. 3/28/1861   M. 2/20/1879   B. 1/19/1856
D. 11/18/1899   D. 12/27/1924

M628221 - Arlington Hicks Neel - Ada Chitwood
B. 2/28/1880   M. _____   B. _____
D. _____   D. _____

M6282211 - Harriet Frances Neel
B. _____
D. _____

x

z

M6282212 - Richard Elgin Neel
  B. _____
  D. _____

M6282213 - Paul Randolph Neel
  B. _____
  D. _____

M6282214 - William Matthias Neel
  B. _____
  D. _____

M628222 - Anna Lane Neel - William Beverly Belchee
B. 9/19/1883   M. _____   B. _____
D. _____   D. _____

M6282221 - Naomi Lucile Belchee
  B. _____
  D. _____

M6282222 - Ruth Carlock Belchee
  B. _____
  D. _____

M6282223 - Mary Lee Belchee - Thomas P. Snodgrass
  B. _____ M. _____   B. _____
  D. _____   D. _____

  M62822231 - Elizabeth Jane Snodgrass
    B. _____
    D. _____

M6282224 - Billie Neel Belchee - W. W. Morgan
  B. _____ M. _____   B. _____
  D. _____   D. _____

M62822241 - Jo Anne Morgan
  B. _____
  D. _____

M628223 - Ora Lee Neel - **M643122** Thomas Edward Nash
  B. 2/2/1885 M. _____   B. _____
  D. _____   D. _____

M6431221 - Claude Witten Nash - Blanche R. Barnes
  B. _____ M. _____   B. _____
  D. _____   D. _____

M64312211 - Philip Barnes Nash
  B. _____
  D. _____

M6431222 - Nancy Ernestine Nash
  B. _____
  D. _____

M6431223 - Anna May Nash
  B. _____
  D. _____

M6431224 - Thomas Edward Nash, Jr.
  B. _____
  D. _____

M628224 - Margaret Barnes Neel - Adam Steven Shannon
  B. 1/9/1888 M. _____   B. _____
  D. _____   D. _____

M6282241 - Wylie Wynne Shannon
  B. _____
  D. _____

M6282242 - Willie Moore Shannon
    B. _____
    D. _____

M6282243 - Margaret Bernice Shannon - Jesse H. Lambert
    B. 7/15/1915   M. 6/7/1935   B. 5/11/1906
    D. 7/22/1984   D. 5/13/1971

    M62822431 – Amelia Elizabeth Lambert – Joseph Kujawa
        B. 1944   M. 12/1/1963   B. 12/1/1934
        D. _____   D. 5/31/1975

    M62822432 – Jessica Susan Lambert – William Brown
        B. 10/26/1946   M. 10/1965   B. _____
        D. 12/22/1978

M6282244 - Adam Steven Shannon, Jr. - Ethel Grubb
    B. 12/29/1917   M. 11/3/1941   B. 3/10/1923
    D. 8/8/1985   D. _____

    *****M62822441** - Linda Jean Shannon - Philip Loring Roof, Jr.
        B. 8/24/1946   M. 3/5/1988   B. 11/25/1941

    *****M62822442** - Daniel Stephen Shannon – Nancy Grocee
        B. 3/31/1949   M. 20/27/1970   B. 2/20/1949

        M628224421 – Cassie Danielle Shannon – Stephen Robert Cooke
            B. 11/11/1975   M. 10/18/2001   B. _____

M6282245 - Annie Neel Shannon - Charles Knill
    B. 9/23/1918   M. _____   B. 11/7/1915
    D. 9/6/1954   D. _____

    M62822451 - Carolyn Moore Knill - Richard Meggitt
        B. 10/18/1940   M. 1/26/1970   B. 5/9/1943

*M62822452 – Christine Keefer Meggitt – John H. Roderiques
B. 3/23/1949   M. 9/7/1975   B. 1/28/1942

M6282246 - James Lee Shannon - Mary Catherine Fry
B. 9/23/1918   M. 9/15/1945   B. 8/31/1925
D. 4/1/1988   D. _____

*M62822461 – Stephen Curtis Shannon – Barbara Jean Winterson
B. 12/9/1948   M. 7/31/1972   B. 1/12/1948

*M628224611 – Joyce Megan Shannon-Winterson
B. 10/19/1981

*M628224612 – Sally Catherine Shannon-Winterson
B. 5/30/1986

*M62822462 – Gregory Lee Shannon – Virginia Ann Mariano
B. 10/8/1952   M. 5/22/1981   B. 10/24/1950

M628224621 - Christopher Louis Shannon
B. 11/7/1984

M628224622 – Jonathan Lee Shannon
B. 10/30/1986

*M62822463 – Kathryn Olivia Shannon – Michael Alan Wible
B. 5/7/1954   M. 11/15/2003   B. 2/14/1956

*M62822464 – Jeffrey Fry Shannon – Terry Lynn Sheckells
B. 7/18/1957   M. _____   B. 12/8/1957

M628224641 - Kristina Lynn Shannon
B. 12/10/1986

M628224642 – Rachel Leigh Shannon
B. 4/28/1991

M62822465 – James Mark Shannon - _____
       B. 12/25/1960   M. _____   B. _____

     M628224651 – Samuel Jacob Shannon
             B. 12/27/1991

*M62822466 – John Laurence Shannon – Lisa K. Knight
       B. 3/15/1963   M. 6/21/1994   B. 4/27/1964

     *M628224661 - Jackson Lee Shannon
             B. 10/12/1995

     *M628224662 – Kelly Lynn Shannon
             B. 1/1/2000

*M6282247 - Clara B. Shannon – Samuel William Wilson, Jr.
     B. 8/17/1923   M. 8/4/1943   B. 8/21/1918
                                      D. 8/2/1987

     *M62822471 - Craig Alan Wilson
     B. 2/12/1956

M6282248 - Jasper Daugherty Shannon - Jane Hilliard
     B. 3/17/1925   M. 6/28/1952   B. 10/1/1929
     D. 11/10/1973

     M62822481 – Jane Ann Shannon – (1) Michael Bennett
          B. 9/23/1957   (1)M _____   B. 3/15/1953
                        (2)M 5/5/1986   D. 3/15/1982

                                  (2) Richard Malinowski
                                        B. 5/4/1955

          M628224811 – (1) Michael Casey Bennett
                    B. 1/28/1981

          M628224812 – (2) Shannon Lee Malinowski
                    B. 1/3/1988

M628225 - Clara B. Neel - William Hoge Buchanan, Jr.
    B. 9/20/1893   M. _____   B. 1887
    D. 10/20/1985   D. 6/25/1960

M628226 - David Elgin Neel - Mollie Kate Hale
    B. 1/22/1885   M. 12/16/ B. 12/4/1892
    D. 8/8/1956   D. 7/17/1975

    *M6282261 - Oreda Mildred Neel - Walter Owen Kaylor
        B. 5/15/1920   M. 6/22/1940   B. 2/16/1918

        *M62822611 - David Owen Kaylor - Linda Karen French
            B. 3/28/1944   M. 1/3/1965 B. _____

            *M628226111 - Katharine Kaylor - Barry S. Slayden
                B. 10/30/1965   M. 6/12/1999   B. _____

            *M628226112 - Kimberly Kristine Kaylor - Scott Wallman
                B. 6/26/1969   M. 7/1/1994 B. _____

                *M62822261121 - Evan Parker Wallman
                    B. 3/12/1997

            *M628226113 - Karaline Kelly Kaylor - Joe Charles Williamson, III
                B. 6/12/1974   M. 1994   B. _____

        *M62822612 - Lewis Hale Kaylor - Masie Romeo
            B. 3/12/1948   M. _____   B. _____

        *M62822613 - Charles William Kaylor - (1)Nanci Pat Engle
            B. 9/12/1956   (1)M. 1978   B. 11/11/1953
                               (2)M. 1985

                            (2)Margaret Elizabeth Byrd
                            B. 2/26/1955

    *M628226131 - (1)Joshua Hale Kaylor
    B. 6/15/1980

    *M628226132 - (2)Sarah Elizabeth Kaylor
    B. 3/24/1986

M62823 - Margaret W. Daugherty - John Harrison Mattox
  B. 3/1/1864   M. 9/7/1892   B. 10/1/1867
  D. _____   D. 6/20/1933

  M628231 - James John Mattox
    B. 6/26/1894
    D. 10/1/1917

  M628232 - Nancy Kate Mattox -Charles Floyd Bedall
    B. 10/1/1896   M. 12/28/1933   B. 3/13/1900
    D. 11/15/1981   D. 5/15/1990

    M6282321 - Charlene Kyle Bedall
    B. 6/9/1938

M62824 - John William Daugherty - Angeline Walker
  B. 6/5/1867 M. 12/25/1884   B. 4/28/1860
  D. 9/23/1895   D. 8/13/1931

  M628241 - Robert Hicks Daugherty - Mabel Alice Woodward
    B. 10/25/1885   M. _____   B. _____
    D. _____   D. _____

    M6282411 - Robert Hicks Daugherty, Jr. - Lou Vera Green
    B. _____   M. _____   B. _____
    D. _____   D. _____

M62824111 - Robert Hicks Daugherty, III
    B. _____
    D. _____

M628242 - Carrie Belle Daugherty
    B. 1886
    D. 1898

M628243 - William Edward Daugherty
    B. 1889
    D. As infant

M628244 - Ethel Marie Daugherty
    B. 8/7/1890
    D. _____

M628245 - Elizabeth May Daugherty - Thomas J. Williamson
    B.5/6/1892 M. _____   B. _____
    D. _____   D. _____

M628246 - Nancy Lee Daugherty - Harry James Martin
    B. 5/15/1894   M. _____   B. _____
    D. _____   D. _____

    M6282461 - Mary Elizabeth Martin - James A. Thompson
        B. _____ M. _____   B. _____
        D. _____   D. _____

    M6282462 - Catharyne Walker Martin
        B. _____
        D. _____

    M6282463 - Harry James Martin, Jr.
        B. _____
        D. _____

M628247 - Johnsie William Daugherty - Robert L. Porter
 B. 2/9/1896 M. _____   B. _____
 D. _____   D. _____

 M6282471 - James William Porter
  B. _____
  D. _____

 M6282472 - Robert L. Porter, Jr.
  B. _____
  D. _____

 M6282473 - John Gordon Porter
  B. _____
  D. _____

 M6282474 - Virginia Lee Porter
  B. _____
  D. _____

M62825 - George Fulton Daugherty - May M. Walker
 B. 8/25/1869 M. 6/24/1889   B. 4/10/1868
 D. 11/12/1936   D. _____

 M628251 - James Sidney Daugherty - Agnes Hawley
  B. 9/22/1891 M. _____ B. _____
  D. 3/16/1922   D. _____

  M6282511 - Olga D. Daugherty
   B. _____
   D. _____

 M628252 - Hubert Allen Daugherty - Nellie Leggin
  B. 1/25/1895 M. _____ B. _____
  D. _____   D. _____

M6282521 - Patricia May Daugherty
    B. _____
    D. _____

M628253 - William Clarence Daugherty - Virginia May Mills
    B. 1/16/1898   M. _____   B. _____
    D. _____   D. _____

M628254 - Elmo Thomas Daugherty
    B. 10/28/1903
    D. _____

M628255 - John Carlisle Daugherty
    B. 9/5/1905
    D. _____

M628256 - Paul Warren Daugherty - Rhenda Mabel Quillen
    B. 1/15/1909   M. _____   B. _____
    D. _____   D. _____

    M6282561 - Michael James Daugherty
        B. _____
        D. _____

    M6282562 - Robert Fulton Daugherty
        B _____
        D. _____

M62826 - Charles R. Daugherty
    B. 8/27/1871
    D. 8/29/1873

M62827 - Nannie May Daugherty - Hugh Allen Green
    B. 1/13/1876   M. 12/1/1896   B. 5/30/1870
    D. _____   D. _____

M628271 - Fred Allen Green
    B. 10/26/1897
    D. _____

M6283   David Whitley Moore (1) - Jane Elizabeth Balch
    B. 6/26/1838   M. 9/19/1871   B. 9/29/1848
    D. 3/30/1885   D. 7/24/1938

M62831 - James Edward Moore - Sarah Delphina Hay
    B. 6/24/1872   M. 10/3/1893   B. 11/13/1869
    D. _____   D. 1/1/1937

M628311 - Clara May Moore - Robert Lee Finch
    B. _____ M. _____ B. _____
    D. _____   D. _____

M628312 - Franklin Earl Moore - Ethel May Olson
    B. _____ M. _____ B. _____
    D. _____   D. _____

M6283121 - James Paul Moore
    B. _____
    D. _____

M6283122 - Dorothy Dean Moore
    B. _____
    D. _____

M6283123 - Robert Benjamin Moore
    B. _____
    D. _____

M628313 - Bessie Gertrude Moore - Harry Denni
    B. _____ M. _____ B. _____
    D. _____   D. _____

M6283131 - Virginia Delphine Denni
    B. _____
    D. _____

M6283132 - Martha Gwynne Denni
    B. _____
    D. _____

M6283133 - Lyda Jane Denni
    B. _____
    D. _____

M628314 - Pearl Nadine Moore - Lyle Darwin Morley
    B. _____   M. _____   B. _____
    D. _____   D. _____

M62832 - Wade Hampton Moore - Sadie May Ayres
    B. 6/14/1876   M. 12/24/1902   B. 2/24/1880
    D. _____   D. _____

M628321 - Virginia Ayres Moore - Leonard S. Bocher
    B. 5/6/1905   M. 4/4/1926   B. 1/4/1901
    D. _____   D. _____

M6283211 - Barbara Ann Bocher
    B. 8/26/1935
    D. _____

M62833 - Mabel Irene Moore - Friend Clark Drake
    B. 2/28/1878   M. 11/8/1899   B. 3/4/1871
    D. _____   D. _____

M628331 - Ruth Bernice Drake - Earl Edward Farris
    B. _____   M. _____   B. _____
    D. _____   D. _____

M62834 - Clifford Ernest Moore
B. 1/14/1885
D. _____

M6283x   Creed F. Moore (1)
B. _____
D. _____

M6284   James K. P. Moore (1) - Anna Rebecca Carzine
B. 3/10/1845   M. 12/24/1877   B. 9/29/1859
D. 3/9/1933   D. 8/8/1891

M62841 - Burtie Mariah Moore - William Davis Eley
B. 1/21/1879   M. 12/24/1900   B. 10/1/1877
D. _____   D. _____

M628411 - Hugh Moore Eley – Thelma Gore
B. 12/1/1902   M. 5/24/1925   B. _____
D. _____   D. _____

M628412 - Howell Davis Eley - Bertha Belt
B. 12/24/1904   M. 3/27/1927   B. _____
D. _____   D. _____

M628413 - James Parrott Eley - Mary Rayfield
B. 8/31/1907   M. 9/30/1930   B. _____
D. _____   D. _____

M6284131 - Billie Ann Eley
B. 5/30/1931

M6284132 - Yevonne Eley
B. 8/31/1937

M628414 - Haskell Frank Eley
B. 8/27/1910
D. _____

M628415 - Grace Mabel Eley - Ora Littlejohn
B. 10/31/1912   M. 5/21/1929   B. _____
D. _____   D. _____

M628416 - Edna Lee Eley - Edwin Parks
B. 11/25/1915   M. 12/21/1935   B. _____
D. _____   D. _____

M6284161 - Edwin David Parks
B. 2/2/1938

M628417 - Jack Burt Eley
B. _____
D. _____

M628418 - Carl Wayne Eley
B. _____
D. _____

M62842 - Hattie Alice Moore - Flournoy Shelton
B. 5/31/1882   M. 8/1909 B. _____
D. 6/23/1914   D. 1918

M62843 - Infant
D. _____

M62844 - Infant
D. _____

M62845 - John William Moore
B. 7/30/1891
D. 8/10/1891

M6285   William Jackson Moore (1) - Mahaley McClure
              B. 3/6/1848   M. 1875   B. _____
              D. 6/10/1918   D. 5/31/1892

M62851 - Minnie Moore
            B. _____
            D. As infant

M62852 - Creed Moore
            B. _____
            D. At eight years

M62853 - Nash Edison Moore - Ollie Gordon Rosser
            B. 12/24/1877   M. 1902   B. 12/24/1879
            D. 5/15/1906   D. _____

   M628531 - Gordon Nash Moore - Cloey Angelas Thomas
                B. 4/4/1904   M. 10/27/1923   B. _____
                D. _____   D. _____

      M6285311 - Helen Yvonne Moore
                    B. 10/5/1924

      M6285312 - Shirley Jeanne Moore
                    B. 10/15/1929

      M6285313 - Kathleen Geneva Moore
                    B. 4/10/1931

      M6285314 - Gordon Robert Moore
                    B. 5/28/1934

   M628532 - Jackson Truston Moore - Thelma Shaw
                B. _____   M. 5/22/1925   B. 3/8/1905
                D. _____   D. _____

M6285321 - Jacqueline Moore
    B. 2/8/1929
    D. 8/1/1932

M6285322 - William Gordon Moore
    B. 8/1/1932
    D. _____

M62854 - Roy Moore
    B. 3/4/1882
    D. _____

M62855 - James Burt Moore - (1) Cora Summers
    B. 3/23/1885   (1)M. 7/25/1907   B. _____
    D. _____   (2)M. 3/1/1921   D. 6/15/1919

                (2) Edna Moheiser
                    B. 7/2/1897
                    D. _____

    M628551 - Wade Jackson Moore (2)
        B. _____
        D. _____

M62856 - Ora Elissa Moore - Nathan B. Forest Anderson
    B. 7/16/1888   M. 8/18/1907   B. 12/29/1881
    D. 7/16/1913   D. _____

    M628561 - Gladys Juanita Anderson - James Claude Sands
        B. 6/27/1908   M. 6/28/1926   B. 8/16/1907
        D. _____   D. _____

    M6285611 - Royce Calvin Sands
        B. 6/30/1927

M6285612 - Carl Vernal Sands
B. 5/24/1929

M628562 - Elgin D. Forest Anderson - Birdie Frances Domdy
B. 6/2/1910 M. 7/23/1930   B. 3/13/1913
D. _____   D. _____

M6285621 - Howard Forest Anderson
B. 7/15/1931

M6285622 - Modena Fay Anderson
B. 10/18/1932

M6285x   Margaret Moore (2)
B. _____
D. _____

M6286   Elizabeth Moore - Edward Vaughan
B. _____   M. _____   B. _____
D. _____   D. _____

M6287   Electra Moore - James Akers
B. _____   M. _____   B. _____
D. _____   D. _____

M6288   Augusta Moore - Luther Graham
B. _____   M. _____   B. _____
D. _____   D. _____

M6289   Lavalette Moore - William F. Graham
B. _____   M. _____   B. _____
D. 1934   D. 6/1952

*__M62891__ - John Wann Graham – Matilda Earls
B. 1877   M. _____   B. _____
D. 1947   D. 11/29/1940

*M628911 - Myrtle Graham
    B. _____
    D. <u>As Infant</u>

*M628912 – Mollie Graham – George Peery
    B. _____   M. _____   B. _____
    D. _____   D. _____

    *M6289121 - Carl Edward Peery
        B. _____
        D. _____

    *M6289122 - Phyllis Peery - _____ Fox
        B. _____   M. _____   B. _____
        D. _____   D. _____

    *M6289123 - A. M. Peery
        B. _____
        D. _____

    *M6289124 - Jimmy Peery
        B. _____

*M628913 – Bill Graham – Rose Stevenson
    B. _____   M. _____   B. _____
    D. _____   D. _____

    *M6289131 – William Graham
        B. _____
        D. _____

    *M6289132 – Shirley Graham - _____ Hart
        B. _____   M. _____   B. _____
        D. _____   D. _____

*M6289133 – Walter Graham
    B. _____
    D. _____

*M6289134 – James Graham
    B. _____
    D. _____

*M6289135 – George C. Graham
    B. _____
    D. _____

*M6289136 – Mike Graham
    B. _____
    C. _____

*M628914 – Frank Graham – Julia Smith
    B. _____   M. _____   B. _____
    D. _____   D. _____

*M628915 – Clarence Graham
    B. _____
    D. 6/27/1927

*M628916 – Shields Graham – Mary Taylor
    B. 10/28/1912
    D. 8/2000

    *M6289161 – Berrnice Graham
        B. _____

    *M6289162 – Altha Graham - _____ Cline
        B. _____   M. _____   B. _____

    *M6289163 – Dale Graham
        B. _____

*M628917 – Gladys Gray Graham – Audrey H. Edmonds
    B. 1/5/1914   M. _____   B. 1/14/1912
    D. _____   D. 10/21/1991

    *M6289171 – Dwight G. Edmonds
        B. 10/17/1935

    *M6289172 – Daniel W. Edmonds
        B. 10/22/1937

    *M6289173 - Alma R. Edmonds - _____ Peery
        B. 8/21/1939   M. _____   B. _____

    *M6289174 - Betty Carol Edmonds - _____ Farmer
        B. 12/10/1941   M. _____   B. _____

*M628918 – George Dewey Graham
    B. 3/2/1918
    D. 11/10/1982

*M628919 – John Bunyan Graham - _____
    B. 9/23/1921   M. _____   B. _____
    D. 2/6/2001

    *M6289191 – Carol Graham
           B. _____
           D. _____

    *M6289192 - Tommy Graham
           B. _____
           D._____

    *M6289193 – Loretta Graham
           B. _____
           D. _____

*M6289194 – Ricky Graham
      B. _____
      D. _____

M62892 - Aaron Sheffy Graham - Mary Elizabeth Shrader
      B. 6/20/1878   M. _____   B. 6/27/1885
      D. 8/8/1962   D. 9/20/1957

    M628921 - Dewey S. Graham
          B. 7/15/1903
          D. 8/15/1932

    M628922 - Albert L. Graham - _____
          B. 4/16/1905   M. _____   B. _____
          D. 8/1974   D. _____

    M628923 - Edna May Graham - _____ Freeman
          B. 5/22/1907   M. _____   B. _____
          D. 1993   D. _____

    M628924 - Julia Grey Graham - Ardel Greer
          B. 5/22/1907   M. _____   B. _____
          D. 8/13/1996   D. _____

    M628925 - John Harrison Graham - Georgia Adeline Sexton
          B. 9/17/1910   M. 4/21/1941   B. 2/25/1924
          D. 3/12/1992   D. 5/23/1980

        M6289251 - William Eugene Graham
              B. 9/19/1941
              D. 9/19/1941

        *M6289252 - John Harrison Graham - (1) Doris Jean Evans
              B. 12/3/1942   (1)M. 8/3/1963   B. _____
                              (2)M. 6/18/   D. 4/10/1997
                              (3)M. 11/18/1992

(2) Wanda Sue Davis (Div)
B. 7/8/1949
D. 11/30/1991

(3) Kathy Delayne Blankenship
B. 8/12/1952

*M62892521 - (1) Elisa Joyce Graham - Brian Robert Nahory
B. 1/24/1964   M. 12/7/1991   B. 10/7/1967
D. 6/27/2002

    *M628925211 - Caleb Scott Nahory
    B. 6/20/1994

    *M628925212 - Alexa Brianna Nahory
    B. 7/27/1995

    *M628925213 - Alysa Marie Nahory
    B. 7/27/1995

*M62892522- (1) Christina Joan Graham - Paul Edgar Brooks
B. 2/2/1968 M. 7/7/1990 B. 9/6/1957

    *M62892521 - Cruiz Aaron Graham
    B. 5/12/1987

    *M628925211 - Cody Ryan Brooks
    B. 2/14/1991

*M62892523 - (2) John Harrison Graham, II - Melissa Ann Dillon
B. 9/12/1972   M. 1/15/1994   B. 5/1/1973

    *M628925231 - Dillon Harrison Graham
    B. 9/6/1997

*M62892524 - (2) Dolly Darline Graham - Mark Wayne Warren
B. 8/3/1974 M. 6/11/1994   B. 3/3/1973

*M628925241 - Terry Wayne Warren
B. 4/12/1992

*M6289253 - Wanda Ellen Graham
B. 7/22/1944

*M6289254 - George Aaron Graham – Zola Ina Darlene Dunford
B. 8/23/1945   M. 1/1/1966   B. 8/14/1946

*M62892541 - John Aaron Graham - Melissa Ann Groseclose
B. 4/15/1966   M. 2/9/1991 B. 2/26/1970

*M628925411 - Scott Aaron Graham
B.12/2/1994

*M62892542 - Dreama Annette Graham - Walter Lee Ashbey
B. 2/10/1968   M. 4/1/1889 B. 10/7/1968

*M628925421 - Dakota Chaning Ashbey
B. 4/8/1985

*M628925422 - Christopher Aaron Ashbey
B. 11/2/1989

*M62892543 - Marty Ray Graham - Sharon Robertson
B. 1/26/1971   M. 8/24/1991   B. 7/21/1972

*M628925431 - Samuel Harrison Graham
B. 4/30/1998

*M6289255 - Mary Belle Graham (1) Charles Arthur Davis
B. 1/17/1947   (1)M. 1/22/1966   B. 7/15/1943
                  (2)M. 6/30/1979   D. 12/25/1976

(2) Kenneth Ray Fowler
B. 12/9/1947

*M62892551 - (1) Mark Steven Davis - Susan Lynn Shrader
B. 11/27/1966   M. 8/26/1989   B. 10/26/1969

*M628925511 - Andrew Steven Davis
B. 6/9/1994

*M62892552 - (1) Michael DeWayne Davis - Amy Carol Castle
B. 8/15/1970   M. 9/7/1991   B. 7/15/1972

*M628925521 - Megan Hope Davis
B. 8/3/1996

M628926 – Ruby Matilda Graham - Henry N. Casey
B. 7/25/1913   M. _____   B. 3/4/1910
D. 3/27/2003   D. 12/23/1973

M6289261 - Bobby Ray Casey - Sue Quesonberry
B. 7/24/1936   M. 5/15/1982   B. _____
D. _____   D. _____

M62892611 - Holly Marie Casey
B. 3/21/1983

M6289262 - Billy E. Casey - _____
B. 5/29/1938   M. _____   B. _____
D. 9/10/1994   D. _____

M62892621 – Billy E. Casey, Jr.
B. _____

M62892622 – Wallace Lee Casey
B. _____
D. 8/2001

M62892623 – Douglas Casey
B. _____

M62892624 – Ricky Casey
B. _____
D. _____

M62892625 – Virginia Casey - _____
B. _____   M. _____   B. _____

M62892626 – Paula Casey - _____
B. _____   M. _____   B. _____

M62892627 – Cindy Casey - _____
B. _____   M._____   B. _____

M62892628 – Nicole Casey
B. _____

M6289263 - Henry N. Casey, Jr. – Carole Sue Cochran
B. 2/2/1940 M. _____   B. _____
D. _____   D. _____

M6289264 - Aaron W. Casey – _____
B. 8/17/1944   M. 9/28/1980   B. _____
D. _____   D. _____

M62892641 – Aaron W. Casey, Jr.
B. 6/30/1983

M6289265 - Georgia B. Casey – Bobby R. Crawford
B. 8/24/1948   M. 10/15/1978   B. 3/12/1947

M62892651 – Carmen R. Crawford - _____
B. 8/19/1974   M. _____   B. _____

M62892652 – Bobbi R. Crawford - _____
    B. 5/1/1979   M. _____   B. _____

*****M6289266** - Clyde M. Casey – Freda B. Coeburn
    B. 6/6/1951 M. 9/28/1978   B. 12/19/1961
    D. 3/10/1998

*****M6289267** - Virginia L. Casey - Gene Shrader
    B. 4/23/1952   M.8/27/1973   B. 3/13/1938
    D. 2/15/2001

*****M6289268** - H. Elwood Casey – Iva Ann Mangus
    B. 4/3/1955 M. 7/16/1974   B. 10/8/1955
    D. 7/23/1979

M628927 - Sally Bell Graham - Albert Troy Harman
    B. 7/26/1916   M. _____   B. 6/25/1913
    D. _____   D. 11/13/1997

*****M6289271** - Eunice Pauline Harman - Ronald James Panciera
    B. 6/18/1934   M. 11/19/1955   B. 12/1/1933

M62892711 - Ronald James Panciera, Jr.- Martha Petrik
    B. 11/11/1956   M. 11/17/1979   B. 9/14/1959

M628927111 - Justin Panciera
    B. 5/6/1982

M628927112 - Joseph Panicera
    B. 5/19/1984

M628927113 - Ronald James Panciera, III
    B. 12/22/1987

M62892712 - Albert Troy Panciera – (1) Karen Johnson (Div)
    B. 3/6/1959   (1)M. 10/1/1988   B. 9/13/1956
                (2)M. 4/26/1903

                           (2) Betty Beverly
                           B. _____

    M628927121 - Melissa Panciera
        B. 2/27/1987

    M628927122 - Amanda Panciera
        B. 8/9/1989

    M62892713 - Gina Marie Panciera - Frank McDonnell (Div)
        B. 5/28/1966   M. 6/23/1990   B. _____

    M628927131 - Ryan Edward McDonnell
        B. 10/23/1993

M628928 - Rosa Katherine Graham - Cammie Kasbin Harman
    B. 10/20/1918   M. _____   B. 1916
    D. 8/18/1968   D. _____

    M6289281 - Shelby Jean Harman - Gordan D. Hagy
        B. 1938   M. _____   B. _____

    M62892811 - Larry Hagy - Shelia Duncan Reedy
        B. 1958   M. _____   B. _____

    M62892812 - Leslie Hagy - David M. Gillespie
        B. 1960   M. _____   B. 1957
                           D. 1998

M628928121 - Tiffany M.Gillespie -Wendell Grizzle
B. 1980   M. 1998   B. 1978

M628928122 - Delores R. Gillespie
B. 1984

M6289282 - Cammie Kasbin Harman, Jr. - Patricia Ann Davidson
B. 1940   M. _____   B. _____

M62892821 - Terri Lynn Harman - Jerry William Wolfe
B. 1960   M. _____   B. 1955

M628928211 - Heather Michelle Wolfe
B. 1983

M628928212 - Brenna Louise Wolfe
B. 1985

M62892822 - Daniel Edward Harman
B. 1962

M62892823 - Jeffrey David Harman - Terry Lynn Tellis
B. 1967   M. _____   B. 1966

M6289283 - Janice Lane Harman - Eugene Randolph Allgood III
B. 1943   M. _____   B. _____

M62892831 - Christy Elaine Allgood - RobertWyche Williams
B. 1965   M. _____   B. 1969

M62892832 - Catherine Glenn Allgood - Jason PaulWillis
B. 1970   M. _____   B. 1976

M628929   Virginia Graham - _____ Holland
   B. 6/27/1920   M. _____   B. _____
   D. 8/1990   D. _____

M62892-10 Bobbie Elizabeth Graham - John Wesley Watts
   B. 9/17/1922   M. _____   B. 5/5/1923
                                           D. 5/11/1978

   M62892-10-1 - John Wesley Watts, Jr. - Ruth Kathleen Springsteen
      B. 1/11/1947   M. 3/27/1982   B. _____

      M62892-10-1-1- Steven Wesley Watts
         B. 2/18/1972

      M62892-10-1-2 - Richard Warren Watts
         B. 7/7/1975

      M62892-10-1-3 - Kristine Michele Watts
         B. 2/13/1978

      M62892-10-1-4 - Mathews Gabriel Watts
         B. 4/4/1979

      M62892-10-1-5 - Adam Joseph Watts
         B. 5/20/1983

   M61892-10-2 - Michael Lee Watts - Cathy Scotch
      B. 11/15/1948   M. _____   B. _____
                                              D. _____

   M62892-10-3 - Diana Lynn Watts - Raymond Lee Linex
      B. 9/9/1952   M. 8/2/1968   B. _____

      M62892-10-3-1 - Raymond Lee Linex, II
         B. 9/23/1969

      M62892-10-3-2 - Stephen Eric Linex
         B. 10/18/1971

M62892-10-3-3 - Tanya Renee Linex
B. 10/25/1973

M62892-10-4 - Kathy Sue Watts - Gary Wayne Enochs
B. 1/18/1955   M. 1/2/1972   B. _____
D. _____

M62892-10-4-1 - Benjamin J. Enochs
B. 10/30/1972

M62892-10-4-2 - Zachary Taylor Enochs
B. 8/2/1975

M62892-10-5 - Mark D'Wayne Watts - Marilyn Barton
B. 7/7/1959   M. 3/11/1999   B. _____

M62892-11 - - William J. Graham
B. 9/10/1923
D. 5/1972

M62893 – Robert Luke Graham – Gertrude Yates
B. 3/23/1884   M. _____   B. 9/4/1888
D. _____   D. 4/14/1975

M628931 – Foster Graham
B. 1/28/1909
D. _____

M628932 – Walter Witten Graham – Evelyn M. _____
B. 3/2/1911   M. _____ B. 1/14/1932
D. 10/27/1976

*M6289321 – Walter Witten Graham, Jr. – Donnetta Cline
B. 1/4/1959   M. _____   B. 9/2/1961

M62893211 – Walter Witten Graham,III
B. 11/15/1980

M62893212 – William Chadwick Graham
B. 2/24/1984

M62893213 - Paige Marie Graham
B. 6/28/1989

M628933 – Dovie Graham – George Washington Repass
B. 12/20/1913   M. _____   B. 6/24/1903
D. 1/5/2001   D. 10/11/1975

*M6289331 – Margaret Louise Repass – James Kulchar
B. 8/5/1930   M. _____   B. 10/1/1925

*M62893311 – Andrew George Kulchar
B. 5/14/1950

*M62893312 - Mary Dovie Kulchar
B. 4/8/1957

*M62893313 – James Byron Kulchar
B. 3/20/1966

*M6289332 - Alfred Jack Repass – Mary Lucille Linkous
B. 12/14/1932   M. _____   B. 8/27/1932

M62893321 - Alfred Jack Repass, II – Kimberley Sue _____
B. 5/22/1959   M. 6/25/1988   B. _____
D. 4/3/2002

*M628933211 - Jared Alexander Repass
B. 5/24/1995

*M6289333 – Roy Douglas Repass – Katherine F. Goss
B. 4/1/1943   M. _____   B. 10/1/1944

*M62893331 - Lisa Marie Repass – Carl Harry
    B. 7/31/1966   M. 10/1/1988   B. _____

    *M628933311 – Chandler Robert Harry
        B. 1/13/1993

*M62893332 – Shelia Repass – Wayne Smith
    B. 11/27/1970   M. 5/10/1999   B. _____

    *M628933321 – Trevor Edwards Smith
        B. _____

*M62893333 – David Wayne Repass – Amanda Roberts
    B. 8/21/1974   M. 9/27/1996   B. _____

*M6289334 – Marshall Graham Repass – June Etta Poskas
    B. 3/24/1946   M. _____   B. 11/28/1949

    *M62893341 – Mara Michelle Repass – Steve Wingo
        B. 7/7/1966   M. 6/21/1984   B. _____

        *M628933411 – Steven Christopher Wingo
            B. 4/3/1986

*M628934 – Janice Viola Graham – James W. Asbury
    B. 10/9/1920   M. _____   B. 10/1/1918

    *M6289341 – Retha Jane Asbury - _____ Thelan (Div)
        B. 6/14/1949   M. _____   B. _____

    *M6289342 – James Miller Asbury
        B. 2/11/1953

M628935 – J. C. Graham
    B. 1/15/1923

30.

The John Shannon Moore Line
Biographical Charts

M62822441
Genealogical Number

Linda Jean Shannon   Port Republic, MD 20676
Name (including maiden name if applicable)   Town of Residence

Washington, D.C.   8/24/1946
Birthplace   Date of Birth   Date of Death   Where Buried

Philip Loving Roof, Jr.   Washington, D.C.   11/24/1941
Name of Spouse   Birthplace   Date of Birth   Date of Death

                                3/5/1988   La Plata, MD
Where Buried   Date of Marriage   Place of Marriage

If married more than once:

Name of Spouse   Birthplace   Date of Birth   Date of Death

Where Buried   Date of Marriage   Place of Marriage

Philip Loving Roof, Sr. - Berth Railsback
Parents of Spouse (with Mother's maiden name) 1st Marriage

Subsequent Marriage (if applicable)

Family Details

Schools attended, dates and degrees: Community, political work, etc.:
Virginia Commonwealth University 1964-1968 BFA   NEA, MSTA, EACC. >Education Associations,
in Art Education. University of MD 1979-1984-   Reach to Recovery Volunteer
MED Education   (Am. Cancer Soc.)
Descendant   Descendant

Prince Georges Com. College 1959-1961
Spouse   Spouse

Basic Employment History: Clubs, Church Affiliations, etc.:
                                                     Trinity United Methodist Church, Prince Frederick
Art Teacher - Charlottesville, VA 1968-1969   MD, John Hanson Chapter-DAR, Alpha Eta
Henry E. Lackey H.S. Charles Co. MD 1969-2003-Retired Chapter of Delta Kappa Gamma Soc. International
Descendant   Descendant
Elevator Mechanic retired - Office of the   Trinity United Methodist Church, Harbor Hills
Architect of the Capitol, Washington D.C.   Citizens Association.
Spouse   Spouse

Military Service:

Descendant   Spouse

M62822442
Genealogical Number

Daniel Stephen Shannon
Name (including maiden name if applicable)   Town of Residence

                              3/31/1949
Birthplace   Date of Birth   Date of Death   Where Buried

Nancy Grocee   2/20/1949
Name of Spouse   Birthplace   Date of Birth   Date of Death

                              10/27/1970
Where Buried   Date of Marriage   Place of Marriage

If married more than once:

Name of Spouse   Birthplace   Date of Birth   Date of Death

Where Buried   Date of Marriage   Place of Marriage

Parents of Spouse (with Mother's maiden name) 1st Marriage

Subsequent Marriage (if applicable)

Family Details

Schools attended, dates and degrees: Community, political work, etc.:

Descendant   Descendant

Spouse   Spouse

Basic Employment History: Clubs, Church Affiliations, etc.:

Descendant   Descendant

Spouse   Spouse

Military Service:

Descendant   Spouse

M62822452
Genealogical Number

Christine Keefer Meggitt   Chatham, Mass
Name (including maiden name if applicable)   Town of Residence

Frederick, MD   3/23/1949
Birthplace   Date of Birth   Date of Death   Where Buried

John H. Roderiques   Chatham, MA   1/28/1942
Name of Spouse   Birthplace   Date of Birth   Date of Death

                          9/7/1975   Comus, MD
Where Buried   Date of Marriage   Place of Marriage

If married more than once:

Name of Spouse   Birthplace   Date of Birth   Date of Death

Where Buried   Date of Marriage   Place of Marriage

Parents of Spouse (with Mother's maiden name) 1st Marriage

Subsequent Marriage (if applicable)

Family Details

Schools attended, dates and degrees: Community, political work, etc.:

Descendant   Descendant

Spouse   Spouse

Basic Employment History: Clubs, Church Affiliations, etc.:

Descendant   Descendant

Spouse   Spouse

Military Service:

Descendant   Spouse

M62822461
Genealogical Number

Stephen Curtis Shannon
Name (including maiden name if applicable)

Kennebunkford, ME
Town of Residence

Frederick, MD
Birthplace

12/9/1948
Date of Birth

Date of Death

Where Buried

Barbara Jean Winterson
Name of Spouse

Leonardtown, MD
Birthplace

1/12/1948
Date of Birth

Date of Death

Where Buried

7/31/1972
Date of Marriage

Leonardtown, MD
Place of Marriage

If married more than once:

Name of Spouse

Birthplace

Date of Birth

Date of Death

Where Buried

Date of Marriage

Place of Marriage

Charles Richey Winterson III and Marion Jean Halstead
Parents of Spouse (with Mother's maiden name) 1st Marriage

Subsequent Marriage (if applicable)

Family Details

Schools attended, dates and degrees:

Community, political work, etc.:

U. of MD 1966-1979, BA History 1971, MA History 1975
University of New England College of Osteopathic Medicine
1982-86, D.O.
Harvard U. School of Public Health 1988-1990, M.P.H.
Descendant

Descendant

U. of MD 1966-1977 BS 1972, PhD 1977
Spouse

Spouse

Basic Employment History:

Clubs, Church Affiliations, etc.:

Physician & Specialty Family Medicine & Preventive
Medicine. Currently: Dean, University of New England
College of Osteopathic Medicine
Descendant

Descendant

Professor of Physiology, University of New England
College of Osteopathic Medicine
Spouse

Sierra Club
Spouse

Military Service:

Descendant

Spouse

M628224611
Genealogical Number

Joyce Megan Shannon-Winterson   Kennebunkford, ME
Name (including maiden name if applicable)   Town of Residence

Portland, ME   10/19/1981
Birthplace   Date of Birth   Date of Death   Where Buried

Name of Spouse   Birthplace   Date of Birth   Date of Death

Where Buried   Date of Marriage   Place of Marriage

If married more than once:

Name of Spouse   Birthplace   Date of Birth   Date of Death

Where Buried   Date of Marriage   Place of Marriage

Parents of Spouse (with Mother's maiden name) 1st Marriage

Subsequent Marriage (if applicable)

Family Details

Schools attended, dates and degrees: Community, political work, etc.:

Kennebunk High School 1999
Colby College, BA, 1999-2003
Descendant   Descendant

Spouse   Spouse

Basic Employment History: Clubs, Church Affiliations, etc.:

Descendant   Descendant

Spouse   Spouse

Military Service:

Descendant   Spouse

M628224612
Genealogical Number

Sally Catherine Shannon-Winterson
Name (including maiden name if applicable)

Kennebunkford, ME
Town of Residence

Portland, ME   5/30/1986
Birthplace   Date of Birth

Date of Death   Where Buried

Name of Spouse   Birthplace   Date of Birth   Date of Death

Where Buried   Date of Marriage   Place of Marriage

If married more than once:

Name of Spouse   Birthplace   Date of Birth   Date of Death

Where Buried   Date of Marriage   Place of Marriage

Parents of Spouse (with Mother's maiden name) 1st Marriage

Subsequent Marriage (if applicable)

Family Details

Schools attended, dates and degrees: Community, political work, etc.:

Kennebunk High School (currently)
Descendant   Descendant

Spouse   Spouse

Basic Employment History: Clubs, Church Affiliations, etc.:

Descendant   Descendant

Spouse   Spouse

Military Service:

Descendant   Spouse

M62822462
Genealogical Number

Gregory Lee Shannon
Name (including maiden name if applicable)

Laurel, MD
Town of Residence

Prince Frederick, MD
Birthplace

10/8/1952
Date of Birth

Date of Death

Where Buried

Virginia Mariano
Name of Spouse

Paterson, NJ
Birthplace

10/24/1950
Date of Birth

Date of Death

Where Buried

5/22/1982
Date of Marriage

Prince Frederick, MD
Place of Marriage

If married more than once:

Name of Spouse

Birthplace

Date of Birth

Date of Death

Where Buried

Date of Marriage

Place of Marriage

Eleanor Traino & Louis Joseph Mariano
Parents of Spouse (with Mother's maiden name) 1st Marriage

Subsequent Marriage (if applicable)

Family Details

Schools attended, dates and degrees:

UMCP - 1969 to 1973 - BS
College Park, MD
Descendant
Wm. Paterson Univ. 1968-1972 - BSN
Wayne, NJ
Spouse

Basic Employment History:
Self employed - G.L. Shannon Realty
Inc.
Descendant

Registered Nurse
Spouse

Military Service:

Descendant

Community, political work, etc.:

Descendant

Spouse

Clubs, Church Affiliations, etc.:

South Columbia Baptist
Descendant

South Columbia Baptist
Spouse

Spouse

M62822463
Genealogical Number

Kathryn Olivia Shannon
Name (including maiden name if applicable)

Prince Ferderick, MD
Town of Residence

Huntingtown, MD
Birthplace

5/7/1954
Date of Birth

Date of Death

Where Buried

Michael Alan Wible
Name of Spouse

Hollywood, MD
Birthplace

2/14/1956
Date of Birth

Date of Death

Where Buried

11/15/2003
Date of Marriage

Hollywood, MD
Place of Marriage

If married more than once:

Name of Spouse

Birthplace

Date of Birth

Date of Death

Where Buried

Date of Marriage

Place of Marriage

Parents of Spouse (with Mother's maiden name) 1st Marriage

Subsequent Marriage (if applicable)

Family Details

Schools attended, dates and degrees:

Community, political work, etc.:

University of Maryland, BS 12/1976
Descendant

Descendant

Spouse

Spouse

Basic Employment History:

Clubs, Church Affiliations, etc.:

Descendant

Descendant

Spouse

Spouse

Military Service:

Descendant

Spouse

M62822464
Genealogical Number

Jeffrey Fry Shannon
Name (including maiden name if applicable)

Huntingtown, MD
Town of Residence

Whiteford, MD
Birthplace

7/18/1957
Date of Birth

Date of Death

Where Buried

Terry Lynn Sheckells
Name of Spouse

Prince Frederick, MD
Birthplace

12/8/1957
Date of Birth

Date of Death

Where Buried

Date of Marriage

Place of Marriage

If married more than once:

Name of Spouse

Birthplace

Date of Birth

Date of Death

Where Buried

Date of Marriage

Place of Marriage

Elliott Gibson Sheckells and Virginia Alberta Dowell
Parents of Spouse (with Mother's maiden name) 1st Marriage

Subsequent Marriage (if applicable)

Family Details

Schools attended, dates and degrees:

Community, political work, etc.:

University of MD (Colege Park) B.S. in Business mgt;
12-79
Descendant

Descendant

York College B.S. in Accounting; 5-79
Spouse

Spouse

Basic Employment History:

Clubs, Church Affiliations, etc.:

First Virginia Banks, Inc. 19 years, Vice President
Descendant
Calvert County Government
Director of Finance
Spouse

Huntingtown United Methodist Church
Descendant

Same
Spouse

Military Service:

Descendant

Spouse

M62822466
Genealogical Number

John Lawrence Shannon
Name (including maiden name if applicable)

St. Leonard, MD
Town of Residence

Baltimore
Birthplace

3/15/1963
Date of Birth

Date of Death

Where Buried

Lisa L. Knight
Name of Spouse

Springfield, PA
Birthplace

4/27/1964
Date of Birth

Date of Death

Where Buried

6/21/1994
Date of Marriage

Key West, Fla
Place of Marriage

If married more than once:

Name of Spouse

Birthplace

Date of Birth

Date of Death

Where Buried

Date of Marriage

Place of Marriage

Donald T. Knight and Nancy C. Maloney
Parents of Spouse (with Mother's maiden name) 1st Marriage

Subsequent Marriage (if applicable)

Family Details

Schools attended, dates and degrees:

Community, political work, etc.:

University of Maryland, Mechanical
Engineering Degree
Descendant
Bowie State University, Western MD College
Education Degree
Spouse

Descendant

Spouse

Basic Employment History:
Mirant Company - Chalk Point,
Generating Station
Descendant

Clubs, Church Affiliations, etc.:

Descendant

Calvert Co. Public Schools
Spouse

Spouse

Military Service:

Descendant

Spouse

M628224661
Genealogical Number

Jackson Lee Shannon _____   St. Leonards, MD _____
Name (including maiden name if applicable)   Town of Residence

_____   10/21/1995
Birthplace   Date of Birth   Date of Death   Where Buried

_____   _____   _____   _____
Name of Spouse   Birthplace   Date of Birth   Date of Death

_____   _____   _____
Where Buried   Date of Marriage   Place of Marriage

If married more than once:

_____   _____   _____   _____
Name of Spouse   Birthplace   Date of Birth   Date of Death

_____   _____   _____
Where Buried   Date of Marriage   Place of Marriage

_____
Parents of Spouse (with Mother's maiden name) 1st Marriage

_____
Subsequent Marriage (if applicable)

Family Details

Schools attended, dates and degrees: Community, political work, etc.:

_____   _____
Descendant   Descendant

_____   _____
Spouse   Spouse

Basic Employment History: Clubs, Church Affiliations, etc.:

_____   _____
Descendant   Descendant

_____   _____
Spouse   Spouse

Military Service:

_____   _____
Descendant   Spouse

M628224662
Genealogical Number

Kelly Lynn Shannon   St. Leonards, MD
Name (including maiden name if applicable)   Town of Residence

                          1/1/2000
Birthplace   Date of Birth   Date of Death   Where Buried

Name of Spouse   Date of Birth   Date of Death

Where Buried   Date of Marriage   Place of Marriage

If married more than once:

Name of Spouse   Birthplace   Date of Birth   Date of Death

Where Buried   Date of Marriage   Place of Marriage

Parents of Spouse (with Mother's maiden name) 1st Marriage

Subsequent Marriage (if applicable)

Family Details

Schools attended, dates and degrees: Community, political work, etc.:

Descendant   Descendant

Spouse   Spouse

Basic Employment History: Clubs, Church Affiliations, etc.:

Descendant   Descendant

Spouse   Spouse

Military Service:

Descendant   Spouse

M6282247
Genealogical Number

Clara B. Shannon   Chevy Chase, MD
Name (including maiden name if applicable)   Town of Residence

Bland County, VA   8/17/1923
Birthplace   Date of Birth   Date of Death   Where Buried

Samuel Wilson, Jr.   Rogers, ARK   8/21/1918   8/2/1987
Name of Spouse   Birthplace   Date of Birth   Date of Death

Rockville, MD   8/4/1943   Alexandria, LA
Where Buried   Date of Marriage   Place of Marriage

If married more than once:

_____   _____   _____   _____
Name of Spouse   Birthplace   Date of Birth   Date of Death

_____   _____   _____
Where Buried   Date of Marriage   Place of Marriage

Samuel & Allie Wilson
Parents of Spouse (with Mother's maiden name) 1st Marriage

_____
Subsequent Marriage (if applicable)

Family Details

Schools attended, dates and degrees: Community, political work, etc.:

Poolesville High School - Strayer Business
School
Descendant   Descendant
University of Texas - University of
MD
Spouse   Spouse

Basic Employment History: Clubs, Church Affiliations, etc.:

Chesapeake & Potomac Telephone Co.   DAR
Descendant   Descendant

National Testing Lab
Spouse   Spouse

Military Service:

US Army - WW2
Descendant   Spouse

M62822471
Genealogical Number

Craig Alan Wilson
Name (including maiden name if applicable)

Thailand
Town of Residence

Washington, DC   2/12/1956
Birthplace   Date of Birth

Date of Death   Where Buried

Name of Spouse   Birthplace   Date of Birth   Date of Death

Where Buried   Date of Marriage   Place of Marriage

If married more than once:

Name of Spouse   Birthplace   Date of Birth   Date of Death

Where Buried   Date of Marriage   Place of Marriage

Parents of Spouse (with Mother's maiden name) 1st Marriage

Subsequent Marriage (if applicable)

Family Details

Schools attended, dates and degrees:

Yale B.A. 1978, Harvard Law School
J.D.; 1981
Descendant

Community, political work, etc.:

Descendant

Spouse

Spouse

Basic Employment History:

General Counsel, Finansa plc
Descendant

Clubs, Church Affiliations, etc.:

Episcopalian
Descendant

Spouse

Spouse

Military Service:

Descendant

Spouse

M6282261
_____
Genealogical Number

Oreda Mildred Neal   Bluefield, W.VA
Name (including maiden name if applicable)   Town of Residence

                            5/15/1920
Birthplace   Date of Birth   Date of Death   Where Buried

Walter Owen Kaylor   2/16/1918
Name of Spouse   Birthplace   Date of Birth   Date of Death

                            6/22/1940
Where Buried   Date of Marriage   Place of Marriage

If married more than once:

Name of Spouse   Birthplace   Date of Birth   Date of Death

Where Buried   Date of Marriage   Place of Marriage

Parents of Spouse (with Mother's maiden name) 1st Marriage

Subsequent Marriage (if applicable)

Family Details

Schools attended, dates and degrees: Community, political work, etc.:

Descendant   Descendant

Spouse   Spouse

Basic Employment History: Clubs, Church Affiliations, etc.:

Descendant   Descendant

Spouse   Spouse

Military Service:

Descendant   Spouse

M62822611
Genealogical Number

David Owen Kaylor
Name (including maiden name if applicable)   Town of Residence

_____   3/28/1944   _____   _____
Birthplace   Date of Birth   Date of Death   Where Buried

Linda Karen French
Name of Spouse   Birthplace   Date of Birth   Date of Death

_____   1/3/1965   _____
Where Buried   Date of Marriage   Place of Marriage

If married more than once:

_____   _____   _____   _____
Name of Spouse   Birthplace   Date of Birth   Date of Death

_____   _____   _____
Where Buried   Date of Marriage   Place of Marriage

Parents of Spouse (with Mother's maiden name) 1st Marriage

Subsequent Marriage (if applicable)

Family Details

Schools attended, dates and degrees: Community, political work, etc.:

_____   _____
Descendant   Descendant

_____   _____
Spouse   Spouse

Basic Employment History: Clubs, Church Affiliations, etc.:

_____   _____
Descendant   Descendant

_____   _____
Spouse   Spouse

Military Service:

_____   _____
Descendant   Spouse

M628226111
Genealogical Number

Katharine Kaylor
Name (including maiden name if applicable)   Town of Residence

_____   10/30/1965   _____   _____
Birthplace   Date of Birth   Date of Death   Where Buried

Barry S. Sladen   _____   _____   _____
Name of Spouse   Birthplace   Date of Birth   Date of Death

_____   6/12/1999   _____
Where Buried   Date of Marriage   Place of Marriage

If married more than once:

_____   _____   _____   _____
Name of Spouse   Birthplace   Date of Birth   Date of Death

_____   _____   _____
Where Buried   Date of Marriage   Place of Marriage

_____
Parents of Spouse (with Mother's maiden name) 1st Marriage

_____
Subsequent Marriage (if applicable)

Family Details

Schools attended, dates and degrees: Community, political work, etc.:

_____   _____
Descendant   Descendant

_____   _____
Spouse   Spouse

Basic Employment History: Clubs, Church Affiliations, etc.:

_____   _____
Descendant   Descendant

_____   _____
Spouse   Spouse

Military Service:

_____   _____
Descendant   Spouse

M628226112
Genealogical Number

Kimberley Kristine Kaylor
Name (including maiden name if applicable)   Town of Residence

                                    6/26/1969
Birthplace   Date of Birth   Date of Death   Where Buried

Scott Wallman
Name of Spouse   Birthplace   Date of Birth   Date of Death

                                    7/1/1944
Where Buried   Date of Marriage   Place of Marriage

If married more than once:

Name of Spouse   Birthplace   Date of Birth   Date of Death

Where Buried   Date of Marriage   Place of Marriage

Parents of Spouse (with Mother's maiden name) 1st Marriage

Subsequent Marriage (if applicable)

Family Details

Schools attended, dates and degrees: Community, political work, etc.:

Descendant   Descendant

Spouse   Spouse

Basic Employment History: Clubs, Church Affiliations, etc.:

Descendant   Descendant

Spouse   Spouse

Military Service:

Descendant   Spouse

M6282261121
Genealogical Number

Evan Parker Wallman
Name (including maiden name if applicable)   Town of Residence

     3/12/1997
Birthplace   Date of Birth   Date of Death   Where Buried

Name of Spouse   Birthplace   Date of Birth   Date of Death

Where Buried   Date of Marriage   Place of Marriage

If married more than once:

Name of Spouse   Birthplace   Date of Birth   Date of Death

Where Buried   Date of Marriage   Place of Marriage

Parents of Spouse (with Mother's maiden name) 1st Marriage

Subsequent Marriage (if applicable)

Family Details

Schools attended, dates and degrees: Community, political work, etc.:

Descendant   Descendant

Spouse   Spouse

Basic Employment History: Clubs, Church Affiliations, etc.:

Descendant   Descendant

Spouse   Spouse

Military Service:

Descendant   Spouse

M628226113
Genealogical Number

Karaline Kelly Kaylor
Name (including maiden name if applicable)　　　　　Town of Residence

_____　6/12/1974　　　　_____　_____
Birthplace　　　Date of Birth　　Date of Death　　Where Buried

Joe Charles Williamson, III
Name of Spouse　　Birthplace　　Date of Birth　　Date of Death

_____　1994　　　　_____
Where Buried　　Date of Marriage　　Place of Marriage

If married more than once:

_____　_____　_____　_____
Name of Spouse　　Birthplace　　Date of Birth　　Date of Death

_____　_____　_____
Where Buried　　Date of Marriage　　Place of Marriage

_____
Parents of Spouse (with Mother's maiden name) 1st Marriage

_____
Subsequent Marriage (if applicable)

Family Details

Schools attended, dates and degrees:　　　Community, political work, etc.:

_____　_____
Descendant　　　　Descendant

_____　_____
Spouse　　　　　Spouse

Basic Employment History:　　　Clubs, Church Affiliations, etc.:

_____　_____
Descendant　　　　Descendant

_____　_____
Spouse　　　　　Spouse

Military Service:

_____　_____
Descendant　　　　Spouse

M62822612
Genealogical Number

Lewis Hale Kaylor
Name (including maiden name if applicable)   Town of Residence

                              3/12/1948
Birthplace   Date of Birth   Date of Death   Where Buried

Name of Spouse   Birthplace   Date of Birth   Date of Death

Where Buried   Date of Marriage   Place of Marriage

If married more than once:

Name of Spouse   Birthplace   Date of Birth   Date of Death

Where Buried   Date of Marriage   Place of Marriage

Parents of Spouse (with Mother's maiden name) 1st Marriage

Subsequent Marriage (if applicable)

Family Details

Schools attended, dates and degrees: Community, political work, etc.:

Descendant   Descendant

Spouse   Spouse

Basic Employment History: Clubs, Church Affiliations, etc.:

Descendant   Descendant

Spouse   Spouse

Military Service:

Descendant   Spouse

M62822613
Genealogical Number

Charles William Kaylor   The Woodlands, Texas
Name (including maiden name if applicable)   Town of Residence

Bluefield, W.VA   9/12/1956
Birthplace   Date of Birth   Date of Death   Where Buried

Margaret Elizabeth Byrd   Houston, Texas   2/26/1955
Name of Spouse   Birthplace   Date of Birth   Date of Death

                             1985   Houston, Texas
Where Buried   Date of Marriage   Place of Marriage

If married more than once:

Nanci Pat Engle   Charleston, W.VA   11/11/1953
Name of Spouse   Birthplace   Date of Birth   Date of Death

                             1978   Buchanan, W.VA
Where Buried   Date of Marriage   Place of Marriage

Damon & JoAnn Engle
Parents of Spouse (with Mother's maiden name) 1st Marriage

Roy & Mable Byrd
Subsequent Marriage (if applicable)

Family Details

Schools attended, dates and degrees: Community, political work, etc.:

B.A. West Virginia Wesleyan College
MBA University of Houston
Descendant   Descendant

Spouse   Spouse

Basic Employment History: Clubs, Church Affiliations, etc.:

Descendant   Descendant

Spouse   Spouse

Military Service:

Descendant   Spouse

M628226131
Genealogical Number

Joshua Hale Kaylor   The Woodlands, Texas
Name (including maiden name if applicable)   Town of Residence

Houston, Texas   6/15/1980
Birthplace   Date of Birth   Date of Death   Where Buried

Name of Spouse   Birthplace   Date of Birth   Date of Death

Where Buried   Date of Marriage   Place of Marriage

If married more than once:

Name of Spouse   Birthplace   Date of Birth   Date of Death

Where Buried   Date of Marriage   Place of Marriage

Parents of Spouse (with Mother's maiden name) 1st Marriage

Subsequent Marriage (if applicable)

Family Details

Schools attended, dates and degrees: Community, political work, etc.:

B.S. Texas A&M University
Descendant   Descendant

Spouse   Spouse

Basic Employment History: Clubs, Church Affiliations, etc.:

Descendant   Descendant

Spouse   Spouse

Military Service:

Descendant   Spouse

M628226132
Genealogical Number

Sarah Elizabeth Kaylor
Name (including maiden name if applicable)

The Woodlands, Texas
Town of Residence

The Woodlands, Texas
Birthplace

3/24/1986
Date of Birth

Date of Death

Where Buried

Name of Spouse

Birthplace

Date of Birth

Date of Death

Where Buried

Date of Marriage

Place of Marriage

If married more than once:

Name of Spouse

Birthplace

Date of Birth

Date of Death

Where Buried

Date of Marriage

Place of Marriage

Parents of Spouse (with Mother's maiden name) 1st Marriage

Subsequent Marriage (if applicable)

Family Details

Schools attended, dates and degrees:

Community, political work, etc.:

Descendant

Descendant

Spouse

Spouse

Basic Employment History:

Clubs, Church Affiliations, etc.:

Descendant

Descendant

Spouse

Spouse

Military Service:

Descendant

Spouse

M62891
Genealogical Number

John Wann Graham
Name (including maiden name if applicable)   Town of Residence

Dry Fork, VA   1877   1947   N. Tazewell, VA
Birthplace   Date of Birth   Date of Death   Where Buried

Matilda Earls   Cliffield, VA   11/29/1940
Name of Spouse   Birthplace   Date of Birth   Date of Death

N. Tazewell, VA
Where Buried   Date of Marriage   Place of Marriage

If married more than once:

Name of Spouse   Birthplace   Date of Birth   Date of Death

Where Buried   Date of Marriage   Place of Marriage

Parents of Spouse (with Mother's maiden name) 1st Marriage

Subsequent Marriage (if applicable)

Family Details

Schools attended, dates and degrees: Community, political work, etc.:

Descendant   Descendant

Spouse   Spouse

Basic Employment History: Clubs, Church Affiliations, etc.:

Descendant   Descendant

Spouse   Spouse

Military Service:

Descendant   Spouse

M628911
Genealogical Number

Myrtle Graham
Name (including maiden name if applicable)   Town of Residence

                                                              Died as infant
Birthplace   Date of Birth   Date of Death   Where Buried

Name of Spouse   Birthplace   Date of Birth   Date of Death

Where Buried   Date of Marriage   Place of Marriage

If married more than once:

Name of Spouse   Birthplace   Date of Birth   Date of Death

Where Buried   Date of Marriage   Place of Marriage

Parents of Spouse (with Mother's maiden name) 1st Marriage

Subsequent Marriage (if applicable)

Family Details

Schools attended, dates and degrees: Community, political work, etc.:

Descendant   Descendant

Spouse   Spouse

Basic Employment History: Clubs, Church Affiliations, etc.:

Descendant   Descendant

Spouse   Spouse

Military Service:

Descendant   Spouse

M628912
_____
Genealogical Number

Mollie Graham
_____   _____
Name (including maiden name if applicable)   Town of Residence

_____   _____   _____   _____
Birthplace   Date of Birth   Date of Death   Where Buried

George Peery
_____   _____   _____   _____
Name of Spouse   Birthplace   Date of Birth   Date of Death

_____   _____   _____
Where Buried   Date of Marriage   Place of Marriage

If married more than once:

_____   _____   _____   _____
Name of Spouse   Birthplace   Date of Birth   Date of Death

_____   _____   _____
Where Buried   Date of Marriage   Place of Marriage

_____
Parents of Spouse (with Mother's maiden name) 1st Marriage

_____
Subsequent Marriage (if applicable)

Family Details

Schools attended, dates and degrees: Community, political work, etc.:

_____   _____
Descendant   Descendant

_____   _____
Spouse   Spouse

Basic Employment History: Clubs, Church Affiliations, etc.:

_____   _____
Descendant   Descendant

_____   _____
Spouse   Spouse

Military Service:

_____   _____
Descendant   Spouse

M6289121
Genealogical Number

Carl Edward Peery
Name (including maiden name if applicable)

Town of Residence

Birthplace   Date of Birth   Date of Death   Where Buried

Name of Spouse   Birthplace   Date of Birth   Date of Death

Where Buried   Date of Marriage   Place of Marriage

If married more than once:

Name of Spouse   Birthplace   Date of Birth   Date of Death

Where Buried   Date of Marriage   Place of Marriage

Parents of Spouse (with Mother's maiden name) 1st Marriage

Subsequent Marriage (if applicable)

Family Details

Schools attended, dates and degrees: Community, political work, etc.:

Descendant   Descendant

Spouse   Spouse

Basic Employment History: Clubs, Church Affiliations, etc.:

Descendant   Descendant

Spouse   Spouse

Military Service:

Descendant   Spouse

M6289122
Genealogical Number

Phyllis Peery
Name (including maiden name if applicable)   Town of Residence

Birthplace   Date of Birth   Date of Death   Where Buried

- Fox
Name of Spouse   Birthplace   Date of Birth   Date of Death

Where Buried   Date of Marriage   Place of Marriage

If married more than once:

Name of Spouse   Birthplace   Date of Birth   Date of Death

Where Buried   Date of Marriage   Place of Marriage

Parents of Spouse (with Mother's maiden name) 1st Marriage

Subsequent Marriage (if applicable)

Family Details

Schools attended, dates and degrees: Community, political work, etc.:

Descendant   Descendant

Spouse   Spouse

Basic Employment History: Clubs, Church Affiliations, etc.:

Descendant   Descendant

Spouse   Spouse

Military Service:

Descendant   Spouse

M6289123
Genealogical Number

A. M. Peery
Name (including maiden name if applicable)   Town of Residence

Birthplace   Date of Birth   Date of Death   Where Buried

Name of Spouse   Birthplace   Date of Birth   Date of Death

Where Buried   Date of Marriage   Place of Marriage

If married more than once:

Name of Spouse   Birthplace   Date of Birth   Date of Death

Where Buried   Date of Marriage   Place of Marriage

Parents of Spouse (with Mother's maiden name) 1st Marriage

Subsequent Marriage (if applicable)

Family Details

Schools attended, dates and degrees: Community, political work, etc.:

Descendant   Descendant

Spouse   Spouse

Basic Employment History: Clubs, Church Affiliations, etc.:

Descendant   Descendant

Spouse   Spouse

Military Service:

Descendant   Spouse

M6289124
Genealogical Number

Jimmy Peery
Name (including maiden name if applicable)

Ohio
Town of Residence

Birthplace
Date of Birth
Date of Death
Where Buried

Name of Spouse
Birthplace
Date of Birth
Date of Death

Where Buried
Date of Marriage
Place of Marriage

If married more than once:

Name of Spouse
Birthplace
Date of Birth
Date of Death

Where Buried
Date of Marriage
Place of Marriage

Parents of Spouse (with Mother's maiden name) 1st Marriage

Subsequent Marriage (if applicable)

Family Details

Schools attended, dates and degrees:

Community, political work, etc.:

Descendant

Descendant

Spouse

Spouse

Basic Employment History:

Clubs, Church Affiliations, etc.:

Descendant

Descendant

Spouse

Spouse

Military Service:

Descendant

Spouse

M628913
Genealogical Number

Bill Graham
Name (including maiden name if applicable)

Town of Residence

Birthplace   Date of Birth   Date of Death   Where Buried

Rose Stevenson
Name of Spouse   Birthplace   Date of Birth   Date of Death

Where Buried   Date of Marriage   Place of Marriage

If married more than once:

Name of Spouse   Birthplace   Date of Birth   Date of Death

Where Buried   Date of Marriage   Place of Marriage

Parents of Spouse (with Mother's maiden name) 1st Marriage

Subsequent Marriage (if applicable)

Family Details

Schools attended, dates and degrees: Community, political work, etc.:

Descendant   Descendant

Spouse   Spouse

Basic Employment History: Clubs, Church Affiliations, etc.:

Descendant   Descendant

Spouse   Spouse

Military Service:

Descendant   Spouse

M6289131
Genealogical Number

William Graham
Name (including maiden name if applicable)

Georgia
Town of Residence

Birthplace   Date of Birth   Date of Death   Where Buried

Name of Spouse   Birthplace   Date of Birth   Date of Death

Where Buried   Date of Marriage   Place of Marriage

If married more than once:

Name of Spouse   Birthplace   Date of Birth   Date of Death

Where Buried   Date of Marriage   Place of Marriage

Parents of Spouse (with Mother's maiden name) 1st Marriage

Subsequent Marriage (if applicable)

Family Details

Schools attended, dates and degrees: Community, political work, etc.:

Descendant   Descendant

Spouse   Spouse

Basic Employment History: Clubs, Church Affiliations, etc.:

Descendant   Descendant

Spouse   Spouse

Military Service:

Descendant   Spouse

M6289132
Genealogical Number

Shirley Graham
Name (including maiden name if applicable)

S. Carolina
Town of Residence

Birthplace   Date of Birth   Date of Death   Where Buried

- Hart
Name of Spouse   Birthplace   Date of Birth   Date of Death

Where Buried   Date of Marriage   Place of Marriage

If married more than once:

Name of Spouse   Birthplace   Date of Birth   Date of Death

Where Buried   Date of Marriage   Place of Marriage

Parents of Spouse (with Mother's maiden name) 1st Marriage

Subsequent Marriage (if applicable)

Family Details

Schools attended, dates and degrees: Community, political work, etc.:

Descendant   Descendant

Spouse   Spouse

Basic Employment History: Clubs, Church Affiliations, etc.:

Descendant   Descendant

Spouse   Spouse

Military Service:

Descendant   Spouse

M6289133
Genealogical Number

Walter Graham   Chicago
Name (including maiden name if applicable)   Town of Residence

Birthplace   Date of Birth   Date of Death   Where Buried

Name of Spouse   Birthplace   Date of Birth   Date of Death

Where Buried   Date of Marriage   Place of Marriage

If married more than once:

Name of Spouse   Birthplace   Date of Birth   Date of Death

Where Buried   Date of Marriage   Place of Marriage

Parents of Spouse (with Mother's maiden name) 1st Marriage

Subsequent Marriage (if applicable)

Family Details

Schools attended, dates and degrees: Community, political work, etc.:

Descendant   Descendant

Spouse   Spouse

Basic Employment History: Clubs, Church Affiliations, etc.:

Descendant   Descendant

Spouse   Spouse

Military Service:

Descendant   Spouse

M6289134
Genealogical Number

James Graham
Name (including maiden name if applicable)

N. Tazewell, VA
Town of Residence

Birthplace   Date of Birth   Date of Death   Where Buried

Name of Spouse   Birthplace   Date of Birth   Date of Death

Where Buried   Date of Marriage   Place of Marriage

If married more than once:

Name of Spouse   Birthplace   Date of Birth   Date of Death

Where Buried   Date of Marriage   Place of Marriage

Parents of Spouse (with Mother's maiden name) 1st Marriage

Subsequent Marriage (if applicable)

Family Details

Schools attended, dates and degrees: Community, political work, etc.:

Descendant   Descendant

Spouse   Spouse

Basic Employment History: Clubs, Church Affiliations, etc.:

Descendant   Descendant

Spouse   Spouse

Military Service:

Descendant   Spouse

M6289135
Genealogical Number

George C. Graham   Bluefield, VA
Name (including maiden name if applicable)   Town of Residence

Birthplace   Date of Birth   Date of Death   Where Buried

Name of Spouse   Birthplace   Date of Birth   Date of Death

Where Buried   Date of Marriage   Place of Marriage

If married more than once:

Name of Spouse   Birthplace   Date of Birth   Date of Death

Where Buried   Date of Marriage   Place of Marriage

Parents of Spouse (with Mother's maiden name) 1st Marriage

Subsequent Marriage (if applicable)

Family Details

Schools attended, dates and degrees: Community, political work, etc.:

Descendant   Descendant

Spouse   Spouse

Basic Employment History: Clubs, Church Affiliations, etc.:

Descendant   Descendant

Spouse   Spouse

Military Service:

Descendant   Spouse

M6289136
Genealogical Number

Mike Graham   Pennsylvania
Name (including maiden name if applicable)   Town of Residence

Birthplace   Date of Birth   Date of Death   Where Buried

Name of Spouse   Birthplace   Date of Birth   Date of Death

Where Buried   Date of Marriage   Place of Marriage

If married more than once:

Name of Spouse   Birthplace   Date of Birth   Date of Death

Where Buried   Date of Marriage   Place of Marriage

Parents of Spouse (with Mother's maiden name) 1st Marriage

Subsequent Marriage (if applicable)

Family Details

Schools attended, dates and degrees: Community, political work, etc.:

Descendant   Descendant

Spouse   Spouse

Basic Employment History: Clubs, Church Affiliations, etc.:

Descendant   Descendant

Spouse   Spouse

Military Service:

Descendant   Spouse

M628914
Genealogical Number

Frank Graham
Name (including maiden name if applicable)   Town of Residence

Birthplace   Date of Birth   Date of Death   Where Buried

Julia Smith
Name of Spouse   Birthplace   Date of Birth   Date of Death

Where Buried   Date of Marriage   Place of Marriage

If married more than once:

Name of Spouse   Birthplace   Date of Birth   Date of Death

Where Buried   Date of Marriage   Place of Marriage

Parents of Spouse (with Mother's maiden name) 1st Marriage

Subsequent Marriage (if applicable)

Family Details

Schools attended, dates and degrees: Community, political work, etc.:

Descendant   Descendant

Spouse   Spouse

Basic Employment History: Clubs, Church Affiliations, etc.:

Descendant   Descendant

Spouse   Spouse

Military Service:

Descendant   Spouse

M628915
Genealogical Number

Clarence Graham
Name (including maiden name if applicable)   Town of Residence

                                                        6/27/1927
Birthplace   Date of Birth   Date of Death   Where Buried

Name of Spouse   Birthplace   Date of Birth   Date of Death

Where Buried   Date of Marriage   Place of Marriage

If married more than once:

Name of Spouse   Birthplace   Date of Birth   Date of Death

Where Buried   Date of Marriage   Place of Marriage

Parents of Spouse (with Mother's maiden name) 1st Marriage

Subsequent Marriage (if applicable)

Family Details

Schools attended, dates and degrees: Community, political work, etc.:

Descendant   Descendant

Spouse   Spouse

Basic Employment History: Clubs, Church Affiliations, etc.:

Descendant   Descendant

Spouse   Spouse

Military Service:

Descendant   Spouse

M628916
Genealogical Number

Shields Graham
Name (including maiden name if applicable)   Town of Residence

_____   10/28/1912   8/2000   _____
Birthplace   Date of Birth   Date of Death   Where Buried

Mary Taylor
Name of Spouse   Birthplace   Date of Birth   Date of Death

Where Buried   Date of Marriage   Place of Marriage

If married more than once:

Name of Spouse   Birthplace   Date of Birth   Date of Death

Where Buried   Date of Marriage   Place of Marriage

Parents of Spouse (with Mother's maiden name) 1st Marriage

Subsequent Marriage (if applicable)

Family Details

Schools attended, dates and degrees: Community, political work, etc.:

Descendant   Descendant

Spouse   Spouse

Basic Employment History: Clubs, Church Affiliations, etc.:

Descendant   Descendant

Spouse   Spouse

Military Service:

Descendant   Spouse

M6289161
Genealogical Number

Berrnie Graham
Name (including maiden name if applicable)

Parkersburg, W.VA
Town of Residence

Birthplace   Date of Birth   Date of Death   Where Buried

Name of Spouse   Birthplace   Date of Birth   Date of Death

Where Buried   Date of Marriage   Place of Marriage

If married more than once:

Name of Spouse   Birthplace   Date of Birth   Date of Death

Where Buried   Date of Marriage   Place of Marriage

Parents of Spouse (with Mother's maiden name) 1st Marriage

Subsequent Marriage (if applicable)

Family Details

Schools attended, dates and degrees:

Community, political work, etc.:

Descendant

Descendant

Spouse

Spouse

Basic Employment History:

Clubs, Church Affiliations, etc.:

Descendant

Descendant

Spouse

Spouse

Military Service:

Descendant

Spouse

M6289162
Genealogical Number

Altha Graham   N. Tazewell, VA
Name (including maiden name if applicable)   Town of Residence

Birthplace   Date of Birth   Date of Death   Where Buried

- Cline
Name of Spouse   Birthplace   Date of Birth   Date of Death

Where Buried   Date of Marriage   Place of Marriage

If married more than once:

Name of Spouse   Birthplace   Date of Birth   Date of Death

Where Buried   Date of Marriage   Place of Marriage

Parents of Spouse (with Mother's maiden name) 1st Marriage

Subsequent Marriage (if applicable)

Family Details

Schools attended, dates and degrees: Community, political work, etc.:

Descendant   Descendant

Spouse   Spouse

Basic Employment History: Clubs, Church Affiliations, etc.:

Descendant   Descendant

Spouse   Spouse

Military Service:

Descendant   Spouse

M6289163
Genealogical Number

Dale Graham   N. Tazewell, VA
Name (including maiden name if applicable)   Town of Residence

Birthplace   Date of Birth   Date of Death   Where Buried

Name of Spouse   Birthplace   Date of Birth   Date of Death

Where Buried   Date of Marriage   Place of Marriage

If married more than once:

Name of Spouse   Birthplace   Date of Birth   Date of Death

Where Buried   Date of Marriage   Place of Marriage

Parents of Spouse (with Mother's maiden name) 1st Marriage

Subsequent Marriage (if applicable)

Family Details

Schools attended, dates and degrees: Community, political work, etc.:

Descendant   Descendant

Spouse   Spouse

Basic Employment History: Clubs, Church Affiliations, etc.:

Descendant   Descendant

Spouse   Spouse

Military Service:

Descendant   Spouse

M628917
Genealogical Number

Gladys Gray Graham
Name (including maiden name if applicable)

N. Tazewell, VA
Town of Residence

Cliffield, VA
Birthplace

1/5/1914
Date of Birth

Date of Death

Where Buried

Audrey H.. Edmonds
Name of Spouse

Ashbury, VA
Birthplace

1/14/1912
Date of Birth

10/21/1991
Date of Death

Where Buried

Date of Marriage

Place of Marriage

If married more than once:

Name of Spouse

Birthplace

Date of Birth

Date of Death

Where Buried

Date of Marriage

Place of Marriage

Parents of Spouse (with Mother's maiden name) 1st Marriage

Subsequent Marriage (if applicable)

Family Details

Schools attended, dates and degrees:

Community, political work, etc.:

Descendant

Descendant

Spouse

Spouse

Basic Employment History:

Clubs, Church Affiliations, etc.:

Descendant

Descendant

Spouse

Spouse

Military Service:

Descendant

Spouse

M6289171
Genealogical Number

Dwight G. Edmonds
Name (including maiden name if applicable)

Live Oaks, Fla.
Town of Residence

10/17/1935

| Birthplace | Date of Birth | Date of Death | Where Buried |

| Name of Spouse | Birthplace | Date of Birth | Date of Death |

| Where Buried | Date of Marriage | Place of Marriage |

If married more than once:

| Name of Spouse | Birthplace | Date of Birth | Date of Death |

| Where Buried | Date of Marriage | Place of Marriage |

Parents of Spouse (with Mother's maiden name) 1st Marriage

Subsequent Marriage (if applicable)

Family Details

Schools attended, dates and degrees:

Community, political work, etc.:

Descendant

Descendant

Spouse

Spouse

Basic Employment History:

Clubs, Church Affiliations, etc.:

Descendant

Descendant

Spouse

Spouse

Military Service:

Descendant

Spouse

M6289172
Genealogical Number

Daniel W. Edmonds   Manly, Iowa
Name (including maiden name if applicable)   Town of Residence

                              10/22/1937
Birthplace   Date of Birth   Date of Death   Where Buried

Name of Spouse   Birthplace   Date of Birth   Date of Death

Where Buried   Date of Marriage   Place of Marriage

If married more than once:

Name of Spouse   Birthplace   Date of Birth   Date of Death

Where Buried   Date of Marriage   Place of Marriage

Parents of Spouse (with Mother's maiden name) 1st Marriage

Subsequent Marriage (if applicable)

Family Details

Schools attended, dates and degrees: Community, political work, etc.:

Descendant   Descendant

Spouse   Spouse

Basic Employment History: Clubs, Church Affiliations, etc.:

Descendant   Descendant

Spouse   Spouse

Military Service:

Descendant   Spouse

M6289173
Genealogical Number

Alma R. Edmonds
Name (including maiden name if applicable)

N. Tazewell, VA
Town of Residence

Birthplace

8/21/1939
Date of Birth

Date of Death

Where Buried

- Peery
Name of Spouse

Birthplace

Date of Birth

Date of Death

Where Buried

Date of Marriage

Place of Marriage

If married more than once:

Name of Spouse

Birthplace

Date of Birth

Date of Death

Where Buried

Date of Marriage

Place of Marriage

Parents of Spouse (with Mother's maiden name) 1st Marriage

Subsequent Marriage (if applicable)

Family Details

Schools attended, dates and degrees:

Community, political work, etc.:

Descendant

Descendant

Spouse

Spouse

Basic Employment History:

Clubs, Church Affiliations, etc.:

Descendant

Descendant

Spouse

Spouse

Military Service:

Descendant

Spouse

M6289174
Genealogical Number

Betty Carol Edmonds   Roanoke, VA
Name (including maiden name if applicable)   Town of Residence

                              12/10/1941
Birthplace   Date of Birth   Date of Death   Where Buried

 - Farmer
Name of Spouse   Birthplace   Date of Birth   Date of Death

Where Buried   Date of Marriage   Place of Marriage

If married more than once:

Name of Spouse   Birthplace   Date of Birth   Date of Death

Where Buried   Date of Marriage   Place of Marriage

Parents of Spouse (with Mother's maiden name) 1st Marriage

Subsequent Marriage (if applicable)

Family Details

Schools attended, dates and degrees: Community, political work, etc.:

Descendant   Descendant

Spouse   Spouse

Basic Employment History: Clubs, Church Affiliations, etc.:

Descendant   Descendant

Spouse   Spouse

Military Service:

Descendant   Spouse

M628918
Genealogical Number

George Dewey Graham
Name (including maiden name if applicable)   Town of Residence

Birthplace   3/2/1918 Date of Birth   11/10/1982 Date of Death   Where Buried

Name of Spouse   Birthplace   Date of Birth   Date of Death

Where Buried   Date of Marriage   Place of Marriage

If married more than once:

Name of Spouse   Birthplace   Date of Birth   Date of Death

Where Buried   Date of Marriage   Place of Marriage

Parents of Spouse (with Mother's maiden name) 1st Marriage

Subsequent Marriage (if applicable)

Family Details

Schools attended, dates and degrees: Community, political work, etc.:

Descendant   Descendant

Spouse   Spouse

Basic Employment History: Clubs, Church Affiliations, etc.:

Descendant   Descendant

Spouse   Spouse

Military Service:

Descendant   Spouse

M628919
Genealogical Number

John Bunyan Graham
Name (including maiden name if applicable)   Town of Residence

_____   9/23/1921   2/6/2001   _____
Birthplace   Date of Birth   Date of Death   Where Buried

_____   _____   _____   _____
Name of Spouse   Birthplace   Date of Birth   Date of Death

_____   _____   _____
Where Buried   Date of Marriage   Place of Marriage

If married more than once:

_____   _____   _____   _____
Name of Spouse   Birthplace   Date of Birth   Date of Death

_____   _____   _____
Where Buried   Date of Marriage   Place of Marriage

_____
Parents of Spouse (with Mother's maiden name) 1st Marriage

_____
Subsequent Marriage (if applicable)

Family Details

Schools attended, dates and degrees: Community, political work, etc.:

_____   _____
Descendant   Descendant

_____   _____
Spouse   Spouse

Basic Employment History: Clubs, Church Affiliations, etc.:

_____   _____
Descendant   Descendant

_____   _____
Spouse   Spouse

Military Service:

_____   _____
Descendant   Spouse

M6289191
Genealogical Number

Carol Graham
Name (including maiden name if applicable)   Town of Residence

Birthplace   Date of Birth   Date of Death   Where Buried

Name of Spouse   Birthplace   Date of Birth   Date of Death

Where Buried   Date of Marriage   Place of Marriage

If married more than once:

Name of Spouse   Birthplace   Date of Birth   Date of Death

Where Buried   Date of Marriage   Place of Marriage

Parents of Spouse (with Mother's maiden name) 1st Marriage

Subsequent Marriage (if applicable)

Family Details

Schools attended, dates and degrees: Community, political work, etc.:

Descendant   Descendant

Spouse   Spouse

Basic Employment History: Clubs, Church Affiliations, etc.:

Descendant   Descendant

Spouse   Spouse

Military Service:

Descendant   Spouse

M6289192
Genealogical Number

Tommy Graham
Name (including maiden name if applicable)

Penn.
Town of Residence

Birthplace

Date of Birth

Date of Death

Where Buried

Name of Spouse

Birthplace

Date of Birth

Date of Death

Where Buried

Date of Marriage

Place of Marriage

If married more than once:

Name of Spouse

Birthplace

Date of Birth

Date of Death

Where Buried

Date of Marriage

Place of Marriage

Parents of Spouse (with Mother's maiden name) 1st Marriage

Subsequent Marriage (if applicable)

Family Details

Schools attended, dates and degrees:

Community, political work, etc.:

Descendant

Descendant

Spouse

Spouse

Basic Employment History:

Clubs, Church Affiliations, etc.:

Descendant

Descendant

Spouse

Spouse

Military Service:

Descendant

Spouse

M6289193
Genealogical Number

Loretta Graham   Penn
Name (including maiden name if applicable)   Town of Residence

Birthplace   Date of Birth   Date of Death   Where Buried

Name of Spouse   Birthplace   Date of Birth   Date of Death

Where Buried   Date of Marriage   Place of Marriage

If married more than once:

Name of Spouse   Birthplace   Date of Birth   Date of Death

Where Buried   Date of Marriage   Place of Marriage

Parents of Spouse (with Mother's maiden name) 1st Marriage

Subsequent Marriage (if applicable)

Family Details

Schools attended, dates and degrees: Community, political work, etc.:

Descendant   Descendant

Spouse   Spouse

Basic Employment History: Clubs, Church Affiliations, etc.:

Descendant   Descendant

Spouse   Spouse

Military Service:

Descendant   Spouse

M6289194
Genealogical Number

Ricky Graham
Name (including maiden name if applicable)

Penn
Town of Residence

Birthplace   Date of Birth   Date of Death   Where Buried

Name of Spouse   Birthplace   Date of Birth   Date of Death

Where Buried   Date of Marriage   Place of Marriage

If married more than once:

Name of Spouse   Birthplace   Date of Birth   Date of Death

Where Buried   Date of Marriage   Place of Marriage

Parents of Spouse (with Mother's maiden name) 1st Marriage

Subsequent Marriage (if applicable)

Family Details

Schools attended, dates and degrees: Community, political work, etc.:

Descendant   Descendant

Spouse   Spouse

Basic Employment History: Clubs, Church Affiliations, etc.:

Descendant   Descendant

Spouse   Spouse

Military Service:

Descendant   Spouse

M6289252
Genealogical Number

John Harrison Graham		Princeton, W.VA	
Name (including maiden name if applicable)		Town of Residence	

Welch, W.VA	12/3/1942		
Birthplace	Date of Birth	Date of Death	Where Buried

Kathy Delayne Blankenship		8/12/1952	
Name of Spouse	Birthplace	Date of Birth	Date of Death

	11/18/1992	Bluefield, W.VA	
Where Buried	Date of Marriage	Place of Marriage	

If married more than once:
2. Wanda Sue Davis
1. Doris Jean Evans

		7/8/1949	11/30/1991
			4/10/1997
Name of Spouse	Birthplace	Date of Birth	Date of Death
	1. 6/18		
	2. 8/3/1963		
Where Buried	Date of Marriage	Place of Marriage	

Parents of Spouse (with Mother's maiden name) 1st Marriage

Subsequent Marriage (if applicable)

Family Details

Schools attended, dates and degrees:	Community, political work, etc.:
Descendant	Descendant
Spouse	Spouse
Basic Employment History:	Clubs, Church Affiliations, etc.:
Descendant	Descendant
Spouse	Spouse
Military Service:	
Descendant	Spouse

M62892521
Genealogical Number

Elisa Joyce Graham   MD
Name (including maiden name if applicable)   Town of Residence

Welch, W.VA   1/24/1964   6/27/2002   Hanover, PA
Birthplace   Date of Birth   Date of Death   Where Buried

Brian Robert Nahory   10/7/1967
Name of Spouse   Birthplace   Date of Birth   Date of Death

                               12/7/1991   MD
Where Buried   Date of Marriage   Place of Marriage

If married more than once:

Name of Spouse   Birthplace   Date of Birth   Date of Death

Where Buried   Date of Marriage   Place of Marriage

Parents of Spouse (with Mother's maiden name) 1st Marriage

Subsequent Marriage (if applicable)

Family Details

Schools attended, dates and degrees: Community, political work, etc.:

Descendant   Descendant

Spouse   Spouse

Basic Employment History: Clubs, Church Affiliations, etc.:

Descendant   Descendant

Spouse   Spouse

Military Service:

Descendant   Spouse

M628925211
Genealogical Number

Caleb Scott Nahory
Name (including maiden name if applicable)

Hanover, PA
Town of Residence

MD
Birthplace

6/20/1994
Date of Birth

Date of Death

Where Buried

Name of Spouse

Birthplace

Date of Birth

Date of Death

Where Buried

Date of Marriage

Place of Marriage

If married more than once:

Name of Spouse

Birthplace

Date of Birth

Date of Death

Where Buried

Date of Marriage

Place of Marriage

Parents of Spouse (with Mother's maiden name) 1st Marriage

Subsequent Marriage (if applicable)

Family Details

Schools attended, dates and degrees:

Community, political work, etc.:

Descendant

Descendant

Spouse

Spouse

Basic Employment History:

Clubs, Church Affiliations, etc.:

Descendant

Descendant

Spouse

Spouse

Military Service:

Descendant

Spouse

M628925212
Genealogical Number

Alexa Brianna Nahory
Name (including maiden name if applicable)

Hanover, PA
Town of Residence

MD
Birthplace

7/27/1995
Date of Birth

Date of Death

Where Buried

Name of Spouse

Birthplace

Date of Birth

Date of Death

Where Buried

Date of Marriage

Place of Marriage

If married more than once:

Name of Spouse

Birthplace

Date of Birth

Date of Death

Where Buried

Date of Marriage

Place of Marriage

Parents of Spouse (with Mother's maiden name) 1st Marriage

Subsequent Marriage (if applicable)

Family Details

Schools attended, dates and degrees:

Community, political work, etc.:

Descendant

Descendant

Spouse

Spouse

Basic Employment History:

Clubs, Church Affiliations, etc.:

Descendant

Descendant

Spouse

Spouse

Military Service:

Descendant

Spouse

M62825213
Genealogical Number

Alysa Marie Nahory

Hanover, PA

Name (including maiden name if applicable)

Town of Residence

MD   7/27/1995

Birthplace   Date of Birth   Date of Death   Where Buried

Name of Spouse   Birthplace   Date of Birth   Date of Death

Where Buried   Date of Marriage   Place of Marriage

If married more than once:

Name of Spouse   Birthplace   Date of Birth   Date of Death

Where Buried   Date of Marriage   Place of Marriage

Parents of Spouse (with Mother's maiden name) 1st Marriage

Subsequent Marriage (if applicable)

Family Details

Schools attended, dates and degrees:

Community, political work, etc.:

Descendant

Descendant

Spouse

Spouse

Basic Employment History:

Clubs, Church Affiliations, etc.:

Descendant

Descendant

Spouse

Spouse

Military Service:

Descendant

Spouse

M62892522
Genealogical Number

Christina Joan Graham   Thorpe, W.VA
Name (including maiden name if applicable)   Town of Residence

Welch, W.VA   2/2/1968
Birthplace   Date of Birth   Date of Death   Where Buried

Paul Edgar Brooks   W.VA   9/6/1957
Name of Spouse   Birthplace   Date of Birth   Date of Death

                            7/7/1990   Conkline Town, W.VA
Where Buried   Date of Marriage   Place of Marriage

If married more than once:

Name of Spouse   Birthplace   Date of Birth   Date of Death

Where Buried   Date of Marriage   Place of Marriage

Paul & Stella Fowler Brooks
Parents of Spouse (with Mother's maiden name) 1st Marriage

Subsequent Marriage (if applicable)

Family Details

Schools attended, dates and degrees: Community, political work, etc.:

Descendant   Descendant

Spouse   Spouse

Basic Employment History: Clubs, Church Affiliations, etc.:

Descendant   Descendant

Spouse   Spouse

Military Service:

Descendant   Spouse

M62825221
Genealogical Number

Cruiz Aaron Graham
Name (including maiden name if applicable)

Thorpe, W.VA
Town of Residence

Welch, W.VA   5/12/1987
Birthplace   Date of Birth

Date of Death   Where Buried

Name of Spouse   Birthplace   Date of Birth   Date of Death

Where Buried   Date of Marriage   Place of Marriage

If married more than once:

Name of Spouse   Birthplace   Date of Birth   Date of Death

Where Buried   Date of Marriage   Place of Marriage

Parents of Spouse (with Mother's maiden name) 1st Marriage

Subsequent Marriage (if applicable)

Family Details

Schools attended, dates and degrees: Community, political work, etc.:

Descendant   Descendant

Spouse   Spouse

Basic Employment History: Clubs, Church Affiliations, etc.:

Descendant   Descendant

Spouse   Spouse

Military Service:

Descendant   Spouse

M628925222
Genealogical Number

Cody Ryan Brooks   Thorpe, W.VA
Name (including maiden name if applicable)   Town of Residence

Welch, W.VA   2/14/1991
Birthplace   Date of Birth   Date of Death   Where Buried

Name of Spouse   Birthplace   Date of Birth   Date of Death

Where Buried   Date of Marriage   Place of Marriage

If married more than once:

Name of Spouse   Birthplace   Date of Birth   Date of Death

Where Buried   Date of Marriage   Place of Marriage

Parents of Spouse (with Mother's maiden name) 1st Marriage

Subsequent Marriage (if applicable)

Family Details

Schools attended, dates and degrees: Community, political work, etc.:

Descendant   Descendant

Spouse   Spouse

Basic Employment History: Clubs, Church Affiliations, etc.:

Descendant   Descendant

Spouse   Spouse

Military Service:

Descendant   Spouse

M62892523
Genealogical Number

John Harrison Graham II
Name (including maiden name if applicable)

Town of Residence

Alexandria, VA   9/12/1972
Birthplace   Date of Birth

Date of Death   Where Buried

Melissa Ann Dillon   5/1/1973
Name of Spouse   Birthplace   Date of Birth   Date of Death

                                    1/15/1994   Coalwood, WV
Where Buried   Date of Marriage   Place of Marriage

If married more than once:

Name of Spouse   Birthplace   Date of Birth   Date of Death

Where Buried   Date of Marriage   Place of Marriage

Parents of Spouse (with Mother's maiden name) 1st Marriage

Subsequent Marriage (if applicable)

Family Details

Schools attended, dates and degrees: Community, political work, etc.:

Descendant   Descendant

Spouse   Spouse

Basic Employment History: Clubs, Church Affiliations, etc.:

Descendant   Descendant

Spouse   Spouse

Military Service:

Descendant   Spouse

M628925231
Genealogical Number

Dillon Harrison Graham   Cedar Point, VA
Name (including maiden name if applicable)   Town of Residence

TN   9/6/1997
Birthplace   Date of Birth   Date of Death   Where Buried

Name of Spouse   Birthplace   Date of Birth   Date of Death

Where Buried   Date of Marriage   Place of Marriage

If married more than once:

Name of Spouse   Birthplace   Date of Birth   Date of Death

Where Buried   Date of Marriage   Place of Marriage

Parents of Spouse (with Mother's maiden name) 1st Marriage

Subsequent Marriage (if applicable)

Family Details

Schools attended, dates and degrees: Community, political work, etc.:

Descendant   Descendant

Spouse   Spouse

Basic Employment History: Clubs, Church Affiliations, etc.:

Descendant   Descendant

Spouse   Spouse

Military Service:

Descendant   Spouse

M62892524
Genealogical Number

Dolly Darline Graham
Name (including maiden name if applicable)

Max Meadows, VA
Town of Residence

Alexandria, VA
Birthplace

8/3/1974
Date of Birth

Date of Death

Where Buried

Mark Wayne Warren
Name of Spouse

Birthplace

3/3/1973
Date of Birth

Date of Death

Where Buried

6/11/1994
Date of Marriage

WV
Place of Marriage

If married more than once:

Name of Spouse

Birthplace

Date of Birth

Date of Death

Where Buried

Date of Marriage

Place of Marriage

Sam & Agnis Winebarger Warren
Parents of Spouse (with Mother's maiden name) 1st Marriage

Subsequent Marriage (if applicable)

Family Details

Schools attended, dates and degrees:

Community, political work, etc.:

Descendant

Descendant

Spouse

Spouse

Basic Employment History:

Clubs, Church Affiliations, etc.:

Descendant

Descendant

Spouse

Spouse

Military Service:

Descendant

Spouse

M628925241
Genealogical Number

Terry Wayne Warren   Max Meadows, VA
Name (including maiden name if applicable)   Town of Residence

Welch, WV   4/12/1992
Birthplace   Date of Birth   Date of Death   Where Buried

Name of Spouse   Birthplace   Date of Birth   Date of Death

Where Buried   Date of Marriage   Place of Marriage

If married more than once:

Name of Spouse   Birthplace   Date of Birth   Date of Death

Where Buried   Date of Marriage   Place of Marriage

Parents of Spouse (with Mother's maiden name) 1st Marriage

Subsequent Marriage (if applicable)

Family Details

Schools attended, dates and degrees: Community, political work, etc.:

Descendant   Descendant

Spouse   Spouse

Basic Employment History: Clubs, Church Affiliations, etc.:

Descendant   Descendant

Spouse   Spouse

Military Service:

Descendant   Spouse

M6289253
Genealogical Number

Wanda Ellen Graham
Name (including maiden name if applicable)

Thorpe, WV
Town of Residence

Welch, WV
Birthplace

7/22/1944
Date of Birth

Date of Death

Where Buried

Name of Spouse

Birthplace

Date of Birth

Date of Death

Where Buried

Date of Marriage

Place of Marriage

If married more than once:

Name of Spouse

Birthplace

Date of Birth

Date of Death

Where Buried

Date of Marriage

Place of Marriage

Parents of Spouse (with Mother's maiden name) 1st Marriage

Subsequent Marriage (if applicable)

Family Details

Schools attended, dates and degrees:

Community, political work, etc.:

Descendant

Descendant

Spouse

Spouse

Basic Employment History:

Clubs, Church Affiliations, etc.:

Descendant

Descendant

Spouse

Spouse

Military Service:

Descendant

Spouse

M6289254
Genealogical Number

George Aaron Graham   Troutdale, VA
Name (including maiden name if applicable)   Town of Residence

Welch, WV   8/23/1945
Birthplace   Date of Birth   Date of Death   Where Buried

Zola Ina Darlene Dunford   Sugar Grove, VA   9/14/1946
Name of Spouse   Birthplace   Date of Birth   Date of Death

                             1/1/1966   Sugar Grove, VA
Where Buried   Date of Marriage   Place of Marriage

If married more than once:

Name of Spouse   Birthplace   Date of Birth   Date of Death

Where Buried   Date of Marriage   Place of Marriage

Dorothy Marie Haulsey Dunford
Samuel Hix Dunford
Parents of Spouse (with Mother's maiden name) 1st Marriage

Subsequent Marriage (if applicable)

Family Details

Schools attended, dates and degrees: Community, political work, etc.:

Descendant   Descendant

Spouse   Spouse

Basic Employment History: Clubs, Church Affiliations, etc.:

Descendant   Descendant

Spouse   Spouse

Military Service:

Descendant   Spouse

M62892541
Genealogical Number

John Aaron Graham
Name (including maiden name if applicable)

Chilhowie, VA
Town of Residence

Marion, VA
Birthplace

4/15/1966
Date of Birth

Date of Death

Where Buried

Melissa Ann Groseclose
Name of Spouse

Wytheville, VA
Birthplace

12/26/1970
Date of Birth

Date of Death

Where Buried

2/9/1991
Date of Marriage

Cripple Creek, VA
Place of Marriage

If married more than once:

Name of Spouse

Birthplace

Date of Birth

Date of Death

Where Buried

Date of Marriage

Place of Marriage

Parents of Spouse (with Mother's maiden name) 1st Marriage

Subsequent Marriage (if applicable)

Family Details

Schools attended, dates and degrees:

Community, political work, etc.:

Descendant

Descendant

Spouse

Spouse

Basic Employment History:

Clubs, Church Affiliations, etc.:

Descendant

Descendant

Spouse

Spouse

Military Service:

Descendant

Spouse

M628925411
Genealogical Number

Scott Aaron Graham
Name (including maiden name if applicable)

Chilhowie, VA
Town of Residence

Arlington, VA
Birthplace

· 12/2/1994
Date of Birth

Date of Death

Where Buried

Name of Spouse

Birthplace

Date of Birth

Date of Death

Where Buried

Date of Marriage

Place of Marriage

If married more than once:

Name of Spouse

Birthplace

Date of Birth

Date of Death

Where Buried

Date of Marriage

Place of Marriage

Parents of Spouse (with Mother's maiden name) 1st Marriage

Subsequent Marriage (if applicable)

Family Details

Schools attended, dates and degrees:

Community, political work, etc.:

Descendant

Descendant

Spouse

Spouse

Basic Employment History:

Clubs, Church Affiliations, etc.:

Descendant

Descendant

Spouse

Spouse

Military Service:

Descendant

Spouse

M62892542
Genealogical Number

Dreama Annette Graham   Chilhowie, VA
Name (including maiden name if applicable)   Town of Residence

Marion, VA   2/10/1968
Birthplace   Date of Birth   Date of Death   Where Buried

Walter Lee Ashbey   Marion, VA   10/7/1968
Name of Spouse   Birthplace   Date of Birth   Date of Death

                            4/1/1989   Chilhowie, VA
Where Buried   Date of Marriage   Place of Marriage

If married more than once:

Name of Spouse   Birthplace   Date of Birth   Date of Death

Where Buried   Date of Marriage   Place of Marriage

Parents of Spouse (with Mother's maiden name) 1st Marriage

Subsequent Marriage (if applicable)

Family Details

Schools attended, dates and degrees: Community, political work, etc.:

Descendant   Descendant

Spouse   Spouse

Basic Employment History: Clubs, Church Affiliations, etc.:

Descendant   Descendant

Spouse   Spouse

Military Service:

Descendant   Spouse

M628925421
Genealogical Number

Dakota Chaning Ashbey
Name (including maiden name if applicable)   Town of Residence

                              4/8/1985
Birthplace   Date of Birth   Date of Death   Where Buried

Name of Spouse   Birthplace   Date of Birth   Date of Death

Where Buried   Date of Marriage   Place of Marriage

If married more than once:

Name of Spouse   Birthplace   Date of Birth   Date of Death

Where Buried   Date of Marriage   Place of Marriage

Parents of Spouse (with Mother's maiden name) 1st Marriage

Subsequent Marriage (if applicable)

Family Details

Schools attended, dates and degrees: Community, political work, etc.:

Descendant   Descendant

Spouse   Spouse

Basic Employment History: Clubs, Church Affiliations, etc.:

Descendant   Descendant

Spouse   Spouse

Military Service:

Descendant   Spouse

M628925422
Genealogical Number

Christopher Aaron Ashbey
Name (including maiden name if applicable)   Town of Residence

                                    14/2/89
Birthplace   Date of Birth   Date of Death   Where Buried

Name of Spouse   Birthplace   Date of Birth   Date of Death

Where Buried   Date of Marriage   Place of Marriage

If married more than once:

Name of Spouse   Birthplace   Date of Birth   Date of Death

Where Buried   Date of Marriage   Place of Marriage

Parents of Spouse (with Mother's maiden name) 1st Marriage

Subsequent Marriage (if applicable)

Family Details

Schools attended, dates and degrees: Community, political work, etc.:

Descendant   Descendant

Spouse   Spouse

Basic Employment History: Clubs, Church Affiliations, etc.:

Descendant   Descendant

Spouse   Spouse

Military Service:

Descendant   Spouse

M62892543
Genealogical Number

Marty Ray Graham   Troutdale, VA
Name (including maiden name if applicable)   Town of Residence

Marion, VA   1/26/1971
Birthplace   Date of Birth   Date of Death   Where Buried

Sharon Robertson   Marion, VA   7/21/1972
Name of Spouse   Birthplace   Date of Birth   Date of Death

                        8/24/1991   Sugar Grove, VA
Where Buried   Date of Marriage   Place of Marriage

If married more than once:

Name of Spouse   Birthplace   Date of Birth   Date of Death

Where Buried   Date of Marriage   Place of Marriage

Parents of Spouse (with Mother's maiden name) 1st Marriage

Subsequent Marriage (if applicable)

Family Details

Schools attended, dates and degrees: Community, political work, etc.:

Descendant   Descendant

Spouse   Spouse

Basic Employment History: Clubs, Church Affiliations, etc.:

Descendant   Descendant

Spouse   Spouse

Military Service:

Descendant   Spouse

M628925431
Genealogical Number

Samuel Harrison Graham
Name (including maiden name if applicable)

Troutdale, VA
Town of Residence

Marion, VA
Birthplace

4/30/1998
Date of Birth

Date of Death

Where Buried

Name of Spouse

Birthplace

Date of Birth

Date of Death

Where Buried

Date of Marriage

Place of Marriage

If married more than once:

Name of Spouse

Birthplace

Date of Birth

Date of Death

Where Buried

Date of Marriage

Place of Marriage

Parents of Spouse (with Mother's maiden name) 1st Marriage

Subsequent Marriage (if applicable)

Family Details

Schools attended, dates and degrees:

Community, political work, etc.:

Descendant

Descendant

Spouse

Spouse

Basic Employment History:

Clubs, Church Affiliations, etc.:

Descendant

Descendant

Spouse

Spouse

Military Service:

Descendant

Spouse

M6289255
Genealogical Number

Mary Belle Graham   Thorpe, W.VA
Name (including maiden name if applicable)   Town of Residence

Welch, W.VA   1/17/1947
Birthplace   Date of Birth   Date of Death   Where Buried

Kenneth Ray Fowler   Welch, W.VA   12/9/1947
Name of Spouse   Birthplace   Date of Birth   Date of Death

                            6/30/1979   Conklen Town, W.VA
Where Buried   Date of Marriage   Place of Marriage

If married more than once:

Charles Arthur Davis   W.VA   7/15/1943   12/25/1976
Name of Spouse   Birthplace   Date of Birth   Date of Death

Woodlawn, Bluefield, W.VA   1/22/1966   MD
Where Buried   Date of Marriage   Place of Marriage

Gaither & Blanch Davis
Parents of Spouse (with Mother's maiden name) 1st Marriage

Boyd & Hattie Goins Fowler
Subsequent Marriage (if applicable)

Family Details

Schools attended, dates and degrees: Community, political work, etc.:

Descendant   Descendant

Spouse   Spouse

Basic Employment History: Clubs, Church Affiliations, etc.:

Descendant   Descendant

Spouse   Spouse

Military Service:

Descendant   Spouse

M62892551
Genealogical Number

Mark Steven Davis
Name (including maiden name if applicable)

Denver, NC
Town of Residence

Bethesda, MD
Birthplace

11/27/1966
Date of Birth

Date of Death

Where Buried

Susan Lynn Shrader
Name of Spouse

W.VA
Birthplace

10/26/1969
Date of Birth

Date of Death

Where Buried

8/26/1989
Date of Marriage

Anawalt, W.VA
Place of Marriage

If married more than once:

Name of Spouse

Birthplace

Date of Birth

Date of Death

Where Buried

Date of Marriage

Place of Marriage

Rufus & Orthia McCoy Shrader
Parents of Spouse (with Mother's maiden name) 1st Marriage

Subsequent Marriage (if applicable)

Family Details

Schools attended, dates and degrees:

Community, political work, etc.:

Descendant

Descendant

Spouse

Spouse

Basic Employment History:

Clubs, Church Affiliations, etc.:

Descendant

Descendant

Spouse

Spouse

Military Service:

Descendant

Spouse

M628925511
Genealogical Number

Andrew Steven Davis
Name (including maiden name if applicable)

Denver, NC
Town of Residence

Charlotte, NC
Birthplace

6/9/1994
Date of Birth

Date of Death

Where Buried

Name of Spouse

Birthplace

Date of Birth

Date of Death

Where Buried

Date of Marriage

Place of Marriage

If married more than once:

Name of Spouse

Birthplace

Date of Birth

Date of Death

Where Buried

Date of Marriage

Place of Marriage

Parents of Spouse (with Mother's maiden name) 1st Marriage

Subsequent Marriage (if applicable)

Family Details

Schools attended, dates and degrees:

Community, political work, etc.:

Descendant

Descendant

Spouse

Spouse

Basic Employment History:

Clubs, Church Affiliations, etc.:

Descendant

Descendant

Spouse

Spouse

Military Service:

Descendant

Spouse

M62892552
Genealogical Number

Michael DeWayne Davis   Zionville, NC
Name (including maiden name if applicable)   Town of Residence

Fairfax, VA   8/15/1970
Birthplace   Date of Birth   Date of Death   Where Buried

Amy Carol Castle   7/15/1972
Name of Spouse   Birthplace   Date of Birth   Date of Death

                                     9/7/1991   Zionvile, NC
Where Buried   Date of Marriage   Place of Marriage

If married more than once:

Name of Spouse   Birthplace   Date of Birth   Date of Death

Where Buried   Date of Marriage   Place of Marriage

Archie Lewis Castle & Carolyn Sanders
Parents of Spouse (with Mother's maiden name) 1st Marriage

Subsequent Marriage (if applicable)

Family Details

Schools attended, dates and degrees: Community, political work, etc.:

Descendant   Descendant

Spouse   Spouse

Basic Employment History: Clubs, Church Affiliations, etc.:

Descendant   Descendant

Spouse   Spouse

Military Service:

Descendant   Spouse

817

M628925521
Genealogical Number

Megan Hope Davis   Zionville, NC
Name (including maiden name if applicable)   Town of Residence

Boone, NC   8/3/1996
Birthplace   Date of Birth   Date of Death   Where Buried

Name of Spouse   Birthplace   Date of Birth   Date of Death

Where Buried   Date of Marriage   Place of Marriage

If married more than once:

Name of Spouse   Birthplace   Date of Birth   Date of Death

Where Buried   Date of Marriage   Place of Marriage

Parents of Spouse (with Mother's maiden name) 1st Marriage

Subsequent Marriage (if applicable)

Family Details

Schools attended, dates and degrees: Community, political work, etc.:

Descendant   Descendant

Spouse   Spouse

Basic Employment History: Clubs, Church Affiliations, etc.:

Descendant   Descendant

Spouse   Spouse

Military Service:

Descendant   Spouse

M6289266
Genealogical Number

Clyde M. Casey
Name (including maiden name if applicable)

Bluefield, W.VA
Town of Residence

Jenkinjones, W.VA
Birthplace

6/6/1951
Date of Birth

Date of Death

Where Buried

Freda B. Coeburn
Name of Spouse

Bluefield, W.VA
Birthplace

12/19/1961
Date of Birth

Date of Death

Where Buried

9/28/1978
Date of Marriage

Tazewell, VA
Place of Marriage

If married more than once:

Name of Spouse

Birthplace

Date of Birth

Date of Death

Where Buried

Date of Marriage

Place of Marriage

Freda Stacey - Walter Coeburn
Parents of Spouse (with Mother's maiden name) 1st Marriage

Subsequent Marriage (if applicable)

Family Details

Schools attended, dates and degrees:

Community, political work, etc.:

Ashland Grade School, Ashland, W.VA
Descendant

Descendant

Spouse

Spouse

Basic Employment History:

Clubs, Church Affiliations, etc.:

Plumber, Coal miner
Descendant

Moose Lodge, Bluefield, W.VA
Descendant

Nursing Aid
Spouse

Spouse

Military Service:

Descendant

Spouse

M6289267
Genealogical Number

Virginia L. Casey
Name (including maiden name if applicable)

Princeton, W.VA
Town of Residence

Jenkinjones, W.VA
Birthplace

4/23/1952
Date of Birth

2/15/2001
Date of Death

Where Buried

Gene Shrader
Name of Spouse

Princeton
Birthplace

3/13/1938
Date of Birth

Date of Death

Where Buried

8/27/1973
Date of Marriage

Pearisburg, VA
Place of Marriage

If married more than once:

Name of Spouse

Birthplace

Date of Birth

Date of Death

Where Buried

Date of Marriage

Place of Marriage

Kathleen L. Tabor - Paris Shrader
Parents of Spouse (with Mother's maiden name) 1st Marriage

Subsequent Marriage (if applicable)

Family Details

Schools attended, dates and degrees:

North Fork -Elkhorn Jr. High
North Fork, W.VA
Descendant
Glenwood High School, Princeton,
W.VA
Spouse

Community, political work, etc.:

Descendant

Spouse

Basic Employment History:

Bluefield Daily Telegraph
Descendant

Owner-operator tractor trailer (18 wheeler)
Spouse

Military Service:

Descendant

Clubs, Church Affiliations, etc.:

Descendant

Spouse

Spouse

M6289268
Genealogical Number

H. Elwood Casey
Name (including maiden name if applicable)

Bluefield, W.VA
Town of Residence

Welch, W.VA
Birthplace

4/3/1955
Date of Birth

7/23/1979
Date of Death

Where Buried

Iva Ann Mangus
Name of Spouse

Bluefield, W.VA
Birthplace

10/8/1955
Date of Birth

Date of Death

Where Buried

7/16/1974
Date of Marriage

Tazewell, VA
Place of Marriage

If married more than once:

Name of Spouse

Birthplace

Date of Birth

Date of Death

Where Buried

Date of Marriage

Place of Marriage

Parents of Spouse (with Mother's maiden name) 1st Marriage

Subsequent Marriage (if applicable)

Family Details

Schools attended, dates and degrees:

Community, political work, etc.:

Descendant

Descendant

Spouse

Spouse

Basic Employment History:

Clubs, Church Affiliations, etc.:

Construction Coal Miner
Descendant

Moose Lodge - Princeton, W.VA
Descendant

Homemaker
Spouse

Spouse

Military Service:

Descendant

Spouse

M6289271
Genealogical Number

Eunice Pauline Harman   Bradenton, Fla.
Name (including maiden name if applicable)   Town of Residence

                          6/18/1934
Birthplace   Date of Birth   Date of Death   Where Buried

Ronald James Panciera   12/1/1933
Name of Spouse   Birthplace   Date of Birth   Date of Death

                          11/19/1955   Skygusty, W.VA
Where Buried   Date of Marriage   Place of Marriage

If married more than once:

Name of Spouse   Birthplace   Date of Birth   Date of Death

Where Buried   Date of Marriage   Place of Marriage

Parents of Spouse (with Mother's maiden name) 1st Marriage

Subsequent Marriage (if applicable)

Family Details

Schools attended, dates and degrees: Community, political work, etc.:

Descendant   Descendant

Spouse   Spouse

Basic Employment History: Clubs, Church Affiliations, etc.:

Descendant   Descendant

Spouse   Spouse

Military Service:

Descendant   Spouse

M6289321
Genealogical Number

Walter Witten Graham, Jr.
Name (including maiden name if applicable)

Tazewell, VA
Town of Residence

Bluefield, W.VA
Birthplace

1/4/1959
Date of Birth

Date of Death

Where Buried

Donnetta Cline
Name of Spouse

Welch, W.VA
Birthplace

9/2/1961
Date of Birth

Date of Death

Where Buried

Date of Marriage

Place of Marriage

If married more than once:

Name of Spouse

Birthplace

Date of Birth

Date of Death

Where Buried

Date of Marriage

Place of Marriage

Parents of Spouse (with Mother's maiden name) 1st Marriage

Subsequent Marriage (if applicable)

Family Details

Schools attended, dates and degrees:

Community, political work, etc.:

Descendant

Descendant

Spouse

Spouse

Basic Employment History:

Clubs, Church Affiliations, etc.:

Descendant

Descendant

Spouse

Spouse

Military Service:

Descendant

Spouse

M6289331
Genealogical Number

Margaret Louise Repass   N. Tazewell, VA
Name (including maiden name if applicable)   Town of Residence

N. Tazewell, VA   8/5/1930
Birthplace   Date of Birth   Date of Death   Where Buried

James Kulchar   Caretta, W.VA   10/1/1925
Name of Spouse   Birthplace   Date of Birth   Date of Death

Where Buried   Date of Marriage   Place of Marriage

If married more than once:

Name of Spouse   Birthplace   Date of Birth   Date of Death

Where Buried   Date of Marriage   Place of Marriage

Parents of Spouse (with Mother's maiden name) 1st Marriage

Subsequent Marriage (if applicable)

Family Details

Schools attended, dates and degrees: Community, political work, etc.:

Descendant   Descendant

Spouse   Spouse

Basic Employment History: Clubs, Church Affiliations, etc.:

Descendant   Descendant

Spouse   Spouse

Military Service:

Descendant   Spouse

M62893311
Genealogical Number

Andrew George Kulchar
Name (including maiden name if applicable)

N. Tazewell, VA
Town of Residence

Bluefield, W.VA
Birthplace

5/14/1950
Date of Birth

Date of Death

Where Buried

Name of Spouse

Birthplace

Date of Birth

Date of Death

Where Buried

Date of Marriage

Place of Marriage

If married more than once:

Name of Spouse

Birthplace

Date of Birth

Date of Death

Where Buried

Date of Marriage

Place of Marriage

Parents of Spouse (with Mother's maiden name) 1st Marriage

Subsequent Marriage (if applicable)

Family Details

Schools attended, dates and degrees:

Community, political work, etc.:

Descendant

Descendant

Spouse

Spouse

Basic Employment History:

Clubs, Church Affiliations, etc.:

Descendant

Descendant

Spouse

Spouse

Military Service:

Descendant

Spouse

M62893312
Genealogical Number

Mary Dovie Kulchar
Name (including maiden name if applicable)

Tazewell, VA
Town of Residence

Bluefield, W.VA
Birthplace

4/8/1957
Date of Birth

Date of Death

Where Buried

Name of Spouse

Birthplace

Date of Birth

Date of Death

Where Buried

Date of Marriage

Place of Marriage

If married more than once:

Name of Spouse

Birthplace

Date of Birth

Date of Death

Where Buried

Date of Marriage

Place of Marriage

Parents of Spouse (with Mother's maiden name) 1st Marriage

Subsequent Marriage (if applicable)

Family Details

Schools attended, dates and degrees:

Community, political work, etc.:

Descendant

Descendant

Spouse

Spouse

Basic Employment History:

Clubs, Church Affiliations, etc.:

Descendant

Descendant

Spouse

Spouse

Military Service:

Descendant

Spouse

M62893313
Genealogical Number

James Byron Kulchar
Name (including maiden name if applicable)

Kuwait
Town of Residence

Bluefield, W.VA   3/20/1966
Birthplace   Date of Birth   Date of Death   Where Buried

Name of Spouse   Birthplace   Date of Birth   Date of Death

Where Buried   Date of Marriage   Place of Marriage

If married more than once:

Name of Spouse   Birthplace   Date of Birth   Date of Death

Where Buried   Date of Marriage   Place of Marriage

Parents of Spouse (with Mother's maiden name) 1st Marriage

Subsequent Marriage (if applicable)

Family Details

Schools attended, dates and degrees: Community, political work, etc.:

Descendant   Descendant

Spouse   Spouse

Basic Employment History: Clubs, Church Affiliations, etc.:

Descendant   Descendant

Spouse   Spouse

Military Service:

Descendant   Spouse

M6289332
Genealogical Number

Alfred Jack Repass   North Tazewell, VA
Name (including maiden name if applicable)   Town of Residence

North Tazewell, VA   12/14/1932
Birthplace   Date of Birth   Date of Death   Where Buried

Mary Lucille Linkous   N. Tazewell   8/27/1932
Name of Spouse   Birthplace   Date of Birth   Date of Death

Where Buried   Date of Marriage   Place of Marriage

If married more than once:

Name of Spouse   Birthplace   Date of Birth   Date of Death

Where Buried   Date of Marriage   Place of Marriage

Parents of Spouse (with Mother's maiden name) 1st Marriage

Subsequent Marriage (if applicable)

Family Details

Schools attended, dates and degrees: Community, political work, etc.:

Descendant   Descendant

Spouse   Spouse

Basic Employment History: Clubs, Church Affiliations, etc.:

Descendant   Descendant

Spouse   Spouse

Military Service:

Descendant   Spouse

M628933211
Genealogical Number

Jared Alexander Repass
Name (including maiden name if applicable)

N. Tazewell, VA
Town of Residence

Birthplace

5/24/1995
Date of Birth

Date of Death

Where Buried

Name of Spouse

Birthplace

Date of Birth

Date of Death

Where Buried

Date of Marriage

Place of Marriage

If married more than once:

Name of Spouse

Birthplace

Date of Birth

Date of Death

Where Buried

Date of Marriage

Place of Marriage

Parents of Spouse (with Mother's maiden name) 1st Marriage

Subsequent Marriage (if applicable)

Family Details

Schools attended, dates and degrees:

Community, political work, etc.:

Descendant

Descendant

Spouse

Spouse

Basic Employment History:

Clubs, Church Affiliations, etc.:

Descendant

Descendant

Spouse

Spouse

Military Service:

Descendant

Spouse

M6289333
Genealogical Number

Roy Douglas Repass

Tazewell, VA

Name (including maiden name if applicable)

Town of Residence

N. Tazewell, VA

4/1/1943

Birthplace

Date of Birth

Date of Death

Where Buried

Katherine F. Goss

Lynchburg, VA

10/1/1944

Name of Spouse

Birthplace

Date of Birth

Date of Death

Where Buried

Date of Marriage

Place of Marriage

If married more than once:

Name of Spouse

Birthplace

Date of Birth

Date of Death

Where Buried

Date of Marriage

Place of Marriage

Parents of Spouse (with Mother's maiden name) 1st Marriage

Subsequent Marriage (if applicable)

Family Details

Schools attended, dates and degrees:

Community, political work, etc.:

Descendant

Descendant

Spouse

Spouse

Basic Employment History:

Clubs, Church Affiliations, etc.:

Descendant

Descendant

Spouse

Spouse

Military Service:

Descendant

Spouse

M62893331
Genealogical Number

Lisa Marie Repass   Tazewell, VA
Name (including maiden name if applicable)   Town of Residence

Bluefield, W.VA   7/31/1966
Birthplace   Date of Birth   Date of Death   Where Buried

Carl Harry
Name of Spouse   Birthplace   Date of Birth   Date of Death

                             10/1/1988   Tazewell, VA
Where Buried   Date of Marriage   Place of Marriage

If married more than once:

Name of Spouse   Birthplace   Date of Birth   Date of Death

Where Buried   Date of Marriage   Place of Marriage

Parents of Spouse (with Mother's maiden name) 1st Marriage

Subsequent Marriage (if applicable)

Family Details

Schools attended, dates and degrees: Community, political work, etc.:

Descendant   Descendant

Spouse   Spouse

Basic Employment History: Clubs, Church Affiliations, etc.:

Descendant   Descendant

Spouse   Spouse

Military Service:

Descendant   Spouse

M628933311
Genealogical Number

Chandler Robert Harry
Name (including maiden name if applicable)

Tazewell, VA
Town of Residence

Birthplace

1/13/1993
Date of Birth

Date of Death

Where Buried

Name of Spouse

Birthplace

Date of Birth

Date of Death

Where Buried

Date of Marriage

Place of Marriage

If married more than once:

Name of Spouse

Birthplace

Date of Birth

Date of Death

Where Buried

Date of Marriage

Place of Marriage

Parents of Spouse (with Mother's maiden name) 1st Marriage

Subsequent Marriage (if applicable)

Family Details

Schools attended, dates and degrees:

Community, political work, etc.:

Descendant

Descendant

Spouse

Spouse

Basic Employment History:

Clubs, Church Affiliations, etc.:

Descendant

Descendant

Spouse

Spouse

Military Service:

Descendant

Spouse

M62893332
Genealogical Number

Shelia R. Repass
Name (including maiden name if applicable)

N. Tazewell, VA
Town of Residence

Bluefield, W.VA
Birthplace

11/27/1970
Date of Birth

Date of Death

Where Buried

Wayne Smith
Name of Spouse

Birthplace

Date of Birth

Date of Death

Where Buried

5/10/1999
Date of Marriage

Tazewell, VA
Place of Marriage

If married more than once:

Name of Spouse

Birthplace

Date of Birth

Date of Death

Where Buried

Date of Marriage

Place of Marriage

Parents of Spouse (with Mother's maiden name) 1st Marriage

Subsequent Marriage (if applicable)

Family Details

Schools attended, dates and degrees:

Community, political work, etc.:

Descendant

Descendant

Spouse

Spouse

Basic Employment History:

Clubs, Church Affiliations, etc.:

Descendant

Descendant

Spouse

Spouse

M628933321
Genealogical Number

Trevor Edwards Smith _____   N. Tazewell, VA _____
Name (including maiden name if applicable)   Town of Residence

_____   _____   _____   _____
Birthplace   Date of Birth   Date of Death   Where Buried

_____   _____   _____   _____
Name of Spouse   Birthplace   Date of Birth   Date of Death

_____   _____   _____
Where Buried   Date of Marriage   Place of Marriage

If married more than once:

_____   _____   _____   _____
Name of Spouse   Birthplace   Date of Birth   Date of Death

_____   _____   _____
Where Buried   Date of Marriage   Place of Marriage

_____
Parents of Spouse (with Mother's maiden name) 1st Marriage

_____
Subsequent Marriage (if applicable)

Family Details

Schools attended, dates and degrees: Community, political work, etc.:

_____   _____
Descendant   Descendant

_____   _____
Spouse   Spouse

Basic Employment History: Clubs, Church Affiliations, etc.:

_____   _____
Descendant   Descendant

_____   _____
Spouse   Spouse

Military Service:

_____   _____
Descendant   Spouse

M62893333
Genealogical Number

David Wayne Repass
Name (including maiden name if applicable)

Tazewell, VA
Town of Residence

Bluefield, W.VA
Birthplace

8/21/1974
Date of Birth

Date of Death

Where Buried

Amanda Roberts
Name of Spouse

Birthplace

Date of Birth

Date of Death

Where Buried

9/27/1996
Date of Marriage

Tazewell, VA
Place of Marriage

If married more than once:

Name of Spouse

Birthplace

Date of Birth

Date of Death

Where Buried

Date of Marriage

Place of Marriage

Parents of Spouse (with Mother's maiden name) 1st Marriage

Subsequent Marriage (if applicable)

Family Details

Schools attended, dates and degrees:

Community, political work, etc.:

Descendant

Descendant

Spouse

Spouse

Basic Employment History:

Clubs, Church Affiliations, etc.:

Descendant

Descendant

Spouse

Spouse

Military Service:

Descendant

Spouse

M6289334
Genealogical Number

Marshall Graham Repass   North Tazewell, VA
Name (including maiden name if applicable)   Town of Residence

Tazewell, VA   3/24/1946
Birthplace   Date of Birth   Date of Death   Where Buried

June Etta Poskas   Tazewell, VA   11/28/1949
Name of Spouse   Birthplace   Date of Birth   Date of Death

Where Buried   Date of Marriage   Place of Marriage

If married more than once:

Name of Spouse   Birthplace   Date of Birth   Date of Death

Where Buried   Date of Marriage   Place of Marriage

Parents of Spouse (with Mother's maiden name) 1st Marriage

Subsequent Marriage (if applicable)

Family Details

Schools attended, dates and degrees: Community, political work, etc.:

Descendant   Descendant

Spouse   Spouse

Basic Employment History: Clubs, Church Affiliations, etc.:

Descendant   Descendant

Spouse   Spouse

Military Service:

Descendant   Spouse

M62893341
Genealogical Number

Mara Michelle Repass
Name (including maiden name if applicable)

Town of Residence

Fairfax County, VA   7/7/1966
Birthplace   Date of Birth   Date of Death   Where Buried

Steven Wingo
Name of Spouse   Birthplace   Date of Birth   Date of Death

                            6/21/1984   Tazewell, VA
Where Buried   Date of Marriage   Place of Marriage

If married more than once:

Name of Spouse   Birthplace   Date of Birth   Date of Death

Where Buried   Date of Marriage   Place of Marriage

Parents of Spouse (with Mother's maiden name) 1st Marriage

Subsequent Marriage (if applicable)

Family Details

Schools attended, dates and degrees: Community, political work, etc.:

Descendant   Descendant

Spouse   Spouse

Basic Employment History: Clubs, Church Affiliations, etc.:

Descendant   Descendant

Spouse   Spouse

Military Service:

Descendant   Spouse

M628933411
Genealogical Number

Steven Christopher Wingo
Name (including maiden name if applicable)

Town of Residence

Tazewell, VA   4/13/1986
Birthplace   Date of Birth   Date of Death   Where Buried

Name of Spouse   Birthplace   Date of Birth   Date of Death

Where Buried   Date of Marriage   Place of Marriage

If married more than once:

Name of Spouse   Birthplace   Date of Birth   Date of Death

Where Buried   Date of Marriage   Place of Marriage

Parents of Spouse (with Mother's maiden name) 1st Marriage

Subsequent Marriage (if applicable)

Family Details

Schools attended, dates and degrees: Community, political work, etc.:

Descendant   Descendant

Spouse   Spouse

Basic Employment History: Clubs, Church Affiliations, etc.:

Descendant   Descendant

Spouse   Spouse

Military Service:

Descendant   Spouse

M628934
Genealogical Number

Janice Viola Graham
Name (including maiden name if applicable)

Tazewell, VA
Town of Residence

Tazewell, VA   10/9/1920
Birthplace   Date of Birth

Date of Death   Where Buried

James W. Asbury   Tazewell, VA   10/1/1918
Name of Spouse   Birthplace   Date of Birth   Date of Death

Where Buried   Date of Marriage   Place of Marriage

If married more than once:

Name of Spouse   Birthplace   Date of Birth   Date of Death

Where Buried   Date of Marriage   Place of Marriage

Parents of Spouse (with Mother's maiden name) 1st Marriage

Subsequent Marriage (if applicable)

Family Details

Schools attended, dates and degrees: Community, political work, etc.:

Descendant   Descendant

Spouse   Spouse

Basic Employment History: Clubs, Church Affiliations, etc.:

Descendant   Descendant

Spouse   Spouse

Military Service:

Descendant   Spouse

M6289341
Genealogical Number

Retha Jane Asbury   Charlottesville, VA
Name (including maiden name if applicable)   Town of Residence

Bluefield, W.VA   6/14/1949
Birthplace   Date of Birth   Date of Death   Where Buried

Thelen (Div)
Name of Spouse   Birthplace   Date of Birth   Date of Death

Where Buried   Date of Marriage   Place of Marriage

If married more than once:

Name of Spouse   Birthplace   Date of Birth   Date of Death

Where Buried   Date of Marriage   Place of Marriage

Parents of Spouse (with Mother's maiden name) 1st Marriage

Subsequent Marriage (if applicable)

Family Details

Schools attended, dates and degrees: Community, political work, etc.:

Descendant   Descendant

Spouse   Spouse

Basic Employment History: Clubs, Church Affiliations, etc.:

Descendant   Descendant

Spouse   Spouse

Military Service:

Descendant   Spouse

M62893332
Genealogical Number

Shelia R. Repass
Name (including maiden name if applicable)

N. Tazewell, VA
Town of Residence

Bluefield, W.VA
Birthplace

11/27/1970
Date of Birth

Date of Death

Where Buried

Wayne Smith
Name of Spouse

Birthplace

Date of Birth

Date of Death

Where Buried

5/10/1999
Date of Marriage

Tazewell, VA
Place of Marriage

If married more than once:

Name of Spouse

Birthplace

Date of Birth

Date of Death

Where Buried

Date of Marriage

Place of Marriage

Parents of Spouse (with Mother's maiden name) 1st Marriage

Subsequent Marriage (if applicable)

Family Details

Schools attended, dates and degrees:

Community, political work, etc.:

Descendant

Descendant

Spouse

Spouse

Basic Employment History:

Clubs, Church Affiliations, etc.:

Descendant

Descendant

Spouse

Spouse

Military Service:

Descendant

Spouse

M6289342
Genealogical Number

James Miller Asbury   Louisa, VA
Name (including maiden name if applicable)   Town of Residence

Tazewell, VA   2/11/1953
Birthplace   Date of Birth   Date of Death   Where Buried

Name of Spouse   Birthplace   Date of Birth   Date of Death

Where Buried   Date of Marriage   Place of Marriage

If married more than once:

Name of Spouse   Birthplace   Date of Birth   Date of Death

Where Buried   Date of Marriage   Place of Marriage

Parents of Spouse (with Mother's maiden name) 1st Marriage

Subsequent Marriage (if applicable)

Family Details

Schools attended, dates and degrees: Community, political work, etc.:

Descendant   Descendant

Spouse   Spouse

Basic Employment History: Clubs, Church Affiliations, etc.:

Descendant   Descendant

Spouse   Spouse

Military Service:

Descendant   Spouse

31.

THE ISAAC QUINN MOORE LINE
GENEALOGICAL CHARTS

M629   *Isaac Quinn Moore - Elizabeth C. Tabor*
B. 2/24/1821   M. 9/28/1848   B. 6/10/1825
D. 12/19/1893   D. 1/10/1889

M6291 Cosby Buenavista Moore - Charles Clinton Wilson
B. 9/2/1849   M. 2/20/1873   B. 7/13/1844
D. 6/12/1933   D. 9/9/1925

    M62911 - Hugh Edward Wilson - **M62522** Ida Marie Moore
        B. 3/17/1874   M. 11/25/1908   B. 4/7/1874
        D. _____   D. _____

        M625221 - Hazel Virginia Wilson
            B. 11/9/1910
            D. _____

        M625222 - Mary Moore Wilson
            B. 6/2/1913
            D. _____

    M62912 - John William Wilson
        B. 5/19/1876
        D. _____

    M62913 - Sarah Elizabeth Wilson - **M6227** Oscar Bascom Moore
        B. 10/11/1878   M. 9/23/1903   B. 1/17/1855
        D. _____   D. 8/24/1944

    For this line, see **M6227**

    M62914 - Sidney Baxter Wilson - (1)Eliza Adams
        B. 10/10/1881   (1)M. 7/17/1910   B. _____
        D. _____   (2)M. 8/6/1924   D. _____

                       (2) Mary Baker
                            B. _____
                            D. _____

*Indicates that a bio is included.

M629141 - (1) Charles Clinton Wilson, Jr.
    B. _____
    D. _____

M62915 - Nancy America Wilson - Charles Clinton Smith
    B. 6/9/1883   M. _____   B. _____
    D. _____   D. _____

    M629151 - Charles Clinton Smith, Jr.
        B. _____
        D. _____

    M629152 - Ward Smith
        B. _____
        D. _____

M62916 - Jennie Rebecca Wilson - **M62233** Grattan Floyd Mustard
    B. 8/7/1886   M. 1/21/1914   B. 3/13/1879
    D. _____   D. _____

For this line, see **M62233**

M62917 - Charles Robert Wilson
    B. 7/6/1888
    D. 11/24/1911

M62918 - Lelia May Wilson - Henry T. Graham
    B. 12/2/1891   M. 10/9/1912   B. _____
    D. 3/28/1933   D. _____

    M629181 - Irene Graham
        B. _____
        D. _____

    M629182 - Mildred Graham
        B. _____
        D. _____

M6292 Mary Jane Moore - **M6252** John Columbus Moore
    B. 10/4/1852   M. 10/15/1874   B. 12/24/1852
    D. 4/23/1937   D. 3/29/1887

For this line, see **M6252**

M6293   - Edward Poage Moore - (1) **M62632** Sarah Rebecca Whitley
    B. 12/19/1854   (1)M. 1/1882   B. 10/9/1856
    D. 1/8/1939   (2)M. 12/25/1921   D. 9/17/1918

                        (2) Myrtle Shawver
                                 B. 8/26/1871
                                 D. 7/3/1932

    M62931 - (1) William Jackson Moore
        B. 11/8/1883
        D. _____

    M62932 - (1) Margaret Elizabeth Moore - Cary Perkins Painter
        B. 1/6/1887   M. 9/21/1910   B. 10/11/1886
        D. 4/30/1976   D. _____

        ***M629321** - Ruth Moore Painter - Grover W. Brown
            B. 7/21/1911   M. 7/18/1933   B. 12/29/1912
                                        D. 8/15/1982

            ***M6293211** - Richard Painter Brown - Geraldine Sue Barber
                B. 4/26/1938   M. 2/4/1961   B. 1/23/1940

                ***M62932111** - Linda Kay Brown-William Andrew Mattson, Jr. (Div.)
                    B. 12/30/1964   M. 5/10/1986   B. 2/24/1960

                    ***M629321111** - Amanda Rae Mattson
                        B. 2/28/1987

                    ***M629321112** - Christopher Brian Mattson
                        B. 8/10/1988

*M629321113 - Gregory Allen Mattson
B. 3/26/1992

*M62932112 - Andrew Patrick Brown - Quadelupe Ramona Ortega
B. 2/13/1968   M. 3/2/1991   B. 5/23/ 1969

*M629321121 - Andrew Scott Brown
B. 9/29/1994

*M629321122 - Alexandra Paige Brown
B. 8/13/1997

M629321123 – Taylor Elizabeth Brown
B. 5/24/2000

*M62932113 - Teressa Lynn Brown - Thomas Quigley
B. 6/5/1972   M. 6/20/1991   B. 11/12/1970

*M629321131 - Riley Thomas Quigley
B. 2/10/1994

*M629321132 – Taylor Matthew Quigley
B. 9/11/1997

*M6293212 - Guy Edward Brown - (1)Ralissa Simonowitz
B. 6/13/1941   (1)M. 2/4/1964   B. 9/14/1943
                     (2)M. 8/15/1984   D. 4/22/1978

                                    (2) Charlene Luy
                                        B. 5/12/1944

*M62932121 - Pauline Theresa Brown(1)
B. 7/4/1964
D. 4/22/1978

*M62932122 - Pamela Ann Brown(1) - William Borguez
B. 10/21/1967   M. 7/18/1992   B. 1/16/1961

*M629321221 - Eva Alicia Borguez
B. 2/12/1993

*M629321222 – Gabriel Aidan Borguez
B. 9/15/1998

*M629322 - Mary Rebecca Painter - John Robert Douthat
B. 11/4/1913   M. 9/30/1935   B. 9/4/1911
D. 11/9/1998   D. 6/22/1984

*M6293221 - Roberta Douthat - (1) Charles Walter Hatcher, Jr.
B. 11/1/1936   (1)M. _____   B. 8/29/1933
               (2)M. _____

               (2) Landon Boice Bellamy
                       B. _____

*M62932211 - (1)Mary Kaye Hatcher - (1) Mark Johnson
B. 12/8/1959   (1)M. 9/20/1981   B. 3/20/1957
               (2)M. 7/2/2000

                       (2) Stephen Layne Moody
                       B. _____
*M629322111 - (1)Mary Nicole Johnson
B. 1/8/1987

*M629322112 - (1)Caitlin Michelle Johnson
B. 9/6/1989

*M629322113 - (1)Mitzi Renee Johnson
B. 12/7/1993

*M62932212 - (1) Kimberly Anne Hatcher – (1) Jack Gelain Surber
B. 8/4/1957   (1)M.4/19/1979   B. 11/9/1956
               (2)M. 3/19/1998

                       (2) Lonnie Blevins
                       B. 8/6/1956

*M629322121 - (1) Candace Leigh Surber – Eric Williams
  B. 5/28/1976   M. 9/29/2001   B. 4/1/1983

    M6293221211 – Chase Lee Williams
      B. 2/7/2002

*M629322122 - (1) Amy Anne Surber - _____ Carter
  B. 1/14/1980   M. _____   B. _____

    M6293221221 - Christen Anne Carter
      B. 3/21/2000

*M629322123 - (1) Ashley Gelain Surber – Brandon Morrell
  B. 6/19/1982   M. 8/16/2003   B. 10/14/1979

*M62932213 - Charles Walter Hatcher, III(1) - Teresa _____
  B. 6/16/61   M. _____   B. _____

  *M629322131 - Megan Nicole Hatcher
      B. _____

  *M629322132 - Tamera Brooke Hatcher
      B. _____

*M6293222 - James Louis Douthat - Sara Willela Kell
  B. 7/4/1939   M. _____   B. 4/3/1946

  *M62932221 - Thomas Anthony Douthat
  B. 5/20/1967

  *M62932222 - Marilee Douthat - Shan Michael Cleland
  B. 1/4/1969   M. 4/30/1994   B. _____

    M629322221 - _____
      B. _____

    *M629322222 – Caroline Grace Cleland
  B. 2/18/2002

*M6293223 - Margaret Frances Douthat - Robert Edward Elam
     B. 8/18/1944   M. _____   B. 4/14/1944
                                       D. 8/27/2000

*M62932231 - Sara Rebecca Elam - John David Hale
     B. 10/9/1970   M. 5/14/1995   B. _____

*M629322311 - Destinee Breanne Hale
     B. 8/13/1994

*M62932232 - Ralph Cary Elam – Eugena M. Rickmon
     B. 5/8/1973   M. 6/9/2001   B. _____

M629323 - Ida Louise Painter - Edward Hampton Gearheart
     B. 3/29/1916   M. 11/1935   B. 7/10/1914
     D. 3/30/1982   D. 9/6/1972

*M6293231 - Peggy Lee Gearheart - (1)Melvin C. Rachel, Jr. (Div)
     B. 2/4/1939   (1)M.11/4/1957   B. 1/14/1939
                (2)M. 7/3/1974

                               (2)Frederick Hal DeGray
                               B. 8/24/1935

*M62932311 - Lindall Eugene Rachel(1) - Lisa Metz
     B. 3/23/1961   M. 1983   B. 9/14/1957

*M629323111 - Shannon Marie Rachel
     B. 5/17/1983

*M629323112 – Brook Lee Rachel
     B. 8/10/1987

*M62932312 - Scott Douglas Rachel(1) - Tammy Gailey (Div.)
     B. 11/14/1962   M. 8/20/1983   B. 5/12/1963

*M629323121 - Shawn Douglas Rachel
     B. 1/25/1985

*M629323122 - Daniel Lee Rachel
B. 10/10/1988

*M62932313 - Kent Allan Rachel(1) – Amy Studer
B. 8/15/1969   M. 10/18/1997   B. 11/15/1970

*M62932314 - Brett Matthew DeGray(2)
B. 10/31/1975

*M6293232 - Mary Lou Gearheart - Edward Robert Heiby
B. 12/19/1941   M. 11/4/1961   B. 11/30/1941
D. 6/4/1999

*M62932321 - Andrea Heiby - Daniel Comstock
B. 4/27/1963   M. 11/8/1989   B. 6/19/1962

*M629323211 - Cody James Comstock
B. 8/30/1991

*M629323212 - Cassidy Taylor Comstock
B. 2/26/1996

*M62932322 - Jeffrey Robert Heiby - Monika _____ (Div.)
B. 2/19/1968   M. 1/22/1994   B. _____

*M629323221 - Hunter Edward Heiby
B. 2/17/1996

*M62932323 - Christopher Edward Heiby - Jennifer Lynne Dodge
B. 5/16/1970   M. 8/7/1993   B. 1/5/1969

*M629323231 - Garrett Allan Heiby
B. 1/14/1995

*M629323232 Braeden Owen Heiby
B. 3/22/2002

*M6293233 - Cary Edward Gearheart - Sandra Kay Cover
B. 1/22/1945   M. 9/4/1965   B. 5/27/1945

*M62932331 - Monica Kay Gearheart
B. 1/10/1967

*M62932332 - Traci Renee Gearheart - Jerry L. Kenison
B. 4/9/1969   M. 10/20/1990   B. 6/3/1968

*M629323321 - Kelsea Cassandra Kenison
B. 4/12/1991

*M629323322 - Kaleb Edward Kenison
B. 10/6/1992

M629323323 – Kinsey Leigh Kenison
B. 7/27/2000

M6293234 - Ralph Allan Gearheart
B. 2/1/1948
D. 5/26/1968

M629324 - Margaret Elizabeth Painter
B. 4/17/1925
D. 7/1943

M62933 - (1)James Archibald Moore
B. 10/28/1889
D. _____

M62934 - (1)Charles Walter Moore - Belle Harman
B. 9/10/1893   M. 7/9/1935   B. 10/25/1894
D. _____   D. _____

M6294 -   John Oscar Moore
B. 11/27/1857
D. 10/7/1885

M6295 - Martha America Moore
    B. 9/9/1860
    D. 4/5/1884

M6296 - William Trigg Moore - (1) Sarah Hess
    B. 5/31/1862   (1)M. _____   B. _____
    D. 1/8/1927   (2)M. 3/9/1893   D. _____

                    (2) Rhoda Caldwell
                        B. 3/5/1872
                        D. _____

(Five by (2) - Bertie only survivor)

    M62961 - (2) Bertie Gertrude Moore *(Never married)*
        B. 1894
        D. _____

M6297 - Laura Moore - Edward Stevens
    B. _____   M. _____   B. _____
    D. _____   D. _____

M6298 - Johnston Hoge Moore - Lydia Compton
    B. 6/21/1873   M. 1893   B. 1869
    D. 12/27/1918   D. 12/26/1936

    M62981 - James Garfield Moore - Tessie May Gray
        B. 4/30/1894   M. 6/1917   B. 6/5/1901
        D. 10/1967   D. _____

        *****M629811** - Gertrude Ann Moore - Homer Birchfield
            B. 7/28/1918   M. 8/17/1935   B. 6/15/1913
            D. _____   D. _____

            M6298111 - Mary Mae Birchfield
                B. 5/10/1936
                D. 5/10/1936

*M6298112 - James Thomas Birchfield - Kathleen Gray Bostic
    B. 4/11/1937   M. _____   B. 8/23/1942
    D. 4/18/1981

    *M62981121 - John Glen Birchfield
        B. 1/1/1963

    *M62981122 - David Andrew Birchfield
        B. 6/8/1964

    *M62981123 - Kathy Ann Birchfield - Kenneth Dwayne Evans
        B. 10/7/1966   M. _____   B. 5/13/1963

        *M62911231 - Joseph Samuel Evans
            B. 4/10/1991

    *M62981124 - Daniel Lee Birchfield - Lora Alice Sneads
        B. 11/17/1973   M. _____   B. 12/17/1965

*M6298113 - Robert Boyd Birchfield - Karen D. Kimbrell
    B. 2/10/1940   M. 1/24/1965   B. 11/13/1942

    *M62981131 - Matthew Boyd Birchfield – Katherine E. Kraker
        B. 11/23/1967   M. 3/29/1998   B. 3/25/1965

        M629811311 – Erin Marie Birchfield
            B. 5/13/2002

    *M62981132 - Weston Dale Birchfield
        B. 8/11/1971

*M6298114 - Constance Marie Birchfield - James Judson Howard
    B. 2/27/1942   M. 4/20/1968   B. 11/14/1943
                                          D/ 12/25/2000

    *M62981141 - Judson Zale Howard - Michelle Marie Robbins
        B. 7/31/1969   M. 4/30/1994   B. 6/10/1971

        M629811411 – Kimberley Marie Howard
            B. 5/2/1999

M629811412 – Kelley Ann Howard
B. 10/28/2002

*M62981142 - Joseph Gale Howard
B. 1/22/1974

*M6298115 - Wilburn Lonnie Birchfield - Francine Louise Chayra
B. 5/5/1944   M. 1969   B. 5/4/1947

*M62981151 - Heath Gilbert Birchfield
B. 8/16/1972

*M62981152 - Michelle Louise Birchfield
B. 5/28/1976

*M62981153 - Frances Marie Birchfield
B. 12/29/1977

M6298115x - Brenda Kay Birchfield
B. 11/6/1947
D. 11/6/1947

*M6298116 - Gloria Dawn Birchfield - (1) James A. Reinhold
B. 12/7/1948   (1)M. _____   B. 2/16/1945
                      (2)M. _____   D. 5/16/1977

                            (2) Floyd Daniel Walton
                            B. 2/23/1937

*M62981161 - James Homer Reinhold(1) - Tina R. White
B. 2/23/1967   M. 8/2/1987   B. _____

*M629811611 - James Wesley Reinhold
B. 11/15/1990

*M629811612 - Krista Lane Reinhold
B. 12/31/1991

*M62981162 - Alice Irene Reinhold(1)
B. 1/5/1969

*M62981163 - Kevin Lynn Reinhold(1)
B. 2/4/1972

*M62981164 - Matthew Daniel Walton(2)
B. 8/8/1979

*M6298117 - Janice Elaine Birchfield - Johnnie Madford Hollandsworth
B. 8/16/1950   M. _____   B. 7/31/1950

    *M62981171 - Marie Dawn Hollandsworth
    B. 7/11/1981

    *M62981172 - Billie Jack Hollandsworth
    B. 7/23/1983

*M6298118 - Verlin Lee Birchfield - (1)Rose Ann Berage
B. 4/26/1952   (1)M. _____   B. 8/7/1953
                (2)M. _____

                         (2) Audrey Louise Vaughan Comer
                         B. _____

    *M62981181 - Verlin Lee Birchfield, Jr.(1) - Yoshike Furosako
    B. 5/24/1972   M. _____   B. 6/15/1963

        *M629811811 - Eliot Sho-ta Birchfield
        B. 12/12/1994

        *M629811812 - Lenie Maria Birchfield
        B. 11/13/1996

*M6298119 - Homer Roscoe Birchfield
    B. 5/9/1953

M6298119x - Sharon Sue Birchfield
    B. 5/22/1957
    D. 5/22/1957

*M6298119y - Paul Franklin Birchfield - Melinda Wooland
    B. 7/10/1958   M. _____   B. _____

*M629812 - Dock M. Moore
    B. 7/22/1920

M629813 - Mary J. Moore
    B. 2/26/1923
    D. 9/22/1924

*M629814 - Walter Sims Moore - Eva Devon Brooks
    B. 7/15/1925   M. 11/21/1946   B. 10/14/1927

    *M6298141 - Glen D. Moore -   (1) Betty B. Read (Div.)
        B. 10/11/1947   (1)M. 6/29/1968   B. 11/3/1949
                           (2)M. _____

                           (2) Jenna Dawn Foster
                              B. 7/4/1956

        *M62981411 - (1) David Wayne Moore
            B. 10/25/1971

        *M62981412 - (2) Eric James Moore
            B. 6/30/1979

        *M62981413 - (2) Travis Michael Moore
            B. 11/26/1982

*M6298142 - Jerry Wayne Moore - Deborah Kathryn Ratcliff
    B. 8/31/1953   M. _____   B. 7/26/1951

  *M62981421 - Jeremy Wayne Moore
      B. 10/28/1977

  *M62981422 - Jonathan Lee Moore
      B. 10/08/1982

*M6298143 – Mary Alice Moore - (1) Ted White (Div)
    B. 8/27/1962   M. _____   B. 10/18/1960
                      M. _____

                      (2) Steven M. Sanders
                                B. 10/18/1946

  *M62981431 - (1) Christopher Patrick White
      B. 5/30/1979

*M629815 - Easter M. Moore - James C. Cook
    B. 12/16/1927   M. 12/31/1948   B. 3/1/1929

  *M6298151 - Tessie Mae Cook - (1) Lawrance Watson (Div)
      B. 12/11/1949   (1)M. 3/8/1968   B. 8/22/1945
                   (2)M. 1978

                    (2) John Frederic Hooker
                            B. 2/7/1941

    *M62981511 - Markus Wayne Watson (1)
        B. 2/11/1969

    *M62981512 - Cheryl Lynn Watson(1) - _____
        B. 10/28/1971   M. _____   B. _____

      *M629815121 - Tiffany Nicole Watson
          B. 3/6/1992

    *M62981513 - Paul Stephen Watson
        B. 12/20/1975

*M6298152 - Dewey Lee Cook - Barbara Brown (Div)
  B. 12/28/1965   M. 7/3/1988   B. 5/7/1960

  *M62981521 - Matthew James Lee Cook
    B. 5/2/1988

*M6298153 - Judy Fay Cook - (1) Kenneth Ammons (Div)
  B. 8/12/1957   (1)M. _____   B. 10/7/1949
                      (2)M. 5/20/1994

                      (2) Ricky Wayne Smallwood
                              B. 12/6/1954

  *M62981531 - Angela Marie Ammons(1) - _____ Mullins
    B. 8/27/1969   M. _____   B. _____

*M6298154 - Gladys Kay Cook - (1)Keith Boehmer (Div)
  B. 11/14/1954   (1)M. 11/23/1973 B. 4/20/1953
                      (2)M. 6/30/1997

                      (2) Audie Chritchley
                              B. 10/30/1957

  *M62981541 - (1)James Michael Boehmer - Melinda Mullenax
    B. 11/18/1972   M. 1/30/1993   B. 12/26/1970

    *M629815411 - Meghan Haley Boehmer
      B. 12/28/1994

    M629815412 – Caleb Shane Boehmer
      B. 7/19/1996

  *M62981542 - (1)Shannon Keith Boehmer
      B. 5/26/1975

  M62981543 - (2) Christine Hannah Critchley
      B. 7/23/1998

*M629816 - James Thomas Moore - Iris Janette Alsup
  B. 3/6/1930   M. 5/22/1954   B. 9/20/1936

  *M6298161 - James Thomas Moore, Jr. - Cynthia Lynn Powers
    B. 3/23/1959   M. 1/5/1981   B. 4/23/1959

    *M62981611 - Jessica Dawn Moore – Justin B. Hall
      B. 12/28/1981   M. 1/24/2004   B. 12/26/1980

  *M6298162 - David Allen Moore - Melissa Ann Smith
    B. 9/13/1962   M. 8/30/1985   B. 10/10/1966

    *M62981621 - David Allen Moore, Jr.
      B. 9/12/1986

    *M62981622 - Amanda Nicole Moore
      B. 5/12/1988

  *M6298163 - Tina Sue Moore - Jerome Krug
    B. 4/5/1968   M. 8/30/1997   B. _____

*M629817 - Hubert L. Moore
  B. 12/26/1932

*M629818 - Laura Lydia Moore - (1) John Walls
  B. 8/20/1935   (1)M. 11/5/1955   B. 4/12/1930
                        (2)M. 1970   D. 2001
                        (3)M. 1976

                                (2) Woodrow Franklin Johnson
                                      B. 4/7/1934
                                      D. 9/12/1974

                                (3) Robert Putze
                                      B. 3/1/1933

  *M6298181 - John Walls, Jr.(1)
    B. 9/6/1956

*M6298182 - Robert D. Walls(1) - Marilyn Ann Armstrong
    B. 9/1/1958   M. 11/27/1980   B. 6/18/1954
                                                    D. 12/19/1993

    *M62981821 - Laura Sue Walls
        B. 2/19/1984
        D. 2/22/1984

*M6298183 - James Joseph Walls(1)
    B. 3/22/1960

*M6298184 - Linda Sue Walls(1) – David James Billingsley
    B. 12/10/1962   M. 12/27/1983   B. 8/30/1948

    M62981841 – Lydia Althea Billingsley
        B. 10/2/1991

    M62981842 – Hudson James Billingsley
        B. 9/16/1993

*M6298185 - Diana Walls(1) - _____ Tate
    B. 8/7/1964   M. _____   B. _____

*M6298186 - Andrew Walls(1)
    B. 8/11/1966

*M6298187 - (2) Woodrow Franklin Johnson, Jr.(2) - Carolynn Trent
    B. 4/4/1970   M.5/21/1996   B. 11/5/1963

    *M62981871 - Abigail Louise Johnson
        B. 5/31/1998

    M62981872 – Hannah Elizabeth Stephanie Johnson
        B. 6/24/2001

*M629819 - Joseph Edward Moore - Sandra Jean Dove
    B. 6/17/1944   M. 2/15/1966   B. 3/5/1950

*M6298191 - Victoria Lee Moore - (1) Dale Lee Buckler (Div.)
    B. 9/12/1966   (1)M. 12/17/1985   B. 6/19/1967
               (2)M. 5/4/2002

                     (2) James David Chedester
                        B. 3/3/1968

    *M62981911 - Candice Lee Buckler
        B. 2/6/1986

    *M62981912 - Dale Lee Buckler, Jr.
        B. 9/9/1991

*M6298192 - Angela Jo Moore – John Charles Smith
    B. 9/4/1970   M. 9/22/2001   B. 1/20/1973

*M6298193 - Joseph Edward Moore, Jr. – Christine Marie Antionette Gentile
    B. 10/25/1973   M. 6/19/1998   B. 10/29/1973

    M62981831 – Ethan Joseph Moore
        B. 5/24/2001

M62982 - Orville V. Moore - Romie E. Hardy
    B. 4/20/1898   M. 8/19/1919   B. 12/9/1900
    D. _____   D. _____

    *M629821 - Dewey E. Moore
        B. 6/2/1920
        D. 1938

    *M629822 - Ada Moore - Charles D. Salyers
        B. 8/3/1922   M. 1945   B. 9/8/1923
                                  D. 7/8/1989

    *M6298221 - Charlie D. Salyers, Jr. - Mary Jane Bentley
        B. 12/25/45   M. 1963   B. 1945
        D. 7/31/1984

*M62982211 Charles D. Salyers, III
        B. _____

M6298222 – Thomas Salyers – (1) Regina Fuller (Div.)
        B. 1952   (1)M. _____   B. _____
                                           (2)M _____

                                  (2) Della Crouse
                                                        B. _____

M62982221 – Gail Salyers
        B. _____

*M62982211 - Douglas Michael Salyers – Kimberly Tyler
        B. 8/31/1968   M. 8/16/1997   B. _____

*M62982212 - Karen Salyers - Darrell Camper (Div.)
        B. 10/2/1971   M. 6/13/1992   B. 12/8/1957

*M629823 - Johnston Henry Moore - Geneva Stanley
    B. 3/29/1924   M. _____   B. 6/23/1929

*M6298231 - Carolyn Moore - _____ Dillon
        B. 4/13/1946   M. _____   B. _____

*M6298232 - Barbara Moore - James Patrick Ray
        B. 12/31/1949   M. _____   B. 8/27/1937

*M6298233 - Audrey Moore - _____ Howell
        B. 3/9/1951   M. _____   B. _____

*M6298234 - Doris Jane Moore - _____ Clark
        B. 6/19/1956   M. _____   B. _____

*M62982341 - Christopher Allen Clark
        B. _____

*M629824 - Harry Elwood Moore - Eva L. Smith
B. 4/30/1926   M. _____   B. 6/27/1931
2 Children

*M6298241 - Deborah Susan Moore - Earl G. Kitts
B. 12/24/1951   M. 2/19/1971   B. _____

*M62982411 - Tiffany Elizabeth Kitts
B. 6/29/1972

*M6298242 - Harry Edward Moore - Chris C. Bowe
B. 9/21/1953   M. 11/5/1970   B. _____

*M62982421 - Brian Keith Moore
B. 5/14/1971

*M629825 - Virginia F. Moore - George G. Lee
B. 4/1/1928   M. _____   B. _____

M629826 – Orville Moore – Cosby Henneger
2 Children

*M62983 - Edward P. Moore - Louise Barnett
B. 3/2/1901   M. _____   B. _____
D. _____   D. _____

*M629831 - Dory Moore
B. _____
D. _____

*M629832 - Margaret Moore
B. _____
D. _____

*M629833 - Bernard Moore
    B. _____
    D. _____

*M629834 - Florence Moore
    B. _____
    D. _____

*M629835 - Thomas Moore
    B. _____
    D. _____

*M62984 - Bessie Moore - Henry Harman
    B. 5/1/1902   M. 7/26/1919   B. 2/18/1900
    D. _____   D. _____

    *M629841 - Ernest Alvin Harman
        B. 6/6/1920

    *M629842 - Garnett Marie Harman
        B. 1/30/1922

    *M629843 - Willie May Harman
        B. 1/18/1924

    *M629844 - Walter Edward Harman
        B. 1/24/1926

    *M629845 - Winifred Reese Harman
        B. 12/19/1928

*M62985 – Grace Moore – Harry Melvin Bennett
    B. 8/8/1906   M. 5/19/1928   B. 12/25/1898
    D. _____   D. _____

32.

THE ISAAC QUINN MOORE LINE
BIOGRAPHICAL CHARTS

M629321
Genealogical Number

Ruth Moore Painter   Saginaw, Mich.
Name (including maiden name if applicable)   Town of Residence

Bluff City, VA   7/21/1911
Birthplace   Date of Birth   Date of Death   Where Buried

Grover William Brown   Radford, VA   12/29/1912   8/15/1982
Name of Spouse   Birthplace   Date of Birth   Date of Death
Acacia Cemetery
Beverly Hills, Michigan   7/18/1933
Where Buried   Date of Marriage   Place of Marriage

If married more than once:

Name of Spouse   Birthplace   Date of Birth   Date of Death

Where Buried   Date of Marriage   Place of Marriage

William Elbert Brown - Mae Lenea Duncan
Parents of Spouse (with Mother's maiden name) 1st Marriage

Subsequent Marriage (if applicable)

Family Details

Schools attended, dates and degrees: Community, political work, etc.:

Descendant   Descendant

Spouse   Spouse

Basic Employment History: Clubs, Church Affiliations, etc.:

Descendant   Descendant

Spouse   Spouse

Military Service:

Descendant   Spouse

M6293211
Genealogical Number

Richard Painter Brown   Saginaw, Mich.
Name (including maiden name if applicable)   Town of Residence

Columbus, Ohio   4/26/1938
Birthplace   Date of Birth   Date of Death   Where Buried

Geraldine Sue Barber   Beaverdam, Ohio   1/23/1940
Name of Spouse   Birthplace   Date of Birth   Date of Death

                            2/4/1961   Birmingham, Mi.
Where Buried   Date of Marriage   Place of Marriage

If married more than once:

Name of Spouse   Birthplace   Date of Birth   Date of Death

Where Buried   Date of Marriage   Place of Marriage

Grant Barber - Carrie Yant
Parents of Spouse (with Mother's maiden name) 1st Marriage

Subsequent Marriage (if applicable)

Family Details

Schools attended, dates and degrees: Community, political work, etc.:

Birmingham Mi. H.S. - . Northern Mi. Univ. - MA Ed. Adm. 71-72   Can. America Games - Saginaw Twp/Cambridge
Central Mich. Univ. 1960-64, BA in Ed. Saginaw Val. Univ   Ontario, Rotary - Past pres., Paul Harris Fellow
Descendant   Descendant
Mich. State Univ. 1959-60
Central Mi. Univ. 1960-62 - B.S.
Spouse   Spouse

Basic Employment History: Clubs, Church Affiliations, etc.:
St. Louis Public Sch. Lakeview Pub. Sch. Gratiot Co. Int.
Schools, Saginaw Twp. Comm. Sch. Hoogerland   Saginaw Valley Rotary,
 Memorial Workshop   2nd Presb. Church
Descendant   Descendant
Farewell Pub. Sch. Lakeview Comm. Sch.   Potter Club
St. Louis Pub. Sch. Sag. Twp. Comm Sch.   2nd Presb. Church
Spouse   Spouse

Military Service:

US Navy   Homeguard
Descendant   Spouse

M62932111
Genealogical Number

Linda Kay Brown   Lake Orion, Mich.
Name (including maiden name if applicable)   Town of Residence

Alma, Mich.   12/30/1964
Birthplace   Date of Birth   Date of Death   Where Buried

William Andrew Mattson, Jr. Sault St. Marie, Mich.   2/24/1960
Name of Spouse   Birthplace   Date of Birth   Date of Death

                             5/10/1986
Where Buried   Date of Marriage   Place of Marriage

If married more than once:

Name of Spouse   Birthplace   Date of Birth   Date of Death

Where Buried   Date of Marriage   Place of Marriage

William Mattson – Shirley –
Parents of Spouse (with Mother's maiden name) 1st Marriage

Subsequent Marriage (if applicable)

Family Details

Schools attended, dates and degrees: Community, political work, etc.:

Descendant   Descendant

Spouse   Spouse

Basic Employment History: Clubs, Church Affiliations, etc.:

Descendant   Descendant

Spouse   Spouse

Military Service:

Descendant   Spouse

M629321111
Genealogical Number

Amanda Rae Mattson
Name (including maiden name if applicable)

Town of Residence

Saginaw, Mich.   2/28/1987
Birthplace   Date of Birth   Date of Death   Where Buried

Name of Spouse   Birthplace   Date of Birth   Date of Death

Where Buried   Date of Marriage   Place of Marriage

If married more than once:

Name of Spouse   Birthplace   Date of Birth   Date of Death

Where Buried   Date of Marriage   Place of Marriage

Parents of Spouse (with Mother's maiden name) 1st Marriage

Subsequent Marriage (if applicable)

Family Details

Schools attended, dates and degrees: Community, political work, etc.:

Descendant   Descendant

Spouse   Spouse

Basic Employment History: Clubs, Church Affiliations, etc.:

Descendant   Descendant

Spouse   Spouse

Military Service:

Descendant   Spouse

M629321112
Genealogical Number

Christopher Brian Mattson
Name (including maiden name if applicable)   Town of Residence

Saginaw, Mich.   8/10/1988
Birthplace   Date of Birth   Date of Death   Where Buried

Name of Spouse   Birthplace   Date of Birth   Date of Death

Where Buried   Date of Marriage   Place of Marriage

If married more than once:

Name of Spouse   Birthplace   Date of Birth   Date of Death

Where Buried   Date of Marriage   Place of Marriage

Parents of Spouse (with Mother's maiden name) 1st Marriage

Subsequent Marriage (if applicable)

Family Details

Schools attended, dates and degrees: Community, political work, etc.:

Descendant   Descendant

Spouse   Spouse

Basic Employment History: Clubs, Church Affiliations, etc.:

Descendant   Descendant

Spouse   Spouse

Military Service:

Descendant   Spouse

M629321113
Genealogical Number

Gregory Allen Mattson
Name (including maiden name if applicable)

Town of Residence

Rochester, Mich.   3/26/1992
Birthplace   Date of Birth   Date of Death   Where Buried

Name of Spouse   Birthplace   Date of Birth   Date of Death

Where Buried   Date of Marriage   Place of Marriage

If married more than once:

Name of Spouse   Birthplace   Date of Birth   Date of Death

Where Buried   Date of Marriage   Place of Marriage

Parents of Spouse (with Mother's maiden name) 1st Marriage

Subsequent Marriage (if applicable)

Family Details

Schools attended, dates and degrees: Community, political work, etc.:

Descendant   Descendant

Spouse   Spouse

Basic Employment History: Clubs, Church Affiliations, etc.:

Descendant   Descendant

Spouse   Spouse

Military Service:

Descendant   Spouse

M62932112
Genealogical Number

Andrew Patrick Brown   Kalera, Mich.
Name (including maiden name if applicable)   Town of Residence

St. Louis, Mich.   2/13/1968
Birthplace   Date of Birth   Date of Death   Where Buried

Guadelupe Ortega   Saginaw, Mich.   5/23/ -
Name of Spouse   Birthplace   Date of Birth   Date of Death

                             3/2/1991
Where Buried   Date of Marriage   Place of Marriage

If married more than once:

Name of Spouse   Birthplace   Date of Birth   Date of Death

Where Buried   Date of Marriage   Place of Marriage

Pedre Ramono Ortega - Mona -
Parents of Spouse (with Mother's maiden name) 1st Marriage

Subsequent Marriage (if applicable)

Family Details

Schools attended, dates and degrees: Community, political work, etc.:

Descendant   Descendant

Spouse   Spouse

Basic Employment History: Clubs, Church Affiliations, etc.:

Descendant   Descendant

Spouse   Spouse

Military Service:

Descendant   Spouse

M629321121
Genealogical Number

Andrew Scott Brown
Name (including maiden name if applicable)

Town of Residence

Saginaw, Mich.   6/29/1994
Birthplace   Date of Birth   Date of Death   Where Buried

Name of Spouse   Birthplace   Date of Birth   Date of Death

Where Buried   Date of Marriage   Place of Marriage

If married more than once:

Name of Spouse   Birthplace   Date of Birth   Date of Death

Where Buried   Date of Marriage   Place of Marriage

Parents of Spouse (with Mother's maiden name) 1st Marriage

Subsequent Marriage (if applicable)

Family Details

Schools attended, dates and degrees: Community, political work, etc.:

Descendant   Descendant

Spouse   Spouse

Basic Employment History: Clubs, Church Affiliations, etc.:

Descendant   Descendant

Spouse   Spouse

Military Service:

Descendant   Spouse

M629321122
Genealogical Number

Alexandra Paige Brown
Name (including maiden name if applicable)   Town of Residence

_____   8/13/1997   _____   _____
Birthplace   Date of Birth   Date of Death   Where Buried

_____   _____   _____   _____
Name of Spouse   Birthplace   Date of Birth   Date of Death

_____   _____   _____
Where Buried   Date of Marriage   Place of Marriage

If married more than once:

_____   _____   _____   _____
Name of Spouse   Birthplace   Date of Birth   Date of Death

_____   _____   _____
Where Buried   Date of Marriage   Place of Marriage

_____
Parents of Spouse (with Mother's maiden name) 1st Marriage

_____
Subsequent Marriage (if applicable)

Family Details

Schools attended, dates and degrees: Community, political work, etc.:

_____   _____
Descendant   Descendant

_____   _____
Spouse   Spouse

Basic Employment History: Clubs, Church Affiliations, etc.:

_____   _____
Descendant   Descendant

_____   _____
Spouse   Spouse

Military Service:

_____   _____
Descendant   Spouse

M62932113
Genealogical Number

Teressa Lynn Brown
Name (including maiden name if applicable)

Saginaw, Mich
Town of Residence

Lakeview, Mich.
Birthplace

6/5/1972
Date of Birth

Date of Death

Where Buried

Thomas Quigley
Name of Spouse

Boston, Mass.
Birthplace

Date of Birth

Date of Death

Where Buried

2/14/1992
Date of Marriage

Place of Marriage

If married more than once:

Name of Spouse

Birthplace

Date of Birth

Date of Death

Where Buried

Date of Marriage

Place of Marriage

Anthony Quigley – Donna Grady
Parents of Spouse (with Mother's maiden name) 1st Marriage

Subsequent Marriage (if applicable)

Family Details

Schools attended, dates and degrees:

Community, political work, etc.:

Descendant

Descendant

Spouse

Spouse

Basic Employment History:

Clubs, Church Affiliations, etc.:

Descendant

Descendant

Spouse

Spouse

Military Service:

Descendant

Spouse

M629321131
Genealogical Number

Thomas Quigley
Name (including maiden name if applicable)

Town of Residence

Boston, Mass.
Birthplace

2/10/1994
Date of Birth

Date of Death

Where Buried

Name of Spouse

Birthplace

Date of Birth

Date of Death

Where Buried

Date of Marriage

Place of Marriage

If married more than once:

Name of Spouse

Birthplace

Date of Birth

Date of Death

Where Buried

Date of Marriage

Place of Marriage

Parents of Spouse (with Mother's maiden name) 1st Marriage

Subsequent Marriage (if applicable)

Family Details

Schools attended, dates and degrees:

Community, political work, etc.:

Descendant

Descendant

Spouse

Spouse

Basic Employment History:

Clubs, Church Affiliations, etc.:

Descendant

Descendant

Spouse

Spouse

Military Service:

Descendant

Spouse

M629321132
Genealogical Number

Taylor Matthew Quigley
Name (including maiden name if applicable)

Town of Residence

<u>9/11/1997</u>
Birthplace   Date of Birth   Date of Death   Where Buried

Name of Spouse   Birthplace   Date of Birth   Date of Death

Where Buried   Date of Marriage   Place of Marriage

If married more than once:

Name of Spouse   Birthplace   Date of Birth   Date of Death

Where Buried   Date of Marriage   Place of Marriage

Parents of Spouse (with Mother's maiden name) 1st Marriage

Subsequent Marriage (if applicable)

Family Details

Schools attended, dates and degrees: Community, political work, etc.:

Descendant   Descendant

Spouse   Spouse

Basic Employment History: Clubs, Church Affiliations, etc.:

Descendant   Descendant

Spouse   Spouse

Military Service:

Descendant   Spouse

M6293212
Genealogical Number

Guy Edward Brown
Name (including maiden name if applicable)

Land O' Lakes, Fla.
Town of Residence

Columbus, Ohio
Birthplace

6/13/1941
Date of Birth

Date of Death

Where Buried

Charlene Luy
Name of Spouse

Birthplace

5/12/1944
Date of Birth

Date of Death

Where Buried

8/15/1984
Date of Marriage

Place of Marriage

If married more than once:

Ralissa Simonowitz
Name of Spouse

Poland
Birthplace

9/14/1943
Date of Birth

4/22/1978
Date of Death

Ludington, Mich.
Where Buried

1/4/1964
Date of Marriage

Place of Marriage

Max Simonowitz - Kate -
Parents of Spouse (with Mother's maiden name) 1st Marriage

Subsequent Marriage (if applicable)

Family Details

Schools attended, dates and degrees:

Community, political work, etc.:

Descendant

Descendant

Spouse

Spouse

Basic Employment History:

Clubs, Church Affiliations, etc.:

Descendant

Descendant

Spouse

Spouse

Military Service:

Descendant

Spouse

M62932121
Genealogical Number

Pauline Theresa Brown
Name (including maiden name if applicable)

Town of Residence

Detroit, Mich.	7/4/1964	4/22/1978	Ludington, Mich.
Birthplace	Date of Birth	Date of Death	Where Buried

Name of Spouse	Birthplace	Date of Birth	Date of Death

Where Buried	Date of Marriage	Place of Marriage

If married more than once:

Name of Spouse	Birthplace	Date of Birth	Date of Death

Where Buried	Date of Marriage	Place of Marriage

Parents of Spouse (with Mother's maiden name) 1st Marriage

Subsequent Marriage (if applicable)

Family Details

Schools attended, dates and degrees:

Community, political work, etc.:

Descendant

Descendant

Spouse

Spouse

Basic Employment History:

Clubs, Church Affiliations, etc.:

Descendant

Descendant

Spouse

Spouse

Military Service:

Descendant

Spouse

M62932122
Genealogical Number

Pamela Ann Brown   Beverly Hills, Mich.
Name (including maiden name if applicable)   Town of Residence

Grand Rapids, Mich.   10/21/1967
Birthplace   Date of Birth   Date of Death   Where Buried

William Borguez   Santiago, Chile   1/16/1961
Name of Spouse   Birthplace   Date of Birth   Date of Death

                          7/18/1992
Where Buried   Date of Marriage   Place of Marriage

If married more than once:

Name of Spouse   Birthplace   Date of Birth   Date of Death

Where Buried   Date of Marriage   Place of Marriage

Guillermo Borguez - Alicia -
Parents of Spouse (with Mother's maiden name) 1st Marriage

Subsequent Marriage (if applicable)

Family Details

Schools attended, dates and degrees: Community, political work, etc.:

Descendant   Descendant

Spouse   Spouse

Basic Employment History: Clubs, Church Affiliations, etc.:

Descendant   Descendant

Spouse   Spouse

Military Service:

Descendant   Spouse

M629321221
Genealogical Number

Eva Alicia Borguez
Name (including maiden name if applicable)

Town of Residence

Royal Oak, Mich.   2/12/1993
Birthplace   Date of Birth   Date of Death   Where Buried

Name of Spouse   Birthplace   Date of Birth   Date of Death

Where Buried   Date of Marriage   Place of Marriage

If married more than once:

Name of Spouse   Birthplace   Date of Birth   Date of Death

Where Buried   Date of Marriage   Place of Marriage

Parents of Spouse (with Mother's maiden name) 1st Marriage

Subsequent Marriage (if applicable)

Family Details

Schools attended, dates and degrees: Community, political work, etc.:

Descendant   Descendant

Spouse   Spouse

Basic Employment History: Clubs, Church Affiliations, etc.:

Descendant   Descendant

Spouse   Spouse

Military Service:

Descendant   Spouse

M629321222
Genealogical Number

Gabriel Aidan Borguez
Name (including maiden name if applicable)   Town of Residence

                                9/15/1998
Birthplace   Date of Birth   Date of Death   Where Buried

Name of Spouse   Birthplace   Date of Birth   Date of Death

Where Buried   Date of Marriage   Place of Marriage

If married more than once:

Name of Spouse   Birthplace   Date of Birth   Date of Death

Where Buried   Date of Marriage   Place of Marriage

Parents of Spouse (with Mother's maiden name) 1st Marriage

Subsequent Marriage (if applicable)

Family Details

Schools attended, dates and degrees: Community, political work, etc.:

Descendant   Descendant

Spouse   Spouse

Basic Employment History: Clubs, Church Affiliations, etc.:

Descendant   Descendant

Spouse   Spouse

Military Service:

Descendant   Spouse

M629322
Genealogical Number

Mary Rebecca Painter
Name (including maiden name if applicable)

Town of Residence

Bluff City, Giles Co., VA   11/4/1913   11/9/1998
Birthplace   Date of Birth   Date of Death   Where Buried

John Robert Douthat   Bluefield, W.VA   9/4/1911   6/22/1984
Name of Spouse   Birthplace   Date of Birth   Date of Death

                          9/30/1935
Where Buried   Date of Marriage   Place of Marriage

If married more than once:

Name of Spouse   Birthplace   Date of Birth   Date of Death

Where Buried   Date of Marriage   Place of Marriage

Parents of Spouse (with Mother's maiden name) 1st Marriage

Subsequent Marriage (if applicable)

Family Details

Schools attended, dates and degrees: Community, political work, etc.:

Descendant   Descendant

Spouse   Spouse

Basic Employment History: Clubs, Church Affiliations, etc.:

Descendant   Descendant

Spouse   Spouse

Military Service:

Descendant   Spouse

M6293221
Genealogical Number

Roberta Douthat   Bluff City, Tenn.
Name (including maiden name if applicable)   Town of Residence

Bluefield, W.VA   11/1/1936
Birthplace   Date of Birth   Date of Death   Where Buried

Charles Walter Hatcher, Jr.   Bristol, Tenn.   8/29/1933
Name of Spouse   Birthplace   Date of Birth   Date of Death

Where Buried   Date of Marriage   Place of Marriage

If married more than once:

Landon Boice Bellamy
Name of Spouse   Birthplace   Date of Birth   Date of Death

Where Buried   Date of Marriage   Place of Marriage

Parents of Spouse (with Mother's maiden name) 1st Marriage

Subsequent Marriage (if applicable)

Family Details

Schools attended, dates and degrees: Community, political work, etc.:

Descendant   Descendant

Spouse   Spouse

Basic Employment History: Clubs, Church Affiliations, etc.:

Descendant   Descendant

Spouse   Spouse

Military Service:

Descendant   Spouse

M62932211
Genealogical Number

Mary Kaye Hatcher
Name (including maiden name if applicable)

Chattanooga, Tenn.
Town of Residence

Bristol, Tenn.
Birthplace

12/8/1959
Date of Birth

Date of Death

Where Buried

Mark Johnson
Name of Spouse

Birthplace

3/20/1957
Date of Birth

Date of Death

Where Buried

7/2/2000
Date of Marriage

Place of Marriage

If married more than once:

Stephen Layne Moody
Name of Spouse

Birthplace

Date of Birth

Date of Death

Where Buried

9/20/1981
Date of Marriage

Place of Marriage

Parents of Spouse (with Mother's maiden name) 1st Marriage

Subsequent Marriage (if applicable)

Family Details

Schools attended, dates and degrees:

Community, political work, etc.:

Descendant

Descendant

Spouse

Spouse

Basic Employment History:

Clubs, Church Affiliations, etc.:

Descendant

Descendant

Spouse

Spouse

Military Service:

Descendant

Spouse

M629322111
Genealogical Number

Mary Nicole Johnson
Name (including maiden name if applicable)

Chattanooga, Tenn.
Town of Residence

1/8/1987

Birthplace | Date of Birth | Date of Death | Where Buried

Name of Spouse | Birthplace | Date of Birth | Date of Death

Where Buried | Date of Marriage | Place of Marriage

If married more than once:

Name of Spouse | Birthplace | Date of Birth | Date of Death

Where Buried | Date of Marriage | Place of Marriage

Parents of Spouse (with Mother's maiden name) 1st Marriage

Subsequent Marriage (if applicable)

Family Details

Schools attended, dates and degrees:

Community, political work, etc.:

Descendant

Descendant

Spouse

Spouse

Basic Employment History:

Clubs, Church Affiliations, etc.:

Descendant

Descendant

Spouse

Spouse

Military Service:

Descendant

Spouse

M629322112
Genealogical Number

Caitlin Michelle Johnson
Name (including maiden name if applicable)

Chattanooga, Tenn.
Town of Residence

	9/6/1989		
Birthplace	Date of Birth	Date of Death	Where Buried

Name of Spouse	Birthplace	Date of Birth	Date of Death

Where Buried	Date of Marriage	Place of Marriage

If married more than once:

Name of Spouse	Birthplace	Date of Birth	Date of Death

Where Buried	Date of Marriage	Place of Marriage

Parents of Spouse (with Mother's maiden name) 1st Marriage

Subsequent Marriage (if applicable)

Family Details

Schools attended, dates and degrees:

Community, political work, etc.:

Descendant

Descendant

Spouse

Spouse

Basic Employment History:

Clubs, Church Affiliations, etc.:

Descendant

Descendant

Spouse

Spouse

Military Service:

Descendant

Spouse

M629322113
Genealogical Number

Mitzi Renee Johnson _____   Chattanooga, Tenn. _____
Name (including maiden name if applicable)   Town of Residence

_____   12/7/1993
Birthplace   Date of Birth   _____   _____
                                                    Date of Death   Where Buried

_____   _____   _____   _____
Name of Spouse   Birthplace   Date of Birth   Date of Death

_____   _____   _____
Where Buried   Date of Marriage   Place of Marriage

If married more than once:

_____   _____   _____   _____
Name of Spouse   Birthplace   Date of Birth   Date of Death

_____   _____   _____
Where Buried   Date of Marriage   Place of Marriage

_____
Parents of Spouse (with Mother's maiden name) 1st Marriage

_____
Subsequent Marriage (if applicable)

Family Details

Schools attended, dates and degrees: Community, political work, etc.:

_____   _____
Descendant   Descendant

_____   _____
Spouse   Spouse

Basic Employment History: Clubs, Church Affiliations, etc.:

_____   _____
Descendant   Descendant

_____   _____
Spouse   Spouse

Military Service:

_____   _____
Descendant   Spouse

M62932212
Genealogical Number

Kimberly Anne Hatcher   Bristol, Tenn.
Name (including maiden name if applicable)   Town of Residence

Bristol, Tenn.   8/4/1957
Birthplace   Date of Birth   Date of Death   Where Buried

Lonnie Blevins   8/6/1956
Name of Spouse   Birthplace   Date of Birth   Date of Death

                                  3/19/1998
Where Buried   Date of Marriage   Place of Marriage

If married more than once:

Jack Gelain Surber   11/9/1956
Name of Spouse   Birthplace   Date of Birth   Date of Death

                                  4/19/1979
Where Buried   Date of Marriage   Place of Marriage

Parents of Spouse (with Mother's maiden name) 1st Marriage

Subsequent Marriage (if applicable)

Family Details

Schools attended, dates and degrees: Community, political work, etc.:

Descendant   Descendant

Spouse   Spouse

Basic Employment History: Clubs, Church Affiliations, etc.:

Descendant   Descendant

Spouse   Spouse

Military Service:

Descendant   Spouse

M629322121
Genealogical Number

Candace Leigh Surber
Name (including maiden name if applicable)   Town of Residence

Bristol, Tenn.   5/28/1976
Birthplace   Date of Birth   Date of Death   Where Buried

Eric Williams   4/1/1983
Name of Spouse   Birthplace   Date of Birth   Date of Death

                                  9/29/2001
Where Buried   Date of Marriage   Place of Marriage

If married more than once:

Name of Spouse   Birthplace   Date of Birth   Date of Death

Where Buried   Date of Marriage   Place of Marriage

Parents of Spouse (with Mother's maiden name) 1st Marriage

Subsequent Marriage (if applicable)

Family Details

Schools attended, dates and degrees: Community, political work, etc.:

Descendant   Descendant

Spouse   Spouse

Basic Employment History: Clubs, Church Affiliations, etc.:

Descendant   Descendant

Spouse   Spouse

Military Service:

Descendant   Spouse

M629322122
Genealogical Number

Amy Anne Surber
Name (including maiden name if applicable)

Town of Residence

Johnson City, Tenn.   1/14/1980
Birthplace   Date of Birth   Date of Death   Where Buried

- Carter
Name of Spouse   Birthplace   Date of Birth   Date of Death

Where Buried   Date of Marriage   Place of Marriage

If married more than once:

Name of Spouse   Birthplace   Date of Birth   Date of Death

Where Buried   Date of Marriage   Place of Marriage

Parents of Spouse (with Mother's maiden name) 1st Marriage

Subsequent Marriage (if applicable)

Family Details

Schools attended, dates and degrees: Community, political work, etc.:

Descendant   Descendant

Spouse   Spouse

Basic Employment History: Clubs, Church Affiliations, etc.:

Descendant   Descendant

Spouse   Spouse

Military Service:

Descendant   Spouse

M629322123
Genealogical Number

Ashley Gelain Surber
Name (including maiden name if applicable)   Town of Residence

Morristown, Tenn.	6/19/1982		
Birthplace	Date of Birth	Date of Death	Where Buried

Brandon Morrell		10/14/1979	
Name of Spouse	Birthplace	Date of Birth	Date of Death

	8/16/2003	
Where Buried	Date of Marriage	Place of Marriage

If married more than once:

Name of Spouse	Birthplace	Date of Birth	Date of Death

Where Buried	Date of Marriage	Place of Marriage

Parents of Spouse (with Mother's maiden name) 1st Marriage

Subsequent Marriage (if applicable)

Family Details

Schools attended, dates and degrees: Community, political work, etc.:

Descendant   Descendant

Spouse   Spouse

Basic Employment History: Clubs, Church Affiliations, etc.:

Descendant   Descendant

Spouse   Spouse

Military Service:

Descendant   Spouse

M62932213
Genealogical Number

Charles Walter Hatcher, III   Bristol, Tenn.
Name (including maiden name if applicable)   Town of Residence

Bristol, Tenn.   6/16/1961
Birthplace   Date of Birth   Date of Death   Where Buried

Teresa
Name of Spouse   Birthplace   Date of Birth   Date of Death

Where Buried   Date of Marriage   Place of Marriage

If married more than once:

Name of Spouse   Birthplace   Date of Birth   Date of Death

Where Buried   Date of Marriage   Place of Marriage

Parents of Spouse (with Mother's maiden name) 1st Marriage

Subsequent Marriage (if applicable)

Family Details

Schools attended, dates and degrees: Community, political work, etc.:

Descendant   Descendant

Spouse   Spouse

Basic Employment History: Clubs, Church Affiliations, etc.:

Descendant   Descendant

Spouse   Spouse

Military Service:

Descendant   Spouse

M629322131
Genealogical Number

Megan Nicole Hatcher
Name (including maiden name if applicable)   Town of Residence

Birthplace   Date of Birth   Date of Death   Where Buried

Name of Spouse   Birthplace   Date of Birth   Date of Death

Where Buried   Date of Marriage   Place of Marriage

If married more than once:

Name of Spouse   Birthplace   Date of Birth   Date of Death

Where Buried   Date of Marriage   Place of Marriage

Parents of Spouse (with Mother's maiden name) 1st Marriage

Subsequent Marriage (if applicable)

Family Details

Schools attended, dates and degrees: Community, political work, etc.:

Descendant   Descendant

Spouse   Spouse

Basic Employment History: Clubs, Church Affiliations, etc.:

Descendant   Descendant

Spouse   Spouse

Military Service:

Descendant   Spouse

M629322132
Genealogical Number

Tamara Brooke Hatcher
Name (including maiden name if applicable)   Town of Residence

Birthplace   Date of Birth   Date of Death   Where Buried

Name of Spouse   Birthplace   Date of Birth   Date of Death

Where Buried   Date of Marriage   Place of Marriage

If married more than once:

Name of Spouse   Birthplace   Date of Birth   Date of Death

Where Buried   Date of Marriage   Place of Marriage

Parents of Spouse (with Mother's maiden name) 1st Marriage

Subsequent Marriage (if applicable)

Family Details

Schools attended, dates and degrees: Community, political work, etc.:

Descendant   Descendant

Spouse   Spouse

Basic Employment History: Clubs, Church Affiliations, etc.:

Descendant   Descendant

Spouse   Spouse

Military Service:

Descendant   Spouse

M6293222
Genealogical Number

James Louis Douthat
Name (including maiden name if applicable)

Signal Mountain, Tenn.
Town of Residence

Mercer County, W.VA
Birthplace

7/4/1939
Date of Birth

Date of Death

Where Buried

Sara Willela Kell
Name of Spouse

Atlanta, GA
Birthplace

4/3/1946
Date of Birth

Date of Death

Where Buried

Date of Marriage

Place of Marriage

If married more than once:

Name of Spouse

Birthplace

Date of Birth

Date of Death

Where Buried

Date of Marriage

Place of Marriage

Parents of Spouse (with Mother's maiden name) 1st Marriage

Subsequent Marriage (if applicable)

Family Details

Schools attended, dates and degrees:

Community, political work, etc.:

Descendant

Descendant

Spouse

Spouse

Basic Employment History:

Clubs, Church Affiliations, etc.:

Descendant

Descendant

Spouse

Spouse

Military Service:

Descendant

Spouse

M62932221
Genealogical Number

Thomas Anthony Douthat
Name (including maiden name if applicable)

Signal Mountain, Tenn.
Town of Residence

Athens, Tenn.
Birthplace

5/20/1967
Date of Birth

Date of Death

Where Buried

Name of Spouse

Birthplace

Date of Birth

Date of Death

Where Buried

Date of Marriage

Place of Marriage

If married more than once:

Name of Spouse

Birthplace

Date of Birth

Date of Death

Where Buried

Date of Marriage

Place of Marriage

Parents of Spouse (with Mother's maiden name) 1st Marriage

Subsequent Marriage (if applicable)

Family Details

Schools attended, dates and degrees:

Community, political work, etc.:

Descendant

Descendant

Spouse

Spouse

Basic Employment History:

Clubs, Church Affiliations, etc.:

Descendant

Descendant

Spouse

Spouse

Military Service:

Descendant

Spouse

M62932222
Genealogical Number

Marilee Douthat
Name (including maiden name if applicable)

Simpsonville, SC
Town of Residence

South Pittsburg
Birthplace

1/4/1969
Date of Birth

Date of Death

Where Buried

Shan Michael Cleland
Name of Spouse

Birthplace

Date of Birth

Date of Death

Where Buried

4/30/1994
Date of Marriage

Place of Marriage

If married more than once:

Name of Spouse

Birthplace

Date of Birth

Date of Death

Where Buried

Date of Marriage

Place of Marriage

Parents of Spouse (with Mother's maiden name) 1st Marriage

Subsequent Marriage (if applicable)

Family Details

Schools attended, dates and degrees:

Community, political work, etc.:

Descendant

Descendant

Spouse

Spouse

Basic Employment History:

Clubs, Church Affiliations, etc.:

Descendant

Descendant

Spouse

Spouse

Military Service:

Descendant

Spouse

M629322222
Genealogical Number

Caroline Grace Cleland
Name (including maiden name if applicable)   Town of Residence

_____   2/18/2002
Birthplace   Date of Birth   Date of Death   Where Buried

Name of Spouse   Birthplace   Date of Birth   Date of Death

Where Buried   Date of Marriage   Place of Marriage

If married more than once:

Name of Spouse   Birthplace   Date of Birth   Date of Death

Where Buried   Date of Marriage   Place of Marriage

Parents of Spouse (with Mother's maiden name) 1st Marriage

Subsequent Marriage (if applicable)

Family Details

Schools attended, dates and degrees: Community, political work, etc.:

Descendant   Descendant

Spouse   Spouse

Basic Employment History: Clubs, Church Affiliations, etc.:

Descendant   Descendant

Spouse   Spouse

Military Service:

Descendant   Spouse

M6293223
Genealogical Number

Margaret Frances Douthat
Name (including maiden name if applicable)

Bluefield, VA
Town of Residence

Bluefield, W.VA
Birthplace

8/18/1944
Date of Birth

Date of Death

Where Buried

Robert Edward Elam
Name of Spouse

Bluefield, W.VA
Birthplace

4/14/1944
Date of Birth

8/21/2000
Date of Death

Where Buried

Date of Marriage

Place of Marriage

If married more than once:

Name of Spouse

Birthplace

Date of Birth

Date of Death

Where Buried

Date of Marriage

Place of Marriage

Parents of Spouse (with Mother's maiden name) 1st Marriage

Subsequent Marriage (if applicable)

Family Details

Schools attended, dates and degrees:

Community, political work, etc.:

Descendant

Descendant

Spouse

Spouse

Basic Employment History:

Clubs, Church Affiliations, etc.:

Descendant

Descendant

Spouse

Spouse

Military Service:

Descendant

Spouse

M62932231
Genealogical Number

Sara Rebecca Elam
Name (including maiden name if applicable)

Bluefield, VA
Town of Residence

Bluefield, W.VA	10/9/1970		
Birthplace	Date of Birth	Date of Death	Where Buried

John David Hale			
Name of Spouse	Birthplace	Date of Birth	Date of Death

	5/14/1995	
Where Buried	Date of Marriage	Place of Marriage

If married more than once:

Name of Spouse	Birthplace	Date of Birth	Date of Death

Where Buried	Date of Marriage	Place of Marriage

Parents of Spouse (with Mother's maiden name) 1st Marriage

Subsequent Marriage (if applicable)

Family Details

Schools attended, dates and degrees:

Community, political work, etc.:

Descendant

Descendant

Spouse

Spouse

Basic Employment History:

Clubs, Church Affiliations, etc.:

Descendant

Descendant

Spouse

Spouse

Military Service:

Descendant

Spouse

M629322311
Genealogical Number

Destinee Breanne Hale   Bluefield, VA
Name (including maiden name if applicable)   Town of Residence

                        8/13/1994
Birthplace   Date of Birth   Date of Death   Where Buried

Name of Spouse   Birthplace   Date of Birth   Date of Death

Where Buried   Date of Marriage   Place of Marriage

If married more than once:

Name of Spouse   Birthplace   Date of Birth   Date of Death

Where Buried   Date of Marriage   Place of Marriage

Parents of Spouse (with Mother's maiden name) 1st Marriage

Subsequent Marriage (if applicable)

Family Details

Schools attended, dates and degrees: Community, political work, etc.:

Descendant   Descendant

Spouse   Spouse

Basic Employment History: Clubs, Church Affiliations, etc.:

Descendant   Descendant

Spouse   Spouse

Military Service:

Descendant   Spouse

M62932232
Genealogical Number

Ralph Cary Elam   Bluefield, VA
Name (including maiden name if applicable)   Town of Residence

Bluefield, W.VA   5/8/1973
Birthplace   Date of Birth   Date of Death   Where Buried

Eugena M. Rickmon
Name of Spouse   Birthplace   Date of Birth   Date of Death

                           6/9/2001
Where Buried   Date of Marriage   Place of Marriage

If married more than once:

Name of Spouse   Birthplace   Date of Birth   Date of Death

Where Buried   Date of Marriage   Place of Marriage

Parents of Spouse (with Mother's maiden name) 1st Marriage

Subsequent Marriage (if applicable)

Family Details

Schools attended, dates and degrees: Community, political work, etc.:

Descendant   Descendant

Spouse   Spouse

Basic Employment History: Clubs, Church Affiliations, etc.:

Descendant   Descendant

Spouse   Spouse

Military Service:

Descendant   Spouse

M6293231
Genealogical Number

Peggy Lee Gearheart   Galion, Ohio
Name (including maiden name if applicable)   Town of Residence

Bluefield, W.VA   2/4/1939
Birthplace   Date of Birth   Date of Death   Where Buried

Frederick Hal DeGray   Galion, Ohio   8/22/1935
Name of Spouse   Birthplace   Date of Birth   Date of Death

                             7/3/1974
Where Buried   Date of Marriage   Place of Marriage

If married more than once:

Melvin C. Rachel, Jr. (Div.)   Bramwell, W.VA   1/14/1939
Name of Spouse   Birthplace   Date of Birth   Date of Death

                                11/4/1957
Where Buried   Date of Marriage   Place of Marriage

Parents of Spouse (with Mother's maiden name) 1st Marriage

Subsequent Marriage (if applicable)

Family Details

Schools attended, dates and degrees: Community, political work, etc.:

Descendant   Descendant

Spouse   Spouse

Basic Employment History: Clubs, Church Affiliations, etc.:

Descendant   Descendant

Spouse   Spouse

Military Service:

Descendant   Spouse

M62932311
Genealogical Number

Lindall Eugene Rachel
Name (including maiden name if applicable)

Galion, Ohio
Town of Residence

Crestline, Ohio
Birthplace

3/23/1961
Date of Birth

Date of Death

Where Buried

Lisa Metz
Name of Spouse

Birthplace

9/14/1957
Date of Birth

Date of Death

Where Buried

1983
Date of Marriage

Place of Marriage

If married more than once:

Name of Spouse

Birthplace

Date of Birth

Date of Death

Where Buried

Date of Marriage

Place of Marriage

Parents of Spouse (with Mother's maiden name) 1st Marriage

Subsequent Marriage (if applicable)

Family Details

Schools attended, dates and degrees:

Community, political work, etc.:

Descendant

Descendant

Spouse

Spouse

Basic Employment History:

Clubs, Church Affiliations, etc.:

Descendant

Descendant

Spouse

Spouse

Military Service:

Descendant

Spouse

M629323111
Genealogical Number

Shannon Marie Rachel
Name (including maiden name if applicable)

Town of Residence

5/17/1983
Birthplace   Date of Birth   Date of Death   Where Buried

Name of Spouse   Birthplace   Date of Birth   Date of Death

Where Buried   Date of Marriage   Place of Marriage

If married more than once:

Name of Spouse   Birthplace   Date of Birth   Date of Death

Where Buried   Date of Marriage   Place of Marriage

Parents of Spouse (with Mother's maiden name) 1st Marriage

Subsequent Marriage (if applicable)

Family Details

Schools attended, dates and degrees: Community, political work, etc.:

Descendant   Descendant

Spouse   Spouse

Basic Employment History: Clubs, Church Affiliations, etc.:

Descendant   Descendant

Spouse   Spouse

Military Service:

Descendant   Spouse

M629323112
Genealogical Number

Brook Lee Rachel
Name (including maiden name if applicable)   Town of Residence

                        8/10/1987
Birthplace   Date of Birth   Date of Death   Where Buried

Name of Spouse   Birthplace   Date of Birth   Date of Death

Where Buried   Date of Marriage   Place of Marriage

If married more than once:

Name of Spouse   Birthplace   Date of Birth   Date of Death

Where Buried   Date of Marriage   Place of Marriage

Parents of Spouse (with Mother's maiden name) 1st Marriage

Subsequent Marriage (if applicable)

Family Details

Schools attended, dates and degrees: Community, political work, etc.:

Descendant   Descendant

Spouse   Spouse

Basic Employment History: Clubs, Church Affiliations, etc.:

Descendant   Descendant

Spouse   Spouse

Military Service:

Descendant   Spouse

M62932312
Genealogical Number

Scott Douglas Rachel   Galion, Ohio
Name (including maiden name if applicable)   Town of Residence

Crestline, Ohio   11/14/1962
Birthplace   Date of Birth   Date of Death   Where Buried

Tammy Gailey (Div.)   5/12/1963
Name of Spouse   Birthplace   Date of Birth   Date of Death

                         8/20/1983
Where Buried   Date of Marriage   Place of Marriage

If married more than once:

Name of Spouse   Birthplace   Date of Birth   Date of Death

Where Buried   Date of Marriage   Place of Marriage

Parents of Spouse (with Mother's maiden name) 1st Marriage

Subsequent Marriage (if applicable)

Family Details

Schools attended, dates and degrees: Community, political work, etc.:

Descendant   Descendant

Spouse   Spouse

Basic Employment History: Clubs, Church Affiliations, etc.:

Descendant   Descendant

Spouse   Spouse

Military Service:

Descendant   Spouse

M629323121
Genealogical Number

Shawn Douglas Rachel
Name (including maiden name if applicable)   Town of Residence

                              1/25/1985
Birthplace   Date of Birth   Date of Death   Where Buried

Name of Spouse   Birthplace   Date of Birth   Date of Death

Where Buried   Date of Marriage   Place of Marriage

If married more than once:

Name of Spouse   Birthplace   Date of Birth   Date of Death

Where Buried   Date of Marriage   Place of Marriage

Parents of Spouse (with Mother's maiden name) 1st Marriage

Subsequent Marriage (if applicable)

Family Details

Schools attended, dates and degrees: Community, political work, etc.:

Descendant   Descendant

Spouse   Spouse

Basic Employment History: Clubs, Church Affiliations, etc.:

Descendant   Descendant

Spouse   Spouse

Military Service:

Descendant   Spouse

M629323122
Genealogical Number

Daniel Lee Rachel
Name (including maiden name if applicable)   Town of Residence

10/10/1988
Birthplace   Date of Birth   Date of Death   Where Buried

Name of Spouse   Birthplace   Date of Birth   Date of Death

Where Buried   Date of Marriage   Place of Marriage

If married more than once:

Name of Spouse   Birthplace   Date of Birth   Date of Death

Where Buried   Date of Marriage   Place of Marriage

Parents of Spouse (with Mother's maiden name) 1st Marriage

Subsequent Marriage (if applicable)

Family Details

Schools attended, dates and degrees: Community, political work, etc.:

Descendant   Descendant

Spouse   Spouse

Basic Employment History: Clubs, Church Affiliations, etc.:

Descendant   Descendant

Spouse   Spouse

Military Service:

Descendant   Spouse

M62932313
Genealogical Number

Kent Allan Rachel
Name (including maiden name if applicable)

Crestline, Ohio
Town of Residence

Crestline, Ohio   8/15/1969
Birthplace   Date of Birth   Date of Death   Where Buried

Amy Studer   11/15/1970
Name of Spouse   Birthplace   Date of Birth   Date of Death

                  10/18/1997
Where Buried   Date of Marriage   Place of Marriage

If married more than once:

Name of Spouse   Birthplace   Date of Birth   Date of Death

Where Buried   Date of Marriage   Place of Marriage

Parents of Spouse (with Mother's maiden name) 1st Marriage

Subsequent Marriage (if applicable)

Family Details

Schools attended, dates and degrees:

Community, political work, etc.:

Descendant   Descendant

Spouse   Spouse

Basic Employment History: Clubs, Church Affiliations, etc.:

Descendant   Descendant

Spouse   Spouse

Military Service:

Descendant   Spouse

M62932314
Genealogical Number

Brett Matthew DeGray   Galion, Ohio
Name (including maiden name if applicable)   Town of Residence

Galion, Ohio   10/31/1975
Birthplace   Date of Birth   Date of Death   Where Buried

Name of Spouse   Birthplace   Date of Birth   Date of Death

Where Buried   Date of Marriage   Place of Marriage

If married more than once:

Name of Spouse   Birthplace   Date of Birth   Date of Death

Where Buried   Date of Marriage   Place of Marriage

Parents of Spouse (with Mother's maiden name) 1st Marriage

Subsequent Marriage (if applicable)

Family Details

Schools attended, dates and degrees: Community, political work, etc.:

Descendant   Descendant

Spouse   Spouse

Basic Employment History: Clubs, Church Affiliations, etc.:

Descendant   Descendant

Spouse   Spouse

Military Service:

Descendant   Spouse

M6293232
Genealogical Number

Mary Lou Gearheart
Name (including maiden name if applicable)

Slidell, LA
Town of Residence

Bluefield, W.VA
Birthplace

12/19/1941
Date of Birth

Date of Death

Where Buried

Edward Robert Heiby
Name of Spouse

Galion, Ohio
Birthplace

11/30/1941
Date of Birth

6/4/1999
Date of Death

Where Buried

Date of Marriage

Place of Marriage

If married more than once:

Name of Spouse

Birthplace

Date of Birth

Date of Death

Where Buried

Date of Marriage

Place of Marriage

Parents of Spouse (with Mother's maiden name) 1st Marriage

Subsequent Marriage (if applicable)

Family Details

Schools attended, dates and degrees:

Community, political work, etc.:

Descendant

Descendant

Spouse

Spouse

Basic Employment History:

Clubs, Church Affiliations, etc.:

Descendant

Descendant

Spouse

Spouse

Military Service:

Descendant

Spouse

M62932321
Genealogical Number

Andrea Heiby
Name (including maiden name if applicable)

Slidell, LA
Town of Residence

Zeist, The Netherlands   4/27/1963
Birthplace   Date of Birth

Date of Death   Where Buried

Daniel Comstock
Name of Spouse   Birthplace

6/19/1962
Date of Birth   Date of Death

Where Buried   11/8/1989
Date of Marriage   Place of Marriage

If married more than once:

Name of Spouse   Birthplace   Date of Birth   Date of Death

Where Buried   Date of Marriage   Place of Marriage

Parents of Spouse (with Mother's maiden name) 1st Marriage

Subsequent Marriage (if applicable)

Family Details

Schools attended, dates and degrees: Community, political work, etc.:

Descendant   Descendant

Spouse   Spouse

Basic Employment History: Clubs, Church Affiliations, etc.:

Descendant   Descendant

Spouse   Spouse

Military Service:

Descendant   Spouse

M629323211
Genealogical Number

Cody James Comstock
Name (including maiden name if applicable)   Town of Residence

                                    8/30/1991
Birthplace   Date of Birth   Date of Death   Where Buried

Name of Spouse   Birthplace   Date of Birth   Date of Death

Where Buried   Date of Marriage   Place of Marriage

If married more than once:

Name of Spouse   Birthplace   Date of Birth   Date of Death

Where Buried   Date of Marriage   Place of Marriage

Parents of Spouse (with Mother's maiden name) 1st Marriage

Subsequent Marriage (if applicable)

Family Details

Schools attended, dates and degrees: Community, political work, etc.:

Descendant   Descendant

Spouse   Spouse

Basic Employment History: Clubs, Church Affiliations, etc.:

Descendant   Descendant

Spouse   Spouse

Military Service:

Descendant   Spouse

M629323212
Genealogical Number

Cassidy Taylor Comstock
Name (including maiden name if applicable)

Town of Residence

2/26/1996

Birthplace   Date of Birth   Date of Death   Where Buried

Name of Spouse   Birthplace   Date of Birth   Date of Death

Where Buried   Date of Marriage   Place of Marriage

If married more than once:

Name of Spouse   Birthplace   Date of Birth   Date of Death

Where Buried   Date of Marriage   Place of Marriage

Parents of Spouse (with Mother's maiden name) 1st Marriage

Subsequent Marriage (if applicable)

Family Details

Schools attended, dates and degrees: Community, political work, etc.:

Descendant   Descendant

Spouse   Spouse

Basic Employment History: Clubs, Church Affiliations, etc.:

Descendant   Descendant

Spouse   Spouse

Military Service:

Descendant   Spouse

M6932322
Genealogical Number

Jeffrey Robert Heiby
Name (including maiden name if applicable)

Slidell, LA
Town of Residence

Galion, Ohio
Birthplace

2/19/1968
Date of Birth

Date of Death

Where Buried

Monika - (Div.)
Name of Spouse

Birthplace

Date of Birth

Date of Death

Where Buried

1/22/1994
Date of Marriage

Place of Marriage

If married more than once:

Name of Spouse

Birthplace

Date of Birth

Date of Death

Where Buried

Date of Marriage

Place of Marriage

Parents of Spouse (with Mother's maiden name) 1st Marriage

Subsequent Marriage (if applicable)

Family Details

Schools attended, dates and degrees:

Community, political work, etc.:

Descendant

Descendant

Spouse

Spouse

Basic Employment History:

Clubs, Church Affiliations, etc.:

Descendant

Descendant

Spouse

Spouse

Military Service:

Descendant

Spouse

M629323221
Genealogical Number

Hunter Edward Heiby
Name (including maiden name if applicable)   Town of Residence

                          2/17/1996
Birthplace   Date of Birth   Date of Death   Where Buried

Name of Spouse   Birthplace   Date of Birth   Date of Death

Where Buried   Date of Marriage   Place of Marriage

If married more than once:

Name of Spouse   Birthplace   Date of Birth   Date of Death

Where Buried   Date of Marriage   Place of Marriage

Parents of Spouse (with Mother's maiden name) 1st Marriage

Subsequent Marriage (if applicable)

Family Details

Schools attended, dates and degrees: Community, political work, etc.:

Descendant   Descendant

Spouse   Spouse

Basic Employment History: Clubs, Church Affiliations, etc.:

Descendant   Descendant

Spouse   Spouse

Military Service:

Descendant   Spouse

M62932323
Genealogical Number

Christopher Edward Heiby
Name (including maiden name if applicable)

Cordova, Tenn.
Town of Residence

Sumter, SC
Birthplace

5/16/1970
Date of Birth

Date of Death

Where Buried

Jennifer Lynne Dodge
Name of Spouse

Birthplace

1/5/1969
Date of Birth

Date of Death

Where Buried

8/7/1993
Date of Marriage

Place of Marriage

If married more than once:

Name of Spouse

Birthplace

Date of Birth

Date of Death

Where Buried

Date of Marriage

Place of Marriage

Parents of Spouse (with Mother's maiden name) 1st Marriage

Subsequent Marriage (if applicable)

Family Details

Schools attended, dates and degrees:

Community, political work, etc.:

Descendant

Descendant

Spouse

Spouse

Basic Employment History:

Clubs, Church Affiliations, etc.:

Descendant

Descendant

Spouse

Spouse

Military Service:

Descendant

Spouse

M629323231
Genealogical Number

Garrett Allan Heiby
Name (including maiden name if applicable)   Town of Residence

                    1/14/1995
Birthplace   Date of Birth   Date of Death   Where Buried

Name of Spouse   Birthplace   Date of Birth   Date of Death

Where Buried   Date of Marriage   Place of Marriage

If married more than once:

Name of Spouse   Birthplace   Date of Birth   Date of Death

Where Buried   Date of Marriage   Place of Marriage

Parents of Spouse (with Mother's maiden name) 1st Marriage

Subsequent Marriage (if applicable)

Family Details

Schools attended, dates and degrees: Community, political work, etc.:

Descendant   Descendant

Spouse   Spouse

Basic Employment History: Clubs, Church Affiliations, etc.:

Descendant   Descendant

Spouse   Spouse

Military Service:

Descendant   Spouse

M629323232
Genealogical Number

Braeden Owen Heiby
Name (including maiden name if applicable)   Town of Residence

                                    3/22/2002
Birthplace   Date of Birth   Date of Death   Where Buried

Name of Spouse   Birthplace   Date of Birth   Date of Death

Where Buried   Date of Marriage   Place of Marriage

If married more than once:

Name of Spouse   Birthplace   Date of Birth   Date of Death

Where Buried   Date of Marriage   Place of Marriage

Parents of Spouse (with Mother's maiden name) 1st Marriage

Subsequent Marriage (if applicable)

Family Details

Schools attended, dates and degrees: Community, political work, etc.:

Descendant   Descendant

Spouse   Spouse

Basic Employment History: Clubs, Church Affiliations, etc.:

Descendant   Descendant

Spouse   Spouse

Military Service:

Descendant   Spouse

M6293233
Genealogical Number

Cary Edward Gearheart
Name (including maiden name if applicable)   Town of Residence

Crestline, Ohio   1/22/1945
Birthplace   Date of Birth   Date of Death   Where Buried

Sandra Kay Cover   Bucyrus, Ohio   5/27/1945
Name of Spouse   Birthplace   Date of Birth   Date of Death

                           9/4/1965
Where Buried   Date of Marriage   Place of Marriage

If married more than once:

Name of Spouse   Birthplace   Date of Birth   Date of Death

Where Buried   Date of Marriage   Place of Marriage

Parents of Spouse (with Mother's maiden name) 1st Marriage

Subsequent Marriage (if applicable)

Family Details

Schools attended, dates and degrees: Community, political work, etc.:

Descendant   Descendant

Spouse   Spouse

Basic Employment History: Clubs, Church Affiliations, etc.:

Descendant   Descendant

Spouse   Spouse

Military Service:

Descendant   Spouse

M62932331
Genealogical Number

Monica Kay Gearheart
Name (including maiden name if applicable)

Crestline, Ohio
Town of Residence

Crestline, Ohio
Birthplace

1/10/1967
Date of Birth

Date of Death

Where Buried

Name of Spouse

Birthplace

Date of Birth

Date of Death

Where Buried

Date of Marriage

Place of Marriage

If married more than once:

Name of Spouse

Birthplace

Date of Birth

Date of Death

Where Buried

Date of Marriage

Place of Marriage

Parents of Spouse (with Mother's maiden name) 1st Marriage

Subsequent Marriage (if applicable)

Family Details

Schools attended, dates and degrees:

Community, political work, etc.:

Descendant

Descendant

Spouse

Spouse

Basic Employment History:

Clubs, Church Affiliations, etc.:

Descendant

Descendant

Spouse

Spouse

Military Service:

Descendant

Spouse

M62932332
Genealogical Number

Traci Renee Gearheart
Name (including maiden name if applicable)

Crestline, Ohio
Town of Residence

Crestline, Ohio
Birthplace

4/6/1969
Date of Birth

Date of Death

Where Buried

Jerry L. Kenison
Name of Spouse

Birthplace

6/3/1968
Date of Birth

Date of Death

Where Buried

10/20/1990
Date of Marriage

Place of Marriage

If married more than once:

Name of Spouse

Birthplace

Date of Birth

Date of Death

Where Buried

Date of Marriage

Place of Marriage

Parents of Spouse (with Mother's maiden name) 1st Marriage

Subsequent Marriage (if applicable)

Family Details

Schools attended, dates and degrees:

Community, political work, etc.:

Descendant

Descendant

Spouse

Spouse

Basic Employment History:

Clubs, Church Affiliations, etc.:

Descendant

Descendant

Spouse

Spouse

Military Service:

Descendant

Spouse

M62932321
Genealogical Number

Kelsea Cassandra Kenison
Name (including maiden name if applicable)

Town of Residence

4/12/1991
Birthplace | Date of Birth | Date of Death | Where Buried

Name of Spouse | Birthplace | Date of Birth | Date of Death

Where Buried | Date of Marriage | Place of Marriage

If married more than once:

Name of Spouse | Birthplace | Date of Birth | Date of Death

Where Buried | Date of Marriage | Place of Marriage

Parents of Spouse (with Mother's maiden name) 1st Marriage

Subsequent Marriage (if applicable)

Family Details

Schools attended, dates and degrees: | Community, political work, etc.:

Descendant | Descendant

Spouse | Spouse

Basic Employment History: | Clubs, Church Affiliations, etc.:

Descendant | Descendant

Spouse | Spouse

Military Service:

Descendant | Spouse

M62932322
Genealogical Number

Kaleb Edward Kenison
Name (including maiden name if applicable)   Town of Residence

                              10/6/1992
Birthplace   Date of Birth   Date of Death   Where Buried

Name of Spouse   Birthplace   Date of Birth   Date of Death

Where Buried   Date of Marriage   Place of Marriage

If married more than once:

Name of Spouse   Birthplace   Date of Birth   Date of Death

Where Buried   Date of Marriage   Place of Marriage

Parents of Spouse (with Mother's maiden name) 1st Marriage

Subsequent Marriage (if applicable)

Family Details

Schools attended, dates and degrees: Community, political work, etc.:

Descendant   Descendant

Spouse   Spouse

Basic Employment History: Clubs, Church Affiliations, etc.:

Descendant   Descendant

Spouse   Spouse

Military Service:

Descendant   Spouse

M629811
Genealogical Number

Gertrude Ann Moore
Name (including maiden name if applicable)   Town of Residence

Boissevain, VA   7/28/1918
Birthplace   Date of Birth   Date of Death   Where Buried

Homer Birchfield   Wyoming County, W.VA   6/15/1913
Name of Spouse   Birthplace   Date of Birth   Date of Death

                          8/17/1935
Where Buried   Date of Marriage   Place of Marriage

If married more than once:

Name of Spouse   Birthplace   Date of Birth   Date of Death

Where Buried   Date of Marriage   Place of Marriage

Thomas Birchfield - Rosiebell McKenney
Parents of Spouse (with Mother's maiden name) 1st Marriage

Subsequent Marriage (if applicable)

Family Details

Schools attended, dates and degrees: Community, political work, etc.:

Descendant   Descendant

Spouse   Spouse

Basic Employment History: Clubs, Church Affiliations, etc.:

Descendant   Descendant

Spouse   Spouse

Military Service:

Descendant   Spouse

M6298112
Genealogical Number

James Thomas Birchfield
Name (including maiden name if applicable)   Town of Residence

_____   4/11/1937   4/2/1981   _____
Birthplace   Date of Birth   Date of Death   Where Buried

Kathleen Bostic   Seebert, W.VA   8/23/1942   _____
Name of Spouse   Birthplace   Date of Birth   Date of Death

_____   _____   _____
Where Buried   Date of Marriage   Place of Marriage

If married more than once:

_____   _____   _____   _____
Name of Spouse   Birthplace   Date of Birth   Date of Death

_____   _____   _____
Where Buried   Date of Marriage   Place of Marriage

_____
Parents of Spouse (with Mother's maiden name) 1st Marriage

_____
Subsequent Marriage (if applicable)

Family Details

Schools attended, dates and degrees: Community, political work, etc.:

_____   _____
Descendant   Descendant

_____   _____
Spouse   Spouse

Basic Employment History: Clubs, Church Affiliations, etc.:

_____   _____
Descendant   Descendant

_____   _____
Spouse   Spouse

Military Service:

_____   _____
Descendant   Spouse

M62981121
Genealogical Number

John Glen Birchfield
Name (including maiden name if applicable)

Staunton, VA
Town of Residence

Marlington, W.VA
Birthplace

1/1/1963
Date of Birth

Date of Death

Where Buried

Name of Spouse

Birthplace

Date of Birth

Date of Death

Where Buried

Date of Marriage

Place of Marriage

If married more than once:

Name of Spouse

Birthplace

Date of Birth

Date of Death

Where Buried

Date of Marriage

Place of Marriage

Parents of Spouse (with Mother's maiden name) 1st Marriage

Subsequent Marriage (if applicable)

Family Details

Schools attended, dates and degrees:

Community, political work, etc.:

Descendant

Descendant

Spouse

Spouse

Basic Employment History:

Clubs, Church Affiliations, etc.:

Descendant

Descendant

Spouse

Spouse

Military Service:

Descendant

Spouse

M62981122
Genealogical Number

David Andrew Birchfield
Name (including maiden name if applicable)

Town of Residence

Marlington, W.VA
Birthplace

6/8/1964
Date of Birth

Date of Death

Where Buried

Name of Spouse

Birthplace

Date of Birth

Date of Death

Where Buried

Date of Marriage

Place of Marriage

If married more than once:

Name of Spouse

Birthplace

Date of Birth

Date of Death

Where Buried

Date of Marriage

Place of Marriage

Parents of Spouse (with Mother's maiden name) 1st Marriage

Subsequent Marriage (if applicable)

Family Details

Schools attended, dates and degrees:

Community, political work, etc.:

Descendant

Descendant

Spouse

Spouse

Basic Employment History:

Clubs, Church Affiliations, etc.:

Descendant

Descendant

Spouse

Spouse

Military Service:

Descendant

Spouse

M62981123
Genealogical Number

Kathy Ann Birchfield
Name (including maiden name if applicable)

Hillsboro, W.VA
Town of Residence

Marlington, W.VA
Birthplace

10/7/1966
Date of Birth

Date of Death

Where Buried

Kenneth Dwayne Evans
Name of Spouse

Hillsboro, W.VA
Birthplace

5/13/1963
Date of Birth

Date of Death

Where Buried

Date of Marriage

Place of Marriage

If married more than once:

Name of Spouse

Birthplace

Date of Birth

Date of Death

Where Buried

Date of Marriage

Place of Marriage

Parents of Spouse (with Mother's maiden name) 1st Marriage

Subsequent Marriage (if applicable)

Family Details

Schools attended, dates and degrees:

Community, political work, etc.:

Descendant

Descendant

Spouse

Spouse

Basic Employment History:

Clubs, Church Affiliations, etc.:

Descendant

Descendant

Spouse

Spouse

Military Service:

Descendant

Spouse

M629811231
Genealogical Number

Joseph Samuel Evans
Name (including maiden name if applicable)   Town of Residence

Maryland   4/10/1991
Birthplace   Date of Birth   Date of Death   Where Buried

Name of Spouse   Birthplace   Date of Birth   Date of Death

Where Buried   Date of Marriage   Place of Marriage

If married more than once:

Name of Spouse   Birthplace   Date of Birth   Date of Death

Where Buried   Date of Marriage   Place of Marriage

Parents of Spouse (with Mother's maiden name) 1st Marriage

Subsequent Marriage (if applicable)

Family Details

Schools attended, dates and degrees: Community, political work, etc.:

Descendant   Descendant

Spouse   Spouse

Basic Employment History: Clubs, Church Affiliations, etc.:

Descendant   Descendant

Spouse   Spouse

Military Service:

Descendant   Spouse

M62981124
Genealogical Number

Daniel Lee Birchfield
Name (including maiden name if applicable)

Hillsboro, W.VA
Town of Residence

Fairlea, W.VA
Birthplace

11/17/1973
Date of Birth

Date of Death

Where Buried

Lora Alice Snead
Name of Spouse

Glen Burnie, MD
Birthplace

12/17/1965
Date of Birth

Date of Death

Where Buried

Date of Marriage

Place of Marriage

If married more than once:

Name of Spouse

Birthplace

Date of Birth

Date of Death

Where Buried

Date of Marriage

Place of Marriage

Parents of Spouse (with Mother's maiden name) 1st Marriage

Subsequent Marriage (if applicable)

Family Details

Schools attended, dates and degrees:

Community, political work, etc.:

Descendant

Descendant

Spouse

Spouse

Basic Employment History:

Clubs, Church Affiliations, etc.:

Descendant

Descendant

Spouse

Spouse

Military Service:

Descendant

Spouse

M6298113
Genealogical Number

Robert Boyd Birchfield   Lewisburg, W.VA
Name (including maiden name if applicable)   Town of Residence

Hotchkiss, W.VA   2/10/1940
Birthplace   Date of Birth   Date of Death   Where Buried

Karen A. Kimbrell   Lafayette, IN   11/13/1942
Name of Spouse   Birthplace   Date of Birth   Date of Death

                         1/24/1965
Where Buried   Date of Marriage   Place of Marriage

If married more than once:

Name of Spouse   Birthplace   Date of Birth   Date of Death

Where Buried   Date of Marriage   Place of Marriage

Gordon Dale Kimbrell - Gladys Anne Daugherty
Parents of Spouse (with Mother's maiden name) 1st Marriage

Subsequent Marriage (if applicable)

Family Details

Schools attended, dates and degrees: Community, political work, etc.:

Descendant   Descendant

Spouse   Spouse

Basic Employment History: Clubs, Church Affiliations, etc.:

Descendant   Descendant

Spouse   Spouse

Military Service:

Descendant   Spouse

M62981131
Genealogical Number

Matthew Boyd Birchfield
Name (including maiden name if applicable)   Town of Residence

Jacksonville Beach, Fla.   11/23/1967
Birthplace   Date of Birth   Date of Death   Where Buried

Name of Spouse   Birthplace   Date of Birth   Date of Death

Where Buried   Date of Marriage   Place of Marriage

If married more than once:

Name of Spouse   Birthplace   Date of Birth   Date of Death

Where Buried   Date of Marriage   Place of Marriage

Parents of Spouse (with Mother's maiden name) 1st Marriage

Subsequent Marriage (if applicable)

Family Details

Schools attended, dates and degrees: Community, political work, etc.:

Descendant   Descendant

Spouse   Spouse

Basic Employment History: Clubs, Church Affiliations, etc.:

Descendant   Descendant

Spouse   Spouse

Military Service:

Descendant   Spouse

M62981132
Genealogical Number

Weston Dale Birchfield
Name (including maiden name if applicable)   Town of Residence

Carmel, California   8/11/1971
Birthplace   Date of Birth   Date of Death   Where Buried

Name of Spouse   Birthplace   Date of Birth   Date of Death

Where Buried   Date of Marriage   Place of Marriage

If married more than once:

Name of Spouse   Birthplace   Date of Birth   Date of Death

Where Buried   Date of Marriage   Place of Marriage

Parents of Spouse (with Mother's maiden name) 1st Marriage

Subsequent Marriage (if applicable)

Family Details

Schools attended, dates and degrees: Community, political work, etc.:

Descendant   Descendant

Spouse   Spouse

Basic Employment History: Clubs, Church Affiliations, etc.:

Descendant   Descendant

Spouse   Spouse

Military Service:

Descendant   Spouse

M6298114
Genealogical Number

Constance Marie Birchfield
Name (including maiden name if applicable)

Buckeye, W.VA
Town of Residence

Hotchkiss, W.VA
Birthplace

2/27/1942
Date of Birth

Date of Death

Where Buried

James Judson Howard
Name of Spouse

Marlington, W.VA
Birthplace

11/14/1943
Date of Birth

Date of Death

Where Buried

4/20/1968
Date of Marriage

Place of Marriage

If married more than once:

Name of Spouse

Birthplace

Date of Birth

Date of Death

Where Buried

Date of Marriage

Place of Marriage

James Wallace Howard - Charlean Alberta Swearergan
Parents of Spouse (with Mother's maiden name) 1st Marriage

Subsequent Marriage (if applicable)

Family Details

Schools attended, dates and degrees:

Community, political work, etc.:

Descendant

Descendant

Spouse

Spouse

Basic Employment History:

Clubs, Church Affiliations, etc.:

Descendant

Descendant

Spouse

Spouse

Military Service:

Descendant

Spouse

M62981141
Genealogical Number

Judson Dale Howard   Manassas, VA
Name (including maiden name if applicable)   Town of Residence

Highpoint, NC   7/31/1969
Birthplace   Date of Birth   Date of Death   Where Buried

Michelle Marie Robbins
Name of Spouse   Birthplace   Date of Birth   Date of Death

                                 4/30/1994
Where Buried   Date of Marriage   Place of Marriage

If married more than once:

Name of Spouse   Birthplace   Date of Birth   Date of Death

Where Buried   Date of Marriage   Place of Marriage

Parents of Spouse (with Mother's maiden name) 1st Marriage

Subsequent Marriage (if applicable)

Family Details

Schools attended, dates and degrees: Community, political work, etc.:

Descendant   Descendant

Spouse   Spouse

Basic Employment History: Clubs, Church Affiliations, etc.:

Descendant   Descendant

Spouse   Spouse

Military Service:

Descendant   Spouse

M62981142
Genealogical Number

Joseph Gale Howard
Name (including maiden name if applicable)   Town of Residence

Highpoint, NC   1/22/1974
Birthplace   Date of Birth   Date of Death   Where Buried

Name of Spouse   Birthplace   Date of Birth   Date of Death

Where Buried   Date of Marriage   Place of Marriage

If married more than once:

Name of Spouse   Birthplace   Date of Birth   Date of Death

Where Buried   Date of Marriage   Place of Marriage

Parents of Spouse (with Mother's maiden name) 1st Marriage

Subsequent Marriage (if applicable)

Family Details

Schools attended, dates and degrees: Community, political work, etc.:

Descendant   Descendant

Spouse   Spouse

Basic Employment History: Clubs, Church Affiliations, etc.:

Descendant   Descendant

Spouse   Spouse

Military Service:

Descendant   Spouse

M6298115
Genealogical Number

Wilburn Lonnie Birchfield   Bakersville, California
Name (including maiden name if applicable)   Town of Residence

Hotchkiss, W.VA   5/5/1944
Birthplace   Date of Birth   Date of Death   Where Buried

Francine Louise Chayra   Santa Maria, California   5/4/1947
Name of Spouse   Birthplace   Date of Birth   Date of Death

Where Buried   Date of Marriage   Place of Marriage

If married more than once:

Name of Spouse   Birthplace   Date of Birth   Date of Death

Where Buried   Date of Marriage   Place of Marriage

Parents of Spouse (with Mother's maiden name) 1st Marriage

Subsequent Marriage (if applicable)

Family Details

Schools attended, dates and degrees: Community, political work, etc.:

Descendant   Descendant

Spouse   Spouse

Basic Employment History: Clubs, Church Affiliations, etc.:

Descendant   Descendant

Spouse   Spouse

Military Service:

Descendant   Spouse

M62981151
Genealogical Number

Heath Gilbert Birchfield
Name (including maiden name if applicable)

Town of Residence

Las Vegas, Nevada   8/16/1972
Birthplace   Date of Birth   Date of Death   Where Buried

Name of Spouse   Birthplace   Date of Birth   Date of Death

Where Buried   Date of Marriage   Place of Marriage

If married more than once:

Name of Spouse   Birthplace   Date of Birth   Date of Death

Where Buried   Date of Marriage   Place of Marriage

Parents of Spouse (with Mother's maiden name) 1st Marriage

Subsequent Marriage (if applicable)

Family Details

Schools attended, dates and degrees: Community, political work, etc.:

Descendant   Descendant

Spouse   Spouse

Basic Employment History: Clubs, Church Affiliations, etc.:

Descendant   Descendant

Spouse   Spouse

Military Service:

Descendant   Spouse

M62981152
Genealogical Number

Michelle Louise Birchfield
Name (including maiden name if applicable)   Town of Residence

Victorville, Calif.   8/16/1976
Birthplace   Date of Birth   Date of Death   Where Buried

Name of Spouse   Birthplace   Date of Birth   Date of Death

Where Buried   Date of Marriage   Place of Marriage

If married more than once:

Name of Spouse   Birthplace   Date of Birth   Date of Death

Where Buried   Date of Marriage   Place of Marriage

Parents of Spouse (with Mother's maiden name) 1st Marriage

Subsequent Marriage (if applicable)

Family Details

Schools attended, dates and degrees: Community, political work, etc.:

Descendant   Descendant

Spouse   Spouse

Basic Employment History: Clubs, Church Affiliations, etc.:

Descendant   Descendant

Spouse   Spouse

Military Service:

Descendant   Spouse

M62981153
Genealogical Number

Frances Marie Birchfield
Name (including maiden name if applicable)

Town of Residence

Austin, Texas   12/29/1977
Birthplace   Date of Birth   Date of Death   Where Buried

Name of Spouse   Birthplace   Date of Birth   Date of Death

Where Buried   Date of Marriage   Place of Marriage

If married more than once:

Name of Spouse   Birthplace   Date of Birth   Date of Death

Where Buried   Date of Marriage   Place of Marriage

Parents of Spouse (with Mother's maiden name) 1st Marriage

Subsequent Marriage (if applicable)

Family Details

Schools attended, dates and degrees: Community, political work, etc.:

Descendant   Descendant

Spouse   Spouse

Basic Employment History: Clubs, Church Affiliations, etc.:

Descendant   Descendant

Spouse   Spouse

Military Service:

Descendant   Spouse

M6298116
Genealogical Number

Gloria Dawn Birchfield
Name (including maiden name if applicable)

Hillsboro, W.VA
Town of Residence

Pocahontas County, W.VA
Birthplace

12/7/1948
Date of Birth

Date of Death

Where Buried

Floyd Daniel Walton
Name of Spouse

Birthplace

2/23/1937
Date of Birth

Date of Death

Where Buried

Date of Marriage

Place of Marriage

If married more than once:

James A. Reinhold
Name of Spouse

Greensboro County, W.VA
Birthplace

2/16/1945
Date of Birth

5/16/1977
Date of Death

Where Buried

Date of Marriage

Place of Marriage

Parents of Spouse (with Mother's maiden name) 1st Marriage

Subsequent Marriage (if applicable)

Family Details

Schools attended, dates and degrees:

Community, political work, etc.:

Descendant

Descendant

Spouse

Spouse

Basic Employment History:

Clubs, Church Affiliations, etc.:

Descendant

Descendant

Spouse

Spouse

Military Service:

Descendant

Spouse

M62981161
Genealogical Number

James Homer Reinhold
Name (including maiden name if applicable)   Town of Residence

Pocahontas County, W.VA   2/23/1967
Birthplace   Date of Birth   Date of Death   Where Buried

Tina R. White
Name of Spouse   Birthplace   Date of Birth   Date of Death

                                 8/2/1987
Where Buried   Date of Marriage   Place of Marriage

If married more than once:

Name of Spouse   Birthplace   Date of Birth   Date of Death

Where Buried   Date of Marriage   Place of Marriage

Parents of Spouse (with Mother's maiden name) 1st Marriage

Subsequent Marriage (if applicable)

Family Details

Schools attended, dates and degrees: Community, political work, etc.:

Descendant   Descendant

Spouse   Spouse

Basic Employment History: Clubs, Church Affiliations, etc.:

Descendant   Descendant

Spouse   Spouse

Military Service:

Descendant   Spouse

M629811611
Genealogical Number

James Wesley Reinhold
Name (including maiden name if applicable)   Town of Residence

                     11/15/1990
Birthplace   Date of Birth   Date of Death   Where Buried

Name of Spouse   Birthplace   Date of Birth   Date of Death

Where Buried   Date of Marriage   Place of Marriage

If married more than once:

Name of Spouse   Birthplace   Date of Birth   Date of Death

Where Buried   Date of Marriage   Place of Marriage

Parents of Spouse (with Mother's maiden name) 1st Marriage

Subsequent Marriage (if applicable)

Family Details

Schools attended, dates and degrees: Community, political work, etc.:

Descendant   Descendant

Spouse   Spouse

Basic Employment History: Clubs, Church Affiliations, etc.:

Descendant   Descendant

Spouse   Spouse

Military Service:

Descendant   Spouse

M629811612
Genealogical Number

Krista Lane Reinhold
Name (including maiden name if applicable)   Town of Residence

_____   12/31/1991   _____   _____
Birthplace   Date of Birth   Date of Death   Where Buried

_____   _____   _____   _____
Name of Spouse   Birthplace   Date of Birth   Date of Death

_____   _____   _____
Where Buried   Date of Marriage Place of Marriage

If married more than once:

_____   _____   _____   _____
Name of Spouse   Birthplace   Date of Birth   Date of Death

_____   _____   _____
Where Buried   Date of Marriage Place of Marriage

Parents of Spouse (with Mother's maiden name) 1st Marriage

Subsequent Marriage (if applicable)

Family Details

Schools attended, dates and degrees: Community, political work, etc.:

_____   _____
Descendant   Descendant

_____   _____
Spouse   Spouse

Basic Employment History: Clubs, Church Affiliations, etc.:

_____   _____
Descendant   Descendant

_____   _____
Spouse   Spouse

Military Service:

_____   _____
Descendant   Spouse

M62981162
Genealogical Number

Alice Irene Reinhold   Hillsboro, W.VA
Name (including maiden name if applicable)   Town of Residence

Pocahontas County, W.VA   1/5/1969
Birthplace   Date of Birth   Date of Death   Where Buried

Name of Spouse   Birthplace   Date of Birth   Date of Death

Where Buried   Date of Marriage   Place of Marriage

If married more than once:

Name of Spouse   Birthplace   Date of Birth   Date of Death

Where Buried   Date of Marriage   Place of Marriage

Parents of Spouse (with Mother's maiden name) 1st Marriage

Subsequent Marriage (if applicable)

Family Details

Schools attended, dates and degrees: Community, political work, etc.:

Descendant   Descendant

Spouse   Spouse

Basic Employment History: Clubs, Church Affiliations, etc.:

Descendant   Descendant

Spouse   Spouse

Military Service:

Descendant   Spouse

M62981163
Genealogical Number

Kevin Lynn Reinhold
Name (including maiden name if applicable)   Town of Residence

Ashland, KY   2/4/1972
Birthplace   Date of Birth   Date of Death   Where Buried

Name of Spouse   Birthplace   Date of Birth   Date of Death

Where Buried   Date of Marriage   Place of Marriage

If married more than once:

Name of Spouse   Birthplace   Date of Birth   Date of Death

Where Buried   Date of Marriage   Place of Marriage

Parents of Spouse (with Mother's maiden name) 1st Marriage

Subsequent Marriage (if applicable)

Family Details

Schools attended, dates and degrees: Community, political work, etc.:

Descendant   Descendant

Spouse   Spouse

Basic Employment History: Clubs, Church Affiliations, etc.:

Descendant   Descendant

Spouse   Spouse

Military Service:

Descendant   Spouse

M62981164
Genealogical Number

Matthew Daniel Walton
Name (including maiden name if applicable)

Town of Residence

Elkins, W.VA   8/8/1979
Birthplace   Date of Birth   Date of Death   Where Buried

Name of Spouse   Birthplace   Date of Birth   Date of Death

Where Buried   Date of Marriage   Place of Marriage

If married more than once:

Name of Spouse   Birthplace   Date of Birth   Date of Death

Where Buried   Date of Marriage   Place of Marriage

Parents of Spouse (with Mother's maiden name) 1st Marriage

Subsequent Marriage (if applicable)

Family Details

Schools attended, dates and degrees: Community, political work, etc.:

Descendant   Descendant

Spouse   Spouse

Basic Employment History: Clubs, Church Affiliations, etc.:

Descendant   Descendant

Spouse   Spouse

Military Service:

Descendant   Spouse

M6298117
Genealogical Number

Janice Elaine Birchfield
Name (including maiden name if applicable)

Staunton, VA
Town of Residence

Raleigh County, W.VA
Birthplace

8/16/1950
Date of Birth

Date of Death

Where Buried

Johnnie Madford Hollandsworth
Name of Spouse

Birthplace

7/31/1950
Date of Birth

Date of Death

Where Buried

Date of Marriage

Place of Marriage

If married more than once:

Name of Spouse

Birthplace

Date of Birth

Date of Death

Where Buried

Date of Marriage

Place of Marriage

Parents of Spouse (with Mother's maiden name) 1st Marriage

Subsequent Marriage (if applicable)

Family Details

Schools attended, dates and degrees:

Community, political work, etc.:

Descendant

Descendant

Spouse

Spouse

Basic Employment History:

Clubs, Church Affiliations, etc.:

Descendant

Descendant

Spouse

Spouse

Military Service:

Descendant

Spouse

M62981171
Genealogical Number

Marie Dawn Hollandsworth
Name (including maiden name if applicable)   Town of Residence

Elkins, W.VA   7/11/1981
Birthplace   Date of Birth   Date of Death   Where Buried

Name of Spouse   ·   Birthplace   Date of Birth   Date of Death

Where Buried   Date of Marriage   Place of Marriage

If married more than once:

Name of Spouse   Birthplace   Date of Birth   Date of Death

Where Buried   Date of Marriage   Place of Marriage

Parents of Spouse (with Mother's maiden name) 1st Marriage

Subsequent Marriage (if applicable)

Family Details

Schools attended, dates and degrees: Community, political work, etc.:

Descendant   Descendant

Spouse   Spouse

Basic Employment History: **Clubs, Church Affiliations, etc.:**

Descendant   Descendant

Spouse   Spouse

Military Service:

Descendant   Spouse

M62981172
Genealogical Number

Billie Jack Hollandsworth
Name (including maiden name if applicable)   Town of Residence

Fairlea, W.VA   7/23/1983
Birthplace   Date of Birth   Date of Death   Where Buried

Name of Spouse   Birthplace   Date of Birth   Date of Death

Where Buried   Date of Marriage   Place of Marriage

If married more than once:

Name of Spouse   Birthplace   Date of Birth   Date of Death

Where Buried   Date of Marriage   Place of Marriage

Parents of Spouse (with Mother's maiden name) 1st Marriage

Subsequent Marriage (if applicable)

Family Details

Schools attended, dates and degrees: Community, political work, etc.:

Descendant   Descendant

Spouse   Spouse

Basic Employment History: Clubs, Church Affiliations, etc.:

Descendant   Descendant

Spouse   Spouse

Military Service:

Descendant   Spouse

M6298118
Genealogical Number

Verlin Lee Birchfield   Hillsboro, W.VA
Name (including maiden name if applicable)   Town of Residence

Pocahontas County, W.VA   4/26/1952
Birthplace   Date of Birth   Date of Death   Where Buried

Audrey Louise Vaughn Comer
Name of Spouse   Birthplace   Date of Birth   Date of Death

Where Buried   Date of Marriage   Place of Marriage

If married more than once:

Rose Ann Berage   Delaware   8/7/1953
Name of Spouse   Birthplace   Date of Birth   Date of Death

Where Buried   Date of Marriage   Place of Marriage

Parents of Spouse (with Mother's maiden name) 1st Marriage

Subsequent Marriage (if applicable)

Family Details

Schools attended, dates and degrees: Community, political work, etc.:

Descendant   Descendant

Spouse   Spouse

Basic Employment History: Clubs, Church Affiliations, etc.:

Descendant   Descendant

Spouse   Spouse

Military Service:

Descendant   Spouse

M62981181
Genealogical Number

Verlin Lee Birchfield, Jr.
Name (including maiden name if applicable)

Danville, VA
Town of Residence

Waynesboro, VA
Birthplace

5/24/1972
Date of Birth

Date of Death

Where Buried

Yoshike Furosako
Name of Spouse

Yokohama, Japan
Birthplace

6/15/1963
Date of Birth

Date of Death

Where Buried

Date of Marriage

Place of Marriage

If married more than once:

Name of Spouse

Birthplace

Date of Birth

Date of Death

Where Buried

Date of Marriage

Place of Marriage

Parents of Spouse (with Mother's maiden name) 1st Marriage

Subsequent Marriage (if applicable)

Family Details

Schools attended, dates and degrees:

Community, political work, etc.:

Descendant

Descendant

Spouse

Spouse

Basic Employment History:

Clubs, Church Affiliations, etc.:

Descendant

Descendant

Spouse

Spouse

Military Service:

Descendant

Spouse

M629811811
Genealogical Number

Eliot Sho-ta Birchfield
Name (including maiden name if applicable)   Town of Residence

Japan   12/12/1994
Birthplace   Date of Birth   Date of Death   Where Buried

Name of Spouse   Birthplace   Date of Birth   Date of Death

Where Buried   Date of Marriage   Place of Marriage

If married more than once:

Name of Spouse   Birthplace   Date of Birth   Date of Death

Where Buried   Date of Marriage   Place of Marriage

Parents of Spouse (with Mother's maiden name) 1st Marriage

Subsequent Marriage (if applicable)

Family Details

Schools attended, dates and degrees: Community, political work, etc.:

Descendant   Descendant

Spouse   Spouse

Basic Employment History: Clubs, Church Affiliations, etc.:

Descendant   Descendant

Spouse   Spouse

Military Service:

Descendant   Spouse

M629811812
Genealogical Number

Lenie Maria Birchfield
Name (including maiden name if applicable)   Town of Residence

Japan   11/13/1996
Birthplace   Date of Birth   Date of Death   Where Buried

Name of Spouse   Birthplace   Date of Birth   Date of Death

Where Buried   Date of Marriage   Place of Marriage

If married more than once:

Name of Spouse   Birthplace   Date of Birth   Date of Death

Where Buried   Date of Marriage   Place of Marriage

Parents of Spouse (with Mother's maiden name) 1st Marriage

Subsequent Marriage (if applicable)

Family Details

Schools attended, dates and degrees: Community, political work, etc.:

Descendant   Descendant

Spouse   Spouse

Basic Employment History: Clubs, Church Affiliations, etc.:

Descendant   Descendant

Spouse   Spouse

Military Service:

Descendant   Spouse

M6298119
Genealogical Number

Homer Roscoe Birchfield   Waynesboro, VA
Name (including maiden name if applicable)   Town of Residence

                              5/9/1953
Birthplace   Date of Birth   Date of Death   Where Buried

Name of Spouse   Birthplace   Date of Birth   Date of Death

Where Buried   Date of Marriage   Place of Marriage

If married more than once:

Name of Spouse   Birthplace   Date of Birth   Date of Death

Where Buried   Date of Marriage   Place of Marriage

Parents of Spouse (with Mother's maiden name) 1st Marriage

Subsequent Marriage (if applicable)

Family Details

Schools attended, dates and degrees: Community, political work, etc.:

Descendant   Descendant

Spouse   Spouse

Basic Employment History: Clubs, Church Affiliations, etc.:

Descendant   Descendant

Spouse   Spouse

Military Service:

Descendant   Spouse

M6298119y
Genealogical Number

Paul Franklin Birchfield
Name (including maiden name if applicable)

Middlebrook, VA
Town of Residence

Birthplace

7/10/1958
Date of Birth

Date of Death

Where Buried

Melinda Wooland
Name of Spouse

Birthplace

Date of Birth

Date of Death

Where Buried

Date of Marriage

Place of Marriage

If married more than once:

Name of Spouse

Birthplace

Date of Birth

Date of Death

Where Buried

Date of Marriage

Place of Marriage

Parents of Spouse (with Mother's maiden name) 1st Marriage

Subsequent Marriage (if applicable)

Family Details

Schools attended, dates and degrees:

Community, political work, etc.:

Descendant

Descendant

Spouse

Spouse

Basic Employment History:

Clubs, Church Affiliations, etc.:

Descendant

Descendant

Spouse

Spouse

Military Service:

Descendant

Spouse

M629812
Genealogical Number

Dock M.Moore
Name (including maiden name if applicable)

Bluefield, VA
Town of Residence

| | 7/22/1920 | | |
| Birthplace | Date of Birth | Date of Death | Where Buried |

| | | | |
| Name of Spouse | Birthplace | Date of Birth | Date of Death |

| | | |
| Where Buried | Date of Marriage | Place of Marriage |

If married more than once:

| | | | |
| Name of Spouse | Birthplace | Date of Birth | Date of Death |

| | | |
| Where Buried | Date of Marriage | Place of Marriage |

Parents of Spouse (with Mother's maiden name) 1st Marriage

Subsequent Marriage (if applicable)

Family Details

Schools attended, dates and degrees:

Community, political work, etc.:

Descendant

Descendant

Spouse

Spouse

Basic Employment History:

Clubs, Church Affiliations, etc.:

Descendant

Descendant

Spouse

Spouse

Military Service:

Descendant

Spouse

M629814
Genealogical Number

Walter Sims Moore
Name (including maiden name if applicable)

Pocahontas, VA
Town of Residence

Slab Fork, W.VA
Birthplace

7/15/1925
Date of Birth

Date of Death

Where Buried

Eva Devon Brooks
Name of Spouse

Boissevain, VA
Birthplace

10/14/1927
Date of Birth

Date of Death

Where Buried

11/21/1946
Date of Marriage

Place of Marriage

If married more than once:

Name of Spouse

Birthplace

Date of Birth

Date of Death

Where Buried

Date of Marriage

Place of Marriage

Parents of Spouse (with Mother's maiden name) 1st Marriage

Subsequent Marriage (if applicable)

Family Details

Schools attended, dates and degrees:

Community, political work, etc.:

Descendant

Descendant

Spouse

Spouse

Basic Employment History:

Clubs, Church Affiliations, etc.:

Descendant

Descendant

Spouse

Spouse

Military Service:

Descendant

Spouse

M6298141
Genealogical Number

Glen D. Moore   Midlothian, VA
Name (including maiden name if applicable)   Town of Residence

Boissevain, VA   10/11/1947
Birthplace   Date of Birth   Date of Death   Where Buried

Janna Dawn Foster   Newport News, VA   7/4/1956
Name of Spouse   Birthplace   Date of Birth   Date of Death

                      8/6/1977
Where Buried   Date of Marriage   Place of Marriage

If married more than once:

Betty B. Read (Div)   Hampton, VA   11/3/1949
Name of Spouse   Birthplace   Date of Birth   Date of Death

                      6/29/1968
Where Buried   Date of Marriage   Place of Marriage

Frank Read - Nancy -
Parents of Spouse (with Mother's maiden name) 1st Marriage

Gerald Vincent Foster - Polly Pomeroy
Subsequent Marriage (if applicable)

Family Details

Schools attended, dates and degrees: Community, political work, etc.:

Descendant   Descendant

Spouse   Spouse

Basic Employment History: Clubs, Church Affiliations, etc.:

Descendant   Descendant

Spouse   Spouse

Military Service:

Descendant   Spouse

M62981411
Genealogical Number

David Wayne Moore
Name (including maiden name if applicable)   Town of Residence

Newport News, VA   10/25/1971
Birthplace   Date of Birth   Date of Death   Where Buried

Name of Spouse   Birthplace   Date of Birth   Date of Death

Where Buried   Date of Marriage   Place of Marriage

If married more than once:

Name of Spouse   Birthplace   Date of Birth   Date of Death

Where Buried   Date of Marriage   Place of Marriage

Parents of Spouse (with Mother's maiden name) 1st Marriage

Subsequent Marriage (if applicable)

Family Details

Schools attended, dates and degrees: Community, political work, etc.:

Descendant   Descendant

Spouse   Spouse

Basic Employment History: Clubs, Church Affiliations, etc.:

Descendant   Descendant

Spouse   Spouse

Military Service:

Descendant   Spouse

M62981412
Genealogical Number

Eric James Moore
Name (including maiden name if applicable)   Town of Residence

Newport News, VA   6/30/1979
Birthplace   Date of Birth   Date of Death   Where Buried

Name of Spouse   Birthplace   Date of Birth   Date of Death

Where Buried   Date of Marriage   Place of Marriage

If married more than once:

Name of Spouse   Birthplace   Date of Birth   Date of Death

Where Buried   Date of Marriage   Place of Marriage

Parents of Spouse (with Mother's maiden name) 1st Marriage

Subsequent Marriage (if applicable)

Family Details

Schools attended, dates and degrees: Community, political work, etc.:

Descendant   Descendant

Spouse   Spouse

Basic Employment History: Clubs, Church Affiliations, etc.:

Descendant   Descendant

Spouse   Spouse

Military Service:

Descendant   Spouse

M62981413
Genealogical Number

Travis Michael Moore
Name (including maiden name if applicable)

Town of Residence

Newport News, VA   11/26/1982
Birthplace   Date of Birth   Date of Death   Where Buried

Name of Spouse   Birthplace   Date of Birth   Date of Death

Where Buried   Date of Marriage   Place of Marriage

If married more than once:

Name of Spouse   Birthplace   Date of Birth   Date of Death

Where Buried   Date of Marriage   Place of Marriage

Parents of Spouse (with Mother's maiden name) 1st Marriage

Subsequent Marriage (if applicable)

Family Details

Schools attended, dates and degrees: Community, political work, etc.:

Descendant   Descendant

Spouse   Spouse

Basic Employment History: Clubs, Church Affiliations, etc.:

Descendant   Descendant

Spouse   Spouse

Military Service:

Descendant   Spouse

M6298142
Genealogical Number

Jerry Wayne Moore
Name (including maiden name if applicable)

Beckley, W.VA
Town of Residence

Bluefield, W.VA
Birthplace

8/31/1953
Date of Birth

Date of Death

Where Buried

Deborah Kathryn Ratcliff
Name of Spouse

Charleston, W.VA
Birthplace

7/26/1951
Date of Birth

Date of Death

Where Buried

Date of Marriage

Place of Marriage

If married more than once:

Name of Spouse

Birthplace

Date of Birth

Date of Death

Where Buried

Date of Marriage

Place of Marriage

Parents of Spouse (with Mother's maiden name) 1st Marriage

Subsequent Marriage (if applicable)

Family Details

Schools attended, dates and degrees:

Community, political work, etc.:

Descendant

Descendant

Spouse

Spouse

Basic Employment History:

Clubs, Church Affiliations, etc.:

Descendant

Descendant

Spouse

Spouse

Military Service:

Descendant

Spouse

M62981421
Genealogical Number

Jeremy Wayne Moore
Name (including maiden name if applicable)

Beckley, W.VA
Town of Residence

Bluefield,W.VA
Birthplace

10/28/1977
Date of Birth

Date of Death

Where Buried

Name of Spouse

Birthplace

Date of Birth

Date of Death

Where Buried

Date of Marriage

Place of Marriage

If married more than once:

Name of Spouse

Birthplace

Date of Birth

Date of Death

Where Buried

Date of Marriage

Place of Marriage

Parents of Spouse (with Mother's maiden name) 1st Marriage

Subsequent Marriage (if applicable)

Family Details

Schools attended, dates and degrees:

Community, political work, etc.:

Descendant

Descendant

Spouse

Spouse

Basic Employment History:

Clubs, Church Affiliations, etc.:

Descendant

Descendant

Spouse

Spouse

Military Service:

Descendant

Spouse

M62981422
Genealogical Number

Jonathan Lee Moore
Name (including maiden name if applicable)

Beckley, W.VA
Town of Residence

10/8/1982
Birthplace   Date of Birth   Date of Death   Where Buried

Name of Spouse   Birthplace   Date of Birth   Date of Death

Where Buried   Date of Marriage   Place of Marriage

If married more than once:

Name of Spouse   Birthplace   Date of Birth   Date of Death

Where Buried   Date of Marriage   Place of Marriage

Parents of Spouse (with Mother's maiden name) 1st Marriage

Subsequent Marriage (if applicable)

Family Details

Schools attended, dates and degrees:

Community, political work, etc.:

Descendant

Descendant

Spouse

Spouse

Basic Employment History:

Clubs, Church Affiliations, etc.:

Descendant

Descendant

Spouse

Spouse

Military Service:

Descendant

Spouse

M6298143
Genealogical Number

Mary Alice Moore
Name (including maiden name if applicable)

Richmond, VA
Town of Residence

Bluefield, W.VA
Birthplace

8/27/1962
Date of Birth

Date of Death

Where Buried

Steven M. Sanders
Name of Spouse

Indianapolis, Indiana
Birthplace

10/18/1946
Date of Birth

Date of Death

Where Buried

Date of Marriage

Place of Marriage

If married more than once:

Ted White (Div.)
Name of Spouse

New York
Birthplace

10/18/1960
Date of Birth

Date of Death

Where Buried

Date of Marriage

Place of Marriage

Parents of Spouse (with Mother's maiden name) 1st Marriage

Subsequent Marriage (if applicable)

Family Details

Schools attended, dates and degrees:

Community, political work, etc.:

Descendant

Descendant

Spouse

Spouse

Basic Employment History:

Clubs, Church Affiliations, etc.:

Descendant

Descendant

Spouse

Spouse

Military Service:

Descendant

Spouse

M62981431
Genealogical Number

Christopher Patrick White   Richmond, VA
Name (including maiden name if applicable)   Town of Residence

Bluefield, W.VA   5/30/1979   _____   _____
Birthplace   Date of Birth   Date of Death Where Buried

_____   _____   _____   _____
Name of Spouse   Birthplace   Date of Birth Date of Death

_____   _____   _____
Where Buried   Date of Marriage   Place of Marriage

If married more than once:

_____   _____   _____   _____
Name of Spouse   Birthplace   Date of Birth Date of Death

_____   _____   _____
Where Buried   Date of Marriage   Place of Marriage

_____
Parents of Spouse (with Mother's maiden name) 1st Marriage

_____
Subsequent Marriage (if applicable)

Family Details

Schools attended, dates and degrees: Community, political work, etc.:

_____   _____
Descendant   Descendant

_____   _____
Spouse   Spouse

Basic Employment History: Clubs, Church Affiliations, etc.:

_____   _____
Descendant   Descendant

_____   _____
Spouse   Spouse

Military Service:

_____   _____
Descendant   Spouse

M629815
Genealogical Number

Easter M. Moore   Bartow, W.VA
Name (including maiden name if applicable)   Town of Residence

Skelton, W.VA   12/16/1927
Birthplace   Date of Birth   Date of Death   Where Buried

James C. Cook   Glen Morris, W.VA   3/1/1929
Name of Spouse   Birthplace   Date of Birth   Date of Death

                                        12/31/1948
Where Buried   Date of Marriage   Place of Marriage

If married more than once:

Name of Spouse   Birthplace   Date of Birth   Date of Death

Where Buried   Date of Marriage   Place of Marriage

Dewey Cook – Lakie –
Parents of Spouse (with Mother's maiden name) 1st Marriage

Subsequent Marriage (if applicable)

Family Details

Schools attended, dates and degrees: Community, political work, etc.:

Descendant   Descendant

Spouse   Spouse

Basic Employment History: Clubs, Church Affiliations, etc.:

Descendant   Descendant

Spouse   Spouse

Military Service:

Descendant   Spouse

M6298151
Genealogical Number

Tessie Mae Cook
Name (including maiden name if applicable)

Somerville, Tenn.
Town of Residence

Hotchkiss, W.VA
Birthplace

12/11/1949
Date of Birth

Date of Death

Where Buried

John Frederick Hooker
Name of Spouse

Eads, Tenn.
Birthplace

2/7/1941
Date of Birth

Date of Death

Where Buried

1978
Date of Marriage

Place of Marriage

If married more than once:

Lawrence Watson (Div. 1977)
Name of Spouse

Memphis, Tenn.
Birthplace

8/22/1945
Date of Birth

Date of Death

Where Buried

3/8/1968
Date of Marriage

Place of Marriage

Jessie Watson - Martha Hopper
Parents of Spouse (with Mother's maiden name) 1st Marriage

Jimmy Hooker - Dot Price
Subsequent Marriage (if applicable)

Family Details

Schools attended, dates and degrees:

Community, political work, etc.:

Descendant

Descendant

Spouse

Spouse

Basic Employment History:

Clubs, Church Affiliations, etc.:

Descendant

Descendant

Spouse

Spouse

Military Service:

Descendant

Spouse

M62981511
Genealogical Number

Markus Wayne Watson
Name (including maiden name if applicable)   Town of Residence

Memphis, Tenn.   2/11/1969
Birthplace   Date of Birth   Date of Death   Where Buried

Name of Spouse   Birthplace   Date of Birth   Date of Death

Where Buried   Date of Marriage   Place of Marriage

If married more than once:

Name of Spouse   Birthplace   Date of Birth   Date of Death

Where Buried   Date of Marriage   Place of Marriage

Parents of Spouse (with Mother's maiden name) 1st Marriage

Subsequent Marriage (if applicable)

Family Details

Schools attended, dates and degrees: Community, political work, etc.:

Descendant   Descendant

Spouse   Spouse

Basic Employment History: Clubs, Church Affiliations, etc.:

Descendant   Descendant

Spouse   Spouse

Military Service:

Descendant   Spouse

M62981512
Genealogical Number

Cheryl Lynn Watson
Name (including maiden name if applicable)

Town of Residence

Memphis, Tenn.
Birthplace

10/28/1970
Date of Birth

Date of Death

Where Buried

Name of Spouse

Birthplace

Date of Birth

Date of Death

Where Buried

Date of Marriage

Place of Marriage

If married more than once:

Name of Spouse

Birthplace

Date of Birth

Date of Death

Where Buried

Date of Marriage

Place of Marriage

Parents of Spouse (with Mother's maiden name) 1st Marriage

Subsequent Marriage (if applicable)

Family Details

Schools attended, dates and degrees:

Community, political work, etc.:

Descendant

Descendant

Spouse

Spouse

Basic Employment History:

Clubs, Church Affiliations, etc.:

Descendant

Descendant

Spouse

Spouse

Military Service:

Descendant

Spouse

M629815121
Genealogical Number

Tiffany Nichole Watson
Name (including maiden name if applicable)

Town of Residence

Elizabethtown, KY   3/6/1992
Birthplace   Date of Birth   Date of Death   Where Buried

Name of Spouse   Birthplace   Date of Birth   Date of Death

Where Buried   Date of Marriage   Place of Marriage

If married more than once:

Name of Spouse   Birthplace   Date of Birth   Date of Death

Where Buried   Date of Marriage   Place of Marriage

Parents of Spouse (with Mother's maiden name) 1st Marriage

Subsequent Marriage (if applicable)

Family Details

Schools attended, dates and degrees: Community, political work, etc.:

Descendant   Descendant

Spouse   Spouse

Basic Employment History: Clubs, Church Affiliations, etc.:

Descendant   Descendant

Spouse   Spouse

Military Service:

Descendant   Spouse

M62981513
Genealogical Number

Paul Stephen Watson
Name (including maiden name if applicable)

                                          Town of Residence

Memphis, Tenn   12/20/1975
Birthplace   Date of Birth   Date of Death   Where Buried

Name of Spouse   Birthplace   Date of Birth   Date of Death

Where Buried   Date of Marriage   Place of Marriage

If married more than once:

Name of Spouse   Birthplace   Date of Birth   Date of Death

Where Buried   Date of Marriage   Place of Marriage

Parents of Spouse (with Mother's maiden name) 1st Marriage

Subsequent Marriage (if applicable)

Family Details

Schools attended, dates and degrees: Community, political work, etc.:

Descendant   Descendant

Spouse   Spouse

Basic Employment History: Clubs, Church Affiliations, etc.:

Descendant   Descendant

Spouse   Spouse

Military Service:

Descendant   Spouse

M6298152
Genealogical Number

Dewey Lee Cook
Name (including maiden name if applicable)

Bartow, W.VA
Town of Residence

Newenberg, Germany
Birthplace

12/27/1965
Date of Birth

Date of Death

Where Buried

Barbara Brown (Div)
Name of Spouse

Covington, VA
Birthplace

5/7/1960
Date of Birth

Date of Death

Where Buried

7/31/1988
Date of Marriage

Place of Marriage

If married more than once:

Name of Spouse

Birthplace

Date of Birth

Date of Death

Where Buried

Date of Marriage

Place of Marriage

Emerson Brown - Alice -
Parents of Spouse (with Mother's maiden name) 1st Marriage

Subsequent Marriage (if applicable)

Family Details

Schools attended, dates and degrees:

Community, political work, etc.:

Descendant

Descendant

Spouse

Spouse

Basic Employment History:

Clubs, Church Affiliations, etc.:

Descendant

Descendant

Spouse

Spouse

Military Service:

Descendant

Spouse

M62981521
Genealogical Number

Matthew James Lee Cook
Name (including maiden name if applicable)   Town of Residence

Covington, VA   5/2/1988
Birthplace   Date of Birth   Date of Death   Where Buried

Name of Spouse   Birthplace   Date of Birth   Date of Death

Where Buried   Date of Marriage   Place of Marriage

If married more than once:

Name of Spouse   Birthplace   Date of Birth   Date of Death

Where Buried   Date of Marriage   Place of Marriage

Parents of Spouse (with Mother's maiden name) 1st Marriage

Subsequent Marriage (if applicable)

Family Details

Schools attended, dates and degrees: Community, political work, etc.:

Descendant   Descendant

Spouse   Spouse

Basic Employment History: Clubs, Church Affiliations, etc.:

Descendant   Descendant

Spouse   Spouse

Military Service:

Descendant   Spouse

M6298153
Genealogical Number

Judy Fay Cook
Name (including maiden name if applicable)

Rineyville, KY
Town of Residence

Hillsboro, W.VA
Birthplace

8/12/1951
Date of Birth

Date of Death

Where Buried

Ricky Wayne Smallwood
Name of Spouse

Rineyville, KY
Birthplace

12/6/1954
Date of Birth

Date of Death

Where Buried

5/20/1994
Date of Marriage

Place of Marriage

If married more than once:

Kenneth Ammons (Div)
Name of Spouse

Rineyville, KY
Birthplace

10/7/1949
Date of Birth

Date of Death

Where Buried

Date of Marriage

Place of Marriage

Bob Ammons - Dorothy -
Parents of Spouse (with Mother's maiden name) 1st Marriage

Herbert Ivan Smallwood - Pauline Bennett
Subsequent Marriage (if applicable)

Family Details

Schools attended, dates and degrees:

Community, political work, etc.:

Descendant

Descendant

Spouse

Spouse

Basic Employment History:

Clubs, Church Affiliations, etc.:

Descendant

Descendant

Spouse

Spouse

Military Service:

Descendant

Spouse

M62981531
Genealogical Number

Angela Marie Ammons
Name (including maiden name if applicable)

Elizabethtown, KY
Town of Residence

8/27/1969
Birthplace   Date of Birth   Date of Death   Where Buried

- Mullins
Name of Spouse   Birthplace   Date of Birth   Date of Death

Where Buried   Date of Marriage   Place of Marriage

If married more than once:

Name of Spouse   Birthplace   Date of Birth   Date of Death

Where Buried   Date of Marriage   Place of Marriage

Parents of Spouse (with Mother's maiden name) 1st Marriage

Subsequent Marriage (if applicable)

Family Details

Schools attended, dates and degrees:

Community, political work, etc.:

Descendant

Descendant

Spouse

Spouse

Basic Employment History:

Clubs, Church Affiliations, etc.:

Descendant

Descendant

Spouse

Spouse

Military Service:

Descendant

Spouse

M6298154
Genealogical Number

Gladys Kay Cook
Name (including maiden name if applicable)

Lansing, W.VA
Town of Residence

Fort Meade, MD
Birthplace

11/14/1954
Date of Birth

Date of Death

Where Buried

Audie Critchley
Name of Spouse

Birthplace

10/30/1957
Date of Birth

Date of Death

Where Buried

6/30/1997
Date of Marriage

Place of Marriage

If married more than once:

Keith Boehmer (Div.)
Name of Spouse

Detroit, Mich.
Birthplace

4/20/1953
Date of Birth

Date of Death

Where Buried

11/23/1973
Date of Marriage

Place of Marriage

Parents of Spouse (with Mother's maiden name) 1st Marriage

Subsequent Marriage (if applicable)

Family Details

Schools attended, dates and degrees:

Community, political work, etc.:

Descendant

Descendant

Spouse

Spouse

Basic Employment History:

Clubs, Church Affiliations, etc.:

Descendant

Descendant

Spouse

Spouse

Military Service:

Descendant

Spouse

M62981541
Genealogical Number

James Michael Boehmer   Bartow, W.VA
Name (including maiden name if applicable)   Town of Residence

Fort Knox, KY   11/18/1972
Birthplace   Date of Birth   Date of Death   Where Buried

Melinda Mullenax   Durbin, W.VA   12/26/1970
Name of Spouse   Birthplace   Date of Birth   Date of Death

                         1/30/1993
Where Buried   Date of Marriage   Place of Marriage

If married more than once:

Name of Spouse   Birthplace   Date of Birth   Date of Death

Where Buried   Date of Marriage   Place of Marriage

Parents of Spouse (with Mother's maiden name) 1st Marriage

Subsequent Marriage (if applicable)

Family Details

Schools attended, dates and degrees: Community, political work, etc.:

Descendant   Descendant

Spouse   Spouse

Basic Employment History: Clubs, Church Affiliations, etc.:

Descendant   Descendant

Spouse   Spouse

Military Service:

Descendant   Spouse

M629815411
Genealogical Number

Meghan Haley Boehmer
Name (including maiden name if applicable)   Town of Residence

Elkins, W.VA   12/28/1994
Birthplace   Date of Birth   Date of Death   Where Buried

Name of Spouse   Birthplace   Date of Birth   Date of Death

Where Buried   Date of Marriage   Place of Marriage

If married more than once:

Name of Spouse   Birthplace   Date of Birth   Date of Death

Where Buried   Date of Marriage   Place of Marriage

Parents of Spouse (with Mother's maiden name) 1st Marriage

Subsequent Marriage (if applicable)

Family Details

Schools attended, dates and degrees: Community, political work, etc.:

Descendant   Descendant

Spouse   Spouse

Basic Employment History: Clubs, Church Affiliations, etc.:

Descendant   Descendant

Spouse   Spouse

Military Service:

Descendant   Spouse

M62981542
Genealogical Number

Shannon Keith Boehmer
Name (including maiden name if applicable)   Town of Residence

Fr. Knox, KY   6/26/1975
Birthplace   Date of Birth   Date of Death   Where Buried

Name of Spouse   Birthplace   Date of Birth   Date of Death

Where Buried   Date of Marriage   Place of Marriage

If married more than once:

Name of Spouse   Birthplace   Date of Birth   Date of Death

Where Buried   Date of Marriage   Place of Marriage

Parents of Spouse (with Mother's maiden name) 1st Marriage

Subsequent Marriage (if applicable)

Family Details

Schools attended, dates and degrees: Community, political work, etc.:

Descendant   Descendant

Spouse   Spouse

Basic Employment History: Clubs, Church Affiliations, etc.:

Descendant   Descendant

Spouse   Spouse

Military Service:

Descendant   Spouse

M629816
Genealogical Number

James Thomas Moore   Abbs Valley, VA
Name (including maiden name if applicable)   Town of Residence

Camp Creek, W.VA   3/6/1930
Birthplace   Date of Birth   Date of Death   Where Buried

Iris Janette Alsup   Boissevain, VA   9/20/1936
Name of Spouse   Birthplace   Date of Birth   Date of Death

                          5/22/1954
Where Buried   Date of Marriage   Place of Marriage

If married more than once:

Name of Spouse   Birthplace   Date of Birth   Date of Death

Where Buried   Date of Marriage   Place of Marriage

Wilson Alsup - Bertha -
Parents of Spouse (with Mother's maiden name) 1st Marriage

Subsequent Marriage (if applicable)

Family Details

Schools attended, dates and degrees: Community, political work, etc.:

Descendant   Descendant

Spouse   Spouse

Basic Employment History: Clubs, Church Affiliations, etc.:

Descendant   Descendant

Spouse   Spouse

Military Service:

Descendant   Spouse

M6298161
Genealogical Number

James Thomas Moore, Jr.   Abbs Valley, VA
Name (including maiden name if applicable)   Town of Residence

Abbs Valley, VA   3/23/1959
Birthplace   Date of Birth   Date of Death   Where Buried

Cynthia Lynn Powers   Washington, DC   4/23/1959
Name of Spouse   Birthplace   Date of Birth   Date of Death

                                1/5/1981
Where Buried   Date of Marriage   Place of Marriage

If married more than once:

Name of Spouse   Birthplace   Date of Birth   Date of Death

Where Buried   Date of Marriage   Place of Marriage

Arthur Powers - Geraldine -
Parents of Spouse (with Mother's maiden name) 1st Marriage

Subsequent Marriage (if applicable)

Family Details

Schools attended, dates and degrees: Community, political work, etc.:

Descendant   Descendant

Spouse   Spouse

Basic Employment History: Clubs, Church Affiliations, etc.:

Descendant   Descendant

Spouse   Spouse

Military Service:

Descendant   Spouse

M62981611
Genealogical Number

Jessica Dawn Moore   Bluefield, VA
Name (including maiden name if applicable)   Town of Residence

Bluefield, W.VA   12/28/1981
Birthplace   Date of Birth   Date of Death   Where Buried

Justin B. Hall   12/26/1980
Name of Spouse   Birthplace   Date of Birth   Date of Death

                         1/24/2004
Where Buried   Date of Marriage   Place of Marriage

If married more than once:

Name of Spouse   Birthplace   Date of Birth   Date of Death

Where Buried   Date of Marriage   Place of Marriage

Parents of Spouse (with Mother's maiden name) 1st Marriage

Subsequent Marriage (if applicable)

Family Details

Schools attended, dates and degrees: Community, political work, etc.:

Descendant   Descendant

Spouse   Spouse

Basic Employment History: Clubs, Church Affiliations, etc.:

Descendant   Descendant

Spouse   Spouse

Military Service:

Descendant   Spouse

M6298162
Genealogical Number

David Allen Moore   York Springs, PA
Name (including maiden name if applicable)   Town of Residence

Pocahontas, VA   9/13/1962
Birthplace   Date of Birth   Date of Death   Where Buried

Melissa Ann Smith   Gettysburg, PA   10/10/1966
Name of Spouse   Birthplace   Date of Birth   Date of Death

     8/30/1985
Where Buried   Date of Marriage   Place of Marriage

If married more than once:

Name of Spouse   Birthplace   Date of Birth   Date of Death

Where Buried   Date of Marriage   Place of Marriage

Paul Smith - Loretta -
Parents of Spouse (with Mother's maiden name) 1st Marriage

Subsequent Marriage (if applicable)

Family Details

Schools attended, dates and degrees: Community, political work, etc.:

Descendant   Descendant

Spouse   Spouse

Basic Employment History: Clubs, Church Affiliations, etc.:

Descendant   Descendant

Spouse   Spouse

Military Service:

Descendant   Spouse

M62981621
Genealogical Number

David Allen Moore, Jr.
Name (including maiden name if applicable) | Town of Residence

Dover Air Force Base, DE   9/12/1986
Birthplace   Date of Birth   Date of Death   Where Buried

Name of Spouse   Birthplace   Date of Birth   Date of Death

Where Buried   Date of Marriage   Place of Marriage

If married more than once:

Name of Spouse   Birthplace   Date of Birth   Date of Death

Where Buried   Date of Marriage   Place of Marriage

Parents of Spouse (with Mother's maiden name) 1st Marriage

Subsequent Marriage (if applicable)

Family Details

Schools attended, dates and degrees: Community, political work, etc.:

Descendant   Descendant

Spouse   Spouse

Basic Employment History: Clubs, Church Affiliations, etc.:

Descendant   Descendant

Spouse   Spouse

Military Service:

Descendant   Spouse

M62981622
Genealogical Number

Amanda Nicole Moore
Name (including maiden name if applicable)   Town of Residence

Dover Air Force Base, DE   5/12/1988
Birthplace   Date of Birth   Date of Death   Where Buried

Name of Spouse   Birthplace   Date of Birth   Date of Death

Where Buried   Date of Marriage   Place of Marriage

If married more than once:

Name of Spouse   Birthplace   Date of Birth   Date of Death

Where Buried   Date of Marriage   Place of Marriage

Parents of Spouse (with Mother's maiden name) 1st Marriage

Subsequent Marriage (if applicable)

Family Details

Schools attended, dates and degrees: Community, political work, etc.:

Descendant   Descendant

Spouse   Spouse

Basic Employment History: Clubs, Church Affiliations, etc.:

Descendant   Descendant

Spouse   Spouse

Military Service:

Descendant   Spouse

M6298163
Genealogical Number

Tina Sue Moore   Waverly, Fla.
Name (including maiden name if applicable)   Town of Residence

West Palm Beach, Fla.   4/5/1968
Birthplace   Date of Birth   Date of Death   Where Buried

Jerome Krug
Name of Spouse   Birthplace   Date of Birth   Date of Death

                               8/30/1997
Where Buried   Date of Marriage   Place of Marriage

If married more than once:

Name of Spouse   Birthplace   Date of Birth   Date of Death

Where Buried   Date of Marriage   Place of Marriage

Parents of Spouse (with Mother's maiden name) 1st Marriage

Subsequent Marriage (if applicable)

Family Details

Schools attended, dates and degrees: Community, political work, etc.:

Descendant   Descendant

Spouse   Spouse

Basic Employment History: Clubs, Church Affiliations, etc.:

Descendant   Descendant

Spouse   Spouse

Military Service:

Descendant   Spouse

M629817
Genealogical Number

Hubert L. Moore
Name (including maiden name if applicable)

Town of Residence

Birthplace

12/26/1932
Date of Birth

Date of Death

Where Buried

Name of Spouse

Birthplace

Date of Birth

Date of Death

Where Buried

Date of Marriage

Place of Marriage

If married more than once:

Name of Spouse

Birthplace

Date of Birth

Date of Death

Where Buried

Date of Marriage

Place of Marriage

Parents of Spouse (with Mother's maiden name) 1st Marriage

Subsequent Marriage (if applicable)

Family Details

Schools attended, dates and degrees:

Community, political work, etc.:

Descendant

Descendant

Spouse

Spouse

Basic Employment History:

Clubs, Church Affiliations, etc.:

Descendant

Descendant

Spouse

Spouse

Military Service:

Descendant

Spouse

M629818
Genealogical Number

Laura Lydia Moore
Name (including maiden name if applicable)

Hillsboro, W.VA
Town of Residence

Slabfork, W.VA
Birthplace

8/20/1935
Date of Birth

Date of Death

Where Buried

(3) Robert Putze
Name of Spouse

Richmond, VA
Birthplace

3/1/1933
Date of Birth

Date of Death

Where Buried

1976
Date of Marriage

Place of Marriage

If married more than once:
(1) John Walls
(2) Woodrow Johnson
Name of Spouse

Sayer, PA
Beckley, W.VA
Birthplace

4/12/1930
4/7/1934
Date of Birth

2001
9/12/1974
Date of Death

(2) Seebert, W.VA
Where Buried

(1) 11/5/1955
(2) 1970
Date of Marriage

Place of Marriage

Parents of Spouse (with Mother's maiden name) 1st Marriage

Subsequent Marriage (if applicable)

Family Details

Schools attended, dates and degrees:

Community, political work, etc.:

Descendant

Descendant

Spouse

Spouse

Basic Employment History:

Clubs, Church Affiliations, etc.:

Descendant

Descendant

Spouse

Spouse

Military Service:

Descendant

Spouse

M6298181
Genealogical Number

John Walls, Jr.   Smithfield, N.C.
Name (including maiden name if applicable)   Town of Residence

Bluefield, W.VA   9/6/1956
Birthplace   Date of Birth   Date of Death   Where Buried

Name of Spouse   Birthplace   Date of Birth   Date of Death

Where Buried   Date of Marriage   Place of Marriage

If married more than once:

Name of Spouse   Birthplace   Date of Birth   Date of Death

Where Buried   Date of Marriage   Place of Marriage

Parents of Spouse (with Mother's maiden name) 1st Marriage

Subsequent Marriage (if applicable)

Family Details

Schools attended, dates and degrees: Community, political work, etc.:

Descendant   Descendant

Spouse   Spouse

Basic Employment History: Clubs, Church Affiliations, etc.:

Descendant   Descendant

Spouse   Spouse

Military Service:

Descendant   Spouse

M6298182
Genealogical Number

Robert D. Walls
Name (including maiden name if applicable)

Aiken, SC
Town of Residence

Munich, Germany
Birthplace

9/1/1958
Date of Birth

Date of Death

Where Buried

Marilyn Ann Armstrong
Name of Spouse

Marlington, W.VA
Birthplace

6/18/1954
Date of Birth

12/19/1993
Date of Death

Buckeye, W.VA
Where Buried

11/27/1980
Date of Marriage

Place of Marriage

If married more than once:

Name of Spouse

Birthplace

Date of Birth

Date of Death

Where Buried

Date of Marriage

Place of Marriage

Parents of Spouse (with Mother's maiden name) 1st Marriage

Subsequent Marriage (if applicable)

Family Details

Schools attended, dates and degrees:

Community, political work, etc.:

Descendant

Descendant

Spouse

Spouse

Basic Employment History:

Clubs, Church Affiliations, etc.:

Descendant

Descendant

Spouse

Spouse

Military Service:

Descendant

Spouse

M62981821
Genealogical Number

Laura Sue Walls
Name (including maiden name if applicable)   Town of Residence

Mobile, Ala.   2/19/1984   2/22/1984   Lucedale, Miss.
Birthplace   Date of Birth   Date of Death   Where Buried

Name of Spouse   Birthplace   Date of Birth   Date of Death

Where Buried   Date of Marriage   Place of Marriage

If married more than once:

Name of Spouse   Birthplace   Date of Birth   Date of Death

Where Buried   Date of Marriage   Place of Marriage

Parents of Spouse (with Mother's maiden name) 1st Marriage

Subsequent Marriage (if applicable)

Family Details

Schools attended, dates and degrees: Community, political work, etc.:

Descendant   Descendant

Spouse   Spouse

Basic Employment History: Clubs, Church Affiliations, etc.:

Descendant   Descendant

Spouse   Spouse

Military Service:

Descendant   Spouse

M6298183
Genealogical Number

James Joseph Walls
Name (including maiden name if applicable)

Daytona Beach, Fla.
Town of Residence

Fort Sill, Okla.
Birthplace

3/22/1960
Date of Birth

Date of Death

Where Buried

Name of Spouse

Birthplace

Date of Birth

Date of Death

Where Buried

Date of Marriage

Place of Marriage

If married more than once:

Name of Spouse

Birthplace

Date of Birth

Date of Death

Where Buried

Date of Marriage

Place of Marriage

Parents of Spouse (with Mother's maiden name) 1st Marriage

Subsequent Marriage (if applicable)

Family Details

Schools attended, dates and degrees:

Community, political work, etc.:

Descendant

Descendant

Spouse

Spouse

Basic Employment History:

Clubs, Church Affiliations, etc.:

Descendant

Descendant

Spouse

Spouse

Military Service:

Descendant

Spouse

M6298184
Genealogical Number

Linda Walls   St. Amant, La.
Name (including maiden name if applicable)   Town of Residence

Ft. Knox, KY   10/10/1962
Birthplace   Date of Birth   Date of Death   Where Buried

-    Billingsley
Name of Spouse   Birthplace   Date of Birth   Date of Death

Where Buried   Date of Marriage   Place of Marriage

If married more than once:

Name of Spouse   Birthplace   Date of Birth   Date of Death

Where Buried   Date of Marriage   Place of Marriage

Parents of Spouse (with Mother's maiden name) 1st Marriage

Subsequent Marriage (if applicable)

Family Details

Schools attended, dates and degrees: Community, political work, etc.:

Descendant   Descendant

Spouse   Spouse

Basic Employment History: Clubs, Church Affiliations, etc.:

Descendant   Descendant

Spouse   Spouse

Military Service:

Descendant   Spouse

M6298185
Genealogical Number

Diana Walls
Name (including maiden name if applicable)   Town of Residence

Ft. Knox, KY   8/7/1964
Birthplace   Date of Birth   Date of Death   Where Buried

- Tate
Name of Spouse   Birthplace   Date of Birth   Date of Death

Where Buried   Date of Marriage   Place of Marriage

If married more than once:

Name of Spouse   Birthplace   Date of Birth   Date of Death

Where Buried   Date of Marriage   Place of Marriage

Parents of Spouse (with Mother's maiden name) 1st Marriage

Subsequent Marriage (if applicable)

Family Details

Schools attended, dates and degrees: Community, political work, etc.:

Descendant   Descendant

Spouse   Spouse

Basic Employment History: Clubs, Church Affiliations, etc.:

Descendant   Descendant

Spouse   Spouse

Military Service:

Descendant   Spouse

M6298186
Genealogical Number

Andrew Walls   Roanoke, VA
Name (including maiden name if applicable)   Town of Residence

Veczena, Italy   8/11/1966
Birthplace   Date of Birth   Date of Death   Where Buried

Name of Spouse   Birthplace   Date of Birth   Date of Death

Where Buried   Date of Marriage   Place of Marriage

If married more than once:

Name of Spouse   Birthplace   Date of Birth   Date of Death

Where Buried   Date of Marriage   Place of Marriage

Parents of Spouse (with Mother's maiden name) 1st Marriage

Subsequent Marriage (if applicable)

Family Details

Schools attended, dates and degrees: Community, political work, etc.:

Descendant   Descendant

Spouse   Spouse

Basic Employment History: Clubs, Church Affiliations, etc.:

Descendant   Descendant

Spouse   Spouse

Military Service:

Descendant   Spouse

M6298187
Genealogical Number

Woodrow Franklin Johnson, Jr.   North Tazewell, VA
Name (including maiden name if applicable)   Town of Residence

Marlington, W.VA   4/4/1970
Birthplace   Date of Birth   Date of Death   Where Buried

Carolynn Trent   Ispwich, England   11/5/1963
Name of Spouse   Birthplace   Date of Birth   Date of Death

                             5/21/1996
Where Buried   Date of Marriage   Place of Marriage

If married more than once:

Name of Spouse   Birthplace   Date of Birth   Date of Death

Where Buried   Date of Marriage   Place of Marriage

Parents of Spouse (with Mother's maiden name) 1st Marriage

Subsequent Marriage (if applicable)

Family Details

Schools attended, dates and degrees: Community, political work, etc.:

Descendant   Descendant

Spouse   Spouse

Basic Employment History: Clubs, Church Affiliations, etc.:

Descendant   Descendant

Spouse   Spouse

Military Service:

Descendant   Spouse

M62981871
Genealogical Number

Abigail Louise Johnson
Name (including maiden name if applicable)

North Tazewell, VA
Town of Residence

Richmond, VA
Birthplace

5/31/1998
Date of Birth

Date of Death

Where Buried

Name of Spouse

Birthplace

Date of Birth

Date of Death

Where Buried

Date of Marriage

Place of Marriage

If married more than once:

Name of Spouse

Birthplace

Date of Birth

Date of Death

Where Buried

Date of Marriage

Place of Marriage

Parents of Spouse (with Mother's maiden name) 1st Marriage

Subsequent Marriage (if applicable)

Family Details

Schools attended, dates and degrees:

Community, political work, etc.:

Descendant

Descendant

Spouse

Spouse

Basic Employment History:

Clubs, Church Affiliations, etc.:

Descendant

Descendant

Spouse

Spouse

Military Service:

Descendant

Spouse

M629819
Genealogical Number

Joseph Edward Moore
Name (including maiden name if applicable)

Brandywine, MD
Town of Residence

6/17/1944
Birthplace   Date of Birth

Date of Death   Where Buried

Sandra Jean Dove
Name of Spouse   Birthplace

3/5/1950
Date of Birth   Date of Death

2/15/1966
Where Buried   Date of Marriage   Place of Marriage

If married more than once:

Name of Spouse   Birthplace   Date of Birth   Date of Death

Where Buried   Date of Marriage   Place of Marriage

Parents of Spouse (with Mother's maiden name) 1st Marriage

Subsequent Marriage (if applicable)

Family Details

Schools attended, dates and degrees:

Community, political work, etc.:

Descendant

Descendant

Spouse

Spouse

Basic Employment History:

Clubs, Church Affiliations, etc.:

Descendant

Descendant

Spouse

Spouse

Military Service:

Descendant

Spouse

M6298191
Genealogical Number

Victoria Lee Moore
Name (including maiden name if applicable)

Brandywine, MD
Town of Residence

Birthplace

9/12/1966
Date of Birth

Date of Death

Where Buried

James David Chedester
Name of Spouse

Birthplace

3/3/1968
Date of Birth

Date of Death

Where Buried

5/4/2002
Date of Marriage

Place of Marriage

If married more than once:

Dale Lee Buckler (Div)
Name of Spouse

Birthplace

6/19/1967
Date of Birth

Date of Death

Where Buried

12/17/1985
Date of Marriage

Place of Marriage

Parents of Spouse (with Mother's maiden name) 1st Marriage

Subsequent Marriage (if applicable)

Family Details

Schools attended, dates and degrees:

Community, political work, etc.:

Descendant

Descendant

Spouse

Spouse

Basic Employment History:

Clubs, Church Affiliations, etc.:

Descendant

Descendant

Spouse

Spouse

Military Service:

Descendant

Spouse

M62981911
Genealogical Number

Candice Lee Buckler   Brandywine, MD
Name (including maiden name if applicable)   Town of Residence

                                7/6/1986
Birthplace   Date of Birth   Date of Death   Where Buried

Name of Spouse   Birthplace   Date of Birth   Date of Death

Where Buried   Date of Marriage   Place of Marriage

If married more than once:

Name of Spouse   Birthplace   Date of Birth   Date of Death

Where Buried   Date of Marriage   Place of Marriage

Parents of Spouse (with Mother's maiden name) 1st Marriage

Subsequent Marriage (if applicable)

Family Details

Schools attended, dates and degrees: Community, political work, etc.:

Descendant   Descendant

Spouse   Spouse

Basic Employment History: Clubs, Church Affiliations, etc.:

Descendant   Descendant

Spouse   Spouse

Military Service:

Descendant   Spouse

M62981912
Genealogical Number

Dale Lee Buckler, Jr.
Name (including maiden name if applicable)   Town of Residence

_____   9/9/1991
Birthplace   Date of Birth   Date of Death   Where Buried

_____
Name of Spouse   Birthplace   Date of Birth   Date of Death

_____
Where Buried   Date of Marriage   Place of Marriage

If married more than once:

_____
Name of Spouse   Birthplace   Date of Birth   Date of Death

_____
Where Buried   Date of Marriage   Place of Marriage

_____
Parents of Spouse (with Mother's maiden name) 1st Marriage

_____
Subsequent Marriage (if applicable)

Family Details

Schools attended, dates and degrees: Community, political work, etc.:

_____   _____
Descendant   Descendant

_____   _____
Spouse   Spouse

Basic Employment History: Clubs, Church Affiliations, etc.:

_____   _____
Descendant   Descendant

_____   _____
Spouse   Spouse

Military Service:

_____   _____
Descendant   Spouse

M6298192
Genealogical Number

Angela Jo Moore
Name (including maiden name if applicable)

Town of Residence

9/4/1970
Birthplace   Date of Birth   Date of Death   Where Buried

John Charles Smith
Name of Spouse   Birthplace

1/20/1973
Date of Birth   Date of Death

9/22/2001
Where Buried   Date of Marriage   Place of Marriage

If married more than once:

Name of Spouse   Birthplace   Date of Birth   Date of Death

Where Buried   Date of Marriage   Place of Marriage

Parents of Spouse (with Mother's maiden name) 1st Marriage

Subsequent Marriage (if applicable)

Family Details

Schools attended, dates and degrees: Community, political work, etc.:

Descendant   Descendant

Spouse   Spouse

Basic Employment History: Clubs, Church Affiliations, etc.:

Descendant   Descendant

Spouse   Spouse

Military Service:

Descendant   Spouse

M6298193
Genealogical Number

Joseph Edward Moore, Jr.
Name (including maiden name if applicable)   Town of Residence

                                10/25/1973
Birthplace   Date of Birth   Date of Death   Where Buried

Christine Marie Antionette Gentile   10/29/1973
Name of Spouse   Birthplace   Date of Birth   Date of Death

                                6/19/1998
Where Buried   Date of Marriage   Place of Marriage

If married more than once:

Name of Spouse   Birthplace   Date of Birth   Date of Death

Where Buried   Date of Marriage   Place of Marriage

Parents of Spouse (with Mother's maiden name) 1st Marriage

Subsequent Marriage (if applicable)

Family Details

Schools attended, dates and degrees: Community, political work, etc.:

Descendant   Descendant

Spouse   Spouse

Basic Employment History: Clubs, Church Affiliations, etc.:

Descendant   Descendant

Spouse   Spouse

Military Service:

Descendant   Spouse

M629821
Genealogical Number

Dewey E. Moore
Name (including maiden name if applicable)

Town of Residence

Boissevain, VA   6/2/1920   1938
Birthplace   Date of Birth   Date of Death   Where Buried

Name of Spouse   Birthplace   Date of Birth   Date of Death

Where Buried   Date of Marriage   Place of Marriage

If married more than once:

Name of Spouse   Birthplace   Date of Birth   Date of Death

Where Buried   Date of Marriage   Place of Marriage

Parents of Spouse (with Mother's maiden name) 1st Marriage

Subsequent Marriage (if applicable)

Family Details

Schools attended, dates and degrees: Community, political work, etc.:

Descendant   Descendant

Spouse   Spouse

Basic Employment History: Clubs, Church Affiliations, etc.:

Descendant   Descendant

Spouse   Spouse

Military Service:

Descendant   Spouse

M629822
Genealogical Number

Ada Moore   Kathleen, Fla.
Name (including maiden name if applicable)   Town of Residence

Boissevain, VA   8/3/1922
Birthplace   Date of Birth   Date of Death   Where Buried

Charles D. Salyers   Castlewood, VA   9/8/1923   7/8/1989
Name of Spouse   Birthplace   Date of Birth   Date of Death

                                  1945
Where Buried   Date of Marriage   Place of Marriage

If married more than once:

Name of Spouse   Birthplace   Date of Birth   Date of Death

Where Buried   Date of Marriage   Place of Marriage

Parents of Spouse (with Mother's maiden name) 1st Marriage

Subsequent Marriage (if applicable)

Family Details

Schools attended, dates and degrees: Community, political work, etc.:

Descendant   Descendant

Spouse   Spouse

Basic Employment History: Clubs, Church Affiliations, etc.:

Descendant   Descendant

Spouse   Spouse

Military Service:

Descendant   Spouse

M6298221
Genealogical Number

Charles D. Salyers, Jr.
Name (including maiden name if applicable)

Town of Residence

Boissevain, VA
Birthplace

12/25/1945
Date of Birth

7/31/1982
Date of Death

Claypool Hill, VA
Greenhills Mem. Cem.
Where Buried

Mary Jane Bentley
Name of Spouse

Birthplace

1945
Date of Birth

Date of Death

Where Buried

1963
Date of Marriage

Place of Marriage

If married more than once:

Name of Spouse

Birthplace

Date of Birth

Date of Death

Where Buried

Date of Marriage

Place of Marriage

Parents of Spouse (with Mother's maiden name) 1st Marriage

Subsequent Marriage (if applicable)

Family Details

Schools attended, dates and degrees:

Community, political work, etc.:

Descendant

Descendant

Spouse

Spouse

Basic Employment History:

Clubs, Church Affiliations, etc.:

Descendant

Descendant

Spouse

Spouse

Military Service:

Descendant

Spouse

M62982211
Genealogical Number

Charles D. Salyers, III
Name (including maiden name if applicable)   Town of Residence

Birthplace   Date of Birth   Date of Death   Where Buried

Name of Spouse   Birthplace   Date of Birth   Date of Death

Where Buried   Date of Marriage   Place of Marriage

If married more than once:

Name of Spouse   Birthplace   Date of Birth   Date of Death

Where Buried   Date of Marriage   Place of Marriage

Parents of Spouse (with Mother's maiden name) 1st Marriage

Subsequent Marriage (if applicable)

Family Details

Schools attended, dates and degrees: Community, political work, etc.:

Descendant   Descendant

Spouse   Spouse

Basic Employment History: Clubs, Church Affiliations, etc.:

Descendant   Descendant

Spouse   Spouse

Military Service:

Descendant   Spouse

M62982211
Genealogical Number

Douglas Michael Salyers   Seymour, Tenn.
Name (including maiden name if applicable)   Town of Residence

                          8/31/1968
Birthplace   Date of Birth   Date of Death   Where Buried

Kimberly Tyler
Name of Spouse   Birthplace   Date of Birth   Date of Death

                          8/16/1997
Where Buried   Date of Marriage   Place of Marriage

If married more than once:

Name of Spouse   Birthplace   Date of Birth   Date of Death

Where Buried   Date of Marriage   Place of Marriage

Parents of Spouse (with Mother's maiden name) 1st Marriage

Subsequent Marriage (if applicable)

Family Details

Schools attended, dates and degrees: Community, political work, etc.:

Descendant   Descendant

Spouse   Spouse

Basic Employment History: Clubs, Church Affiliations, etc.:

Descendant   Descendant

Spouse   Spouse

Military Service:

Descendant   Spouse

M62982212
Genealogical Number

Karen Salyers   Rural Retreat, VA
Name (including maiden name if applicable)   Town of Residence

                              10/2/1971
Birthplace   Date of Birth   Date of Death   Where Buried

Darrell Camper (Div)   12/8/1957
Name of Spouse   Birthplace   Date of Birth   Date of Death

                              6/13/1992
Where Buried   Date of Marriage   Place of Marriage

If married more than once:

Name of Spouse   Birthplace   Date of Birth   Date of Death

Where Buried   Date of Marriage   Place of Marriage

Parents of Spouse (with Mother's maiden name) 1st Marriage

Subsequent Marriage (if applicable)

Family Details

Schools attended, dates and degrees: Community, political work, etc.:

Descendant   Descendant

Spouse   Spouse

Basic Employment History: Clubs, Church Affiliations, etc.:

Descendant   Descendant

Spouse   Spouse

Military Service:

Descendant   Spouse

M629823
Genealogical Number

Johnston Henry Moore   Bluefield, VA
Name (including maiden name if applicable)   Town of Residence

Tazewell County, VA   3/29/1924
Birthplace   Date of Birth   Date of Death   Where Buried

Geneva Stanley   McDowell County, W.VA   6/23/1929
Name of Spouse   Birthplace   Date of Birth   Date of Death

Where Buried   Date of Marriage   Place of Marriage

If married more than once:

Name of Spouse   Birthplace   Date of Birth   Date of Death

Where Buried   Date of Marriage   Place of Marriage

Parents of Spouse (with Mother's maiden name) 1st Marriage

Subsequent Marriage (if applicable)

Family Details

Schools attended, dates and degrees: Community, political work, etc.:

Descendant   Descendant

Spouse   Spouse

Basic Employment History: Clubs, Church Affiliations, etc.:

Descendant   Descendant

Spouse   Spouse

Military Service:

Descendant   Spouse

M6298231
Genealogical Number

Carolyn Moore
Name (including maiden name if applicable)

Boissevain, VA
Town of Residence

Birthplace

4/13/1946
Date of Birth

Date of Death

Where Buried

\- Dillon
Name of Spouse

Birthplace

Date of Birth

Date of Death

Where Buried

Date of Marriage

Place of Marriage

If married more than once:

Name of Spouse

Birthplace

Date of Birth

Date of Death

Where Buried

Date of Marriage

Place of Marriage

Parents of Spouse (with Mother's maiden name) 1st Marriage

Subsequent Marriage (if applicable)

Family Details

Schools attended, dates and degrees:

Community, political work, etc.:

Descendant

Descendant

Spouse

Spouse

Basic Employment History:

Clubs, Church Affiliations, etc.:

Descendant

Descendant

Spouse

Spouse

Military Service:

Descendant

Spouse

M6298232
Genealogical Number

Barbara Jean Moore
Name (including maiden name if applicable)

Princeton, W.VA
Town of Residence

Tazewell County, VA
Birthplace

12/31/1949
Date of Birth

Date of Death

Where Buried

James Patrick Ray
Name of Spouse

Mercer County, W.VA
Birthplace

8/27/1937
Date of Birth

Date of Death

Where Buried

Date of Marriage

Place of Marriage

If married more than once:

Name of Spouse

Birthplace

Date of Birth

Date of Death

Where Buried

Date of Marriage

Place of Marriage

Parents of Spouse (with Mother's maiden name) 1st Marriage

Subsequent Marriage (if applicable)

Family Details

Schools attended, dates and degrees:

Community, political work, etc.:

Descendant

Descendant

Spouse

Spouse

Basic Employment History:

Clubs, Church Affiliations, etc.:

Descendant

Descendant

Spouse

Spouse

Military Service:

Descendant

Spouse

M6298233
Genealogical Number

Audrey Moore
Name (including maiden name if applicable)

Bluefield, VA
Town of Residence

3/9/1951

| Birthplace | Date of Birth | Date of Death | Where Buried |

- Howell

| Name of Spouse | Birthplace | Date of Birth | Date of Death |

| Where Buried | Date of Marriage | Place of Marriage |

If married more than once:

| Name of Spouse | Birthplace | Date of Birth | Date of Death |

| Where Buried | Date of Marriage | Place of Marriage |

Parents of Spouse (with Mother's maiden name) 1st Marriage

Subsequent Marriage (if applicable)

Family Details

Schools attended, dates and degrees:

Community, political work, etc.:

Descendant

Descendant

Spouse

Spouse

Basic Employment History:

Clubs, Church Affiliations, etc.:

Descendant

Descendant

Spouse

Spouse

Military Service:

Descendant

Spouse

M6298234
Genealogical Number

Doris Jane Moore
Name (including maiden name if applicable)

Bluefield, VA
Town of Residence

6/19/1956

| Birthplace | Date of Birth | Date of Death | Where Buried |

- Clark

| Name of Spouse | Birthplace | Date of Birth | Date of Death |

| Where Buried | Date of Marriage | Place of Marriage |

If married more than once:

| Name of Spouse | Birthplace | Date of Birth | Date of Death |

| Where Buried | Date of Marriage | Place of Marriage |

Parents of Spouse (with Mother's maiden name) 1st Marriage

Subsequent Marriage (if applicable)

Family Details

Schools attended, dates and degrees:

Community, political work, etc.:

Descendant

Descendant

Spouse

Spouse

Basic Employment History:

Clubs, Church Affiliations, etc.:

Descendant

Descendant

Spouse

Spouse

Military Service:

Descendant

Spouse

M62982341
Genealogical Number

Christopher Allen Clark
Name (including maiden name if applicable)

Town of Residence

Birthplace

Date of Birth

Date of Death

Where Buried

Name of Spouse

Birthplace

Date of Birth

Date of Death

Where Buried

Date of Marriage

Place of Marriage

If married more than once:

Name of Spouse

Birthplace

Date of Birth

Date of Death

Where Buried

Date of Marriage

Place of Marriage

Parents of Spouse (with Mother's maiden name) 1st Marriage

Subsequent Marriage (if applicable)

Family Details

Schools attended, dates and degrees:

Community, political work, etc.:

Descendant

Descendant

Spouse

Spouse

Basic Employment History:

Clubs, Church Affiliations, etc.:

Descendant

Descendant

Spouse

Spouse

Military Service:

Descendant

Spouse

M629824
Genealogical Number

Harry Elwood Moore
Name (including maiden name if applicable)

Bluefield, VA
Town of Residence

Boissevain, VA
Birthplace

4/30/1926
Date of Birth

Date of Death

Where Buried

Eva L. Smith
Name of Spouse

Big Vein, VA
Birthplace

6/27/1931
Date of Birth

Date of Death

Where Buried

Date of Marriage

Place of Marriage

If married more than once:

Name of Spouse

Birthplace

Date of Birth

Date of Death

Where Buried

Date of Marriage

Place of Marriage

Parents of Spouse (with Mother's maiden name) 1st Marriage

Subsequent Marriage (if applicable)

Family Details

Schools attended, dates and degrees:

Community, political work, etc.:

Descendant

Descendant

Spouse

Spouse

Basic Employment History:

Clubs, Church Affiliations, etc.:

Descendant

Descendant

Spouse

Spouse

Military Service:

Descendant

Spouse

M6298241
Genealogical Number

Deborah Susan Moore
Name (including maiden name if applicable)

Bluefield, W.VA
Town of Residence

Bluefield, W.VA
Birthplace

12/21/1951
Date of Birth

Date of Death

Where Buried

Earl G. Kitts
Name of Spouse

Birthplace

Date of Birth

Date of Death

Where Buried

2/19/1971
Date of Marriage

Place of Marriage

If married more than once:

Name of Spouse

Birthplace

Date of Birth

Date of Death

Where Buried

Date of Marriage

Place of Marriage

Parents of Spouse (with Mother's maiden name) 1st Marriage

Subsequent Marriage (if applicable)

Family Details

Schools attended, dates and degrees:

Community, political work, etc.:

Descendant

Descendant

Spouse

Spouse

Basic Employment History:

Clubs, Church Affiliations, etc.:

Descendant

Descendant

Spouse

Spouse

Military Service:

Descendant

Spouse

M62982411
Genealogical Number

Tiffany Elizabeth Kitts
Name (including maiden name if applicable)

Bluefield, W.VA
Town of Residence

Princeton, W.VA
Birthplace

6/29/1972
Date of Birth

Date of Death

Where Buried

Name of Spouse

Birthplace

Date of Birth

Date of Death

Where Buried

Date of Marriage

Place of Marriage

If married more than once:

Name of Spouse

Birthplace

Date of Birth

Date of Death

Where Buried

Date of Marriage

Place of Marriage

Parents of Spouse (with Mother's maiden name) 1st Marriage

Subsequent Marriage (if applicable)

Family Details

Schools attended, dates and degrees:

Community, political work, etc.:

Descendant

Descendant

Spouse

Spouse

Basic Employment History:

Clubs, Church Affiliations, etc.:

Descendant

Descendant

Spouse

Spouse

Military Service:

Descendant

Spouse

M6298242
Genealogical Number

Harry Edward Moore   Bluefield, VA
Name (including maiden name if applicable)   Town of Residence

Bluefield, W.VA   9/21/1953
Birthplace   Date of Birth   Date of Death   Where Buried

Chris C. Bowe
Name of Spouse   Birthplace   Date of Birth   Date of Death

                         11/5/1970
Where Buried   Date of Marriage   Place of Marriage

If married more than once:

Name of Spouse   Birthplace   Date of Birth   Date of Death

Where Buried   Date of Marriage   Place of Marriage

Parents of Spouse (with Mother's maiden name) 1st Marriage

Subsequent Marriage (if applicable)

Family Details

Schools attended, dates and degrees: Community, political work, etc.:

Descendant   Descendant

Spouse   Spouse

Basic Employment History: Clubs, Church Affiliations, etc.:

Descendant   Descendant

Spouse   Spouse

Military Service:

Descendant   Spouse

M62982421
Genealogical Number

Brian Keith Moore
Name (including maiden name if applicable)

Town of Residence

Bluefield, W.VA   5/14/1971   6/7/1993
Birthplace   Date of Birth   Date of Death   Where Buried

Name of Spouse   Birthplace   Date of Birth   Date of Death

Where Buried   Date of Marriage   Place of Marriage

If married more than once:

Name of Spouse   Birthplace   Date of Birth   Date of Death

Where Buried   Date of Marriage   Place of Marriage

Parents of Spouse (with Mother's maiden name) 1st Marriage

Subsequent Marriage (if applicable)

Family Details

Schools attended, dates and degrees: Community, political work, etc.:

Descendant   Descendant

Spouse   Spouse

Basic Employment History: Clubs, Church Affiliations, etc.:

Descendant   Descendant

Spouse   Spouse

Military Service:

Descendant   Spouse

M629825
Genealogical Number

Virginia F. Moore   Charleston, SC
Name (including maiden name if applicable)   Town of Residence

Tazewell, VA   4/1/1928
Birthplace   Date of Birth   Date of Death   Where Buried

George G. Lee   Norfolk, VA
Name of Spouse   Birthplace   Date of Birth   Date of Death

Where Buried   Date of Marriage   Place of Marriage

If married more than once:

Name of Spouse   Birthplace   Date of Birth   Date of Death

Where Buried   Date of Marriage   Place of Marriage

Parents of Spouse (with Mother's maiden name) 1st Marriage

Subsequent Marriage (if applicable)

Family Details

Schools attended, dates and degrees: Community, political work, etc.:

Descendant   Descendant

Spouse   Spouse

Basic Employment History: Clubs, Church Affiliations, etc.:

Descendant   Descendant

Spouse   Spouse

Military Service:

Descendant   Spouse

M62983
Genealogical Number

Edward P. Moore
Name (including maiden name if applicable)   Town of Residence

_____   3/2/1901   _____   _____
Birthplace   Date of Birth   Date of Death   Where Buried

Louise Barnett
Name of Spouse   Birthplace   Date of Birth   Date of Death

_____   _____   _____
Where Buried   Date of Marriage   Place of Marriage

If married more than once:

_____   _____   _____   _____
Name of Spouse   Birthplace   Date of Birth   Date of Death

_____   _____   _____
Where Buried   Date of Marriage   Place of Marriage

Parents of Spouse (with Mother's maiden name) 1st Marriage

Subsequent Marriage (if applicable)

Family Details

Schools attended, dates and degrees: Community, political work, etc.:

_____   _____
Descendant   Descendant

_____   _____
Spouse   Spouse

Basic Employment History: Clubs, Church Affiliations, etc.:

_____   _____
Descendant   Descendant

_____   _____
Spouse   Spouse

Military Service:

_____   _____
Descendant   Spouse

M629831
Genealogical Number

Dory Moore
Name (including maiden name if applicable)   Town of Residence

Birthplace   Date of Birth   Date of Death   Where Buried

Name of Spouse   Birthplace   Date of Birth   Date of Death

Where Buried   Date of Marriage   Place of Marriage

If married more than once:

Name of Spouse   Birthplace   Date of Birth   Date of Death

Where Buried   Date of Marriage   Place of Marriage

Parents of Spouse (with Mother's maiden name) 1st Marriage

Subsequent Marriage (if applicable)

Family Details

Schools attended, dates and degrees: Community, political work, etc.:

Descendant   Descendant

Spouse   Spouse

Basic Employment History: Clubs, Church Affiliations, etc.:

Descendant   Descendant

Spouse   Spouse

Military Service:

Descendant   Spouse

M629832
Genealogical Number

Margaret Moore
Name (including maiden name if applicable)   Town of Residence

Birthplace   Date of Birth   Date of Death   Where Buried

Name of Spouse   Birthplace   Date of Birth   Date of Death

Where Buried   Date of Marriage   Place of Marriage

If married more than once:

Name of Spouse   Birthplace   Date of Birth   Date of Death

Where Buried   Date of Marriage   Place of Marriage

Parents of Spouse (with Mother's maiden name) 1st Marriage

Subsequent Marriage (if applicable)

Family Details

Schools attended, dates and degrees: Community, political work, etc.:

Descendant   Descendant

Spouse   Spouse

Basic Employment History: Clubs, Church Affiliations, etc.:

Descendant   Descendant

Spouse   Spouse

Military Service:

Descendant   Spouse

M629833
Genealogical Number

Bernard Moore
Name (including maiden name if applicable)   Town of Residence

Birthplace   Date of Birth   Date of Death   Where Buried

Name of Spouse   Birthplace   Date of Birth   Date of Death

Where Buried   Date of Marriage   Place of Marriage

If married more than once:

Name of Spouse   Birthplace   Date of Birth   Date of Death

Where Buried   Date of Marriage   Place of Marriage

Parents of Spouse (with Mother's maiden name) 1st Marriage

Subsequent Marriage (if applicable)

Family Details

Schools attended, dates and degrees: Community, political work, etc.:

Descendant   Descendant

Spouse   Spouse

Basic Employment History: Clubs, Church Affiliations, etc.:

Descendant   Descendant

Spouse   Spouse

Military Service:

Descendant   Spouse

M629834
Genealogical Number

Florence Moore
Name (including maiden name if applicable)   Town of Residence

Birthplace   Date of Birth   Date of Death   Where Buried

Name of Spouse   Birthplace   Date of Birth   Date of Death

Where Buried   Date of Marriage   Place of Marriage

If married more than once:

Name of Spouse   Birthplace   Date of Birth   Date of Death

Where Buried   Date of Marriage   Place of Marriage

Parents of Spouse (with Mother's maiden name) 1st Marriage

Subsequent Marriage (if applicable)

Family Details

Schools attended, dates and degrees: Community, political work, etc.:

Descendant   Descendant

Spouse   Spouse

Basic Employment History: Clubs, Church Affiliations, etc.:

Descendant   Descendant

Spouse   Spouse

Military Service:

Descendant   Spouse

M629835
Genealogical Number

Thomas Moore
Name (including maiden name if applicable)   Town of Residence

Birthplace   Date of Birth   Date of Death   Where Buried

Name of Spouse   Birthplace   Date of Birth   Date of Death

Where Buried   Date of Marriage   Place of Marriage

If married more than once:

Name of Spouse   Birthplace   Date of Birth   Date of Death

Where Buried   Date of Marriage   Place of Marriage

Parents of Spouse (with Mother's maiden name) 1st Marriage

Subsequent Marriage (if applicable)

Family Details

Schools attended, dates and degrees: Community, political work, etc.:

Descendant   Descendant

Spouse   Spouse

Basic Employment History: Clubs, Church Affiliations, etc.:

Descendant   Descendant

Spouse   Spouse

Military Service:

Descendant   Spouse

M62984
Genealogical Number

Bessie Moore
Name (including maiden name if applicable)

Town of Residence

Birthplace | 5/1/1902 Date of Birth | Date of Death | Where Buried

Henry Harman
Name of Spouse | Birthplace | 2/18/1900 Date of Birth | Date of Death

Where Buried | 7/26/1919 Date of Marriage | Place of Marriage

If married more than once:

Name of Spouse | Birthplace | Date of Birth | Date of Death

Where Buried | Date of Marriage | Place of Marriage

Parents of Spouse (with Mother's maiden name) 1st Marriage

Subsequent Marriage (if applicable)

Family Details

Schools attended, dates and degrees:

Community, political work, etc.:

Descendant

Descendant

Spouse

Spouse

Basic Employment History:

Clubs, Church Affiliations, etc.:

Descendant

Descendant

Spouse

Spouse

Military Service:

Descendant

Spouse

M629841
Genealogical Number

Ernest Alvin Harman
Name (including maiden name if applicable)   Town of Residence

                                    6/6/1920
Birthplace   Date of Birth   Date of Death   Where Buried

Name of Spouse   Birthplace   Date of Birth   Date of Death

Where Buried   Date of Marriage   Place of Marriage

If married more than once:

Name of Spouse   Birthplace   Date of Birth   Date of Death

Where Buried   Date of Marriage   Place of Marriage

Parents of Spouse (with Mother's maiden name) 1st Marriage

Subsequent Marriage (if applicable)

Family Details

Schools attended, dates and degrees: Community, political work, etc.:

Descendant   Descendant

Spouse   Spouse

Basic Employment History: Clubs, Church Affiliations, etc.:

Descendant   Descendant

Spouse   Spouse

Military Service:

Descendant   Spouse

M629842
Genealogical Number

Garnett Marie Harman
Name (including maiden name if applicable)   Town of Residence

                              1/30/1922
Birthplace   Date of Birth   Date of Death   Where Buried

Name of Spouse   Birthplace   Date of Birth   Date of Death

Where Buried   Date of Marriage   Place of Marriage

If married more than once:

Name of Spouse   Birthplace   Date of Birth   Date of Death

Where Buried   Date of Marriage   Place of Marriage

Parents of Spouse (with Mother's maiden name) 1st Marriage

Subsequent Marriage (if applicable)

Family Details

Schools attended, dates and degrees: Community, political work, etc.:

Descendant   Descendant

Spouse   Spouse

Basic Employment History: Clubs, Church Affiliations, etc.:

Descendant   Descendant

Spouse   Spouse

Military Service:

Descendant   Spouse

M629843
Genealogical Number

Willie May Harman
Name (including maiden name if applicable)   Town of Residence

                              1/18/1924
Birthplace   Date of Birth   Date of Death   Where Buried

Name of Spouse   Birthplace   Date of Birth   Date of Death

Where Buried   Date of Marriage   Place of Marriage

If married more than once:

Name of Spouse   Birthplace   Date of Birth   Date of Death

Where Buried   Date of Marriage   Place of Marriage

Parents of Spouse (with Mother's maiden name) 1st Marriage

Subsequent Marriage (if applicable)

Family Details

Schools attended, dates and degrees: Community, political work, etc.:

Descendant   Descendant

Spouse   Spouse

Basic Employment History: Clubs, Church Affiliations, etc.:

Descendant   Descendant

Spouse   Spouse

Military Service:

Descendant   Spouse

M629844
Genealogical Number

Walter Edward Harman
Name (including maiden name if applicable)   Town of Residence

_____   1/24/1926   _____   _____
Birthplace   Date of Birth   Date of Death   Where Buried

_____   _____   _____   _____
Name of Spouse   Birthplace   Date of Birth   Date of Death

_____   _____   _____
Where Buried   Date of Marriage   Place of Marriage

If married more than once:

_____   _____   _____   _____
Name of Spouse   Birthplace   Date of Birth   Date of Death

_____   _____   _____
Where Buried   Date of Marriage   Place of Marriage

_____
Parents of Spouse (with Mother's maiden name) 1st Marriage

_____
Subsequent Marriage (if applicable)

Family Details

Schools attended, dates and degrees: Community, political work, etc.:

_____   _____
Descendant   Descendant

_____   _____
Spouse   Spouse

Basic Employment History: Clubs, Church Affiliations, etc.:

_____   _____
Descendant   Descendant

_____   _____
Spouse   Spouse

Military Service:

_____   _____
Descendant   Spouse

M629845
Genealogical Number

Winifred Reese Harman
Name (including maiden name if applicable)   Town of Residence

12/19/1928
Birthplace   Date of Birth   Date of Death   Where Buried

Name of Spouse   Birthplace   Date of Birth   Date of Death

Where Buried   Date of Marriage   Place of Marriage

If married more than once:

Name of Spouse   Birthplace   Date of Birth   Date of Death

Where Buried   Date of Marriage   Place of Marriage

Parents of Spouse (with Mother's maiden name) 1st Marriage

Subsequent Marriage (if applicable)

Family Details

Schools attended, dates and degrees: Community, political work, etc.:

Descendant   Descendant

Spouse   Spouse

Basic Employment History: Clubs, Church Affiliations, etc.:

Descendant   Descendant

Spouse   Spouse

Military Service:

Descendant   Spouse

M62985
Genealogical Number

Grace Moore
Name (including maiden name if applicable)

Town of Residence

8/8/1906
Birthplace   Date of Birth   Date of Death   Where Buried

Harry Melvin Bennett   12/25/1898
Name of Spouse   Birthplace   Date of Birth   Date of Death

5/19/1928
Where Buried   Date of Marriage   Place of Marriage

If married more than once:

Name of Spouse   Birthplace   Date of Birth   Date of Death

Where Buried   Date of Marriage   Place of Marriage

Parents of Spouse (with Mother's maiden name) 1st Marriage

Subsequent Marriage (if applicable)

Family Details

Schools attended, dates and degrees: Community, political work, etc.:

Descendant   Descendant

Spouse   Spouse

Basic Employment History: Clubs, Church Affiliations, etc.:

Descendant   Descendant

Spouse   Spouse

Military Service:

Descendant   Spouse

33.

THE ISAAC QUINN MOORE LINE
PICTURES

Edward Poage Moore
(M6293)   B. 12/19/1854   D. 1/8/1939

Edward Poage Moore Family
(M6293)   B. 12/19/1854   D. 1/8/1939

Margaret E. Moore
(M62932)   B. 1/6/1887   D. 4/30/1976

Family of Margaret Elizabeth Moore Painter
(M62932)   B. 1/6/1887   D. 4/30/1976

Painter Sisters
Ruth Moore (Painter) Brown (M629321) B. 7/21/1911 D.
Mary Rebecca (Painter) Douthat (M629321) B. 11/4/1913 D. 11/9/1998
Ida Louise (Painter) Gearheart (M629323) B. 3/29/1916 D. 3/30/1982

34.

THE JAMES HARVEY MOORE LINE

The James Harvey Moore Line

James Harvey Moore (M641) was the first child of Joseph Moore (M64) who was the younger brother of James Moore, the "Captive" and fourth child of Captain James Moore. He married his first cousin, Jane Shannon Moore (M627) daughter of James Moore, the "Captive" and Nancy Shannon. They had three children, Mary Keziah, Samuel Lycurgus , and Sarah Christine.

I am indebted to Gretchen Miller (M6412142) great-granddaughter of Samuel Lycurgus, for the obituary of her father, Jesse Ward Moore (M641214), an outstanding Professor at Virginia Tech, part of which is reproduced below:

> Jesse Ward Moore, 97, of Blacksburg, passed away Monday, May 19, 2003. He was born in Tazewell County, Va. on May 22, 1905, the son of the late Sam Houston and Mary Grace Whitman Moore. He was also preceded in death by his wife, Mina Ray Munsey Moore. He was educated at Bluefield College, the University of Virginia, and Virginia Polytechnic Institute and was a retired Mathematics Professor from Virginia Tech, having taught there from 1936 to 1971. He was a graduate of VPI Class of 1931 and a member of the "Old Guard." He was a member of Pi Mu Epsilon fraternity and the Fincastle Rifles, Sons of Confederate Veterans. He was a lifelong horseman who was dedicated to the development and enhancement of the American Saddlebred Horse. He is survived by a son, Samuel H. Moore II and daughter, Gretchen M. and son-in-law, Will Miller of Roanoke; grandsons, Stuart H. Moore and wife Louise, of Richmond and B. Hunter Miller of Roanoke, granddaughter, Courtney V. Moore of Baltimore; sister-in-law, Joyce G. Moore of Tazewell; and several nieces and nephews.

I am also indebted to Mrs. Peyton M. Moore, who was married to Peyton (M6412515) for 47 years when he was called home, on July 9, 2001, for the obituary of her husband. He was the Pastor of Lamar Baptist Church of Arlington, Texas and greatly beloved by his congregation.

> Mr. Moore, a native of Meridian, Miss., had served in a variety of ministerial roles before coming to Lamar Baptist Church, including a 15-year term as a Southern Baptist missionary in Vietnam that ended with the American evacuation of Saigon in1975.

His son, Greg Moore of The Woodlands, said condolences have come from all over the world since the news of his father's death.

> Mr. Moore is survived by his wife; two sons, Terry Moore and his wife, Susan, of Grand Prairie, and Greg Moore and his wife, Jill, of The Woodlands; a daughter, Celia Anne Wofford and her husband, Mark, of Martinez, Calif., six grandchildren, Christopher and Heather Moore, Graham and Kaylee Moore and Peyton and Tess Wofford; his brothers Edd Moore and wife, Ouida, of Tennessee and Jim Moore and wife, Jeanette of Mississippi.

Biographical information on other James Harvey Moore descendants is in the bio sheets following.

M641 ***James Harvey Moore - M627 Jane Shannon Moore***
    B. _____   M. 9/11/1832   B. 7/9/1812
    D. 1846   D. 12/12/1900

  M6411 - Mary Keziah Moore - John Elias Hale
     B. 7/8/1833   M. 6/2/1852   B. 10/10/1830
     D. 8/18/1888   D. 8/30/1882

    M64111 - Elias John Hale - Melissa Catherine Bailey
       B. 9/12/1853   M. 1887   B. 2/24/1859
       D. 3/19/1899   D. 1/20/1923

      M641111 - John Hale - Mary Tuggle
         B. _____   M. _____   B. _____
         D. _____   D. _____

        M6411111 - _____ Hale (F) _____ Shumate
           B. _____   M. _____   B. _____
           D. _____   D. _____

  M6412 - Samuel Lycurgus Moore - Martha Margaret Shannon
     B. 3/11/1835   M. 2/8/1860   B. 12/26/1841
     D. _____   D. 9/16/1893

    M64120 – Infant
       B. 2/13/1861
       D. 3/10/1861

    M64120x - Sarah Rebecca Moore
       B. 3/21/1862
       D. 12/11/1881

    M64121 - Samuel Houston Moore - Mary Grace Whitman
       B. 10/31/1864   M. 3/31/1897   B. 8/19/1872
       D. _____   D. _____

*Indicates that a bio is included.

M641211 - Perry Alexander Moore
B. 2/4/1898
D. 8/27/1899

M641212 - Martha Louise Moore
B. 8/25/1900
D. 4/6/1901

M641213 - John Houston Moore - Gladys Marie Myers
B. 8/27/1902   M. 6/21/1936   B. 7/18/1906
D. 11/21/1983   D. 1/31/1988

    M6412131 - Virginia Marie Moore
    B. 6/7/1942
    D. _____

    M6412132 - Marie Louise Moore - James Doherty
    B. 8/4/1943   M. _____   B. 10/15/1941

        M64121321 - James Moore Doherty
        B. 3/14/1982

        M64121322 - John Houston Doherty
        B. 5/26/1984

*M641214 - Jesse Ward Moore - Mina Ray Munsey
B. 5/22/1905   M. 12/02/1944   B. 11/2/1916
D. 5/19/2003   D. 11/13/1979

    *M6412141 - Samuel Houston Moore, II - (1) Norma Owen (Div)
    B. 10/2/1947   (1)M. 1970   B. 1/7/1947
               (2)M. 8/11/2001

                    (2) Dolly Spradlin
                    B. 9/19/1946

*M64121411 - (1) Stuart Hargrove Moore – Louise Adamson
B. 8/21/77   M. 5/4/2002   B. 1/5/1970

M64121412 - Courtney Virginia Moore
B. 12/5/1977

*M6412142 - Gretchen Howard Moore - Clarence Wilfred Miller
B. 10/14/1950   M. _____   B. 6/7/1940

*M64121421 - Brandon Hunter Miller
B. 3/9/1986

M641215 - Samuel Lycurgus Moore, II - Joyce Gullett
B. 5/5/1916   M. 10/1954   B. 5/19/1933
D. 3/15/2002

M6412151 - Samuel Lycurgus Moore, III – Sharon Kay Moore (Div)
B. 8/15/1955   M. 9/25/1976   B. 4/29/1957

M64121511 – Jessica Moore – Clarence Eugene Hoops
B. 8/12/1978   M. 1997   B. _____

M641215111 - Gavin Hoops
B. 8/4/2002

M641216 - Mary Mildred Moore - **M624624** Glenn Baldwin Mullin
B. 8/12/1908   M. 6/12/1936   B. 7/3/1904
D. _____   D. _____

M6246241 - James Oscar Mullin
B. 10/23/1940
D. _____

M641217 - Allie Mae Moore - Robert Elmore Buchanan
    B. 10/29/1910   M. 10/18/1930   B. 4/13/1905
    D. 6/10/1998   D. _____

M64122 - Mary Marie Moore - Charles William McDowell
    B. 10/20/1866   M. 7/28/1886   B. 2/13/1862
    D. _____   D. 6/27/1924

M641221 - Lelia McDowell - Russell Bane Compton
    B. 6/23/1887   M. 12/24/1905   B. 3/10/1879
    D. _____   D. _____

    M6412211 - Mary Frances Muset Compton - Shirley Mitchum
        B. 2/10/1911   M. 1/3/1932   B. 2/11/1911
        D. _____   D. _____

        M64122111 - Arnold Russell Mitchum
            B. 11/5/1932

        M64122112 - Shirley Gretta Mitchum
            B. 3/3/1934

        M64122113 - Ferdie Lowell Mitchum
            B. 8/24/1935

    M6412212 - Bane Gormon Compton
        B. 6/7/1916
        D. _____

M641222 - Infant
    B. 7/28/1890
    D. 7/28/1890

M641223 - Infant
    B. 9/6/1891
    D. 9/6/1891

M641224 - Burt McDowell
B. 7/2/1892
D. 12/14/1928

M641225 -Trula McDowell
B. 1/24/1900
D. _____

M641226 - Vivian Etheldra McDowell
B. 6/8/1904
D. 6/27/1906

M641227 - Dana Moore McDowell
B. 5/28/1907
D. 11/29/1915

M64123 - Ferdinand Dunn Moore
B. 7/19/1868
D. 6/17/1883

M64124 - Robert B. Moore
B. 12/6/1870
D. 10/1/1881

M64125 - James William Moore - Mollie V Coats
B. 11/22/1872   M. 4/30/1896   B. 2/22/1875
D. 1/28/1933   D. _____

M641251 - Ferdinand Lycurgus Moore - (1)Pearl Mullins
B. 2/11/1899   (1)M. 2/21/1920 B. _____
D. 2/19/1938   (2)M. 1924   D. _____

(2)Katie Edna Sullivan
B. _____
D. 7/18/1933

*M6412511 – (2) Ferdinand Lycurgus Moore, Jr. - Lois Burt
   B. 9/22/1925   M. 7/3/1943   B. 10/10/25
   D. 11/21/1994

   M64125111 - Freddie Lois Moore - Jim Raley
      B. 10/31/1944   M. _____   B. _____

         M641251111 - David Raley
            B. 10/16/1970

   *M64125112 - Mary Joleen Moore
      B. 8/7/1946

   *M64125113- Ferdinand Lycurgus Moore, III -Mary Ellen Hodgin
            B. 3/19/1948   M. 2/27/1972   B. 5/14/1954

      *M641251131 - Ferdinand Lycurgus Moore, IV-Rebecca
                                              Lynn Ridout
            B. 10/22/1974   M. 1/18/2003   B. 7/27/1979

      *M641251132 - Emily Graham Moore
            B. 2/27/1979

   *M64125114 - Alphus Burt Moore - Sherri Cade
      B. 10/17/1953   M. 11/12/1983   B. 1/13/1953

      *M641251141 - Matthew Burt Moore
         B. 11/22/1988

*M6412512 – (2) James William Moore - Janet Louise Evans
   B. 9/25/1926   M. 7/4/1952   B. 5/16/1934

M64125121 - Catherine Aline Moore - Virgil Lester Fulcher
   B. 8/26/1953   M. 6/2/1973   B. 8/14/1953

   M641251211 - Stuart Clayton Fulcher
      B. 10/24/1982

*M64125122 - Michael Logan Moore - Regina Lynn Salzman
   B. 2/10/1957   M. 6/11/1983   B. 3/19/1958

   M641251221 - Mindy Lynn Moore
      B. 10/25/1985

   M641251222 - Melissa Louise Moore
      B. 12/26/1989

   M641251223 – Mary Lynn Moore
      B. 5/27/1996

M64125123 - William Henry Moore – Jacki Crow (Div)
   B. 11/26/1959   M. _____   B. _____
   D. 8/2/1991

   *M641251231– Jacqueline Nicole Moore – Darnell Roberts
      B. 1/12/1978   M. 9/30/2000   B. 6/23/1970

      *M6412512311 - Madison Grace Roberts
         B. 3/15/2000

      *M6412512312 – Reese Nicole Roberts
         B. 7/1/2002

*M64125124 -James Nicholas Moore - Kathleen Marie McGovern
   B. 10/21/1961   M. 5/3/1980   B. 5/15/1960

*M641251241-Nicholas Andrew Moore–Amber Rose Rabito
        B. 10/31/1980   M. 4/6/2002   B. 2/21/1981

        M6412512411 – Savanna Rose Moore
        B. 8/28/2002

        M641252412 – Madeline Marie Moore
        B. 8/28/2002

    *M641251242 - Coley Edward Sullivan Moore
        B. 4/25/1988

M6412513 – **(2)** Charles Emmitt Moore
        B. _____   Died as infant
        D. _____

M6412514 – **(2)**Edwin LaVegie Moore - Ouida Kathryn Yates
        B. 12/26/1928   M. _____   B. 7/26/1933

    M64125141 - Pamela Claire Moore - Gregory Wayne Elliott
        B. 12/8/1954   M. _____   B. 2/7/1960

    M64125142 - Edward LaVegie Moore, Jr.- Debra Louise Rose
        B. 8/27/1956   M. _____   B. 10/2/1956

        M641251421 - Laura Michelle Moore
        B. 8/31/1980

        M641251422 - Matthew Edward Moore
        B. 8/20/1984

    *M64125143 - Suzanne Kathleen Moore - James Michael
                                            Rominger
        B. 6/26/1963   M. 5/16/1992   B. 2/18/1963

*M641251431 - Austin Brooks Rominger
B. 6/6/1996

*M641251432 - Britt Michael Rominger
B. 6/11/1998

*M641251433 – McKenna Reese Rominger
B. 2/28/2002

*M641251434 - Riley McLain Rominger
B. 5/26/2003

*M6412515 – (2)Peyton Matterson Moore - Celia Torres
B. 8/10/1930   M. _____   B. 6/11/1929
D. 7/9/2001

*M64125151 - Terry Morelle Moore - Susan Hicks
B. 5/15/1955   M. 7/22/1978   B. 10/25/1954

*M641251511 - Christopher Peyton Moore
B. 3/31/1982

*M641251512 - Heather Michelle Moore
B. 1/24/1985

*M64125152 - Ralph Gregory Moore - Jill DeMello
B. 2/21/1958   M. 9/30/1995   B. 1/31/1965

*M641251521 – Graham Austin Moore
B. 1/17/1998

*M641251522 – Kaylee Lauren Moore
B. 12/1/1999

*M64125153 - Celia Anne Moore - Mark Woffard
B. 8/29/1963   M. 9/4/1993   B. 12/3/1963

M641251531 – Samuel Peyton Woffard
    B. 12/31/1996

M641251532 – Celia Tess Wofford
    B. 9/2/2000

M64126 - Charles Francis Moore - Mae Coats
    B. 5/10/1874   M. 8/2/1903   B. _____
    D. 3/13/1910   D. _____

M641261 - Charles Francis Moore, Jr.
    B. 7/16/1908
    D. _____

M64127 - Olive Virginia Moore
    B. 11/14/1876
    D. 6/4/1894

M64128 - John Walton Moore
    B. 5/3/187S
    D. 4/18/1902

M64129 - Margaret M. Moore
    B. 10/7/1882
    D. 10/7/1882

M6413 - Sarah Christine Moore - Charles Tiffany Gillespie
    B. 6/17/1843   M. 1/16/1867   B. 3/15/1838
    D. 5/21/1902   D. 7/18/1911

M64131 - Tiffany Lee Gillespie – (1) Permelia Daniel
    B. 11/8/1867   (1)M. _____   B. _____
    D. _____   (2)M. _____   D. _____

(2) Molly Vance
B. _____
D. _____

M641311 – (1) Edward Gillespie
B. _____
D. _____

M641312 – (1) Wade Gillespie
B. _____
D. _____

M641313 – (1) John Gillespie
B. _____
D. _____

M641314 – (1) Minnie Gillespie - _____ Fugate
B. _____   M. _____   B. _____
D. _____   D. _____

M641315 – (1) Stella Gillespie
B. _____
D. _____

M64132 - Edwin Browne Gillespie - Mollie Vaughan
B. 7/15/1869   M. 10/7/1893   B. 10/7/1869
D. _____   D. _____

M641321 - Warren L. Gillespie
B. _____
D. _____

M641322 - Raymond D. Gillespie
B. _____
D. _____

M641323 - Blanche Gillespie
        B. _____
        D. _____

M64133 - Harvey Ernest Gillespie - Clara May Osborne
        B. 12/21/1871   M. 4/4/1919   B. 10/29/1871
        D. _____   D. _____

M64134 - Mary Jane Gillespie - _____ Napier
        B. _____   M. _____   B. _____
        D. _____   D. _____

    M641341 - Bernice Napier
            B. _____
            D. _____

M64135 - Nannie Marie Gillespie - Joseph Hopkins
        B. 1/1/1877   M. 4/26/1905   B. 3/2/1877
        D. _____   D. _____

    M641351 - Sally Christine Hopkins - Curtis Holmes
            B. 7/23/1906   M. 12/26/1927   B. 4/15/1907
            D. _____   D. _____

        M6413511 - Donald Dean Holmes
            B. 3/4/1929

        M6413512 - Billie Raymond Holmes
            B. 10/13/1930

    M641352 - Will Chapman Hopkins
        B. 5/18/1909
        D. _____

M641353 - Rosalie Ernestine Hopkins
   B. 3/31/1912
   D. _____

M641354 - Mary Elizabeth St.Clair Hopkins
   B. 6/13/1915
   D. _____

M641355 - Herma Lou Hopkins
   B. 8/19/1921
   D. _____

M641356 - Wanda Charlene Hopkins
   B. 7/10/1923
   D. _____

M64136 - Charles Samuel Gillespie - Emma Lawson Dew
   B. 4/25/1879   M. 9/21/1902   B. 2/27/1881
   D. _____   D. _____

   M641361 - Vivian Gillespie - Augustus Goodman
      B. 1/7/1904   M. 1933   B. _____
      D. _____   D. _____

   M641362 - Carl Gillespie
      B. 1/16/1906
      D. 7/31/1906

   M641363 - Hugh Gillespie - _____
      B. 5/2/1907   M. _____   B. _____
      D. 5/21/1922   D. _____

M64137 - Bettie St.Clair Gillespie - Peter Andrew Loar
   B. 7/19/1881   M. 5/30/1906   B. 7/9/1879
   D. _____   M. _____   D. _____

M64138 - Rees Bowen Gillespie
 B. _____
 D. _____

M64139 - Isaac Fudge Gillespie
 B. _____
 D. _____

35.

THE JAMES HARVEY MOORE LINE
BIOGRAPHICAL SHEETS

M641214
Genealogical Number

Jesse Ward Moore
Name (including maiden name if applicable)   Town of Residence

Tazewell County, VA   5/22/1905   5/19/2003   Tazewell, VA
Birthplace   Date of Birth   Date of Death   Where Buried

Mina Ray Munsey   Floyd, VA   11/2/1916   11/13/1979
Name of Spouse   Birthplace   Date of Birth   Date of Death

Floyd, VA   12/2/1944   Floyd, VA
Where Buried   Date of Marriage   Place of Marriage

If married more than once:

Name of Spouse   Birthplace   Date of Birth   Date of Death

Where Buried   Date of Marriage   Place of Marriage

John Hargrove Munsey - Gretchen Amanda Howard
Parents of Spouse (with Mother's maiden name) 1st Marriage

Subsequent Marriage (if applicable)

Family Details

Schools attended, dates and degrees: Community, political work, etc.:
Bluefield College, 1928/V.P.I., B.S. 1932/
V.P.I. M.S. 1936 Chemical
Engineering
Descendant   Descendant

Radford College/National Business College
Spouse   Spouse

Basic Employment History: Clubs, Church Affiliations, etc.:

Math Professor, V.P.I. 1936-1971   Presbyterian
Descendant   Descendant

Housewife
Spouse   Spouse

Military Service:

Descendant   Spouse

M6412141
Genealogical Number

Samuel Houston Moore, II   Salem, VA
Name (including maiden name if applicable)   Town of Residence

Roanoke, VA   10/2/1947
Birthplace   Date of Birth   Date of Death   Where Buried

Dolly Spradlin   Christiansburg, VA   9/19/1946
Name of Spouse   Birthplace   Date of Birth   Date of Death

                                            8/11/2001   Virginia Beach, VA
Where Buried   Date of Marriage   Place of Marriage

If married more than once:

Norma Owen (Div)   Greensboro, NC   1/7/1947
Name of Spouse   Birthplace   Date of Birth   Date of Death

                                            1970   Greensboro, NC
Where Buried   Date of Marriage   Place of Marriage

Woodrow Wilson Owen, Virginia Young
Parents of Spouse (with Mother's maiden name) 1st Marriage

Raymond Spradlin, Leona Hale
Subsequent Marriage (if applicable)

Family Details

Schools attended, dates and degrees: Community, political work, etc.:
Guildford College, Greensboro NC,
B.S. Business Admin.

Descendant   Descendant

New River and Wytheville Community College - L.P.N.
Spouse   Spouse

Basic Employment History: Clubs, Church Affiliations, etc.:
VA Dept. of Transportation & Land Acquisition   Certified General Real Estate
Specialist   Appraiser
Descendant   Descendant
Hospital Emergency Room and Private
Practice Physician Nurse
Spouse   Spouse

Military Service:

Descendant   Spouse

M64121411
Genealogical Number

Stuart Hargrove Moore   Salem, VA
Name (including maiden name if applicable)   Town of Residence

Highpoint, NC   8/21/1972
Birthplace   Date of Birth   Date of Death   Where Buried

Louise Adamson   Richmond, VA   1/5/1970
Name of Spouse   Birthplace   Date of Birth   Date of Death

                                 5/4/2002   Richmond, Virginia
Where Buried   Date of Marriage   Place of Marriage

If married more than once:

Name of Spouse   Birthplace   Date of Birth   Date of Death

Where Buried   Date of Marriage   Place of Marriage

Vincent Cassel Adamson - Pearl Gurkin Riggin
Parents of Spouse (with Mother's maiden name) 1st Marriage

Subsequent Marriage (if applicable)

Family Details

Schools attended, dates and degrees: Community, political work, etc.:

Cove Spring High - Roanoke, VA - Grad May 1990
Roanoke College - Salem, VA - Grad May 1995
Descendant   Descendant
Washington & Lee -Lexington VA - Grad May 1992
VCU - Richmond VA - Grad May 1994
Mercer University - Macon GA - Grad May 1997
Spouse   Spouse

Basic Employment History: Clubs, Church Affiliations, etc.:
Sales after college - Custom Home Builder   Member - Woodlawn UMC -
1996 - Present   Roanoke, VA
Descendant   Descendant
Attorney - Adamson and Adamson   Member St. Stephens Episcopal
1997 - Present   Richmond, VA
Spouse   Spouse

Military Service:

Descendant   Spouse

M6412142
Genealogical Number

Gretchen Howard Moore
Name (including maiden name if applicable)

Roanoke, VA
Town of Residence

Roanoke, VA
Birthplace

10/14/1950
Date of Birth

Date of Death

Where Buried

Clarence Wilfred Miller
Name of Spouse

Lexington, VA
Birthplace

6/7/1940
Date of Birth

Date of Death

Where Buried

Date of Marriage

Place of Marriage

If married more than once:

Name of Spouse

Birthplace

Date of Birth

Date of Death

Where Buried

Date of Marriage

Place of Marriage

Clarence Little Miller - Mabel Irene Jarvis
Parents of Spouse (with Mother's maiden name) 1st Marriage

Subsequent Marriage (if applicable)

Family Details

Schools attended, dates and degrees:

Community, political work, etc.:

Guilford College, BA 1972/Radford
University, MS 1978
Descendant

Descendant

National Business College 1958-1960
Spouse

Spouse

Basic Employment History:

Clubs, Church Affiliations, etc.:

Private Music Teacher
Descendant
Field Rep.; Equifax Services, 1964-1995
Field Rep - Choicepoint 1995-present
Spouse

Presbyterian
Descendant

Presbyterian
Spouse

Military Service:

Descendant

National Guard Reserves 1962-1968
Spouse

M64121421
Genealogical Number

Brandon Hunter Miller   Roanoke, VA
Name (including maiden name if applicable)   Town of Residence

Roanoke, VA   3/9/1986
Birthplace   Date of Birth   Date of Death   Where Buried

Name of Spouse   Birthplace   Date of Birth   Date of Death

Where Buried   Date of Marriage   Place of Marriage

If married more than once:

Name of Spouse   Birthplace   Date of Birth   Date of Death

Where Buried   Date of Marriage   Place of Marriage

Parents of Spouse (with Mother's maiden name) 1st Marriage

Subsequent Marriage (if applicable)

Family Details

Schools attended, dates and degrees: Community, political work, etc.:

Hidden Valley High School will
graduate 2004
Descendant   Descendant

Spouse   Spouse

Basic Employment History: Clubs, Church Affiliations, etc.:

                                               Presbyterian
Descendant   Descendant

Spouse   Spouse

Military Service:

Descendant   Spouse

M6412511
Genealogical Number

Ferdinand Lycurgus Moore, Jr.
Name (including maiden name if applicable)   Town of Residence

Meridian, MS	9/22/1925	11/21/1994	Meridian, MS
Birthplace	Date of Birth	Date of Death	Where Buried

Lois Burt	Meridian, MS	10/10/1925	
Name of Spouse	Birthplace	Date of Birth	Date of Death

	7/3/1943	Meridian, MS
Where Buried	Date of Marriage	Place of Marriage

If married more than once:

Name of Spouse	Birthplace	Date of Birth	Date of Death

Where Buried	Date of Marriage	Place of Marriage

Alphus E. Burt - Myrtle Mae Lewis
Parents of Spouse (with Mother's maiden name) 1st Marriage

Subsequent Marriage (if applicable)

Family Details

Schools attended, dates and degrees: Community, political work, etc.:

Meridian Public High School
Descendant

Meridian C. College Board
Descendant

Meridian Public High School
Spouse

Spouse

Basic Employment History: Clubs, Church Affiliations, etc.:

Self-employed - Liquor Store
Descendant

East End Methodist
Descendant

Liquor Store
Spouse

Spouse

Military Service:

Army - WWII Sergeant
Descendant

Spouse

M64125112
Genealogical Number

Mary Joleen Moore   Meridian, MS
Name (including maiden name if applicable)   Town of Residence

Meridian, MS   8/7/1946
Birthplace   Date of Birth   Date of Death   Where Buried

Name of Spouse   Birthplace   Date of Birth   Date of Death

Where Buried   Date of Marriage   Place of Marriage

If married more than once:

Name of Spouse   Birthplace   Date of Birth   Date of Death

Where Buried   Date of Marriage   Place of Marriage

Parents of Spouse (with Mother's maiden name) 1st Marriage

Subsequent Marriage (if applicable)

Family Details

Schools attended, dates and degrees: Community, political work, etc.:

Meridan Public Schools -
Univ. of Southern MS
Descendant   Descendant

Spouse   Spouse

Basic Employment History: Clubs, Church Affiliations, etc.:

Lauderdale County School   Methodist
Descendant   Descendant

Spouse   Spouse

Military Service:

Descendant   Spouse

M64125113
Genealogical Number

Ferdie Lycurgus Moore, III
Name (including maiden name if applicable)

Meridian, MS
Town of Residence

Meridian, MS   3/19/1948
Birthplace   Date of Birth

Date of Death   Where Buried

Mary Ellen Hodgin   Meridian, MS   5/14/1954
Name of Spouse   Birthplace   Date of Birth   Date of Death

Where Buried   2/27/1972
Date of Marriage   Lauderdale County, MS
Place of Marriage

If married more than once:

Name of Spouse   Birthplace   Date of Birth   Date of Death

Where Buried   Date of Marriage   Place of Marriage

Arthur Killen Hodgin, Mary Ann Combs
Parents of Spouse (with Mother's maiden name) 1st Marriage

Subsequent Marriage (if applicable)

Family Details

Schools attended, dates and degrees:

Community, political work, etc.:

Miss. State U. B.S. Business
Descendant

Descendant

Spouse

Spouse

Basic Employment History:

Clubs, Church Affiliations, etc.:

Descendant

Descendant

Spouse

Spouse

Military Service:

Descendant

Spouse

M641251131
Genealogical Number

Ferdinand Lycurgus Moore, IV
Name (including maiden name if applicable)

Meridian, MS
Town of Residence

Meridian, MS
Birthplace

10/22/1974
Date of Birth

Date of Death

Where Buried

Rebecca Lynn Ridout
Name of Spouse

Neshoba County, MS
Birthplace

7/27/1979
Date of Birth

Date of Death

Where Buried

1/18/2003
Date of Marriage

Decatur, MS
Place of Marriage

If married more than once:

Name of Spouse

Birthplace

Date of Birth

Date of Death

Where Buried

Date of Marriage

Place of Marriage

Rodney Ridout & Cathy Smith
Parents of Spouse (with Mother's maiden name) 1st Marriage

Subsequent Marriage (if applicable)

Family Details

Schools attended, dates and degrees:

Community, political work, etc.:

Descendant

Descendant

Spouse

Spouse

Basic Employment History:

Clubs, Church Affiliations, etc.:

Descendant

Descendant

Spouse

Spouse

Military Service:

Descendant

Spouse

M641251132
Genealogical Number

Emily Graham Moore
Name (including maiden name if applicable)

Virginia Beach, Virginia
Town of Residence

Meridian, MS
Birthplace

2/27/1979
Date of Birth

Date of Death

Where Buried

Name of Spouse

Birthplace

Date of Birth

Date of Death

Where Buried

Date of Marriage

Place of Marriage

If married more than once:

Name of Spouse

Birthplace

Date of Birth

Date of Death

Where Buried

Date of Marriage

Place of Marriage

Parents of Spouse (with Mother's maiden name) 1st Marriage

Subsequent Marriage (if applicable)

Family Details

Schools attended, dates and degrees:

Community, political work, etc.:

Descendant

Descendant

Spouse

Spouse

Basic Employment History:

Clubs, Church Affiliations, etc.:

Descendant

Descendant

Spouse

Spouse

Military Service:

Descendant

Spouse

M64125114
Genealogical Number

Alphus Burt Moore
Name (including maiden name if applicable)

Laurel, MS
Town of Residence

Meridian, MS
Birthplace

10/17/1953
Date of Birth

Date of Death

Where Buried

Sherri Cade
Name of Spouse

Greenwood, MS
Birthplace

1/13/1953
Date of Birth

Date of Death

Where Buried

11/12/1983
Date of Marriage

Greenwood, Le Flore Co., MS
Place of Marriage

If married more than once:

Name of Spouse

Birthplace

Date of Birth

Date of Death

Where Buried

Date of Marriage

Place of Marriage

Parents of Spouse (with Mother's maiden name) 1st Marriage

Subsequent Marriage (if applicable)

Family Details

Schools attended, dates and degrees:

Meridian H.S., Auburn Univ, B.S. Miss. State Univ
1975, Post grad Univ of Mississippi
Descendant

Community, political work, etc.:

Volunteer United Way 26 years
Bd. Press. 2003 Pine Belt Region
Descendant

Spouse

Spouse

Basic Employment History:

UPS, Sanderson Farms, Inc.
Descendant

Clubs, Church Affiliations, etc.:
Bd. Pres. Christian Food Mission Inc.
Westminster Presbyterian Church,
Elder Laurel Christian School,
Descendant

Spouse

Spouse

Military Service:

Descendant

Spouse

M641251141
Genealogical Number

Matthew Burt Moore
Name (including maiden name if applicable)

Laurel, MS
Town of Residence

Amory, MS   11/22/1988
Birthplace   Date of Birth   Date of Death   Where Buried

Name of Spouse   Birthplace   Date of Birth   Date of Death

Where Buried   Date of Marriage   Place of Marriage

If married more than once:

Name of Spouse   Birthplace   Date of Birth   Date of Death

Where Buried   Date of Marriage   Place of Marriage

Parents of Spouse (with Mother's maiden name) 1st Marriage

Subsequent Marriage (if applicable)

Family Details

Schools attended, dates and degrees: Community, political work, etc.:

Laurel Christian School - 9th Grade
Descendant   Descendant

Spouse   Spouse

Basic Employment History: Clubs, Church Affiliations, etc.:

Descendant   Descendant

Spouse   Spouse

Military Service:

Descendant   Spouse

M6412512
Genealogical Number

James William Moore   Moss Point, Miss.
Name (including maiden name if applicable)   Town of Residence

Meridian, MS   9/25/1926
Birthplace   Date of Birth   Date of Death   Where Buried

Janet Louise Evans   Meridian, MS   5/16/1934
Name of Spouse   Birthplace   Date of Birth   Date of Death

                 7/4/1952   Meridian, MS
Where Buried   Date of Marriage   Place of Marriage

If married more than once:

Name of Spouse   Birthplace   Date of Birth   Date of Death

Where Buried   Date of Marriage   Place of Marriage

George Alexander Evans - Louise Covington
Parents of Spouse (with Mother's maiden name) 1st Marriage

Subsequent Marriage (if applicable)

Family Details

Schools attended, dates and degrees: Community, political work, etc.:

Descendant   Descendant

Spouse   Spouse

Basic Employment History: Clubs, Church Affiliations, etc.:

Descendant   Descendant

Spouse   Spouse

Military Service:

Descendant   Spouse

M64125122
Genealogical Number

Michael Logan Moore
Name (including maiden name if applicable)

Salina, KS
Town of Residence

Meridian, MS
Birthplace

2/10/1957
Date of Birth

Date of Death

Where Buried

Regina Lynn Salzman
Name of Spouse

Salina, KS
Birthplace

3/19/1958
Date of Birth

Date of Death

Where Buried

6/11/1983
Date of Marriage

Salina, KS
Place of Marriage

If married more than once:

Name of Spouse

Birthplace

Date of Birth

Date of Death

Where Buried

Date of Marriage

Place of Marriage

Parents of Spouse (with Mother's maiden name) 1st Marriage

Subsequent Marriage (if applicable)

Family Details

Schools attended, dates and degrees:

Community, political work, etc.:

Descendant

Descendant

Spouse

Spouse

Basic Employment History:

Clubs, Church Affiliations, etc.:

Descendant

Descendant

Spouse

Spouse

Military Service:

Descendant

Spouse

M641251231
Genealogical Number

Jacqueline Nicole Moore
Name (including maiden name if applicable)   Town of Residence

_____   1/12/1978   _____   _____
Birthplace   Date of Birth   Date of Death   Where Buried

Darrell Roberts   _____ 6/23/1970   _____
Name of Spouse   Birthplace   Date of Birth   Date of Death

_____   _____ _____
Where Buried   Date of Marriage Place of Marriage

If married more than once:

_____   _____ _____   _____
Name of Spouse   Birthplace   Date of Birth   Date of Death

_____   _____ _____
Where Buried   Date of Marriage Place of Marriage

_____
Parents of Spouse (with Mother's maiden name) 1st Marriage

_____
Subsequent Marriage (if applicable)

Family Details

Schools attended, dates and degrees: Community, political work, etc.:

_____   _____
Descendant   Descendant

_____   _____
Spouse   Spouse

Basic Employment History: Clubs, Church Affiliations, etc.:

_____   _____
Descendant   Descendant

_____   _____
Spouse   Spouse

Military Service:

_____   _____
Descendant   Spouse

M6412512311
Genealogical Number

Madison Grace Roberts
Name (including maiden name if applicable)   Town of Residence

_____ 3/15/2000   _____ _____
Birthplace   Date of Birth   Date of Death   Where Buried

_____   _____   _____ _____
Name of Spouse   Birthplace   Date of Birth   Date of Death

_____   _____   _____
Where Buried   Date of Marriage Place of Marriage

If married more than once:

_____   _____   _____ _____
Name of Spouse   Birthplace   Date of Birth   Date of Death

_____   _____   _____
Where Buried   Date of Marriage Place of Marriage

Parents of Spouse (with Mother's maiden name) 1st Marriage

Subsequent Marriage (if applicable)

Family Details

Schools attended, dates and degrees: Community, political work, etc.:

_____   _____
Descendant   Descendant

_____   _____
Spouse   Spouse

Basic Employment History: Clubs, Church Affiliations, etc.:

_____   _____
Descendant   Descendant

_____   _____
Spouse   Spouse

Military Service:

_____   _____
Descendant   Spouse

M6412512312
Genealogical Number

Reese Nicole Roberts
Name (including maiden name if applicable)   Town of Residence

                          7/1/2002
Birthplace   Date of Birth   Date of Death   Where Buried

Name of Spouse   Birthplace   Date of Birth   Date of Death

Where Buried   Date of Marriage   Place of Marriage

If married more than once:

Name of Spouse   Birthplace   Date of Birth   Date of Death

Where Buried   Date of Marriage   Place of Marriage

Parents of Spouse (with Mother's maiden name) 1st Marriage

Subsequent Marriage (if applicable)

Family Details

Schools attended, dates and degrees: Community, political work, etc.:

Descendant   Descendant

Spouse   Spouse

Basic Employment History: Clubs, Church Affiliations, etc.:

Descendant   Descendant

Spouse   Spouse

Military Service:

Descendant   Spouse

M64125124
Genealogical Number

James Nicholas Moore
Name (including maiden name if applicable)

Moss Point, Miss.
Town of Residence

Pascagoula, Miss.
Birthplace

10/21/1961
Date of Birth

Date of Death

Where Buried

Kathleen Marie McGovern
Name of Spouse

Birthplace

5/15/1960
Date of Birth

Date of Death

Where Buried

5/3/1980
Date of Marriage

Place of Marriage

If married more than once:

Name of Spouse

Birthplace

Date of Birth

Date of Death

Where Buried

Date of Marriage

Place of Marriage

Parents of Spouse (with Mother's maiden name) 1st Marriage

Subsequent Marriage (if applicable)

Family Details

Schools attended, dates and degrees:

Community, political work, etc.:

Descendant

Descendant

Spouse

Spouse

Basic Employment History:

Clubs, Church Affiliations, etc.:

Descendant

Descendant

Spouse

Spouse

Military Service:

Descendant

Spouse

M641251241
Genealogical Number

Nicholas Andrew Moore   Covington, LA
Name (including maiden name if applicable)   Town of Residence

Pascagoula, MS   10/31/1980
Birthplace   Date of Birth   Date of Death   Where Buried

Amber Rose Rabito   2/21/1981
Name of Spouse   Birthplace   Date of Birth   Date of Death

                        4/6/2002   New Orleans, LA
Where Buried   Date of Marriage   Place of Marriage

If married more than once:

Name of Spouse   Birthplace   Date of Birth   Date of Death

Where Buried   Date of Marriage   Place of Marriage

Parents of Spouse (with Mother's maiden name) 1st Marriage

Subsequent Marriage (if applicable)

Family Details

Schools attended, dates and degrees: Community, political work, etc.:

Descendant   Descendant

Spouse   Spouse

Basic Employment History: Clubs, Church Affiliations, etc.:

Descendant   Descendant

Spouse   Spouse

Military Service:

Descendant   Spouse

M641251242
Genealogical Number

Coley Edward Sullivan Moore
Name (including maiden name if applicable)

Moss Point, MS
Town of Residence

Pascagoula, MS
Birthplace

4/25/1988
Date of Birth

Date of Death

Where Buried

Name of Spouse

Birthplace

Date of Birth

Date of Death

Where Buried

Date of Marriage

Place of Marriage

If married more than once:

Name of Spouse

Birthplace

Date of Birth

Date of Death

Where Buried

Date of Marriage

Place of Marriage

Parents of Spouse (with Mother's maiden name) 1st Marriage

Subsequent Marriage (if applicable)

Family Details

Schools attended, dates and degrees:

Community, political work, etc.:

Descendant

Descendant

Spouse

Spouse

Basic Employment History:

Clubs, Church Affiliations, etc.:

Descendant

Descendant

Spouse

Spouse

Military Service:

Descendant

Spouse

M64125143
Genealogical Number

Suzanne Kathleen Moore   Chattanooga, TN
Name (including maiden name if applicable)   Town of Residence

Titusville, FL   6/26/1963
Birthplace   Date of Birth   Date of Death   Where Buried

James Michael Rominger   Kansas City, Miss.   2/18/1963
Name of Spouse   Birthplace   Date of Birth   Date of Death

                                    5/16/1992   Chattanooga, TN
Where Buried   Date of Marriage   Place of Marriage

If married more than once:

Name of Spouse   Birthplace   Date of Birth   Date of Death

Where Buried   Date of Marriage   Place of Marriage

James Edward Rominger and Gretchen Rita Oberndorfer
Parents of Spouse (with Mother's maiden name) 1st Marriage

Subsequent Marriage (if applicable)

Family Details

Schools attended, dates and degrees: Community, political work, etc.:

Univ. of TN at Chattanooga 1981 -BS Business Adm:
                    1985   Marketing
Descendant   Descendant

Covenant College - BS Business Adm: Management
Spouse   Spouse

Basic Employment History: Clubs, Church Affiliations, etc.:

                                                          Baptist
Descendant   Descendant

W.R. Grace   Baptist
Spouse   Spouse

Military Service:

Descendant   Spouse

M641251431
Genealogical Number

Austin Brooks Rominger   Chattanooga, Tenn.
Name (including maiden name if applicable)   Town of Residence

Chattanooga, TN   6/6/1996
Birthplace   Date of Birth   Date of Death   Where Buried

Name of Spouse   Birthplace   Date of Birth   Date of Death

Where Buried   Date of Marriage   Place of Marriage

If married more than once:

Name of Spouse   Birthplace   Date of Birth   Date of Death

Where Buried   Date of Marriage   Place of Marriage

Parents of Spouse (with Mother's maiden name) 1st Marriage

Subsequent Marriage (if applicable)

Family Details

Schools attended, dates and degrees: Community, political work, etc.:

Descendant   Descendant

Spouse   Spouse

Basic Employment History: Clubs, Church Affiliations, etc.:

Descendant   Descendant

Spouse   Spouse

Military Service:

Descendant   Spouse

M641251432
Genealogical Number

Britt Michael Rominger   Chattanooga, Tenn.
Name (including maiden name if applicable)   Town of Residence

Chattanooga, TN   6/11/1998
Birthplace   Date of Birth   Date of Death   Where Buried

Name of Spouse   Birthplace   Date of Birth   Date of Death

Where Buried   Date of Marriage   Place of Marriage

If married more than once:

Name of Spouse   Birthplace   Date of Birth   Date of Death

Where Buried   Date of Marriage   Place of Marriage

Parents of Spouse (with Mother's maiden name) 1st Marriage

Subsequent Marriage (if applicable)

Family Details

Schools attended, dates and degrees: Community, political work, etc.:

Descendant   Descendant

Spouse   Spouse

Basic Employment History: Clubs, Church Affiliations, etc.:

Descendant   Descendant

Spouse   Spouse

Military Service:

Descendant   Spouse

M641251433
Genealogical Number

McKenna Reese Rominger
Name (including maiden name if applicable)

Chattanooga, TN
Town of Residence

Chattanooga, TN
Birthplace

2/28/2002
Date of Birth

Date of Death

Where Buried

Name of Spouse

Birthplace

Date of Birth

Date of Death

Where Buried

Date of Marriage

Place of Marriage

If married more than once:

Name of Spouse

Birthplace

Date of Birth

Date of Death

Where Buried

Date of Marriage

Place of Marriage

Parents of Spouse (with Mother's maiden name) 1st Marriage

Subsequent Marriage (if applicable)

Family Details

Schools attended, dates and degrees:

Community, political work, etc.:

Descendant

Descendant

Spouse

Spouse

Basic Employment History:

Clubs, Church Affiliations, etc.:

Descendant

Descendant

Spouse

Spouse

Military Service:

Descendant

Spouse

M641251434
Genealogical Number

Riley McLain Rominger   Chattanooga, TN
Name (including maiden name if applicable)   Town of Residence

Chattanooga, TN   5/26/2003
Birthplace   Date of Birth   Date of Death   Where Buried

Name of Spouse   Birthplace   Date of Birth   Date of Death

Where Buried   Date of Marriage   Place of Marriage

If married more than once:

Name of Spouse   Birthplace   Date of Birth   Date of Death

Where Buried   Date of Marriage   Place of Marriage

Parents of Spouse (with Mother's maiden name) 1st Marriage

Subsequent Marriage (if applicable)

Family Details

Schools attended, dates and degrees: Community, political work, etc.:

Descendant   Descendant

Spouse   Spouse

Basic Employment History: Clubs, Church Affiliations, etc.:

Descendant   Descendant

Spouse   Spouse

Military Service:

Descendant   Spouse

M6412515
Genealogical Number

Peyton Matterson Moore
Name (including maiden name if applicable)

Town of Residence

Meridian, Miss.	8/10/1930	7/9/2001	Arlington, TX
Birthplace	Date of Birth	Date of Death	Where Buried

Cela Torres		6/11/1929	
Name of Spouse	Birthplace	Date of Birth	Date of Death

Where Buried	Date of Marriage	Place of Marriage	

If married more than once:

Name of Spouse	Birthplace	Date of Birth	Date of Death

Where Buried	Date of Marriage	Place of Marriage	

Parents of Spouse (with Mother's maiden name) 1st Marriage

Subsequent Marriage (if applicable)

Family Details

Schools attended, dates and degrees:

Community, political work, etc.:

Descendant

Descendant

Spouse

Spouse

Basic Employment History:

Clubs, Church Affiliations, etc.:

Descendant

Descendant

Spouse

Spouse

Military Service:

Descendant

Spouse

M64125151
Genealogical Number

Terry Morelle Moore   Grand Prairie, Texas
Name (including maiden name if applicable)   Town of Residence

Fort Worth, Texas   5/15/1955
Birthplace   Date of Birth   Date of Death   Where Buried

Susan Hicks   10/25/1954
Name of Spouse   Birthplace   Date of Birth   Date of Death

                           7/22/1978
Where Buried   Date of Marriage   Place of Marriage

If married more than once:

Name of Spouse   Birthplace   Date of Birth   Date of Death

Where Buried   Date of Marriage   Place of Marriage

Parents of Spouse (with Mother's maiden name) 1st Marriage

Subsequent Marriage (if applicable)

Family Details

Schools attended, dates and degrees: Community, political work, etc.:

Descendant   Descendant

Spouse   Spouse

Basic Employment History: Clubs, Church Affiliations, etc.:

Descendant   Descendant

Spouse   Spouse

Military Service:

Descendant   Spouse

M641251511
Genealogical Number

Christopher Peyton Moore
Name (including maiden name if applicable)

Grand Prairie, Texas
Town of Residence

3/31/1982
Birthplace   Date of Birth   Date of Death   Where Buried

Name of Spouse   Birthplace   Date of Birth   Date of Death

Where Buried   Date of Marriage   Place of Marriage

If married more than once:

Name of Spouse   Birthplace   Date of Birth   Date of Death

Where Buried   Date of Marriage   Place of Marriage

Parents of Spouse (with Mother's maiden name) 1st Marriage

Subsequent Marriage (if applicable)

Family Details

Schools attended, dates and degrees: Community, political work, etc.:

Descendant   Descendant

Spouse   Spouse

Basic Employment History: Clubs, Church Affiliations, etc.:

Descendant   Descendant

Spouse   Spouse

Military Service:

Descendant   Spouse

M641251512
Genealogical Number

Heather Michelle Moore   Grand Prairie, Texas
Name (including maiden name if applicable)   Town of Residence

                          1/24/1985
Birthplace   Date of Birth   Date of Death   Where Buried

Name of Spouse   Birthplace   Date of Birth   Date of Death

Where Buried   Date of Marriage   Place of Marriage

If married more than once:

Name of Spouse   Birthplace   Date of Birth   Date of Death

Where Buried   Date of Marriage   Place of Marriage

Parents of Spouse (with Mother's maiden name) 1st Marriage

Subsequent Marriage (if applicable)

Family Details

Schools attended, dates and degrees: Community, political work, etc.:

Descendant   Descendant

Spouse   Spouse

Basic Employment History: Clubs, Church Affiliations, etc.:

Descendant   Descendant

Spouse   Spouse

Military Service:

Descendant   Spouse

M64125152
Genealogical Number

Ralph Gregory Moore
Name (including maiden name if applicable)

The Woodlands, TX
Town of Residence

Waco, Texas
Birthplace

2/21/1958
Date of Birth

Date of Death

Where Buried

Jill DeMello
Name of Spouse

Birthplace

Date of Birth

Date of Death

Where Buried

9/30/1995
Date of Marriage

Place of Marriage

If married more than once:

Name of Spouse

Birthplace

Date of Birth

Date of Death

Where Buried

Date of Marriage

Place of Marriage

Parents of Spouse (with Mother's maiden name) 1st Marriage

Subsequent Marriage (if applicable)

Family Details

Schools attended, dates and degrees:

Community, political work, etc.:

Descendant

Descendant

Spouse

Spouse

Basic Employment History:

Clubs, Church Affiliations, etc.:

Descendant

Descendant

Spouse

Spouse

Military Service:

Descendant

Spouse

M641251521
_____
Genealogical Number

Graham Austin Moore
_____   The Woodlands, TX
Name (including maiden name if applicable)   Town of Residence

Newport Beach, CA   1/17/1998
Birthplace   Date of Birth   Date of Death   Where Buried

_____ _____ _____ _____
Name of Spouse   Birthplace   Date of Birth   Date of Death

_____ _____ _____
Where Buried   Date of Marriage   Place of Marriage

If married more than once:

_____ _____ _____ _____
Name of Spouse   Birthplace   Date of Birth   Date of Death

_____ _____ _____
Where Buried   Date of Marriage   Place of Marriage

_____
Parents of Spouse (with Mother's maiden name) 1st Marriage

_____
Subsequent Marriage (if applicable)

Family Details

Schools attended, dates and degrees: Community, political work, etc.:

_____   _____
Descendant   Descendant

_____   _____
Spouse   Spouse

Basic Employment History: Clubs, Church Affiliations, etc.:

_____   _____
Descendant   Descendant

_____   _____
Spouse   Spouse

Military Service:

_____   _____
Descendant   Spouse

M6412515212
Genealogical Number

Kaylee Lauren Moore   The Woodlands, TX
Name (including maiden name if applicable)   Town of Residence

Spring, TX   12/1/1999
Birthplace   Date of Birth   Date of Death   Where Buried

Name of Spouse   Birthplace   Date of Birth   Date of Death

Where Buried   Date of Marriage   Place of Marriage

If married more than once:

Name of Spouse   Birthplace   Date of Birth   Date of Death

Where Buried   Date of Marriage   Place of Marriage

Parents of Spouse (with Mother's maiden name) 1st Marriage

Subsequent Marriage (if applicable)

Family Details

Schools attended, dates and degrees: Community, political work, etc.:

Descendant   Descendant

Spouse   Spouse

Basic Employment History: Clubs, Church Affiliations, etc.:

Descendant   Descendant

Spouse   Spouse

Military Service:

Descendant   Spouse

M64125153
Genealogical Number

Celia Anne Moore ("C'Anne")   Heidelberg, Germany
Name (including maiden name if applicable)   Town of Residence

Houston, Texas   8/29/1963
Birthplace   Date of Birth   Date of Death   Where Buried

Mark Wofford   Lubbock, TX   12/3/1963
Name of Spouse   Birthplace   Date of Birth   Date of Death

                 9/4/1993   Dallas, Texas
Where Buried   Date of Marriage   Place of Marriage

If married more than once:

Name of Spouse   Birthplace   Date of Birth   Date of Death

Where Buried   Date of Marriage   Place of Marriage

H. Sam Wofford & Jane Wyche
Parents of Spouse (with Mother's maiden name) 1st Marriage

Subsequent Marriage (if applicable)

Family Details

Schools attended, dates and degrees: Community, political work, etc.:

Palm Beach Atlantic college:
Baylor U. '95 BBA Marketing
Descendant   Descendant

Univ. of Texas '96 E.E.
Spouse   Spouse

Basic Employment History: Clubs, Church Affiliations, etc.:

Stay at home Mom
Descendant   Descendant

Siemens Medical Systems
Spouse   Spouse

Military Service:

Descendant   Spouse

36.

The James Harvey Moore Line
Pictures

Mary Grace & Sam Houston Moore (1) with Sam H., II (2)
(1)   (M64121)   B. 10/31/1864   D. ---
(2)   (M6412141)   B. 10/2/1947

John (1), Sam (2) & Jesse (3) Moore

1) (M641213) B. 8/27/1902 D. 11/21/1983
2) (M641215) B. 5/5/1916 D. 3/15/2002
3) (M641214) B. 5/11/1905 D. 5/19/2003

37.

The Martha Poage Moore Line
Genealogical Chart

Martha Poage Moore - M624 Joseph Addison Moore

B. 5/11/1811   M. 8/30/1831   B. 9/29/1805

D. 8/7/1890   D. 11/1882

(See M624)

37.

The Mary Brown Moore Line
Genealogical Charts

M643   *Mary Brown Moore - William V. Shannon*
B. _____   M. 1829   B. 12/18/1806
D. 4/23/1881   D. 11/7/1891

M6431 - Elizabeth Shannon - John T. Nash
B. _____   M. 1/18/1853   B. _____
D. _____   D. _____

M64311 - Andrew Jackson Nash - Naomi John Summers
B. 1/27/1853   M. 11/16/1875   B. _____
D. 3/2/1942   D. 11/14/1941

M643111 - Lou Emma Nash
B. 10/17/1876
D. 1895

M643112 - Mary Jettie Nash - Lewis Edgar Walker
B. 10/3/1878   M. 11/17/1897   B. 5/15/1873
D. _____   D. 5/18/1936

M6431121 - Ruth Inez Walker - Frank Shuler Suthers
B. 11/7/1902   M. 6/17/1924   B. 2/5/1898
D. _____   D. _____

M6431122 - Fred Randolph Walker - Dorothy Ann Jonas
B. 1/26/1909   M. 6/25/1938   B. 7/14/1917
D. _____   D. _____

M64311221 - Randolph William Walker
B. 8/28/1940

M6431123 - Ralph Edward Walker
B. 9/27/1918
D. _____

*Indicates that a bio is included.

M643113 - Wade Marvin Nash - India Jane Wagner
    B. _____   M. 10/14/1903   B. _____
    D. _____   D. _____

M6431131 - Charles Edward Nash - Blanche Vivian Whitt
    B. 8/21/1904   M. 7/21/1926   B. 8/21/1904
    D. 2/24/1973   D. 1/28/1983

*M64311311- Charles Edward Nash, Jr.- Elizabeth Carnefix Ward
    B. 7/27/1927   M. 6/13/1954   B. 7/28/1929

*M643113111 - Sarah Elizabeth Nash - Richard Chaffin
                                        (Div)
       B. 6/2/1955   M. 6/3/1978   B. 4/14/1953

*M6431131111 - Grace Olivia Chaffin
       B. 8/28/1989

M643113112 - Emily Annette Nash - Jefferson
                                   Oakley Sword
       B. 3/4/1957   M.8/2/1980   B. _____

M6431131121 - Charles Jefferson Sword
       B. 7/13/1983

M6431131122 - Sarah Elizabeth Sword
       B. 12/16/1988

*M64311312 - Nancy Annette Nash
       B. 8/19/1930

*M64311313 - Richard Carson Nash - (1)Glenna Halsey(Div)
    B. 5/5/1936   (1)M. _____   B. _____
    D. 11/12/1988 (2)M. _____

                  (2)Charlotte Davis Jackson
                  (Div)
                  B. _____

*M6431132 - Roy Swanson Nash - Rebecca Wallace
    B. 11/5/1905   M. 9/1/1938   B. 5/10/1910
    D. 9/1989   D. 1/31/1970

*M64311321 - Ella Margaret Nash - Thomas L. Williamson
    B. 4/7/1939   M. 1/14/1961   B. 4/20/1933

*M643113211 - Tammy Sue Williamson-Derald Dean
                      Ortloff, II
    B. 1962   M. 3/22/1994   B. 1/1/1963

*M6431132111 – Derald Dean Ortloff, III
    B. 7/4/1997

*M643113212 - Lee Ann Williamson – (1) Steve Smith
    B. 1964   (1)M. 1985   B. _____
            (2)M. 2001

                  (2) Dennis Hayes
                  B. 9/14/1964

M6431132121 – (1) Chelsea N. Smith
    B. 8/7/1991

*M643113213 - Darrell Dwight Williamson
    B. 2/1970
    D. 8/1992

M64311322 - Donna Sue Nash - Wayne Hansford Arnold
    B. 12/5/1941   M. 11/2/1963   B. _____

    M643113221 - Evelyn Grace Arnold
        B. 1965
        D. 1983

    M643113222 - Carol Sue Arnold
        B. 1968

*M6431133 - Mack Mays Nash - Lora L. Garrett
    B. 10/31/1909   M. 4/17/1938   B. 2/11/1917
    D. 3/31/1994   D. 2/8/1990

    *M64311331 - Jane Garrett Nash - Joseph Paul Gaino, Jr.
        B. 12/28/1943   M. 8/8/1964   B. 10/6/1942

        M643113311 - Joseph Paul Gaino, III
            B. 11/16/1969
            D. 9/11/1992

        M643113312 – Mary Garret Gaino
            B. 5/19/1973

    M64311332 - Kenneth Mack Nash - Nancy Yonce
        B. 2/15/1949   M. 4/5/1975   B. 11/9/1947

*M6431134 - Ella Maye Nash - H. Edward Steele
    B. 6/18/1911   M. 4/29/1933   B. 8/24/1906
    D. 1978   D. 6/27/2003

M6431135 - Wade Marvin Nash, Jr. - Marie Stowers
    B. 1/20/1913   M. 6/26/1948   B. _____
    D. 1986   D. _____

M64311351 - Gail Nash - Michael Graham
    B. _____   M. _____   B. _____
    D. _____   D. _____

M643113511 - Angela Gail Graham
    B. _____
    D. _____

M64311352 - Betty Mae Nash - Charlie Blevins
    B. _____   M. _____   B. _____
    D. _____   D. _____

*M6431136 - Naomi Frances Nash - George Stephen Melcher
    B. 11/18/1914   M. 7/21/1937   B. 5/9/1913
    D. _____   D. _____

M64311361-Wade Stephen Melcher–(1)Pamela Gay Epperson (Div)
    B. _____   (1)M. 11/17/1971   B. _____
    D. _____   (2)M. _____   D. _____

                              (2) Martha _____
                              B. _____

M643113611 - Ryan Melcher
    B. 12/1976

M643113612 - Leslie Melcher
    B. 1980

M6431137 - Virginia Blanche Nash - Patrick Henry McNulty, Jr.
    B. 10/3/1916   M. 8/1941   B. _____
    D. _____   D. _____

    M64311371 - Patrick Henry McNulty, III - Katherine _____
        B. _____   M. _____   B. _____
        D. _____   D. _____

        M643113711 - Mary Kate McNulty- Michael _____
            B. _____   M. _____   B. _____

    *M64311372 - Vivian Lea McNulty - Daniel F. Sullivan, III
        B.8/19/1947   M. 6/27/1970   B. 4/12/1944

        M643113721 - Daniel F. Sullivan, IV
            B. 9/4/1977

        M643113722 – Virginia Emily Sullivan
            B. 4/25/1981

M6431138 - Lucian Fred Nash - Mabel Leona Durham
    B. 3/8/1919   M. 12/20/1955   B. 11/10/1925
    D. 4/2001   D. _____

    *M64311381 - Sheri Lynn Nash - Gerald Blaine Pugh (Div)
        B. 1/15/1956   M. 6/5/1976   B. 11/9/1948
                                                D. 2/17/2001

        *M643113811 - Stacy Ann Pugh – Rick Wellons (Div)
            B. 10/20/1976   M. _____   B. _____

*M643113812 -Michael Wayne Pugh – Nora Dunford Catron
          B. 4/28/1977   M. 9/30/2000   B. 4/1/1977

       *M6431138121 – Michael Freddy Pugh
               B. 2/13/2001

*M643113813 - Stephen William Pugh
          B. 2/1/1980

*M643113814 - Timothy Pugh
          B. 1/28/1983

M64311382 - Eve Ellen Nash - Joe Allen Shrader
          B. 11/5/1957   M. _____   B. _____

       M643113821 - Adam Nicholas Shrader
               B. 3/30/1982

       M643113822 - Christopher Pyott Shrader
               B. 8/19/1983

       M643113823 - Kimberly Marie Shrader
               B. 5/1/1987

M64311383 - Mark Anthony Nash - (1) Bonnie Kidd (Div)
          B. 12/31/1959   (1)M. _____ B. _____
                                (2)M. _____

(2) Brenda Amburn
                    B. _____

M643113831 - Craig Allen Nash
        B. 4/25/1978

M643113832 - Benjamin Ray Nash – Martha _____
        B. 11/4/1980   M. _____   B. _____

    M6431138321 – Devon Nash
            B. 2001

M64311384 – Keith Douglas Nash
        B. _____

M6431139 - Janet Ruth Nash - Nicholas Hodock
        B. 3/23/1923   M. 12/13/1942   B. _____
        D. 4/25/2003

M643113-10 - William Shannon Nash - Dorothy Sluss
        B. 3/2/1924   M. 12/2/1950   B. _____
        D. 8/19/1985   D. _____

    M643113-10-1 - Shannon Kay Nash - Daniel Beckett
            B. 11/8/1951   M. 9/15/1972   B. 6/26/1951
            D. _____   D. _____

        M643113-10-1-1 - Michael John Beckett
                B. 6/7/1974

M643113-10-1-2 - Gary Allen Beckett - Monica Gandy

?

B. 7/31/1976   M. 7/31/1993   B. _____

M643113-10-1-2-1 - Hillary Renee Beckett

?

B. 4/5/1993

*****M643113-10-2** - Virginia Sue Nash - Ronald Baker

B. 9/24/1953   M. 5/30/1973   B. 7/18/1950

*****M643113-10-2-1** - Chrystal Renee Baker - Frank Long

B. 3/5/1974   M. 7/17/1993   B. _____

*****M643113-10-3** - Elizabeth Marie Nash – Harry Phipps

B. 11/11/1954   M. 6/1972   B. 9/20/1954

*****M643113-10-4** - William Raymond Wade Nash - Debra Kay

Hawley

B. 1/24/1955   M. 12/24/1982   B. 9/24/1955

*****M643113-10-4-1** - William Shannon Nash, II

B. 12/16/1982

*****M643113-10-5** - Frances Eileen Nash - Alex Samuel Blizzard

B. 5/1/1958   M. _____   B. 7/31/1956

*****M6431131-10-5-1**- Samuel Alex Blizzard

B. 10/26/1974

*M6431131-10-5-2- Heather Blizzard
B. 5/31/1978

*M643113-10-6 - Nancy Ruth Nash - Charles K. Howard, III
B. 12/30/1959   M. _____   B. _____

*M643113-10-6-1 - Jessica Shannon Howard
B. 10/11/1984

M643114 - Lavi Gertrude Nash - W.L. Shawver
B. 8/18/1883   M. 2/28/1903   B. _____
D. 3/20/1937   D. _____

M6431141 - Paul H. Shawver – (1) Evelyn Mae Griffith
B. 11/25/1903   (1)M. _____   B. _____
D. 1972   (2)M. 9/2/1926   D. _____

                 (2) Alice Neal
                                   B. _____

M64311411 – (2) Paul Richard Shawver
B. 12/24/1930
D. 2/26/1944

M6431142 - William Edward Shawver – Clara Kinser
B. 1908   M. _____   B. _____
D. 9/10/64   D. _____

M64311421 – Mildred Sawver
B. _____
D. _____

M64311422 – Eugene Shawver
    B. _____
    D. _____

M64311423 – Aline Shawver - _____ Peery
    B. _____   M. _____   B. _____
    D. _____   D. _____

M64311424 – Donald Shawver
    B. _____
    D. _____

M64311425 – Edward Shawver
    B. _____
    D. _____   Twins
M64311426 - William Shawver
    B. _____
    D. _____

M64311427 Mary Sue Shawver
    B. _____
    D. _____

M64311428 - Alice Mead Shawver
    B. _____
    D. _____

M6431143 - Bessie Shawver – Buford Bourne
    B.7/27/1912   M. _____   B. _____
    D. _____   D. _____

M64311431 – William Thomas Bourne – Dorothy Still
    B. 8/19/1931   M. _____   B. _____

M643114311 – Jeffrey T. Bourne
B. 3/28/1959

M643114312 – Anna L. Bourne
B. 12/7/1960

M643114313 – William T. Bourne, Jr.
B. 9/24/1964

M64311432 – Robert Eugene Bourne – Norma Lou Cyphen
B. 1/19/1934   M. ___ _   B. _____

M643114321 – Michael E. Bourne
B. 3/25/1956

M643114322 – Robert N. Bourne
B. 6/1/1971

M6431144 - Clyde Jackson Shawver
B. 2/2/1917
D. 9/23/1963

M6431145 – Fred Francis Shawver
B. 3/3/1925

M643115 - Blanche Nash - R.L. Helms
B. 7/10/1886   M. 9/14/1910   B._____
D. 1/27/1973   D._____

M643116 - Frank William Nash - Mary Ann Hunnell
B. 2/24/1890   M. 10/7/1914   B. 4/6/1888
D. _____   D. _____

M6431161 - Hattie Emanda Nash - Paul Alexander Carter
B. 8/1/1915   M. 3/19/1933   B. 6/6/1915
D. _____   D. _____

M64311611 - Naomi Sebra Carter – James Curby Medlin
B. 1/25/1934   M. _____   B. _____

    M643116111 - Paul N. Medlin
    B. 7/1/1955

    M643116112 – Paula A. Medlin
    B.12/19/1957

    M643116113 – Amanda F. Medlin
    B. 8/7/1965

    M643116114 – Donna Lou Medlin
    B. 1/16/1969

M64311612 - Otis Jackson Carter – Phyllis Ann Williams
B. 12/19/1935   M. 5/24/1957   B. _____

    M643116121 - Rosemary Carter
    B. 11/30/1958

    M643116122 – Susanna Carter
    B. 12/9/1962

M64311613 - Betty Lee Carter – Lloyd French
B. 3/24/1939   M. _____   B. _____

    M643116131 – Lloyd Fletcher French, Jr.
    B. 3/30/1970

M64311614 - Margaret Alberta Carter – Roy Melvin Medlin
B. 3/25/1941   M. 10/3/1960   B. _____

M643116141 – Ralph Earl Medlin
B. 5/30/1963

M643116142 – Pamela Ann Medlin
B. 12/12/1964

M643116143 - Angela Lou Medlin
B. 12/12/1964

M643116144 – Bruce Wayne Medlin
B. 3/15/1966

M64311615 – James Shanklin Carter – (1) Connie Jean Bailey
B. 4/14/1945   (1)M. 6/28/1967 B. _____
                  (2)M. _____

                              (2) Patricia Ann Blankenship
                              B. _____

M643116151 - (1) James Lee Carter
B. 8/24/1964

M64311616 – Priscilla Lane Carter – Howard Alan Leedy
B. 6/23/1947   M. 6/6/1971   B. _____

M64311617 – Mary Ellen Carter – Glen Miles
B. 4/24/1950   M. 611/27/1969 B. _____

M643116171 - Carrie Miles
B. 8/22/1970

M6431162 - Mary Helen Nash
    B. 5/1/1917
    D. 10/26/1917

M6431163 - Margaret Louemma Nash - Warren Geryal Hypes
    B. 12/1/1919   M. 5/12/1940   B. 11/30/1919
    D. _____   D. _____

M6431164 - Frank Pyott Nash
    B. 12/5/1922

M6431165 - Elberta May Nash
    B. 1/30/1925

M6431166 - Robert Shannon Nash
    B. 1/30/1929

M643117 - Annie Frances Nash - Glenn R. Mahood
    B. 1/6/1893   M. 6/15/1914   B. 3/21/1888
    D. _____   D. _____

    M6431171 - Miriam Frances Mahood - Harold Hoots Garner
        B. 4/13/1915   M. 4/5/1939   B. 9/3/1916
        D. _____   D. _____

        M643161711 – Harold Hoots Garner, Jr. – Patricia Ann Finks
            B. _____   M. _____   B. _____

            M64311617111 – Samuel Glen Garner
                B. _____

M6431172 - Eugene Ray Mahood - Irene Magdalene Myers
    B. 11/27/1917   M. 3/10/1940   B. _____
    D. _____   M. _____   D. _____

    M64311721 – Gail Elizabeth Mahood – H. Lester Morris, Jr.
        B. _____   M. _____   B. _____

        M643117211 – H. Lester Morris, III
            B. _____

    M64311722 – Kathie Glenn Mahood – William E. Neal, Jr.
        B. _____   M. _____   B. _____

        M643117221 – Jacob Shore Neal
            B. _____

M6431173 - Naomi Elizabeth Mahood
    B. 10/28/1919
    D. _____

M6431174 - Bobby Nash Mahood
    B. 9/24/1924
    D. 6/23/1966

M6431175 - Lucille Greever Mahood – Paul W. Spain
    B. 10/13/1925   M. 4/28/1956   B. _____

M6431176 - Betty Joan Mahood – Paul Vincent Powers
    B. 4/6/1932   M. 6/19/1954   B. _____

    M64311761 - Susan Lynn Powers
        B. 12/29/1955

M64311762 - Paul Vincent Powers, Jr.
B. 9/5/1959

M643118 - Fred Thomas Nash - Ruth Smithdeal
B. 10/3/1895   M. 10/7/1927   B. _____
D. 8/5/1962   D. _____

M643119 - George R. Nash - Isabel Ellen Brown
B. 3/26/1899   M. 2/23/1934   B. 5/9/1898
D. _____   D. _____

    M6431191 - Jack Brown Nash – Phyllis Irene Wilson
    B. 2/28/1925   M. 8/20/1972   B. _____

        M64311911 – Jackie Wilson Nash
        B. 6/16/1950

        M64311912 - Phyllis Gail Nash
        B. 8/29/1952

        M64311913 - Pamela Kay Nash
        B. 9/26/1955

    M6431192 - Ray Alexander Nash – Barbara V. Smith
    B. 7/7/1927   M. _____   B. _____

        M64311921 – Timothy Allen Nash
        B. 8/8/1960

        M64311922 - Theresa Lyn Nash
        B. 5/21/1963

    M6431193 - Paul Sexton Nash – June G. Crowell
    B. 12/18/1929   M. 8/9/1951   B. _____

M64311931 – Paul Steven Nash
B. 9/17/1954

M64311932 – George Raymond Nash
B. 4/23/1958

M6431194 - Alvin Nash – Gloria McLain
B. 9/20/1933   M. _____   B. _____

M64311941 – Kristin Lynn Nash
B. 11/8/1966

M64312 - George Washington Nash - Charlotte Priscilla Tiller
B. 11/27/1853   M. 7/1875   B. 7/20/1856
D. 1896   D. _____

M643121 - Nancy Elizabeth Nash - Mosby Edward Tabor
B. 8/13/1875   M. 9/27/1894   B. _____
D. 12/6/1959   D. 1931

M6431211 - Aletha Florence Tabor - Joseph Stupalsky
B. 6/24/1895   M. 10/2/1913   B. _____
D. 6/24/1920   D. _____

Changed name to Tabor
M64312111 - Joseph Stupalsky, Jr. – Vivian Sayers
B. _____   M. 4/21/1951   B. _____
D. _____

M64312112- Edward DeWitt (Stupalsky) Tabor – Virginia R. Yost
B. _____   M. 7/20/1940   B. _____
D. _____   D. _____

M6431212 - Harold Johnson Tabor - Ollie Browning Deaton
    B. 1/22/1900   M. 7/28/1923   B. _____
    D. _____   D. _____

M64312121 - Evelyn Tabor – George Edward Mann
    B. 5/30/1924   M. 6/16/1950   B. _____
    D. _____   D. _____

        M643121211 - Diana Lynn Mann
        B. 1/10/1954

M64312122 – Anna Louise Tabor – Sebe James Reynolds
    B. 12/18/1925   M. _____   B. _____
    D. _____   D. _____

        M643121221 – Rebecca Ann Reynolds
        B. 11/10/1958

M64312123 - Billie Marie Tabor – James Floyd DeHart
    B. 7/27/1927   M. 6/9/1951   B. _____
    D. _____   D. _____

        M643121231 – Debra Carol DeHart – Robert Elmore Evans
        B. 12/12/1953   M. 8/13/1973   B. _____

M6431213 - Buenos Tabor - Margie Wallace
    B. 1900   M. 1919   B. _____
    D. _____   D. _____

M64312131 - Elmer W. Tabor – Dorcas A. Anderson
    B. 7/31/1923   M. 1/16/1946   B. _____
    D. 5/4/1971   D. _____

M64313121311 – Elmer W. Tabor, Jr.
B. _____

M64313121312 – Jennifer Joy Tabor
B. _____

M643122 - Thomas Edward Nash - Ora Lee Neel
B. 2/8/1877   M. 5/27/1903   B. 2/2/1885
D. 5/30/1935   D. 3/17/1975

M6431221 - Claude Witten Nash - Blanche Richmond Barnes
B. 10/28/1904   M. 8/3/1933   B. 11/24/1907
D. 7/25/1987   D. 4/2/1982

*M64312211 - Philip Barnes Nash – Gail Thais Prescott
B. 4/4/1938   M. 11/30/1963   B. 12/10/1940

M643122111 – Prescott Barnes Nash
B. 10/22/1966

M643122112 – Alexis Richmond Nash
B. 9/11/1969

M643122113 – Alicia Bennett Nash
B. 1/11/1971

*M64312212 – Charlotte Priscilla Nash – Searborn Flournoy
                                          Brown
B.6/10/1940   M. 4/21/1962   B. 10/12/1939

*M643122121 – Evan Heywood Brown
B. 2/22/1973

M6431222 - Nancy Earnestine Nash
B. 5/4/1906
D. 8/18/1990

M6431223 - Anna May Nash
    B. 4/10/1909
    D. 2/20/1920

M6431224 - Thomas Edward Nash, Jr.
    B. 11/13/1915
    D. 12/20/1993

M643123 – May Ruth Nash
    B. 10/15/1878
    D. 4/15/1901

M643124 - Hallie Lavinia Nash - Charles Crockett Bailey
    B. 5/5/1880   M. 12/25/1901   B. _____
    D. 1917   D. 4/1944

    M6431241 - Willie Corinne Bailey – Skelton Earl Layne
        B. 11/10/1902   M. 5/30/1925   B. _____
        D. _____   D. _____

        M64312411 - Skelton Earl Layne, Jr. – Mary F. Murphy
            B. 10/16/1926   M. _____   B. _____
            D. _____   D. _____

            M643124111 – Marcus Stephen Layne
                B. 6/26/1957

            M643124112 – Ronald Joseph Layne
                B. 2/16/1959

    M6431242 - Charles Glenn Bailey – Ann Northern Wiley
        B. 12/4/1903   M. 11/25/1926   B. _____
        D. 1/6/1965   D. _____

        M64312421 - Freddy Ann Bailey – Wendall John Clark
            B. 10/6/1931   M. _____   B. _____

THE MARY BROWN MOORE LINE

M643124211 – Michael Glenn Clark
B. 3/22/1957

M643124212 – David Wendall Clark
B. 11/20/1963

M643124213 – Emily Alexandra Clark
B. 11/30/1968

M64312422 – Glenna Carolyn Bailey
B. 7/26/1934

M6431243 – Frederick Rounds Bailey – Dorothy Matthews
B. 8/19/1905   M. 8/19/1933   B. _____
D. _____   D. _____

M64312431 – William Sheffey Bailey – Liesolotte Else Borchard
B. 9/26/1934   M. 12/11/1954   B. _____

M643124311 – Michael Fred Bailey
B. 5/30/1955

M643124312 – Julia Lynn Bailey
B. 5/19/1956

M643124313 – Kathleen Ann Bailey
B. 10/13/1957

M64312432 – Judith Bailey – (1) Aubrey T. Gray
B. 1/7/1936   (1)M. 1961   B._____
                   (2)M. 10/9/1970

(2) John Curtis Holland
B. _____

1127

M643124321 - (1) Rebella Shaun Gray
           B. _____

M643124322 – (1) Kevin Thomas Gray
           B. _____

M643124323 - (1) Jennifer Gray
           B. _____

M6431244 - Jay Bigelow Bailey - Genevieve Clubb
    B. 12/16/1906   M. 12/24/1933   B. _____
    D. _____   D. _____

M64312441 - Mary Sue Bailey – Earl Cook
    B. _____   M. 12/19/1946   B. _____

M643124411 – James Jay Cook
        B. _____

M643124412 – Victoria Michelle Cook
        B. _____

M643124413 – Traly Ray Cook
        B. _____

M6431245 - Thomas Crockett Bailey – Edna May Harless
    B. 11/11/1908   M. _____   B. _____
    D. _____   D. _____

M64312451 - Thomas C. Bailey, Jr. – Toni Jean Melodia
    B. 4/21/1947   M. 6/9/1973   B. _____

M643124512 – Betty Jo Bailey - Donald Lynn Roberts
    B. 1/5/1949   M. _____   B. _____

23

M6431245121 - Christy Lynn Roberts
B. 9/18/1969

M6431245122 - Misty Leigh Roberts
B. 9/24/1970

M643124513 – Marcus Wayne Bailey
B. 3/4/1951

M643124514 – James Bigelow Bailey
B. 9/20/1952

M6431246 - Eugene Cassidy Bailey - Mabel Clare Cooper
B. 5/26/1911   M. 9/6/1934   B. _____
D. _____   D. _____

M64312461 - Jane Ann Bailey – Alan Wendel Derthick
B. 2/2/1936   M. 12/21/1958   B. _____

M643124611 – Mark Alan Dethick
B. 9/24/1960

M643124612 - Steven John Dethick
B. 5/21/1962

M64312462 – John Charles Bailey – Jeanne Bell
B. 11/5/1937   M. _____   B. _____

M643124621 – John Charles Bailey, Jr.
B. 9/23/1963

M643124622 – Janice Carmen Bailey
B. 3/2/1966

24

M6431247 – Samuel Sheffey Bailey – Rosemary J. Fiala
    B. 7/15/1913   M. 11/12/1938   B. _____
    D. _____   D. _____

M64312471 – John Vincent Bailey – Loretta Fay Baker
      B. 11/5/1939   M. 4/21/1967   B. _____

    M643124711 – Linda Carmela Bailey
        B. _____

    M643124712 – Lori Catherine Bailey
        B. _____

M64312472 – Barbara Ann Bailey – Wayne Yengst
      B. 5/23/1942   M. 2/3/1963   B. _____

    M643123721 – Lisa Lynn Yengst
        B. _____

M64312473 – Robert Charles Bailey – Becky L. Wheat
      B. 9/21/1946   M. _____   B. _____

M6431248 – Guy Havens Bailey – Virginia W. Schrader
    B. 9/4/1915   M. 7/10/___   B. _____
    D. _____   D. _____

M64312481 – Anne Havens Bailey
    B. 8/11/1959

M64312482 – Lynne Corinne Bailey
    B. 9/1/1960

M64312483 – Thomas Wayne Bailey
    B. 5/28/1962

M643125 - Grace Elma Nash - William Jackson Duncan
    B. 3/21/1882   M. 5/1/1906   B. 3/17/1881
    D.1971   D. _____

M6431251 - Charlotte Elizabeth Duncan - Fitch Edward Wallace
    B. 4/22/1907   M. 8/24/1938   B. 2/3/1904
    D. _____   D. _____

M64312511 - Charlotte Ruth Wallace – Ronald J. Smiczek
    B. 6/28/1939   M. 12/5/1959   B. _____

M643125111 – Catherine Ann Smiczek
    B. _____

M643125112 - Jeanne Elizabeth Smiczek
    B. _____

M6431252 - Hallie Ruth Duncan
    B. 4/9/1909
    D. _____

M6431253 – William Jackson Duncan, Jr. - Helen Rose Franz
    B. 3/22/1911   M. 4/8/1937   B. 1/29/1915
    D. _____   D. _____

M64312531 - Janice Rose Duncan
    B. 2/27/1938
    D. _____

M6431254 - Edward Morton Duncan
    B. 1/29/1914
    D. 1/31/1968

M6431255 – Horace Milton Duncan – Nancy K. Thomas
    B. 11/12/1915   M. 10/1949   B. _____
    D. _____   D. _____

M6431256 – Paul Nash Duncan - May Mildred Trumbo
    B. 11/19/1918   M. 1/28/1940   B. 9/24/1920
    D. 4/5/1946   D. _____

        M64312561 – Kellie Duncan
                B. _____

        M64312562 – Shannon Duncan
                B. _____

        M64312563 – Erin Duncan
                B. _____

M643126 – Guy Henry Nash - Elizabeth Bailey
    B. 9/4/1891   M. 6/1923   B. _____
    D. 2/23/1968   D. _____

M643127 – Sallie Ruth Nash
    B. 12/10/1894
    D. 12/10/1895

M643128 – Harriet Zane Nash – (1) Harrison M. Thompson
    B. 3/10/1896   (1)M. 6/10/1913 B. _____
    D. _____   (2)M. _____ D. 1930

                    (2) George Fox
                        B. _____
                        D. _____

M6431281 - (1) Harrison M. Thompson, Jr. – Renna Carol Keyes
B. 3/10/1916   M. 2/3/1940   B. _____
D. _____   D. _____

    M64312811 – Carol Zane Thompson – James E. Hill
        B. 10/3/1941   M. 6/29/1963   B. _____

        M643128111 – Kathryn Courtney Hill
            B. 6/3/1967

        M643128112 – Lauren Hunter Hill
            B. 3/22/1970

        M643128113 – James Patrick Hill
            B. 4/27/1973

M6431282 - (1) Elma Zane Thompson - Edwin W. Kaye
B. 5/23/1918   M. 5/6/1938   B. _____
D. _____   D. _____

    M64312821 – George Edwin Kaye – Mary Jane Bocock
        B. 3/4/1941   M. 12/26/1962   B. _____
        D. 2/19/1974

        M643128211 – Thomas Lee Kaye
            B. _____

        M643128212 – Maria Christine Kaye
            B. _____

        M643128213 - Susan Lynn Kaye
            B. _____

    M64312822 - Jack Nash Thompson – Trula V. Call
        B. 11/13/1946   M. 5/25/1967   B. _____

M64312823 – Mary Ann Thompson – William Edward Carver
    B. 4/5/1949   M. 2/22/1971   B. _____

    M643128231 - William Scott Carver
        B. _____

    M64312824 – Robert Lewis Thompson
        B. 10/22/1954

    M64312825 – Betty Leigh Thompson
        B. 4/15/1958

M6431283 - (1) William Jackson Thompson – Lewis Jane Calloway
    B. 8/26/1920   M. 7/12/1945   B. _____
    D. _____

M6431284 - (1) Robert Henry Thompson
    B. 3/2/1923
    D. 7/29/1929

M64313 - Henry Melvin Nash – Sue Southern Phillips
    B. 11/9/1857   M. _____   B. _____
    D. 10/6/1942   D. _____

    M643131 – Daughter
        B. _____

M64314 - Rhoda Nash - Robert Harry
    B.1/14/1863   M. 11/11/1885   B. _____
    D. 11/12/1945   D. _____

    M643141 - Ata Ula Harry – Claude W. Johnston
        B. 11/5/1886   M. 10/9/1907   B. _____

M6431411 – Herbert Scott Johnston – Evelyn Ruth Lipes
    B. 7/22/1909   M. 3/9/1937   B. _____
    D. 12/16/1964   D. _____

    M64314111 – Judith Ann Johnston
        B. 3/14/1938

    M64314112 – Herbert Scott Johnston, Jr. – Janet Gail Nash
        B. 3/15/1945   M. _____   B. _____

M6431412 – Marie Barnes Johnston – Charles Gearing
    B. 5/12/1911   M. 10/18/1934   B. _____
    D. 4/29/1935   D. _____

M643142 – John Calvin Harry – Margaret Ruth Dishman
    B. 5/23/1888   M. 9/28/1923   B. _____
    D. _____   D. _____

    M6431421 – John Calvin Harry, Jr. – Eleanor Gibson
        B. 9/24/1924   M. _____   B. _____

        M64314211 – Deborah Harry
            B. _____

    M6431422 – James A. Harry – Dorothy Givens
        B. 9/12/1928   M. _____   B. _____

        M64314221 - Gail Harry
            B. _____

    M6431423 - Robert K. Harry
        B 5/2/1930

M643143 – Grover William Harry
> B. 12/15/1889
> D. 12/22/1966

M64315 - William Lane Nash - _____
> B. _____   M. _____   B. _____
> D. _____   D. _____

> **M643151** - William Lane Nash, Jr.
>> B. _____
>> D. _____

M64316 - Harriet Nash - T. B. Drinkard
> B. _____   M. _____   B. _____
> D. _____   D. _____

M64317 - John Shannon Nash
> B. _____
> D. _____

M64318 - Sidney R. Nash - Anna Walker
> B. _____   M. _____   B. _____
> D. _____   D. _____

> **M643181** - Hazel Nash - George Wilburn
>> B. _____   M. _____   B. _____
>> D. _____   D. _____

M6432 - Mary Ann Shannon - Jesse Bailey
> B. _____   M. 12/15/1859   B. 7/7/1837
> D. _____   M. _____   D. 3/12/1901

M64321 - William Edward Bailey - Clementine Mahood
       B. _____   M. _____   B. _____
       D. _____   D. 11/1938

M64322 - Fannie Bailey - J. Edward Wagner
       B. _____   M. _____   B. _____
       D. 5/1939   D. _____

      M643221 - E. Morton Wagner - _____
            B. _____   M. _____   B. _____
            D. _____   D. _____

M64323 - Julia Bailey - Edward E. Tiller
       B. _____   M. _____   B. _____
       D. _____   D. _____

M64324 - James Catlett Bailey
       B. 8/24/1868
       D. 6/28/1877

M64325 - Mollie Bailey - George Deaton
       B. _____   M. _____   B. _____
       D. _____   D. _____

M64326 - Samuel Abner Bailey
       B. 3/23/1874
       D. 3/24/1895

M64327 - Virginia Bailey - _____ Williams
       B. _____   M. _____   B. _____
       D. _____   D. _____

M64328 - Grattan M. Bailey
    B. _____
    D. _____

M6433 – James Catlett Shannon
    B. _____
    D. _____

M6434 - Joseph B. Shannon - Mary F. Hambrick
    B. 1/2/1840   M. 3/22/1866   B. 4/30/1843
    D. 9/8/1905   D. _____

    M64341 - Laura B. Shannon - Charles Hale, Jr.
        B. 2/7/1867   M. _____   B. _____
        D. 1/24/1924   D. _____

    M64342 - Margaret Ella Shannon - Charles P. Stimson
        B. 11/14/1868   M. 2/15/1893   B. 11/3/1867
        D. _____   D. 6/15/1925

        M643421 - William V. Stimson - Lillian Dixon
            B. _____   M. _____   B. _____
            D. _____   D. _____

            M6434211 - William V. Stimson, Jr.
                B. "c" 1927

            M6434212 - Francis Stimson
                B. "c" 1934

        M643422 - Joseph Stimson - Martha Hopkins
            B. _____   M. _____   B. _____
            D. _____   D. _____

M643423 - Mary Ruth Stimson
    B. 12/23/1925

M64343 - John William Shannon - Eva Belle Gibson
    B. 6/15/1870   M. 11/6/1906   B. _____
    D. 3/22/1932   D. _____

    M643431 - Mary Kate Shannon
        B. 11/20/1910
        D. _____

M64344 - Mary Virginia Shannon
    B. 7/19/1876
    D. 10/24/1888

38.

THE MARY BROWN MOORE LINE
BIOGRAPHICAL CHARTS

M64311311
Genealogical Number

Charles Edward Nash, Jr.   Tazewell, VA
Name (including maiden name if applicable)   Town of Residence

Amonate, VA   7/27/1927
Birthplace   Date of Birth   Date of Death   Where Buried

Elizabeth Carnefix Ward   Tazewell, VA   7/29/1929
Name of Spouse   Birthplace   Date of Birth   Date of Death

                          6/13/1954   Tazewell, VA
Where Buried   Date of Marriage   Place of Marriage

If married more than once:

Name of Spouse   Birthplace   Date of Birth   Date of Death

Where Buried   Date of Marriage   Place of Marriage

Herbert & Estelle Moore Ward
Parents of Spouse (with Mother's maiden name) 1st Marriage

Subsequent Marriage (if applicable)

Family Details

Schools attended, dates and degrees: Community, political work, etc.:

King College 1970
Columbia Theological Sem. - 1971
Descendant   Descendant

Spouse   Spouse

Basic Employment History: Clubs, Church Affiliations, etc.:

Presbyterian Minister   Presbyterian
Descendant   Descendant

Spouse   Spouse

Military Service:

Navy, WWII
Descendant   Spouse

M643113111
Genealogical Number

Sarah Elizabeth Nash
Name (including maiden name if applicable)

Wytheville, VA
Town of Residence

Tazewell, VA
Birthplace

6/2/1955
Date of Birth

Date of Death

Where Buried

Richard L. Chaffin (Div)
Name of Spouse

Lebanon, VA
Birthplace

11/14/1953
Date of Birth

Date of Death

Where Buried

6/3/1978
Date of Marriage

Place of Marriage

If married more than once:

Name of Spouse

Birthplace

Date of Birth

Date of Death

Where Buried

Date of Marriage

Place of Marriage

James and Betsey Clark Chaffin
Parents of Spouse (with Mother's maiden name) 1st Marriage

Subsequent Marriage (if applicable)

Family Details

Schools attended, dates and degrees:

Community, political work, etc.:

BSW Radford University, MSW Virginia
Commonwealth University
Descendant

Descendant

Spouse

Spouse

Basic Employment History:

Clubs, Church Affiliations, etc.:

Descendant

Descendant

Spouse

Spouse

Military Service:

Descendant

Spouse

M6431131111
Genealogical Number

Grace Olivia Chaffin
Name (including maiden name if applicable)

Wytheville, VA
Town of Residence

Wytheville, VA
Birthplace

8/28/1989
Date of Birth

Date of Death

Where Buried

Name of Spouse

Birthplace

Date of Birth

Date of Death

Where Buried

Date of Marriage

Place of Marriage

If married more than once:

Name of Spouse

Birthplace

Date of Birth

Date of Death

Where Buried

Date of Marriage

Place of Marriage

Parents of Spouse (with Mother's maiden name) 1st Marriage

Subsequent Marriage (if applicable)

Family Details

Schools attended, dates and degrees:

Community, political work, etc.:

George Wythe High School
Descendant

Descendant

Spouse

Spouse

Basic Employment History:

Clubs, Church Affiliations, etc.:

Descendant

Children of the American Revolution
Descendant

Spouse

Spouse

Military Service:

Descendant

Spouse

M64311312
Genealogical Number

Nancy Annette Nash
Name (including maiden name if applicable)

N. Tazewell, VA
Town of Residence

Amonate, VA
Birthplace

8/19/1930
Date of Birth

Date of Death

Where Buried

Name of Spouse

Birthplace

Date of Birth

Date of Death

Where Buried

Date of Marriage

Place of Marriage

If married more than once:

Name of Spouse

Birthplace

Date of Birth

Date of Death

Where Buried

Date of Marriage

Place of Marriage

Parents of Spouse (with Mother's maiden name) 1st Marriage

Subsequent Marriage (if applicable)

Family Details

Schools attended, dates and degrees:

Texas Christian U. 1960 BA
Texas Christian U. 1961 MA
Descendant

Community, political work, etc.:

Descendant

Spouse

Spouse

Basic Employment History:

Clubs, Church Affiliations, etc.:

Medical Laboratory Supervisor
Descendant

Episcopalian
Descendant

Spouse

Spouse

Military Service:

Descendant

Spouse

M64311313
Genealogical Number

Richard Carson Nash   Houston, TX
Name (including maiden name if applicable)   Town of Residence

Amonate, VA   5/5/1936   11/12/1988   Tazewell, VA
Birthplace   Date of Birth   Date of Death   Where Buried

Glenna Halsey (Div)   Mouth of Wilson, VA
Name of Spouse   Birthplace   Date of Birth   Date of Death

                                                    North Carolina
Where Buried   Date of Marriage   Place of Marriage

If married more than once:

Charlotte Davis Jackson (Div) Oklahoma
Name of Spouse   Birthplace   Date of Birth   Date of Death

                                                    Texas
Where Buried   Date of Marriage   Place of Marriage

Parents of Spouse (with Mother's maiden name) 1st Marriage

Subsequent Marriage (if applicable)

Family Details

Schools attended, dates and degrees: Community, political work, etc.:

VA Polytechnic Inst. 1956 BS
Descendant   Descendant

Spouse   Spouse

Basic Employment History: Clubs, Church Affiliations, etc.:
Group Manager, Lincoln
National Life Insurance   Methodist
Descendant   Descendant

Spouse   Spouse

Military Service:

Descendant   Spouse

M6431132
Genealogical Number

Roy Swanson Nash
Name (including maiden name if applicable)

Bailey Switch, VA
Town of Residence

Bailey Switch, VA   11/5/1905   9/1989   Grandview Cemetery
Birthplace   Date of Birth   Date of Death   Bluefield, VA
                                                             Where Buried

Rebecca Wallace   Springville, VA   5/10/1910   1/1970
Name of Spouse   Birthplace   Date of Birth   Date of Death

Grandview Cemetery
Bluefield, VA   9/1/1938
Where Buried   Date of Marriage   Place of Marriage

If married more than once:

Name of Spouse   Birthplace   Date of Birth   Date of Death

Where Buried   Date of Marriage Place of Marriage

Parents of Spouse (with Mother's maiden name) 1st Marriage

Subsequent Marriage (if applicable)

Family Details

Schools attended, dates and degrees: Community, political work, etc.:

Descendant   Descendant

Spouse   Spouse

Basic Employment History: Clubs, Church Affiliations, etc.:

Employed by Appalachian Power Company   Methodist
Descendant   Descendant

Spouse   Spouse

Military Service:

Descendant   Spouse

M64311321
Genealogical Number

Ella Margaret Nash   N. Tazewell, VA
Name (including maiden name if applicable)   Town of Residence

Bluefield, W.VA   4/7/1939
Birthplace   Date of Birth   Date of Death   Where Buried

Thomas L. Williamson   Bishop, VA   4/20/1933
Name of Spouse   Birthplace   Date of Birth   Date of Death

Where Buried   Date of Marriage   Place of Marriage

If married more than once:

Name of Spouse   Birthplace   Date of Birth   Date of Death

Where Buried   Date of Marriage   Place of Marriage

Thomas and Helen Asbury Williamson
Parents of Spouse (with Mother's maiden name) 1st Marriage

Subsequent Marriage (if applicable)

Family Details

Schools attended, dates and degrees: Community, political work, etc.:

Bluefield Sanitarium School of X-Ray
Tech.
Descendant   Descendant

Spouse   Spouse

Basic Employment History: Clubs, Church Affiliations, etc.:
Bluefield Sanitarium & Tazewell Comm.
Radiology Dept.   Adria Advent Church
Descendant   Descendant
N.S.R.R. Co. Brakeman, Conductor   Mason, Scottish Rite, Kazim Temple
and Yard Master   Past Pres Russell, Tazewell Shrine Club
Spouse   Spouse

Military Service:

Air Force - 4 Years Korea 1952-1956
Descendant   Spouse

M643113211
Genealogical Number

Tammy Sue Williamson
Name (including maiden name if applicable)

Homestead, Fla.
Town of Residence

Bluefield, W.VA	1962		
Birthplace	Date of Birth	Date of Death	Where Buried

Derald Dean Ortloff, II	Anchorage, Alaska	1/1/1963	
Name of Spouse	Birthplace	Date of Birth	Date of Death

	3/22/1994	Bluefield, VA	
Where Buried	Date of Marriage	Place of Marriage	

If married more than once:

Name of Spouse	Birthplace	Date of Birth	Date of Death

Where Buried	Date of Marriage	Place of Marriage	

Derald Dean Ortloff & Margarette Faye Ketchem
Parents of Spouse (with Mother's maiden name) 1st Marriage

Subsequent Marriage (if applicable)

Family Details

Schools attended, dates and degrees:
Graduated Tazewell High 1980
Southwest Virginia Community College 1982
Associate degree in science
Descendant

Community, political work, etc.:

Descendant

Tazewell High 1981
Spouse

Spouse

Basic Employment History:
Tazewell Hospital, Bluefield Regional Medical
Center & Homemaker
Descendant
United States Air Force 21 years
Air Force Reserves 1 year
Spouse

Clubs, Church Affiliations, etc.:

Descendant

Spouse

Military Service:

Descendant

Spouse

M643113211
_____
Genealogical Number

Derald Dean Ortloff, III
_____   _____
Name (including maiden name if applicable)   Town of Residence

                                            7/4/1997
_____   _____   _____   _____
Birthplace   Date of Birth   Date of Death   Where Buried

_____   _____   _____   _____
Name of Spouse   Birthplace   Date of Birth   Date of Death

_____   _____   _____
Where Buried   Date of Marriage   Place of Marriage

If married more than once:

_____   _____   _____   _____
Name of Spouse   Birthplace   Date of Birth   Date of Death

_____   _____   _____
Where Buried   Date of Marriage   Place of Marriage

_____
Parents of Spouse (with Mother's maiden name) 1st Marriage

_____
Subsequent Marriage (if applicable)

Family Details

Schools attended, dates and degrees: Community, political work, etc.:

_____   _____
Descendant   Descendant

_____   _____
Spouse   Spouse

Basic Employment History: Clubs, Church Affiliations, etc.:

_____   _____
Descendant   Descendant

_____   _____
Spouse   Spouse

Military Service:

_____   _____
Descendant   Spouse

M643113212
Genealogical Number

Lee Ann Williamson
Name (including maiden name if applicable)

_____
Town of Residence

Bluefield, W.VA
Birthplace

1964
Date of Birth

_____
Date of Death

_____
Where Buried

Dennis Hayes
Name of Spouse

Richmond, VA
Birthplace

9/14/1964
Date of Birth

_____
Date of Death

_____
Where Buried

2001
Date of Marriage

Tazewell, VA
Place of Marriage

If married more than once:

Steve Smith
Name of Spouse

_____
Birthplace

_____
Date of Birth

_____
Date of Death

_____
Where Buried

1985
Date of Marriage

_____
Place of Marriage

Raymond J. Hayes & Judith Ann Karnes
Parents of Spouse (with Mother's maiden name) 1st Marriage

_____
Subsequent Marriage (if applicable)

Family Details

Schools attended, dates and degrees:

Community, political work, etc.:

Tazewell High School 1982
Descendant

_____
Descendant

Tazewell High School 1982
Spouse

_____
Spouse

Basic Employment History:
Pyott-Boone Quality Assurance
Inspector
Descendant
Assistant Vice-President
First Sentinel Bank
Spouse

Clubs, Church Affiliations, etc.:

Adria Advent Church
Descendant

Adria Advent Church (Treasurer)
Spouse

Military Service:

_____
Descendant

_____
Spouse

M643113213
Genealogical Number

Darrell Dwight Williamson
Name (including maiden name if applicable)   Town of Residence

			Grandview Memory
Bluefield, W.VA	Feb 1970	Aug 1992	Gardens, Bluefield, W.VA
Birthplace	Date of Birth	Date of Death	Where Buried

| | | | |
| Name of Spouse | Birthplace | Date of Birth | Date of Death |

| | | |
| Where Buried | Date of Marriage | Place of Marriage |

If married more than once:

| | | | |
| Name of Spouse | Birthplace | Date of Birth | Date of Death |

| | | |
| Where Buried | Date of Marriage | Place of Marriage |

Parents of Spouse (with Mother's maiden name) 1st Marriage

Subsequent Marriage (if applicable)

Family Details

Schools attended, dates and degrees: Community, political work, etc.:

| | |
| Descendant | Descendant |

| | |
| Spouse | Spouse |

Basic Employment History: Clubs, Church Affiliations, etc.:

| | |
| Descendant | Descendant |

| | |
| Spouse | Spouse |

Military Service:

| | |
| Descendant | Spouse |

M6431133
Genealogical Number

Mack Mays Nash   Bluefield, VA
Name (including maiden name if applicable)   Town of Residence

			Bluefield, VA
	10/31/1909	3/31/1994	Grandview
Birthplace	Date of Birth	Date of Death	Where Buried

Lora L. Garrett   Duhring, W.VA   2/11/1917   2/8/1990
Name of Spouse   Birthplace   Date of Birth   Date of Death

Grandview, Bluefield, VA   4/17/1938   Tazewell, VA
Where Buried   Date of Marriage   Place of Marriage

If married more than once:

Name of Spouse   Birthplace   Date of Birth   Date of Death

Where Buried   Date of Marriage   Place of Marriage

Edward Garrett & Edith Wall
Parents of Spouse (with Mother's maiden name) 1st Marriage

Subsequent Marriage (if applicable)

Family Details

Schools attended, dates and degrees: Community, political work, etc.:

Descendant   Descendant

Spouse   Spouse

Basic Employment History: Clubs, Church Affiliations, etc.:

Descendant   Descendant

Spouse   Spouse

Military Service:

Descendant   Spouse

M64311331
Genealogical Number

Jane Garrett Nash   Gaffney, S.C.
Name (including maiden name if applicable)   Town of Residence

Bluefield, W.VA   12/28/1943
Birthplace   Date of Birth   Date of Death   Where Buried

Joseph Paul Gaino, Jr.   Wilmington, DE   10/6/1942
Name of Spouse   Birthplace   Date of Birth   Date of Death

                         8/8/1964   Bluefield, W. VA
Where Buried   Date of Marriage   Place of Marriage

If married more than once:

Name of Spouse   Birthplace   Date of Birth   Date of Death

Where Buried   Date of Marriage   Place of Marriage

Joseph & Olga Gaino
Parents of Spouse (with Mother's maiden name) 1st Marriage

Subsequent Marriage (if applicable)

Family Details

Schools attended, dates and degrees: Community, political work, etc.:
                                            Community Foundation, Red Cross,
Radford College, Radford, VA 1964   Cancer Assoc., Hospital Volunteer,
B.S. History   Meals on Wheels
Descendant   Descendant
VA Tech, Blacksburg, VA 1964
B.S. Civil Engineering
Spouse   Spouse

Basic Employment History: Clubs, Church Affiliations, etc.:

Volunteer/housewife
Descendant   Descendant
Millikens Co. (20 years). Then own
business Garment Technology (1987-present)
Spouse   Spouse

Military Service:

Descendant   Spouse

M6431134
Genealogical Number

Ella Maye Nash
Name (including maiden name if applicable)　　　　Town of Residence

	6/18/1911	1978	Bluefield, W.VA
Birthplace	Date of Birth	Date of Death	Where Buried

H. Edward Steele	Steelesburg, VA	8/24/1906	6/27/2003
Name of Spouse	Birthplace	Date of Birth	Date of Death

Bluefield, W.VA	4/29/1933	
Where Buried	Date of Marriage	Place of Marriage

If married more than once:

Name of Spouse	Birthplace	Date of Birth	Date of Death

Where Buried	Date of Marriage	Place of Marriage

J. Beverley Steele & Lula Brown
Parents of Spouse (with Mother's maiden name) 1st Marriage

Subsequent Marriage (if applicable)

Family Details

Schools attended, dates and degrees:　　　　Community, political work, etc.:

Descendant　　　　Descendant

Spouse　　　　Spouse

Basic Employment History:　　　　Clubs, Church Affiliations, etc.:

Descendant　　　　Descendant

Spouse　　　　Spouse

Military Service:

Descendant　　　　Spouse

M6431136
Genealogical Number

Naomi Frances Nash   Bluefield, VA
Name (including maiden name if applicable)   Town of Residence

Bailey Switch, Bluefield, VA   11/28/1914
Birthplace   Date of Birth   Date of Death   Where Buried

George Stephen Melcher   Bluefield, W.VA   5/9/1913
Name of Spouse   Birthplace   Date of Birth   Date of Death

Where Buried   Date of Marriage   Place of Marriage

If married more than once:

Name of Spouse   Birthplace   Date of Birth   Date of Death

Where Buried   Date of Marriage   Place of Marriage

John Roy Melcher & Beulah Frances Hypes
Parents of Spouse (with Mother's maiden name) 1st Marriage

Subsequent Marriage (if applicable)

Family Details

Schools attended, dates and degrees: Community, political work, etc.:

Descendant   Descendant

Spouse   Spouse

Basic Employment History: Clubs, Church Affiliations, etc.:

Descendant   Descendant

Spouse   Spouse

Military Service:

Descendant   Spouse

M64311372
Genealogical Number

Vivian Lea McNulty
Name (including maiden name if applicable)

Massapequa, NY
Town of Residence

Bluefield, W.VA	8/19/1947		
Birthplace	Date of Birth	Date of Death	Where Buried

Daniel F. Sullivan, III	Washington DC	4/12/1944	
Name of Spouse	Birthplace	Date of Birth	Date of Death

	6/27/1970	Bluefield, W. VA
Where Buried	Date of Marriage	Place of Marriage

If married more than once:

Name of Spouse	Birthplace	Date of Birth	Date of Death

Where Buried	Date of Marriage	Place of Marriage

Daniel F. Sullivan & Virginia Campbell Proctor
Parents of Spouse (with Mother's maiden name) 1st Marriage

Subsequent Marriage (if applicable)

Family Details

Schools attended, dates and degrees:
1965-69 Concord College, Athens BS
1972-74 Hofstra University, MA
Queens College MA - ADA/SDA
Descendant

Community, political work, etc.:

Descendant

1965-68 Concord College BS
Spouse

Spouse

Basic Employment History:
Valley Street High School District
Teacher/Career & Tech. Ed. Dept. Head
Descendant

Clubs, Church Affiliations, etc.:

St. Martin of Tours, Amityville, NY
Descendant

Asst. Head Custodian Farmingdale H.S. District
Spouse

St. Martin of Tours, Amityville, NY
Spouse

Military Service:

Descendant

Spouse

M64311381
Genealogical Number

Sheri Lynn Nash   Bluefield, W.VA
Name (including maiden name if applicable)   Town of Residence

Bluefield, W.VA   11/15/1956
Birthplace   Date of Birth   Date of Death   Where Buried

Gerald Blaine (Jerry) Pugh Bluefield, W.VA   11/9/1948   2/17/2001
Name of Spouse   Birthplace   Date of Birth   Date of Death
Grandview Memory Gardens   Bailey United Methodist Church
Bluefield, W.VA   6/5/1976   Bailey, VA
Where Buried   Date of Marriage   Place of Marriage

If married more than once:

Name of Spouse   Birthplace   Date of Birth   Date of Death

Where Buried   Date of Marriage   Place of Marriage

Parents of Spouse (with Mother's maiden name) 1st Marriage

Edith Brewster & William Blaine (Buck) Pugh
Subsequent Marriage (if applicable)

Family Details

Schools attended, dates and degrees: Community, political work, etc.:
Dudley & Logan St. Elem - Bluefield, VA.
Springville Elem - N. Tazewell, VA
Graham Jr. & Graham High-Bluefield Grad. June 1975
Tazewell Co. Vocational Center - Tazewell Grad. June 1975
National Business College, Bluefield - Grad. June 1996   Graham Historical Society
Descendant   Tazewell Co. Historical Society
Wade Elementary-Bluefield, W.VA   Descendant
Bluefield Jr. & Bluefield High School-Bluefield VA
Spouse   Spouse

Basic Employment History: Clubs, Church Affiliations, etc.:
National Business College - Bluefield, VA
Retired & Senior Volunteer Program of Clinch Valley
Community Action, Tazewell, VA   Bailey United Methodist-Bailey VA
Glenn Moore Transport, Carlisle, PA
Descendant   Descendant
Hart Electric - Bluefield, W.VA
Joy Service Center - Bluefield, VA   Bailey United Methodist-Bailey VA
Spouse   Spouse

Military Service:

                                               Vietnam War
Descendant   Spouse

M643113811
Genealogical Number

Stacy Ann Pugh
Name (including maiden name if applicable)

N. Tazewell, VA
Town of Residence

Bluefield, W.VA
Birthplace

10/20/1976
Date of Birth

Date of Death

Where Buried

Rick Wellons (Div.)
Name of Spouse

Bluefield, W.VA
Birthplace

Date of Birth

Date of Death

Where Buried

Date of Marriage

Bluefield, W.VA
Place of Marriage

If married more than once:

Name of Spouse

Birthplace

Date of Birth

Date of Death

Where Buried

Date of Marriage

Place of Marriage

Parents of Spouse (with Mother's maiden name) 1st Marriage

Subsequent Marriage (if applicable)

Family Details

Schools attended, dates and degrees:
Springville Elem. - N. Tazewell, VA
Wade Elem - Bluefield, VA
Graham Middle & Graham High - Bluefield, VA
Descendant

Community, political work, etc.:

Retired Senior Volunteer Programs
MS Walkathon
Descendant

Spouse

Spouse

Basic Employment History:
Bladyes Eye Clinic-Bluefield, VA
Food Lion, Bluefield, VA
Town & County Veterinary - Tazewell, VA
Descendant

Clubs, Church Affiliations, etc.:

Bailey United Methodist Church
Appalachian Artists Association
Descendant

Spouse

Spouse

Military Service:

Descendant

Spouse

M643113812
Genealogical Number

Michael Wayne Pugh   Bluefield, W.VA
Name (including maiden name if applicable)   Town of Residence

Bluefield, W.VA   4/28/1977
Birthplace   Date of Birth   Date of Death   Where Buried

Nora Dunford Catron   Bluefield, W.VA   4/1/1977
Name of Spouse   Birthplace   Date of Birth   Date of Death

                                                Bailey United Methodist
                         9/30/2000   Church, Bailey, VA.
Where Buried   Date of Marriage   Place of Marriage

If married more than once:

Name of Spouse   Birthplace   Date of Birth   Date of Death

Where Buried   Date of Marriage   Place of Marriage

Freddie Dunford
Parents of Spouse (with Mother's maiden name) 1st Marriage

Subsequent Marriage (if applicable)

Family Details

Schools attended, dates and degrees: Community, political work, etc.:
Wade Elem. - Bluefield VA
Springville Elem. – N. Tazewell, VA
Bluefield Middle - Bluefield, VA
Graham Middle & Graham High-Bluefield, VA
Descendant   Descendant

Montcalm HS - Montcalm, W.VA
Spouse   Spouse

Basic Employment History: Clubs, Church Affiliations, etc.:
Acme Markets, Food City, Wal-Mart -Bluefield, VA
Ryan's Restaurant & Kwik Kafe - Bluefield, VA   Bailey UM Church - Bailey, VA
Descendant   Descendant
Ryan's Restaurant - Bluefield VA.
Westwood Medical Center- Bluefield, VA
Spouse   Spouse

Military Service:

Descendant   Spouse

M6431138121
Genealogical Number

Michael Freddy Pugh
Name (including maiden name if applicable)   Town of Residence

                                    2/13/2001
Birthplace   Date of Birth   Date of Death   Where Buried

Name of Spouse   Birthplace   Date of Birth   Date of Death

Where Buried   Date of Marriage   Place of Marriage

If married more than once:

Name of Spouse   Birthplace   Date of Birth   Date of Death

Where Buried   Date of Marriage   Place of Marriage

Parents of Spouse (with Mother's maiden name) 1st Marriage

Subsequent Marriage (if applicable)

Family Details

Schools attended, dates and degrees: Community, political work, etc.:

Descendant   Descendant

Spouse   Spouse

Basic Employment History: Clubs, Church Affiliations, etc.:

Descendant   Descendant

Spouse   Spouse

Military Service:

Descendant   Spouse

M643113813
Genealogical Number

Stephen William Pugh   Bluefield, W. VA
Name (including maiden name if applicable)   Town of Residence

Bluefield, W.VA	2/1/1980		
Birthplace	Date of Birth	Date of Death	Where Buried

Name of Spouse	Birthplace	Date of Birth	Date of Death

Where Buried	Date of Marriage	Place of Marriage

If married more than once:

Name of Spouse	Birthplace	Date of Birth	Date of Death

Where Buried	Date of Marriage	Place of Marriage

Parents of Spouse (with Mother's maiden name) 1st Marriage

Subsequent Marriage (if applicable)

Family Details

Schools attended, dates and degrees: Community, political work, etc.:
Springville Elem. - N. Tazewell, VA
Graham Intermediate, Graham Middle &
Graham High - Bluefield, W.VA
Tazewell Co. VoTech - N. Tazewell, VA
Descendant   Descendant

Spouse   Spouse

Basic Employment History: Clubs, Church Affiliations, etc.:
Asplundt Tree Service - Bluefield, W.VA. Hood Excavating
Bluefield, W.VA. Brown Construction-N. Tazewell, VA.
Bob Woods Masonry Contracting-N. Tazewell, VA   Bailey United Methodist Church
Descendant   Descendant

Spouse   Spouse

Military Service:

Descendant   Spouse

M643113814
Genealogical Number

Timothy Pugh
Name (including maiden name if applicable)

Bluefield, W. VA
Town of Residence

Bluefield, W.VA
Birthplace

1/28/1983
Date of Birth

Date of Death

Where Buried

Name of Spouse

Birthplace

Date of Birth

Date of Death

Where Buried

Date of Marriage

Place of Marriage

If married more than once:

Name of Spouse

Birthplace

Date of Birth

Date of Death

Where Buried

Date of Marriage

Place of Marriage

Parents of Spouse (with Mother's maiden name) 1st Marriage

Subsequent Marriage (if applicable)

Family Details

Schools attended, dates and degrees:
Springville Elem - N. Tazewell, VA
Graham Middle & High - Bluefield, W.VA
Tazewell Votech - N. Tazewell, VA
Descendant

Community, political work, etc.:

MS Walkathon
Descendant

Spouse

Spouse

Basic Employment History:
Super Clean Car Wash & Food City
Bluefield, W.VA
Descendant

Clubs, Church Affiliations, etc.:

Bailey United Methodist Church
Descendant

Spouse

Spouse

Military Service:

Descendant

Spouse

M643113-10-2
Genealogical Number

Virginia Sue Nash
Name (including maiden name if applicable)

Town of Residence

Bluefield, W.VA
Birthplace

9/24/1953
Date of Birth

Date of Death

Where Buried

Ronald Baker
Name of Spouse

Birthplace

7/18/1950
Date of Birth

Date of Death

Where Buried

5/30/1973
Date of Marriage

Place of Marriage

If married more than once:

Name of Spouse

Birthplace

Date of Birth

Date of Death

Where Buried

Date of Marriage

Place of Marriage

John and Mildred Baker
Parents of Spouse (with Mother's maiden name) 1st Marriage

Subsequent Marriage (if applicable)

Family Details

Schools attended, dates and degrees:

Community, political work, etc.:

Descendant

Descendant

Spouse

Spouse

Basic Employment History:

Clubs, Church Affiliations, etc.:

Descendant

Descendant

Spouse

Spouse

Military Service:

Descendant

Spouse

M643113-10-2-1
Genealogical Number

Crystal Renee Baker
Name (including maiden name if applicable)

Town of Residence

Bluefield, W.VA	3/5/1974		
Birthplace	Date of Birth	Date of Death	Where Buried

Frank Long			
Name of Spouse	Birthplace	Date of Birth	Date of Death

	7/17/1993		
Where Buried	Date of Marriage	Place of Marriage	

If married more than once:

Name of Spouse	Birthplace	Date of Birth	Date of Death

Where Buried	Date of Marriage	Place of Marriage	

Frank Long and -
Parents of Spouse (with Mother's maiden name) 1st Marriage

Subsequent Marriage (if applicable)

Family Details

Schools attended, dates and degrees:

Community, political work, etc.:

_____
Descendant

_____
Descendant

_____
Spouse

_____
Spouse

Basic Employment History:

Clubs, Church Affiliations, etc.:

_____
Descendant

_____
Descendant

_____
Spouse

_____
Spouse

Military Service:

_____
Descendant

_____
Spouse

M643113-10-3
Genealogical Number

Elizabeth Marie Nash
Name (including maiden name if applicable)   Town of Residence

Bluefield, W.VA   11/11/1954
Birthplace   Date of Birth   Date of Death   Where Buried

Harry Phipps   9/20/1954
Name of Spouse   Birthplace   Date of Birth   Date of Death

                         6/1972
Where Buried   Date of Marriage   Place of Marriage

If married more than once:

Name of Spouse   Birthplace   Date of Birth   Date of Death

Where Buried   Date of Marriage   Place of Marriage

Parents of Spouse (with Mother's maiden name) 1st Marriage

Subsequent Marriage (if applicable)

Family Details

Schools attended, dates and degrees: Community, political work, etc.:

Descendant   Descendant

Spouse   Spouse

Basic Employment History: Clubs, Church Affiliations, etc.:

Descendant   Descendant

Spouse   Spouse

Military Service:

Descendant   Spouse

M643113-10-4
_____
Genealogical Number

William Raymond Wade Nash
_____
Name (including maiden name if applicable)   Town of Residence

Bluefield, W.VA   1/24/1955
_____   _____   _____   _____
Birthplace   Date of Birth   Date of Death   Where Buried

Debra Kay Hawley   9/24/1955
_____   _____   _____
Name of Spouse   Birthplace   Date of Birth   Date of Death

_____   12/24/1982   _____
Where Buried   Date of Marriage   Place of Marriage

If married more than once:

_____   _____   _____   _____
Name of Spouse   Birthplace   Date of Birth   Date of Death

_____   _____   _____
Where Buried   Date of Marriage   Place of Marriage

- and Maggie Hawley
_____
Parents of Spouse (with Mother's maiden name) 1st Marriage

_____
Subsequent Marriage (if applicable)

Family Details

Schools attended, dates and degrees: Community, political work, etc.:

_____   _____
Descendant   Descendant

_____   _____
Spouse   Spouse

Basic Employment History: Clubs, Church Affiliations, etc.:

_____   _____
Descendant   Descendant

_____   _____
Spouse   Spouse

Military Service:

_____   _____
Descendant   Spouse

M643113-10-4-1
Genealogical Number

William Shannon Nash, II
Name (including maiden name if applicable)   Town of Residence

Bluefield, W.VA   12/16/1982
Birthplace   Date of Birth   Date of Death   Where Buried

Name of Spouse   Birthplace   Date of Birth   Date of Death

Where Buried   Date of Marriage   Place of Marriage

If married more than once:

Name of Spouse   Birthplace   Date of Birth   Date of Death

Where Buried   Date of Marriage   Place of Marriage

Parents of Spouse (with Mother's maiden name) 1st Marriage

Subsequent Marriage (if applicable)

Family Details

Schools attended, dates and degrees: Community, political work, etc.:

Descendant   Descendant

Spouse   Spouse

Basic Employment History: Clubs, Church Affiliations, etc.:

Descendant   Descendant

Spouse   Spouse

Military Service:

Descendant   Spouse

M643113-10-5
Genealogical Number

Frances Eileen Nash
Name (including maiden name if applicable)

Town of Residence

Bluefield, W.VA   5/1/1958
Birthplace   Date of Birth   Date of Death   Where Buried

Alex Samuel Blizzard   7/31/1956
Name of Spouse   Birthplace   Date of Birth   Date of Death

Where Buried   Date of Marriage   Place of Marriage

If married more than once:

Name of Spouse   Birthplace   Date of Birth   Date of Death

Where Buried   Date of Marriage   Place of Marriage

Floyd and Betty Blizzard
Parents of Spouse (with Mother's maiden name) 1st Marriage

Subsequent Marriage (if applicable)

Family Details

Schools attended, dates and degrees: Community, political work, etc.:

Descendant   Descendant

Spouse   Spouse

Basic Employment History: Clubs, Church Affiliations, etc.:

Descendant   Descendant

Spouse   Spouse

Military Service:

Descendant   Spouse

M643113-10-5-1
Genealogical Number

Samuel Alex Blizzard
Name (including maiden name if applicable)

Falls Mills, VA
Town of Residence

Bluefield, W.VA
Birthplace

10/26/1974
Date of Birth

Date of Death

Where Buried

Name of Spouse

Birthplace

Date of Birth

Date of Death

Where Buried

Date of Marriage

Place of Marriage

If married more than once:

Name of Spouse

Birthplace

Date of Birth

Date of Death

Where Buried

Date of Marriage

Place of Marriage

Parents of Spouse (with Mother's maiden name) 1st Marriage

Subsequent Marriage (if applicable)

Family Details

Schools attended, dates and degrees:

Community, political work, etc.:

Descendant

Descendant

Spouse

Spouse

Basic Employment History:

Clubs, Church Affiliations, etc.:

Descendant

Descendant

Spouse

Spouse

Military Service:

Descendant

Spouse

M643113-10-5-2
_____
Genealogical Number

Heather Blizzard
_____   _____
Name (including maiden name if applicable)   Town of Residence

Bluefield, W.VA_____   5/31/1978_____
Birthplace   Date of Birth   Date of Death   Where Buried

_____   _____   _____   _____
Name of Spouse   Birthplace   Date of Birth   Date of Death

_____   _____   _____
Where Buried   Date of Marriage   Place of Marriage

If married more than once:

_____   _____   _____   _____
Name of Spouse   Birthplace   Date of Birth   Date of Death

_____   _____   _____
Where Buried   Date of Marriage   Place of Marriage

_____
Parents of Spouse (with Mother's maiden name) 1st Marriage

_____
Subsequent Marriage (if applicable)

Family Details

Schools attended, dates and degrees: Community, political work, etc.:

_____   _____
Descendant   Descendant

_____   _____
Spouse   Spouse

Basic Employment History: Clubs, Church Affiliations, etc.:

_____   _____
Descendant   Descendant

_____   _____
Spouse   Spouse

Military Service:

_____   _____
Descendant   Spouse

M643113-10-6
Genealogical Number

Nancy Ruth Nash   Florence, SC
Name (including maiden name if applicable)   Town of Residence

Bluefield, W.VA   12/30/1959
Birthplace   Date of Birth   Date of Death   Where Buried

Charles K. Howard, III
Name of Spouse   Birthplace   Date of Birth   Date of Death

Where Buried   Date of Marriage   Place of Marriage

If married more than once:

Name of Spouse   Birthplace   Date of Birth   Date of Death

Where Buried   Date of Marriage   Place of Marriage

Charles and Jewell Howard
Parents of Spouse (with Mother's maiden name) 1st Marriage

Subsequent Marriage (if applicable)

Family Details

Schools attended, dates and degrees: Community, political work, etc.:

Descendant   Descendant

Spouse   Spouse

Basic Employment History: Clubs, Church Affiliations, etc.:

Descendant   Descendant

Spouse   Spouse

Military Service:

Descendant   Spouse

M643113-10-6-1
Genealogical Number

Jessica Shannon Howard
Name (including maiden name if applicable)

Town of Residence

Florence, S.C.
Birthplace

10/11/1984
Date of Birth

Date of Death

Where Buried

Name of Spouse

Birthplace

Date of Birth

Date of Death

Where Buried

Date of Marriage

Place of Marriage

If married more than once:

Name of Spouse

Birthplace

Date of Birth

Date of Death

Where Buried

Date of Marriage

Place of Marriage

Parents of Spouse (with Mother's maiden name) 1st Marriage

Subsequent Marriage (if applicable)

Family Details

Schools attended, dates and degrees:

Community, political work, etc.:

Descendant

Descendant

Spouse

Spouse

Basic Employment History:

Clubs, Church Affiliations, etc.:

Descendant

Descendant

Spouse

Spouse

Military Service:

Descendant

Spouse

M64312211
Genealogical Number

Philip Barnes Nash
Name (including maiden name if applicable)

Denver, Colorado
Town of Residence

Cleveland, Ohio
Birthplace

4/4/1938
Date of Birth

Date of Death

Where Buried

Gail T. Prescott
Name of Spouse

New City, NY
Birthplace

12/10/1940
Date of Birth

Date of Death

Where Buried

11/30/1963
Date of Marriage

Suffern, NY
Place of Marriage

If married more than once:

Name of Spouse

Birthplace

Date of Birth

Date of Death

Where Buried

11/30/2023
Date of Marriage

Suffern, NY
Place of Marriage

Raymond Prescott & Olive Wagner
Parents of Spouse (with Mother's maiden name) 1st Marriage

Subsequent Marriage (if applicable)

Family Details

Schools attended, dates and degrees:

Community, political work, etc.:

University of North Carolina 1961
Descendant

Descendant

University of North Carolina 1962
Spouse

Spouse

Basic Employment History:
Commercial Airline Pilot
Continental Airlines 1965-2002
Descendant

Clubs, Church Affiliations, etc.:

Descendant

Paralegal 1985-2003
Spouse

Spouse

Military Service:

US Air Force: 1961-1965
Descendant

Spouse

M64312212
Genealogical Number

Charlotte Priscilla Nash
Name (including maiden name if applicable)

Sarasota, Fla.
Town of Residence

Cleveland, Ohio
Birthplace

6/10/1940
Date of Birth

Date of Death

Where Buried

Seaborn Flournoy Brown
Name of Spouse

Richmond, VA
Birthplace

10/12/1939
Date of Birth

Date of Death

Where Buried

4/21/1962
Date of Marriage

Bristol, Virginia
Place of Marriage

If married more than once:

Name of Spouse

Birthplace

Date of Birth

Date of Death

Where Buried

Date of Marriage

Place of Marriage

Parents of Spouse (with Mother's maiden name) 1st Marriage

Subsequent Marriage (if applicable)

Family Details

Schools attended, dates and degrees:

Community, political work, etc.:

Descendant

Descendant

Spouse

Spouse

Basic Employment History:

Clubs, Church Affiliations, etc.:

Descendant

Descendant

Spouse

Spouse

Military Service:

Descendant

Spouse

M643122121
Genealogical Number

Evan Haywood Brown
Name (including maiden name if applicable)   Town of Residence

2/22/1973
Birthplace   Date of Birth   Date of Death   Where Buried

Name of Spouse   Birthplace   Date of Birth   Date of Death

Where Buried   Date of Marriage   Place of Marriage

If married more than once:

Name of Spouse   Birthplace   Date of Birth   Date of Death

Where Buried   Date of Marriage   Place of Marriage

Parents of Spouse (with Mother's maiden name) 1st Marriage

Subsequent Marriage (if applicable)

Family Details

Schools attended, dates and degrees: Community, political work, etc.:

Descendant   Descendant

Spouse   Spouse

Basic Employment History: Clubs, Church Affiliations, etc.:

Descendant   Descendant

Spouse   Spouse

Military Service:

Descendant   Spouse

38.

THE MARY BROWN MOORE LINE
PICTURE

Mary Brown (Moore) Shannon (M643)   D. 4/23/1881 and William V. Shannon Home

Moore Genealogy Index*

*Womens are maiden names only.

Adams, Abraham Alvah - M62171
Adams, Edward Phillips - M62172
Adams, Edward J. - M62176
Adams, Elmer - M62177
Adams, Emerson Still - M621752
Adams, Frederick Vernon - M62175
Adams, Hester - M62174
Adams, Margaretta - M621772
Adams, Martha E. - M62173
Adams, Parks Madden - M621751
Adams, Stephen Andrews - M621753
Adams, Wilbur - M621771
Adams, Jr., Parks Madden - M6217511
Adamson, John William - M62425131
Adkins, Elizabeth Chase - M62744112
Adkins, Mary Virginia - M6263472
Adkins, Robert Walter - M6263471
Adkins, Samuel Edward - M6263473
Adkins, William Earl - M6263474
Adkins, III, Stephen Girard - M62744111
Adkins, Jr., Chase Morison - M6274411
Akens, Chyna - M6242151111
Allen, Cynthia Ann - M621161111
Allen, Lisa Kay - M621161112
Allen, Mark Clarke - M621161113
Allen, Mary Paige - M62362121111
Allen, Thomas David - M62362121112
Allgood, Catherine Glenn - M62892832
Allgood, Christy Elaine - M62892831
Ammons, Angela Marie - M62981531
Anderson, Elgin D. Forest - M628562
Anderson, Gladys Juanita - M628561
Anderson, Howard Forest - M6285621
Anderson, Modena Fay - M6285622
Anderson, Stephanie Irene - M621533111
Anthony, Alice Annette - M624251612
Anthony, Amy Lynn - M624251611
Anthony, Jeffrey Lynn - M62425161
Arnold, Carol Sue - M643113222
Arnold, Evelyn Grace - M643113221
Aron, Amanda - M621531222
Arthur, James Frederick - M624222311
Arthur, James - M6242223111
Arthur, Joel - M6242223113
Arthur, John - M624222313
Arthur, Judith Lynn - M624222312
Arthur, Justin - M6242223112
Asbury, James Miller - M6289342
Asbury, Retha Jane - M6289341
Ashbey, Christopher Aaron - M628925422
Ashbey, Dakota Chaning - M628925421
Atkinson, Helena May - M6215422

Atkinson, Phayre Grace - M6215421
Bailey, Alma Sue - M624253
Bailey, Anne Havens - M64312481
Bailey, Arthur Wendell - M62423221
Bailey, Barbara Ann - M6242342
Bailey, Barbara Ann - M64312472
Bailey, Ben Tom - M62426221
Bailey, Betty Jo - M643124512
Bailey, Betty - M62426213
Bailey, Carrie Elizabeth Taylor - M6242326
Bailey, Charles David - M6242334
Bailey, Charles Glenn - M6431242
Bailey, Dallas T. - M6242324
Bailey, Darrell - M62423311
Bailey, Donald P. - M6242325
Bailey, Ellis Pyott - M6242322
Bailey, Eugene Cassidy - M6431246
Bailey, Fannie - M64322
Bailey, Frances Arnett - M6242626
Bailey, Frances - M6242611
Bailey, Frank Gray - M6242624
Bailey, Frank - M624235
Bailey, Frank - M62426241
Bailey, Freddy Ann - M64312421
Bailey, Frederick Rounds - M6431243
Bailey, Gabriel - M624236
Bailey, George Alexander - M624261
Bailey, Glen Robert - M6242332
Bailey, Glenna Carolyn - M64312422
Bailey, Grattan M. - M64328
Bailey, Guy Havens - M6431248
Bailey, James Bigelow - M643124514
Bailey, James Catlett - M64324
Bailey, James Elwood - M624233
Bailey, James William - M62425
Bailey, Jane Ann - M64312461
Bailey, Janet Annabel - M62421
Bailey, Janice Carmen - M643124622
Bailey, Jay Bigelow - M6431244
Bailey, John Charles - M64312462
Bailey, John Vincent - M64312471
Bailey, Joseph Garland - M62423
Bailey, Joseph Garland - M6242321
Bailey, Judith - M64312432
Bailey, Julia Lynn - M643124312
Bailey, Julia - M64323
Bailey, Kathleen Ann - M643124313
Bailey, Kermit Carter - M6242613
Bailey, Laleen Opie - M6242323
Bailey, Lee Stuart - M6242622
Bailey, Linda Carmela - M643124712
Bailey, Lois Eve - M6242343

Bailey, Lori Catherine - M643124712
Bailey, Lynne Corinne - M64312482
Bailey, Marcus Wayne - M643124513
Bailey, Margaret A. - M62424
Bailey, Margaret Isabel - M624255
Bailey, Martha Alice - M62422
Bailey, Mary J. - M62420
Bailey, Mary Jackson - M6242625
Bailey, Mary Sue - M64312441
Bailey, Michael Allan - M62423411
Bailey, Michael Fred - M643124311
Bailey, Minnie Gertrude - M624251
Bailey, Mollie - M64325
Bailey, Paris Johnson - M624231
Bailey, Paul Allen - M6242341
Bailey, Paul - M624234
Bailey, Pauline - M6242612
Bailey, Peggy - M62426212
Bailey, Robert Charles - M64312473
Bailey, Ron - M624262141
Bailey, Samuel Abner - M64326
Bailey, Samuel Sheffey - M6431247
Bailey, Sherry - M624262112
Bailey, Tammy Michelle - M62423412
Bailey, Terry W. - M62423222
Bailey, Thomas Brown - M62426
Bailey, Thomas Crockett - M6431245
Bailey, Thomas Wayne - M64312483
Bailey, Virginia Catherine - M624631
Bailey, Virginia - M64327
Bailey, Wanda Jeanette - M6242333
Bailey, Wanda - M62426242
Bailey, William Edward - M64321
Bailey, William George - M6242623
Bailey, William Lee - M624262
Bailey, William Paul - M624254
Bailey, William Sheffey - M64312431
Bailey, William Tracie - M624232
Bailey, Willie Corinne - M6431241
Bailey, Willie Mabel - M624252
Bailey, Jr., Ben Tom - M62426211
Bailey, Jr., James Elwood - M6242331
Bailey, Jr., John Charles - M643124621
Bailey, Jr., Paris Johnson - M6242311
Bailey, Jr., Thomas C. - M64312451
Bailey, III, Ben Tom - M624262111
Baker, Chrystal Renee - M643113-10-2-1
Balderson, Kathryn L. - M624216431
Bantn, Megan Elizabeth - M62262142
Banton, Anthony Reed - M62262141
Barbour, Alfred Dunnington - M62116153
Barbour, Anna Christina - M621161531

Barbour, Mary Louise - M62116152
Barbour, Melissa Anna - M62116151
Barnett, Alvin Lee - M6214223
Barnett, Barbara Rosa - M621424
Barnett, Catherine Goldie - M621425
Barnett, Donald Arthur - M6214221
Barnett, Doris Elizabeth - M6214222
Barnett, Leta Winifred - M621423
Barnett, Samuel Arthur - M621422
Barnett, Wilbur Carlyle - M621421
Beadle, Suzanne Doshia - M62422-16-1
Beamer, Asa Brown - M6224534
Beamer, Asa Glen - M622456
Beamer, Byron Linwell - M622451
Beamer, Charles Madison - M622452
Beamer, Margaret Anita - M6224533
Beamer, Mary Moore - M622455
Beamer, Rachael Rogers - M62245311
Beamer, Robert Anderson - M622453
Beamer, Robert Arthur - M6224531
Beamer, Sara Kay - M6224532
Beamer, William Andrew - M6224535
Beamer, William Taylor - M622454
Beatty-Jarrard, Brittany Nicole - M624117442
Beatty-Jarrard, Kyle Lamarr - M624117441
Beavers, Allie Mae - M623642
Beavers, Annie Gertrude - M623644
Beavers, Bertram Bruce - M6236402
Beavers, Betty - M6236481
Beavers, Carlisle - M6236431
Beavers, Cecil - M6236417
Beavers, Charles Claude - M623645
Beavers, Charles Paris - M62367
Beavers, Curtis - M6236415
Beavers, David - M6236418
Beavers, Dexter Estel - M62364
Beavers, Edward Stanley - M62369x
Beavers, Edwin Howard - M6236482
Beavers, Elaine - M6236435
Beavers, Eleanor P. - M62362
Beavers, Eliza Pearl - M623631
Beavers, Eliza Pearl - M623121
Beavers, Elmer Lee - M628132
Beavers, Elmer - M6236401
Beavers, Ernest - M6236414
Beavers, Ethel Glenn - M623647
Beavers, Eugene Bertram - M623640
Beavers, Eugene - M6236453
Beavers, Eva Gray - M623649
Beavers, Gallie Leo - M62368
Beavers, George Francis - M62365
Beavers, Glenn - M6236433

Beavers, Helen P. - M6236432
Beavers, Lillian Grey - M6236413
Beavers, Loraine - M6236452
Beavers, Lucille - M6236403
Beavers, Mary Virginia - M6236416
Beavers, Mary - M623671
Beavers, Mildred - M6236412
Beavers, Otis Howard - M623648
Beavers, Robert G. - M628131
Beavers, Roy Kent - M6236411
Beavers, Sarah Lavine - M62361
Beavers, Sterling Price - M62366
Beavers, Summerfield Still - M62369
Beavers, Virgie Irene - M623646
Beavers, Virginia Katherine - M6236434
Beavers, Walter Summerfield - M623641
Beavers, Wilford - M623681
Beavers, William Grattan - M62363
Beavers, William Grattan - M623643
Beavers, William Grattan - M62312
Beavers, II, H. Wade - M6281311
Beavers, Jr., Charles Claude - M6236451
Beckett, Gary Allen - M643113-10-1-2
Beckett, Hillary Renee - M643113-10-1-2-1
Beckett, Michael John - M643113-10-1-1
Bedall, Charlene Kyle - M6282321
Belchee, Billie Neel - M6282224
Belchee, Mary Lee - M6282223
Belchee, Naomi Lucile - M628222
Belchee, Ruth Carlock - M6282222
Belcher, Michele Ranee - M62245521
Belcher, Todd McNeil - M62245522
Bennett, Martin - M62426263
Bennett, Michael Casey - M628224811
Bennett, Michael - M62426261
Bennett, Terry Ward - M62426262
Berg, Michelle Tiffany - M62744431
Berg, Sean Sven - M62744432
Bertram, James Porter - M62332712
Bertram, Patricia Jean - M62332711
Betita, Kevin Anthony - M621521211
Biddle, Kathleen - M62154712
Biddle, Linda - M62154711
Biddle, William - M62154713
Billingsley, Hudson James - M62981842
Billingsley, Lydia Althea - M62981841
Billips, Alice - M6263422
Billips, Margaret - M6263421
Bingeman, Jodi - M62153313
Bingeman, Lea Naomi - M62153311
Bingeman, Sue - M62153312
Birchfield, Brenda Kay - M6298115x

Birchfield, Constance Marie - M6298114
Birchfield, Daniel Lee - M62981124
Birchfield, David Andrew - M62981122
Birchfield, Eliot Sho-ta - M629811811
Birchfield, Erin Marie - M629811311
Birchfield, Frances Marie - M62981153
Birchfield, Gloria Dawn - M6298116
Birchfield, Heath Gilbert - M62981151
Birchfield, Homer Roscoe - M6298119
Birchfield, James Thomas - M6298112
Birchfield, Janice Elaine - M6298117
Birchfield, John Glen - M62981121
Birchfield, Kathy Ann - M62981123
Birchfield, Lenie Maria - M629811812
Birchfield, Mary Mae - M6298111
Birchfield, Matthew Boyd - M62981131
Birchfield, Michelle Louise - M62981152
Birchfield, Paul Franklin - M6298119y
Birchfield, Robert Boyd - M6298113
Birchfield, Sharon Sue - M6298119x
Birchfield, Verlin Lee - M6298118
Birchfield, Weston Dale - M62981132
Birchfield, Wilburn Lonnie - M6298115
Birchfield, Jr., Verlin Lee - M62981181
Bise, Daryle Ester - M6236491
Bise, Earl Saxton - M6236492
Bise, Frank - M6236494
Bise, Ralph - M6236493
Bixby, Lillian McCollum - M621911
Black, Andrew Glen - M62543
Black, Barbara Beryl - M625452
Black, Bruce Beverly - M625451
Black, Charles Clinton - M62545
Black, Mary Jane Moore - M62544
Black, Ora Lee - M62542
Black, William Arthur - M62541
Blizzard, Heather - M6431131-10-5-2
Blizzard, Samuel Alex - M6431131-10-5-1
Bocher, Barbara Ann - M6283211
Boehmer, Caleb Shane - M629815412
Boehmer, James Michael - M62981541
Boehmer, Meghan Haley - M629815411
Boehmer, Shannon Keith - M62981542
Boggess, Betty - M623621312
Boggess, Bill Johnny - M62362131
Bondshu, Coby Ann - M621161212
Bondshu, Frank Albert - M621161213
Bondshu, Krista Sue - M621161214
Bondshu, William Harold - M621161211
Borguez, Eva Alicia - M629321221
Borguez, Gabriel Aidan - M629321222
Borkey, Elizabeth Cameron - M62467121

Borkey, John Franklin - M62467122
Borkey, Karen Leigh - M6246711
Borkey, Jr., Walter Franklin - M6246712
Bourne, Anna L. - M643114312
Bourne, Jeffrey T. - M643114311
Bourne, Michael E. - M643114321
Bourne, Robert Eugene - M64311432
Bourne, Robert N. - M643114322
Bourne, William Thomas - M64311431
Bourne, Jr., William T. - M643114313
Bowers, William Thomas - M6242121111
Bowman, Judy - M6215821
Bowman, Mary Katelyn - M62467111
Bowman, Mently - M6215823
Bowman, Patti - M6215822
Bramblett, Kristopher Travis - M624117411
Bramblett, Marc Mahlon - M624117412
Brazil, Christopher Shane - M62182111
Brazil, Melina A. - M621821111
Breazeale, IV, Allissa Genevieve - M624683212
Breazeale, IV, Ples John - M624683211
Brie, Sharon - M622332222
Bright, Nancy Ellen - M622681
Brooks, Cody Ryan - M628925211
Brown, Alexandra Paige - M629321122
Brown, Andrew Patrick - M62932112
Brown, Andrew Scott - M629321121
Brown, Banner B. - M624116
Brown, Banner, Jr. B. - M6241161
Brown, Barbara Brenda - M6241162
Brown, Barbara Kent - M6241191
Brown, Blanche Louise - M624115
Brown, Caleb Fulcher - M62468211
Brown, Candice Michele - M62744421
Brown, Charles Fudge - M624111
Brown, Charles Luther - M6241185
Brown, Christie Michelle - M62468321
Brown, Clara Rebecca - M624114
Brown, Clara Rebecca - M62411432
Brown, Ernest - M6241132
Brown, Evan Heywood - M643122121
Brown, Frances - M6241181
Brown, Grace Reeves - M624112
Brown, Guy Edward - M6293212
Brown, Hayter Crockett - M624118
Brown, Jacqueline St.Clair - M6274441
Brown, James Elwood - M624683
Brown, Joan - M62411321
Brown, Linda Kay - M62932111
Brown, Mary Joe - M6241131
Brown, Mary Louise - M6241183
Brown, Mattie Lou - M624112x

Brown, Michael Fortunato - M6246832
Brown, Nancy Tiffany - M6274443
Brown, Nelson Clark - M624682
Brown, Pamela Ann - M62932122
Brown, Pauline Theresa - M62932121
Brown, Richard Painter - M6293211
Brown, Robert Adair - M6241192
Brown, Robert Daniel - M6241184
Brown, Robert Luther - M624113
Brown, Robert Michael - M62468322
Brown, Robin Taylor - M6246822
Brown, Steven James - M62468311
Brown, Taylor Elizabeth - M629321123
Brown, Teressa Lynn - M62932113
Brown, Vivian Gertrude - M624117
Brown, Vivian Gertrude - M6241174
Brown, III, Malcolm Marvin - M62411431
Brown, IV, Malcolm Marvin - M624114311
Brown, Jr., Heyter Crockett - M6241182
Brown, Jr., James Elwood - M6246831
Brown, Jr., James Roy - M624681
Brown, Jr., Kenneth John - M6274442
Brown, Jr., Nelson Clark - M6246821
Brown, Jr., Robert Daniel - M624119
Browning, Leota Vocile - M6214231
Browning, Robert Lee - M6214233
Browning, Virgil Lee - M6214232
Bruce, Frank L. - M623111
Bruce, Garland S. - M62311
Brunemeyer, Thomas Andrew - M6215432232
Brunemeyer, Timothy Allen - M6215432231
Brunk, Charlotte Delia Judith - M62122211
Brunk, Guy Edward - M62122221
Brunk, Guy George - M6212222
Brunk, William Summerfield - M6212221
Bucchi, Amy Lynn - M624232312
Bucchi, Jena Marie - M624232314
Bucchi, John Stevens - M624232311
Bucchi, Michael Paul - M624232313
Buchanan, Donnie E. - M62422-17-1
Buchanan, Mary Elizabeth - M6245812
Buchanan, Jr., William A. - M6245811
Buckler, Candice Lee - M62981911
Buckler, Jr., Dale Lee - M62981912
Bundy, Eunice Jean - M6263153
Bundy, Henry Carter - M6263152
Bundy, Margaret Naomi - M6263151
Bundy, Mary Candler - M6263154
Bundy, Jr., Walter Edward - M6263155
Byrge, Robert Earl - M62421321
Carr, Ella Sue - M6242232
Carr, John Elias - M6242231

Carter, Amelia Suzanne - M62362711
Carter, Amy M. - M624216212
Carter, Beatrice Frazier - M6242161
Carter, Ben Reese - M6242165
Carter, Betty Lee - M64311613
Carter, Christen Anne - M6293221221
Carter, Daniel J. - M624216213
Carter, Debra S. - M62421652
Carter, Francis Gray - M6247112
Carter, Gloria D. - M62421622
Carter, Harry Lee - M6242167
Carter, James Edward - M6242163
Carter, James Lee - M643116151
Carter, James Shanklin - M64311615
Carter, Jennifer E. - M624216511
Carter, Jenny L. - M62421644
Carter, Jodi - M624216211
Carter, Loann M. - M624216214
Carter, Margaret Alberta - M64311614
Carter, Mary Ann - M6242166
Carter, Mary E. - M62421643
Carter, Mary Ellen - M64311617
Carter, Michael D. - M624216412
Carter, Michael R. - M624216512
Carter, Michael T. - M62421642
Carter, Naomi Sebra - M64311611
Carter, Otis Jackson - M64311612
Carter, Priscilla Lane - M64311616
Carter, Roger Dale - M62421621
Carter, Rosemary - M643116121
Carter, Shirley Ann - M6247111
Carter, Susanna - M643116122
Carter, William D. - M62421641
Carter, William E. - M624216411
Carter, William Henry - M62362712
Carter, William Kyle - M6242164
Carter, Jr., Ben Reese - M62421651
Carter, Jr., Daniel R. - M6242162
Carver, William Scott - M643128231
Cary, Cameron Mary Ellen - M62254131
Cary, Sara Michelle - M62254132
Casey, Aaron W. - M6289264
Casey, Billy E. - M6289262
Casey, Bobby Ray - M6289261
Casey, Cindy - M62892627
Casey, Clyde M. - M6289266
Casey, Douglas - M62892623
Casey, Georgia B. - M6289265
Casey, H. Elwood - M6289268
Casey, Holly Marie - M62892611
Casey, Nicole - M62892628
Casey, Paula - M62892626

Casey, Rick - M62892624
Casey, Virginia L. - M6289267
Casey, Virginia - M62892625
Casey, Wallace Lee - M62892622
Casey, Jr., Aaron W. - M62892641
Casey, Jr., Billy E. - M62892621
Casey, Jr., Henry N. - M6289263
Caudill, Angela J. - M62421822
Caudill, Craig E. - M62421824
Caudill, David Franklin - M6242183
Caudill, Gene B. - M6242182
Caudill, M. Ann - M6242184
Caudill, Mark S. - M62421823
Caudill, Teresa L. - M62421821
Caudill, Jr., Robert L. - M6242181
Chaffin, Grace Olivia - M6431131111
Chambers, Amanda - M624221313
Chambers, Kimberly - M624221311
Chambers, Tracy - M624221312
Chapin, Betty Lou - M6236474
Chapin, Edna Cleo - M6236471
Chapin, Emma Miller - M6236475
Chapin, Jennings - M6236473
Chapin, Joseph Mongul - M6236477
Chapin, Nancy Caroline - M6236476
Chapin, William - M6236472
Childress, Rebecca Jane - M624321511
Chrisman, Cindy Marie - M624222412
Chrisman, Craig Michael - M624222411
Chrisman, Mark Allen - M624222413
Chrisman, Nancy Gray - M62422242
Chrisman, III, Campbell Houston - M62422241
Christian, Homer T. - M624541
Churchman, Nora Irene - M6265541
Clark, Andrew Still - M62181
Clark, Christopher Allen - M62982341
Clark, David Wendall - M643124212
Clark, Earl Finley - M62183
Clark, Emily Alexandra - M643124213
Clark, Marovia Eldora - M621831
Clark, Michael Glenn - M643124211
Clark, Pearl Amy - M62182
Cleland, Caroline Grace - M629322222
Cline, Eric T. - M624216221
Cline, Whitney M. - M624216222
Coe, Curtis Craig - M6212422
Coe, Mary Edna - M6212421
Coe, Virginia - M6212423
Coen, Brittany Elizabeth Warren - M6263431121
Collins, Melinda Lou - M62634321
Compton, Bane Gormon - M6412212
Compton, Mary Frances Muset - M6412211

Daugherty, Robert Hicks - M628241
Daugherty, Sarah Elizabeth - M62821
Daugherty, William Clarence - M628253
Daugherty, William Edward - M628243
Daugherty, III, Robert Hicks - M62824111
Daugherty,Jr., Robert Hicks - M6282411
Daughter, - M643131
Davies, Edward Ivan - M6215431
Davies, Elva Birma Florence - M621546
Davies, Gayle Aruna - M6215473
Davies, Harold Allen - M621544
Davies, Helena Adelaide - M621542
Davies, Horatio Chalmers - M621543
Davies, Joan Adelaide - M6215472
Davies, Mary Alene - M6215474
Davies, Nelson Edward - M621541
Davies, Thomas Albert - M621545
Davies, Virginia Maxie - M6215471
Davies, Jr., Albert Horace Minguay - M621547
Davies, Jr., Horatio Chalmers - M6215432
Davis, Allison Sue - M6211612231
Davis, Andrew Steven - M628925511
Davis, Grant Louise - M6211612232
Davis, Mark Steven - M62892551
Davis, Megan Hope - M628925521
Davis, Michael DeWayne - M62892552
Day, Ashley L. - M624216521
Day, Devin C. - M624216522
DeGray, Brett Matthew - M62932314
DeHart, Debra Carol - M643121231
Denni, Lyda Jane - M6283133
Denni, Martha Gwynne - M6283132
Denni, Virginia Delphine - M6283131
Dennison, Cecia Mare - M626362111
Dennison, Diane K. - M62636213
Dennison, Nathan Ward - M626362112
Dennison, Virginia - M62636212
Dennison, Jr., Noland Edward - M62636211
Denny, Brandon Taylor - M6242511121
Denslow, Amy Denise - M62139131
Denslow, Jacob Stedman - M621391321
Denslow, Jacquiline Michail - M62139121
Denslow, Jennifer Catherine - M62139122
Denslow, John William - M62139123
Denslow, Madalyn Faith - M621391322
Denslow, Martha Stedman - M6213911
Denslow, Michael Alan - M62139132
Denslow, Michael Taylor - M6213912
Denslow, Peter Ross - M6213913
Dethick, Mark Alan - M643124611
Dethick, Steven John - M643124612
Dillon, James Moore - M6243114

Dillon, Martha Moore - M62431131
Dillon, Samuel Jesse - M6243115
Dillon, Sarah India - M6243112
Dillon, Jr., Bunyan Webster - M6243113
Dimberg, Cody Douglas - M621391312
Dimberg, Jena Leigh - M621391311
Dinges, Jennifer Elizabeth - M621161222
Dinges, Kristan Suzanne - M621161221
Dinges, Pamela Mitchell - M621161223
Doherty, James Moore - M64121321
Doherty, John Houston - M64121322
Douthat, James Louis - M6293222
Douthat, Margaret Frances - M6293223
Douthat, Marilee - M62932222
Douthat, Roberta - M6293221
Douthat, Thomas Anthony - M62932221
Downs, Al - M62154722
Downs, Tom - M62154721
Drake, Ruth Bernice - M628331
Duncan, Barry Allyn - M62422161
Duncan, Charlotte Elizabeth - M6431251
Duncan, Edward Morton - M6431254
Duncan, Erin - M64312563
Duncan, Hallie Ruth - M6431252
Duncan, Horace Milton - M6431255
Duncan, Janice Rose - M64312531
Duncan, Kellie - M64312561
Duncan, Paul Nash - M6431256
Duncan, Shannon - M64312562
Duncan, Stephen Kent - M62422162
Duncan, Jr., William Jackson - M6431253
Dunlap, Glenna Ruth - M6281731
Dunnington, Angela Marie - M621161242
Dunnington, Annette - M62116113
Dunnington, Carl Still - M621161
Dunnington, Cheryl Emma - M621161241
Dunnington, Edward William - M621161233
Dunnington, Ellen Still - M6211613
Dunnington, Glenn Walter - M62116124
Dunnington, Kathleen Elizabeth - M621161232
Dunnington, Marjorie Sue - M62116122
Dunnington, Mary Louise - M6211615
Dunnington, Melissa Ann - M621161231
Dunnington, Patricia Louise - M62116111
Dunnington, Rachel Ann - M62116121
Dunnington, Robert Clarke - M6211611
Dunnington, Roberta - M62116112
Dunnington, Warren Harvey - M62116123
Dunnington, William Glenn - M6211612
Dustin, - M624262131
Easterline, Charles Still - M6213541
Edmonds, Alma R. - M6289173

Garlinghouse, Robert Orestes - M621822
Garlinghouse, Sarah McCall - M62182311
Garlinghouse, Jr., Richard Earl - M6218231
Garner, Samuel Glen - M64311617111
Garner, Jr., Harold Hoots - M643161711
Garrou, Daniel D. - M6243211123
Garrou, James M. - M6243211122
Garrou, Thomas S. - M6243211121
Gearheart, Cary Edward - M6293233
Gearheart, Mary Lou - M6293232
Gearheart, Monica Kay - M62932331
Gearheart, Peggy Lee - M6293231
Gearheart, Ralph Allan - M6293234
Gearheart, Traci Renee - M62932332
Gerst, Christopher - M621531211
Gerst, Dawn - M62153123
Gerst, Linda - M62153122
Gerst, Randy - M62153121
Gerst, Shelby Marie - M621531212
Gill, Aneva Alice - M6247242
Gill, Betty Ann - M6247232
Gill, Charles Henry - M624723
Gill, David Buchanan - M6247235
Gill, Douglas Leon - M6247221
Gill, Douglas Leon - M6281811
Gill, George Ronald - M6247222
Gill, Howard Hounsell - M624722
Gill, James Howard - M6247223
Gill, Lena Mariah - M624721
Gill, Mary - M6247234
Gill, Peggy - M6247231
Gill, Sam William - M624724
Gill, Sam William - M6247241
Gill, Sue Ellen - M6247243
Gill, Jr., Charles Henry - M6247233
Gillespie, Bettie St.Clair - M64137
Gillespie, Blanche - M641323
Gillespie, Carl - M641362
Gillespie, Charles Samuel - M64136
Gillespie, Delores R. - M628928122
Gillespie, Edward - M641311
Gillespie, Edwin Browne - M64132
Gillespie, Harvey Ernest - M64133
Gillespie, Hugh - M641363
Gillespie, Isaac Fudge - M64139
Gillespie, John - M641313
Gillespie, Mary Jane - M64134
Gillespie, Minnie - M641314
Gillespie, Nannie Marie - M64135
Gillespie, Raymond D. - M641322
Gillespie, Rees Bowen - M64138
Gillespie, Stella - M641315

Gillespie, Tiffany Lee - M64131
Gillespie, Tiffany M. - M628928121
Gillespie, Vivian - M641361
Gillespie, Wade - M641312
Gillespie, Warren L. - M641321
Gilreath, Daniel Jeffery - M62744311
Gilreath, Kate Elizabeth - M62744312
Glanville, Barbara Ann - M6214641
Glanville, Jane Themaine - M6214642
Goode, Caleb - M62263143
Goode, Isaac - M62263144
Goode, Joshua - M62263141
Goode, Zachary - M62263142
Gorman, Thurston White - M6263143
Graham, Aaron Sheffy - M62892
Graham, Albert L. - M628922
Graham, Alice Ann - M6263121
Graham, Altha - M6289162
Graham, Angela Gail - M643113511
Graham, Bernice - M6289161
Graham, Bill - M628913
Graham, Bobbie Elizabeth - M62892-10
Graham, Carol - M6289191
Graham, Christina Joan - M62892522
Graham, Clarence - M628915
Graham, Cruiz Aaron - M62892521
Graham, Dale - M6289163
Graham, Dewey S. - M628921
Graham, Dillon Harrison - M628925231
Graham, Dolly Darline - M62892524
Graham, Dovie - M628933
Graham, Dreama Annette - M62892542
Graham, Edith Barbia - M621413
Graham, Edna May - M628923
Graham, Edward - M621411
Graham, Elisa Joyce - M62892521
Graham, Finley Vaughan - M621414
Graham, Foster - M628931
Graham, Frank - M628914
Graham, George Aaron - M6289254
Graham, George C. - M6289135
Graham, George Dewey - M628918
Graham, Gladys Gray - M628917
Graham, Irene - M629181
Graham, J. C. - M628935
Graham, James William - M626311
Graham, James - M6289134
Graham, Janice Viola - M628934
Graham, John Aaron - M62892541
Graham, John Bunyun - M628919
Graham, John Harrison - M628925
Graham, John Harrison - M6289252

Harry, Gail - M64314221
Harry, Grover William - M643143
Harry, James A. - M6431422
Harry, John Calvin - M643142
Harry, Lisa D. - M624218213
Harry, Lynn M. - M624218212
Harry, Nancie Ann - M6281661
Harry, Robert K. - M6431423
Harry, Steven K. - M624218211
Harry, Jr., John Calvin - M6431421
Harvey, III, Thomas Biddle - M62743121
Hatch, Dorothy Henrietta - M6215231
Hatch, Helen Alice - M6215232
Hatch, Willard Leslie - M6215233
Hatcher, Elizabeth Ann - M624216112
Hatcher, James Edward - M62421613
Hatcher, Jenny Lynn - M62421612
Hatcher, John Thomas - M624216113
Hatcher, Jonathan Randall Clark - M6242161131
Hatcher, Kimberly Anne - M62932212
Hatcher, Kristen Noel - M624216133
Hatcher, Mary Kathryn - M624216111
Hatcher, Mary Kaye - M62932211
Hatcher, Megan Nicole - M629322131
Hatcher, Tamera Brooke - M629322132
Hatcher, Tara D. - M624216132
Hatcher, Thomas Clark - M62421611
Hatcher, III, Charles Walter - M62932213
Hatcher, Jr., James Edward - M624216131
Hatherly, Celine Michelle - M6243232211
Hatvany, Thomas Charles - M621161521
Heiby, Andrea - M62932321
Heiby, Braeden Owen - M629323232
Heiby, Christopher Edward - M62932323
Heiby, Garrett Allan - M629323231
Heiby, Hunter Edward - M629323221
Heiby, Jeffrey Robert - M62932322
Hendrickson, Annie Wells - M624731
Hendrickson, Binnie Frazier - M62472
Hendrickson, Charles Maurice - M624736
Hendrickson, Cora Janet - M6247351
Hendrickson, Effie Virginia - M62471
Hendrickson, Frank Erwin - M6247352
Hendrickson, Frank James - M624735
Hendrickson, James Moore - M62473
Hendrickson, Jaqueline Lee - M6247353
Hendrickson, John Robert Moore - M624732
Hendrickson, Mary Isabel - M624733
Hendrickson, Mildred Lee - M624737
Hendrickson, Jr., Charles Maurice - M6247361
Henry, Courtney Robyn - M622171224
Henry, Jason Charles - M622171222

Henry, Kristin Kay - M622171221
Henry, Ryan Patrick - M622171223
Higginboth, Jr., William Moore - M622621
Higginbotham, Barbara Letitia - M62263
Higginbotham, Charles Andrew - M6226213
Higginbotham, Charles Russell - M62262131
Higginbotham, Clynta LeVici - M62269
Higginbotham, India Allen - M62268
Higginbotham, Joshua Moore - M62262132
Higginbotham, Laura Matilda - M62264
Higginbotham, Lavinia Brown - M62266
Higginbotham, Lucy Virginia - M6226214
Higginbotham, Margaret Elizabeth - M6226212
Higginbotham, Mary Amanda - M62261
Higginbotham, Oscar Donald - M62267
Higginbotham, Sally Alice - M62265
Higginbotham, William M. - M62262
Higginbotham, William Moore - M62262
Higginbotham, III, William Moore - M6226211
Higginbotham, Jr., William Moore - M622621
Hill, James Patrick - M643128113
Hill, Kathryn Courtney - M643128111
Hill, Lauren Hunter - M643128112
Hodock, Brett A. - M6242141113
Hodock, Donald - M624214112
Hodock, Tanya J. - M6242141112
Hodock, Timothy W. - M6242141111
Hodock, II, Thomas J. - M62421411
Hodock, III, Thomas J. - M624124111
Hogg, Barbara Virginia - M6248221
Hoilman, Annie Lucille - M6263433
Hoilman, Hazel Audrine - M6263431
Hoilman, Margaret Sue - M6263432
Hollandsworth, Billie Jack - M62981172
Hollandsworth, Marie Dawn - M62981171
Holmes, Billie Raymond - M6413512
Holmes, Donald Dean - M6413511
Holt, Rush Madison - M62245322
Holt, Tristan Asa - M62245323
Holt, IV, John Andrew Broaddus - M62245321
Hoops, Gavin - M641215111
Hopkins, Herma Lou - M641355
Hopkins, Mary Elizabeth St.Clair - M641354
Hopkins, Rosalie Ernestine - M641353
Hopkins, Sally Christine - M641351
Hopkins, Wanda Charlene - M641356
Hopkins, Will Chapman - M641352
Horton, Jennifer Josephine - M6236212141
Horton, John Bowen - M6236212143
Horton, William Clay - M6236212142
Hounshell, Billie Reeves - M624832
Hounshell, Howard Andrew - M624831

Karr, Charles Robert - M62461

Kitts, Elizabeth Louvenia - M6281711

Karr, Frank King - M62466

Kitts, Homer Morton - M628178

Karr, James Wirt - M62465

Kitts, Nancy Ethel M268175

Karr, Jesse Moore - M62467

Kitts, Newell Jane - M628174

Karr, Margaret Frazier - M62463

Kitts, Robert Ernest - M628171

Karr, Mary Moore - M624671

Kitts, Ruth Alice - M628173

Karr, Nida Jane - M62468

Kitts, Tiffany Elizabeth - M62982411

Karr, Sarah Poage - M62462

Kitts, William Moore - M628176

Karr, William Luther - M62464

Kitts, Jr., Charles Frank - M628177

Katz, Cameron Robert - M622332211

Klappenbach, Andrew Bean - M627424131

Katz, Cayla Alexis - M622332212

Klappenbach, Brian Dale - M62742412

Katz, Erica Lynne - M62233222

Klappenbach, Bruce Douglas - M62742413

Katz, Robert Douglas - M62233221

Klappenbach, Charles Mitchell - M627424132

Kaye, George Edwin - M64312821

Klappenbach, David Edward - M62742411

Kaye, Maria Christine - M643128212

Klappenbach, Elliott Boone - M627424133

Kaye, Susan Lynn - M643128213

Klappenbach, Preston Michael - M627424111

Kaye, Thomas Lee - M643128211

Knapp, Ezra John - M624323133

Kaylor, Charles William - M62822613

Knapp, Jacob Samuel - M624323131

Kaylor, David Owen - M62822611

Knapp, Jennifer Marie - M624323132

Kaylor, Joshua Hale - M628226131

Knill, Carolyn Moore - M62822451

Kaylor, Karaline Kelly - M628226113

Knill, Christine Keefer - M62822452

Kaylor, Katharine - M628226111

Kulchar, Andrew George - M62893311

Kaylor, Kimberly Kristine - M628226112

Kulchar, James Byron - M62893313

Kaylor, Lewis Hale - M62822612

Kulchar, Mary Dovie - M62893312

Kaylor, Sarah Elizabeth - M628226132

Lambert, Amelia Elizabeth - M62822431

Keister, Blanchard Osborne - M626362

Lambert, Jessica Susan - M62822432

Keister, Emmy Jean - M6263621

Larson, Michael Collins - M626343212

Keister, Louise Gay - M62661

Larson, M.D., Kelly Michelle - M626343211

Keister, Phyllis Carolyn - M6263622

Laughlin, Anne Lisabeth - M6213922

Kempf, Aaron Matthew - M62139224

Laughlin, George Andrew - M621392

Kempf, Joshua Paul - M62139222

Laughlin, Mary Jane - M621391

Kempf, Nathan Andrew - M62139221

Laughlin, Patrick Andrew - M6213921

Kempf, Rachael Anne - M62139223

Laughlin, Susan Denise - M6213923

Kenison, Kaleb Edward - M629323322

Lawlor, Claire Rebecca - M6241141111

Kenison, Kelsea Cassandra - M629323321

Layne, Marcus Stephen - M643124111

Kenison, Kinsey Leigh - M629323323

Layne, Ronald Joseph - M643124112

Kennedy, Barbara Jane - M621464

Layne, Jr., Skelton Earl - M64312411

Kennedy, Elaine - M6214613

Leedy, Chris Elizabeth - M62425143

Kennedy, Harold Douglas - M621461

Leedy, Doris Jean - M6242516

Kennedy, James Cronin - M6214612

Leedy, Janet - M62425142

Kennedy, Karen Ann - M6214631

Leedy, Jimmy Eleanor - M6242515

Kennedy, Karl Leander - M621463

Leedy, John Clark - M6242514

Kennedy, Ken - M6214621

Leedy, John Robert - M62425144

Kennedy, Mary Frances - M6214611

Leedy, Lois Annette - M6242512

Kennedy, Murray Vaughan - M621462

Leedy, Margaret Baugh - M6242517

Kidd, Charlotte Ann - M6226312

Leedy, Mary Alice - M6242511

Kidd, Linda Jane - M6226311

Leedy, Melissa - M624215111

Kidd, Sara Louise - M6226313

Leedy, Patricia Jean - M62425141

Kidd, Susan Rebecca - M6226314

Leedy, Ruth Greer - M6242513

Kitchings, James Alan - M62254141

Leffel, Will Tom - M6243111

Kitchings, Joshua David - M62254142

Lester, Adam Keith - M624234122

Kitts, David Roscoe - M628172

Lester, Michael L. - M62233231

McGraw, Janet Irene   -   M6241155
McGraw, Lyle Gillespie   -   M6241154
McGraw, Mary Moore   -   M6241153
McGraw, Michael   -   M6241151
McKenzie, Alice Lynn   -   M62422122
McKenzie, Margaret Eugenia   -   M62422121
McMichael, Caroline Rae   -   M62274221
McMurray, Louis T.   -   M623312
McMurray, Lulora H.   -   M623311
McMurray, Rufus J.   -   M623313
McNeil, Barbara Jean   -   M6224552
McNeil, Charles Richard   -   M6224551
McNulty, Mary Kate   -   M643113711
McNulty, Vivian Lea   -   M64311372
McNulty, III, Patrick Henry   -   M64311371
McThenia, Emma Grace   -   M622311222
McThenia, Mary Amanda   -   M6223111
McThenia, Paige Barns   -   M62231121
McThenia, Whitley Wolf   -   M622311221
McThenia, William Talmadge   -   M62231123
McThenia, III, Andrew Wolf   -   M62231122
McThenia, Jr., Andrew Wolf   -   M6223112
Medlin, Amanda F.   -   M643116113
Medlin, Angela Lou   -   M643116143
Medlin, Bruce Wayne   -   M643116144
Medlin, Donna Lou   -   M643116114
Medlin, Pamela Ann   -   M643116142
Medlin, Paul N.   -   M643116111
Medlin, Paula A.   -   M643116112
Medlin, Ralph Earl   -   M643116141
Meggitt, Christine Keefer   -   M62822452
Melander, Carolyn Grace   -   M62154224
Melander, Dorothy Jean   -   M62154225
Melander, Erlc John   -   M621542213
Melander, Harold William   -   M62154221
Melander, Kimberley Paige   -   M6215422123
Melander, Marilyn Louise   -   M62154223
Melander, Matthew   -   M6215422121
Melander, Michael William   -   M621542212
Melander, Milton John   -   M62154222
Melander, Stephen Michael   -   M6215422122
Melander, Susan Carole   -   M621542211
Melcher, Leslie   -   M643113612
Melcher, Ryan   -   M643113611
Melcher, Wade Stephen   -   M64311361
Merchant, Christopher Scott   -   M62468222
Merchant, Jeffrey Thompson   -   M62468221
Miles, Carrie   -   M643116171
Miller, Brandon Hunter   -   M64121421
Miller, Julia St.Clair   -   M6274452
Miller, Katherine Jaspers   -   M62744511
Miller, Linda Elaine   -   M6227121

Miller, Robert D.   -   M6274451
Miltenberger, Sharon Ann   -   M624321112
Miltenberger, William Martin   -   M624321111
Mintz, Aaron Barns   -   M622312211
Mintz, Anna Johnston   -   M622312212
Miquelle, Dana Lisa   -   M62252232
Miquelle, Jessica George   -   M62252231
Mitchell, Eldred Duane   -   M6245233
Mitchell, Iris Elaine   -   M6245231
Mitchell, Richard Earl   -   M6245232
Mitchum, Arnold Russell   -   M64122111
Mitchum, Ferdie Lowell   -   M64122113
Mitchum, Shirley Gretta   -   M64122112
Moore, Ada   -   M629822
Moore, Alexandra Wilson   -   M62252322
Moore, Allie Mae   -   M641217
Moore, Alphus Burt   -   M64125114
Moore, Alyson Adams   -   M62252221
Moore, Amanda Nicole   -   M62981622
Moore, Andrew Edward   -   M62521
Moore, Andrew Perry   -   M625
Moore, Angela Jo   -   M6298192
Moore, Ann Huston   -   M6225233
Moore, Attila   -   M6245X
Moore, Audrey   -   M6298233
Moore, Augusta   -   M6288
Moore, Augustus Fulton   -   M6241
Moore, Barbara Elvira   -   M62244
Moore, Barbara Jane   -   M6228
Moore, Barbara Rebecca   -   M622712
Moore, Barbara   -   M6298232
Moore, Barnes Thompson   -   M62254
Moore, Bernard   -   M629833
Moore, Bertie Gertrude   -   M62961
Moore, Bessie Gertrude   -   M628313
Moore, Bessie   -   M62984
Moore, Bettie   -   M62413
Moore, Brian Keith   -   M62982421
Moore, Burtie Mariah   -   M62841
Moore, Buse Harman   -   M62415
Moore, Carolyn   -   M6298231
Moore, Catherine Aline   -   M64125121
Moore, Celia Anne   -   M64125153
Moore, Charles Emmitt   -   M6412513
Moore, Charles Francis   -   M64126
Moore, Charles Walter   -   M62934
Moore, Christopher James   -   M62252242
Moore, Christopher Peyton   -   M641251511
Moore, Clara May   -   M628311
Moore, Clifford Ernest   -   M62834
Moore, Clinton Barnes   -   M6228x
Moore, Coley Edward Sullivan   -   M641251242

Moore, Cosby Buenavista   -   M6291
Moore, Countney Virginia   -   M64121412
Moore, Creed F.   -   M6283x
Moore, Creed   -   M62852
Moore, David Allen   -   M6298162
Moore, David Wayne   -   M62981411
Moore, David Whitley   -   M6283
Moore, Deborah Susan   -   M6298241
Moore, Dewey E.   -   M629821
Moore, Dock M.   -   M629812
Moore, Doris Jane   -   M6298234
Moore, Dorothy Dean   -   M6283122
Moore, Dory   -   M629831
Moore, Easter M.   -   M629815
Moore, Edward P.   -   M62983
Moore, Edward Poage   -   M6293
Moore, Edward LaVegie   -   M6412514
Moore, Electra   -   M6287
Moore, Eliz Jane   -   M6281
Moore, Elizabeth Brown   -   M622414
Moore, Elizabeth Margaret   -   M62252111
Moore, Elizabeth Tennessee   -   M6247
Moore, Elizabeth   -   M6286
Moore, Ella Brown   -   M62246
Moore, Elliott Nauman   -   M62252351
Moore, Elvira H.   -   M6221x
Moore, Elvira   -   M62414
Moore, Emily Graham   -   M641251132
Moore, Eric James   -   M62981412
Moore, Eric St.Clair   -   M6225235
Moore, Erika Kehding   -   M6225231
Moore, Ethan Joseph   -   M62981831
Moore, Ferdinand Dunn   -   M64123
Moore, Ferdinand Lycurgus   -   M641251
Moore, Flavins Joseph   -   M6251
Moore, Florence   -   M629834
Moore, Franklin Earl   -   M628312
Moore, Freddie Lois   -   M64125111
Moore, George Montraville   -   M6253
Moore, George Walker StClair   -   M622522
Moore, Gertrude Ann   -   M629811
Moore, Glen D.   -   M6298141
Moore, Gordon Nash   -   M62853
Moore, Gordon Robert   -   M6285314
Moore, Grace   -   M62985
Moore, Graham Austin   -   M641251521
Moore, Gretchen Howard   -   M6412142
Moore, Haley Corrine   -   M6243231121
Moore, Harry Edward   -   M6298242
Moore, Harry Elwood   -   M629824
Moore, Hattie Alice   -   M62842
Moore, Heather Michelle   -   M641251512

Moore, Helen Yvonne   -   M6285311
Moore, Hubert L.   -   M629817
Moore, Ida Marie   -   M62522
Moore, India   -   M62251
Moore, Isaac Quinn   -   M629
Moore, Jackson Truston   -   M628532
Moore, Jacob Reynolds   -   M62252352
Moore, Jacqueline Nicole   -   M641251231
Moore, Jacqueline   -   M6285321
Moore, James Archibald   -   M62933
Moore, James Burt   -   M62855
Moore, James Edward   -   M62831
Moore, James Garfield   -   M62981
Moore, James Harvey   -   M641
Moore, James Herbert   -   M62523
Moore, James K.   -   M6284
Moore, James Nicholas   -   M64125124
Moore, James Paul   -   M6283121
Moore, James Thomas   -   M629816
Moore, James Tivis   -   M6243
Moore, James William   -   M64125
Moore, James William   -   M6412512
Moore, James Charles   -   M6224
Moore, James Milton   -   M622413
Moore, James Rutherford   -   M622523
Moore, Jane Shannon   -   M627
Moore, Jeffrey Taylor   -   M6227111
Moore, Jeremy Wayne   -   M62981421
Moore, Jerry Wayne   -   M6298142
Moore, Jesse Ward   -   M641214
Moore, Jessica Dawn   -   M62981611
Moore, Jessica   -   M64121511
Moore, John Clinton   -   M622415
Moore, John Columbus   -   M6252
Moore, John Columbus   -   M6252
Moore, John Freeman   -   M62273
Moore, John Houston   -   M641213
Moore, John Oscar   -   M6294
Moore, John Shannon   -   M628
Moore, John Walton   -   M64128
Moore, John William   -   M62845
Moore, Johnston Henry   -   M629823
Moore, Johnston Hoge   -   M6298
Moore, Jonathan Lee   -   M62981422
Moore, Jonathan Tyler   -   M62252241
Moore, Joseph Addison   -   M624
Moore, Joseph Addison   -   M624
Moore, Joseph Edward   -   M629819
Moore, Joseph Luther   -   M6249
Moore, Julia Ann   -   M6248
Moore, June Archer   -   M622541
Moore, Katharine Tierney   -   M6225234

Moore, Kathleen Geneva - M6285313
Moore, Kaylee Lauren - M641251522
Moore, Laura Lydia - M629818
Moore, Laura Michelle - M641251421
Moore, Laura - M6297
Moore, Lavalette - M6289
Moore, Lavinia Walker - M6221
Moore, Levicie Barnes - M6226
Moore, Luther - M624X1
Moore, Mabel Irene - M62833
Moore, Madelina Marie - M641252412
Moore, Margaret Elizabeth - M62932
Moore, Margaret Emory - M62432
Moore, Margaret M. - M64129
Moore, Margaret St.Clair - M622524
Moore, Margaret StClair - M6225223
Moore, Margaret Virginia - M62243
Moore, Margaret - M6285x
Moore, Margaret - M629832
Moore, Marie Louise - M6412132
Moore, Martha Amanda - M6242
Moore, Martha America - M6295
Moore, Martha Christine - M6245
Moore, Martha India - M62431
Moore, Martha Poage - M621
Moore, Martha Poage - M642
Moore, Mary Alice - M6298143
Moore, Mary B. - M626
Moore, Mary Berkeley - M6225221
Moore, Mary Brown - M643
Moore, Mary Eliza - M6229
Moore, Mary Elizabeth - M62272
Moore, Mary Ellen - M62253
Moore, Mary India - M62242
Moore, Mary J. - M629813
Moore, Mary Jane - M6292
Moore, Mary Joleen - M64125112
Moore, Mary Keziah - M6411
Moore, Mary Louise - M62411
Moore, Mary Lynn - M641251223
Moore, Mary Marie - M64122
Moore, Mary Mildred - M641216
Moore, Martha Louise - M641212
Moore, Matilda Peery - M6223
Moore, Matthew Burt - M641251141
Moore, Matthew Edward - M641251422
Moore, Melissa Louise - M641251222
Moore, Michael Logan - M64125122
Moore, Milton Ladd - M624X
Moore, Mindy Lynn - M641251221
Moore, Minnie - M62851
Moore, Nancy Ellen - M622416

Moore, Nancy Jane - M6244
Moore, Nancy Rose - M6282
Moore, Nash Edison - M62853
Moore, Nicholas Andrew - M641251241
Moore, Octavia Columbus - M6246
Moore, Olive Virginia - M64127
Moore, Ora Elissa - M62856
Moore, Ora Virginia - M62433
Moore, Orville V. - M62982
Moore, Orville - M629826
Moore, Oscar Barnes - M62275
Moore, Oscar Bascom - M6227
Moore, Oscar Bascom - M6227
Moore, Pamela Claire - M64125141
Moore, Pearl Nadine - M628314
Moore, Perry Alexander - M641211
Moore, Peyton Matterson - M6412515
Moore, Princess Palmyra - M6254
Moore, Ralph Gregory - M64125152
Moore, Rebecca - M62412
Moore, Robert B. - M64124
Moore, Robert Barns - M6225224
Moore, Robert Benjamin - M6283123
Moore, Robert Henry - M6222
Moore, Robert Henry - M62252
Moore, Robert Taylor - M622411
Moore, Rose McDonald - M62274
Moore, Roy - M62854
Moore, Sallie Matilda - M62245
Moore, Sally Lain - M623
Moore, Samuel Houston - M64121
Moore, Samuel Lycurgus - M6412
Moore, Sarah Rebecca - M6252
Moore, Sarah Rebecca - M6420x
Moore, Savanna Rose - M6412512411
Moore, Shirley Jeanne - M6285312
Moore, Stuart Hargrove - M64121411
Moore, Suzanne Kathleen - M64125143
Moore, Terry Morelle - M64125151
Moore, Thomas - M629835
Moore, Tina Sue - M6298163
Moore, Travis Michael - M62981413
Moore, Turner Cronin - M6225212
Moore, Victoria Lee - M6298191
Moore, Virginia Ayres - M628321
Moore, Virginia F. - M629825
Moore, Virginia Marie - M6412131
Moore, Virginia - M624X3
Moore, Wade Hampton - M62832
Moore, Wade Jackson - M628551
Moore, Walter Sims - M629814
Moore, William Gordon - M6285322

Mustard, Mary Matilda - M622311
Mustard, Mary Virginia - M622361
Mustard, Nancy Barnes - M6223312
Mustard, Oscar Jasper - M62235
Mustard, Rebecca Glyn - M6223311
Mustard, Robert Clinton - M62232
Mustard, Samuel Elbert - M62236
Mustard, Sharon Lynne - M6223322
Mustard, William Mustard - M62231
Mustard, Jr., Clinton Luther - M6223324
Mustard, Jr., Grattan Floyd - M622333
Nahory, Alexa Brianna - M628925212
Nahory, Alysa Marie - M628925213
Nahory, Caleb Scott - M628925211
Napier, Bernice - M641341
Nash, Alexis Richmond - M643122112
Nash, Alicia Bennett - M643122113
Nash, Alvin - M6431194
Nash, Andrew Jackson - M64311
Nash, Anna May - M6431223
Nash, Anna May - M6431223
Nash, Annie Frances - M643117
Nash, Benjamin Raymond - M643113832
Nash, Betty Mae - M64311352
Nash, Blanche - M643115
Nash, Charles Edward - M6431131
Nash, Charlotte Priscilla - M64312212
Nash, Claude Witten - M6431221
Nash, Claude Witten - M6431221
Nash, Craig Allen - M643113831
Nash, Devon - M6431138321
Nash, Donna Sue - M64311322
Nash, Elberta May - M6431165
Nash, Elizabeth Marie - M643113-10-3
Nash, Ella Margaret - M64311321
Nash, Ella Maye - M6431134
Nash, Emily Annette - M643113112
Nash, Eve Ellen - M64311382
Nash, Frances Eileen - M643113-10-5
Nash, Frank Pyott - M6431164
Nash, Frank William - M643116
Nash, Fred Thomas - M643118
Nash, Gail - M64311351
Nash, George R. - M643119
Nash, George Raymond - M64311932
Nash, George Washington - M64312
Nash, Grace Elma - M643125
Nash, Guy Henry - M643126
Nash, Hallie Lavinia - M643124
Nash, Harriet Zane - M643128
Nash, Harriet - M64316
Nash, Hattie Emanda - M6431161

Nash, Hazel - M643181
Nash, Henry Melvin - M64313
Nash, Jack Brown - M6431191
Nash, Jackie Wilson - M64311911
Nash, Jane Garrett - M64311331
Nash, Janet Ruth - M6431139
Nash, John Shannon - M64317
Nash, Keith Douglas - M64311384
Nash, Kenneth Mack - M64311332
Nash, Kristin Lynn - M64311941
Nash, Lavi Gertrude - M643114
Nash, Lou Emma - M643111
Nash, Lucian Fred - M6431138
Nash, Mack Mays - M6431133
Nash, Margaret Louemma - M6431163
Nash, Mark Anthony - M64311383
Nash, Mary Helen - M6431162
Nash, Mary Jettie - M643112
Nash, May Ruth - M643123
Nash, Nancy Annette - M64311312
Nash, Nancy Earnestine - M6431222
Nash, Nancy Elizabeth - M643121
Nash, Nancy Ernestine - M6431222
Nash, Nancy Ruth - M643113-10-6
Nash, Naomi Frances - M6431136
Nash, Pamela Kay - M64311913
Nash, Paul Sexton - M6431193
Nash, Paul Steven - M64311931
Nash, Philip Barnes - M64312211
Nash, Philip Barnes - M64312211
Nash, Phyllis Gail - M64311912
Nash, Prescott Barnes - M643122111
Nash, Ray Alexander - M6431192
Nash, Rhoda - M64314
Nash, Richard Carson - M64311313
Nash, Robert Shannon - M6431166
Nash, Roy Swanson - M6431132
Nash, Sallie Ruth - M643127
Nash, Sarah Elizabeth - M643113111
Nash, Shannon Kay - M643113-10-1
Nash, Sheri Lynn - M64311381
Nash, Sidney R. - M64318
Nash, Theresa Lynn - M64311922
Nash, Thomas Edward - M643122
Nash, Thomas Edward - M643122
Nash, Timothy Allen - M64311921
Nash, Virginia Blanche - M6431137
Nash, Virginia Sue - M643113-10-2
Nash, Wade Marvin - M643113
Nash, William Lane - M64315
Nash, William Raymond Wade - M643113-10-4
Nash, William Shannon - M643113-10

Peery, Maggie C.   - M623625
Peery, Margaret   - M6236223
Peery, Mary Bowen   - M623621214
Peery, Michael David   - M6236212112
Peery, Michael Thompson   - M623621211
Peery, Nan   - M62362117
Peery, Nan   - M6261236
Peery, Phyllis   - M6289122
Peery, Ruth Christian   - M6236214
Peery, Samuel Clay   - M6236212121
Peery, Sarah Elizabeth   - M6236212113
Peery, Stephen Preston   - M623621213
Peery, Stuart Samuel   - M6236212132
Peery, Treulean Ann   - M62362111
Peery, Trula Ann   - M6261231
Peery, William Whitley   - M62362113
Peery, William Whitley   - M62362116
Peery, William Whitley   - M6261233
Peery, III, Charles Henry   - M6236243
Peery, Jr., Charles David   - M62362114
Peery, Jr., Charles David   - M6261234
Peery, Jr., Charles Henry   - M623624
Peery, Jr., Glen Clay   - M62362121
Peery, Jr., Stephen Preston   - M6236212131
Perkins, Gordon St.Clair   - M6274221
Perkins, Walter Douglas Dow   - M622332221
Philistine, Kristen Rose   - M62274131
Philistine, Kyle James   - M62274132
Phillips, Margaret   - M6225131
Pidgeon, Juvenne Elizabeth   - M62373111
Pilawski, Chad Louis   - M62744412
Pilawski, Renee Dawn   - M62744411
Porter, Eliza   - M628154
Porter, James William   - M6282471
Porter, John Gordon   - M6282473
Porter, Nancy Letitia   - M628152
Porter, Robert Minister   - M628151
Porter, Thadryl Trevell   - M6281531
Porter, Virginia Lee   - M6282474
Porter, William Benjamin   - M628153
Porter, Jr., Robert L.   - M6282472
Pouier, Jenny   - M624216441
Powell, Dorothy Lee   - M6247123
Powell, Emma Virginia   - M6247121
Powell, George Robert   - M6247122
Powell, Harley Ray   - M6247125
Powell, Joy Ann   - M6247124
Powers, Susan Lynn   - M64311761
Powers, Jr., Paul Vincent   - M64311762
Preston, Irene Brown   - M6241143
Preston, Isabella Moore   - M6241141
Preston, Jack   - M62411423

Preston, Judith Ann   - M62411424
Preston, Mary Helen   - M62411421
Preston, Thomas Ballard   - M6241142
Preston, Thomas Montgomery   - M62411422
Price, Robert Henry   - M62252312
Price, Jr., Frederick Ward   - M62252311
Puckett, Bruce Allen   - M624262523
Puckett, Erinn Michelle   - M624262521
Puckett, John Franklin   - M62426251
Puckett, Kelly Nicole   - M624262512
Puckett, Mary Kristen   - M624262511
Puckett, Michael   - M624262522
Puckett, Jr., Lee Ed   - M62426251
Pugh, Michael Freddy   - M6431138121
Pugh, Michael Wayne   - M643113812
Pugh, Stacy Ann   - M643113811
Pugh, Stephen William   - M643113813
Pugh, Timothy   - M643113814
Pupello, Marcia Ann   - M6223521
Quigley, Riley Thomas   - M629321131
Quigley, Taylor Matthew   - M629321132
Rachel, Brook Lee   - M629323112
Rachel, Daniel Lee   - M629323122
Rachel, Kent Allan   - M62932313
Rachel, Lindall Eugene   - M62932311
Rachel, Scott Douglas   - M62932312
Rachel, Shannon Marie   - M629323111
Rachel, Shawn Douglas   - M629323121
Rackley, Paul William   - M6243232222
Rackley, Sarah Catherine   - M6243232221
Rader, Virginia June   - M622631
Raglin, Bradley Ronald   - M624327111
Raglin, Jonathan Travis   - M624327112
Raley, David   - M641251111
Rannabarger, Annie Fields   - M622173
Rannabarger, Arthur   - M622172
Rannabarger, Charles Edward   - M6221723
Rannabarger, Glen Russell   - M6221724
Rannabarger, Juanita Joanne   - M6221725
Rannabarger, Marvin Ray   - M6221727
Rannabarger, Mary Lavenia   - M622171
Rannabarger, Mary Lou   - M6221726
Rannabarger, Richard Arthur   - M6221721
Rannabarger, Robert Lee   - M6221722
Rawlings, Chase   - M6242223124
Rawlings, Genevieve   - M6242223123
Rawlings, Loren   - M6242223122
Rawlings, Louis   - M6242223121
Rebuck, Allen Wayne   - M62421841
Rebuck, John Wallace   - M62421842
Reinhold, Alice Irene   - M62981162
Reinhold, James Homer   - M62981161

Reinhold, James Wesley   -   M629811611
Reinhold, Kevin Lynn   -   M62981163
Reinhold, Krista Lane   -   M629811612
Repass, Alfred Jack   -   M6289332
Repass, David Wayne   -   M62893333
Repass, Jared Alexander   -   M628933211
Repass, Lisa Marie   -   M62893331
Repass, Mara Michelle   -   M62893341
Repass, Margaret Louise   -   M6289331
Repass, Marshall Graham   -   M6289334
Repass, Roy Douglas   -   M6289333
Repass, Shelia   -   M62893332
Repass, II, Alfred Jack   -   M62893321
Reynolds, Benjamin Mason   -   M62744521
Reynolds, Edric Scott   -   M62744522
Reynolds, Rebecca Ann   -   M643121221
Richardson, Scott   -   M624224222
Richardson, Todd Carl   -   M624224221
Ripley, Huston   -   M6225242
Ripley, St.Clair   -   M6225241
Ripley, Timothy Regan   -   M6225243
Ritchey, Frances Arlene   -   M6212512
Ritchey, Leslie McCaw   -   M6212511
Roberts, Christy Lynn   -   M6431245121
Roberts, Madison Grace   -   M6412512311
Roberts, Misty Leigh   -   M6431245122
Roberts, Reese Nicole   -   M6412512312
Roden, Christina Doreen   -   M62532112
Roden, Matthew Christian   -   M62532111
Roden, Sharon Lynn   -   M62153212
Roden, William Christian   -   M62153211
Rodgers, Brian Frank   -   M62263113
Rodgers, Robert Earl   -   M62263112
Rodgers, William Thornton   -   M62263111
Rojo, Kristen Bailey   -   M622681111
Rominger, Austin Brooks   -   M641251431
Rominger, Britt Michael   -   M641251432
Rominger, McKenna Reese   -   M641251433
Rominger, Riley McLain   -   M641251434
Roncella, Anthony J.   -   M624216122
Roncella, Crystal S.   -   M6242161211
Roncella, Frank   -   M624216121
Roncella, Stephanie N.   -   M6242161221
Roncella, Tara L.   -   M6242161212
Rose, J. T.   -   M62332411
Rose, Leah Nan   -   M623324112
Rose, Lynnelle Renee   -   M623324113
Rose, Melanie Ann   -   M623324111
Rosen, Mary Gay   -   M62425173
Rosen, Rebecca Dawn   -   M62425172
Rosen, Trudy Susan   -   M62425171
Rosen, Wendy Gail   -   M62425174

Ruble, A. W.   -   M6242152
Ruble, Charles Ervin   -   M62421512
Ruble, Charles   -   M6242151
Ruble, Sandra Mae   -   M62421511
Russell, Ruth   -   M6213152
Russell, Zella   -   M6213151
Rutherford, Martha Lou   -   M62634311
Salyers, Douglas Michael   -   M62982211
Salyers, Gail   -   M62982221
Salyers, Karen   -   M62982212
Salyers, Thomas   -   M6298222
Salyers, III, Charles D.   -   M62982211
Salyers, Jr., Charlie D.   -   M6298221
Sanchez, Eli Gabriel   -   M627423132
Sanchez, Jon Marco   -   M627423131
Sands, Carl Vernal   -   M6285612
Sands, Royce Calvin   -   M6285611
Saunders, Jessica Nicole   -   M624251721
Saunders, Sara Amanda   -   M624251722
Schall, Barbara Jo   -   M62411744
Scheel, Alexander Mason Reynolds   -   M627445211
Schildwachter, Brooke Anne   -   M62746111
Schildwachter, Hayes St.Clair   -   M62746113
Schildwachter, Meredith Donnel   -   M62746112
Scott, Judith Ann   -   M62432322
Scott, Algene Stewart   -   M624327
Scott, Amy Towers   -   M624321212
Scott, Andrew Jonathon   -   M6243232122
Scott, Brad   -   M62432612
Scott, Cynthia Rose   -   M62432323
Scott, David Christopher   -   M62432821
Scott, David Moore   -   M6243213
Scott, Deborah Ruth   -   M62432122
Scott, Delores Jean   -   M62432133
Scott, Dwight Barker   -   M62432134
Scott, Frances Kay   -   M62432131
Scott, Grace Morgan   -   M6243232121
Scott, Hubert Emory   -   M6243261
Scott, James Muncy   -   M6243231
Scott, James Rudolph   -   M624328
Scott, John Tivis   -   M624321
Scott, Keith Conn   -   M62432152
Scott, Kelly Leigh   -   M624323211
Scott, Kelly   -   M62432613
Scott, Lois Ann   -   M6243242
Scott, Luther George   -   M624324
Scott, Lynda Marie   -   M62432312
Scott, Margaret Ellen   -   M6243211
Scott, Matthew Emory   -   M624326
Scott, Patricia Ann   -   M6243271
Scott, Paul Mitchell   -   M624325

Scott, Rachael Elizabeth - M624321213
Scott, Robert Twining - M6243282
Scott, Rosemary Corrine - M624232112
Scott, Russell E. - M6243241
Scott, Ruth Diane - M62432313
Scott, Sarah Ann - M6243283
Scott, Sara Shannon - M624321211
Scott, Sidney Martin - M624323
Scott, Steven Michael - M62432123
Scott, Susan Elaine - M62432151
Scott, Suzanne Elizabeth - M62432822
Scott, Thomas Bennett - M6243215
Scott, Tracy - M62432611
Scott, William Bennett - M6243214
Scott, Willie Gladys - M624322
Scott, III, James Muncy - M624323111
Scott, III, John Tivis - M62432121
Scott, III, Sidney Martin - M62432321
Scott, IV, Sidney Martin - M624323212
Scott, Jr., David Moore - M62432132
Scott, Jr., James Muncy - M62432311
Scott, Jr., James Rudolph - M6243281
Scott, Jr., John Tivis - M6243212
Scott, Jr., Paul Mitchell - M6243251
Scott, Jr., Sidney Martin - M6243232
Seay, Jonathan Bransford - M62233131
Self, Christina Rene - M624323221
Self, Michelle Leigh - M624323222
Sells, Clinton Edward - M624251131
Sells, James Edward - M62425113
Sells, John Paul Alexander - M624251111
Sells, John Paul Rutledge - M62425111
Sells, Mary Amy - M624251113
Sells, Mary Lori - M624251112
Sells, Thomas Michael - M62425112
Shackelfod, Lavenia Kay - M62217122
Shackelford, Donald William - M6221713
Shackelford, Kenneth Lee - M6221712
Shackelford, Marjorie Lou - M6221714
Shackelford, Mary Genevieve - M6221711
Shackelford, Stephen Roy - M62217123
Shackelford, Jr., Kenneth Lee - M62217121
Shanahan, Bridget Katherine - M621533113
Shanahan, Tara Rose - M621533112
Shannon, Annie Neel - M6282245
Shannon, Cassie Danielle - M628224421
Shannon, Christopher Louis - M628224621
Shannon, Clara B. - M6282247
Shannon, Daniel Stephen - M62822442
Shannon, Elizabeth - M6431
Shannon, Gregory Lee - M62822462
Shannon, Jackson Lee - M628224661

Shannon, James Catlett - M6433
Shannon, James Lee - M6282246
Shannon, James Mark - M62822465
Shannon, Jane Ann - M62822481
Shannon, Jasper Daugherty - M6282248
Shannon, Jeffery Fry - M62822464
Shannon, John Laurence - M62822466
Shannon, John William - M64343
Shannon, Jonathon Lee - M628224622
Shannon, Joseph B. - M6434
Shannon, Joyce Megan - M628224611
Shannon, Kathryn Olivia - M62822463
Shannon, Kelly Lynn - M628224662
Shannon, Kristina Lynn - M628224641
Shannon, Laura B. - M64341
Shannon, Linda Jean - M62822441
Shannon, Margaret Bernice - M6282243
Shannon, Margaret Ella - M64342
Shannon, Mary Ann - M6432
Shannon, Mary Kate - M643431
Shannon, Mary Virginia - M64344
Shannon, Rachel Leigh - M628224642
Shannon, Sally Catherine - M628224612
Shannon, Samuel Jacob - M628224651
Shannon, Stephen Curtis - M62822461
Shannon, Willie Moore - M6282242
Shannon, Wylie Wynne - M6282241
Shannon, Jr., Adam Steven - M6282244
Sharpe, Audrey Marquith - M62117112
Sharpe, Constance Lucille - M62117111
Shawver, Alice Mead - M64311428
Shawver, Aline - M64311423
Shawver, Bessie - M6431143
Shawver, Clyde Jackson - M6431144
Shawver, Donald - M64311424
Shawver, Edward - M64311425
Shawver, Eugene - M64311422
Shawver, Fred Francis - M6431145
Shawver, Mary Sue - M64311427
Shawver, Mildred - M64311421
Shawver, Paul H. - M6431141
Shawver, Paul Richard - M64311411
Shawver, William Edward - M6431142
Shawver, William - M64311426
Shelton, Francis Witten - M6263341
Shelton, Kent Fulton - M6263343
Shelton, William Reese - M6263342
Shrader, Adam Nicholas - M643113821
Shrader, Christopher Pyott - M643113822
Shrader, Kimberly Marie - M643113823
Sither, Marea Nicole - M627411211
Smiczek, Catherine Ann - M643125111

Smiczek, Jeanne Elizabeth - M643125112
Smith, Carl Gene - M62116131
Smith, Glenn Robert - M621161313
Smith, Harold Whitley - M6263311
Smith, Holley Sue - M621161314
Smith, Jack Still - M62116132
Smith, Joetta Still - M621161322
Smith, Kelvin Gene - M621161323
Smith, Laura Ellan - M62261311
Smith, Lee Anna - M621161312
Smith, Lee - M621161332
Smith, Lois Ann - M621161331
Smith, N. Chelsea - M6431132121
Smith, Nancy Ellen - M62116134
Smith, Trevor Edwards - M628933321
Smith, Ward - M629152
Smith, William Clarke - M62116133
Smith, Zetta Loyce - M621161321
Smith, Jr., Charles Clinton - M629151
Smith, Jr., William Clarke - M621161333
Snodgrass, Charles Brown - M6241121
Snodgrass, Elizabeth Jane - M62822231
Snodgrass, Harold William - M6241123
Snodgrass, Mary Brown - M62411231
Snodgrass, Sandra Jane - M62411232
Snodgrass, Jr., Robert Hutton - M6241122
Snyder, Michael William - M62262122
Snyder, Natalie Elizabeth - M622621211
Snyder, Jr., Stephen Douglas - M62262121
Sparks, Blenna Rae - M62233121
Sparks, Jenna Katherine - M622331222
Sparks, Monroe Spencer - M622331221
Sparks, Jr., Lanny Leck - M62233122
St.Clair, Allison Leigh - M6274611
St.Clair, Amy (Amey) Rowe - M6274622
St. Clair, Beverly Virginia - M62741111
St.Clair, Catherine Cecil - M627471
St.Clair, Charles Tiffany - M62741
St.Clair, Charles Wade - M627462
St.Clair, Elizabeth Armstrong - M6274311
St.Clair, Frank Sterling - M6274811
St.Clair, Frank Tabler - M62745
St.Clair, Glenn Moore - M62744
St.Clair, Glenn - M627445
St.Clair, Jacqueline Pendleton - M627444
St.Clair, Jane Elwood - M627423
St.Clair, Jane Pryor - M6274621
St.Clair, John Alexander - M62742
St.Clair, Joseph Davis - M62741113
St.Clair, Judean Annette - M6274812
St.Clair, Julia Tiffany - M627441
St.Clair, Kathryn Tiffany - M6274821

St.Clair, Marea Norvell - M6274112
St.Clair, Maria Tiffany - M627421
St.Clair, Martha Jane - M62747x
St.Clair, Mary Archer - M6274312
St.Clair, Nancy Harman - M627424
St.Clair, Otis Eugene - M62746
St.Clair, Pauline Bittle - M627443
St.Clair, Richard Otis - M627461
St.Clair, Rob Roy - M62747
St.Clair, Rosalinda Blow - M627442
St.Clair, Rosalinda Blow - M62749x
St.Clair, Sarah Elizabeth - M627422
St.Clair, Sarah Maria - M62749
St.Clair, Virginia Beverly - M62741111
St.Clair, Wade Hampton - M62743
St.Clair, Wade Tiffany - M627482
St.Clair, II, Alexander Armstrong - M627432
St.Clair, III, Alexander - M62748
St.Clair, III, Alexander - M62748
St.Clair, III, Charles Tiffany - M6274111
St.Clair, IV, Alexander - M627481
St.Clair, IV, Charles Tiffany - M62741112
St.Clair, Jr., Charles Tiffany - M627411
St.Clair, Jr., Frank Tabler - M627451
St.Clair, Jr., Rob Roy - M627472
St.Clair, Jr., Wade Hampton - M627431
Stafford, Carrie Lucille - M624563
Stafford, Charles Draper - M6245221
Stafford, Crystal Mae - M6245223
Stafford, Dailey Van Buren - M62457
Stafford, David Orville - M624564
Stafford, Dewey Chapman - M624513
Stafford, Elizabeth Dora Lee - M62455
Stafford, Ellen Jane - M6245222
Stafford, Grace Pearl - M62459x
Stafford, Hazel Irene - M624562
Stafford, Ida Faith - M624523
Stafford, James Addison - M62451
Stafford, James William - M624515
Stafford, Laura Mae - M624521
Stafford, Margaret Julia - M62454
Stafford, Margie Kathleen - M624561
Stafford, Nellie Grant - M62458
Stafford, R.C. Allen - M624511
Stafford, Robert Lee - M62452121
Stafford, Robert Luther Brown - M62456
Stafford, Roberta Jane - M62453
Stafford, Roy Edward - M624522
Stafford, S.M. Flanagan - M624512
Stafford, Stacy Pink - M62459
Stafford, Tyler Hoge - M62452
Steffey, Allison Leigh - M624117141

Steffey, Cassandra Gene - M62411713
Steffey, James Porter - M62411712
Steffey, Stephen Early - M62411714
Stephans, Ottie Mabel - M624711
Stephens, Ada Lee - M624717
Stephens, Binnie Catherine - M624713
Stephens, Carrie Lee - M624712
Stephens, Robert Roosevelt - M624715
Stephens, Sidney Beltrans - M624716
Stephens, William Edward - M624714
Still, Abraham Craig - M621591
Still, Abraham Price - M62132
Still, Abram Allen - M62152
Still, Adaiah - M62161
Still, Adam Hamilton - M62137213
Still, Allan Alvin - M6215212
Still, Allen Burt - M6212522
Still, Amanda - M62159314
Still, Andrew Taylor - M6213
Still, Andrew Taylor - M621353
Still, Andrew Taylor - M6213711
Still, Ann Taylor - M62137215
Still, Annie Christine - M621141
Still, Aruna Grant - M62154
Still, Barbara Jane Poage - M6214
Still, Birma Harriet - M62158
Still, Blanch Jean - M6211713
Still, Boaz Alexander - M62137214
Still, Carolyn - M6215911
Still, Carrie Anne - M62159224
Still, Cassandra Elliott - M6219
Still, Charles Edward - M62135
Still, Charles Shelton - M6213551
Still, Clarence Percy - M621521
Still, Dara C. - M62159312
Still, Delia Frank - M621222
Still, Della Jean - M621172
Still, Doreen - M6215321
Still, Dudley Turner - M62134
Still, Duncan Ross - M6215923
Still, Edith Dorothy - M621523
Still, Edward Clark - M621171
Still, Edward Cox - M6211
Still, Edward M. - M6215322
Still, Edward Marsden - M62153
Still, Ellen Lelia - M621533
Still, Elva Nadine - M625211
Still, Ernest Mently - M621532
Still, Eugene Updyke - M621361
Still, Fleetwood Churchill - M62111
Still, Frank Alva - M6211712
Still, Fred Mix - M621371

Still, Fred - M62138
Still, Frederick George - M6215922
Still, George Anderson - M621221
Still, George W. - M62132x
Still, Gladys Mary - M621142
Still, Grace - M621531
Still, Harold Rider - M621351
Still, Harry Mix - M62137
Still, Harry Stanley - M6213712
Still, Helen Dorothy - M621176
Still, Helen Gladys - M621352
Still, Herman Taylor - M62136
Still, Iva May - M62163
Still, James Abram - M62125
Still, James Edward - M62115
Still, James Moore - M6212
Still, Jennie Tyler - M62162
Still, Jerold Marcus - M62117123
Still, Joanne Elizabeth - M6212521
Still, John Jay - M62114
Still, John Marquith - M62117122
Still, John Wesley - M6216
Still, Joseph Maclise - M62113
Still, Katie Marie - M62159224
Still, Katrina Susanne - M62159228
Still, Keith Michael - M62159223
Still, Kelly Beth - M62159226
Still, Kendra Michael - M62159229
Still, Kevin Natheniel - M62159221
Still, Kimberly Joy - M62159227
Still, Kristy Noel - M621592-10
Still, Kyle Christopher - M62159222
Still, Lorenzo Waugh - M62133x
Still, Mabel Alvena - M6211711
Still, Marcia Ione - M62134x
Still, Marilyn Ann - M62152121
Still, Mark Lanza - M62137212
Still, Marovia Marsden - M6218
Still, Martha Elizabeth - M62121
Still, Martha Helen Blanche - M62139
Still, Marusha Hale - M62131
Still, Mary Elizabeth - M621354
Still, Mary Gertrude - M621251
Still, Mary Jane Findley - M62124
Still, Mary Margaret - M621175
Still, Mary Margarette - M6217
Still, Mently Frederick - M62159
Still, Noah - M62159313
Still, Orthor Simpson - M62156
Still, Patricia Ann - M6215933
Still, Paul Anthony - M62159211
Still, Richard Harry - M621372

Still, Robert Edward - M62117121
Still, Robert John - M6215932
Still, Ruphus King - M62155
Still, Ruth Jane - M621174
Still, Sarah Margaretta - M62116
Still, Sharon Lee - M62152122
Still, Summerfield Saunders - M62122
Still, Susan B. - M62133
Still, Susan Sorepta - M62123
Still, Susan - M6215912
Still, Theodore Andrew - M6211714
Still, Thomas Abraham - M62117
Still, Thomas Chalmers - M6215
Still, Thomas Chalmers - M6215921
Still, Thomas Clerill - M621592
Still, Thomas Eugene - M621173
Still, Virgil Farris - M621252
Still, William Leonard - M62151
Still, William Leonard - M621593
Still, William Moore - M62112
Still, William S. - M62159311
Still, William Thomas - M6215931
Still, III, Richard Harry - M62137211
Still, Jr., Charles Edward - M621355
Still, Jr., Eugene Updyke - M6213611
Still, Jr., Herman Taylor - M621362
Still, Jr., Richard Harry - M6213721
Still, Jr., Thomas Chalmers - M62157
Stille, Charlene Louise - M6254211
Stille, Charles Henry - M625421
Stimson, Francis - M6434212
Stimson, Joseph - M643422
Stimson, Mary Ruth - M643423
Stimson, William V. - M643421
Stimson, Jr., William V. - M6434211
Stine, Carolyn Ashley - M623672121
Stine, Kathryn Lynn - M6236272122
Stuckey, Kimberly Dawn - M621161121
Sullivan, Virginia Emily - M643113722
Sullivan, IV, Daniel F. - M643113721
Surber, Amy Ann - M629322122
Surber, Ashley Gelain - M629322123
Surber, Candace Leigh - M629322121
Sutherland, Katheryn Marea - M62741123
Sutherland, Linden Crockett - M627411221
Sutherland, Marjorie St.Clair - M62741121
Sutherland, Nathalie Lynn - M627411223
Sutherland, Rebecca Lindsey - M627411222
Sutherland, III, George Dudley - M62741122
Sutich, Travis - M621533121
Sutphin, Lettitia Louise - M62362751
Sutton, Nora Barbour - M621161511

Sutton, Roberta Barbour - M621161512
Sweet, Linda Rebecca - M62411411
Sword, Charles Jefferson - M6431131121
Sword, Sarah Elizabeth - M6431131122
Szabad, George M. - M621542241
Tabler (Newson), Elroy - M6215332
Tabler (Newson), Joyce Bell - M6215331
Tabor, Aletha Florence - M6431211
Tabor, Anna Louise - M64312122
Tabor, Billie Marie - M64312123
Tabor, Buenos - M6431213
Tabor, Elmer W. - M64312131
Tabor, Evelyn - M64312121
Tabor, Harold Johnson - M6431212
Tabor, Irving Moore - M624331
Tabor, Jennifer Joy - M64313121312
Tabor, Kenneth - M6242142
Tabor, Lillian B. - M6242141
Tabor (Stupalsky), Edward DeWitt - M64312112
Tabor (Stupalsky), Joseph - M64312111
Tabor, Jr., Elmer W. - M64313121311
Taylor, Rebecca Eleanor - M624251531
Thomas, David Joseph - M6241171313
Thomas, Mary Alexandra - M624117132
Thomas, Megan Elizabeth - M6241171311
Thomas, Morgan Alexandria - M6241171312
Thomas, Robert Brown - M624117131
Thomas, William Gerald - M624117133
Thompson, Alicia Ann - M62432833
Thompson, Betty Leigh - M64312825
Thompson, Bradley William - M62432832
Thompson, Carol Zane - M64312811
Thompson, Elma Zane - M6431282
Thompson, Geneva Anne - M62631462
Thompson, Jack Nash - M64312822
Thompson, Laura Elizabeth - M62432831
Thompson, Mary Ann - M64312823
Thompson, Neva Jean - M6214711
Thompson, Robert Henry - M6431284
Thompson, Robert Lewis - M64312824
Thompson, William Jackson - M6431283
Thompson, William S. - M62631461
Thompson, Jr., Harrison M. - M6431281
Tidy, Robert Harris - M623624111
Tiffany, Maria Jane - M6274
Tiggs, Deanna Kethry - M6215422112
Tiggs, Jonathan Karl - M6215422111
Tiller, III, Jason Pyott - M62426212
Todd, James Samuel - M6215852
Todd, Leonard MacLane - M6215851
Todd, Lounis - M6215853
Traynham, Ann Tiffany - M6274241

1205

Traynham, Nancy St.Clair - M6274243
Traynham, III, John Edward - M6274242
Trimble, Donald - M6247331
Trimble, Markley - M6247332
Trimble, Pauline Maud - M624734
Trott, Allison Tyler - M624224232
Trott, Lynn - M624224231
Turner, Rebecca Sue - M62634331
VanO'Linda, Calvin - M621391111
VanO'Linda, Christopher Allen - M62139111
VanO'Linda, Jessee Roy - M621391112
VanO'Linda, Katherine Rose - M621391113
Vaughan, Abram Still - M62147
Vaughan, Barbara Ann Frances - M62146
Vaughan, Catherine Connor - M62142
Vaughan, Clara Caroline - M621471
Vaughan, Dudley Still - M62142x
Vaughan, Frederick Philemon - M62144
Vaughan, Gerald Ralph - M6214731
Vaughan, Icypheon Gertrude - M62148
Vaughan, Ida Geneva - M621472
Vaughan, James Bradley Findley - M62143
Vaughan, Martha Moore - M62141
Vaughan, Sarah C. - M62143y
Vaughan, William - M62143x
Vaughan, Winifred Marovia - M62145
Vaughan, Jr., Abram Still - M621473
Vawter, Margaret Cosby - M6261222
Vawter, Nancy Rose - M6261221
Vest, Clara Lucille - M624581
Votgelsanger, James - M621531221
Wagner, Albert Carl - M6242242
Wagner, Alice Kathryn - M62422423
Wagner, Amanda Ella - M624214
Wagner, Amanda - M62422-10-1-1
Wagner, Amy Elizabeth - M624213112
Wagner, Barbara Ann - M624224211
Wagner, Barbara Lee - M62422-15-3
Wagner, Bernice Mescal - M6242224
Wagner, Betty Ann - M62422133
Wagner, Beverly Ann - M624224222
Wagner, Carlton Lee - M62422421
Wagner, Charles Davis - M62422-15-7
Wagner, Charles Deaton - M62422-11
Wagner, Charles Edward - M62421311
Wagner, Charlotte Ann - M62422-15-2
Wagner, Claude - M624226
Wagner, Curtis Pierce - M6242243
Wagner, David Franklin - M62422-15-5
Wagner, Debra Jo - M624224213
Wagner, E. Morton - M643221
Wagner, Edward Mustard - M624213

Wagner, Eleanor - M6242216
Wagner, Ella Sue - M62422-15-4
Wagner, Eula Green - M62422-13
Wagner, Frances Lacine - M62422-17
Wagner, Frances St.Clair - M6242222
Wagner, Gary Lee - M624224212
Wagner, Helen - M6242214
Wagner, James Edward - M6242133
Wagner, James Hoge - M624211
Wagner, James Paul - M6242215
Wagner, James Pierce - M624224
Wagner, Janella Lee - M6242241
Wagner, Jason - M624213114
Wagner, Jean Merle - M6242223
Wagner, Jeanie Pearl - M6242216
Wagner, Jefferson Calhoun - M62421312
Wagner, Jennifer - M624213113
Wagner, John Randolph - M62422-15-8
Wagner, Joseph Dell - M62422132
Wagner, Joseph Green - M6242213
Wagner, Julia Alice - M6242212
Wagner, Kathryn - M6242132
Wagner, Lena Flournoy - M624218
Wagner, Lillie Mae - M624215
Wagner, Linda Sue - M62422131
Wagner, Mae Brown - M62422-14
Wagner, Mariah Clarica - M624227
Wagner, Martha Alice - M624229
Wagner, Mary Frances - M62422-15-6
Wagner, Michael Lamar - M624213121
Wagner, Mildred Harrison - M6242221
Wagner, Myrtle Addington - M62422-12
Wagner, Nancy Georgia - M624228
Wagner, Ozella Gray - M624223
Wagner, Patricia Sue - M624221511
Wagner, Paul Keith - M6242134
Wagner, Rebecca Hope - M62422-15-9
Wagner, Robert Charles - M6242131
Wagner, Robert Charles - M624213111
Wagner, Robert King - M62422-15
Wagner, Roger Wolson - M62422-10-1
Wagner, Rosa Mariah - M624217
Wagner, Ruth - M6242217
Wagner, Samuel Oscar - M624222
Wagner, St.Clair - M62422-10
Wagner, Steven Andrew - M624213122
Wagner, Sue Georgia - M624212
Wagner, Tyler Frazier - M624225
Wagner, Ule - M62422-11-2
Wagner, Virginia Belle - M62422-15-11
Wagner, Virginia Bogle - M62422-16
Wagner, William David - M624221

Wagner, William Garnet - M6242211
Wagner, William Thomas - M62422-15-10
Wagner, Jr., James Paul - M62422151
Wagner, Jr., Robert King - M62422-15-1
Wajick, Alice Ruth - M62425153
Wajick, Brian David - M624251523
Wajick, Leslie Michelle - M624251521
Wajick, Margaret Ann - M62425151
Wajick, Stephanie Lynn - M624251522
Wajick,II, Carl Johnny - M62425152
Walker, Freddie Randolph - M6431122
Walker, Ralph Edward - M6431123
Walker, Randolph William - M64311221
Walker, Ruth Inez - M6431121
Wallace, Andrew Still - M621631
Wallace, Charlotte Ruth - M64312511
Wallin, Miriam - M6215311
Wallin, Pauline - M6215312
Wallman, Evan Parker - M62822261121
Walls, Andrew - M6298186
Walls, Diana - M6298185
Walls, James Joseph - M6298183
Walls, Laura Sue - M62981821
Walls, Linda Sue - M6298184
Walls, Robert D. - M6298182
Walls, Jr., John - M6298181
Walton, Matthew Daniel - M62981164
Wamsley, Kyle Hunter - M6242515121
Wamsley, Travis Reed - M624515122
Waqner, Jack - M62422-11-1
Ward, Everett St.Clair - M62742311
Ward, Jane Ketner - M627423111
Ward, Janet Elizabeth - M6211423
Ward, Kimberly Ann - M62742313
Ward, Margaret - M6211421
Ward, Owen Jay - M6211422
Ward, Stacey Tinnel - M62742312
Ward, Wallace Ward - M627423123
Ward, III, Lilburn Everett - M6274231
Ward,Jr., Everett St.Clair - M627423112
Warren, Brad - M624251423
Warren, Hazel Marie - M626343112
Warren, Kenny - M624251422
Warren, Scott - M62451421
Warren, Terry Wayne - M628925241
Warren, Becky Jo - M626343111
Watson, Cheryl Lynn - M62981512
Watson, Markus Wayne - M62981511
Watson, Paul Stephen - M62981513
Watson, Tiffany Nicole - M629815121
Watts, Adam Joseph - M62892-10-1-5
Watts, Diana Lynn - M62892-10-3

Watts, Kathy Sue - M62892-10-4
Watts, Kristine Michele - M62892-10-1-3
Watts, Mark D'Wayne - M62892-10-5
Watts, Mathews Gabriel - M62892-10-1-4
Watts, Michael Lee - M62892-10-2
Watts, Richard Warren - M62892-10-1-2
Watts, Steven Wesley - M62892-10-1-1
Watts, Jr., John Wesley - M62892-10-1
White, Arnold Brown - M6263144
White, Buford Thompson - M6263145
White, Christopher Patrick - M62981431
White, Clair Graham - M6263141
White, Frances Nan - M6233241
White, Hubert Stuart - M6263142
White, Mary Rachel - M6263146
White, Orville Brown - M6263141
White, Robert - M62631431
White, Thomas - M62631451
White, Jr., Hubert Stuart - M62631421
Whitley, Amy - M623322211
Whitley, Annie Cora - M62651
Whitley, Annie - M62343
Whitley, Barbara J. - M6237
Whitley, Beulah B. - M623323
Whitley, Captain Loyd - M623321
Whitley, Charles H. - M62357
Whitley, Charles Tiffany - M62332
Whitley, Cora Elizabeth - M6233271
Whitley, Cora - M623332
Whitley, Dorothy - M626554
Whitley, Ebb Keister - M626337
Whitley, Elgan Lane - M6261
Whitley, Elgan Lane - M62654
Whitley, Elizabeth Ann - M62332721
Whitley, Ella Jackson - M62611
Whitley, Ellen Mary - M626534
Whitley, Emmaline V. - M62661
Whitley, Fannie Ann - M626121
Whitley, Florence Jeannette - M62636
Whitley, George Lockhart - M626553
Whitley, George - M623333
Whitley, Henry H. - M62358
Whitley, Hugh J - M62464
Whitley, Hugh Price - M62652
Whitley, Irene Patterson - M6263382
Whitley, James Robert - M626333
Whitley, James Shannon - M6263
Whitley, James Oliver - M623327
Whitley, James Rufus - M62333
Whitley, James S. - M62341
Whitley, James Samuel - M62351
Whitley, Jana Grace - M6263362

Whitley, Janie Florence - M626335
Whitley, John David - M626533
Whitley, John H. - M6265
Whitley, John L. - M62334
Whitley, John Whitman - M62653
Whitley, Joseph Garnett - M626338
Whitley, Kirby G. - M62352
Whitley, Louisa - M62635
Whitley, Loyd George - M6233223
Whitley, Margaret Catherine - M626331
Whitley, Margaret E. - M62634
Whitley, Margaret May - M626123
Whitley, Martha - M623326
Whitley, Mary Alice - M62631
Whitley, Mary Blanche - M626332
Whitley, Mary L. - M62331
Whitley, Mary Naomi - M62656
Whitley, Mary P. - M6238
Whitley, Mary Price - M62622
Whitley, Mary - M623322212
Whitley, Matilda B. - M6232
Whitley, Milton - M623331
Whitley, Minnie - M62658
Whitley, Nancy J. - M62356
Whitley, Nancy Lane - M6231
Whitley, Nannie Belle - M626124
Whitley, Nannie Rose - M626531
Whitley, Nellie Rose - M626122
Whitley, Nellie Rose - M62657
Whitley, Norman S. - M6234
Whitley, Paul - M623335
Whitley, Peggy (Margaret) - M6236
Whitley, Phyllis Brook - M6263372
Whitley, Polly - M62621
Whitley, Rees B. - M6235
Whitley, Reese Jackson - M62633
Whitley, Robert Owen - M6233221
Whitley, Rosalyn - M626339
Whitley, Rufus C. - M6233
Whitley, Rufus Joseph - M62332231
Whitley, Sarah Fanny - M62353
Whitley, Sarah L. - M62342
Whitley, Sarah Rebecca - M62632
Whitley, Sarah Virginia - M626334
Whitley, Sharon Rose - M6263361
Whitley, Stewart French - M626532
Whitley, Theron Jennings - M626551
Whitley, Thomas F. - M62355
Whitley, Vesta Elizabeth - M623324
Whitley, Virginia Ellen - M626555
Whitley, Virginia Geraldine - M6265521
Whitley, Virginia - M623336

Whitley, Walter - M626336
Whitley, Wesley Price - M6262
Whitley, William A. - M6239
Whitley, William Addison - M62612
Whitley, William E. - M62354
Whitley, William Gerald - M626552
Whitley, William Loyd - M62332221
Whitley, William Neel - M62655
Whitley, William Reese - M626332x
Whitley, William Rufus - M623322
Whitley, William - M623334
Whitley, II, Reese Jackson - M6263381
Whitley, Jr., Charles T. - M623325
Whitley, Jr., E. Lane - M626541
Whitley, Jr., Ebb Keister - M6263373
Whitley, Jr., James Robert - M6263331
Whitley, Jr., James Oliver - M6233272
Whitley, Jr., Loyd George - M62332232
Whitley, Jr., William Rufus - M6233222
Whitt, Richard Darrell - M6223511
Williams, Annabelle - M6242123
Williams, Bobbie Joe - M62421231
Williams, Brandon Burke - M624212232
Williams, Chase Lee - M6293221211
Williams, Dana Wagner - M6242122
Williams, Danny Grattan - M62421222
Williams, Emily Marie - M624212234
Williams, Eva Sue - M62421211
Williams, Garnet Porter - M6242125
Williams, Georgia H. - M6242124
Williams, Holly Opal - M624212231
Williams, Leslie Kenneth - M62421223
Williams, Mark Jason - M624212312
Williams, Max Justin - M624212313
Williams, Michael Joseph - M624212311
Williams, Mildred M. - M6242126
Williams, Roy J. - M6242121
Williams, Valerie Blanch - M624212233
Williams, Virginia Ruth - M62421221
Williams, Jr., Garnet Porter - M62421251
Williamson, Darrell Dwight - M643113213
Williamson, Lee Ann - M643113212
Williamson, Tammy Sue - M643113211
Wilson, Charles Edwin - M6226811
Wilson, Charles Robert - M62917
Wilson, Craig Alan - M62822471
Wilson, Hazel Virginia - M625221
Wilson, Hazel Virginia - M625221
Wilson, Hugh Edward - M62911
Wilson, Jennie Rebecca - M62916
Wilson, Jesse Price - M62268112
Wilson, John Wilson - M62912